MW00748406

A Black Studies Primer

Heroes and Heroines of the African Diaspora

Keith A. P. Sandiford

TO: ELYSE

Very best wishes

[signature]

22/5/11

H
HANSIB

HANSIB PUBLICATIONS
London and Hertfordshire UK

Published by Hansib Publications in 2008
London & Hertfordshire

Hansib Publications Limited
P.O. Box 226, Hertford, Hertfordshire, SG14 3WY, UK

Email: info@hansib-books.com
Website: www.hansib-books.com

A catalogue record of this book is
available from the British Library

ISBN 978-1-906190-06-4

© Keith A. P. Sandiford

All rights reserved. No part of this publication may be
reproduced, stored in or introduced into a retrieval system,
or transmitted in any form, or by any means, electronic,
mechanical, photocopying, recording, or otherwise,
without the prior permission of the publisher.

Cover designed by Pam Taylor
Printed and bound by The Alden Press, Oxford, UK

To Lorraine, Gary and Shelley
three unsung black stalwarts who deserve a
much larger book devoted entirely to themselves

PREFACE

This *Black Studies Primer* is a direct response to urgent requests from several African, American, British, Canadian and Caribbean organizations and individuals for a compendium of heroes and heroines who have demonstrated black excellence in the past. There still persists in the public mind, especially in the western world, the fallacious notion that Blacks have been unable to contribute constructively to the evolution of modern civilization, except in the fields of music and sport. That is an offspring of the North American myth that Whites compensate for their physical inferiority by having certain innate advantages in intellect and intelligence.

This study should dispel that kind of nonsense forever. It reveals that there is hardly a field of human endeavour in which Blacks have failed to demonstrate excellence. Despite a great deal of editing and exclusion, still present here is a wonderful array of black activists, actors, administrators, artists, athletes, authors, businessmen, educators, engineers, entrepreneurs, inventors, journalists, jurists, lawyers, mathematicians, musicians, philanthropists, philosophers, photographers, physicians, pioneers, politicians, priests, scientists, scholars, sculptors, singers, soldiers, statesmen, teachers and theologians. There is also considerable evidence of African ingenuity before, during, and after the tragic interlude of European colonization.

I have been much encouraged in this enterprise by the members of the Afro-Caribbean Association of Manitoba (ACAM), the Barbados Association of Winnipeg (BAW), the Black Educators' Association of Manitoba (BEAM), the Black History Month Celebration Committee of Winnipeg, the Manitoba Association for Multicultural Education (MAME), the Caribbean Seniors of Manitoba and Hansib Publishers of London (UK). Special assistance has also been willingly offered by Mr Noel Alleyne (UK), Dr Hilary Beckles (Barbados), Dr Selwyn Carrington (USA), Her Excellency Ms June Clarke (Canada), Ms Sonia Dechausay (Canada), Professor Donald K. Gordon (Canada), Professor John Kendle (Canada), Ms Angela King (USA), Dr James Millette (USA), Mr Sheldon Millette (Canada), Dr Kathleen Phillips-Lewis (USA), Ms Hyrol Springer (Canada) and Ms Dawn Williams (Canada). To these individuals and organizations I offer warm and sincere thanks.

Keith A.P. Sandiford, Winnipeg, Manitoba

INTRODUCTION

This *Black Studies Primer* has been compiled to fill a gaping hole in secondary school curricula in most parts of the world. Black teachers and children, especially in the western hemisphere, have long been clamouring for suitable texts dealing fairly with the black experience. All of the recommended readings have thus far been found wanting for one reason or another. Too many of them have been written by white authors who sometimes fail to show the necessary sensitivity in the handling of such delicate issues as exploitation, racism and slavery. The bulk of the available literature displays too obvious a Eurocentric bias and leaves young black readers without a proper appreciation for their roots, heritage and culture. Hopefully, this effort, which is an offspring of *A Black Historical Calendar*, published by the Afro-Caribbean Association of Manitoba (ACAM) in Winnipeg during 1973-94, will provide teenagers of all races with an understanding of the black experience and help them to appreciate the important contributions made by Blacks over the years to the development of modern civilization.

The need for a work such as this becomes immediately obvious when considering the fact that, while white performers are idolized by the western media, black innovators remain curiously concealed, as it were, in the shadows of history. Every literate North American, for instance, is familiar with the name of Alexander Graham Bell, but all too few have ever heard of such creative black engineers as Latimer Lewis and Granville T. Woods who did so much to ensure that Bell's telephone system actually worked. Almost unknown to the whole continent of Europe is the fact that most of the systems and devices that the world has now become accustomed to, and takes for granted, were the products of black genius and ingenuity. Such simple gadgets as ironing boards, folding chairs, lawn mowers, ironing combs, dust pans, elevator shafts, golf tees, light bulbs, stop signs, refrigerators and fountain pens, to name but a few, have been invented and/or perfected by Blacks. The modern world would not have been the same without their significant contributions to computer science and nuclear technology. The Blacks have left an indelible mark on such disciplines as agriculture, chemistry, engineering, literature, mathematics, medicine, music, philosophy and physics. This is seldom emphasized, or even noticed, by conventional historians and sociologists.

The book appears in the form of an encyclopaedia to facilitate easy reference. It offers skeletal pieces of information on a variety of individual stars in the hope that students and teachers alike will be inspired to pursue further research on their own favourite subjects and themes. It has tried, wherever possible, to provide exact dates of birth and death to facilitate the preparation of 'Black Historical Calendars' which teachers in the province of Manitoba have found so useful in stimulating interest in Black Studies. It has also tried to cover as many fields as possible, deliberately to correct that pernicious myth (so prevalent in North America) that Blacks have traditionally succeeded only in the areas of music and sport. This study demonstrates that there is hardly a field of human endeavour on which the Black race has failed to make an enormous impact. It also proves quite conclusively that there has been a solid corpus of native African literature during the last two centuries. If the study appears to focus too narrowly on Africa, the North American mainland, the United Kingdom and the West Indian islands, it is simply because this is where the majority of Blacks have lived and worked. Despite the remarkable African diaspora over the past two centuries, Blacks have thus far been generally excluded from most parts of Asia, Europe and the South Pacific.

This list of black heroes and heroines is, by its very nature, selective and arbitrary. It is certainly not intended to be viewed as complete and exhaustive. There are so many potential entries that a number of delicate decisions had to be made with respect to omissions and inclusions. How can a compiler include, say, an Ella Fitzgerald, and exclude similar heroines such as Pearl Bailey and Sarah Vaughan? Such decisions in the end depend upon peculiarities of taste and considerations of space. There is an incredibly long list of African-American stars in the fields of music and sport. This *Black Studies Primer* tries to identify the greatest innovators and the most influential among them. Literally hundreds of them are consequently excluded. The same is true of distinguished black African and Caribbean authors and politicians. Careful editing is necessary if a certain balance is to be achieved. The most that any compiler can hope to do is to draw attention to a fraction of them to show how crucial and varied was the black contribution to African and Caribbean politics, literature and philosophy.

In the preparation of this study, several sources were invaluable. The internet proved to be a gold mine with its remarkable volume of information on characters who find so little space in the traditional printed texts. Albeit slightly out of date, the *Encyclopaedia of Black America*, edited by W. Augustus Low and Virgil A. Clift (1984), drew attention to hundreds of African-Americans who would otherwise have remained unknown. Peter Fryer's excellent *Staying Power: The History of Black People in Britain* (1984) filled another void and is supplemented by the recent effort to discover the 100 Greatest Black Britons (2003). The attempt to rescue Canadian Blacks from the mists of history began with Robin Winks' magisterial *The Blacks in Canada* (1971) and was continued by James Walker with his three seminal studies during the 1980s. *Towards Freedom: The African-Canadian Experience*, by Ken Alexander and Avis Glaze in 1996; *Some Missing Pages*, recently launched by the Quebec Board of Black Educators; Sheldon Taylor's *Many Rivers to Cross: The African-Canadian Experience* (1992); and Dawn P. Williams' *Who's Who in Black Canada* (2006) have all been very useful. These works very clearly show that Blacks have made a significant contribution over the years to the development of modern Canada, even though the bulk of white writers, unfortunately, still continue to neglect this important feature of Canadian history.

The greatest difficulty in producing this *Black Studies Primer* springs from the slippery definition of the word 'black' itself. For many people, especially West Indians, black is simply a generic term for non-white. In this study, however, the final decision was to restrict the definition of black to those of ethnic Sub-Saharan African descent and to preserve a sharp distinction between Blacks on the one hand and Browns and Yellows on the other. There are therefore no Indian, Berber, Aboriginal or Amerindian personalities here. Nor did this entirely solve the problem. How do you treat a Michael Norman Manley, whose mother was a white Anglo-Saxon, or a Bessie Head whose mother was a white South African with Afrikaner roots? Where also does this leave Eldrick 'Tiger' Woods, whose mother is distinctly oriental? The final decision was to allow the subjects, in a manner of speaking, to choose for themselves. So far as everyone knows, Head, Manley and Woods, like the celebrated William Edward Burghardt DuBois before them, have all considered themselves black and that is good enough for the author. On the other hand, there is no evidence that Alexandre Dumas, one of the most prolific and most popular of French authors of the nineteenth century, ever did so. His father, a soldier in Napoleon's army, was the illegitimate son of the marquis de La Pailleterie and Marie Cessette Dumas, a black lady from San Domingo. Consequently, both Dumas (1802-70) and his son of the same name, who was simply known as Dumas Fils (1824-95), have been omitted, despite their enormous contributions to French literature.

The recent effort to determine the greatest of the black Britons was most welcome indeed. The results have drawn attention to some important but largely forgotten characters, such as George Bridgetower, Olaudah Equiano, Ignatius Sancho, Mary Seacole and Henry Sylvester Williams, who had hitherto been confined to oblivion. But the final collection included many questionable entries, such as the mythical George of Lydda, Queen Charlotte, Queen Philippa and Septimus Severus who, as far as can be ascertained, did not consider themselves black and were certainly not regarded as black by their contemporaries.

AARON, Hank

Henry Louis Aaron is famous for registering more home runs than any other player in the history of major-league baseball in North America. The mark of 755 he set while playing for the Milwaukee Braves, Atlanta Braves and Milwaukee Brewers during 1954-75 is still standing. Born on 5 February 1934, in Mobile, Alabama, Aaron played with the Indianapolis Clowns of the Negro American League until he was signed by the Boston Braves to a minor league contract in 1952. By the time he was promoted to the majors, the Braves had moved to Milwaukee. One of the few power hitters who could maintain a .300 batting average while consistently registering more than 30 home runs per season, Aaron won the National League batting championship with a .328 average in 1956 and was named that league's most valuable player in 1957. He ended his career with the remarkable overall average of .310. When, on 8 April 1974, he broke Babe Ruth's career record of 714 home runs that had stood for 39 years, he became the recipient of much racist hate mail. A reliable all-round player, who could catch, field, throw and run the bases very well, Hank Aaron never received the credit or the salary that his enormous talents would seem to have deserved. Following his retirement as a player, he became one of the first Blacks in major league baseball's upper-level management as Atlanta's vice-president of player development. He is also active for Turner Broadcasting (TBS) as a corporate vice-president of community relations and a member of its board of directors. In 1982 he was inducted into the Baseball Hall of Fame and in 2002 he received the Presidential Medal of Freedom, America's highest civilian honour. His autobiography, *I Had a Hammer*, was published in 1990.

ABABA ARAGAY

Ras Ababa Aragay was a noted Ethiopian soldier and politician who distinguished himself during the war against the Italians (1935-41) when he used guerilla tactics to frustrate the invaders. Born in Salalé on 18 August 1903, he began his military career as a lieutenant in Emperor Haile Selassie's bodyguard before becoming chief of police in Addis Ababa. After the withdrawal of Italian troops from Ethiopia, Ras Ababa Aragay's rise was rapid. A devoted servant of the emperor, he acted in turn as governor of Addis Ababa (1941), governor of Sidamo (1941-42) and of Tegré (1943-47). He also served as minister of war (1942-43), minister of the interior (1949-55) and minister of defence (1955-60). He was occupying the important post of chairman of the Council of Ministers when killed on 15 December 1960 in an abortive coup.

ABACHA, Sani

Born in Kano on 20 September 1943, Sani Abacha joined the Nigerian Army and rose all the way to the rank of brigadier by 1980 after having been trained in American, British and Nigerian military schools. He participated in three consecutive military coups d'etat before himself taking charge of the Nigerian state as well as the army in 1993. Despite his pledge to restore democracy as soon as possible, he muzzled the press, eliminated all elected institutions and assemblies, dismissed the majority of old army leaders, established a personal body guard of some 2,000 soldiers and ruled Nigeria tyrannically. He embezzled huge sums of public money while executing and imprisoning his most dangerous rivals and opponents. Abacha died of an apparent heart attack at Abuja on 9 June 1998.

ABAYOMI-COLE, John Augustus

Born of Sierra Leonean parents at Ilorin in Nigeria in 1848, Revd John Augustus Abayomi-Cole left his mark as priest, politician, author and administrator after a very lengthy career. He was educated in Sierra Leone before furthering his studies in the United States and being ordained a priest in the American Wesleyan Methodist Church. He returned to Sierra Leone and took over the superintendence of the Maroon Chapel in 1887 but resigned after differences with his congregation. In 1905, Abayomi-Cole founded his own church, the Gospel Mission Hall, where various ethnic groups came to worship. A renowned herbalist, he produced effective antidotes against rheumatic pains, skin diseases, nervous ailments and mental disorders. Shrewdly combining agriculture with science, he distilled spirits, manufactured soap, transformed molasses into sugar and extracted various foods from corn. Apart from ginger, which was then in great demand in Europe, he cultivated cassava, cocoa, corn, vegetables and yams while also participating in the lucrative palm-oil trade. Had he received adequate government support in those days he might well have led Sierra Leone in a timely and effective diversification of its staple food crops. His firm belief in the value of the soil led to the founding in 1922 of the Sierra Leone Farmers' Association which he served for many years as president. Abayomi-Cole was associated with almost every progressive movement of the day, devoting much of his time and energy particularly to the National Congress of British West Africa (NCBWA). His versatility was amazing. Sierra Leone lost a truly original thinker when he died in 1943 at the advanced age of ninety-five.

ABBOTT, Anderson

Dr Anderson Ruffin Abbott, the son of a successful businessman, was born in Toronto, Ontario, in 1837. Educated at Toronto Academy and Oberlin

College in Ohio, he proceeded to study medicine at the University of Toronto from which he obtained his degree in 1861. He was the first black graduate from the Toronto Medical College. Two years later, he was appointed a surgeon in the Northern army during the American Civil War. He returned to Ontario in 1865 to open his private practice in Chatham, where he became president of the Wilberforce Educational Institute during 1873-80. He became coroner for Kent County in 1874 and was associate editor of the British Methodist Episcopal Church's mouthpiece, *The Messenger*, as well as a writer for the *Planet*. Abbott moved to Chicago in 1894 to take up the post of surgeon-general at the Provident Hospital and Training School, the first such institution for African-Americans. Following his retirement, he returned to Toronto, where he died in 1913. He is best remembered as one of the earliest black physicians in Canadian history and as a vocal critic of segregation in the Ontario public schools. He wrote numerous articles on a variety of subjects ranging from Darwinism, politics, and history to education and poetry.

ABBOTT, Diane

Diane Julie Abbott is a British Labour Party member of parliament. She was the first black woman ever elected to the House of Commons and remained the only one until she was joined in 1997 by Oona King (who lost her seat in the general election of 2005). Born on 27 September 1953 of Jamaican parents in Paddington, London, she was educated at Harrow County Grammar School before emerging with an MA in History from Cambridge University. A journalist by profession, she worked as an administrative trainee with the Home Office; Race Relations Officer with the National Council for Civil Liberties; a researcher and reporter with TV AM and Thames Television; Public Relations Officer with the Greater London Council and Head of Lambeth Council's Press Office. Her political career began in 1982 when she was elected to the Westminster City Council, one of the first black women councillors in the United Kingdom. Five years later she was elected to the House of Commons as MP for Hackney North and Stoke Newington. Active for many years in the trades union movement, particularly on race equality issues, Ms. Abbott served briefly as Britain's first black female officer in the Association of Cinematographers Television and Allied Technicians. A committed social and political activist, she was a founder member of the Black Media Workers' Organization, a keen supporter of the Organization of Women of African and Asian Descent (OWAAD) and president of Black Women Mean Business.

ABBOTT, Wilson

Wilson Ruffin Abbot was born of an Irish father and free African-American mother in Richmond, Virginia, in 1801. After an apprenticeship as a carpenter, he served briefly on a Mississippi steamer before opening a grocery store in Mobile, Alabama. Driven from his prosperous store by envious Whites, he emigrated in 1835 to Toronto, where he became a thriving real estate broker. By 1870, he owned several properties in Toronto, Hamilton and Owen Sound. Always keen on local politics, Wilson Abbott gave support to the Crown during the uprising of 1837 and helped to found the Coloured Wesleyan Methodist Church of Toronto in 1838. During the 1840s, he joined the Anti-Slavery Society of Canada, was elected to the Toronto City Council, and served as a member of the Reform Central Committee. He died in 1876, after seeing his son, Anderson Ruffin Abbott, become the first Canadian-born Black to qualify as a doctor and receive a license to practise in Toronto.

ABEDI, Sheikh

Sheikh Kaluta bin Amri Abedi, a noted Swahili poet, was born in Ujiji, in Tanganyika, in 1924. He attended the Tabora Secondary School before studying to be a missionary. He was elected to parliament in 1959 and served as mayor of Dar es Salaam. In 1962 he was appointed Regional Commissioner and in 1963 became minister of justice for Tanzania. His collection of poems, *Sheria Za Kuyunga Mashairi, Na Diwani Ya Amri (The Rules and Versification of the Poems of Amri)*, was published in 1954. Sheikh Abedi died on 15 October 1964.

ABIOLA, Moshood

One of the wealthiest magnates in African history, Moshood Kashimawo Olawale Abiola was born in Abeokuta on 24 August 1937. A scholarship took him to Scotland where he studied accounting at the University of Glasgow and returned to serve as an accountant for ITT Nigeria in 1968. By 1971 he had become its chief executive and chairman and occupied these posts until 1988. During these years he amassed an immense private fortune and was able to purchase, among other things (including 21 wives), an airline, a publishing house and a newspaper syndicate. As he also made enormous contributions for the building of schools and other philanthropic causes, he became very popular and was elected president of Nigeria in 1993 by a huge majority when democratic elections were held in his country for the first time in many years. But the military junta annulled the elections and imprisoned Abiola in 1994. He remained in jail, despite the protests of the international community, until his death in very strange circumstances on 7 July 1998.

ABRAHAMS, Peter

Peter Lee Abrahams was born at Vrededorp, near Johannesburg in South Africa, on 19 March 1919. He became an outstanding novelist, short-story writer and journalist. After attending St Peter's Secondary School in Johannesburg, he emigrated to England in 1939 and worked for the *London Observer* while writing several radio scripts for the BBC's Third Programme during the 1950s. He then settled in Jamaica, British West Indies, where he worked for the rest of his days as a journalist and broadcaster while editing the *West Indian Economist*. His numerous books included *Dark Testament*, a collection of short stories published in 1942; *Song of the City* (1945); *Mine Boy* (1946); *The Path of Thunder* (1948); *Wild Conquest* (1951); *Tell Freedom* (1954); *A Wreath for Udomo* (1956); *Jamaica: An Island Mosaic* (1957); *A Night of Their Own* (1965); *This Island Now* (1966) and *A View from Coyaba* (1985). *Mine Boy* established him as one of the leading African novelists, though *Wild Conquest* was perhaps the finest of all his fiction. Abrahams' writing did much to draw international attention to the harsh realities of black life in South Africa during the days of apartheid and most of his books have been translated into many languages.

ABUBAKAR III

Born in Sokoto, Nigeria, on 15 March 1903, Abubakar III became one of the most famous of all modern African religious leaders. By the time of his death on 1 November 1988, he had become the spiritual leader of an estimated 50 million Muslims in Nigeria and its neighbourhood. The most powerful Islamic figure in sub-Saharan Africa, Abubakar III was appointed scribe of the Denge district in 1929 and succeeded his uncle, Hassan, as sultan in 1938. During World War II he fought on the British side in Burma and was knighted for his services in 1954. Throughout his rule, he emphasized the importance of education, even for girls, and encouraged the older Muslim students to further their studies in Europe, although he tried to discourage them from abandoning their African heritage. A devout ascetic, Abubakar III created a positive impression on all those with whom he came into contact and is perhaps best remembered for offering free private tuition in his own library to the poor children of his district. Such was the nobility of his character that he commanded the respect of Christians as well as Muslims and of Europeans as well as Africans.

ABUBAKAR, Abdusalam

Major General Abdusalam Abubakar, Nigeria's defence chief of staff, was sworn in as that country's president on 9 June 1998, following the sudden death of the previous military ruler, Major General Sani Abacha. Born in Minna in north central Nigeria, on 13 June 1942, he attended a secondary school in the neighbouring town of Bida before entering the Kaduna Technical Institute in 1963. He served briefly in the air force and joined the national army in 1975, rising rapidly up the ranks. In 1981, he commanded Nigeria's contingent of the UN peacekeeping forces in Lebanon and by 1993 had risen to the rank of defence chief of staff. Abubakar promised to restore civilian rule as soon as possible and he freed a number of political prisoners but he inherited so many economic and social problems that it seemed unlikely that he would ever be able to solve them. He oversaw the transition of a democratically elected government and the establishment of a new constitution in 1999.

ABUBAKAR, Alhaji

Better known as Sir Tafawa Balewa, this Nigerian author, linguist and statesman was born in Bauchi Province in northern Nigeria in 1912. He was educated in various Nigerian schools before attending the London School of Education in England. He returned to Nigeria as an education officer but soon entered politics. He was appointed to the first Northern House of Assembly and then elected to the Federal House of Representatives in Lagos. After serving as chief minister since 1957, Sir Tafawa Balewa became the first federal prime minister of independent Nigeria in 1960. He was assassinated in 1966. His works included *Nigeria Speaks* (1964) and *Shaihu Umar*, a Hausa novel, which was eventually translated into English and published in 1967, twelve years after its original appearance.

ACHEBE, Chinua

This celebrated Nigerian author, critic, teacher and diplomat was born at Ogidi in eastern Nigeria on 16 November 1930. The son of one of the first Ibo Mission teachers, he was educated at the Church Missionary Society School and the Government College in Umuahia before attending Ibadan University. Achebe worked as a broadcaster with the Nigerian Broadcasting Company in 1954 and became its first director of external broadcasting in 1961. Five years later, he resigned in order to devote more time to his writing. During the Biafran struggle for independence (1967-69), he served as a Biafran diplomat. Achebe then lectured widely in Europe and North America and became Director of African Studies at the University of Nigeria. He began editing *Okike*, a literary journal, in 1971. His works include such novels as *Things Fall Apart* (1958), *No Longer at Ease* (1960), *Arrow of God* (1964) and *A Man of the People* (1966). His poetry appeared in such collections as *Beware, Soul Brothers* (1971), *Christmas at Biafra and Other Poems* (1973) and *Collected Poems* (2004). His short stories were published in such collections as *The Sacrificial Egg* (1962), and *Girls at War and Other Stories* (1973). He also wrote a children's tale, *Chike and the River* (1966). Considered by many critics to be one of Africa's greatest writers, Achebe's *Things Fall Apart* has sold over 10 million copies around the world and has been translated into fifty languages. His novels deal mainly with the psychological disorientation accompanying the imposition of Western customs and values upon traditional African society. His treatise of literary criticism, *An Image of Africa: Racism in Conrad's Heart of Darkness*, has become one of the most controversial essays of its kind. Achebe is an Honorary Fellow of the Modern Language Association of America (1975); a Fellow of the Royal Society of Literature of London (1981); and a Fellow of the American Academy of Arts and Letters (1982). In 2004, he was awarded the prestigious Peace Prize of the German Book Trade. He is also the recipient of over thirty honorary degrees from universities in Canada, England, Nigeria, Scotland, South Africa and the United States and his works have won numerous prizes and awards. In 2004, however, he refused to accept the Commander of the Federal Republic, Nigeria's highest honour, in protest over the state of affairs in his native country.

ACQUAAH, Gaddiel

A Methodist educator and scholar, who played a major role in the translation of the Christian Bible into the Fante language, Revd Gaddiel Acquaah was born at Anomabu in 1884 in the Gold Coast (later known as Ghana). Himself the son of a Methodist minister, he became a teacher and eventually headmaster of a Wesleyan school at Shama. He was ordained a priest in 1912 and appointed chairman of the Methodist Bible Translation Committee. His famous Fante Bible was eventually published in 1944. Acquaah became vice-principal of the Methodist Training College at Aburi (some 20 miles north of Accra). In 1949, he was appointed a member of the Coussey Committee on Constitutional Reform and was awarded the OBE by the British government for his service to the church and state. He published several books, including *Fante Proverbs* and *John Wesley*. His best-known novel, *The Morning After*, appeared in 1961. His poetry was published in such collections as *Oguaa Aban* (1939), and *Nsem A Wonyin* (1939). He was also the author of numerous pamphlets, many of them (like some of his books) in Fante. Also in Fante was the collection of hymns for children, *Mbofraba Asorye Ndwom*, published in 1929. Revd Gaddiel Acquaah died in Accra on 25 March 1954.

ADAMA, Modibbo

Modibbo Adama was the famous Fulani warrior and scholar who founded the emirate of Adamawa in eastern Nigeria during the early years of the nineteenth century. In 1809 he began a jihad (holy war) against various non-Muslim peoples in western Africa and created a powerful Islamic state that eventually extended over parts of present-day Nigeria and most of northern Cameroon. In 1841, he established his capital at Yola, which still remains the headquarters of the emirate. Adama died in 1848.

ADAMS, Grantley

Born in Barbados on 28 April 1898, the Rt Excellent Sir Grantley Herbert Adams was the first and only prime minister of the British West Indian Federation which collapsed after only four years (1958-62). Educated at Harrison College, Barbados, and the University of Oxford, England, he became one of the most successful lawyers in Barbados. He played a prominent role in the formation of the Barbados Labour Party (BLP) and the Barbados Workers' Union (BWU) and was instrumental in bringing about a number of social, economic and constitutional reforms. A firm advocate of universal suffrage, local autonomy and Caribbean unity, Adams did more than any other single individual to extend the Barbadian franchise and to establish the principle of collective bargaining during the 1940s. As the leader of the majority party in 1954, he became the first premier of Barbados when that colony established a system of ministerial self-government. He overhauled the unfair fiscal system that had left the burden of taxation on the poorest sections of the society and initiated such useful reforms as workmen's compensation and a peasant loan system, before resigning in 1958 to lead the British West Indian Federation. He was knighted in 1957. Adams died on 28 November 1971 and was named a National Hero by the BLP government in April 1998. The international airport at Seawell in Christ Church, Barbados, has also been named after him and his birthday is now being celebrated as a national holiday in his native island.

ADAMS, Leonard

Dr Leonard Adams, internationally known for his contributions to the study of 18th century French literature, was born in Trinidad and educated at the University of the West Indies (BA 1958), McMaster University (MA 1967) and the University of London (PhD 1971). He taught at the University of Guelph, Ontario, from 1967 until 1996 and was elevated to the status of Professor Emeritus when he retired. He is best known for his seven-volume edition of *William Wake's Gallican Correspondence and Related Documents 1716-1731* which appeared during 1988-93. In addition to numerous scholarly articles, Adams also wrote *Coyer and the Enlightenment* which is volume 123 of *Studies on Voltaire and the Eighteenth Century* (1974). An accomplished musician, he has won prizes for his singing and has given recitals in several Caribbean islands.

ADAMS, Tom

Jon Michael Geoffrey Manningham Adams, the son of Sir Grantley, was born in Barbados, West Indies, on 14 September 1931. Educated at Harrison College, he won a Barbados Scholarship in 1950 and proceeded to study law in England. He worked for some years as a freelance broadcaster and producer for the British Broadcasting Corporation (BBC) and Independent Television (ITV) in London before returning to Barbados in 1962. He was elected to the Barbados House of Assembly in 1966 and held his seat in that legislature until his death. In 1971 he became leader of the Barbados Labour Party (BLP) which won the general elections of 1976 and 1981. Adams became prime minister of Barbados in 1976 and was still in office when he died suddenly on 11 March 1985, after having generated a great deal of controversy by supporting the United States intervention in Grenada in 1983. His tenure of office witnessed considerable economic prosperity and a consolidation of the social programmes that the Errol Barrow government had initiated. Tom Adams was one of the most eloquent of all Barbadian parliamentary debaters.

ADEMOLA, Adetokunbo

Sir Adetokunbo Adegboyega Ademola was a distinguished Nigerian jurist who became the first indigenous chief justice of the Nigerian Supreme Court (1958-72) and was a cofounder of the Nigerian Law School. Born in Abeokuta on 1 February 1906, Adetokunbo was the son of Sir Ladapo Ademola II, the paramount ruler (1920-63) of the Egba people in southern Nigeria. He attended King's College in Lagos and Selwyn College, Cambridge, England, before studying law at the Middle Temple in London and being called to the bar in 1934. Following his return to Nigeria, Ademola worked in the civil service, practised law and served as a magistrate (1939-49) and a puisne judge (1949-55). He was appointed to the Nigerian Supreme Court by the British authorities in 1949 and named chief justice of the Western Region in 1955. He became chancellor of the University of Nigeria in 1975 and chairman of the Commonwealth Foundation in 1978. Ademola was knighted in 1957 and made a privy counsellor in 1963. He died on 29 January 1993.

ADJETEY, Cornelius

Cornelius Frederick Adjetey was the first Ghanaian martyr to the cause of national independence. He was killed when British troops opened fire on a peaceful demonstration - an event that hastened the British withdrawal from the Gold Coast, as it was then called. Born in 1893, Adjetey fought bravely in both World Wars. In the first, he saw action in East Africa, and in the second he took part in expeditions to Burma. He was promoted to the rank of sergeant in 1944 and decorated for his service to the British Empire. He was protesting against post-war conditions in the Gold Coast when fatally shot on 28 February 1948. This incident led to widespread rioting and looting in Accra and forced the British government to establish a Royal Commission to investigate the cause of the disturbances. Sergeant Adjetey and his two slain comrades had a monument erected in their memory where they had fallen at the Osu crossroads.

ADOULA, Cyrille

Son of Bangala middle-class parents in what was then the Belgian Congo, Cyrille Adoula was born on 13 September 1921 in Léopoldville. After studying at the Roman Catholic St Joseph's Institute, he enjoyed a successful career in banking until 1956 when he became general secretary of the Belgian-sponsored General Federation of Workers. Two years later, he helped to organize the Mouvement National Congolais (MNC), the first modern political party in the Congo. In 1959, Adoula broke with Patrice Lumumba, Congo's first prime minister upon independence, and formed an opposition party known as MNC-Kalonji. After Lumumba's overthrow, Adoula was named interior minister before rising to the office of prime minister in 1961. But he faced a number of crises, including the attempted secession of Katanga under Moise Tshombe. With the help of UN forces, Adoula suppressed the rebellion only to be replaced by Tshombe in July 1964. He later served as ambassador to Belgium and to the United States and as foreign minister briefly prior to his retirement in 1970. He died on 24 May 1978 in Lausanne, Switzerland.

ADU BOFO

Adu Bofo was an Asante general who served also as treasurer to the local chieftain and is best remembered for his staunch opposition to the British in West Africa. But all of his plans to thwart the British advance ultimately failed. He died in 1883. He is now revered as a great Ghanaian patriot.

AFFAWAR GABRA IYASUS

A relative of the Empress Taytu Betul, this noted Ethiopian artist, poet, novelist and diplomat was born on 10 July 1868. He studied art in Italy and returned to decorate the Church of Raguel in Entoto, the former capital of Ethiopia. He wrote the first Amharic novel, Lebb Wallad Tarik (A Story Born Out of Fantasy) in 1908. This novel and his famous Amharic grammar texts gave Affawar Gabra Iyasus a prominent place in Ethiopian language and literature. He wrote three Italian works on the Amharic language, including the important Il Verbo Amarico. He also published a fine biography of Emperor Menilek II in 1909. In 1918 Affawar was sent to the United States as head of an Ethiopian trade mission and later served (1931-35) as Ethiopia's ambassador to Italy. His reputation for tact, diplomacy and scholarship eventually led to his appointment as president of the Special Court established in Addis Ababa to settle disputes between Ethiopian nationals and foreigners. During the Italian occupation (1935-41), he was promoted to the highest position in the Ethiopian Court system. But his well-known sympathy for Italians led to his political downfall after 1941. He died in exile on 25 September 1947.

AFONSO I
Born Muemba Nzinga around 1461, this famous Congolese chief came to power soon after the arrival of the Portuguese in that region. Adopting the Christian religion and other forms of Europeanization, he changed his name to Afonso to impress the Portuguese. Afonso I ruled as the sixth mwene-Kongo from 1506 to 1543 and tried his best to modernize his state along European lines. He used Portuguese weapons to defeat his brother, a rival claimant to the throne, and to discourage his neighbours. He founded schools and sent the sons of aristocrats to study in Portugal. His own son, later known as Dom Henrique, studied there and was consecrated as the first African Catholic bishop. Afonso also used Portuguese advisers, artisans and builders to remodel his empire and to renovate the architecture of his capital. His alliance with Portugal, however, steadily backfired. Not only did the Portuguese have their own agenda but Afonso's subjects were displeased by the edicts banning traditional customs. The Portuguese ignored his commercial regulations and began the intensive African-European trading of slaves that was destined to have disastrous effects for Kongo and its neighbours. Afonso is remembered as a great builder and a sincere Christian ruler with vision and foresight, but he was outwitted by the Europeans and his own violent seizure of the throne in 1506 had set too tempting an example for others to follow.

AFRICA
Africa is the second largest continent in the world, being smaller only than Asia. It is about 11.7 million square miles in extent, i.e. about three times the size of Europe, and covers about one fifth of the total land space in the world. Its population currently (2006) is estimated at about 890 million, which is about 13.7% of the overall total. Africa can therefore be described as relatively underpopulated. This is largely because the great Sahara desert (about 3.5 million square miles) occupies about one third of the whole continent.

The ancestors of all black people on earth came from Africa. This continent has left its mark on their behaviour even though many black families have no immediate connection with their original homeland. There is something distinctly African about black art, sculpture, language, literature, music, religion, and sport which makes black culture different from others.

For many years, white scholars tried to leave the impression that Africa was inhabited by savages and remained uncivilized until the Europeans conquered it during the nineteenth century. Recent scholarship has shown, however, that several vibrant civilizations existed there long before the white people arrived. In fact, African history is marked by the genius of several individual rulers and the success of many huge empires from ancient times onwards.

Today, African culture has become partially Europeanized after a century of foreign domination. Most African literature, for instance, is written in English, French, Portuguese or Spanish, and most African peoples speak at least one European language. But such native African languages as Amharic, Ewe, Fante, Ga, Swahili, Twi, Xhosa and Zulu still hold their own in many countries and several African authors have been publishing useful texts in their native tongues. Africans have learnt to merge their traditional patterns with European models and this has been clearly reflected not only in their language and literature but in their art, music, science, philosophy and religion.

Africa's geography is so harsh that the continent remains the poorest on earth. Africa is mainly a mixture of desert, lakes, swamps, marshes, jungles and mountains. Hence the relative sparseness of its population. Apart from areas in Egypt, Nigeria, South Africa and Zimbabwe, the land is often too sandy and rocky to be suitable for agriculture on a grand scale. Nor is the general inadequacy of the agricultural soil accompanied by a generous supply of precious metals and minerals (apart from diamonds and gold in South Africa). Even Ghana, once known as the Gold Coast, is now but a shadow of its former self after centuries of European exploitation and exhaustion of its rich mineral reserves. Some oil is found in Nigeria, but Sub-Saharan Africa, generally speaking, is by no means as fortunate in this respect as most of the countries in the Middle East. Alternate heat, drought and floods then combine to add to the general discomfort.

Africa also suffers from its history. After centuries of fierce internal competition for limited resources, the continent was badly administered by Europeans who established too few schools, hospitals or industries during the colonial period. Thus too many African countries were basically too poor to stand on their own economically after having achieved their political independence in the 1950s and 1960s. Even those countries with some potential for industrial development often lacked the necessary financial reserves to take full advantage of their mineral and other resources. To make matters worse, the African political boundaries drawn arbitrarily and whimsically by the Europeans in the nineteenth century paid too little attention to the actual traditions of the inhabitants. Most of the modern African states therefore are not really nations at all. They are little more than unwieldy combinations of multicultural and multiethnic units of competing peoples who find it difficult to cooperate for a common cause.

While the last several decades have consequently witnessed much physical violence, economic hardship and political unrest in most parts of Africa, that continent still continues to produce an incredible amount of excellent art, sculpture, literature, music and philosophy.

AFRICA IN THE TWENTY-FIRST CENTURY: QUO VADIS?

Africa remains in shambles at the dawn of the twenty-first century after almost fifty years of decolonization. This continent is politically the most unstable and financially the most feeble. There are social, economic and public health problems in almost every country in Africa. All Blacks, even those of the diaspora, must now seek explanations for this tragedy in the hope of creating a brighter tomorrow.

Africa's misfortunes spring partly from her harsh geography and her unhappy past. She is not as liberally supplied with precious metals and mineral resources as are other continents. Deserts, rivers, lakes, jungles, swamps, mountains and rocky soils also reduce her opportunities for profitable agriculture. The climate is generally too hot and humid, even for comfortable living. Alternating floods and drought wreak havoc with local farming and such countries as Ethiopia, Mozambique and Somalia face occasional starvation. Apart from Egypt, Nigeria and South Africa, the continent is relatively sparsely populated. Although it is almost three times the size of Europe, it contains only about 890 million people. In other words, Africa occupies about 20% of the world's land space but its population is less than 14% of the world's total.

Such unkind geography has left a profound impact on African history and psychology. Several ethnic groups developed there almost as isolated pockets of civilization because of the nature of the terrain. The struggles for the limited supplies of pure water, arable land and precious metals have always therefore been keen and bitter. African history has consequently been one of conflict rather than co-operation. These conflicts have been sharpened by ethnic, linguistic and cultural differences.

It was this, as much as anything else, which gave the Europeans their enormous advantage in the nineteenth century when they began their mad scramble for African territory. Had the Africans been able to compose their differences and unite against the white invaders, it is unlikely that the latter would have succeeded, despite their technological superiority. But traditional enemies sought to gain an advantage by allying with the newcomers, sometimes to their everlasting regret.

This competitive tradition has remained alive and militated against the successful and peaceful evolution of the African multiethnic 'nations' which the Europeans had selfishly and callously manufactured for their own convenience just over 100 years ago. There is hardly a single natural political entity throughout the length and breadth of Africa today. Even such relatively small countries as Côte d'Ivoire, the Gambia, Guinea, Liberia and Malawi contain a remarkable variety of ethnolinguistic groups.

Difficulties have arisen in almost every African state during the period of Independence precisely because of the continuing struggle for empowerment among the ethnic communities that have been forced into unnatural (and sometimes untenable) unions. The perennial conflict continues in Nigeria, for example, among Yoruba (17.5%) Hausa (17.2%), Ibo (13.3%) Fulani (10.7%) Ibibio (4.1%), Kanuri (3.6%), Egba (2.9%), Tiv (2.6%),Bura (1.1%),Nupe (1.0%), Edo (1.0%) and other peoples (25%), according to the most recent estimates. The situation in Uganda is the same, with its composition in 2002 analysed by UNESCO in the following manner: Ganda 17.3%, Nkole 9.8%, Soga 8.6%, Kiga 7.0%, Teso 6.6%, Lango 6.2%, Acholi 4.8% and Gisu 4.7%. And, as everyone knows, Rwanda has also been consistently torn apart by intense rivalries among the Hutu (85%), the Tutsi (14%) and the Twa (1%).

Some of the frustration springs, too, from the economic situation in which the majority of African countries found themselves when the European imperialists withdrew after World War II. The African colonies had for the most part been ruralized deliberately as the colonizers searched relentlessly for raw materials to manufacture at home. Very few African industries were developed by the imperial powers and even the gold supplies of Ghana were practically exhausted by the time that the British abandoned what they had called the Gold Coast, after many decades of exploitation. African colonies had been used simply as appendages to the imperial economy without any thought about the future.

Emerging African countries were thus left to compete on uneven terms with the older nations of the developed world and a gulf was promptly established between the so-called North and the so-called South. The industrialized nations routinely set prices both for their own goods and for those of others, thus widening the gap between the rich and poor countries. The value of African currency was often determined quite cavalierly by international agencies with their headquarters in Europe and North America.

This was the burden of President Julius Nyerere's complaint in 1981, when he addressed the United Nations in a memorable plea for economic justice. He could not but lament that, while the prices of manufactured goods continued to soar, the world markets were offering to pay less and less for such items as bananas, cashew nuts, cassava, coconuts, coffee, corn, cotton, millet, plantains, sweet potatoes and tobacco which were then being produced by Tanzania. The Tanzanians, he observed, were forever selling cheap and buying dear.

Nyerere was speaking here on behalf of the entire South. The Africans had been exploited in one fashion during the age of imperialism and now they were being exploited in another in the age of decolonization. Any such financial help as they were offered by the Super Seven came inevitably with crippling strings attached, and the kinds of reforms recommended by the developed countries were western in conception and origin and often proved inappropriate when attempted in Africa.

The result of these developments was that many African countries were unable to generate revenues that would permit meaningful programmes to improve their public health, transportation, education and other systems. The initial lack of infrastructures meant that it was almost impossible for them to compete against their industrialized neighbours.

These were the realities of 20th century Africa long after the Europeans had withdrawn. Blacks everywhere hoped that the Age of Independence would spawn a host of progressive and unselfish Messiahs bent on undoing the mischief of geography and history. Some able leaders did emerge, and no one can question the abilities of such individuals as Hastings Banda, Jomo Kenyatta, Kwame Nkrumah, Léopold Senghor and others. But while these patriots were most effective in destroying a colonial empire or two, they seldom succeeded in the vital matter of national construction.

Some apologists might argue that the African leaders of the mid-century were facing insoluble problems and that, in any case, the birth of new nations inevitably entail post-natal pangs. But most of the early nationalists were too impatient and often too dictatorial. Some ethnic minorities became too fearful of the misuse of authority and Africa consequently witnessed one bloody coup after another. Some leaders, too, found themselves caught in unsavoury ethnic politics and tended occasionally to favour their own community at the expense of others. To make matters worse, some African leaders unfortunately embezzled public funds that could have been more appropriately used to build roads, libraries, schools and hospitals.

Africa has thus been faced with a chronic crisis of leadership. Dictators have wantonly destroyed most of the democratic structures that the early nationalists tried so desperately to establish. In too many cases, the military became the dominant force and well-meaning politicians found themselves at the mercy of unscrupulous generals. The sad fact is that the tradition of military dictatorship is much stronger on this continent than is the western tradition of democracy. Monarchical absolutism has historically been the African norm, with the ruler dominating the witch-doctor priests (church), the local chiefs (state) and the armed forces.

So the picture of Africa at the threshold of the twenty-first century is an ugly one: a continent torn by civil strife, abject poverty and chronic misgovernment; a continent still left firmly in the financial, industrial and economic grip of the so-called developed world.

It is in this critical analysis of the situation that the solutions to the problems lie. It is clear that the continent needs a different type of leadership. Less trust must be placed in the ability of military minds. A greater effort has to be made to ensure the subordination of the army to the requirements of the state. Rule by fear and by force is seldom a satisfactory method of developing a national spirit and consciousness. Nationalism is one of the strongest forces in modern history and the Africans need to remember that the evolution of the national spirit takes time and effort. Ethnicity can eventually become submerged in the national flood, and this is more easily and effectively accomplished when policies of linguistic, cultural and political equality are honestly pursued.

Very few of the great nations in existence today began as single ethnic entities. It took a long and tortuous process of Russification, for example, to mould a variety of Slavic communities into the modern nation of Russia. The unification of Japan was finalized only in the sixteenth century after a long tradition of fragmentation. England arose after a patient fusion of Angles, Saxons, Celts, Jutes, Danes and Normans. Interestingly enough, it was the Normans who imposed a centralized system upon this motley collection from which modern England ultimately sprang. After five centuries of the so-called 'Norman Yoke', the English emerged with a powerful sense of national purpose which permitted them to defy the papacy as well as the Great Powers of Europe in the sixteenth century with impunity. The United States itself is a curious amalgam of European and other peoples but its powerful sense of nationalism has served as an awesome motivating impulse. It is obvious, then, that huge ethnic and linguistic barriers can be overcome in due course with patience and understanding.

Africans must aim at making constructive use of the centralizing agencies which the Europeans left in place. They have to learn to forget the pre-European phase of their history and strive more effectively for policies of co-operation and unity. Their leaders must abandon parochial approaches, attitudes and mentalities. Above all, they must be committed to the national cause and not to personal agendas. The first prerequisite is the forging of a national spirit and identity. Ethnolinguistic barriers must be destroyed at all costs and this can only be done by peaceful means if all ethnic minorities are treated with justice and respect. No longer should the Ibo feel superior to the Yoruba or vice versa. No longer should the Hutu see the need to lord it over the Tutsi or the Twa. No longer should the citizens of Burkina Faso make sharp distinctions among their Bobo, Fulani, Grosi, Gurma, Lobi, Mande, Mossi, Senufo and Tuareg descendants.

The second prerequisite is the grim determination of all African governments to improve the socioeconomic condition of the nation as a whole. Emphasis must be placed on three areas in particular: education, public health and technology. An educated community generally makes good political decisions and is not easily swayed by demagoguery. A solid education system has the merit also of providing the state with well-trained administrators, ambassadors, artists, bureaucrats, doctors, engineers, lawyers, nurses, politicians, priests and teachers.

African literacy rates, which are currently among the lowest in the world, must be improved. It is unacceptable that only 51% of adults in Burundi are literate and less than 30% in Burkina Faso. These statistics make very sad reading indeed. Even in Nigeria, which produced so many literary giants in the 20th century, the literacy rate was estimated in 2002 at no better than 64%. African governments must seriously and deliberately aim at training every member of their communities. Even their farming practices will profit from such a policy.

A healthy community is the primary precondition for all other kinds of growth There is no point in preparing the youth for academic, political or any other form of service if they are destined to live feebly and to die young. The physical vigour of a community is invariably a reflection of its overall well-being. Africans must therefore be prepared to invest more heavily in the building of hospitals for the care of the sick and injured and the erection of schools for the proper training of their nurses, physicians and surgeons.

And, of course, the development of modern technology gives hope for competing more successfully in this technological age. Africa must make every effort to reduce the technological gap between herself and the developed countries. She must never forget that it was largely Europe's lead in this department that allowed that continent to dominate the greater portion of the earth for almost 400 years.

What all of this means is that considerably less money and effort should therefore be devoted to military institutions and purposes. Unfortunately, most African nations in the period of Independence have exaggerated the need for defence and have created stronger armies than necessary. The soldiers in almost every African country have proved a greater threat to the security of their own state than anything posed by outsiders!

The third prerequisite is a strengthening or reconstruction of the

Organization of African Unity. The OAU was potentially an important force capable of exerting almost as much pressure as the European Common Market and the Organization of American States. That is to say, African leaders of the 21st century have to be more committed to a continental programme which provides a useful umbrella under which all member states can seek shelter. The recently established African Union (AU) is therefore a very welcome development indeed. Hopefully, it will be allowed to implement its ambitious programmes. Its major aims are to bring an end to the costly international wars that the continent has witnessed during the Age of Independence, to eliminate ethnic strife and conflict, to remove military rule and political oppression, to improve the quality of life of the impoverished millions of Africans and to establish a single African common market and economy. It can only succeed, however, with the full cooperation of its 53 member states.

The lesson here was effectively taught by the Arabs during the 1970s. They formed a cartel to control and monitor the production and distribution of their oil. OPEC gave them the sort of clout that they had previously lacked. The West could no longer determine the price of oil in unscrupulous and unilateral ways. Such a salutary lesson as this ought never to be ignored. African products may not be as vital to the West as Arab oil, but it is far better for all African farmers to work cooperatively than to compete foolishly and selfishly with each other in this difficult age of increasing globalization.

The recently established AU, if properly administered, can serve as an economic union and community in the same way that CARICOM is intended to operate in the West Indies. It can also monitor the behaviour of individual rulers to prevent aggressive acts by one African state at the expense of another. It can become, so to speak, the United Nations of the African Continent. But such an ideal can only be implemented if individual states are prepared to pursue peaceful policies and to surrender a small portion of their sovereignty.

One of the major problems thus far is that most African leaders have been prepared simply to blame their countries' misery on the behaviour of the imperialising powers who left the continent unprepared for self-government after the chaos resulting from the Great Scramble. No one can deny that the scars of empire went deep. But it is time to accept some responsibility for the scars of the present.

Far too many mistakes have been made by recent African leaders who have tended to multiply (rather than solve) the difficulties they inherited. There are too many examples of corruption and cruelty and these are totally unrelated to European forms of imperialism in a bygone generation. The proverbial buck, as they say in modern parlance, must now stop at

African leadership in the 21st century.

One very promising feature of African history in the last decade of the 20th century was the almost miraculous emergence of Nelson Mandela as the first democratically elected president of the Republic of South Africa. He did not begin on the premise that the Blacks should immediately and vindictively proceed to right the notorious wrongs committed during the age of apartheid. He promised a general amnesty to those who had cruelly oppressed his people and pledged himself to support the basic principles of racial equality and social justice. He saw racial, cultural and social harmony as an essential precondition for the creation of a powerful and healthy state. This great Messiah stressed forbearance, forgiveness, patience and generosity of spirit. By so doing, he was able (at least temporarily) to avoid the crippling disasters that have befallen Robert Mugabe in neighbouring Zimbabwe. There is, quite obviously, a crucial message here for all Africans as they prepare for the 21st century and beyond.

AFRICAN METHODIST EPISCOPAL CHURCH

This was the very first organization of any kind established by American Blacks. It began in 1786 as a small prayer band in St George's Church in Philadelphia, Pennsylvania. Its founder was Richard Allen (1760-1831). It inspired the appearance of several independent black Methodist churches all across the United States. Many local churches eventually became affiliated with the African Methodist Episcopal Church (AMEC) which controlled about 4,500 branches by the early 1970s when its total membership exceeded one million. More than 6,000 ordained clergymen are now attached to this organization, which published its own hymnal early in the nineteenth century. There are AMEC branches today in at least fourteen African countries, Canada, the Caribbean and South America. Once every four years, the AMEC holds a general conference to discuss matters of common concern.

AFRICAN UNION

Established in 2001, the African Union (AU) is an international organization consisting of fifty-three African member states. It is essentially an amalgamation of the older Organization of African Unity (OAU) and the African Economic Community (AEC). All the African states are represented with the solitary exception of Morocco which declined to enter. Eventually, the AU aims to have a single currency and a single integrated defence force, as well as other institutions of state, including a cabinet for the AU head of state. The purpose of the union is to help secure Africa's democracy, human rights and a sustainable economy, especially by bringing an end to ethnic conflicts and creating an effective common market. The

AU was officially launched when it held its first annual session in Durban on 9 July 2002 under the presidency of South Africa's Thabo Mbeki. The AU has a number of official bodies, of which the chief are: the Pan African Parliament; the Assembly of the African Union; the African Commission; the African Court of Justice; the Peace and Security Council; and the Economic, Social and Cultural Council. In addition there are three institutions to control the continental monetary system: the African Central Bank; the African Monetary Fund and the African Investment Bank. The major difficulties confronting the AU at its inception were health issues such as combatting malaria and the AIDS/HIV epidemic; political issues such as confronting undemocratic regimes; mediating in the many civil wars; and economic issues such as improving the standard of living of impoverished and illiterate Africans.

AGANAW ENGEDA

Born in 1903, Aganaw Engeda was an eminent Ethiopian artist and poet. He painted several murals in Addis Ababa and decorated the important church of Qachané Madhani Alam. After studying art in Paris, he returned to decorate the Ethiopian parliament at Addis Ababa, where he founded Ethiopia's first Art School. Aganaw Engeda was killed in an automobile accident in 1948. Several of his poems were published posthumously.

AGGREY, J.E.K.

Dr James Emman Kwegyir Aggrey, whose wise sayings are still quoted as proverbs in Ghana, was a pioneer of higher education for Africans. Born at Anomabu, just east of Cape Coast, on 18 October 1875, this son of a king's chief counsellor, was sent to the Cape Coast Methodist School at a young age and was appointed a teacher in charge of a small school at Abura Dunkwa when he was only fifteen. He received top honours in the Teachers' Certificate examination in 1895 and was awarded a prize by the Gold Coast Executive Council. A fierce opponent of British oppression, he joined the Aborigines' Rights Protection Society (ARPS) and took part in the agitation against the notorious Lands Bill of 1897. He became secretary of ARPS as well as the editor of its newspaper, the *Gold Coast Methodist Times*. In 1898 he left for the United States on a scholarship to the African Methodist Episcopal Zion (AMEZ) Church in New York City. He emerged with his BA in 1902, winning the Gold Medal as the best graduate that year and in 1912 was awarded a PhD from Hood Theological Seminary in Charlotte, North Carolina. After teaching for some years at Livingstone College in Salisbury, North Carolina, he was appointed a member of the Commission established in 1920 to enquire into education in Africa. Three years later he was also a member of the body which investigated educational conditions in East

Africa. Aggrey finally returned to the Gold Coast to help establish Achimota College near Accra, but he died shortly afterwards on 30 July 1927. He was deeply mourned throughout Africa, Europe and the United States. Achimota College named a Memorial Chapel and a House after him. A staunch believer in interracial harmony, he often made the remark that "You can play a tune of sorts on the white piano keys, and you can play a tune of sorts on the black keys, but for harmony you must use both the black and the white". His symbol of the black and white keys became the emblem of Achimota College. A private school, the Aggrey Studio in Barbados, West Indies, was also named after him. Publishing surprisingly little himself, his ideas appear mainly in various biographical studies and it is a reflection of his enormous reputation that his life has inspired so many biographies.

AGGREY, John

Born in 1808, John Aggrey was the first of the traditional chiefs to organize systematic protests against British administration in West Africa. He challenged the imperial parliament by establishing his own tribunal for Cape Coast, arguing that the British courts had no authority to interfere with purely African affairs. Convinced that the British were violating the terms of the Anglo-Fante alliance of 1844, he persisted with his hostility until his health failed. Aggrey was right to point out that the 'Bond' had not invested the British with any authority beyond helping the local chiefs in the conduct of certain judicial processes. He died, much lamented, in 1869 and is remembered now as an early Ghanaian nationalist.

AHIDJO, Ahmadou

Alhaji Ahmadou Ahidjo was the first elected president of independent Cameroon which he governed from 1960 until his voluntary retirement in 1982. He was born in Garoua on 24 August 1924 and educated in local schools. He served for some years as a radio operator before entering politics in 1946. In 1947 he was elected to a regional representative assembly and was re-elected in 1952 and 1956. He served as president of the assembly during 1956-57 and then as deputy prime minister (1957-58). Ahidjo founded his own party, the African Union Camerounaise, in 1958 and was proclaimed president of the Republic of Cameroon in 1960. In 1966 he formed another party, the Union Nationale Camerounaise, and declared Cameroon a one-party state. He then had no difficulty being re-elected president four times in succession. His rule was characterized by political stability and economic progress, but when he was accused by his successor and protégé, Paul Biya, of trying to regain power in 1983, he was condemned to death in absentia by a military tribunal. Ahidjo spent his last years in exile in southern France and in Senegal, where he died (at Dakar) on 30 November 1989.

AIDOO, Ama Ata

Christina Ama Ata Aidoo, a distinguished Ghanaian author and educator, was born on 23 March 1942. A graduate of the University of Ghana in 1964, she was appointed research fellow of the Institute of African Affairs before studying creative writing at Stanford University in the United States. Ama Ata Aidoo, who served for several years as a Professor of English at the University of Ghana, is an accomplished novelist, short story writer and playwright. Many of her short stories have been published in *Black Orpheus* and *Okyeame*. Among her plays, *Anowa*, has probably been her most successful. First published in 1970, it was produced to great acclaim in the United Kingdom in 1991. It is a symbolic dramatization of a nineteenth century Ghanaian legend about a young girl who rejects her parents' choice of a husband to marry a man of her own choosing. Aidoo's finest short-stories appear in the collection, *No Sweetness Here*, published in 1969, and her best-known plays include *Dilemma of a Ghost* (1965). In 1977, she published a semi-autobiographical novel, *Our Sister Killjoy; or Reflections from a Black-eyed Squint*. Her second novel, *Changes*, won the Commonwealth Writers Prize for the African Region in 1993. She also produced two collections of poems, *Someone Talking to Sometime* (1986) and *Birds and Other Poems* (1987). In addition, she wrote a children's book, *The Eagle and the Chicken* in 1987. Most of Aidoo's writing adroitly examines the clash of urban and rural cultures in modern Ghana and much of it has been reprinted in African anthologies. She moved to Zimbabwe in 1983 and worked for the Curriculum Development Unit of the Ministry of Education. She has also been a keen supporter of the Zimbabwe Women Writers Group.

AILEY, Alvin

Born on 5 January 1931 in Rogers, Texas, Alvin Ailey became an innovative dancer, director and choreographer who helped to establish modern dance as a popular art form in the United States. He founded the Alvin Ailey American Dance Theatre in 1958 and directed such choreographic masterpieces as *Blues Suite* (1958), *Revelations* (1960), *Quintet* (1968), *Masekela Language* (1969), *Cry* (1971) and *The Lark Ascending* (1972). One of the greatest male dancers of his generation, Ailey began his career as a member of the Lester Horton company and made his Broadway début in *House of Flowers* (1954). After dancing in the movie, *Carmen Jones*, Ailey decided to concentrate on choreography and began to synthesize elements of classical ballet, jazz dance and African-Caribbean dance with the more traditional styles and forms. His company soon became a showcase for such black choreographers as Talley Beatty, George Faison and Donald McKayle. His troupe, which began as exclusively black, gradually became multiracial during the 1960s. It served as a cultural ambassador and made numerous tours to Africa, Australia, Europe and the Far East. Ailey's influence on modern dance was simply enormous and this was recognized by such institutions as Cedar Crest College and Princeton University from which he received honorary doctorates of fine arts. He died on 1 December 1989. Many of his seventy-nine works are still being performed by such companies as the American Ballet Theatre, the Paris Opera Ballet, the English National Ballet, and the Royal Danish Ballet.

AKANDE, Zanana

In 1990, Zanana L. Akande, a Toronto native born in 1937, became the first black woman to be elected to the Ontario provincial parliament and represented the riding of St Andrew/St Patrick until 1994, after having taught for many years. She was appointed minister of community and social services and later served as parliamentary assistant to the premier. She became involved in several ministerial committees and was largely instrumental in establishing the programme which created over 5,000 summer jobs for youths across the province between 1991 and 1994. After her retirement from politics, she was elected president of Toronto's Urban Alliance on Race Relations. An active community servant, Zanana Akande has sat on numerous boards and committees and lectured to various groups, schools and organizations on such subjects as equity, effective communication and social change. She was also the co-founder of *Tiger Lily*, a magazine catering to the needs and interests of so-called 'Visible Minority' women. She has been the recipient of many prestigious awards.

AKAR, John Joseph

John Joseph Akar of Sierra Leone was a noted actor, broadcaster, diplomat, journalist, and author. Born at Rotifunk on 20 May 1927, he was educated at the Evangelical United Brethren Day School and the Albert Academy in Freetown, before furthering his studies in the United States at Oberlin College and the University of California at Berkeley. He then went on to the London University School of Economics (LSE) in England. Akar became director of broadcasting in Sierra Leone during 1960-66 and composed Sierra Leone's national anthem in 1961. He organized (and directed) the National Dance Troupe in Sierra Leone which soon established a worldwide reputation. Akar was appointed Sierra Leone's ambassador to the United States in 1969 but resigned when his country declared itself a republic in 1971. He spent his last years in Jamaica, West Indies, writing for the *Daily Gleaner*. He died there on 23 June 1975. His two best known plays were *Valley Without Echo* and *Cry Tamba*.

AKE, Claude

Born on 18 February 1939, Claude Ake was a noted Nigerian political scientist and activist who was an expert on African politics and economics. He founded the Centre for Advanced Social Sciences in Port Harcourt and served for many years as its director. A highly respected scholar, he was once invited to serve as a visiting professor at Yale University in the United States. In 1995 he resigned from a Shell Oil commission to protest the execution of Ken Saro-Wiwa and eight other activists by the Nigerian government. He died on 8 July 1996.

AKLILU HABTA-WOLD

Son of a Shawa clergyman, Aklilu Habta-Wold was born in Addis Ababa on 12 March 1912. He studied in academic institutions in Egypt and France and returned to Ethiopia after 1941 to give staunch support to Emperor Haile Selassie. He was largely instrumental in securing the Anglo-Ethiopian Agreement of 1944 and it was he who signed the UN Charter on behalf of Ethiopia in 1945. Aklilu Habta-Wold served as minister for foreign affairs for much of the period 1949-61 and did most to unite Ethiopia and Eritrea in 1952. One of the emperor's leading advisers throughout the 1960s, he paid the supreme penalty when Haile Selassie was overthrown. He was assassinated on 24 November 1974. Aklilu had done a great deal to modernize Ethiopia during the critical period which followed the Italian occupation (1935-41).

AKROFI, Clement Anderson

Born on 1 July 1901 at Aripede (about thirty miles north of Accra), Clement Anderson Akrofi became a noted educator, theologian and linguist. A leading authority on Twi, he advocated its adoption as Ghana's official language. He was educated at Basel Mission schools and the Akuporon Training College, where he returned as a teacher in 1923. His famous grammar text, *Twi Kasa Mmara*, was published in 1938. After his retirement from teaching in 1956, he devoted his energy to the Presbyterian church and produced a modern Twi Bible in 1965. Akrofi was honoured by the British Government with an MBE in 1944 and received an honorary doctorate from the Johannes Gutenberg University of Mainz, West Germany, in 1960. He remained a staunch supporter of Ghanaian independence and was often consulted on political matters by such Ghanaian leaders as Joseph Danquah and Kwame Nkrumah. He died on his 66th birthday in 1967.

AKU, Andreas

Revd Andreas Aku was a notable Ghanaian author and theologian who became the first indigenous head of the Ewe Presbyterian Church in 1922.

Born at Adaklu in 1863, he attended the Bremen Mission School at Waya before teaching at Keta during 1882-95. He then opened a new mission school at Lomé in Togo and was ordained a pastor there in 1910. Aku was the first scholar to translate the Bible into the Ewe language and he also completed an Ewe translation of John Bunyan's *Pilgrim's Progress*. In addition, he wrote a few biographies. He died in 1931 and is still remembered as one of Ghana's brightest individuals.

AKUFFO, F.W.K.

Frederick William Kwasi Akuffo was a paramount chief of Akuapem, a state in what is now southern Ghana, during the period 1895-1927. Educated at Basel Mission Schools and the Theological Seminary in Akuporon, he became a classical scholar and orator of note. He then served as an accountant before being installed as the omanhene of his state. His sympathy for the British produced some dissatisfaction among his people and he was 'destooled' in 1907. In 1920, however, he was reinstated. He built a great palace at Akuporon after the manner of European monarchs and urged his people to adopt European styles and systems. An ardent cocoa farmer, he encouraged the development of this industry by instituting prizes for farmers. Akuffo became a member of the Gold Coast Legislative Council in 1926 and of the newly created Joint Provincial Council of Chiefs in 1927, just before his death.

AKUFO-ADDO, Edward

Edward Akufo-Addo, a prominent Ghanaian lawyer and politician in the period after World War II, was born in Akuapem in 1906 and educated at Oxford University in England, where he studied mathematics. He then pursued a degree in law at the Middle Temple in London and was called to the bar in 1940. Returning to the Gold Coast, he quickly established a flourishing private practice in Accra and served briefly as a member of the Legislative Council, but was exiled for a period following the riots of 1948. After the Gold Coast achieved its political independence and changed its name to Ghana, Akufo-Addo served as a Supreme Court judge under President Kwame Nkrumah. In 1964, however, he was dismissed. When Nkrumah's regime was toppled in 1966, he was appointed chief justice of Ghana by the leaders of the military coup and was elected president in 1970 when civilian government was restored. But on 13 January 1972 Akufo-Addo's administration was overthrown by another military coup.

ALCINDOR, John

John Alcindor was born in Port-of-Spain, Trinidad, in 1873 and was educated at St Mary's College where he won an Island Scholarship which enabled him to pursue medical studies at the University of Edinburgh, Scotland. Following his graduation in 1899, he moved to London and worked in several hospitals. A highly respected physician who fought tirelessly to prevent the spread of tuberculosis and syphilis in Great Britain, he became senior district medical officer of the Metropolitan Borough of Paddington in 1917. He is still fondly remembered as the black doctor of Paddington who gave free medical treatment to his poorest patients. Alcindor was also an active community servant who preached a gospel of racial equality and was instrumental in the formation of the African Progress Union (APU) in 1918. He served as president of the APU from 1921 until his death in 1924. He also participated actively in the second Pan African Congress which met in 1921. He was one of the most eloquent spokesmen for the deliverance of the African and West Indian colonies from the European yoke.

ALDRIDGE, Ira

Ira Frederick Aldridge was born in New York on 24 July 1807 and became a leading Shakespearean actor in Britain and Europe. After attending the African Free School in New York City, he furthered his education in Glasgow, Scotland, and began a stage career that lasted from 1826 to 1865. He gave command performances before, and was honoured by, the monarchs of Austria, Prussia, Russia and Sweden. Billed as the 'African Roscius', after the great Roman comic actor, he made triumphant tours of Europe in several Shakespearean roles, including Othello, King Lear and Macbeth. Generally despised by the British press (especially in London), he played (after 1853) mostly on the continent, where he was revered. He was honoured with the title, Chevalier Ira Aldridge, Knight of Saxony. This great actor never had the opportunity to perform in his native country. Aldridge died in Poland, on 10 August 1867, while making arrangements for his first American tour.

ALEXANDER, Archie

The son of a janitor and a coachman, Archie Alphonso Alexander was born in Ottumwa, Iowa, on 14 May 1888. He became a very successful design and construction engineer after graduating in 1912 from the University of Iowa (where he had been the only black student). Denied access because of his race to any engineering post for which he applied, he worked as the foreman for a bridge-building company before opening his own business in 1917. In 1928 he founded Alexander and Repass which built several bridges, freeways, airfields, railroad trestles and power plants all across North America. Among Alexander's most famous legacies were the heating plant and powerhouse at the University of Iowa, a sewage treatment plant in Grand Rapids, an airfield in Tuskegee and the Whitehurst Freeway in Washington, D.C. In 1934 he was appointed one of the twelve commissioners who investigated the social and economic conditions in Haiti and in 1954 he became the first black governor of the United States Virgin Islands. In 1928 he was awarded the Spingarn Medal by the National Association for the Advancement of Colored People (NAACP) for his success in business, and in 1946 he received an honorary doctorate from Howard University. Alexander died on 4 January 1958 and left substantial sums in his will to provide engineering scholarships for needy students to attend Howard University, the University of Iowa and the Tuskegee Institute in Alabama.

ALEXANDER, Dounne

Born in Trinidad, Dounne Alexander emigrated with her parents to Britain in 1962 and worked for some years as a chemical/bacteriological technician and housing officer. In the 1980s, with no formal training or experience, she established her herbal food manufacturing business, 'GRAMMAS', named in memory of her grandmother. Displaying exceptional marketing skills, she convinced most of the leading supermarket chains to sell and distribute her products. She has won numerous national awards, including one for most outstanding British small business and another as 'Black Businesswoman of the Millennium'.

ALEXANDER, Lincoln

On 20 September 1985, when His Excellency Lincoln MacCaulay Alexander was installed as the Lieutenant Governor of Ontario, he became the first black person to hold a vice-regal office in Canada. Born in Toronto, Ontario, on 21 January 1922, he served as a radio operator in the Royal Canadian Air Force during World II before furthering his studies at McMaster University in Hamilton, Ontario (BA, 1949), and at Osgoode Law School in Toronto (LLB, 1953). He practised as a criminal lawyer in Hamilton and was given the honorary title of Queen's Counsel by the Ontario government in 1965. Entering politics in the late 1960s, Alexander became the first black member of the Canadian parliament when he was the only Conservative candidate elected from an Ontario urban centre in 1968. As the representative of Hamilton West, he served the opposition party as its spokesman on such important matters as housing, immigration, labour and welfare. He was also designated observer to the United Nations in 1976 and 1978. When Joe Clark served briefly as prime minister of Canada in 1979, Alexander was a member of his cabinet. In 1980 he resigned his parliamentary seat to become chairman of the Ontario Workmen's Compensation Board. He received the Man of the Year Award from the Ethnic Press Council of Canada in 1982 and was made a Commander of the Order of St John in 1983. He served as Lieutenant Governor of Ontario until 1992. His duties included summoning and dissolving the provincial legislature, giving assent to its bills, and reading the speech from the throne at the opening of each legislative session. To commemorate his term as Lieutenant Governor, the province of Ontario established the Lincoln Alexander Awards in 1993. In 1991, he was appointed Chancellor of the University of Guelph. Alexander's numerous awards and distinctions include no fewer than seven honorary doctorates and three schools and one highway have been named in his honour. He was awarded the Order of Ontario and made a Companion of the Order of Canada.

ALEXIS, Jacques Stéphen

Jacques Stéphen Alexis was born in Gonaïves, Haiti, on 22 April 1922. After studying in local schools and in Paris, he qualified as a medical doctor but was much more interested in politics and literature. After contributing to the overthrow of the Haitian government in 1946, he spent several years travelling extensively in China, the Middle East and the Soviet Union. He slipped back into Haiti secretly in 1961 but promptly vanished and is presumed to have been assassinated for political reasons. Alexis was an excellent writer of novels, such as *Compère Général Soleil* (1955), *Les Arbres musiciens* (1957), and *L'Espace d'un cillement* (1959). His numerous essays, short stories and critical works appeared in a variety of journals during the 1950s.

ALI, Muhammad

Born Cassius Marcellus Clay on 17 January 1942 in Louisville, Kentucky, this famous boxer first came to prominence when he won the light-heavyweight championship at the Rome Olympics in 1960. He became heavyweight champion of the world by defeating Sonny Liston in 1964. A convert to Islam, he refused induction into the US Army on religious grounds and was promptly stripped of his title in 1967. Successfully defying the establishment and refusing to take part in the Vietnam War, he regained his boxing license in 1970 and proceeded to become the first heavyweight champion to hold the title three times. Altogether, he won no fewer than 56 of his 61 professional bouts. A magnetic personality, Muhammad Ali was a popular and spectacular fighter who revolutionized his sport by adding speed and finesse to the heavyweight division. Generally regarded as the greatest of all heavyweight boxers, he is also well-known for his generous donations to charitable causes. During the 1960s, Muhammad Ali was one of the central figures in the fight for racial equality in the United States.

ALLEN, Lillian

Lillian Allen is an award-winning playwright, poet and writer of short stories. She is one of the important pioneers in the writing and performing of dub poetry, a highly politicized medium which is often set to music. She won Juno awards in the late 1980s for her recordings, *Revolutionary Tea Party* and *Conditions Critical*. Born in Jamaica on 5 April 1951, Lillian Allen immigrated to Canada in 1969 and has spent many years writing, publishing and performing in this country as well as Europe and the United States. She has also worked in film not only as a featured artist but as a co-producer and co-director. Her works include: *De Dub Poets* (a recording, 1984); *Curfew inna BC (*cassette, 1985); *If You See Truth* (1987); *Why Me* (1991); *Nothing But a Hero* (1992); *Women Do This Every Day* (1993); *Freedom and Dance* (CD, 1999); and *Psychic Unrest* (2000). Allen's best-known plays are *Art and Motherhood* (1985), *Love and Other Strange Things* (1991, 1993) and *Marketplace* (radio, 1995). A leading expert on cultural diversity and culture in Canada, Lillian Allen has been a consultant and advisor to all levels of government as well as community groups. She has also served as writer-in-residence at the University of Windsor and a professor at the Ontario College of Arts and Design.

ALLEN, Richard

This outstanding American religious leader was born into slavery in Delaware on 14 February 1760. He became a zealous Methodist preacher and succeeded in converting his own master who eventually sold him his freedom. Settling in Philadelphia in the late 1780s, he created a separate church for Blacks and eventually established the famous African Methodist Episcopal Church (AMEC) which is still in existence today. It began as the Methodist Bethel Church and gradually attracted a huge congregation with Allen as its pastor. In 1799, he became the first Black to be officially ordained in the ministry of the Methodist Episcopal Church and in 1816 became the first black bishop in America when elected by AMEC to assume this role. The Free African Society, which Allen and Revd Absalom Jones founded in 1787, was one of the first official organizations of African-Americans. A strong and consistent supporter of the anti-slavery movement, Revd Allen presided over the first Negro Convention and wrote several articles to the first African-American newspaper, *Freedom's Journal*. He died on 26 March 1831 but his African Methodist Episcopal Church remains the oldest and largest of all African-American organizations today.

ALLEYNE, George

Born in Barbados, West Indies, on 7 October 1932, Sir George Allenmore O'Garren Alleyne is one of the brightest medical minds ever produced by the Caribbean archipelago. After a brilliant career at Harrison College, a Barbados Scholarship took him to the University of the West Indies (UWI), from which he graduated as the gold medallist in medicine in 1957. During the early 1960s he completed a Doctorate in Medicine in the Tropical Metabolism Research Unit at the UWI, where he was appointed Professor of Medicine in 1972, rising to the chairmanship of his department by 1976. In 1977 Dr Alleyne was awarded the prestigious Sir Arthur Sims Commonwealth Travelling Professorship which involved lecturing in medical schools throughout Canada and the British Isles. Four years later, he was appointed Chief of the Research Unit at the Pan-American Health Organization (PAHO) and in 1983 became PAHO's Area Director of Health Programs Development. In 1990, Dr Alleyne was selected as the Assistant Director of PAHO and was unanimously elected Director of the whole organization in 1994, a position he held until his retirement in 2003. He was the first Caribbean person to hold this post. For his outstanding services to medicine and public health, Sir George Alleyne was knighted in 1990 and in 2001 he was awarded the Order of the Caribbean Community, the highest honour that can be conferred on a Caribbean national. He is currently Chancellor of the University of the West Indies and is the first graduate of the UWI to hold this title. His major concerns, as expressed in his numerous reports, speeches and publications, are equity in health care, health and development, and health care problems throughout the Caribbean. Dr Alleyne was elected Fellow of the Royal College of Physicians (London, England) and an Honorary Fellow of the American College of Physicians. He has also been offered honorary doctorates from various universities. Although officially retired, he continues (2006) to be the leader of an important Commission, established recently by the CARICOM governments to examine health issues confronting the region, including HIV/AIDS and their impact on national economies.

ALLSOPP, Herbert
Dr W. Herbert L. Allsopp has been the honorary consul for Ghana in British Columbia since 1991. He is also the principal fisheries development specialist of Smallwood Fishery Consultants, a company he created in 1983 and which has already undertaken almost 100 assignments for such agencies as the World Bank, Asian Development Bank, CIDA and FAO. Born in Guyana, Dr Allsopp emigrated to Canada in 1972 and has spent most of the last fifty years travelling to all parts of the world introducing techniques of fishery management to more than 100 countries. He began his career as the senior officer in charge of fisheries in Guyana during 1949-61. Working with the FAO, he then served as fishery development advisor to Togo during 1961-65, marine biologist and development advisor to Belize in 1965-66, and first senior regional fishery officer for Africa during 1966-72 when he was based in Ghana. In 1972 he was appointed fisheries associate director in Canada. Dr Allsopp conducted original

research on Manatees for control of aquatic weeds in Guyana, Florida and western Africa; established the very first shrimp culture production in South America in 1958; established a model resource management programme for tropical spiny lobsters in Belize; introduced Brazilian fish breeding systems to southeastern Asian aquaculture during the 1970s; and devised prototype programmes for the recovery of fish inadvertently caught in trawling for high-valued target species. Dr Allsopp, who has written more than sixty reports for publication by CIDA, FAO and numerous other organizations, has been honoured by several countries, including Belize, Djibouti, Guyana and Togo and by such institutions as the FAO, IDRC, and the University of Wisconsin.

ALUKO, Timothy

Timothy Mofolorunso Aluko, a noted Nigerian novelist, was born in Ilesha in western Nigeria on 14 June 1918. He attended elementary and secondary schools in his native district before furthering his education at the Government College in Ibadan. He studied civil engineering and town planning at the University of London, England, during 1946-50 and became the chief Town Engineer at Lagos. Aluko was then promoted to the post, which he held for many years, of director of public works for Nigeria's western region. He also taught engineering at the University of Lagos. His novels included *One Man, One Wife* (1959); *One Man, One Matchet* (1964); *Kinsman and Foreman* (1966) and *Chief, the Honourable Minister* (1970). These works paint a vivid picture of ordinary Africans struggling to cope with problems springing from the confusing clash of cultures in the twentieth century.

AMADI, Elechi

This fine Nigerian novelist, poet, playwright and teacher, born on 12 May 1934, was educated at the Government College at Umuahia and at Ibadan University where he earned a BA in mathematics and physics. He worked briefly as a land surveyor before being commissioned in the Nigerian army. In 1965, he shifted to teaching but entered politics in the 1970s and served as head of the Ministry of Information and the Ministry of Education. From 1984 to 1987 he was writer-in-residence and Dean of the Faculty of Arts at the College of Education in Port Harcourt. His best known novels are *The Concubine* (1966); *The Great Ponds* (1969); *The Slave* (1978) and *Estrangement* (1986). His plays include *Isiburu* (1973); *Road to Ibadan* (1977); *Pepper Soup* (1977) and *Dancer of Johannesburg* (1979). Amadi's *Sunset in Biafra* (1973) deals with his experiences during the civil war of 1967-70 in which he sympathised with the federalists despite his Ibo roots.

AMO, Anton Wilhelm

Anton Wilhelm Amo became famous as one of the earliest black scholars and philosophers to gain recognition in Europe. Born around 1703, he was just about four years old when presented as a gift from a Dutch trader to the Duke of Brunswick-Wolfenbuttel. The duke's son, however, accepted him as a toy rather than a slave and had him properly treated and educated. The precocious Amo quickly became proficient in several languages, including Dutch, French, German, Greek, Hebrew and Latin. He studied, and later taught, at the Universities of Halle, Jena and Wittenberg. He became a member of several learned societies in Europe and lectured on such subjects as astronomy, geomancy, logic, metaphysics, palmistry and physiology. Amo returned to West Africa in 1753 and worked briefly as a goldsmith He died on 3 March 1756. His fame in eighteenth century Europe was rare for an African and helped to arouse interest in Africa among the educated élite there.

AMOS, Baroness

Valerie Ann Amos, Baroness Amos, created history in the United Kingdom in 2004 when she became the first black female member of the British cabinet and the first Black to become Leader of the House of Lords and Lord President of the Council. During 2001-03, she had served as parliamentary undersecretary for foreign and Commonwealth affairs. Previously she had been a Government Whip in the House of Lords and a spokesperson on social security, international development and women's issues. Born in Guyana on 13 March 1954, she emigrated to the United Kingdom and was educated at Townley Grammar School for Girls before completing a degree in sociology at Warwick University, a master's degree in cultural studies at Birmingham University and doctoral research at the University of East Anglia. Lady Amos began her career in local government, working in various London boroughs during the 1980s. She was chief executive of the Equal Opportunities Commission from 1989 to 1994 and then director of Amos Bernard during 1995-98. She was chair of the Runnymede Trust, a trustee of the Institute of Public Policy Research, a trustee of Voluntary Services Overseas, and chair of the Alfya Trust. She was also very active in Project Hope, a non-profit organization which promotes healthcare. Her charity works have involved being the chair of the board of governors at the Royal College of Nursing Institute (1994-98) and one of the directors of Hampstead Theatre. She was created a Life Peer in August 1997 as Baroness Amos of Brondesbury in the London Borough of Brent. She has been the recipient of numerous awards, including honorary doctorates from the Universities of Leicester and Warwick and an honorary professorship at Thames Valley University in 1995 in recognition of her work on equality and social justice. She is only the third woman in history to lead the upper house of parliament in the United Kingdom.

ANDERSON, Marian

One of the most popular American singers of her generation, Marian Anderson was born in Philadelphia, Pennsylvania, on 17 February 1902. This remarkable contralto became (in 1955) the first black person to perform at the Metropolitan Opera. She gave royal command performances for the kings of Denmark and Sweden during the 1930s. Because of her race, however, the Daughters of the American Revolution (DAR) refused to allow her to sing at Constitution Hall in Washington, D.C. In protest, Eleanor Roosevelt, the first lady, resigned from DAR and arranged for Anderson to present a free Easter Sunday concert, on 9 April 1939, at the Lincoln Memorial, where an estimated 75,000 admirers flocked to hear her sing such spirituals as 'My Soul is Anchored in the Lord' and 'Gospel Train' as well as Schubert's 'Ave Maria'. Anderson toured India and the Far East in 1957 as an emissary of the United States government and was named an American delegate to the 13th General Assembly of the United Nations in 1958. She was awarded the Spingarn Medal in 1939, the Presidential Medal of Freedom in 1963, a Kennedy Center Honor in 1978, and the National Arts Medal in 1986. In 1980 her image was minted on a congressional gold medal. Marian Anderson died on 8 April 1993. Her autobiography, *My Lord, What a Morning*, was published in 1956. Her legacy includes the annual Marian Anderson Award, established since 1942, to provide scholarships to promising young singers.

ANDERSON, Michael

Lt Col Michael Philip Anderson was one among a handful of Blacks selected by NASA to join a crew of astronauts. He was a member of the Space Shuttle *Columbia* that crashed sixteen minutes prior to its scheduled landing on 1 February 2003, killing all aboard. Born in Plattsburg, New York, on 25 December 1959, he studied physics and astronomy at the University of Washington and Creighton University. He joined the United States Air Force, in which he held many important posts, including that of an aircraft commander and instructor pilot in the 920th Air Refuelling Squadron, Wurtsmith Air Force Base, Michigan. He logged about 3000 hours in various types of aircraft before being selected by NASA in 1994 to join the space programme. His flight experience prior to the fatal crash included a nine-day trip aboard *Endeavour* in January 1998 during which Anderson travelled 3.6 million miles in 138 orbits of the earth. He was posthumously awarded the Congressional Space Medal of Honour, the NASA Space Flight Medal, the NASA Distinguished Medal and the Defence Distinguished Service Medal.

ANDERSON, Viv

Born to West Indian parents in Nottingham, England, on 29 July 1956, Vivian Alexander Anderson became the first black football player to represent England in international competition when he made his début against Czechoslovakia in 1978. During a long and stellar career, he led many English clubs to league and division championships. He played for Nottingham Forest, Arsenal, Manchester United, Sheffield Wednesday, Barnsley and Middlesbrough between 1974 and 1995. He managed Barnsley briefly before serving as an assistant to Bryan Robson at Middlesborough until his retirement in 2001. He was inducted into the English Football Hall of Fame in 2004. Anderson was also awarded an MBE by the British Government for his services to football.

ANDRADE, Mario

Mario Coelho Pinto de Andrade was an outstanding Angolan writer and nationalist leader. Born in Golungo Alto on 21 August 1928, he was the founder and former president (1960-62) of the Popular Movement for the Liberation of Angola (MPLA) and the editor of several collections of Portuguese-language African poems. He attended the University of Lisbon where he met such notable African nationalists as Agostinho Neto (who later became Angola's first president) and Amilcar Cabral (the future president of Guinea-Bissau). Andrade also studied at the Sorbonne in Paris where he wrote some acrid anticolonialist poetry and joined the staff of the cultural review, *Présence Africaine*. He co-operated with Neto at first and played a key role in the early development of the MPLA but later seceded from the party and founded his own opposition group, Revolta Activa. Andrade eventually migrated to Guinea-Bissau and served as a cabinet minister under Cabral. Fluent in two languages, his works included such anthologies as *Letteratura Negra* (1961) and *La Poésie Africaine d'Espression Portugaise* (1969). He died on 26 August 1990.

ANGELOU, Maya

This distinguished poet, best-selling author, dancer, educator, civil rights activist, director and producer was born in St Louis, Missouri, in 1928. After studying dance under Martha Graham, Ann Halprin and Pearl Primus, she spent sixteen years as a professional dancer and entertainer. As part of the US State Department tour in 1954-55, she visited twenty-two countries performing and teaching dance. During the early 1960s, Maya Angelou wrote several songs for B.B. King and numerous articles for the *African Review* in Ghana and the *Arab Observer* in Egypt. The story of her unhappy childhood was told in her best-selling autobiography, *I Know Why the Caged Bird Sings*, first published in 1970. Another best-seller is the more recent *A Song Flung Up to Heaven*. Angelou eventually produced three more autobiographical works: *Gather Together in My Name* (1974), *Singin' and Swingin' and Gettin' Merry Like Christmas* (1976) and *The Heart of a Woman* (1981). One of her latest novels is the much acclaimed *I Wouldn't Take Nothing for My Journey Now* (1993). She has also written five collections of poetry: *Just Give Me a Cool Drink of Water 'Fore I Diiie*; *Oh Pray My Wings are Gonna Fit Me Well*; *And Still I Rise*; *I Shall Not Be Moved*; and *Shaker, Why Don't You Sing?* In film and television, Angelou authored the original screenplay and musical score for *Georgia, Georgia*, and wrote and produced a ten-part series on African traditions in American life. She served for some years as the Northern Co-ordinator for the Southern Christian Leadership Conference (SCLC) and in 1975 received the *Ladies' Home Journal* Woman of the Year Award. The recipient of several honours, awards and honorary degrees, Maya Angelou was appointed by President Gerald R. Ford to the American Revolution Bicentennial Advisory Council and by President Jimmy Carter to the National Commission on the Observance of International Women's Year. In 1993, she became only the second poet in the history of the United States to have the honour of writing and reciting original work at the Presidential Inauguration. She is on the board of trustees of the American Film Institute and one of the few women members of the Directors Guild. Mayo Angelou has also served as Reynolds Professor at Wake Forest University in Winston-Salem, North Carolina.

ANIONWU, Elizabeth

Professor Elizabeth Anionwu is a nurse and Head of the Mary Seacole Centre for Nursing Practice at Thames Valley University and Honorary Professor of the London School of Hygiene and Tropical Medicine. She is also the vice-chairperson and treasurer of the Mary Seacole Memorial Statue Appeal. Her specialty is the treatment of sickle cell and thalassaemia on which she has published numerous articles in medical journals as well as chapters in scholarly books. Her role model and major source of inspiration is the legendary Mary Seacole about whom she wrote a biography in 2005. Professor Anionwu is a Fellow of the Royal College of Nursing.

ANNAN, Kofi

On 1 January 1997, Kofi Atta Annan of Ghana became the first person from sub-Saharan Africa to be elected secretary-general of the United Nations. He was also the first secretary-general to rise through the ranks of the UN organization to its highest office. He had joined the UN in 1962 as a budget officer for the World Health Organization (WHO) in Geneva. By 1990 he had become assistant secretary-general and controller for programme planning, budget and finance. In 1993 he was promoted to under-secretary-general of peacekeeping operations. Born on 8 April 1938 in Kumasi, Gold Coast, Kofi Annan was the son of the governor of Ashanti province and a hereditary chief of the Fante people. He was educated at the University of Science and Technology in Kumasi, at Macalester College in Minnesota, and at the Massachusetts Institute of Technology. In 1977 he proposed a plan for the restructuring of the UN bureaucracy not only to make it more efficient but to improve relations with the United States, its host nation. He was faced twenty years later with the monumental task of streamlining the UN bureaucracy, rethinking its basic role as an international organization, and persuading the United States to remit its membership dues then more than $1.5 billion in arrears. Fluent in several languages, he has tried his best to make the UN a respected and powerful force in world politics but has not always received the co-operation of the United States. Among his particular concerns are HIV/AIDS, terrorism, poverty and inequality. In 1998, he was awarded an honorary doctorate by the University of the West Indies. Since then he has received many similar awards from other academic institutions in Africa, Asia, Europe and North America. Annan shared the Nobel Peace Prize in 2001 and was re-appointed by the UN Member States to a second term as secretary general in 2002.

ANOZIE, Sunday
Sunday Ogbonna Anozie, a noted Nigerian critic and scholar, whose works appeared both in English and French, was born in 1942. He was educated in local schools before earning a BA from the University of Nsukka (Nigeria) in 1963. Pursuing further studies at the Sorbonne Paris (France), he achieved a doctorate in sociology and returned briefly to his native country where he edited the Biafran journal, *Conch*, devoted to African culture and literature. Emigrating to the United States, Anozie then taught English at the University of Texas. His best known books are *Sociologie du Roman Africain* (1970) and *Christopher Okigbo: Creative Rhetoric* (1972), an excellent study of that Nigerian poet.

ANTHONY, Michael
Michael Anthony is a noted Trinidadian author and journalist. Born in Mayaro on 10 February 1932, he was educated in his native island before spending 14 years in London, England, where he worked at Reuters. He returned to Trinidad in 1970 to join the staff of the Ministry of Culture. Anthony has written a number of short stories, but much better known are his novels, which include *The Games Were Coming* (1963); *The Year in San Fernando* (1965); *Green Days by the River* (1967); *Streets of Conflict* (1976); *Bright Road to El Dorado* (1981) and *A Better and Brighter Day* (1987).

APPELT, Pamela

In 1987, Judge Pamela Appelt became the first black woman to be appointed to the Court of Canadian Citizenship, a position she held until 2000. Born in Jamaica, she completed her education in microbiology and biochemistry in the United Kingdom before emigrating to Canada in 1966. She worked for some years as a biochemist in Montreal and a researcher in medical biochemistry at McGill University. An enthusiastic community servant, she has delivered several speeches to groups and organizations on violence against women and children. Her known concern for human rights, especially as they relate to women and youth, led in 1999 to her appointment by the province of Ontario as a member of the Custody Review Board and the Child and Family Review Board. Pamela Appelt is also an artist who specializes in three-dimensional découpage. Her works have been exhibited in Canada, Jamaica and the United States. In 1981 she became the first non-American to open at the Recreation Centre, where she featured the *Jamaican Hibiscus* and the *Humming Bird* in her display.

ARCHER, John

The son of a Barbadian father and an Irish mother, John Richard Archer was born in Liverpool on 8 June 1863. After working for many years as a seaman, he settled in Battersea to run a small photographic studio. In 1906 he became the first black person to be elected to public office in Britain when he was elected to the Battersea Borough Council. An ardent liberal, he campaigned successfully for an increased minimum wage for council workers and was re-elected in 1912. One year later, he was elected mayor of Battersea, the first black person to attain such an office in the United Kingdom. Moving further to the left, he joined the Labour Party but failed to win a parliamentary seat in 1919. He became president of the African Progress Union, working for black empowerment and equality. In 1919 he was a British delegate to the Pan-African Congress in London. Archer served as a governor of Battersea Polytechnic, president of the Nine Elms Swimming Club, chair of the Whitley Council Staff Committee and a member of the Wandsworth Board of Guardians. At the time of his death in July 1932, he was deputy leader of Battersea council. When he attended the second Pan African Congress in 1921, he became the first British-born black person to represent his country at an international conference abroad.

ARMAH, Ayi Kwei

Born in 1938, Ayi Kwei Armah has become a distinguished Ghanaian poet, short-story writer, novelist and journalist. Educated at local schools initially, he proceeded to attend Harvard University in the United States to achieve his BA. He then worked for some years as a French-English translator,

English teacher, and television scriptwriter before joining the academic staff at the University of Massachusetts. Armah has written several articles and short stories in both American and African periodicals. He published such fine novels as *The Beautiful Ones Are Not Yet Born* (1968), *Fragments* (1970) and *Why Are We So Blest?* (1971). His short stories include *Yaw Manu's Charm*, which appeared in *Atlantic* (1968), and *The Offal Kind*, published in *Harper's Magazine* (1969). His best known poem perhaps is *Aftermath* which was reprinted in 1971 in an anthology, entitled *Messages from Ghana*. In all of his works, Armah has remained a violent critic of the political leadership since independence in Ghana and other African countries.

ARMATRADING, Joan

An outstanding singer, guitarist and songwriter, Joan Anita Barbara Armatrading was born in Basseterre, St Kitts, on 9 December 1950 and raised in Birmingham, England. Her uncanny ability to range from folk to pop to rock and jazz and even to reggae had won her two Grammy nominations, 18 gold records and 10 platinum albums in seven countries by 1980 before she was thirty years old. Her biggest UK hit songs perhaps have been *Love and Affection*; *Me, Myself and I*, and *Drop the Pilot*. Her most successful albums include *Track Record* (1983); *The Very Best of Joan Armatrading* (1991); *Love and Affection; Best of Joan Armatrading* (1999), and *Love and Affection: Classics* (2003).

ARMATTOE, Raphael

Dr Raphael Ernest Grail Glikpo Armattoe, born on 13 August 1913, became a Togolese poet and historian of some note although he began his career as an anthropologist and finished up being a medical doctor. Two collections of his poetry were printed: *Between the Forest and the Sea* (1950) and *Deep Down the Black Man's Mind* (1954). They did not, however, include *Servant Kings*, perhaps his very best poem, which was republished in 1967 in *West African Verse*. A staunch supporter of Togolese unity and independence, Dr Armattoe led a delegation to the United Nations in 1953 seeking international support for a union between British and French Togo. He died on 12 December that same year.

ARMSTRONG, Bromley

Bromley Armstrong immigrated from Jamaica to Canada in 1947 and has been a most active community servant ever since. He was one of the leaders of the United Auto Workers Union during the 1950s and was the youngest member of the famous delegation which went to Ottawa in 1954 to protest Canada's racist immigration policies. He was also involved in the struggle to enforce the Employment and Accommodation Acts of the 1960s.

Armstrong was a founding member of numerous community organizations, including BIG Investments, the Jamaican Canadian Credit Union, the National Council of Jamaican and Supportive Organizations in Canada and the Urban Alliance Race Relations Committee. In the meantime, he served on several boards and committees, including the Ontario Labour Relations Board, the Ontario Human Rights Commission and the Ontario Advisory Council on Multiculturalism. Armstrong has been the recipient of numerous honours and distinctions, including the Harry Jerome Award for Community Service, 1990; the Order of Distinction, Jamaica, 1983; the Order of Ontario, 1992 and the Order of Canada, 1994.

ARMSTRONG, Louis

Better known as Satchmo, Daniel Louis Armstrong was born in New Orleans, Louisiana, on 4 July 1900. He became one of the most influential of all jazz musicians. The series of recordings he made between 1925 and 1928, with his Hot Five and Hot Seven ensembles, established the pre-eminence of the virtuoso soloist. His mode of singing and handling the trumpet led to the evolution of the swing band during the 1930s and 1940s. With his instrumental range and extroverted style, Armstrong brought jazz to millions of people who had previously cared little for the music. He made several goodwill tours to Europe during the inter-war years and appeared in a number of films, including *Pennies from Heaven* (1936), *Cabin in the Sky* (1943), *The Glenn Miller Story* (1953) and *Hello Dolly* (1969). A very popular band-leader, film star, composer and comedian, Louis Armstrong died on 6 July 1971.

ARNOLD, Jennette

Born in Montserrat, West Indies, Jennette Arnold emigrated to the United Kingdom and pursued a successful career in nursing. She then worked as an industrial relations officer and as regional director of services and special adviser (Equalities) to the general secretary of the Royal College of Nursing. She later became one of the driving forces with Beacon Associates, a training and organizational development consultancy. Jennette Arnold has been instrumental in facilitating, motivating and enabling a large number of black professionals to maximise their potential through personal development, mentorship and management training. She has also been the mayor's cabinet advisor, a London Assembly member and co-founder of the London Black Women Council.

ARTHUR, Owen Seymour

The Hon Owen Seymour Arthur, who has served as prime minister of Barbados since 1994, was born in that Caribbean island on 12 October

1949. Educated at All Saints' Boys' School, Coleridge-Parry School and Harrison College, he achieved two degrees in economics from the University of the West Indies (UWI). He began his career as an economist in Jamaica during the early 1970s and soon rose to the post of Chief Economic Planner at the National Planning Agency there. Between 1979 and 1981, Arthur served as Director of Economics at the Jamaica Bauxite Institute. He represented Jamaica on UNCTAD's Inter-Governmental Group of Exports on the Transfer of Technology in 1975 and 1976 and was a member of the OAS Task Force on Technology Transfer in the Caribbean later in that decade. Returning to Barbados in 1981, Arthur took up the post of Chief Project Analyst in the Ministry of Finance and Planning and was appointed to the Barbados Senate in 1983. One year later, he won a seat in the national parliament and soon became one of the leaders of the Barbados Labour Party (BLP) which he led to a signal triumph on 6 September 1994. The success of his social and economic policies produced the most one-sided election in his country's history in January 1999 when the Democratic Labour Party (DLP), which had governed with sizeable majorities from 1986 to 1994, was suddenly limited to a single seat. His party won again in the general elections of 2005. Arthur is not only a successful politician. He is a well-known consultant and economist, whose publications include: *The Commercialisation of Technology in Jamaica* (1979); *Energy and Mineral Resource Development in the Jamaica Bauxite Industry* (1981); and *The IMF and Economic Stabilisation Policies in Barbados* (1984). For some years he served also as a part-time lecturer in the Department of Management at the UWI and has been a member of several important Boards of Directors in Barbados.

ASAFU-ADJAYE, Edward

Sir Edward Okyere Asafu-Adjaye was the very first Asante lawyer. Descended from an Asante royal family, he was born in 1903 and educated at the Kumasi Government Boys' School before attending the University of London, England, where he won the prestigious Profumo Prize and was called the bar in 1927. He set up his private practice in Accra and took an active interest in local and national politics. He became a firm supporter of Ghanaian nationalism during the 1930s. He was a member of the Kumasi Town Council and of the so-called Confederacy Council for many years. During the early 1950s he served under Kwame Nkrumah first as minister of local government (1951-54) and then as minister of trade and labour in 1955. In 1957, he was appointed an ambassador to France and, in the early 1960s, was a member of the United Nations Committee which investigated apartheid in South Africa. His international reputation as a lawyer and a diplomat led to his being appointed also to the commission established by

Great Britain to enquire into the disturbances that had occurred in British Guiana. He later served as chairman of the commission which exposed the conditions prevailing in Ghana's prisons during Nkrumah's administration. In addition to his legal and political assignments, Asafu-Adjaye was a director of Barclay's Bank (Ghana) Ltd, Mobil Oil (Ghana Ltd) and the Consolidated African Selection Trust Ltd. He also served as president of the African Liberal Council in Accra. Sir Edward Asafu-Adjaye died on 27 February 1976. He had been knighted for his services to Ghana and is best remembered perhaps as his country's first High Commissioner to the United Kingdom after its achievement of political independence in 1957.

ASAMOA, Erasmus

Revd Erasmus Awuko Asamoa was an educator and religious leader who advocated the use of African languages in Ghanaian schools. Born in 1901, he studied at the Presbyterian Training College in Akuporon before attending the Basel Missenhaus in Switzerland. He proceeded to the University of Edinburgh (Scotland) where he obtained his MA in moral philosophy in 1954. He became the first African principal of the St Andrews Training College at Mampon (1956-62) and was then appointed principal of the Presbyterian Training College at Akuporon. He was the first African to achieve this distinction. He died in 1965.

ASANTE, David

Revd David Asante became a missionary with the Basel Lutheran Mission and helped to make Twi the powerful literary language that it became in the twentieth century. Born in Akuporon on 23 December 1834, Asante was converted to Christianity at an early age and was among the first African students to attend the Akuporon Basel Mission Seminary. He then studied at institutions in Basel during 1857-62. He eventually did great missionary work at Larteh and Gyadam, promoting the use of Twi as well as English, and founded a Christian School at Kukurantumi. He did much to revive Christianity in Anum as well as certain parts of Togoland. Asante was instrumental in producing a Twi translation of the Bible and produced several books in Twi and a number of translations. He also wrote a Twi hymn and coined several new Twi words. He died at Akuporon on 13 October 1892.

ASANTEWA, Yaa

Yaa Asantewa is one of the most famous of all Ghanaian heroines. She is best remembered for her unrelenting hostility to the British, whose arrogance she despised. She incited numerous rebellions against the new régime during the 1880s and 1890s, culminating in the great revolt of 1900 when the British governor, Sir Frederick Hodgson, was besieged in the fort at Kumasi and had to be rescued by a British expeditionary force. As one of the ring-leaders of this uprising, Yaa Asantewa was exiled to the Seychelles Islands in the Indian Ocean. She died there in the early 1920s but has not yet been forgotten by her compatriots.

ASHE, Arthur

Born in Richmond, Virginia, on 10 July 1943, Arthur Ashe was the first black tennis player to gain selection to an American Davis Cup team (1963). He graduated from UCLA in 1966 after having led his team to the NCAA championship in 1965. Ashe became the first African-American male to win such major tennis titles as the US amateur championship in 1968, the Australian Open in 1970 and the men's singles at Wimbledon in 1975. In 1985 he was inducted into the International Tennis Hall of Fame. He published an autobiography, *Off the Court* (1981), and the three-volume *A Hard Road to Glory: A History of the African-American Athlete* (1988). Ashe died on 6 February 1993. He was a noted political and social activist who devoted much of his time and energy to such causes as the anti-apartheid movement in South Africa, the plight of Haitian refugees and inner-city youth in the United States, and the education of people about AIDS, the disease that claimed his life. Part of his legacy was the organization of the Arthur Ashe Foundation for the Defeat of AIDS. At Flushing Meadows, New Jersey, where the United States Tennis Association (USTA) annually holds its open championship, the Arthur Ashe Stadium has been named for him.

ASKIA DAUD

The great Songhai Empire in northwestern Africa reached its zenith during the reign of Askia Daud, a remarkably able ruler (1549-82) and a direct descendant of Muhammad Touré (another famous Songhai emperor). A brilliant general as well as an efficient administrator, Askia Daud stretched his dominion from the Atlas Mountains of northern Africa to the tropical Cameroon forests. It embraced literally thousands of ethnic groups and cultures and was one of the most expansive empires of that day. It thus required considerable skill to keep it intact and, shortly after Askia Daud's death, his system began to fall apart. His immediate successors lacked both his strength and his tact. A Hausa revolt seriously weakened the empire in the 1580s and its collapse was completed by a series of Moroccan invasions after 1591, from which the Songhai Empire has not yet recovered.

ATABIA

One of the greatest of all West African chiefs, Na Atabia governed Mamprusi, in what is now northeastern Ghana, for more than half a century (1688-1741). He transformed a very small princedom into a huge territorial empire through his skill as a soldier, an administrator and a diplomat. He provided such efficient government that the region enjoyed several years of tranquillity and prosperous trade. He also offered protection to the Muslims whom he placed in positions of authority. Thus, by the time of his death, Mamprusi had become a highly centralized and Islamic state.

ATTOH-AHUMA, S.R.B.

Revd Samuel Richard Brew Attoh-Ahuma was born on 22 December 1863 in Cape Coast where, in turn, he attended the Wesleyan Elementary School, the Wesleyan High School and Richmond College. He was ordained a Methodist priest but was expelled for his virulent criticisms of the Lands Bill of 1897. He became a member of the Aborigines' Rights Protection Society (ARPS), eventually served as its secretary and edited its newspaper, *The Gold Coast Nation*, for many years. Returning to the Methodist Church in 1920, he founded a number of religious clubs and Sunday Schools. A bitter opponent of the colonial system, Attoh-Ahuma wrote several books promoting the principle of racial equality and justice for native Africans. His most notable works were *Memoirs of West African Celebrities* (1903), *The Gold Coast Nation and National Consciousness* (1911), *Cruel as the Grave* (1913), and *His Quest and Conquest* (1917). He died on 15 December 1921.

AUGUSTA, Alexander

Dr Alexander Thomas Augusta was born on 8 March 1825 in Norfolk, Virginia. Denied access to medical training in the United States, he began his career as a barber before moving to Canada in the hope of studying medicine at the University of Toronto. Gaining acceptance, he qualified as a doctor and established a successful private practice in Canada. He returned to the United States in 1863 and became the first black surgeon in the US army during the Civil War. In 1865, he was promoted to the rank of Lieutenant Colonel, the first Black ever to gain this stature. After the Civil War, Dr Augusta continued private practice in Washington, D.C. and taught in the newly-founded Howard University Medical Department. He retired from Howard University in 1877 but continued to practise medicine until his death in 1890.

AUGUSTINE, Jean

A West Indian by birth, the Hon Dr Jean Augustine is an eminent Canadian educator and politician who served for many years as the president of the Congress of Black Women in Canada. After emigrating from Grenada in 1960, she received the degrees of BA, MEd and an honorary LLD from the University of Toronto. In 1993 she was among the first black women ever to be elected to the Canadian House of Commons and was re-elected twice afterwards. In that forum she continued for many years to advocate the principles of racial and gender equality. She chaired the Canadian Association of Parliamentarians on Population and Development, the Microcredit Summit Council of Canadian Parliamentarians, the National Liberal Women's Caucus and the all-party National Sugar Caucus. In addition, she was an active member of the Standing Committee on Foreign Affairs and International Trade and the Standing Committee on Citizenship and Immigration. In 2002, she was appointed secretary of state (multiculturalism and status of women), becoming the first black woman to serve in the Canadian cabinet. She was responsible for having February declared nationally as Black History Month. She retired from politics in 2005. An outstanding community servant, Dr Augustine has received the Kay Livingstone Award for Commitment to Black Women's Issues, the YWCA Women of Distinction Award for Community Service, the Women on the Move Award from *The Toronto Sun,* Ontario's Volunteer Award and Pin, the Caribana Achievement Award, the Bob Marley Award for her service to the Caribbean community in Canada and the 1994 Canadian Black Achievement Award. Before her entry into politics, she was an elementary school principal with the Toronto District Catholic School Board and served as chair of the Metro Toronto Housing Authority. For several years, Dr Augustine has served on a variety of other important Boards, including the York University Board of Governors. Through fund-raising, she supports the Jean Augustine Scholarship Fund which assists single mothers to undertake post-secondary study at George Brown College.

AWOLOWO, Obafemi

Born at Ijebu-Remo in western Nigeria on 6 March 1909, Chief Obafemi Awolowo attended Anglican and Methodist schools in Ikene and Abeokuta before he became a largely self-taught journalist and trader. He organised the Nigerian Motor Transport Traders Association while he was working as an editor of the *Nigerian Worker* and founded the Trade Union Congress of Nigeria in 1943. While in England studying law during 1944-47, Awolowo founded the Yoruba cultural and political group, known as the Egbe Omo Oduduwa and published his *Path to Nigerian Freedom* (1947), recommending a federation in which each ethnic group enjoyed a certain measure of local autonomy. He returned to Ibadan to practice law while launching himself into local politics. His Egbe Omo Oduduwa became a powerful force in western Nigeria, sweeping the elections of 1951 and carrying Awolowo himself to victory in his native constituency (Ijebu-Remo). He became premier of the Western region in 1954 and headed the federal opposition in 1959. Political squabbles in western Nigeria during the early 1960s led to

Awolowo's imprisonment but he was re-elected as soon as he was released from jail. In 1966 he was formally elected chief of the Yoruba. He not only played a prominent role in Nigerian politics for many years but was a prolific writer. His books included *The Autobiography of Chief Obafemi Awolowo* (1960), *My Early Life* (1968), *Thoughts on the Nigerian Constitution* (1967), *The People's Republic* (1968), and *The Strategy and Tactics of the People's Republic of Nigeria* (1970). He died on 9 May 1987.

AWOONOR, Kofi

Son of a Sierra Leonean father and a Togolese mother, Kofi Awoonor was born in the Gold Coast on 13 March 1935. He was educated in Ghanaian schools, including Achimota College and the Institute of African Studies, before proceeding to the University of London, England, where he achieved his MA in 1968. He returned to Ghana to edit the very influential literary journal, *Okyeame*, encouraging several young Africans by publishing their works. Awoonor eventually emigrated to the United States where he became chairman of the comparative literature programme at the Stony Brook campus of the State University of New York (SUNY). A prolific writer himself, he produced numerous poems, some of which appeared in *Rediscovery and Other Poems* (1964); the *New Sum of Poetry* from the *Negro World* (1966); *Messages: Poems from Ghana (*1970); *Night of My Blood* (1971); *Elegy for the Revolution* (1978); *The House by the Sea* (1978); *A Harvest of Our Dreams* (1984) and *Ancestral Logic and Caribbean Blues* (1993). Awoonor also wrote an important play, *Ancestral Power* (1970) and two novels, *This Earth, My Brother* (1971) and *Comes the Voyager at Last* (1992). In 1975 he published *The Breast of the Earth: A Study of the Cultures and Literatures of Africa*. His writings mainly deal with the sad state of Africa in the twentieth century as a result of European imperialism and African corruption. He served for some years as Ford Foundation Writer-in-Residence at Columbia University, producer and host of the African Heritage television series and as president of the African Literature Association.

AWOONOR-RENNER, Bankole

This prominent Gold Coast journalist and politician was an ardent African nationalist. Born around 1907, he was educated at the Tuskegee Institute in Alabama and the Carnegie Institute of Technology in Pittsburgh, Pennsylvania. He eventually became the first African to be admitted to the Institute of Journalists in the United Kingdom. He also became a member of the Association of Writers in Moscow. For many years, Awoonor-Renner edited the *Gold Coast Leader* before becoming assistant editor of the *Times of West Africa*. Throughout the inter-war period, he contributed poems and articles to all of the newspapers in British West Africa, promoting the cause of African independence. A collection of his poems, entitled *This Africa*, appeared in 1928. Awoonor-Renner was elected the first president of the militant Pan-African Council and was a member of such organizations as the West African Youth League and the Friends of the Asante Freedom Society. He became an avowed Communist during the 1930s and published *The West African Soviet Union* in 1946. He served on the Accra Town Council during 1942-44 and joined Kwame Nkrumah's Convention People's Party (CPP) after World War II. He broke away from the CPP and joined the Moslem Association Party in 1954, but played only an insignificant role afterwards as he was dogged by persistent ill health in his later years. Bankole Awoonor-Renner died on 27 May 1970.

AYLESTOCK, Addie

Revd M. Addie Aylestock, the first woman ever to be ordained by the British Methodist Episcopal Church (BME), was born in September 1909 in the village of Glen Allan, near Elmira, in Ontario, Canada. After leaving elementary school, she worked for some time as a domestic while attending Toronto's Central Technical School in the evenings. She later enrolled at the Toronto Bible College, from which she graduated in 1945. Following many years of service as a deaconess in such cities as Halifax, Montreal and Toronto, she was ordained in 1951 and assigned to the BME Church in North Buxton. Aylestock devoted most of her life to community service throughout southern Ontario and became a most influential and effective religious administrator in that region. She has served as a wonderful source of inspiration to several generations of black Canadian women.

AZIKIWE, Nnamdi

Born in Zungeru, in Northern Nigeria, on 16 December 1904, Dr Benjamin Nnamdi Azikiwe became one of the most highly respected figures in modern Africa. He had the distinction of being elected the first president of the Nigerian Republic in 1963. Generally known as 'Zik', this outstanding west African nationalist and author was educated at various schools in Onitsha and Lagos before stowing away on a ship to the United States where he studied at (and graduated from) Lincoln College in Pennsylvania. He then spent some years in London, England, before moving to the Gold Coast where he edited the *Africa Morning Post*. In 1937, Azikiwe returned to his native colony, joined the Nigerian Youth Movement and became the leading spokesman for Ibo interests. He started a chain of newspapers in Ibadan, Kano, Port Harcourt and Onitsha, among which the most important was the *West Africa Pilot*. He was one of the founders of the National Council of Nigeria and the Cameroons and became a member of the Nigerian Legislative Council in 1948. Azikiwe was one of Nigeria's leading politicians during its early years of independence and served as its first Governor General during 1960-63 but, after the military coup of 1969, he retired for a time to his home in Nsukka where he had helped to establish the University of Nigeria. During the late 1970s he became a leader of the new Nigerian People's Party and campaigned unsuccessfully for the presidency in 1979 and 1983. He died on 11 May 1996. A noted historian and political scientist, Azikiwe wrote several important books, including *Liberia in World Affairs* (1934), *Renascent Africa* (1937), and *My Odyssey* (1970). Also published in 1961 was *Zik: A Selection from the Speeches of Nnamdi Azikiwe.*

BÂ, Mallam Amadou

Born around 1920, Mallam Amadou Hampaté Bâ was a famous Mali scholar and theologian, generally known as the 'Sage of Bamako'. He published many important works in the fields of Islamic theology and African religions. He also developed a satisfactory Arabic script for the modern Fulani language. His best-known scholarly works are *L'Empire Peul du Macina* 1818-53 and a biography, *Tierno Bokar: Le Sage de Bandiagara.* Bâ, who worked for many years with the Institut Français d'Afrique Noire in Dakar, also wrote poetry, some of which appeared in *Koumen: Texte Iniatique des Pasteurs Peuls* (1961) and *Kaidara* (1965).

BABU, Abdul

Abdul Rahman Mohammed Babu was the Tanzanian politician who, as the champion of Pan-Africanism in the mid-20th century, laid the ideological foundations for the Zanzibar Revolution of 1964 which led to the union of Tanganyika and Zanzibar. Babu was born on 22 September 1924. He died on 5 August 1996.

BAILEY, Donovan

The Canadian track-star, Donovan Bailey, was born in Manchester, Jamaica, on 16 December 1967. He moved to Oakville, Ontario, to live with his father in 1981 and attended Sheridan College where he studied economics. After receiving a diploma in business administration, he started his own marketing and investment-consulting business and did not really take athletics seriously until the early 1990s. Encouraged by Dan Pfaff, an American coach, he drastically overhauled his technique, improved his starts and became one of the leading sprinters in the world. Bailey led the Canadian 4 x 100 metre relay team to victory in the 1995 world championships and then fulfilled his personal dream by winning the 100 metre dash in the Atlanta Olympics in the world record time of 9.84 seconds. He then anchored the Canadian quartet to this country's first gold medal in an Olympic relay competition. Bailey has shown other youth that it is possible to combine a professional

career in business with competitive athletics at the highest level. He also
created the Donovan Bailey Foundation, committed to supporting Canadian
amateur athletes.

BAKER, George

Better known as Father Divine, this very popular religious leader was born
in 1880 of share-cropping parents on a rice plantation in Georgia. He
opened his own mission for the distribution of aid and alms to the needy
around the turn of the century. In 1919, he founded a communal
community in Sayville, which his followers called 'Heaven'. By the 1940s
there were several such 'Heavens' scattered across the United States. He
attracted such an exceptionally large following that, by the 1960s, his
Kingdom of Peace movement controlled property whose value was
estimated in excess of $10 million. Father Divine's peace missions were
established in many states, providing low-priced or free food for
impoverished Blacks, especially during the bleak days of the Depression. In
addition to their charitable works, the missions tried to rehabilitate
criminals. But after Father Divine's death on 10 September 1965, the
movement appears to have languished.

BAKER, Josephine

This celebrated singer and dancer was born in St Louis, Missouri, on 3 June
1906. Her reputation as an entertainer was actually made in France,
especially after her performance in *La Revue Nègre*, an American jazz review,
which played in Paris in 1925. She became a French citizen and was
awarded the French Legion of Honour for her work during World War II.
Josephine Baker is also remembered for her philanthropy. During the 1920s
she raised a number of orphan children of many races. After World war II,
she purchased Les Milandes, an estate in southwestern France, which
became a home for her 'rainbow family', which then numbered twelve
orphans of various nationalities. To maintain this orphanage, she came out
of retirement and staged triumphant shows all over the world. During the
1960s, she also supported the civil rights movement in the United States and
actively participated in the great March on Washington in August 1963.
Josephine Baker died on 12 April 1975. *Remembering Josephine*, a biography
written by Stephen Papich, was published in 1976. Her own *Mémoires* had
appeared in 1949.

BALDWIN, James

A noted American author, James Arthur Baldwin was born in Harlem, New
York City, on 2 August 1924. His earliest writing was in the form of articles
published in such newspapers as the *Nation*, *New Leader* and *Commentary*.

Some of them reappeared in such collections of essays as *Notes of a Native Son* (1955), *Nobody Knows My Name* (1961), and *The Fire Next Time* (1963). His novels included *Go Tell It on the Mountain* (1953), *Giovanni's Room* (1956), *Another Country* (1962), *Tell Me How Long the Train's Been Gone* (1968), *If Beale Street Could Talk* (1974), *Just Above My Head* (1979), and *The Evidence of Things Not Seen* (1985). Baldwin also wrote some very good plays, such as *Blues for Mister Charlie* and *The Amen Corner*, and a variety of essays for such magazines as *Harper's*, *Partisan Review*, and *The Reporter*. A collection of his non-fiction, *The Price of a Ticket*, also appeared in 1985. His writing won him a number of awards, including a Eugene Saxon Fellowship in 1945, a prize from the National Institute of Arts and Letters in 1956 and a Ford Foundation grant in 1959. Baldwin served as a member of the national advisory board of the Congress of Racial Equality (CORE) and was made a Commander of the Legion of Honour by the French government in 1986. A firm believer in nonviolence, he was, in his own quiet way, a staunch supporter of the civil rights movement in the United States. He died on 30 November 1987.

BALLANTA-TAYLOR, N.J.G.

Born in Freetown in 1893, Professor Nicholas Julius George Ballanta-Taylor was an eminent Sierra Leonean composer, organist and musicologist. He was educated at the Church Missionary Society Grammar School and at Fourah Bay College in Freetown. After serving briefly in the civil service in Gambia, he travelled throughout western and central Africa researching traditional forms of music. He then went to the United States to further his musical studies at Boston College from which he graduated in 1924. His famous *The Aesthetics of African Music* was published in the early 1930s. Ballanta-Taylor returned to Sierra Leone in 1933 to teach music. In addition to a concert overture, he wrote and produced three successful operas: *Afiwa, Boima, and Effuah*. A great pioneer in the field of African forms, his work became much more valued after his death in 1962.

BAMBAFARA

This famous chief of Nieni, a state in what is now northeastern Sierra Leone, was born in the early 1830s. Bambafara ruled for close to 50 years, extending the area he had inherited from his father in the early 1870s and administering it with great skill, despite serious challenges from the British as well as Samori Touré, the great Mandinka warrior-king. Although the British reduced Bambafara's power towards the turn of the century, they acknowledged him as king of the Nieni and frequently invoked his authority when trying to settle disputes in the area. Chief Bambafara died on 7 July 1921, highly respected by Africans and Europeans alike for his ability, charm and intelligence.

BANANA, Canaan

Born on 5 March 1936 in Esiphezini, Matabeleland, Revd Canaan Sodindo Banana was a Zimbabwean Methodist minister, theologian and statesman who made a significant contribution to the achievement of his country's independence in 1980. He served as the first prime minister of the new republic during 1980-87. He was later convicted of homosexuality and other 'unnatural acts' in a highly controversial case which led to a brief imprisonment. He died on 10 November 2003.

BANCROFT, George

Professor Emeritus George W. Bancroft began his teaching career in his native British Guiana before immigrating to Canada in 1948 and teaching at several levels in Ontario. While lecturing at the University of Toronto (where he achieved his doctorate in 1960), he was seconded in 1980 to the Ontario Ministry of Citizenship and Culture where he served for three years as executive director. In 1988 he was appointed Commissioner of the Ontario Human Rights Commission and held that post until 1991. In addition to numerous articles in scholarly journals, Dr Bancroft's published works include *They Came From Abroad*; *The Novice and The Newcomer*; and *A Place to Stand*.

BANDA, Hastings

Dr Hastings Kamuzu Banda was the first president of an independent Malawi. Born on 14 May 1906 in Nyasaland, he was educated at North American and British universities, eventually emerging with degrees in history and political science as well as medicine. Between 1937 and 1952 he practised successfully as a doctor in England while co-operating with other Pan-Africanists in supporting various independence movements. He worked in Kwame Nkrumah's Ghana during 1953-58 before returning home to lead the Malawi nationalists. Banda succeeded in destroying the Central African Federation and establishing an independent Malawi in 1964. As the leader of this new republic, he distinguished himself by refusing to join the majority of African governments in their denunciation of Rhodesia and South Africa during the 1960s and 1970s. He ignored the strict boycott maintained by the Organization of African Unity (OAU) and insisted that the best hope of changing the political systems of these racist states was through political and social dialogue. He revised the constitution in 1971 when he was declared president of Malawi for life. In matters of morality, Banda remained very puritanical. He outlawed short skirts and pants on women, forbade male tourists with long hair to enter Malawi, and even went so far as to ban television. His strict and autocratic rule gradually alienated him from his people (particularly the younger generation) and he was voted out of office in 1994. He was given a state funeral, however, when he died on 25 November 1997.

BANKOLE-BRIGHT, Herbert Christian

Dr Herbert Christian Bankole-Bright was a controversial Sierra Leonean politician for almost 40 years. Born on 23 August 1883 at Okrika in what is now Nigeria, he was the son of a prosperous merchant who settled eventually in Freetown after his retirement. Bankole-Bright was educated at the Methodist Boys' School in Freetown before studying medicine at the University of Edinburgh in Scotland. He qualified as a doctor and returned in 1911 to Sierra Leone where he ran a nursing home and established such newspapers as *Aurora* and the *Evening Despatch*, through which he consistently expressed his radical views calling, among other things, for a West African Court of Appeal, workmen's compensation, extension of the franchise and elimination of racial discrimination. He became a member of the Legislative Council of Sierra Leone and gave staunch support to the National Congress of British West Africa (NCBWA), which was founded in 1920. His arrogance, however, made him increasingly unpopular among both Africans and Europeans, and his influence gradually diminished during the 1950s. Bankole-Bright died on 12 December 1958.

BANNEKER, Benjamin

Born on 9 November 1731 in Ellicott Mills, Maryland, Benjamin Banneker was one of the outstanding American scholars of any age. When only twenty-two, he built the very first wooden clock ever made in the United States. It kept perfect time for over forty years and attracted tourists to Baltimore from all parts of the world. Banneker was an important mathematician, astronomer, inventor and scientist. He began making astronomical calculations for almanacs during the early 1770s and accurately predicted an eclipse in 1789. From 1792 to 1802 he published a yearly almanac for farmers, then the first scientific studies published by an African-American. He published a treatise on bees and computed the cycle of the 17-year locust. In 1790 he also assisted in the survey of the District of Columbia. Banneker became a national hero for Blacks and a number of schools have been named in his honour. He died on 9 October 1806. A much acclaimed biography, *The Life of Benjamin Banneker*, was published by Silvio A. Bedini in 1972.

BANNERMAN, C.E.W.

Charles Edward Woolhouse Bannerman was born in Accra on 12 October 1884 and became the first native African to be appointed a judge of the Supreme Court of the Gold Coast. He studied law in England during 1913-15 and returned to practice in Accra where he also took an active part in public life. He served as police magistrate in the Supreme Court from 1920 to 1935 and was appointed circuit judge for Asante and the northern territories in 1934. In 1935 he was promoted to the office of puisne judge. Bannerman established a fine reputation as a jurist and received many honours and distinctions. He was awarded an OBE in 1924, a King George V Silver Jubilee Medal in 1935 and a King George VI Coronation Medal in 1937. He died on 10 November 1943.

BARBER, Francis

Francis Barber was born a slave on a Jamaican plantation in 1735 and was brought to England by his owner in 1750. In 1754, the plantation owner died and left Barber £12 and his freedom. For a while, he served as Samuel Johnson's valet until he ran away to sea in 1758. On his return in 1760 he rejoined Johnson's staff as a butler. Johnson encouraged him to attend Bishop's Stortford Grammar School, after which Barber served as his secretary. He arranged trips, received documents and kept Johnson's diary as the latter became increasingly dependent upon him. When Johnson died in 1784, he left Barber with an annuity of £70 and a gold watch. Barber moved to Lichfield, Staffordshire, and later became a teacher in Burntwood. He died in 1801. Barber was perhaps the first Black to teach in a British school.

BARNES, Emery

In 1972, Emery Barnes was, along with Rosemary Brown, among the first two Blacks to be elected to the provincial legislature in British Columbia, Canada. He proceeded to establish a record as the longest-serving member of that body. By 22 March 1994, when he was elected its Speaker, he had already become Dean of the House. He was the first Black to be elected Speaker in any Canadian legislature. Born in New Orleans, Louisiana on 15 December 1929, Barnes had begun his career as an Olympic high jumper and a professional footballer in the Canadian Football League (CFL) and the National Football League (NFL) but is best remembered now as a successful politician who was always a firm advocate of social justice and racial equality. He died on 1 July 1998.

BARNES, John

Born in Kingston, Jamaica, on 11 November 1963, John Barnes emigrated to the United Kingdom and became a football star for Watford, Liverpool, Newcastle United and Charlton Athletic during 1981-1999. He scored 12 goals in 78 appearances for England, thus earning more English caps than any other player of African descent. After a brief stint as head coach of Celtic, he became a highly respected commentator and match analyst of

ITV's coverage of international and domestic football. A keen community servant, Barnes serves as an ambassador for Save the Children and has recently made trips to such places as Kenya and Ethiopia.

BARNETT, Claude

Claude A. Barnett, the journalist who founded the Associated Negro Press (ANP) in 1919, was born in Sanford, Florida, on 16 September 1889. He graduated from the Tuskegee Institute with a degree in engineering in 1906 but seems to have put those qualifications to little use. He worked for some time as a clerk for the US Post Office in Chicago, Illinois, and later became an advertising salesman for the *Chicago Defender*. During World War II, Barnett served as a special assistant to the US Secretary of Agriculture, advising on the problems facing black farmers. His ANP, in the meantime, steadily expanded, supplying wire service to more than 300 newspapers and magazines at its peak. Before it was discontinued in 1963, the ANP went far towards building and stabilizing the African-American press. Barnett died on 2 August 1967.

BARRETT, Lindsay

C. Lindsay Barrett was born on 15 September 1941 in Jamaica, West Indies. He is a noted novelist, poet, playwright, journalist and teacher. After leaving school, he began his career as a reporter for *The Daily Gleaner*, Jamaica's leading newspaper, and then served as news editor of the Jamaica Broadcasting Corporation (JBC). In 1961 he moved to England where he worked for the British Broadcasting Corporation (BBC) and the Transcription Centre. For some years he then travelled throughout Europe and Africa as a journalist and feature writer. He lectured briefly, among other places, at Fourah Bay College in Sierra Leone and at the University of Ibadan. His militant poems, plays and essays deal mainly with racial prejudice. Among his plays the best known are *Jump Kookoo Makka* (1967), *Sigh of a Slave Dream* (1967), and *After This We Heard of Fire* (1973). His finest novel, *Song for Mumu*, was published in 1967. *His Veils of Vengeance Falling* appeared in 1985. Barrett won the Conrad Kent Award (a US prize) in 1970 for his poem *In My Eye and Heart* which dealt with racial prejudice and violence in Alabama during the 1960s. His important works of non-fiction include *The State of Black Desire* (1966); *Danjuma: The Making of a General* (1979); and *Agbada to Khaki: Reporting a Change of Government in Nigeria* (1985). Two collections of his poems have been published in Nigeria and the United Kingdom. Barrett is also a famous broadcaster on both radio and television. He eventually settled down in Nigeria where he married a leading actress, Beti Okotie. He was the founder and associate editor of *Afriscope Magazine*.

BARROW, Errol

The Rt Excellent Errol Walton Barrow was the politician who led Barbados into independence and became its first prime minister in 1966. Born on 21 January 1920, he was educated at Combermere School and Harrison College, Barbados, before joining the Royal Air Force and flying more than fifty missions over western Europe during World War II. After the war, he studied at the London School of Economics and at Lincoln's Inn, emerging with two degrees before returning to Barbados in 1950. Barrow joined the Barbados Labour Party (BLP), then led by Grantley Adams, and was elected to the local legislature in 1951. But he swiftly lost faith in the older black leaders, whom he regarded as too conservative, and founded his own Democratic Labour Party (DLP) in 1955. He led this group to a surprising triumph in the general elections of 1961, when he first became premier, and they retained their majority until 1976. After ten years in opposition (1976-86), the DLP completely swept aside the BLP (24-3) in the elections of 1986 and Barrow returned as prime minister, holding that post until his sudden death on 1 June 1987. A keen advocate of regional integration, he was influential in the establishment of the Caribbean Free Trade Association (CARIFTA), which gradually evolved into the Caribbean Community and Common Market (CARICOM) which is still in existence today. His social and economic reforms during 1961-76 laid the foundations of modern Barbados with education, communications and public health systems unmatched in the so-called 'Third World'. Consistently viewing the aggressiveness of the United States as a threat to Caribbean independence, Barrow was one of the few West Indian political leaders who denounced their intervention in the Grenada crisis of October 1983. He was elevated to the status of a National Hero by the Government of Barbados in 1998.

BARROW, Jocelyn

Dame Jocelyn Barrow is the director for UK Development at Focus Consultancy Ltd. She was the first black woman to be a governor of the British Broadcasting Corporation (BBC) and was founder and deputy chair of the Broadcasting Standards Council. A vigorous supporter of racial equality and social justice, she was a founding member and general secretary of the Campaign Against Racial Discrimination (CARD), the organization most instrumental in promoting the Race Relations legislation of 1968. As a senior teacher and a teacher-trainer at London University in the 1960s, she pioneered the introduction of multi-cultural education, stressing the needs of the various ethnic groups in the country. She also played a key role in the establishment of the North Atlantic Slavery Gallery and the Maritime Museum in Liverpool. She was a trustee of the National Museums and Galleries on Merseyside and a governor of the British Film

Institute. For her work in the field of education and community relations, she was awarded the Order of the British Empire in 1972. She became a Dame of the British Empire in 1992 for her work in broadcasting and her contribution to the work of the European Union as the UK member of the Social and Economic Committee. Her enormous value to British society is reflected in the fact that, at various points, she served in the following capacities: Governor of the Commonwealth Institute; council member of Goldsmith's College, University of London; vice-president of the United Nations Association in the UK and Northern Ireland; trustee to the Irene Taylor Trust providing music in prisons; and national vice-president of the Townswomen's Guild.

BARROW, Nita

Dame Ruth Nita Barrow, the sister of Errol Barrow, was one of the truly outstanding women of the twentieth century. She left an indelible mark on Caribbean nursing, public health, education, politics, religion and diplomacy. Born on 15 November 1916 in St Lucy, Barbados, she trained as a nurse at the Barbados General Hospital before furthering her education at the University of Toronto (Canada), Edinburgh University (Scotland), and Columbia University (United States). She worked as a public health nurse and nursing teacher in Barbados and Jamaica for many years before joining the staff of the World Heath Organization (WHO) in 1964. She served as nursing adviser to the Pan American Health Organization (PAHO) from 1967 to 1971 and became medical commissioner (1971-80) and a president (1983) of the World Council of Churches (WCC). Barrow was president (1975-83) of the World YWCA, health consultant (1981-86) to WHO, president (1982-90) of the International Council for Adult Education (ICAE) and Barbadian ambassador (1986-90) to the United Nations. In 1985 she presided over the International Women's Conference at Nairobi, Kenya, and was the only woman named later that year to the Eminent Persons Group (EPG) of seven established to investigate racism in South Africa. In 1988 she campaigned vainly for the presidency of the UN General Assembly but reached the pinnacle of an extraordinary career when, in 1990, she was appointed Governor General of Barbados, the first woman to be accorded that honour. The recipient of numerous honorary doctorates from reputable universities, she was made Dame of the Order of St Andrew in 1980. She died on 19 December 1995, just a few weeks after the launching of her biography, *Dame Nita: Caribbean Woman, World Citizen*, by Francis W. Blackman. She was perhaps the most highly respected and most sincerely loved Barbadian of her generation. A devout Christian, she devoted a long and multi-faceted life to such causes as social justice, racial equality and women's rights.

BASIE, Count

Always affectionately known as the 'Count', William Basie was an innovative jazz pianist and leader of one of the 'swingingest' bands in the United States for what seemed like an eternity. He was a brilliant organiser who transformed swing from a solo effort to a group phenomenon with an explosive orchestra that thrilled music fans from the 1930s until the 1970s. Basie was born in Hollywood, Florida, on 21 August 1904. For some years he played as an accompanist for travelling vaudeville shows until, in 1935, he formed his own band which proceeded to record one smash hit after another. In 1957, they became the first American band to play a royal command performance for the Queen of England. Basie composed most of their pieces and received numerous awards and distinctions but none more moving perhaps than the tribute paid to him in the 1982 gala at Radio City Music Hall sponsored by the Black Music Association. His best known works were *One O'Clock Jump*, *Taxi War Dance*, *Tickle Toe* and *Swinging the Blues*. He died on 26 April 1984.

BASSEY, Shirley

Dame Shirley Veronica Bassey was born in Tiger Bay, Cardiff, to a Nigerian father and an English mother on 8 January 1937. After attending Moorland Primary School in Cardiff, she worked in odd jobs while supplementing her meagre wages by singing in local nightclubs. Her first single, *Burn My Candle*, released in 1956, was banned by the BBC because of its suggestive lyrics, but it sold well nonetheless. Her first big hit, *Banana Boat Song*, came in 1958. This was followed by a lengthy sequence of successful and popular recordings. Between 1970 and 1979, Dame Bassey had eighteen hit albums in the United Kingdom and starred in two highly-rated BBC TV series. With 31 hits in the UK singles chart over the span of 42 years, plus 35 hit LPs in the corresponding albums chart, Dame Bassey has become Britain's most successful female singer of all time. She is the only performer to have recorded more than one James Bond theme song, having done so for *Goldfinger* (1964), *Diamonds Are Forever* (1971) and *Moonraker* (1979). In 1999, she was created a Dame Commander of the British Empire, the equivalent of a Knight Commander. In 2002 she was invited to sing at Buckingham Palace during the celebrations of Queen Elizabeth II's Golden Jubilee. She was also awarded the prestigious Légion d'Honneur, France's top honour, in recognition of her contribution to the culture of France. She now resides in Monaco, having sold her London apartment and auctioned its furnishings for charity.

BATES, Daisy Lee

Daisy Lee Gaston Bates played a crucial role in the civil rights movements of the 1950s and 1960s in the United States. She and her husband (L.C.

Bates) were largely responsible for the desegregation of schools in Arkansas in defiance of the efforts of the conservative white majority, led by Governor Orval Faubus. They relentlessly pursued the matter in their weekly newspaper, the *Arkansas State Press*, and sought the help of the National Association for the Advancement of Colored People (NAACP) as well as the federal government to enforce the desegregation laws that had recently been enacted. Daisy Lee Bates was herself then the president of the local Arkansas chapter of the NAACP. Although the long-term effect was the admission of black students to schools that had formerly been white, the immediate result was that the Bates's home was vandalized and their newspaper paralysed by loss of advertisements and subscriptions. Bates then focussed entirely on community service and various civil rights activities. In 1962 she published a book about her experiences, *The Long Shadow of Little Rock*, to which Eleanor Roosevelt graciously supplied a foreword. When it was reprinted in 1986, it became the first reprint to be honoured with an American Book Award. Daisy Lee Bates died on 4 November 1999.

BATH, Patricia

Dr Patricia Bath, an innovative ophthalmologist, surgeon, inventor and keen activist for patients' rights was born in Harlem, New York, in 1942. She graduated from the Howard University School of Medicine in 1968 and completed specialty training in ophthalmology and corneal transplant at New York University and Columbia University. In 1975 she became the first African-American woman surgeon at the University of California at Los Angeles (UCLA) Medical Center and the first female faculty member of the UCLA Jules Stein Eye Institute. In 1976, she co-founded the American Institute for the Prevention of Blindness (AIPB). In 1981, Dr Bath conceived the invention for which she has become so famous, the Laserphaco Probe, a surgical tool that uses a laser to vaporize cataracts. This surgical technique was immeasurably safer and more effective than all previous forms of invasive surgery. In 1988, she became the first African-American female doctor to receive a patent for a medical discovery. Her second invention, superior to the first, was patented in 1998 and permitted the restoration of sight to people who had been blind for more than thirty years. Dr Bath also holds patents in Canada, Europe and Japan. In 1983, she became the first woman to be named chair of the Ophthalmology Residency Training Program at Drew/UCLA. Dr Bath was elected to the Hunter College Hall of Fame in 1988 and named Howard University Pioneer in Academic Medicine in 1993. She retired from the UCLA Medical Center in 1993 but continues to advocate telemedicine, direct the AIPB and devote her time and energy to the prevention, treatment and cure of blindness.

BATSON, Brendon

Born in St George's, Grenada, on 1 February 1953, Brendon Batson emigrated to the United Kingdom with his parents when he was nine years old. He became such a fine young football player that he was signed by Arsenal while still at school and was the first Black to play for the Gunners. After playing for Arsenal and Cambridge United, Batson moved to West Bromwich Albion in 1978 where he joined two other black stars, Cyrille Regis and Laurie Cunningham. This was the first time that any professional football club in England had signed three players of African descent. The 'Three Degrees', as they became known, challenged the established racism of British football and paved the way for the generation of black players that followed. Batson's career was curtailed by a serious injury in 1982 but he soon became an able administrator with the Professional Footballers Association, rising to the post of chief executive, responsible for developing the organization into one of the most important trade unions. In 2000 he was awarded an MBE for his services to the sport and in 2002 he became managing director of West Bromwich Albion, his old team.

BAYLIS, Gloria

A registered nurse by training, Gloria L. Baylis is the founder of Baylis Medical Company (BMC) in Montreal, Quebec, in 1983. Born in Barbados in 1927 (née Clarke), she immigrated to Canada in 1953. Her company began as a home office, importing and distributing a range of medical instruments for neurosurgery. It has since grown into a leading developer and manufacturer of high-tech medical products in cardiology, pain management and radiology with annual sales in excess of $5 million and offices in Montreal and Toronto. In addition to a telemedicine device for monitoring patients directly in their homes, the BMC has developed a radio frequency generator and cardiac catheter that is used by cardiologists for creating perforations in the heart. The Baylis Medical was the first company to introduce temperature monitored cardiac ablation to the North American market.

BEARD, Andrew

Andrew Beard was born a slave in Jefferson County, Alabama, in 1849. After his emancipation, he became a farmer, a carpenter, a blacksmith, a railroad worker, a most creative inventor and finally a successful businessman. In 1881, he patented a new form of plough, his first notable invention, and sold the patent rights for $4,000 in 1884. In 1887 he invented a superior plough and sold the patent for $5,200. He invested the money he made from these devices and established a profitable real-estate business. In 1892, he invented a rotary engine. Five years later came his most significant discovery, the Jenny coupler, which did the dangerous job of hooking railroad cars together more effectively. Beard's coupler, which brought him $50,000 for the patent rights, is the forerunner of today's automatic coupler. This innovative genius died in 1921.

BEBEY, Francis

Born on 15 July 1929 in Douala, Francis Bebey became a celebrated Cameroonian poet, novelist, musician and musicologist. He was educated in local Cameroonian schools before attending the Sorbonne and New York University where he studied French literature and music. He then served for many years with the Information Office of UNESCO in Paris. His major works included *Embarras et Cie, nouvelles et poèmes* (1968); *Le Roi Albert d'Effidi* (1973); and a novel, *Le Fils d'Agatha Moudio* (1967), which won the Grand Prix Littéraire de l'Afrique Noire. In the area of musicology, Bebey is best known for *La Musique Africaine Moderne* (1963) and *Musique de l'Afrique* (1967). He experimented with jazz and classical guitar trying to effect a synthesis of European and African rhythms. He recorded and performed in many countries, singing in English, French and Douala. Chief among his own musical recordings perhaps were *Spirituals du Cameroon; Pièce pour Guitare; Concerts pour un vieux mosque;* and *Le Chant d'Ibadan: Black Tears.* He also wrote *La Radiodiffusion en Afrique Noire* (1963). His writing has appeared in a number of journals and anthologies on African music and literature. Bebey died on 28 May 2001.

BECHET, Sidney

Sidney Bechet was born in New Orleans, Louisiana, on 14 May 1891. He became an excellent jazz clarinetist, soprano saxophonist and composer. A child prodigy, he was able to play the clarinet by the age of six, and he was still very young when he played for such bands as Jack Carey's and Buddy Petit's. He toured Europe with the Southern Syncopated Orchestra during the 1920s. Bechet was the first jazzman to achieve recognition as a serious musician, especially after he started to concentrate on the soprano saxophone. As a composer, his best known songs included *Petite Four, The Fishseller, As-tu LaCafard, Viper Mad, Southern Sunset, Delta Mood,* and *The Broken Windmill.* Bechet died on 14 May 1959. He is still considered in many quarters as the greatest of all soprano saxophonists. His autobiography, *Treat It Gentle,* appeared in 1960.

BECKLES, Hilary

Dr Hilary McDonald Beckles was born in Barbados, West Indies, on 11 August 1955. He emigrated with his family to the United Kingdom in 1969 and completed his education at secondary schools in Birmingham and the

University of Hull, from which he achieved his PhD in economic and social history in 1980. Since then he has served the University of the West Indies in several important capacities and is currently a pro-vice chancellor and the principal of the Cave Hill Campus in Bridgetown. In addition to being an able administrator and educator, he is a vigorous political activist, a prolific author and a committed community servant. Considered by many to be one of the brightest scholars thus far produced by Barbados, Professor Beckles has edited and published an extremely long list of significant books, reports and articles. His major works include *European Settlement and Rivalry in the Caribbean 1492-1972* (1983); *Black Rebellion in Barbados: The Struggle Against Slavery, 1627-1838* (1984); *White Servitude and Black Slavery in Barbados 1627-1715* (1989); *Corporate Power in Barbados: Economic Injustice in a Political Democracy: The Mutual Affair* (1989); *A History of Barbados: From Amerindian Society to Nation State* (1990); and *The Development of West Indies Cricket* (1998, which many critics have judged one of the finest books ever to appear on the sociology of this sport). Dr Beckles is the recipient of numerous honours and awards, including an honorary doctorate from the University of Hull.

BELAFONTE, Harry

Harold George Belafonte was born in New York of Jamaican parents on 1 March 1927. He became a very popular actor and singer, while being actively involved in the US civil rights movement during the 1960s. He appeared in such motion pictures as *Bright Road* and *Carmen Jones*. His calypsos are still popular throughout the United States and the Caribbean.

BÉLANCE, Réné

Born on 28 September 1915 in Corail, Haiti, Réné Bélance became one of his country's most accomplished poets. After attending and teaching at local schools in Port-au-Prince, he emigrated to the United States where he taught for several years at Brown University in Rhode Island. His major works included *Rythmes de mon coeur* (1940), *Luminaire (poèmes)* (1941), *Pour célébrer l'absence* (1943), *Survivances* (1944), and *Nul ailleurs* (1978).

BENKA-COKER, Salako

Sir Salako Ambrosius Benka-Coker, the first native Sierra Leonean to become a Chief Justice (1960-63), was born on 16 June 1900. Educated at the Church Missionary Society Grammar School and at Fourah Bay College in Freetown, he proceeded to study law in England and was called to the bar in 1926. Before returning to Sierra Leone in 1935, he practised quite successfully in the Gambia for nine years. He was appointed Crown Counsel in 1943 and held that post for ten years until his promotion to the office of Solicitor General in 1953. Benka-Coker became an acting puisne judge in 1957 before serving as acting Chief Justice in 1959. In 1961, he was knighted and awarded an honorary doctorate of civil law from the University of Durham, England. While Chief Justice of Sierra Leone, Sir Salako Benka-Coker frequently acted as Governor General. He died on 7 December 1965. An avid sports fan, he had also served as the vice-chairman of the Sierra Leone Sports Council (1956-58) and as chairman of the Sierra Leone Football Association (1961).

BENJAMIN, Floella

Floella Benjamin was born in Trinidad on 23 September 1949 and emigrated with her family to the United Kingdom in 1960. She worked briefly as an actress and participated in the film, *Within These Walls*. In the 1980s she began presenting children's television programmes such as *Play School* and *Playaway*. She now runs her own production company and is also the chairperson of the film and television organization, BAFTA. She was awarded an OBE in 2001 for her services to broadcasting. Her autobiography, *Coming to England*, was published in 1997. In 2006 she was appointed chancellor of the University of Exeter. Floella has promoted the Commonwealth around the world and sits on the government's Millennium Commission.

BENN, Nigel

Born in Ilford on 22 January. 1964, Nigel Benn is a former boxing champion who held world titles in two divisions. He finished with a record of 42 wins, 5 losses and 1 draw, with 35 wins by knockout as a professional boxer. Considered by many pundits still one of the hardest punchers, pound for pound, his amateur record (41-1) was even more spectacular. A flamboyant performer, he dominated the middleweight and super middleweight divisions during the 1980s and 1990s. The turning point of his career came when he almost killed one of his opponents, Gerald McClellan, in a championship bout. That seemed to have taken all the fighting spirit out of Benn. He shortly retired from boxing and became a successful deejay and is still something of a TV celebrity in Britain.

BENNETT, Lerone, Jr

An outstanding journalist, educator and historian, Lerone Bennett, Jr was born in Clarksdale, Mississippi, on 17 October 1928. After graduating from Morehouse College (Atlanta) in 1949, he joined the Johnson Publishing Company in Chicago, Illinois, as an associate editor of *Jet*. He later became senior editor of *Ebony*. Bennett's important works include *Before the Mayflower: A History of the Negro in America 1619-1962* (1963); *What Manner of Man: A Biography of Martin Luther King, Jr* (1964); *Black Power USA: The Human Side of Reconstruction, 1867-1877* (1968); *Pioneers in Protest* (1968); *The Challenge of*

Blackness (1973); and *Great Moments in Black History*. Lerone Bennett, Jr became chairman of the Black Studies Program at Northwestern University (Evanston, Illinois) in 1973. He has also served as advisor and consultant to national organizations and commissions, including the National Advisory Commission on Civil Disorders.

BENNETT, Louise

The Honourable Dr Louise Simone Bennett-Coverley was one of Jamaica's best known personalities. This popular actress, folklorist, singer, entertainer, poetess and radio personality was born on 7 September 1919. Affectionately known as 'Miss Lou', she dominated the Jamaican Christmas Pantomime for many years. Her comic poetry, written mostly in the local dialect, is often a serious social commentary masked in humour and irony. She gave respectability to local Jamaican idioms and accents by her regular use of 'labrish' in commercials on the radio and on television. During the 1970s, she hosted a popular TV programme, *Ring Ding*, which allowed children from all parts of the country to showcase their talents in the performing arts. She lectured extensively in the United Kingdom and the United States on Jamaican folklore and music and represented Jamaica all over the world. 'Miss Lou' won numerous awards, including the Musgrave Silver Medal, an MBE, honorary doctorates from the University of the West Indies and York University (Toronto) and the Order of Jamaica. In 2001, she was appointed a Member of the Order of Merit by the Government of Jamaica for her distinguished contribution to the development of the Arts and Culture. Her poems and short stories appeared in such anthologies as *Verses in Jamaican Dialect* (1942), *Jamaican Dialect Poems* (1948), *Anancy Stories and Dialect Verse* (1957), *Laugh With Louise* (1961), *Jamaica Labrish* (1966), *Anancy and Miss Lou* (1979) and *Selected Poems* (1982). On 26 July 2006, Louise Bennett-Coverley died in Toronto, Ontario, where she had spent the last ten years of her life.

BENTSI-ENCHILL, Kwamena

One of the leading jurists in the history of Ghana, Kwamena Bentsi-Enchill was born at Salpond on 22 September 1919. A graduate of Achimota College and Oxford University, he became a brilliant scholar and a very able advocate. After his expulsion from the Convention People's Party (CPP) in the early 1950s, he completed a doctorate at the University of Chicago and became a professor of law at the University of Ghana and later served as Dean of the Faculty of Law at the University of Zambia (1966-70) where he established the *Zambia Law Journal* and was its first editor. He became the first director of the Law Practice Institute of Zambia. Bentsi-Enchill wrote numerous scholarly articles and his arguments in Ghana Law Reports have served as legal bases ever since. His seminal *Land Law in Ghana* (1964) is still the definitive text on that subject. He was elected Fellow of the Ghana Academy of Arts and Sciences in 1969 and appointed a Supreme Court Judge in Ghana in 1971. He served on the Council of the Ghana Academy and was a member of the Law Reform Commission. He died on 21 October 1974.

BEOKU-BETTS, Ernest Samuel

Born on 15 March 1895, Ernest Samuel Beoku-Betts was one of the first Africans to be elected to the Legislative Council of Sierra Leone (1924-27) and became its vice-president in 1927. The son of an enterprising Krio hardware merchant, he was educated at the Leopold Educational Institute and at Fourah Bay College before studying law in England and being called to the bar in 1917. He soon established a thriving private practice in Freetown while becoming an influential politician, serving as a member of the Freetown City Council during 1919-26 and as mayor of Freetown (1925-26). He became the first native Sierra Leonean police magistrate in 1937 and was appointed a puisne judge in 1945. One year later, he was made a judge of the West African Court of Appeal. He was knighted in 1957, only the second native Sierra Leonean to have been so honoured. A staunch critic of the British colonial system, Beoku-Betts gave active support to the National Congress of British West Africa (NCBWA) and openly sympathized with the railway strikers in 1926. Throughout his career, he remained opposed to racism and European forms of injustice. He died on 23 September 1957. Sir Ernest is also remembered as a keen sportsman who played cricket, football and tennis with more than average competence. He served for many years until his death as president of the Sierra Leone Football Association and president of the Sierra Leone Cricket Association.

BERTLEY, Leo

A native of Trinidad and Tobago, Dr Leo W. Bertley immigrated to Canada in 1960 and completed his education at McGill University, Ottawa University and Concordia University. A career educator, he taught at various levels in Canada, the United Kingdom, the United States and the West Indies. In 1960, when he was appointed Principal of St Michael's College, he became the first person of African descent to head a major public school in Quebec. After 1971 he served for more than thirty years as a professor of history at Vanier College in St Laurent, Quebec. An ardent preacher of the gospel of black excellence, Dr Bertley was a founding member of the Garvey Institute, established in Montreal in 1981 to promote the study of the contributions made by Blacks to the development of modern civilization. He authored numerous articles, books and pamphlets. His major works include *Black Tiles in the Mosaic* (1974); *Montreal's*

Oldest Black Congregation (1976); *Canada and Its People of African Descent* (1977); and *This Noble and Apostolic Work: The Presentation Brothers in the Caribbean* (1998). Professor Bertley was also a pioneer in community journalism in Montreal where he established and edited *Afro-Can* and its successor, *The Afro-Canadian*, two monthly newspapers that addressed issues of major concern to Blacks in Quebec during 1981-94.

BEST, Carrie

Born on 4 March 1903 in New Glasgow, Nova Scotia, Dr Carrie Best enjoyed a truly remarkable career as author, historian, journalist, philanthropist and community activist. She devoted her entire life to the establishment of a tolerant and egalitarian society in Canada. In 1946 she founded the *Clarion*, the first black-owned and published newspaper in Nova Scotia. It later became the *Negro Citizen*. In 1952, she started a radio show, *The Quiet Corner*, which aired for twelve years. From 1968 to 1975, Carrie Best was a columnist for *The Pictou Advocate*, using this medium as a platform for her crusades against racism, gender inequality and social injustice. In 1977, she published an autobiography, *That Lonesome Road*. In 1985, at the age of eighty-two, she founded the Harambee Centres, Canada, while still serving as the president of the Kay Livingstone Visible Minority Women's Society of Nova Scotia. For many years she was an exemplary role model and a source of inspiration to Canadian Blacks and women. Dr Carrie Best received numerous awards and honours, including honorary doctorates from St Francis Xavier University and the University of King's College. She was made a member of the Order of Canada in 1974 and was promoted to Officer in 1979. She died on 24 July 2001 at the great age of ninety-eight.

BETHUNE, Mary McLeod

The daughter of former slaves, Mary McLeod Bethune was born near Mayesville, South Carolina, on 10 July 1875. After studying at Scotia College in North Carolina and the Moody Bible Institute in Chicago, she graduated in 1895 and taught briefly in Georgia and South Carolina. Following her marriage to Albertus Bethune, she moved to Florida and founded an industrial school for young Negro women at Daytona Beach in 1904. This evolved, from modest beginnings, into the Bethune-Cookman College, over which Mary herself presided until 1947. By 1923 it was a flourishing institution with 600 students, 32 teachers and a large campus. In the meantime, she also helped to found such organizations as the National Association of Colored Women's Clubs and the National Council of Negro Women. She became a member of the Hoover Committee for Child Welfare and was a director of the National Business League, of the National Urban League, and the Commission on Interracial Cooperation. The first black woman to head a federal office, Mary McLeod Bethune was honoured with a national memorial in Washington, D.C. some nineteen years after her death on 18 May 1955.

BÉTI, Mongo

Using the pseudonym Mongo Béti, Alexandre Biyidi, who was born at Mbalmayo in Cameroon on 30 June 1932, is generally regarded as one of the greatest of all the African Francophone writers. He was a serious critic of Europeanization which, he was convinced, did untold harm to African culture and values. He became a staunch Marxist critic of independent Cameroon and chose to live in self-imposed exile in France, where he taught for many years. His chief novels are *Ville Cruelle* (1954), *Le Pauvre Christ de Bomba* (1956), *Mission Terminée* (1957), and *Le Roi Miraculé: Chronique des Assazam* (1958). The popularity of Mongo Béti's works is reflected in the fact that they have been translated into many languages. His *Pauvre Christ* is a biting satire on the destructive influence of the missionary activities of the Roman Catholic Church in Cameroon, and his *Mission Terminée*, which won the Prix Saint-Beuve in 1958, attacks in comic fashion the effects of French assimilation on Cameroonian village life. His *Maine basse sur le Cameroun* (1972) was banned in both France and Cameroon but *La Ruine presque cocasse d'un polichinelle* (1979) and *Les Deux Mères de Guillaume* (1982) were not. All of Béti's works reflect a sincere concern for the betterment of modern African society. In 1978, with his French-born wife, he founded *Peuples Noirs/Peuples Africains*, a journal committed to the destruction of neocolonialism in Africa. He returned to Cameroon in the 1990s and died there on 8 October 2001.

BEY, Salome

Born in Newark, New Jersey, Salome Bey immigrated to Toronto, Ontario, in 1964 and became internationally known as 'Canada's First Lady of the Blues'. She has appeared in a wide variety of productions ranging from children's theatre, international jazz festivals and Broadway shows to royal command performances. She has enjoyed a successful career and won several awards as an actress, singer and playwright. Her best known play, *Madame Gertrude*, is one in which she herself performed. Her major recordings include *Christmas Blues*; *I Like Your Company*; and *Tears Are Not Enough*.

BHÉLY-QUÉNUM, Olympe

The son of a teacher, Olympe Bhély-Quénum, who became an eminent author, was born in Dahomey on 26 September 1928. He studied at local schools before going to France to further his education and to teach. The Institut des Hautes Études d'Outre-Mer awarded him a certificate in diplomatic studies in 1962 after which he studied sociology at the Sorbonne

and then at the Academy of International Law at the Hague. Bhély-
Quénum then served in the French consular service in Italy for many years
before returning to Paris as a member of the staff of UNESCO. He became
editor of *La Vie Africaine* and contributed stories himself to several journals
in Canada, France, Italy and Switzerland. Apart from numerous short
stories, his writings included such novels as *Un piège sans fin* (1960) and *Le
Chant du Lac*, and a novelette, *Liaison d'un été*.

BIKILA, Abebe

Born around 1927, this famous Ethiopian athlete became the first African
to win an Olympic gold medal when he triumphed in the men's marathon
at Rome in 1960. He repeated this feat at Tokyo four years later, breaking
the world record in that event despite having undergone surgery to remove
his appendix only five weeks before. In 1969, he was paralysed as a result of
a serious car accident, but took up archery while confined to a wheelchair
and competed in the paraplegic Olympics. He died on 25 October 1973.
Abebe Bikila, who had served in Emperor Haile Selassie's household guard,
is still regarded as a legend in Ethiopia and continues to be a source of
inspiration to disadvantaged African athletes.

BIRD, Lester

Born on 21 February 1938, Lester Bryant Bird was the son of Vere
Cornwall Bird who led Antigua and Barbuda to Independence and then
served as prime minister of those islands for what seemed like an eternity.
When his father resigned in 1993, Lester Bird succeeded him as prime
minister and remained at the helm until 2004. He was chairman of the
Antigua Labour Party during 1971-93. In his youth he had been an
outstanding athlete.

BIRD, Vere

Easily the most outstanding figure in the history of Antigua and Barbuda is
Vere Cornwall Bird, who was born in one of the islands' worst slums on 7
December 1909. He became, in 1981, at the advanced age of seventy-two,
the first prime minister of the independent nation of Antigua and Barbuda.
He was the last of the old school of Caribbean politicians who had fought for
racial equality and regional self-determination during the inter-war years.
The victim of the social circumstances which then prevailed, he was limited
to an elementary education at St John Boys' School. He joined the Salvation
Army when still in his teens and served as one of its social workers throughout
the Caribbean, but he eventually broke with that organization when he
realised that no black person could hope to gain meaningful promotion in it.
He was one of the founding members of the Antigua Trades and Labour

Union in 1939 and was easily elected to the Legislative Council in 1945. In 1951 he founded the Antigua Labour Party (ALP) and became the island's first chief minister in 1960 and its first premier when Antigua achieved associated statehood in 1967. The ALP lost the elections in 1971, but Bird led it to resounding victories in 1976, 1980, 1984 and 1989. It was he therefore who conducted the final negotiations leading to the establishment of Antigua and Barbuda as a single independent entity in 1981. The Antiguan grassroots still fondly remember how Vere Bird defended their interests as an aggressive trade union leader for many years, and his peculiar brand of populism made the ALP almost impregnable. When he finally stepped down as leader, his son, Lester Bird, succeeded him to the leadership of the ALP and took over as prime minister of Antigua when the party triumphed again in the elections of 7 March 1994. From behind the scenes, however, it was well-known that Vere Bird continued to dominate Antiguan life and politics. He did so indeed until he died on 28 June 1999.

BISHOP, Maurice

Born on 29 May 1944, Maurice Bishop emerged as the leader of Grenada in the West Indies after the overthrow of Sir Eric Gairy's repressive government in the revolution of March 1979. Although he and his family had suffered much at the hands of Gairy's infamous 'Mongoose Gang', he showed unusual leniency in his treatment of the previous administrators. An avowed socialist, Bishop never earned the respect or support of the western leaders and his alliances with Cuba and other Communist governments alarmed the United States in particular. Just when he seemed bent on softening his attitude towards the West, however, he was assassinated in very strange circumstances on 19 October 1983. Bishop was always a friend of the poor and a firm supporter of workers and their civil rights, but once in power he stifled the press and did his best to limit political opposition. He also promised to hold free, fair and general elections, but never did. Educated at Presentation College in Grenada and the University of London, England, he qualified as a lawyer and returned home to practice in 1970. He founded an opposition party, the New Jewel Movement, organized workers' strikes, and became more determined to put an end to Gairy's régime after his own father was killed in suspicious circumstances in 1974. For four years, Bishop provided Grenada with a certain measure of social tranquillity and some economic prosperity. He also built new roads (thanks to Soviet and Cuban aid). There were therefore mixed feelings throughout the Caribbean when his government fell. He had promised much in 1979 and there were definite signs of material progress but his autocratic methods disappointed many of his supporters.

BIYA, Paul

Paul Biya succeeded Ahmadou Ahidjo as Cameroon's president in 1982 after having served as the latter's right-hand man for fifteen years. Born on 13 February 1933, in the Sangmelima district of what was then French West Africa, he was educated in local Catholic schools before furthering his studies at the University of Paris, France. Following his return to Cameroon in 1962, Biya entered politics and enjoyed a sequence of rapid promotions which took him in five years to the post of director of Ahidjo's cabinet. In 1968 he was named minister of state and secretary-general of the presidency. When the office of prime minister was created by the adoption of a new constitution in 1975, Biya was appointed to it and he remained prime minister until he became president. Ahidjo had expected to become the power behind the throne after his voluntary retirement, but Biya immediately showed his independence by silencing the former president and stamping his own personality on Cameroonian politics and policy. He put an end to the one-party political system that Ahidjo had introduced and made Cameroon a multi-party state in 1990. A sequence of re-elections has kept him in power for twenty-four years. Although he has many critics within his own country, particularly from the Anglophone segment which feels marginalised, he remains highly respected elsewhere. His various honours, for instance, include the Grand Croix de La Légion d'Honneur (French Republic); KCMG (Government of Great Britain); Grand-Cross of Exceptional Class (Federal Republic of Germany); Grand Collier of the Order of Ouissam Mohammadi (Kingdom of Morocco); Great Commander of the Order of Nigeria (Federal Republic of Nigeria); Grand-Croix of the National Order of Merit (Republic of Senegal); Commander of the Tunisian National Order; and Honorary Professor of the University of Beijing. Paul Biya is the author of a political essay, *Communal Liberalism* (1987) which has been translated into English, German and Hebrew.

Black Language and Literature in the Twentieth Century

One of the sociological marvels of the twentieth century was the emergence of vigorous and delightful black literature in many quarters of the globe. Writers of African descent made an indelible mark in this field, often showing a versatility lacking among their white counterparts. While most white writers were able to articulate ideas only in their native tongues, many black authors succeeded in writing brilliantly both in the language of their homeland and in that of former European colonisers.

For many years, the language and forms of African literature depended almost entirely upon European grammar and European models. Thus British West Africans, led by such great authors as Chinua Achebe (1930-?), Cyprian Ekwensi (1921-?) and Wole Soyinka (1934-?), produced an abundance of excellent English literature, while the black intelligentsia in Gabon, Senegal and elsewhere wrote beautiful French.

Initially, there were two deterrents to the production of African literature. In the first place, the tradition on that continent had been an oral rather than a literary one. Fables, legends and folk songs had been passed verbally from generation to generation. History, jurisprudence, philosophy and theology had all been stored in the collective memory in this fashion. Secondly, once colonised, the natives were effectively discouraged from speaking or writing in their native tongues. All across Africa, a particular European language, depending upon the imperial centre, became the only official medium of communication. Africans had perforce to learn Dutch, English, French, German, Italian, Portuguese and Spanish.

The Europeans, in typically snobbish and racist fashion, assumed that Africans lacked distinct languages and were capable of using only dialects. The imperialists quickly came to the conclusion that there were sharp distinctions to be drawn between a perfect language and an imperfect dialect, especially since the latter was used only in verbal communication and was unintelligible to the invaders. They insisted that the African (and other) dialects lacked the four basics of any language: phonology, vocabulary, syntax and semantic meaning. Such nonsense prevailed as linguistic orthodoxy until the decolonization of Africa in the decades immediately following World War II.

Trained in missionary schools at home, and later at universities in Europe, African scholars began to write in every conceivable discipline and established newspapers in almost every urban centre on their continent. Journalism encouraged the spread of European literacy among the colonists, who shortly recognized that fluency in the conqueror's language was an avenue to social acceptance and economic mobility. Long after the Europeans had withdrawn from Africa, however, the natives continued to speak and write in the medium encouraged by the former imperialists. Nigeria, for instance, produced an incredible sequence of able writers of English during the second half of the twentieth century, and Senegal (led by Léopold Sédar Senghor and the famous Diop brothers) established an enviable reputation for magnificent French verse as well as prose.

During the age of independence, African scholars and linguists set out to provide their native tongues with basic texts formalising their syntax and grammar. Such languages as Amharic, Comorian, Ewe, Fante, Fulani, Gaa, Malagasy, Ndebele, Pedi (Northern Sotho), Rundi, Rwanda, Sango, Shona, Somali, Sotho, Swahili, Swazi, Tsonga, Tswana (Western Sotho), Twi, Venda, Xhosa, Yoruba and Zulu, all previously stigmatized as dialects, gradually gained a grudging promotion. African intellectuals also began to serve as translators, rendering into African languages such western classics as the Bible and the works of Shakespeare. African politicians, especially in Kenya, Tanzania and

Zaire, began to promote local language as an essential feature of African nationalism. Swahili, for instance, was declared one of the official languages of Kenya during the 1970s, the same decade in which Mobutu Sese Seko was doing his utmost to de-europeanize Zaire completely. Swahili has since become the national language of Kenya and Tanzania as well. Comorian is used as the national language in the Federal Islamic Republic of the Comoros, while Sango prevails in the Central African Republic, Rundi in Burundi, Rwanda in Rwanda, Sotho in Lesotho, and Tswana in Botswana. Since 1990, too, several of the Bantu languages have become acceptable throughout South Africa.

The Use of Amharic and Ge'ez in Ethiopia
The African language which seems to have found earliest acceptance among Europeans was Amharic, which Ethiopians had long been using as a form of local communication even though they were traditionally fluent in such European tongues as English, French and Italian. The first Amharic novel, *Lebb Wallad Tarik* (A Story Born Out of Fantasy), was published in 1908. It was authored by Affawar Gabra Iyasus (1868-1947), a renowned Ethiopian artist, poet, historian and diplomat, who also wrote three Italian works on the Amharic language, including the important *Il Verbo Amarico*. Affawar was fluent in several European languages, but it was his classic grammar texts which helped to provide Amharic with respectability and international acceptance.

The traditional approach to Amharic, even among the Ethiopians themselves, had been a negative one. Gabra Selasse Walda Aragay (1844?-1912), for instance, regarded it only as a local dialect. This noted administrator and historian wrote an important history of Ethiopia in both Amharic and French. The French version was published posthumously in 1930, but the Amharic original did not see the light of day until 1966.

Much more forthright in his promotion of Amharic as the official language of Ethiopia was Heruy Walda Selasse (1878-1938), a brilliant linguist and diplomat, who established his own printing press at Addis Ababa and published some thirty books on a variety of subjects. His Amharic works included histories, novels, poetry, hymns, travel books and translations revealing a fierce patriotism while also stressing the social and religious responsibilities of Ethiopians. Heruy is generally regarded as the father of modern Amharic literature and is also believed to have translated the Bible into Ge'ez (a lesser known Ethiopian language). He was among the first to preach the modern gospel of linguistic equality.

Emergence of Lingala, Rwanda and Swahili in East Africa
South of Ethiopia, the African language which first found forceful expression on the printed page was Swahili. Muyaka Bin Haji Al-Ghassaniy (1776-1840) was a pioneer secular poet who wrote beautiful verses in the

Swahili language. His numerous stanzas addressed a wide array of themes ranging from dialogue verse to love poems, and from poems on domestic life to political commentary. During most of the colonial era, his works remained unknown, but they were carefully collected and published in 1962 under the title of *Diwani ya Muyaka* (Poetry of Muyaka).

It was Revd Kajiga Balihuta (1922-76) of Zaire who did more perhaps than any other single individual to establish Swahili as an important language in its own right, even though he himself wrote mainly in French. Convinced that Africans would learn a lot more quickly if taught in languages they understood, he produced a number of classics on Swahili grammar and tried his utmost to promote the use of both Lingala and Swahili. He was one of the staunchest advocates of the adoption of African national languages. His scholarly works, including *Conscience Professionelle* (1963), *Pour une Langue Nationale Congolaise* (1967), *Initiation à la Culture Ntu: Grammaire Swahili* (1967), *Langue d'Enseignement et Culture Nationale* (1971), *Lugha Ya Kiswahili* (1972) and *Dictionnaire Swahili-Français, Français-Swahili* (1975), made significant contributions to Zairean language, literature and philosophy.

The Swahili author who gained unarguably the greatest measure of respect from western critics was Robert Shaaban (1909-62), a truly brilliant Tanzanian poet, essayist and novelist, who is almost universally considered the most distinguished of all east African writers. It was he who introduced the essay (insha) into Swahili literature and left to posterity such masterpieces as *Pambo la lugha* (1947), *Kielezo cha fasili* (1954), *Insha na mashairi* (1959) and *Masomo yenye adili* (1959). Some of his finest poetry appeared in *Pambo la lugha* (1947), *Marudi mema* (1952), *Almasi za Africa* (1960), *Ashiki kitabu hiki* (1968), *Masomo yenye adili* (1968), *Utenzi wa Vita vya uhuru* (1968) and *Koja la lugha* (1969). Among his major novels were *Kusadikika, nchi iliyo angani* (1951) and *Siku ya watenzi wote* (1960). Shaaban also wrote several novelettes, including *Adili na nduguze* (1952) and *Utoboro mkulima* (1968), and a biography, *Wasifu wa Siti Binti Saad, mwimbaji wa Ugoja* (1955). His own autobiography, *Maisha yangu naBaada ya miaka hamshini*, appeared in 1949. A fervent Muslim and African nationalist, he always lamented the cruelties of European colonialism and the tendency towards the suppression of African values and traditions.

Another noted Swahili poet was Sheikh Abedi (1924-64) of Tanzania. His collection of poems, *Sheria Za Kuyunga Mashari, Na Diwani Ya Amri* (The Rules and Versification of the Poems of Amri), was published in 1954. Sadly, he died too young to leave a more lasting impression on native African literature.

The role of political leaders in promoting the use of native language at all levels in modern Africa is perhaps best exemplified by the career of Julius Nyerere (1922-99), the first president of Tanzania. It is not often remembered that he was a Swahili scholar of no mean distinction. He personally translated Shakespeare's *Julius Caesar* (1963) and *Merchant of Venice* (1969) into Swahili and himself wrote *Uhuru na Ujama* which was translated into English and published as *Freedom and Socialism* in 1968. Nyerere's writings, which appear in both English and Swahili, are mostly collected essays based on his experiences in African politics.

The major promoter of Rwanda, which has since become one of the official languages of that country was Abbé Alexis Kagame (1912-81), a celebrated poet, historian and ethnographer. Although he studied in French and Italian schools, he remained very keen on the language and culture of his people. He thus wrote mainly in the Rwandan language in which he published several short stories as well as poems. His major works included a history, *Iganif Karinga* (1943), and three volumes of poetry, *Isoko y'amäjyambere* (1949-51). Kagame produced his own translations of his poems in *La divine pastorale: I and II - La naissance de l'univers.* He also wrote a few critical commentaries in French on the literature of the Tutsi.

The Rise of Xhosa in Southern Africa
While Amharic and Swahili enjoyed a richer heritage, Xhosa did not find literate promoters until the beginning of the nineteenth century. Among the first of them was the Revd Tiyo Soga (1829?-71), an eminent journalist, minister, translator, composer of hymns and collector of Bantu fables and customs. Soga is especially famous for having produced in 1866 an excellent translation of John Bunyan's *Pilgrim's Progress*, which had a profound effect on the evolution of the Xhosa language. He was the first African minister to be ordained in Great Britain (Glasgow, 1856). During the 1860s, he contributed regularly to *Indaba* (The News), addressing a wide range of issues in a humorous and intelligent manner. He also composed a large number of Christian hymns in Xhosa, which continue to be sung in several South African churches today. Soga's influence upon subsequent generations of Xhosa writers was enormous.

A similar pioneer was John Knox Bokwe (1855-1922), the outstanding Xhosa poet, song-writer, musician, preacher and teacher, who played a key role in the founding of the South African Native College at Fort Hare in 1916. He too advocated the promotion of native African languages and helped to found the Xhosa newspaper, the *Imvo zabantsundu* (Opinion of the Blacks), which he edited for several years. His famous book of Xhosa hymns, *Amaculo ase Rabe*, was published in 1885. Bokwe translated several works from English into Xhosa and wrote one classic biography, *Ibali Lika Ntsikana*, in 1914. By the time of his death, Xhosa had become one of the better known languages of southern Africa.

To this development a significant contribution was made by John Tengo Jabavu (1859-1921), an eminent South African journalist, teacher and politician. After editing the *Isigidimi sama Xosa* for some years, he helped Bokwe to found the *Imvo zabantsundu* which he served for almost forty years as managing editor, chief reporter, advertising salesman, copyreader, composer and clerk. Jabavu himself must have written more than two thousand articles of all kinds to keep this newspaper afloat. His role in establishing the Native College at Fort Hare was so substantial that for many years it was known simply as Jabavu's College.

Bokwe and Jabavu found a staunch ally in William Gqoba (1840-88), a Bantu pastor, poet and teacher, who was another famous translator of English and Xhosa. During the last four years of his relatively short life, Gqoba edited the *Isigidimi sama Xosa* (Kaffir Express) which often included his own articles on Xhosa history and culture.

Such ardent Xhosa pioneers as Bokwe, Gqoba, Jabavu and Soga laid the foundations upon which modern writers like Archibald Jordan (1906-68) and Samuel Mqhayi (1875-1945) were able to build so spectacularly. The former was an outstanding novelist, poet, scholar and educator. His first novel, *Ingqumbo Yeminyanya* (The Death of the Ancestral Spirits) is still generally regarded as the classic of modern Xhosa writing. Much of his prose and poetry was left unpublished at the time of his death and he is perhaps best remembered for his *Practical Xhosa Course for Beginners* (1965). His scholarly articles, although mainly written in English while he served as a professor in the department of African Languages at the University of Wisconsin in the United States, threw much useful light on Xhosa proverbs and riddles and did much to promote the work of previous Bantu writers.

Samuel Edward Krune Loliwe Mqhayi is easily the most famous of all Xhosa poets. Some of his most beautiful poetry appeared in such works as *Ama-gora e-Mendi* (1920), *I-Bandla labantu* (1923), *Imihobe nemi-Bongo* (1927), *Yoko-Fundwa ezikolweni* (1937) and *I-Nzuzo* (1942). Mqhayi was a prolific writer of prose also. His first Xhosa novel, *Ityala lamaWele*, was published in 1914 and proved a great success. He also wrote such fine biographies as *U-bomi bom-Fundisi u J.K. Bokwe* (1925), *U-Sogqumahashe* (1927), and *Isikhumbuzo sika Ntsikana* (1930). His autobiography, *U-Mqhayi wase- Ntab' ozuko*, appeared in 1939. Mqhayi also translated several European works into Xhosa and made valuable contributions to Jabavu's newspaper, *Imvo zabantsundu*, while himself editing *Izwi labantu* (The Voice of the People).

The Blossoming of Zulu Literature

The Zulus, too, have been writing in their own language for almost 100 years. It was in 1903 that John Langalibalele Dubé (1871-1946), a famous educator, statesman and novelist, helped to found the *Ilanga lase Natal* (The Natal Sun) which was the first Zulu newspaper. Very anxious to preserve Zulu traditions and to promote native culture, Dubé collected thousands of

Zulu folk songs and folk tales and himself wrote often in the Zulu language. His major Zulu works included a novel, *Ujeqe insila ka Tshaka* (1933), and two biographies, *U-Shembe* (1935) and *Ukuziphaina kahle* (1935).

Dubé's *U-Shembe* was a memorial to that great African prophet, Isaiah Shembe (1860?- 1935), who had seceded from the Anglican church late in the nineteenth century and founded his own mission, the Ama-Nazaretha, near Durban. Shembe composed his own hymns, some two hundred of them, and his enthusiastic apostles used them as the basis for *Izihlabelelo zaNazarethe*, an important Zulu hymnal, published in 1940, some five years after Shembe himself had died.

Dubé's work was heartily supported by the Dhlomo brothers (Herbert and Rolfus), both of whom made important contributions to the *Ilanga lase Natal* and wrote beautifully in English as well as Zulu. Herbert Dhlomo (1903-56) produced a number of popular dramas in addition to some charming verse and is remembered as one of the finest authors among South African writers of English. But while Herbert published mainly in the language of the imperialists, Rolfus Dhlomo (1901-?) specialized in Zulu historical novels. His major works included *Izikhali Zanamuhla* (1935), *U-Dingane ka Senzangakhona* (1935), *U-Shaka* (1936), *Ukwazi kiyathuthukisa* (1936), *U-Mpande ka Senzangakhona* (1936), *U-Nomalanga ka Ndengezi* (1946), *U-Cetshwayo* (1952), and *U-Dinuzulu ka Cetshwayo* (1968).

The first great expert on Bantu languages and one of the finest of all Zulu poets was Benedict Vilakazi (1906-47). A prolific writer, he contributed numerous articles in both English and Zulu to such journals as *African Studies*, *Bantu Studies*, *The Native Teachers' Journal* and *The Forum*. Countless poems of his also appeared in *Ilanga lase Natal*, *UmAfrika*, *The Bantu World* and *The Star*. Vilakazi's *Inkondlo kaZulu* was the first collection of Zulu songs to be published. It was selected by Witwatersrand University in 1935 to be the lead volume of its *Bantu Treasury Series*. Vilakazi also produced a collection of Zulu verse in *Amal'eZulu* (1945). His novels included *Nje nempela* (1933), *Noma Nini* (1935) and *U-Dingiswayo ka Jobe* (1939).

The first of the great Zulu playwrights of the modern era was Nimrod Ndebele (1913-2000), whose celebrated *Ugubdudele namazimuzimu* was published in 1941. Composed in the 1930s, it had won the Esther May Bedford Prize for Drama in 1937. It was republished as Volume VI of the *Bantu Treasury Series* in 1959.

The outpouring of Zulu literature during the second half of the twentieth century owed much to the foresight and determination of James Nxumalo (1908-?), a distinguished educator and novelist, who remained convinced that Africans would learn much faster if taught in their native tongues rather than in the language of their European masters. To this end, he produced an important Zulu grammar, *Umtapo wolwazi lwesiZulu*, in 1951. Then came such valuable works as *Isangoma somcwebo wolimi lwesiZulu* (1951), *Igugu lkaZulu* (1953), and *Umthombo wegugu likaZulu* (1953). He also published a Zulu novel, *UZwelonke*, in 1950. Nxumalo thus did a great deal to encourage the use of Zulu in Bantu schools and to formalize it as a modern African language.

Triumph of Sotho, Tswana and Pedi in the South

Just as James Nxumalo was moved to promote the use of Zulu in local schools, Zakea Mangoaela (1883-1963) felt the need to translate English works into Sotho and to produce a collection of Sotho tales and folklore to ensure the preservation of Sotho culture. His famous anthology, *Har'a libatana le linyamat'-sane*, appeared in 1912. Earlier he had published three graded readers, including the renowned *Lipaliso tsa Sesotho*, in 1903. Mangoaela's *Tsoelopela ea Lesotho* was published in 1911. He presented the world with the very first collection of Southern Sotho songs, *Lithoko tsa marena a Basotho*, in 1921.

The stage for Mangoaela's work was actually set by Thomas Mofolo (1875-1948), one of the greatest of all South African vernacular novelists. He is generally regarded as the first important African novelist of the twentieth century and foremost among Bantu authors. Writing in the traditional language of Lesotho, Mofolo published a successful novel, *Moeti oa bochabela*, in 1906, and his much acclaimed *Pitseng* in 1910. His classic, *Chaka*, appeared in 1925. All of these works have since been translated into English.

Among the greatest of Sotho authors was Bennett Khaketla (1915-2000), a distinguished playwright, poet, educator and journalist, who founded the outspoken magazine, *Mohlabani* (The Soldier), in 1956. Always interested in the traditional culture and values of his people, he published his *Sebopheho sa puo*, a very important grammar of the Sotho language, in 1957. He also wrote a number of plays, including *Moshoeshoe le baruti* (1947), *Tholoana tsa sethepu* (1954), *Thoalana tsa boikakaso* (1954) and *Bulane* (1958). Khaketla's major novels included *Meokho ea thabo* (1951) and *Mosali a nkhola* (1960). He also published some fine poetry in *Lipshamate* (1954) and a popular song, *Likenkeng*. He is now best remembered as a fervent Southern Sotho nationalist determined to throw off the European yoke and to give his native language a certain measure of respectability.

Meanwhile, Epafras Ramaila (1897-1962) tried equally valiantly to gain respect for Northern Sotho language and literature. Often called the father of Pedi, he edited the journal, *Mogwara wa babaso*, for several years. His major works included such short stories as *Molomatsebe* (1951) and *Taukobong* (1953); a novel, *Tsakata* (1953); a biography, *Tsa bophelo bya moruti Abraham*

Serote 1865-1930 (1931); two historical studies, *Ditaba tsa South Africa* (1938) and *Setloxo sa batau* (1938); and some excellent poetry in *Direto* (1956) and *Seriti sa Thabantsho* (1960).

Tswana was fortunate in having such a vigorous and unrelenting champion as Solomon Plaatje (1878-1932) whose linguistic skills enabled him to serve as a useful interpreter and signalman for the British Army during the Boer War. From 1901 to 1908, he edited the weekly journal, *Koranta ea beloana* (The Tswana Gazette). He later edited and published the *Tsala ea batho* (Friend of the People). A prolific and scholarly writer in English, Plaatje also translated several Shakespeare plays into Tswana.

The Flourishing of Yoruba and Hausa in Nigeria

West Africans were no less resolute in their determination to promote native language and literature during the colonial era. Revd Samuel Crowther (1807?-91), the first African to be ordained by the Christian Missionary Society, fell foul of the imperial administration when he attempted to preserve traditional values by publishing *A Grammar and Vocabulary of the Yoruba Language in* 1852. He taught Nigerians the importance of respecting their roots even after he himself had risen to high office in the Anglican Church. Crowther was the first black priest to achieve the rank of bishop.

Chief Daniel Olorunfemi Fagunwa (1910-63), a famous Nigerian educator and author, continued Crowther's important crusade by collecting and editing folk tales, which he translated into English. He also wrote several books himself in the Yoruba language. His best-known novel, *Ogboju ode Ninu Igbo Irunmale* (1939), was translated into English and published in 1968 as *The Forest of a Thousand Daemons*. His other works included *Alaye fun Oluko Nipa Lilo Iwe Taiwo ati Kehinde* (1949), *Irinago apa Kini* (1949), *Ireke Onibudo* (1949), *Irinkerindo Ninu Igbo Elegbeje* (1954), *Asayan itan* (1959) and *Adiitu Olodumare* (1961).

Hubert Ogunde (1916-90) was as keen on traditional Yoruba music as on traditional Yoruba drama and theatre. It was he who established the African Music and Dance Research Party which became the first professional theatrical company in Nigeria. An innovative pioneer in the field of Nigerian folk opera, he succeeded wonderfully well in merging traditional Yoruba folk songs with Christian elements in his compositions. In addition to Yoruba songs, Ogunde also wrote some fine Yoruba plays, including *Yoruba Ronu* (1964), *O tito koro* (1965), *Aropin n't`enia* (1967) and *Ologbu dudu* (1967).

Duro Ladipo (1931-78) was another skilful Nigerian playwright, actor and producer who did a great deal to popularize the folk operas and traditions of the Yoruba people. After helping to found the Mbari Mbayo Club in Oshogbo, he established the Duro Ladipo Theatre Company in 1962. His early plays, *Oba Moro* (The King of Ghosts, 1962), *Oba Koso* (The King Did

Not Hang, 1963) and *Oba Waja* (The King Is Dead, 1964) have all become classics of the Yoruba stage and have introduced Yoruba dramatic ideas and conventions to a worldwide audience. A later work, *Eda*, gave further evidence of the validity of his decision to intellectualize Yoruba folk-opera. Ladipo had begun as a composer of Yoruba church music and it was his successful adaptation of Bible stories for the stage that led him to found his own theatre group. The most popular of his productions was *Oba Koso*, which won the Nigerian federal government award for the most significant contribution to culture in 1963, was highly successful at the Berlin Theatre Festival in 1964, and was presented at the Commonwealth Theatre Festival at London, England, in 1967.

Better known as Sir Tafawa Balewa, who became the first federal prime minister of independent Nigeria in 1960, Alhaji Abubakar (1912-66) was also an important linguist and author. He was anxious to promote the use of Hausa in Nigerian schools and himself produced a fine Hausa novel, *Shaihu Umar*, which was eventually translated into English and published in 1967, some twelve years after its original appearance.

Survival of Ewe, Fante, Fulani and Twi in Western Africa

Fante, a Gold Coast medium of communication, found two notable grammarians during the nineteenth century. Joseph Peter Brown (1843-1932) was instrumental in popularizing the use of this language, a grammar of which he published in 1875 and revised in 1913. His son, E.J.P. Brown (1875-1929), wrote several books in English but also published Fante grammars and primers as well as the *Gold Coast and Ashante Reader: a collection of folk tales, proverbs, customs and manners*, which appeared just before his death.

But it was Gaddiel Acquaah (1884-1954) who was the first West African to write mainly in Fante. His famous *Fante Bible* was eventually published in 1944. His poetry appeared in such collections as *Oguaa Aban* (1939) and *Nsem A Wonyin* (1939). His collection of hymns for children, *Mbofraba Asorye Ndwom*, was published in 1929. Among his other major works were *Fante Proverbs* and *John Wesley*, and a popular novel, *The Morning After*, which appeared some years after his death.

Ewe, meanwhile, found its strongest early supporters in Andreas Aku (1863-1931) and Dr Ferdinand Kwasi Fiawoo (1891-1969). The former was a notable Ghanaian author and theologian who became the first indigenous head of the Ewe Presbyterian Church in 1922. He was the first scholar to translate the Bible into Ewe and he also completed an Ewe translation of Bunyan's *Pilgrim's Progress*. Fiawoo became a distinguished Ewe playwright, educator and politician, who popularized the Ewe language after producing his famous *Toko Atolia*, an Ewe drama, in 1932. He aimed constantly and resolutely at the fusion of Christian education with the best in African culture.

David Asante (1834-92) was another keen West African convert to Christianity who tried valiantly to spread that gospel in Anum and Togoland. He was largely instrumental in producing a Twi translation of the Bible while writing several books in Twi and providing his countrymen with a number of other valuable translations. Asante also wrote a Twi hymn and coined several new Twi words. His contribution to the development of modern Twi language and literature is almost beyond calculation.

Twi was eventually furnished in 1938 with its most famous grammar text, *Twi Kasa Mmara*, by Clement Anderson Akrofi (1901-67), a noted educator, theologian and linguist. A leading authority on Twi, he advocated its adoption as Ghana's official language and published a modern Twi Bible in 1965.

Dr Joseph Boakye Danquah (1895-1965), a brilliant Ghanaian scholar and lawyer, is best known perhaps for such classics as *Akan Laws and Customs* (1928), *Cases in Akan Law* (1928), *The Akan Doctrine of God* (1944) and *Revelation of Culture in Ghana* (1961). He was also one of the earliest of the modern Twi playwrights. His dramas included *Nyankonsem* (Heavenly Tales) and *Biribi Wo Baabi* (There is More Beyond). An accomplished poet, historian and dramatist, Dr Danquah was able to write superbly on a variety of interesting subjects both in English and in Akupem-Twi.

This tradition was continued by Kwabena Nkeita (1921-?), an outstanding Assante-Twi scholar, novelist, playwright and musicologist. Publishing numerous seminal books in both English and Twi, he left a huge impact on West African music and literature. Some of his important contributions to musicology appeared in *African Music in Ghana* (1955), *Drumming in the Akan Communities of Ghana* (1955), *Funeral Dirges of the Akan People* (1955) and *Folk Songs of Ghana* (1963). Nkeita also wrote a successful novel, *Kwabena Amoa* (1953) and some fine poetry in *Anwonsen 1944-1949* (1952), *Akwansosem bi* (1967) and a much acclaimed play, *Ananwoma* (1951), which went through six editions within the space of twelve years.

Fulani found its ablest advocate in Mallam Amadou Bâ (1920?-?), a famous Mali scholar and theologian, generally known as the 'Sage of Bamako'. It was he who first developed a satisfactory Arabic script for the modern Fulani language. His major works, however, appeared in French and he is better known in the west for his *L'Empire Peul du Macina 1818-53* and a biography, *Tierno Bokar: Le Sage de Bandiagara*. Bâ also wrote poetry, some of which appeared in *Koumen: Texte Iniatique des Pasteurs Peuls* (1961) and *Kaidara* (1965).

Mainly English, French and Spanish in the Western Hemisphere

This remarkable upsurge of native African literature in the second half of the twentieth century was an integral feature of the rise of modern African nationalism. Pride in traditional customs and values was much encouraged in the period of decolonization. European culture was all too reminiscent of white oppression of local Blacks. Interestingly enough, however, the history of creole or patois in the Caribbean and elsewhere was markedly different. The major media of black communication in the western hemisphere have been English, French and Spanish, in which some of the very best writing has been done by the products of the diaspora. Although that remarkable Jamaican poetess and entertainer, Louise Bennett (1919-2006), has shown the possibilities of local creole, the majority of black writers in the west have continued to write in the European languages. Even though Kamau Brathwaite often uses what he terms 'nation language' - the language of servants and slaves who had been transported from Africa - the base of his prose and verse is still largely English.

In the United States alone, the list of outstanding African-American authors is enormous. Every genre has spawned black geniuses throughout the twentieth century. Great dramatists such as Lorraine Hansberry (1930-65) and Langston Hughes (1902-67); historians such as John Hope Franklin (1915-?), Charles Harris Wesley (1891-1987) and Carter G. Woodson (1875-1950); novelists such as Maya Angelou (1928-), James Baldwin (1924-87), Arna Wendell Bontemps (1902-73), Ralph Waldo Ellison (1914-94), Alex Haley (1921- 92), Toni Morrison (1931-?) and Richard Wright (1908-60); philosophers and theologians such as Alain Locke (1886-1954) and Howard Thurman (1900-81); poets such as Gwendolyn Brooks (1917-2000), Countee Cullen (1903-46), Paul Dunbar (1872-1906), Georgia Johnson (1886-1966) and James Weldon Johnson (1871-1938); and sociologists such as W.E.B. Du Bois (1868-1963), Franklin Frazier (1894-1962), Charles Spurgeon Johnson (1893-1956) and Kelly Miller (1863-1939) have all flourished.

The Caribbean has also produced literary giants at an astonishing rate. The lengthy list of notable English authors from that region includes Edward Brathwaite (1912-?), Kamau Brathwaite (1930-?), Jan Carew (1925-?), Austin Clarke (1932-?), Cecil Foster (1954-?), Errol Hill (1921-2003), C.L.R. James (1901-89), Errol John (1924-88), George Lamming (1927-?), Clare McFarlane (1923-62), Claude McKay (1890-1948), Andrew Salkey (1928-95) and Derek Walcott (1930-?).

No less prolific have been the black Francophone authors in the Caribbean. It is almost a miracle that Haiti and Martinique, two of the poorest communities in the world, have been able to produce so many literary geniuses. That small island of Martinique, which measures less than 450 square miles and still remains an overseas department of France, gave the world the magnificent writings of Aimé Césaire (1913-?), Frantz Fanon (1925-61), Édouard Glissant (1928-?), René Maran (1887-1960) and Joseph Zobel (1915-2006). Aimé Césaire was one of the finest writers of French in the twentieth century. One of the founders of the movement known as négritude (Black is Beautiful), he left a profound impression on all African French authors, especially those in Senegal. His works have been translated into many languages (both African and European) and have left an indelible impact on modern black thinking. Equally important is Dr Frantz Fanon's philosophy as expressed in such acrid and searching works as *Peau noire, masques blancs* (Black Skin, White Masks, 1952), *L'An V de la révolution algérienne* (1959), *Les Damnés de la terre* (The Wretched of the Earth, 1961) and *Pour la révolution africaine* (posthumously in 1964).

Black Haiti's literary output in the twentieth century was simply monumental. Devastated as it was by a series of political crises and natural disasters, that unfortunate country nevertheless produced authors of the quality of Jacques Stéphen Alexis (1922-?), Réné Bélance (1915-?), Jean Fernand Brierre (1909-1992), Roussan Camille (1912-61), René Depestre (1926-?), Anténor Joseph Firmin (1851-1911), Louis-Joseph Janvier (1855-1911), Jean Price-Mars (1876-1969) and Jacques Roumain (1907-44), among a host of others. Haitian literature has been such a well kept secret, even from neighbours in the Caribbean, that it is not very well known that François Duvalier (1907-71), arguably the leading Haitian politician of the twentieth century, left a solid corpus of literature on politics, sociology and medicine. Apart from his monumental *Oeuvres essentielles*, which appeared in four volumes 1958, his miscellaneous writings included *Politique étrangère; histoire diplomatique* (1968), *Politique frontérale, géographie politique* (1968) and *Hommage au Marron Inconnu* (1969). Duvalier was also the co-author, among other works, of the important *Les tendances d'une génération* (1934), *Le problème des classes à travers l'histoire d'Haiti* (1948), and *L'avenir du pays et l'action néfaste de M. Foisset* (1949). He was very influential in shifting Haitian literature and philosophy away from their French models by making local authors increasingly conscious of their debt to African patterns and influences.

As Richard L. Jackson has shown, in his seminal *Black Writers of Latin America*, the Western Hemisphere has spawned a good number of African-American Spanish writers too. Even when it was dangerous, in the nineteenth century, for freed Blacks to write in support of abolition, almost every Latin American society produced its quota of local activists supporting the black cause in eloquent Spanish verse and prose. The classic example in the twentieth century was Cuba's Nicolás Guillén whose celebrated *Motivos de son* left an indelible impact on white and black Cubans alike.

Much More to Blackness than Song and Dance

During the twentieth century, as is very well-known, Blacks became famous the world over for their significant contributions to modern music and sport. In a disparaging manner, some Whites dismissed them simply as too keen on 'play, song and dance'. A careful study of modern language and literature, however, will clearly show that Blacks have done incredibly good work in these fields as well.

BLACKBURN, Thornton

Thornton Blackburn, a fugitive slave who fled from Kentucky to Toronto in 1833, is famous for having designed, built and operated the first taxicab in Upper Canada. Although he was illiterate, he noted trends in public transportation in other cities. He obtained the pattern of a cab from Montreal and gave the commission for its construction to Paul Bishop who delivered the completed vehicle to Blackburn in 1837. The yellow and red cab, named 'The City', was drawn by one horse. It held four passengers together with the driver who sat at the front. Blackburn's business was so successful that many others shortly copied his example.

BLACKMAN, Courtney

Since 1995, His Excellency Courtney Newlands McLaurin Blackman has been Barbados' ambassador to the United Nations and its permanent representative to the Organization of American States (OAS). Born in Barbados in 1933, he was educated at Foundation School and Harrison College before proceeding to the University College of the West Indies (UCWI) in Mona, Jamaica, on a Government Scholarship in 1952. Following his graduation with a BA (Hons) in modern history, he worked as an administrative trainee and then personnel officer with Alcan Jamaica. He then taught for some years in Barbados, Ghana and Jamaica before resuming his studies at the Inter-American University in Puerto Rico and Columbia University in the United States and achieving his PhD in 1969. After lecturing briefly at Hofstra University in Long Island, New York, Dr Blackman returned to his native island to become the first governor of the Barbados Central Bank in 1972, a post he held with distinction for many years. He contributed enormously to his country's reputation as having one of the best managed economies in the developing world. Dr Blackman has been a consultant on international business for several governments and corporations in the West Indies. He has also delivered numerous lectures throughout the Caribbean. In addition to *The Theory and Practice of Central Banking: A Small State's Perspective*, a collection of his essays, and *The Practice of Persuasion*, a collection of his speeches, Blackman has published many articles in scholarly journals. For his services he was awarded his country's Gold Crown of Merit (GCM) and the Barbados Central Bank honoured him in 1998 by establishing the Courtney Blackman Chair in Finance on the Cave Hill campus of the University of the West Indies (UWI). The latter institution also recognized Dr Blackman as one of its Distinguished Graduates when it celebrated its 50th anniversary in July 1998.

BLAIR, Henry

Born in Maryland around 1807, Henry Blair was only the second African-American to receive a patent. He did so in 1834 when he invented a seed planter. Two years later, he patented his famous cotton planter. These two devices were destined to be routinely used throughout the American South during the second half of the nineteenth century. The fact that Blair remained illiterate throughout his life makes his inventions all the more noteworthy. He had to sign his patents with an 'X'. He died in 1860.

BLAIZE, Herbert

Herbert A. Blaize was a prominent figure in Grenadian politics for more than three decades. Born on 26 February 1918, in Carriacou, he was the founder of the Grenada National Party (GNP) in 1953. After taking a Law Society correspondence course, he became a solicitor and was elected to the legislature in 1957. He was appointed chief minister in 1960 but was defeated in 1961 by his main rival, Eric Gairy, then the leader of the Grenada United Labour Party. Blaize was returned to office in 1962 when Gairy was removed by the British government following accusations of corruption. Grenada achieved internal self-government during Blaize's tenure, but Gairy's party was returned to power in 1967. For the next seventeen years Blaize retired from the centre stage but re-emerged in 1984 to lead a coalition government after the overthrow of Maurice Bishop's revolutionary régime. He died on 19 December 1989.

BLAKE, Eubie

James Hubert Blake was one of the greatest and most versatile of all American musicians during the twentieth century. He was a pianist, singer, composer, vaudeville performer, musical director, recording artist, concert and jazz-festival performer, record-company founder, and talk-show guest. As late as the 1980s, when he was almost 100 years old, he was still performing occasionally in public. He made his last professional appearance in 1982 at the age of ninety-nine. Born in Baltimore, Maryland, on 7 February 1883, Eubie Blake was the son of former slaves. A precocious pianist and organist, he made his first public appearance when he was only fifteen. He then toured the vaudeville circuit for many years and produced an outstanding triumph, *Shuffle Along*, in 1921. It was the first Broadway musical to be composed, produced, directed, and performed solely by Blacks. Blake and Noble Sissle also combined to produce such successful musicals as *Elsie* in 1923 and *Chocolate Dandies* in 1924. With a revival of interest of this kind of music some thirty and forty years later, Blake was able to make a triumphant return to Broadway in 1978 with *Eubie*! He was awarded the US Medal of Freedom in 1981 and died, on 12 February 1983, just five days after celebrating his own centennial.

BLANKSON, George Kuntu

An outstanding Gold Coast merchant, soldier, diplomat and statesman, George Kuntu Blankson, the son of Chief Kuntu of Egya, was born at Sodufu in 1809. He was the first native African to be invited to serve on the Gold Coast Legislative Council (1861-73). He worked briefly as a missionary before becoming a full-time trader. His ventures were so successful that he could afford to contribute huge sums towards the building of Ebenezer Church at Anomabu and a school at Mankoadze. But his support of the British during the Asante Wars made him most unpopular in West Africa where his plantations were plundered and his crops destroyed during the 1870s. Blankson became a devout Christian and spent his last years in isolation. He died on 23 August 1898.

BLIZZARD, Stephen

Dr Stephen V. Blizzard is a physician specializing in aviation medicine. He is also a military jet pilot and a flying instructor. Born in Trinidad, he emigrated to Canada in 1958 after studying in the United Kingdom. He joined the Royal Canadian Air Force in 1960, rising to the rank of major in the late 1970s. In 1982 he was deputy commanding officer with the National Defence Medical Detachment and later served as chief of the Civil Aviation Medical Unit with the Department of Civil Aviation Medicine. In 2000 he was appointed a senior consultant of marine medicine with Transport Canada. Dr Blizzard is the author of numerous seminal papers on aviation medicine and the recipient of several awards and distinctions, including a Canadian Forces Decoration (1977), a UN Peacekeeping Force Medal (1979) and a Canadian Peacekeeping Medal (2001). His major works include *The Role of the Doctor in Civil Defence*, *Clinical Aspects of Brucellosis in Man*, *Patient Care in Flight*, and *Photo Chromic Lenses in the Aviation Environment*.

BLUFORD, Guion

Born on 22 November 1942 in Philadelphia, Lt Col Guion Stewart Bluford became the first African-American to travel in space with the lift-off of the STS-8 Orbiter Challenger on 30 August 1983. He graduated from Pennsylvania State University in 1964 and enrolled in the United States Air Force while continuing his studies and earning a PhD in engineering. He made three additional trips into space, altogether clocking almost 700 hours orbiting the earth, before retiring from NASA in 1993. Bluford became vice-president and general manager of the Federal Data Corporation's Science and Engineering Group, Aerospace Sector. He is also programme manager of NASA's Glenn Research Center Microgravity Research, Development and Operations Contract in Cleveland, Ohio. He became a member of the Colorado-based Space Foundation's board of directors in 2000. He was inducted into the International Space Hall of Fame in 1997.

BLYDEN, Edward

Edward Wilmot Blyden was a Liberian educator, scholar, activist, diplomat and statesman who did more than any other figure to lay the foundation for West African nationalism and Pan Africanism. He was born in St Thomas, Virgin Islands, on 3 August 1832 and immigrated to the United States in 1850 with the hope of becoming a clergyman. Disillusioned by the racial barriers he encountered there, he moved to Liberia in 1851 and continued his formal education at Alexander High School in Monrovia. Despite the fact that Blyden was largely self-taught, he became an accomplished linguist, classicist, theologian, historian and sociologist. From 1862 to 1871, he served as professor of classics at the newly opened Liberia College. During 1864-66, in addition to his professorial duties, he acted as secretary of state for Liberia. While living in Sierra Leone briefly during the early 1870s, he edited *Negro*, the first pan-African journal in West Africa. Returning to Liberia, he served that country as its ambassador to Britain and France. He later became the president of Liberia College. Blyden then spent a few years in Nigeria where he wrote regularly for the *Lagos Weekly Record*, one of the earliest promoters of Nigerian and West African nationalism, and in Sierra Leone where he assisted in founding (and helping to edit) the influential *Sierra Leone News* and also the *West African Reporter*. In Sierra Leone, he taught English and 'Western subjects' to young Muslims with the view of building a bridge between the Christian and Muslim communities. Blyden flatly rejected the notion of black inferiority and sought to prove that Africans have a worthy history and culture. As a champion and defender of his race, he published numerous articles, pamphlets and books. His major works included *A Voice From Bleeding Africa* (1856), *Liberia's Offering* (1862), *The Negro in Ancient History* (1869), *The West African University* (1872), *From West Africa to Palestine* (1873), *Christianity, Islam and the Negro Race* (1887), *The Jewish Question* (1898), *West Africa Before Europe* (1905); and *Africa Life and Customs* (1908). Blyden died in Freetown on 7 February 1912.

BOAKYE, Kwasi

Son of Kwaku Dua I, a prominent West African chief, Kwasi Boakye was born on 29 April 1827. He was educated in the Netherlands where he studied mining and engineering and became a convert to Christianity. Accepting employment with the Dutch East India Company he was posted to Java, where he studied the geological structure of the coal-beds and published his findings in Dutch and German journals. He also became a wealthy coffee-planter in Java, where he died at Buitzenzorg on 9 July 1904 after having been made an honorary member of the Society of (Delft) Civil Engineers.

BOATENG, Ozwald

Ozwald Boateng is a famous fashion designer who was born in Ghana in the late 1960s and raised in London, England. The first tailor to stage a catwalk show in Paris, he began making 'bespoke suits' in 1990 and is widely credited with having introduced Savile Row tailoring to a new generation. He was appointed creative director of Givenchy menswear in 2003 and was awarded the Order of the British Empire (OBE) in 2006.

BOATENG, Paul

The Rt Honourable Paul Yaw Boateng was born in Ghana on 14 June 1951 to a Ghanaian father and Scottish mother. His family emigrated to the United Kingdom after the 1966 coup that toppled Kwame Nkrumah's government. Paul was educated at Apsley Grammar School and the University of Bristol. He became a famous civil rights lawyer who persistently denounced the British police for their brutal treatment of African and Asian communities. He was elected to the Greater London Council in1981 and continued his crusade on behalf of racial equality. He gained a seat in the House of Commons in 1987 and held it until his resignation in 2005 to serve as the UK ambassador to South Africa. He became the first Black to serve as a cabinet member in the United Kingdom when he was appointed chief secretary to the treasury in 2002. In 1997 he had also made history when, as undersecretary of state in the department of health, he became the first black politician to hold ministerial office in Great Britain.

BOKASSA, Jean-Bédel

Born at Bobangui in French Equatorial Africa on 22 February 1921, Jean-Bédel Bokassa had originally intended to study for the priesthood, but when World War II broke out, he joined the French army instead and fought in Indochina, where he rose to the rank of captain and was awarded the Croix de Guerre. After the Central African Republic became independent in 1960, he was appointed chief of staff of its small army while his cousin, David Dacko, served as president. He became commander in chief of the Central African Army in 1963 and was appointed to various ministerial posts while retaining his military command. He ousted Dacko in a bloodless military coup on 1 January 1966. Bokassa proceeded to rule his country in a ruthless and autocratic manner and, on 4 December 1977, crowned himself emperor of the new Central African Empire. His rule, characterized by greed and brutality, came to an end in 1979 when he was overthrown by a French military coup and driven into exile. When he returned home in 1986, he was tried for the murders he had caused to be committed while he was emperor and given a life sentence in prison. He died on 22 April 1996.

BOKWE, John Knox

This outstanding Xhosa poet, song-writer, musician, preacher and teacher was born near Lovedale in South Africa on 15 March 1855. Himself the son of a former teacher, he was ordained a minister in 1899 and helped to construct a new church building and thirteen new mission stations in such districts as Maclear, Tsolo and Ugie. He was also instrumental in the founding of the South African Native College at Fort Hare. Revd.John Knox Bokwe was a fine pianist who had earlier begun to write words and music for Xhosa hymns. The result was the publication of the well-known *Amaculo ase Rabe* in 1885. He also became editor of the *Imvo Zabantsundu*, which published items in both English and Xhosa. His Xhosa biography, *Ibali Lika Ntsikana*, appeared in 1914. Bokwe died on 22 February 1922.

BONDS, Barry

The son of Bobby Bonds, a former all-star baseball player, Barry Lamar Bonds was born in Riverside, California, on 24 July 1964. He was a brilliant centre fielder in his youth and shone for the Pittsburgh Pirates even as a rookie in the baseball major league in 1986. His phenomenal ability as a hitter led to his selection as the most valuable player (MVP) in the National League in 1990 and 1991 and to the offer in 1992 by the San Francisco Giants of a six-year contract worth $43,750,000, then the highest for any baseball player. He later extended his contract with the Giants for five years in 2002 for the phenomenal sum of $90 million. He has thus already (2006) earned more than $150 million and is one of baseball's highest-paid players. Bonds continued to star with his new team, winning MVP awards again in 1997 and 2001, scoring a sensational 73 home runs in the latter year. This established a new record for major league baseball in the United States. Bonds also enjoyed some successful play-off series in 2002, erasing previous doubts about his ability to perform well in world series competition. One of the greatest of all baseball players, his magnificent batting has often overshadowed his fielding prowess and pundits do not always remember that he has earned several Golden Glove awards. In 2005, he became only the third hitter, following Babe Ruth (714) and Hank Aaron (755) to exceed 700 home runs in a major league career. He currently stands in second place with 731. He is the only player to exceed 500 home runs and 500 stolen bases in a major league career and holds every conceivable record for walks, of which he has accumulated more than 600 of the intentional variety. Within the last few seasons, however, he has become involved in the infamous Balco scandal and there are suspicions that he has been the beneficiary of performing-enhancing substances, although he has never once tested positive for the use of illegal drugs.

BONGO, Omar

Albert Bernard Bongo, a member of the Bateko, a Gabonese ethnic minority group, was born on 30 December 1935 in the Franceville region of French Equatorial Africa. Educated at the Brazzaville Technical College, he worked briefly in the public service before entering the French Air Force. In 1960, when Gabon gained its political independence, he was appointed assistant director of the ministry of foreign affairs. In 1966 he became deputy prime minister and was elected vice-president of the republic in 1967. After the death of Gabon's first president, Léon M'ba, later that same year, Bongo succeeded to the presidency. He established a one-party state in 1968 and converted to Islam in 1973, when he adopted the name Omar. His policy of state-directed private enterprise and promotion of foreign investments appears to have succeeded since Gabon enjoyed a fair degree of economic prosperity during the first decades of his administration. Abroad, he tightened the Gabonese alliance with France while doing his best to support the goals of the Organization of African Unity (OAU) over which he presided in 1977 when its annual conference was held in Libreville, his own capital city. Bongo has remained president of Gabon until today (2006) and is the longest-serving leader on the African continent. He tries often to mediate disputes in neighbouring countries and is highly respected as the 'Grand Old Man' of west African politics.

BONTEMPS, Arna Wendell

Arna Wendell Bontemps was born in Alexandria, Louisiana, on 13 October 1902. After graduating from Union Pacific College in 1923, he became a leading figure in the Harlem Renaissance and soon established an enviable reputation as an author and critic. He was librarian at Fisk University (Nashville, Tennessee) from 1943 to 1965, professor at the University of Chicago during 1966-69, lecturer and curator in the Beinecke Rare Book and Manuscript Library at Yale University in 1969, and in 1970 was named writer in residence at Fisk. His novels included *God Sends Sunday* (1931), *Black Thunder* (1936), *Chariot in the Sky* (1951) and *Great Slave Narratives* (1969). Bontemps also assisted in the writing of W.C. Handy's autobiography, *Father of the Blues* (1941). With Langston Hughes, he edited *The Poetry of the Negro*

1746-1949 (1949) and *The Book of Negro Folklore* (1958). In addition, he wrote biographies of Frederick Douglass and George Washington Carver, while serving as a critic for *The American Scholar* and the *Saturday Review*. Bontemps' works succeeded in demonstrating that black art, music and poetry have a rich heritage of their own. They brought him numerous prizes and awards, including the Crisis Poetry Prize and the Alexander Pushkin Prize, both in 1926, and the Jane Addams Children's Book Award in 1956. Arna Wendell Bontemps died on 4 June 1973.

BORDEN, George

Captain George Borden was born in New Glasgow, Nova Scotia. He served in the Royal Canadian Air Force (now the Canadian Forces) from 1953 to 1985. When, in the latter year, he was appointed executive assistant to the provincial Minister of Social Services, he became the first Black to hold such a position in his native province. An accomplished poet and songwriter, Captain Borden wrote the lyrics for the *Easter Suite*, a cantata of ten original gospel songs, performed in 1999. He is also an author of some merit, having published a useful trilogy on the Black Experience: *Canaan Odyssey* (1988); *Footprints, Images* and *Reflections* (1993); and *A Mighty Long Way* (2000). An active community servant, George Borden served as Executive Director of the Black United Front for Nova Scotia in 1984 and was Executive Director of the Black Cultural Society of Nova Scotia during 1993-94.

BOSTON, H.J.H.

Sir Henry Josiah Lightfoot Boston became the first Governor General of Sierra Leone (1962-67) after a distinguished legal career. Born on 19 August 1898, he graduated from Fourah Bay College with an MA in 1920 before studying law in England, where he achieved his LLB and BCL from Durham University. He returned in 1926 to establish his private practice at Freetown and was appointed a Justice of the Peace in 1935 and a police magistrate in 1946. Boston rose to the posts of registrar general of the Supreme Court in 1954 and senior police magistrate in 1955. In 1957 he became speaker of the newly constituted House of Representatives. Five years later, he received a knighthood and was asked to serve as Sierra Leone's first Governor General. He was ousted during the military coup of 1967 but received a state burial when he died on 11 January 1969.

BOURNE, Maurice Eugene

Dr Maurice Eugene Bourne was Montreal's very first black dentist. He practised successfully there from 1950 to 1985. He had previously served in the Dental Corps during World War II. He established a free dental clinic at the Negro Community Centre and was an active member of the

Montreal Negro Alumni Group and the Montreal Dental Centre. Dr Bourne was also a dental consultant to the Sun Life Insurance Company.

BOYKIN, Otis

Otis Boykin was born in Dallas, Texas, on 20 August 1920. After graduating from Fisk University and the Illinois Institute of Technology, he worked as a laboratory assistant testing automatic controls for aircraft. He later worked as a consultant for several firms while inventing a number of new devices. He invented an improved electrical resistor used in computers, radios and television sets. He also created a new type of variable resistor that came to be used in guided missile parts, a burglar-proof cash register and a chemical air filter. His innovations in resistor design considerably reduced the cost of producing electronic controls for radio and television. Among his 28 electronic devices, Boykin is best remembered for his invention of the pacemaker which has already saved and/or prolonged millions of lives. He died in Chicago, Illinois, in 1982. The supreme irony is that the inventor of a gadget to stimulate heart action, himself succumbed to heart failure at the age of sixty-two.

BRADLEY, Thomas

Born on 29 December 1917 in Calvert, Texas, but raised in Los Angeles, California, Thomas Bradley, the son of a sharecropper, showed exceptional promise as a track star and attended the University College of Los Angeles (UCLA) on an athletic scholarship. He joined the Los Angeles police department and rose to the rank of lieutenant before qualifying as a lawyer and entering private practice in 1961. In 1963, he became the first black man to be elected to the Los Angeles City Council. Ten years later, Bradley became the first African-American to be elected mayor of Los Angeles. He pledged, among other things, to control street crime, to establish a rapid transit system, and to revive the city's core by attracting private investment. During his lengthy tenure as mayor (1973-93), Los Angeles experienced massive growth and became the second largest city in the United States. Largely instrumental in forging alliances between business and government, Bradley played a key role in the huge success of the 1984 Olympic Games which were held in his city. He died on 29 September 1998.

BRADSHAW, Robert

Robert Llewellyn Bradshaw was the first prime minister of St Kitts-Nevis-Anguilla in 1967 when the three West Indian islands became an independent state in association with the United Kingdom. Born on 16 September 1916, in St Kitts, he was educated at the St Paul's Anglican School there. He worked as a machinist in the central sugar factory from 1922 to 1940 before founding the St Kitts Labour Party and the St Kitts Trade and Labour Union. In 1946 he became a member of the Legislative Council and began his campaign for increased civil liberties, local autonomy and West Indian federation. He became a member of the regional parliament when the British West Indian Federation was established in 1958 and served as its minister of finance. When the federation was dissolved in 1962, Bradshaw returned to St Kitts as minister without portfolio until 1966, when he became chief minister. He led the three islands to independence in 1967 and remained their chief minister until his death on 24 May 1978.

BRAITHWAITE, Edward

Born on 27 June1912 in Georgetown, British Guiana, Edward R. Braithwaite gained immediate fame when his popular novel, *To Sir With Love*, became the subject of a major film, with Sidney Poitier as leading actor, in 1973. After graduating with a BS from City College, New York, in 1940, Braithwaite joined the Royal Air Force during World War II and then completed his MSc in physics at Cambridge University in 1949. He taught in London, England, from 1950 to 1957 before serving as a London Council welfare officer during 1958-60. He was Human Rights Officer in the Veterans' Foundation in Paris (1960-63) before being appointed Lecturer and Education Officer with UNESCO (1963-66). Following Guyana's achievement of political independence in 1966, Braithwaite joined its diplomatic service and was appointed its permanent representative to the United Nations. In addition to *To Sir With Love*, which won the Anisfield-Wolf Award in 1960, he published such other novels as *A Kind of Homecoming* (1962), *A Choice of Straws* (1965), *Paid Servant* (1968), *Reluctant Neighbours* (1972) and *Honorary White* (1975).

BRAITHWAITE, F. Carlton

A native of Jamaica, Dr F. Carlton Braithwaite, a well-known scholar-athlete, immigrated to Canada in 1962 after graduating from the University of the West Indies with a BA in mathematics and economics. He earned an MA from McMaster University and a PhD in economics from Queen's University. From 1966 to 1982, he worked with the federal government first as chief, Econometric Research Division, Statistics Canada, and then as senior economist, Economic Council of Canada. During this time, he wrote several articles which led to changes in the policies and methodologies of Statistics Canada and the Economic Council. He also wrote two influential books, *An Econometric Analysis of the Determinants of Investment in Canadian Manufacturing* (1971) and *The Impact of Investment Incentives on Canada's Economic Growth* (1983).

He consequently became recognized as one of the leading economists on investment in Canada. In 1983, Dr Braithwaite retired from the federal service and founded the highly successful Uniprop Group of Companies which invested mainly in real estate and high-tech industries. Within a few years, the group amassed over $100 million. In 1987, he co-founded the Commonwealth Club of Ottawa which later became known as Commonwealth Club International. During 1995-97, he served on the Board of Directors of the Ontario Realty Corporation. He has recently become an independent distributor for Miranda Inc., a leading natural health and wellness network marketing company. Despite his active professional life, he has remained an enthusiastic community servant in Ottawa.

BRAITHWAITE, Leonard

Leonard Austin Braithwaite, who was born in Toronto on 23 October 1923 to West Indian parents, is best remembered as the first black man to be elected to the Ontario legislature. A graduate of the University of Toronto, the Harvard School of Business Administration and the Osgoode Law School in Toronto, he practised as a barrister and solicitor and was named a Queen's Counsel in 1971. He was elected in 1963 as a member of the provincial Liberal Party to represent the upper middle-class suburb of Etobicoke and served in that capacity until 1975. He did not see himself as primarily a civil rights activist, but he spoke eloquently in favour of racial equality and encouraged other Canadian Blacks to participate actively in local and federal politics. An effective speaker in the legislature, he was instrumental in destroying traditional patterns of segregation in Ontario public schools. He was awarded the Order of Canada in 1997 and the Order of Ontario in 2005.

BRAITHWAITE, Rella Aylestock

Born in Listowel, Ontario, Rella Aylestock Braithwaite has devoted her major energies to the study of the black experience in Canada. In 1973, she co-authored a booklet, *Women of Our Times*, for the first Black Women's Congress. Since then, in addition to numerous articles in ethnic journals, she has written *The Black Woman in Canada* (1975); *Some Black Women* (1993); and *Some Black Men* (1999). She has addressed many audiences on the subject of Canadian Blacks and has amassed a huge collection of black memorabilia.

BRAND, Dionne

Dionne Brand is a distinguished Canadian academic, essayist, poet and documentary film-director and is arguably the loudest and most eloquent voice in support of black Canadian women's quest for freedom and equality.

In 1991, her excellent book of poems, *No Language is Neutral*, was nominated
for the Governor General's Award. Her popular and successful film-
documentaries include *Older, Stronger, Wiser* and *Sisters in the Struggle*. Brand was
born in the West Indies but has lived for many years in Toronto, Ontario.
Among her major publications is *No Burden to Carry* (1991).

BRATHWAITE, Edward Kamau

Edward Kamau Brathwaite, a distinguished West Indian scholar, poet,
playwright, literary critic and teacher, was born in Barbados on 11 May
1930. Educated at Harrison College, he won the prestigious Barbados
Scholarship in 1949, and proceeded to earn his BA in History from
Cambridge University, England, in 1953. After working for some time in
Ghana and the West Indies, he completed his PhD at the University of
Sussex, England, in 1968. Brathwaite, who served for many years as extra-
mural tutor of the University of the West Indies in St Lucia, has also
lectured in many North American universities. His poems have appeared
in such publications as *Rights of Passage* (1967), *Masks* (1968), *Islands* (1969),
The Arrivants (1973), *Mother Poems* (1977), *Barbados Poetry* (1979), *Jamaica
Poetry* (1979), *Third World Poems* (1983), *X/Self* (1987) and *The Zea Mexican
Diary* (1993). His *Born to Slow Horses* (2005) won the 2006 International
Griffin Poetry Prize. Brathwaite has also written some fine plays, including
Odale's Choice (1967) and *Four Plays for Primary Schools* (1964). In addition he
published *The Folk Culture of Jamaican Slaves* (1969) and *Creole Society in
Jamaica 1770-1820* (1971). He has been a major proponent of the use of
what he calls 'nation language' - the kind of language spoken by the slaves
and servants.

BRATHWAITE, Harold

Harold Brathwaite was born in Barbados, West Indies, on 1 June 1940.
After attending St Giles' Boys' School and Harrison College, he graduated
with a BA from the University of the West Indies and then travelled to
France, where he achieved a diploma in education from the University of
Bordeaux. Brathwaite immigrated to Canada and completed his MA from
McMaster University (Hamilton, Ontario) in 1968. A well-known teacher
and education administrator, he is the first black person to be appointed
director of an important board of education in Canada. For many years he
served the Peel Board of Education (Ontario) in this capacity.

BREW, James Hutton

Generally remembered as the pioneer of West African journalism, James
Hutton Brew was an early advocate of Gold Coast independence. Born on
13 July 1844, he was educated in England where he qualified as a solicitor

in 1861 and became one of the first Gold Coast lawyers. A staunch supporter of African rights, he was once jailed for his activities on behalf of the Fante Federation. Brew established several newspapers in West Africa, including the *Gold Coast Times* (1874), the *Western Echo* (1885) and the *Gold Coast Echo* (1888). His agitation led to the appointment of native Africans to the Gold Coast Legislative Council and he was one of the leading critics of the notorious Lands Bill of 1897 which had to be withdrawn. He spent his last years in London, England, where he died on 14 April 1915.

BREWSTER, Yvonne

Yvonne Brewster, a native of Jamaica, first went to the United Kingdom in the 1950s to study drama, speech and mime at the Rose Bruford College and the Royal Academy of Music. She returned to Jamaica where she taught drama and produced her own radio and television shows, while co-founding The Barn, Jamaica's first professional theatre company. She participated then in such memorable films as *The Harder They Come*, *Smile Orange* and *The Marijuana Affair*. Brewster later emigrated to Britain to work extensively in radio, television and directing for Stage Productions. In 1985, with financial help from the Greater London Council, she jointly founded Talawa Theatre Company which has become one of the leading black theatre companies in the world. She has directed a succession of ground-breaking productions for Talawa and her skills have been employed by companies throughout Europe and North America. Yvonne has served on the British Council's Drama and Dance Advisory Board, the Gulbenkian Enquiry into Director Training in Britain and on boards of the Black Theatre Forum and The Theatres Trust. She is a Fellow of the Royal Society of Arts and has been the recipient of several honours and distinctions, including the Living Legend Award from the National Black Theatre Festival in Winston Salem, North Carolina, and an Arts Council Woman of Achievement Award. In 1993 she was awarded an OBE for her services to the arts and in 2001 she was granted an honorary degree from the Open University. She published her memoirs, *The Undertaker's Daughter*, in 2004.

BRIDGETOWER, George

George Augustus Polgreen Bridgetower is regarded by some historians as comparable with the immortal Mozart as a child prodigy. Born in Poland in 1778 to a Barbadian father who was then working as a personal servant to a German prince, he showed extraordinary musical talent from earliest childhood. His first performance was at the age of nine in Paris where he played a violin concerto to great acclaim. There followed a series of successful concerts in London, Bath and Bristol. In 1791, he came under the protection of the Prince of Wales (later King George IV) who engaged famous musicians to teach him musical theory and he eventually achieved a degree in music from Cambridge University in 1811. He held the post of the Prince's first violin in his private band for fourteen years. Seeking leave from his royal patron, Bridgetower played his violin brilliantly all over Europe for many years and met the great Beethoven with whom he sometimes performed on stage. He eventually settled in England and died there in poverty on 29 February 1860, in Peckham, south London.

BRIERRE, Jean Fernand

Jean Fernand Brierre was one of the best poets and most prolific writers produced by Haiti. Born on 28 September 1909 in Jérémie, he attended local schools before becoming a teacher and later a principal of a rural school in Chatard, in the northern part of Haiti. Brierre then studied law and practised journalism, founding the opposition newspaper, *La Bataille*. After holding several posts in the public service and being an ambassador to the United States, Brierre emigrated to Senegal where he became an important member of the ministry of cultural affairs. He took a very active part in the World Festival of Negro Arts at Dakar in 1966. Some of his best poetry appeared in *Chansons secrètes* (1933), *Gerbes pour deux amis* (1945), *Nous garderons le dieu* (1945), *Dessalines nous parle* (1953), *Images d'or* (1959), and *Aux champs pour Occide, sur un clavier bleu et rouge* (1960). Brierre's major plays included *Le Drapeau de demain* (1931), *Au milieu des flammes* (1953) and *Gorée 'Son et lumière'* (1966). He also wrote a very fine novel, *Les horizons sans ciel*, published in 1953. He died on 25 December 1992.

BROODHAGEN, Karl

The outstanding artist and sculptor in the West Indies during the twentieth century was Dr Karl Rupert Broodhagen, who was born in Demerara (now Guyana) on 4 July 1909. He emigrated to Barbados when quite young and remained there until his death in August 2002. Largely self-taught, he had already produced many paintings, portraits and sculptures when he attended Goldsmith College in London, England, during 1950-52 at the request of the governing body of Combermere School, whose teaching staff he had joined in 1949. Broodhagen remained the senior art teacher at that institution until 1995 at the age of eighty-six. He taught almost all of the leading artists and sculptors that Barbados has produced in the last fifty years. Most of the busts in Barbadian public places were produced by Broodhagen who continued to work at his various crafts beyond the age of ninety. His last masterpiece was a statue erected to honour the Rt Excellent Sir Garfield Sobers in April 2002. He received a number of awards and distinctions, including the Gold Crown of Merit (GCM) from the Government of Barbados and a DLitt from the University of the West Indies.

BROODHAGEN, Virgil

The son of a famous Caribbean sculptor and artist, Virgil Lancelot Broodhagen was born in Barbados, West Indies, on 1 September 1943. He was educated at Combermere School and the Barbados Technical Institute, where he performed extremely well in sculpture and mechanical drafting. Emigrating to Canada in 1966, he worked for some years as a mechanical draughtsman in Ottawa, Ontario, before serving the department of Indian and Northern Affairs as an architectural draughtsman. During 1978-88, Broodhagen was a restoration designer/draughtsman for Environment Canada Parks in Winnipeg, Manitoba. He then served Public Works Canada in Winnipeg in a similar capacity from 1988 to 1997. Like his father (Karl), Virgil has become an internationally known artist whose works are exhibited in countries as far apart as Barbados, Belgium, Canada, England, Germany, Holland, Jamaica and the United States. Broodhagen is one of the finest artists thus far produced by the West Indies. He specializes in oils and acrylics and paints beautiful landscapes, although one of his most popular creations is *Tootalik*, an excellent portrait of an Inuit, which he painted in 1978. In 2002, he collaborated with his father to produce the magnificent statue of Sir Garfield Sobers in St Michael, Barbados.

BROOKE, Edward

Edward William Brooke was born in Washington, D.C. on 26 October 1919. After serving as an infantry officer in World War II, he studied law at Boston University from which he earned both the LLB and LLM degrees. He rose to prominence as chairman of the Boston Finance Committee (from 1961). Brooke was elected attorney general of the Commonwealth of Massachusetts in 1962 and, four years later, became the first African-American to be elected to the US Senate by a popular vote. He held that seat until 1978. He was awarded the Presidential Medal of Freedom in 2004.

BROOKS, Angie

This distinguished lawyer and diplomat was born in Virginia, Liberia, on 24 August 1928. The daughter of a clergyman, she was educated at local schools before furthering her studies at various institutions in the United States. She achieved a BA from Shaw University, an LLB and an MSc from Washington University, and doctorates from Shaw and Howard Universities. She also did graduate work in international law at the University of London, England, and was awarded a doctor of civil law degree from Liberia University. In 1954, Dr Brooks became Liberia's permanent representative at the United Nations and contributed enormously to a number of UN committees before being elected president of the UN General Assembly in 1969. She established a reputation as a fervent advocate of the rights of African people and of gender equality.

BROOKS, Gwendolyn

This celebrated poet and educator was born in Topeka, Kansas, on 7 June 1917. Her first collection of poems, *A Street in Bronzeville*, was published in 1945, when *Mademoiselle* named her one of its ten Women of the Year. In 1946, she won an award from the American Academy of Arts and Letters and the first of two consecutive Guggenheim fellowships. In 1950, she became the first black woman to win a Pulitzer Prize after the appearance of her second volume of verse, *Annie Allen*, in 1949. She was named poet laureate of Illinois in 1968 and promptly offered an annual prize for young black writers of prose and poetry. In 1976, she became the first African-American to be elected to the National Institute of Arts and Letters. Brooks left an indelible imprint on the writing of American poetry, of which she published six excellent collections, but she also wrote a well-known short novel, *Maud Martha* (1963), an autobiography, *Report from Part One* (1972), and a children's book, *Bronzeville Boys and Girls*. She was a frequent speaker on college campuses and taught English at several schools in Chicago. Gwendolyn Elizabeth Brooks had the rare talent of making the humdrum lives of everyday urban Blacks appear extraordinary. She consistently made them the subjects of both her poetry and her prose. During her career, she was the recipient of more than fifty honorary degrees. She died in Chicago, Illinois, on 3 December 2000.

BROOKS, John

Dr C. John Brooks was born in Jamaica, West Indies. Ever since his immigration to Canada, he has devoted his major energies to assisting seniors and infants. The John Brooks Community Foundation and Development Fund was established in 1981 to help young people access higher education and it encourages them to achieve academic, artistic and athletic excellence. Dr Brooks has also participated in fund-raising drives for famine relief in Africa. For his humanitarian efforts, he has received numerous awards and honours, including the Ontario Medal for Good Citizenship, Jamaica's Order of Distinction, the Macdonald-Cartier Achievement Award, the Harry Jerome Award, the Civic Order of Merit and the Governor General's Award.

BROOKS, Wilson

Born in Windsor, Ontario, in 1925, Wilson O. Brooks joined the Royal Canadian Air Force and became a bomber pilot during the Second World War. He later taught in several schools before being appointed principal of

Shaw Junior Public School and Glen Senior Public School in Toronto between 1956 and 1966. He is thought to be the first black teacher in an Ontario public school and most certainly the first principal in that province.

BROWN, Aaron

Aaron Brown was born in Pensacola, Florida, in 1906. A graduate of Atlanta University and the University of Chicago, he served as head of the science department at LeMoyne College in Memphis (1928-32), principal of Moultrie High School (1933-35), and president of Albany State College in Georgia (1943-54). Brown was also an influential author in the field of education. His best-known works included *An Evaluation of the Secondary Schools for Negroes in the South* (1943), *The Albany Negro* (1948) and *Ladders to Improvement* (1960).

BROWN, E.J.P.

Born in 1875, Emmanuel Joseph Peter Brown became a noted Gold Coast author, lawyer, journalist, and nationalist. He studied law in England and returned to practice in his native country. He became one of the leaders of the Aborigines' Rights Protection Society (ARPS) which had been founded in response to the harsh measures of the British imperial government. He edited its newspaper, *The Gold Coast Nation*, for many years and used its columns to protest against British injustice. He served as a member of the Gold Coast Legislative Council during 1916-27. In addition to his political and legal activities, Brown wrote several books, including Fante grammars and primers and the *Gold Coast and Ashante Reader: a collection of folk tales, proverbs, customs and manners* (1929). He died on 18 May 1929.

BROWN, Errol

Errol Brown was born in Jamaica and emigrated to the United Kingdom with his family when he was twelve years old. He has since become the popular songwriter and lead singer of the famous disco band, Hot Chocolate. After producing such hit songs as *It Started with a Kiss, You Sexy Thing* and *Everyone's a Winner*, the Hot Chocolate were invited by Prince Charles and Lady Diana to their wedding reception in 1981. After some years in the doldrums, Hot Chocolate enjoyed a revival when their first hit, *You Sexy Thing*, was featured in the film, *The Full Monty*. In 2003, Brown was awarded an MBE for his services to popular music.

BROWN, George

Born in Lawrence, Kansas, in 1925, George L. Brown was destined to become (in 1974) the first black Lieutenant Governor of the state of Colorado. He had earlier won four successive elections to the State Senate during 1956-72. In 1965 he was appointed assistant executive director of the Denver Housing Authority and, four years later, was selected as the first executive director of the Metro-Denver Urban Coalition. A journalist by profession, Brown also served for several years on the staff of the *Denver Post.*

BROWN, Jim
Born on 17 February 1936 in St Simons Island, Georgia, James Nathaniel Brown began his career as a very successful professional athlete before devoting his considerable skills to acting. After graduating from Syracuse University in 1956, he dominated the National Football League (NFL) by leading it in rushing in eight of the nine seasons he played for the Cleveland Browns (1957-65). Generally considered the greatest running back in the history of the NFL, he left several outstanding records. His 12,312 career yards in 2,359 attempts, for an average of 5.22 yards per carry, and 126 career touchdowns remained untouched for more than two decades after his retirement. Jim Brown then proceeded to star in such films as *Rio Conchos*, *The Dirty Dozen*, *Slaughter* and *Black Gunn*. He has also devoted much of his energy towards increasing black participation in US business and industry.

BROWN, Joseph Peter
Born on 16 April 1843, Joseph Peter Brown was a Fante teacher, scholar and politician who staunchly defended African rights and interests during the colonial period. Educated at schools in the Gold Coast and Sierra Leone, he became a teacher at the Wesleyan Elementary School at Cape Coast in 1864. He joined the British Army in 1873 and fought against the Asante before joining the British trading firm of F. and A. Swanzy. He later became one of the founders of the Aborigines' Rights Protection Society (ARPS) and a severe critic of the Lands Bill of 1897. He tried his utmost to prevent the passage of obnoxious laws and assumed the presidency of ARPS from 1928 until his death. Brown was also instrumental in popularising the use of Fante, a grammar of which he published in 1875 and revised in 1913. He died on 23 September 1932.

BROWN, Ron
When, on 10 February 1989, Ronald Harmon Brown was elected to the chairmanship of the Democratic Party National Committee, he had created history by becoming the first Black to chair a major US political party. Born on 1 August 1941, in Washington, D.C., this only child of two Howard University graduates was educated at Hunter College Elementary School and Middlebury College in Vermont. He joined the US Army in 1962 and rose to the rank of captain. In 1967 he left the army to work with the National Urban League by day, while studying law by night, and achieved

his law degree in 1970. In 1971, Brown was elected district leader of the Democratic Party in Mount Vernon, New York. Eight years later, he became deputy manager of Senator Edward Kennedy's presidential campaign. In 1980 he was named chief counsel of the Senate Judiciary Committee. Brown did most to unite and resuscitate the Democratic Party and served during the 1990s as one of the most influential of President Bill Clinton's advisers. As secretary of commerce he travelled widely securing trading partners for the US, especially among the emerging nations. He was killed in a plane crash near Dubrovnik in Croatia on 3 April 1996.

BROWN, Rosemary

Rosemary Brown was born in Jamaica, West Indies, on 17 June 1930. She was educated at Westwood School, Wolmer's High School for Girls in Kingston, and McGill University in Montreal, Quebec. Following her graduation from McGill in 1955, she moved to Vancouver, British Columbia (B.C.), where she remained until her death in April 2003. She became an active member of the B.C. Association for the Advancement of Colored People (BCAACP), lobbying vigorously for the introduction of provincial laws prohibiting racial discrimination in the areas of housing, education and employment. Entering politics herself, she joined the provincial New Democratic Party (NDP) and won a seat in the B.C. legislature in 1972, becoming the first black woman ever to do so. An eloquent and persuasive speaker, she campaigned for the leadership of the federal NDP in 1975 and came second to Ed Broadbent in a surprisingly close contest. A member of the B.C. legislature for many years, she remained a powerful speaker on behalf of black equality and women's rights. In 1987 she hosted the TV Ontario 6-part series on *Women and Politics*. One year later, she was featured in the NFB film, *No Way, Not Me!* In 1989 she was also appointed executive director of MATCH International, a development agency working with women in the so-called Third World. The Ruth Wyn Woodward Professor in Women's Studies at Simon Fraser University, Brown was also an executive member of the South African Educational Trust Fund and the Canadian Women's Foundation. Her autobiography, *Being Brown: A Very Public Life*, was published in 1989. She died on 27 April 2003.

BROWN, William Wells

William Wells Brown was among the first African-Americans to condemn slavery and its attendant evils in a huge body of literature which he managed to produce in the face of enormous difficulties. Born on 16 November 1814 in Lexington, Kentucky, he escaped from slavery when he was about twenty years old and sought refuge in Ohio. Largely self-taught, he lectured for anti-slavery societies in New York and Massachusetts while serving as an agent of the Underground Railroad (1843-49). Travelling to Europe during 1849-54 Brown delivered countless speeches against slavery before returning to the United States in 1854 to continue his crusade on the side of the abolitionists. During the American Civil War (1861-65), he very actively recruited black soldiers for the Union Army. Wells Brown wrote the first novel by an African-American, *Clotel; Or, the President's Daughter*. It was published in England in 1853 but, because of its delicate subject matter, did not appear in the United States until 1969. He was also the first black American to publish a play. It was called *The Escape; Or, a Leap for Freedom*. Among his other major works were *Narrative of William W. Brown, A Fugitive Slave* (1847), *The Black Man* (1863), and *The Rising Son* (1874). All of his writing illuminated the horrors of slavery and was deliberately intended to show that, far from being inferior humans, the Blacks were capable of achieving excellence, if given a fair chance. Wells Brown died on 6 November 1884.

BROWNE, Christene

Born in St Kitts in 1965, Christene Adina Browne came to Canada with her parents in 1970 and later entered the Film Studies Program at Ryerson University in Toronto, Ontario. She has since become a well-known director, producer and film-maker. One of her most successful efforts, *Another Planet*, released in 1999, made her the first black woman in Canada to write and direct a dramatic feature film. It was adjudged the best film by Black International Cinema that year. Another film, *Them That's Not*, also won a special Jury Prize in 1994. Her initial films included *Brothers in Music*, depicting the jazz scene in Canada and *No Choice*, featuring the delicate subject of abortion as it relates to women living in abject poverty. Christene Browne's experience in the film and television industry is unique. In addition to producing, directing, writing and researching, she has also acted as film programmer, curator and arts instructor.

BRUTUS, Dennis

Dennis Vincent Brutus was born of 'coloured' parents in Southern Rhodesia on 28 November 1924. He was educated at schools in Fort Elizabeth and at the Fort Hare University College in South Africa from which he graduated with a BA in 1946. He later studied law at the University of Witwatersrand. During 1948-62, Brutus taught English and Afrikaans at several high schools in South Africa but was eventually dismissed for his vocal criticism of apartheid. His unrelenting opposition to the system led to his imprisonment and then to his exile in 1966. In the years that followed, he undertook a variety of assignments in Australia, England,

India, New Zealand and the United States, while organizing world opinion against apartheid. He also served as director of the World Campaign for the Release of South African Prisoners. These activities led to the exclusion of Rhodesia and South Africa from several Olympic competitions. Throughout all of this, Brutus continued to produce excellent poetry. His best verses appeared in *Sirens, Knuckles, Boots* (1963), *Letters to Martha and Other Poems from a South African Prison* (1968) and *Poems from Algiers* (1970). In 1971 he became professor of African literature at Northwestern University in Illinois, US. His poems are still being widely read and are published in a variety of collections and anthologies.

BUKASA, Léon

Born around 1925 in Jadotville in the province of Katanga, Léon Bukasa became one of Zaire's leading poets and musicians. After trying his hand at a series of odd jobs and occupations, he devoted his life to music, composing and playing songs on both wind and stringed instruments. His songs and verses dealt mainly with the theme of national independence. His most famous composition perhaps was the song *Ngoo, Zaire Na Biso*, published in 1960. He died on 16 January 1974.

BUNCHE, Ralph Johnson

This famous political scientist, educator and diplomat was born of very poor parents in the slums of Detroit, Michigan, on 7 August 1904. When both his father and mother died young, he was raised by his grandmother, a former slave. An athletic scholarship took him to the University of California where he graduated with honours in 1927. Bunche pursued graduate studies at Harvard University where he achieved his MA degree in 1928 and the PhD in 1934. After teaching at Howard University for some years and serving as the chairman of its political science department, he entered government service in 1941. Distinguishing himself as a statesman and diplomat, he was invited to help draw up portions of the UN Charter and gradually became one of the leading officials in the United Nations, rising to the rank of undersecretary general in 1957. In 1948 he headed the commission that brought a temporary halt to the Arab-Israeli war and was awarded the Nobel Peace Prize in 1950 as a result. He was the first African-American to receive this prestigious honour. In 1956, he planned for the UN Emergency Force that succeeded in keeping the peace in the Middle east for more than ten years. In 1960 he was appointed the special UN representative to the Congo and was sent on a similar mission to Yemen three years later. In 1963, he received the Presidential Medal of Freedom. Some years earlier, he had also been a recipient of the NAACP Spingarn Medal. Dr Ralph Bunche was a much revered US citizen when he died on

11 October 1971. His legacy included *A World View of Race*, published in 1936, and (in collaboration with Gunnar Myrdal of Sweden) *An American Dilemma*, which appeared in 1944.

BURLEIGH, Harry Thacker

Harry Thacker Burleigh was born in Erie, Pennsylvania, on 2 December 1866. He became a noted soloist and composer, singing for more than fifty years with the choir of the St George's Episcopal Church in New York. He was one of the first performers to specialize in Negro spirituals and rescued a number of these songs from oblivion by arranging and rewriting more than 100 of them. Burleigh also composed more than 250 songs, ballads, anthems and violin pieces. In 1916 he won the Spingarn Medal for the highest achievement by an African-American. He became (in 1941) the first Black to serve on the board of directors of the American Society of Composers, Authors and Publishers. He died on 12 September 1949, but is still remembered as one of the most important of all American musicians.

BURNHAM, Forbes

Lindon Forbes Sampson Burnham was the politician who led Guyana to its political independence in 1966 and administered the country for the next 19 years. Born on 20 February 1923 at Kitty, East Coast, Demerara, he was educated in local schools in British Guiana before qualifying as a lawyer at the University of London, England. He was one of the founders of the People's Progressive Party (PPP) in 1949 but seceded in 1957 to form his own People's National Congress (PNC). Burnham served as mayor of Georgetown (1959 and 1964) and minister of education in 1953 before his famous split with the PPP, then led by Cheddi Jagan. After the elections of 1964, he formed a coalition with the United Force Party (UFP) to oust the Jagan administration and thus became prime minister. He revised the constitution in 1980 to create the Republic of Guyana and served as its first president until his death on 6 August 1985. Forbes Burnham left a reputation as a ruthless leader who manipulated the elections and suppressed democratic freedoms. His reign proved even more disastrous in a material sense. Guyanese standards of living fell drastically as the country's basic exports (bauxite, sugar and rice) declined in value and production while the price of imports spiralled and the Guyanese currency grew increasingly worthless in foreign markets.

BUSHIRI

Born in Orientale Province around 1911, Bushiri became a famous Zairean prophet in the Kitawalan tradition. Although he was illiterate, he preached the Christian gospel in a uniquely African manner in which the Blacks were portrayed as the meek who would inherit the earth after the acquisitive Europeans had suffered their merited punishment. He founded his own church and openly advocated rebellion against European oppression. He was executed for his role in the Masiri Rebellion of 1944 in the province of Kivu, but his death (on 23 June 1945) only seemed to inspire the Kitawalan Movement in Zaire and elsewhere. His martyrdom gave a stimulus to independence movements all over Africa.

BUSIA, Kofi Abrefa

Descended from a royal family in what is now northwestern Ghana, Kofi Abrefa Busia was born on 11 July 1913. He graduated with a BA from Achimota College before furthering his studies at Oxford University in England. He became a professor of African studies at the University of the Gold Coast and assumed the leadership of the Ghana Congress Party (GCP) in 1952. Throughout the 1950s he led the opposition to Kwame Nkrumah's radical politics and autocratic conduct and became the leader of the coalition (United Party) in 1957. When Nkrumah began to persecute and imprison his critics, Busia went into voluntary exile in 1959 and returned to Ghana when that president was overthrown in 1966. Offered a triumphant welcome on his return, Busia became prime minister of Ghana with the restoration of civilian government. But he found himself exiled again when his administration was overthrown in 1972. After that, he remained in England and lectured in sociology for some years at Oxford University. Busia was not only a prominent Ghanaian politician. He was also a distinguished west African scholar whose major works included *Social Survey of Sekondi-Takoradi* (1948), *The Position of the Chief in the Modern Political System of the Ashanti* (1951), *The Challenge of Africa* (1962), *Purposeful Education for Africa* (1964), and *Africa in Search of Democracy* (1967). He died in Oxford, England, on 28 August 1978. Kofia Busia was another classic and tragic example of superior Ghanaian skills being wasted or stifled during Kwame Nkrumah's chequered administration (1951-1966).

BUSIMBA MIKARARABGE

Monsignor Busimba Mikararabge was the first bishop of the diocese of North Kivu in Zaire and was most influential in helping to develop that region during the first decade of independence. Born in 1912 in Rutshuru, Busimba studied philosophy and theology at seminaries in Rwanda and was ordained a priest in 1940. He was selected as bishop when an autonomous diocese was established in North Kivu in 1960. He continued to show his concern for community welfare throughout his life and his diocese developed sound scholastic, medical, agricultural and social services during his tenure. He died on 7 September 1974.

BUSSA

The Rt Excellent Bussa was named one of the ten National Heroes of Barbados in 1998. He was the African slave who had masterminded the dangerous rebellion against white owners in April 1816. The revolt resulted in the loss of about a quarter of the island's sugarcane crop, almost £200,000 of property and more than 200 lives, but it failed to win the slaves their freedom. Even so, it helped to expedite the total abolition of slavery throughout the British Empire and remained of great symbolic importance to subsequent generations of Barbadian Blacks. Bussa, who was himself killed in the attempt, has ever since been regarded as a martyr and a huge statue was erected in his honour in Bridgetown in 1985.

BUSTAMANTE, William Alexander

One of the most famous and colourful politicians in the history of Jamaica, West Indies, Sir William Alexander Bustamante was born in Blenheim, in the parish of Hanover, on 24 February 1884. The son of a poor Irish planter and a Jamaican mother, he assumed the name of the Spanish officer who adopted him. He emigrated to the United States in the 1920s and apparently made a small fortune by investing wisely during the stock market crash. Returning to Jamaica in 1932, he began his crusade for the poor among his people, organized an Industrial Trade Union, and founded the Jamaica Labour Party (JLP). Supported enthusiastically by the grassroots, especially in the rural districts, the JLP soon came to dominate Jamaican politics and Bustamante served as his country's chief minister from 1944 to 1955. An ardent apostle of collective bargaining, social justice and Jamaican independence, he helped to draft the constitution that made Jamaica an independent nation. He became his country's first prime minister in 1962 but ill health forced him to resign in 1967, at the age of eighty-three. His American sympathies made him a firm opponent of Cuba's Fidel Castro and his patriotism did most to dismantle the British West Indian Federation in 1962. He died on 6 August 1977.

BUTHELEZI, Gatsha Mangosuthu

Chief Gatsha Mangosuthu Buthelezi, a descendant of the royal line of Zulu warriors, was born on 27 August 1928 at Mahlabatini, where his father was a Shenge ruler. Raised in Nongoma, the KwaZulu capital, he was educated at Fort Hare University College in South Africa. In 1953, he was elected acting KwaZulu chief before assuming the reins of full chieftaincy in 1958. After serving for sixteen years as the chief councillor to Paramount Chief Cyprian, Buthelezi became chief executive councillor for the KwaZulu homeland in 1972. He decided to co-operate as much as possible with the South African government, while advocating a programme of equal rights for all South Africans - preferably in some form of federation. This separated Buthelezi from the more militant African National Congress (ANC), led by Nelson Mandela. He was a prolific writer and an eloquent orator who commanded respect both within and outside the African continent. A devoted member of the Anglican Church, he was one of the three diocesan delegates from Zululand to the World Anglican Congress that was held in Toronto in 1963. In 1974, he revived Inkatha, which his grandfather, King Dinizulu, had founded in 1924 as a Zulu cultural movement but, as it appealed only to Zulus, it remained outside the other African nationalist movements of the period. When offered the kind of limited independence that other homelands accepted from South Africa in the early 1980s, Buthelezi refused as he disagreed with the introduction of a tricameral parliament from which Blacks were excluded. He campaigned instead for a fully democratic constitution based on universal suffrage. When the ban was lifted from the ANC, Inkatha continued for some years to compete (rather than co-operate) with it. This made Buthelezi's position as an African nationalist leader much more precarious during the 1990s.

BUYOYA, Pierre

Born on 24 November 1949, Major Pierre Buyoya is a military and political leader who has ruled twice over Burundi, from 1983 to 1987 and from 1996 to 2003. In September 1987 he led a military coup against the Second Republic of Burundi and ousted Jean-Baptiste Bagaza, installing himself as the first president of the Third Republic. He pledged to halt the conflict between the Hutu and Tutsi ethnic groups but failed, largely because he proceeded to establish a mainly Tutsi junta which governed the republic oppressively. He did, however, make provisions for a democratic election in 1992 which resulted in the elevation of Melchior Ndadaye, a Hutu, to the presidency. The ethnic conflict continued and Buyoya returned to power in another coup, successfully staged in 1996. He relinquished office in 2003 as required by the constitution. Both of his terms as president were disastrous. They were marked by chronic instability and violence and tens of thousands of lives were lost. Burundi's social, economic and ethnic problems were left for his successor, Domitien Ndayizeye, a Hutu, to address.

CABRAL, Amilcar

Amilcar Cabral, a prominent nationalist leader in Portuguese Guinea, was born at Bafata in 1921. He was one of the founders of the African Party for the Independence of Guinea and Cape Verde (PAIGC) in 1956 and served as its secretary-general for many years. He also helped to form the Popular Movement for the Liberation of Angola (MPLA). In 1963, under his leadership, the PAIGC initiated one of the most successful of the guerilla campaigns against Portuguese colonial power in Africa. In 1972, Cabral established a Guinean People's National Assembly as a step towards independence but was assassinated in Conakry shortly afterwards (on 20 January1973).

CALLENDER, Murchison

Dr Murchison G. Callender, who taught optometry at the University of Waterloo for almost thirty years, was elevated to the rank of Professor Emeritus when he retired in 1996. Born in Trinidad, he came to Canada as a student in 1958 and earned the degrees of BSc from Concordia University and MSc from the University of Waterloo. He completed his doctorate in optometry at Birmingham University in England. He published several seminal papers on the physiology of the eye in contact with lens wear and has become acknowledged internationally as an expert in this field. He thus serves as a consultant to many manufacturers and medical associations on matters pertaining to contact lenses. Dr Callender has remained very actively involved in research, clinical teaching and vision care programmes in the Caribbean.

CAMILLE, Roussan

Born on 27 August 1912 in Jacmel, Roussan Camille became one of Haiti's finest poets. Educated at the Christian Brothers' School, the Lycée Pinchinat of Jacmel and the Tippenhauer College in Port-au-Prince, he began his career as a journalist and soon became director of *Haiti-Journal*. Entering the public service, he was named secretary of the Haitian legation to Paris before being appointed chef-de-division of the department of public instruction. Camille served briefly as Haitian vice-consul in New York and then returned home to become secretary general at the ministry of public health. Apart from his activities as diplomat and administrator, Camille published several excellent poems and was awarded the Dumarsais Estimé poetry prize for his collection of poems, *Multiple présence*, in 1945. He died on 7 December 1961.

CAMPBELL, Clifford

Sir Clifford Clarence Campbell, who became the first black Governor General of Jamaica when that island achieved its political independence in 1962, was born on 28 June 1892. After leaving Petersfield School, he attended Mico Training College, became a teacher, and then served as headmaster of several schools before entering politics. As a prominent member of the Jamaica Labour Party (JLP), he was first elected to the national House of Representatives in 1944 and was appointed speaker of that legislature in 1950. Campbell later served as President of the Senate.

Knighted in 1963, Sir Clifford finally resigned from the governorship of Jamaica in 1973. He died on 28 September 1991 at the great age of 99.

CAMPBELL, Constantine

Dr Constantine A. Campbell is recognized internationally as one of the leading specialists in soil organic matter. He is especially renowned for his study of nitrogen in American prairie soils. Born on 18 January 1934 in Montego Bay, Jamaica, he immigrated to Canada in 1959 and completed his education at the Universities of Toronto and Saskatchewan. He worked with Agriculture Canada for over thirty years until his retirement in 1998. His research conclusively demonstrated that soil organic matter is a key environmental indicator of the health of prairie soils. He has made numerous presentations on such topics as tillage management, crop response to fertilizers, snow-trapping, water use efficiency, organic farming and soil degradation. He was among the first scientists to radio-carbon date soil organic matter and his 1967 paper on that subject is still cited as a landmark in the discipline. Dr Campbell has authored and/or co-authored almost 200 scientific publications and is the recipient of numerous awards and distinctions, including the Saskatchewan Order of Merit and the Order of Canada.

CAMPBELL, Naomi

Naomi Campbell, the famous British supermodel, actress, singer and author was born to Jamaican parents in Streatham, south London, on 22 May 1970. She studied at the London Academy For Performing Arts and the Italia Conti Academy. She made her first public appearance in 1978 when she played the role of a pupil in a music video with the great Jamaican reggae singer, Bob Marley. She switched from acting to modelling and soon became the first black supermodel to grace the cover of *Vogue*. She modelled for several international designers and forged for twelve years (1987-99) a very close relationship with *Versace*. She created a company, NC Connect, and launched a fragrance, named after herself, in 2000. Naomi also appeared in a few films, including *Miami Rhapsody* and *Prêt-à-Porter*. A ghost-written novel, entitled *Swan*, was published under her name in 1996. She has done a great deal of charity work for the children and people of Africa and participated in a 'Fashion Relief' for Hurricane Katrina victims in 2005 which raised over a million dollars.

CAMPBELL, Simms

Elmer Simms Campbell, who became the first black artist to contribute regularly to US periodicals of general circulation, was born in 1906 in St Louis, Missouri. He was educated at the University of Chicago and the Chicago Art Institute. His syndicated cartoons were carried in more than

100 newspapers without many of the readers knowing that Campbell was black. He specialized in the representation of voluptuous women and contributed frequently to such magazines as *Cosmopolitan, Ebony, Esquire,* the *New Yorker* and *Playboy.* Campbell, who is best remembered for his 'Cuties', was especially skilful in working with pen, pencil and water colours. His work has been exhibited at the Harmon Foundation, New York, the Gallery of Washington, D.C. and at the Art of the American Negro, Chicago, Illinois. He died in 1971.

CAREW, Jan

Born in Agricola, British Guiana, on 24 September 1925, Jan Rynveld Carew is an influential critic, teacher, playwright, poet and editor. Educated at Berbice High School and several universities in Europe and the United States, he became professor of African-American Studies at Northwestern University after teaching for some years at Princeton University. He has edited a number of journals, including *Cotopaxi,* a review of Third World literature and current events, *De Kim* (Holland), *The Kensington Post* (England), and *The African Review* (Ghana). Carew is also a prolific writer himself. His novels include *Black Midas* (1958), *The Last Barbarian* (1961), *Moscow is Not My Mecca* (1964), and *The Wild Coast* (1968). His children's books include *The Third Gift* (1972), *Sons of the Flying Wind* (1970), *Children of the Sin* (1976) and *The Twins of Ilora* (1977). Among his best-known plays are *The Baron of South Boulevard* (1963), *University of Hunger* (1966), *Gentlemen Be Seated* (1967), and *Black Horse, White Rider* (1969). Carew's poems and short stories have also appeared in various journals and anthologies.

CARLISLE, James

Sir James Beethoven Carlisle has been the Governor General of Antigua and Barbuda since 10 June 1993. He was born in the village of Bolans, Antigua, on 5 August 1937 and attended Bolans Public School before continuing his studies at Northampton College of Technology in England and achieving a degree in dentistry from the University of Dundee in Scotland. While in the United Kingdom, he served in the Royal Air Force during 1961-66 and was later commissioned in the Royal Antigua and Barbuda Defence Force. In 1991, he graduated from the American School of Laser Dentistry. Sir James practised in Antigua and England and became actively involved in such organizations as the Medical Board and the Antigua and Barbuda Dental Association. He joined the International Society of Laser Dentists and the British Dental Association. He also developed a fluoride programme for children, gave dental lectures, and instituted a free dental service for seniors and children. He was named a

Fellow of the Royal College of Surgeons of Edinburgh and awarded an honorary doctorate by the Andrews University in Michigan. Sir James was elevated to a knighthood in 1993 and admitted to the Royal Order of the Intare of Rwanda.

CARMICHAEL, Stokely

Born in Port-of-Spain, Trinidad, on 29 June 1941, Stokely Carmichael emigrated with his parents to the United States when he was eleven years old. A black militant nationalist, he originated the term 'Black Power' and urged African-Americans to use force in their struggle for equality and social justice. After graduating from Harvard University, he founded the Student Nonviolent Co-ordinating Committee (SNCC) to challenge the racist laws in the southern states and to persuade Blacks to register for the polls. As a result of SNCC's campaigns, the black voters in Lowndes County in Alabama rose from 70 to 2,600 by 1966. Although Carmichael was aiming largely at desegregation and racial equality, his rhetoric became inflammatory enough to alarm the white majority. He left the United States in 1969, moved to Guinea and focussed more sharply on Pan-Africanism which he saw as a possible panacea for the problems facing Blacks both in Africa and the diaspora. He compiled his speeches in *Stokely Speaks: Black Power Back to Pan-Africanism* (1971) and, with Charles V. Hamilton, wrote *Black Power: The Politics of Liberation in America* (1967). He died in Conakry, Guinea, on 15 November 1998.

CARRINGTON, Edwin

Dr Edwin Carrington, a native of Trinidad and Tobago, is the longest serving secretary- general of the Caribbean Community, a position he has held since 1992. An economist by profession, he began his career in 1964 as an administrative cadet in the economic planning unit of the office of the prime minister of Trinidad and Tobago. He joined the CARICOM secretariat in 1970 and was also his country's High Commissioner to Guyana during 1991-92. Carrington worked with the African, Caribbean and Pacific Group of States (ACP) secretariat in Brussels, serving as its secretary-general between 1985 and 1990. During his tenure at CARICOM, he has been a driving force behind the establishment of the Caribbean Court of Justice and the Caribbean Single Market and Economy (CSME). Dr Carrington has been the recipient of several honours, including the Chaconia Gold Medal (1987), the Order of Distinction of Belize (2001), the Companion of Honour of Barbados (2002), the Order of Jamaica (2003), the Cacique Crown of Honour, Guyana (2003) and the Trinity Cross (2005).

CARSON, Benjamin
Born of very poor parents in a Detroit ghetto in 1950, Dr Benjamin Carson created a sensation when, in 1987, he became the first neurosurgeon to perform a successful separation of Siamese twins who had been joined at the back of the head. Scholarships took him to Yale University where he graduated in 1973. He proceeded to study medicine at the University of Michigan and completed his medical training at John Hopkins University in the late 1970s. After spending a year in Australia (1982-83) performing intricate brain operations, he returned to the United States to serve as the chief paediatric surgeon at John Hopkins University at the tender age of thirty-three and gained international attention by successfully performing a hemispherectomy in 1985. Within a few years he had performed about two dozen of these complex operations with outstanding results. A bold and imaginative surgeon he has performed delicate craniectomies that older and more conservative doctors had thought impracticable. Though still a relatively young physician, his reputation is enormous. Virtually singlehanded, he has extended the boundaries of neurosurgery within the past two decades.

CARTER, George
Mr Justice George Carter, who was born in Toronto of Barbadian parents, graduated with an LLB from the University of Toronto in 1945. After several years of private practice, mainly in civil law, he was appointed a Queen's Counsel in 1969. Ten years later, he was sworn in as an Ontario Provincial Court Judge. He retired from the Bench in 1996.

CARTER, Gwendolyn
Gwendolyn Margaret Carter was among the first African-Canadian women to achieve a doctoral degree. Born in Hamilton, Ontario, in 1906, she received her academic training at the University of Toronto, Oxford University in England and Radcliffe College in Cambridge, Massachusetts. After teaching at McMaster University in the early 1930s, she taught at several colleges in the United States before settling down at Smith College in Northampton, Massachusetts, from 1943 to 1964. An expert in African affairs, Carter was placed on the advisory council for the African Bureau in the US Department of State in 1962. She moved on to Northwestern University in Evanston, Illinois, where she directed the African Studies Program during 1964-74. She taught at Indiana University from 1974 to 1984 and was on the faculty at the University of Florida from 1984 until her retirement at the age of eighty in 1987. Professor Carter was one of the founders of African Studies in the United States and was among the most widely known scholars of African affairs in the twentieth century. Her major

works included *The Politics of Inequality: South Africa Since 1948* (1958), *Independence for Africa* (1960), *South Africa's Transkei: The Politics of Domestic Colonialism* (1967) and *Which Way is South Africa Going?* (1980). She died on 20 February 1991.

CARVER, George Washington

One of the most creative of all American minds, George Washington Carver was born in 1864 and spent some time in slavery in Arkansas. He achieved his BS and MS degrees from Iowa Agricultural College in the 1890s when he was the very first Black to graduate from this institution. In 1896 he joined Booker T. Washington as an instructor at the Tuskegee Institute in Alabama, where he taught for more than forty years. Carver eventually concentrated his research on the industrial uses of the peanut, sweet potato, soybean, pecan, and cotton. His discoveries went far towards improving the agricultural industry in the southern states. Planters there had previously exhausted and impoverished the soil by focussing too narrowly on the cultivation of cotton. Carver persuaded them to improve the quality of their land by diversifying their crops. His amazing research programme developed 300 derivative products from peanuts - among them cheese, coffee, cosmetics, dyes, flour, ink, linoleum, medicinal oils, milk, plastics, soap, and wood stains - and 118 from sweet potatoes, including flour, ink, molasses, vinegar, a synthetic rubber, and postage stamp glue. He also succeeded in making synthetic marble from wood pulp. More interested in science than in money, Carver never attempted to patent his inventions. Others therefore profited more from his work than he himself did. His reward came in the form of sundry distinctions, even after his death on 5 January 1943. A postage stamp, for instance, was issued in his honour and the Carver National Monument was erected for the same purpose. He was named a Fellow of the London Royal Society for the Encouragement of Arts, Manufactures, and Commerce in 1916, awarded the Spingarn Medal by the NAACP in 1923, and the Roosevelt Medal for distinguished service to science in 1939. The Carver Museum was established at Tuskegee University. In 1973, he was elected to the New York University Hall of Fame, and in 1977, George Washington Carver was finally enshrined in the Hall of Fame for Great Americans. He is now universally recognized as one of the finest scientists the world has ever known. His name has been appropriated by countless black clubs, schools, lodges, movie theatres, banks and insurance companies. His efforts brought about a significant advance in American agriculture and, at the same time, considerably enhanced the influence and reputation of Tuskegee Institute.

CASE, David

Air Commodore David Case is the highest ranking black officer in the Royal Air Force (RAF) and the highest ranking black officer ever to serve in Britain's armed forces. Born in Guyana, he emigrated with his family to the United Kingdom when he was five years old. He attended Beckenham Grammar School and learnt to fly on a Flying Scholarship even before he had graduated from that institution. Case joined the RAF as a nineteen-year-old cadet and read aeronautical engineering at The Queen's University of Belfast. He received his commission in 1975 and was awarded the distinguished Sword of Honour, bestowed every year on the top cadet officer.

CATO, Milton

Robert Milton Cato was the first prime minister of St Vincent and the Grenadines when those West Indian islands achieved their political independence in 1979. Born on 3 June 1915, he was educated at the St Vincent Grammar School and later at the University of London, England. After serving in the Canadian Army during World War II, he returned to practise law in St Vincent and became actively involved in local and Caribbean politics. He was one of the founders of the St Vincent Labour Party (SLVP) in 1955 and was elected to the West Indian federal parliament in 1958. In 1967, as leader of the SLVP, Cato became chief minister when that island was still a British dependency. He served as prime minister of St Vincent and the Grenadines until 1984. He died on 10 February 1997.

CÉSAIRE, Aimé

Aimé Césaire was one of the finest writers of French in the twentieth century. He was born in Basse-Pointe, in the Caribbean island of Martinique, on 26 June 1913. Educated at the Lycée Schoelcher in Fort-de-France (Martinique's capital city), he was its top student in English, French, Latin and History and thus won a scholarship in 1931 to further his studies in Paris, France. There he combined with Léopold Senghor of Senegal to found *L'Étudiant Noir*, a student newspaper, which published about six issues during the mid-1930s before it was torpedoed by lack of funds and the opposition of the French authorities. During World War II, Césaire taught at his alma mater, the Lycée Schoelcher in Martinique and helped to produce the influential journal, *Tropiques*, which the political leaders tried vainly to suppress. Partly to combat his radical politics, the government sent Césaire to Haiti as a cultural ambassador in 1943. But he returned to Martinique in 1945, entered politics, dazzled the local community with the excellence of his oratory, and was elected mayor of Fort-de-France as well as a member of the Assemblée Nationale Constituante which met in Paris to administer the French Empire. He became a convert to communism but was so dissatisfied with the French Communist Party's neglect of Martiniquan problems that he founded his own organization, the Parti progressiste Martiniquais, in 1958. Notwithstanding his huge contribution to Martiniquan politics over many decades, Césaire is best remembered for his impact on modern literature. He was one of the founders of the movement known as *négritude*, which stressed the virtues of the African heritage and popularized the notion, whose best English translation perhaps is 'Black is Beautiful'. A truly prolific writer, he left posterity with an enormous volume of poetry as well as prose. *Oeuvres complètes*, containing the bulk of his poetry and miscellaneous writings, appeared in three huge volumes in 1976 under the headings of *I. Poésie, II. Théâtre, III. Oeuvre Historique et politique*. Some of his finest verses had previously been published in *Cahier d'un retour au pays natal* (1939-47), *Les Armes miraculeuses* (1946), *Soleil cou coupé* (1948), and *Ferrements* (1960). Some of his later verse appeared in *Moi, laminaire* (1982) and *Collected Poetry* (1983). Among Césaire's best-known plays were *Et les chiens se taisaient* (1946), *La Tragédie du roi Christophe* (1963), *Une saison au Congo* (1966) and *Une tempête* (1968). His other works included *Discourse sur le colonialism* (1955) and *Toussaint Louverture: La Révolution française et le problème colonial* (1962). One of the most remarkable authors of his generation, Césaire's works have been translated into many languages (both African and European) and have created a significant impact on modern black thinking. Not only was his own output prodigious but his character, writing and philosophy have themselves been the subject of literally countless books and articles.

CETSHWAYO

Born around 1826 near Eshowe, in Zululand, Cetshwayo was the last of the great Zulu warrior-kings. Inspired by the feats of his famous uncle, Shaka, he developed a powerful military machine of some 40,000 well-trained soldiers and restored the glory of the Zulu Empire that had fallen upon rather lean times during the reign of Mpande, his more peaceful father. Cetshwayo disapproved of the manner in which Mpande was catering to the wishes of the Europeans, whom he himself distrusted. He seized the throne in 1857 but was not acknowledged by the British as king of the Zulus until after Mpande's death in 1873. He refused to follow the dictates of either the Boers or the British and was ultimately defeated by the latter at the battle of Ulundi. A few months before, however, Cetshwayo had earned everlasting fame by destroying an entire British regiment in a surprise attack at Isandhlwana on 22 January 1879. This was one of the very few occasions on which an African army, using African weapons, had triumphed over a European force. After being deprived of his chieftaincy by the British, Cetshwayo pleaded his case with great force and dignity before an imperial court in London and was restored as ruler of Zululand in 1883. But several of the new local chiefs refused to accept him as their overlord and he died of a heart attack (some say a broken heart) on 8 February 1884. Cetshwayo remains a national hero to modern Zulus, who guarded his grave deep in Nkanda Forest for many years.

CHAMBERLAIN, Wilt

Wilton Norman Chamberlain was one of the greatest players and most prolific scorers in professional basketball. Born on 21 August 1936 in Philadelphia, Pennsylvania, he grew to 7 ft. 2 in. tall and dominated the game at every level. He was the first player to amass more than 30,000 points in National Basketball Association (NBA) competition and set the NBA record of 100 points in a single game. He led the league in scoring on seven occasions and eleven times in rebounding. He scored 50 or more points in a single game 118 times (an NBA record at the time of his retirement). Chamberlain played in thirteen All Star Games and was inducted into the Basketball Hall of Fame in 1978. A man of several parts, 'Wilt the Stilt' spoke four languages and was also a proficient volley ball player. He died on 12 October 1999.

CHAMBERS, George

Born in Trinidad on 4 October 1928, George Chambers became the second prime minister of Trinidad and Tobago when he succeeded Dr Eric Williams in 1981. Poverty in childhood limited him to a rudimentary education as he was forced to leave school at an early age and to work as an office boy with a local firm of lawyers. But Chambers showed his determination and strength of character by reading voraciously and taking correspondence courses. He entered politics in 1966 as a keen supporter of the People's National Movement (PNM) and gradually became one of Dr Williams' most trusted advisers. He held several different portfolios during the 1970s and emerged as the successor to the PNM leadership when Williams died. Emphasizing the need for continuity, Chambers led the PNM to a surprising triumph in the 1981 elections, reshuffled his cabinet, and embarked on a new style of politics without necessarily changing the direction that Williams had mapped out. While his predecessor was arrogant and aloof, Chambers was self-effacing and people-friendly. He spoke pleasantly to the local media and to the electorate while also re-opening more cordial dialogue with his Caribbean neighbours. He lost the election in 1986 but it is generally agreed that the policy of restraint he pursued during the early 1980s had much to do with the republic's economic recovery in the decade that followed. Chambers died on 4 November 1997.

CHARLES, Eugenia

Dame Mary Eugenia Charles was born on 15 May 1919 in Pointe Michel, Dominica, the West Indian island over which she became the first female Caribbean prime minister in 1980. After attending schools in Dominica and Grenada, she completed her education in Canada, where she graduated with a law degree from the University of Toronto in 1949, and thus became Dominica's first female lawyer. Returning to her native island, she entered local politics and founded the Dominica Freedom Party (DFP) in 1968. She won election to the House of Assembly in 1970 and served from 1975 to 1980 as an effective leader of the opposition. Dame Eugenia Charles remained at Dominica's helm until the DFP's defeat at the polls in 1995. She had led her party to an unprecedented three consecutive electoral triumphs. In 1991 she was elevated to the rank of Dame Commander of the British Empire. In addition to her political activities and her legal practice, she was for many years a director of the Fort Young Hotel and Dominica Cooperative Bank. Although she was generally cautious and conservative in her politics, she remained a consistent advocate of social welfare programmes and limited state intervention. She died on 6 September 2005.

CHARLES, Maurice

Mr Justice Maurice A. Charles has the unique distinction of having been a judge in Guyana, Ghana and Canada during a distinguished career in the practice of law. Born in Guyana, he passed his solicitor's certificate in 1944 and completed his LLB at the University of London in 1952 before immigrating to Canada in 1967. As a member of Britain's Overseas Judicial Service, he exercised civil and criminal jurisdiction in Guyana during 1952-56 before his transfer to Ghana. In 1959, he was promoted to the post of judge in Ghana's High Court where he served until 1967. After qualifying as a barrister and solicitor of the Law Society of Upper Canada in 1969, Mr Justice Charles was appointed to the Ontario provincial judiciary and became the first black criminal court judge in that province. He retired in 1995 but continues to practise criminal law and to act in an advisory capacity on difficult cases.

CHARLES, Pierre

Born on 30 June 1954 in Grand Bay, Pierre Charles was the politician chosen to take over as prime minister of Dominica in 2000 when Roosevelt Douglas suddenly died. He began his career as a teacher before entering politics and drawing attention to himself by denouncing the invasion of Grenada by the United States in 1983. As prime minister he had to deal with a serious and prolonged economic slump. He introduced a series of austerity measures calculated to mollify the International Monetary Fund

(IMF). They resulted in labour strikes but also prompted the IMF in 2003 to approve a special three-year credit to be used to combat poverty. Charles died on 6 January 2004.

CHARLES, Ray

This gifted singer, composer and pianist was born in Albany, Georgia, on 23 September 1930. Blind from glaucoma when very young, he soon learnt to read and write braille and to play the clarinet and the piano. He organized his own rhythm and blues group which became very successful in the early 1950s. His first hit, *I Got a Woman*, was recorded in 1956 and new record sales were established in 1959 by his *Georgia on My Mind*. For many years, Ray Charles was considered America's leading male vocalist and won several awards from the National Academy of Recording Arts and Sciences. He died on 10 June 2004.

CHILEMBWE, John

John Chilembwe, who is often considered the father of Malawi nationalism, was born during the 1860s in the former British colony of Nyasaland. He travelled with Joseph Booth, the fundamentalist missionary, to the United States towards the end of the nineteenth century and received a degree from a Negro theological college. Returning to Nyasaland in 1900, he undertook missionary work and established the Providence Industrial Mission to improve the lot of his black compatriots. Becoming increasingly disenchanted with the oppressiveness of European colonialism, Chilembwe wrote a stern protest in the *Nyasaland Times* in 1914. He was not only critical of British administration in Africa but sceptical of the value of black sacrifices in what essentially was a white man's war. When the British ignored his protest, he led a suicidal and largely symbolic rebellion against their rule and was promptly killed on 3 February 1915. Chilembwe's revolt, of course, was futile. But it drew attention to European injustice in Africa and his martyrdom gave a considerable fillip to African nationalist movements in the generations that followed.

CHILUBA, Frederick

Born on 30 April 1943, Frederick Jacob Titus Chiluba was the second president of Zambia (1991-2002). He was educated at the Kawambwa Secondary School before studying economics in the United States and former Communist countries. Returning to Zambia, he joined the National Union of Building, Engineering and General Workers (NUBEGW) and shortly became its chairman. He later became chairman of the Zambia Congress of Trade Unions (ZCTU) also. In 1990 he co-founded the Movement for Multiparty Democracy which won the elections of 1991 and brought an end to the lengthy reign of Kenneth Kaunda. He was re-elected in 1996 but had to step down on 2 January 2002 as the constitution did not allow presidents to serve three consecutive terms. Chiluba was then elected chairman of the Organization of African Unity (OAU). He had failed to stop escalating crime and poverty in Zambia, as he had promised. His desperate efforts to amend the constitution, albeit in vain, to prolong his own tenure cost him considerable support. After his presidency, he was charged with the embezzlement of huge amounts of money, but many of these charges have been dropped.

CHINAMANO, Josiah

One of the leading African nationalists of the post-war period, Josiah Chinamano was born near Salisbury, in Southern Rhodesia, on 19 October 1922. Educated by missionaries and at Fort Hare University in South Africa, he became a teacher and an administrator in Southern Rhodesia. Always actively involved in the struggle against racist régimes in southern Africa, he was frequently detained and imprisoned by the authorities. He became vice-president of Joshua Nkomo's opposition party, the Zimbabwe African People's Union (ZAPU) and was appointed minister of transport in Robert Mugabe's first cabinet when Rhodesia became the independent state of Zimbabwe in 1980. He was dismissed in 1982 on charges that he was plotting, with other ZAPU members, to overthrow the government, but he remained a member of parliament until his death on 1 October 1984, when he was declared a national hero.

CHISHOLM, Shirley

Shirley Anita St Hill Chisholm was born into poverty in Brooklyn, New York, on 30 November 1924. After achieving her BA from the City University of New York in 1946, she gained her MA from Columbia University in 1952. She worked for many years as a nursery school teacher before beginning her political career as a member of the New York state assembly in 1964. She became the first black woman ever elected to Congress in 1968 and held her seat in this legislature for several terms. In 1971, she boldly entered the race for the Democratic Party's presidential nomination, forcing the party to take more seriously a representative of Blacks and women, who had previously been ignored in these campaigns. In 1972 she was invited to serve on the House Education and Labor Committee, having established herself as a fervent advocate of civil rights and gender equality. She published two interesting books, *Unbought and Unbossed* and *The Good Fight*. After making a huge impact on local and national politics for almost two decades, Chisholm returned to the teaching profession in 1983 and served as a visiting scholar at Spelman College in Atlanta, Georgia, in 1985. She died on 1 January 2005.

CHITEPO, Herbert

Herbert Wiltshire Tfumaindini Chitepo, a prominent African nationalist, was born in Bonda, Rhodesia, on 5 June 1923. He was an outspoken critic of the racist governments in Rhodesia and South Africa and devoted his energies towards their destruction. He achieved a law degree at Fort Hare University College in South Africa and was the first black barrister produced by his country. In 1962 he went into voluntary exile in Tanganyika and masterminded the activities of the militant Zimbabwe African National Union (ZANU) from his headquarters there. In 1966, he moved to Zambia where he was made a senior official of the African National Congress (ANC). But before any of these revolutionary activities could bear positive fruit, Chitepo was killed by a bomb blast in Lusaka on 18 March 1975.

CHRISTIAN, Barbara

A well-known Caribbean American educator and critic, Barbara Christian was born in St Thomas, US Virgin Islands, on 12 December 1943. She became a noted professor of African-American studies and a leading figure in the field of modern literary feminism. She received her BA from Marquette University in 1963, and her PhD from Columbia University in 1970. From 1971 until her death on 25 June 2000, Christian was a professor at the University of California, Berkeley, where she was instrumental in establishing the department of African-American studies. A prolific author and editor, her legacy includes *Black Women Novelists: The Development of a Tradition 1892-1976* (1980), a *Teaching Guide to Accompany Black Foremothers* (1980), *Black Feminist Criticism: Perspectives on Black Women Writers* (1985); *From the Inside Out: Afro-American Women's Literary Tradition and the State* (1987); and *Alice Walker's 'The Colour Purple' and Other Works: A Critical Commentary* (1987). Christian also contributed articles to several scholarly journals.

CHRISTIAN, Elder

Elder Washington Christian was born in Virginia in 1776. He was ordained in the Abyssinia Baptist Church of New York in 1822 and served briefly as a missionary in Boston and Connecticut before deciding, in 1825, to work among the refugee slaves in Canada. In 1826 he accordingly organized the first Baptist Church in Canada. It was also the very first institution catering for Blacks in Canada. Elder Christian founded a number of other Baptist Churches in Ontario but remained the pastor of Toronto First Baptist Church until his death in July 1850.

CHRISTIE, Linford

Linford Christie was born in St Andrew, Jamaica, on 2 April 1960. In 1967, he followed his parents to the United Kingdom where they had emigrated five years before. He attended Henry Compton Secondary School in Fulham and excelled in physical education, but did not specialize in athletics until he was almost twenty. He became a very successful sprinter and in 1993 was the first track star ever to hold simultaneously the Olympic, World, European and Commonwealth titles in the 100 metres. Altogether he finished with 23 medals, more than any other British male athlete before or since. He was awarded an MBE in 1990 and an OBE in 1998 for his services to athletics. Away from the track, Christie hosted the BBC television series *Record Breaker* for a time before its cancellation in 2001. In 2006 he was named a senior mentor for athletes on the British national team.

CHRISTOPHE, Henri

Born on 6 October 1767, Henri Christophe is one of the greatest heroes in the history of Haiti. One of Toussaint Louverture's most trusted lieutenants, he played a very significant role in completing the task that his mentor had begun. He helped to ensure that Haitians would never again be subjects of the French monarchy and he himself was crowned King of Haiti on 2 June 1812. After defeating the French, Christophe had to cope with a serious rebellion, led by Alexandre Sabès Pétion, who (with British help) was able to restore Spanish rule over that portion of the island now known as Santo Domingo. Christophe consolidated the position of the ex-slaves in Haiti by distributing plantations to the military chiefs, restoring peasants to their former occupations, and maintaining a general prosperity. He built the famous *Citadelle Laferrière*, a fortress just south of his capital at Cap-Haïtien, and a truly spectacular palace, Sans Souci. But Christophe committed suicide on 8 October 1820, in the face of mounting opposition from some of the peasants, whom he had forced to labour on the plantations, and from the soldiers within his own army. His political enemies then promptly abolished the monarchy and established the new republic of Haiti.

CLARK, John Pepper

This renowned poet, playwright, short-story writer and teacher, was born in the Niger delta in western Nigeria on 6 April 1935. He was educated at schools in Okrika and Yeremi before graduating from the University of Ibadan with a BA (Hons) in English. For some years, he worked in Ibadan as a journalist with the *Daily Express* and helped to found the Society of Nigerian Authors as well as *The Horn*, a magazine of student poetry. He later became a professor of English at Lagos University. John Pepper Clark is remembered for such fine plays as *Songs of a Goat* (1961), *The Masquerade* (1964) and *The Raft* (1964). He wrote beautiful poetry in *Poems* (1962), *A Reed in the Tide* (1965), and *Casualties: Poems 1966-68* (1970). He produced a quaint satire, *America, Their America*, in 1964, as well as an important work of literary criticism, *The Example of Shakespeare* (1970). Clark has done extensive research into traditional Ijaw myths and legends and has written a number of essays on African poetry.

CLARKE, Austin

Austin Ardinel Chesterfield Clarke, better known as 'Tom', is one of the most famous and most influential of all Caribbean-Canadian writers. Born in Barbados on 26 July 1932, he was educated at Combermere School and Harrison College before teaching briefly at Coleridge Parry School in his native island. He emigrated to Toronto in 1955 and spent the next twenty years there writing numerous plays, short stories and novels. He worked for some time in the late 1970s with the Caribbean Broadcasting Corporation (CBC) in Barbados but then returned to Toronto to continue his remarkable output of fascinating literature. His much acclaimed novels deal mainly with the experiences of Caribbean immigrants in Canada and he has managed to mix the Bajan dialect with formal English in a most effective manner. His major works include *The Survivors of the Crossing* (1964), *Among Thistles and Thorns* (1965), *The Meeting Point* (1967), *Storm of Fortune* (1973), *The Impuritans* (1974), *The Bigger Light* (1975), *The Prime Minister* (1977), *Growing Up Stupid Under the Union Jack* (1980), *Proud Empires* (1986), *A Passage Back Home* (1994), and *The Origin of Waves* (1997). In 2002 he won the prestigious Giller Prize for his much acclaimed *The Polished Hoe*. He has also published numerous short stories in such collections as *When He Was Young and Free and Used to Wear Silks* (1971), *When Women Rule* (1985), *Nine Men Who Laughed* (1986), *In This City* (1992), and *There Are No Elders* (1993). He has also written a few poems and a number of fine plays, including *Son of Learning: A Play in Three Acts* (1974). Clarke's reputation has led to several invitations to serve as writer-in-residence in such prestigious institutions as Brandeis University, Duke University, Indiana University, the University of Guelph, the University of Texas, the University of Toronto, the University of Western Ontario, Williams College, and Yale University. In addition to his writing, Clarke was a founding member of the Writers' Union of Canada, a vice-chairman of the Ontario Film Review Board and a member of Canada's Immigration and Refugee Board. He has won many awards and distinctions culminating in his being invested with the Order of Canada in 1998 and honorary doctorates by the University of Toronto and the University of the West Indies.

CLARKE, Ellis

Sir Ellis Emmanuel Innocent Clarke, who was the second Governor-General of Trinidad and Tobago, was elected unopposed as president when that country declared itself a republic in 1976. Born in Belmont on 28 December 1917, he attended St Mary's College and won the prestigious

Island Scholarship in mathematics. This took him to London, England, where he qualified in law and was called to the bar in 1941. In that year he returned to Trinidad where he practised privately until 1954. He became solicitor-general during 1954-57, deputy colonial secretary 1956-57, attorney-general and constitutional adviser to the cabinet 1957-1962. After Trinidad and Tobago achieved their independence, Sir Ellis Clarke served as ambassador to the United States, Canada and Mexico and permanent representative to the United Nations. In 1972 he was offered a knighthood and named Governor-General of Trinidad and Tobago, a post he held until 1987. An internationally known expert in constitutional law, Sir Ellis remained active in solving diplomatic and constitutional disputes abroad and in dispute resolution and constitutional matters at home. He was one of the first recipients of his country's highest honour, the Trinity Cross, and also received Venezuela's highest national award, *El Gran Cordon*.

CLARKE, George

Professor George Elliott Clarke is one of Canada's outstanding poets and playwrights. Born in Nova Scotia in 1960, he received his BA from the University of Waterloo in 1984, his MA from the University of Dalhousie in 1989 and PhD from Queen's University in 1993. He taught English and Canadian Studies at Duke University, North Carolina, during 1994-99 before being appointed the Visiting Seagram's Chair in Canadian Studies at McGill University. Currently he is professor of English at the University of Toronto. Dr Clarke's poetry appears in such collections as *Saltwater Spirituals and Deeper Blues* (1983); *Provençal Songs* (1993); *Lush Dreams, Blue Exile* (1994); *Gold Indigoes* (2000); *Execution Poems* (2001); and *Illuminated Verse* (2005). He has also published two verse plays, a verse novel and literary criticism. His works bring attention to the rich historical and cultural traditions of Blacks in the Maritimes. His verse novel, *Whylah Falls*, was adapted for radio and aired on the Canadian Broadcasting Corporation (CBC) in 1997. His verse play, *Beatrice Clancy*, was made into an opera, performed on stage and broadcast on CBC television. He also wrote the screenplay for the film, *One Heart Broken into Song*. In 2002, he published *Odysseys Home: Mapping African-Canadian Literature*. Dr Clarke, who has already been awarded honorary doctorates by two Canadian universities, won the Portia White Prize for Artistic Achievement in 1998 and the Canadian Governor General Award for English Poetry in 2001.

CLEMENTS, George

Revd George Clements, a civil rights activist and social reformer of unusual courage, drew international attention to himself in the 1980s by waging a crusade against the distribution of illegal drugs in Chicago's inner-city and persuading both the Illinois state legislature and the US Congress to pass laws against the sale of drug paraphernalia. He had earlier gained some notoriety by becoming, in 1981, the first Catholic priest to adopt a child. In defiance of his local superior, he founded One Church, One Child, an adoption programme dedicated to finding black adoptive parents for black children. When Pope John Paul II overruled Clements' superior, he adopted three more sons and was featured in *The Father Clements Story*, a two-hour television drama, in 1987. Born in Chicago on 26 January 1932, Clements became the first black person to graduate from Quigley Preparatory Seminary. He furthered his studies at St Mary of the Lake Seminary in Mundelein, Illinois, and was ordained a diocesan priest in 1957. Twelve years later he became pastor of Holy Angels Church, where he distinguished himself by establishing a highly rated school in a poor inner-city neighbourhood. In 1977 he was honoured by the Association of the Chicago Priests and presented with the Pope John XXIII Award as the Priest of the Year. A fervent advocate of racial equality and social justice, Revd Clements participated with Dr Martin Luther King, Jr in the march at Selma, Alabama, in 1965.

COBB, Montague

Dr W. Montague Cobb, noted physician and editor, was born in Washington, D.C. in 1904. He received his BA from Amherst College in 1925, his MD from Howard University Medical College in 1929, and his PhD from Case Western Reserve University in 1932. A famous teacher of anatomy, Cobb became president of such organizations as the National Medical Association, the American Association of Physical Anthropologists, and the Anthropological Society of Washington, D.C. He also edited the *Journal of the National Medical Association* for many years after 1949. He is generally remembered as the 'principal historian of the Negro in medicine'. His work went far towards demolishing old myths about anatomical and biological differences based on race.

COLE, Nat King

Born Nathaniel Adams Coles in Montgomery, Alabama, on 17 March 1919, Nat 'King' Cole became one of the most popular and successful singers and jazz pianists in North America. He first came to prominence during the 1930s as the leader and pianist of the King Cole Trio. Instrumentalist at first, the group later featured Cole as vocalist. In 1941 it made a triumphant tour of the United States and made its first recording two years later with Capitol Records. That hit was *Straighten Up and Fly Right*, which Cole himself had first written in 1937. It sold more than 500,000 records and was the beginning of a long sequence of commercial successes.

Cole became the first black performer with his own network radio programme and, in 1956, the first black entertainer with his own national television show. He also appeared in a number of motion pictures, including *Small Town Girl*, *The Blue Gardenia*, *Istanbul*, and *China Gate*. He played the feature role of W.C. Handy in *St Louis Blues* and naturally starred in *The Nat King Cole Story*. His most successful songs perhaps were *It's Only a Paper Moon*, *The Christmas Song*, *Nature Boy*, *Route 66*, *Too Young*, *Walking My Baby Back Home*, and *Unforgettable*. Nat King Cole died on 15 February 1965.

COLE, William Randolph

William Randolph Cole, better known as 'Cozy', was a versatile jazz percussionist, the highlight of whose drumming career was the 1958 hit, *Topsy*, the first drum solo ever to sell more than one million records. Born in East Orange, New Jersey, on 17 October 1909, Cole performed in the 1930s with several major bands, including Cab Calloway's and Stuff Smith's comedy jazz group. He became one of the first black musicians on a network musical staff when (in 1942) he was engaged by CBS radio to play with Raymond Scott's orchestra. In 1943 he appeared in the Broadway musical, *Carmen Jones*. In 1945 he played with Benny Goodman's Quintet in *Seven Lively Arts*, another musical, before touring with Louis Armstrong's All Stars during 1949-53. In 1962 Cole was sent with his band by the US Department of State on a tour of Africa. He later became artist in residence and student lecturer at Capital University in Columbus, Ohio. He died on 29 January 1981.

COLEMAN, Bessie

Bessie Coleman was the very first black female pilot. Born in Atlanta, Texas, on 26 January 1893, she was prevented by poverty from proceeding towards a college education after graduating from high school. She worked at a number of odd jobs before travelling to France in 1920 and attending a school for pilots. Following her graduation, she returned to the United States and performed spectacularly at the Chicago air show, sponsored by the *Chicago Defender*, in 1922. She then began to give flying lessons, lectures and shows throughout the country. Sadly, however, she died in a plane crash in 1926. On every Memorial Day, black American pilots still remember the brave young lady who encouraged so many members of her race and her gender to take up flying as an occupation.

COLEMAN, William T. Jr

William T. Coleman, Jr was born in Philadelphia, Pennsylvania, in 1920. After receiving his BA degree from the University of Pennsylvania in 1941, he studied law as well as business at Harvard University. A senior partner in the firm of Dilworth, Paxson, Kalish, and Coleman of Philadelphia, he also became a director for such major corporations as Pan American World Airways, Penn Mutual Insurance Co., First Penn Corp., First Penn Banking and Trust Co., and Brookings Institute. Coleman also served as president of the National Association for the Advancement of Colored People (NAACP) Legal and Education Fund. During President Ford's tenure (1974-76), he was appointed secretary of transportation, after more than 25 federal and state appointments to positions of authority and importance.

COLERIDGE-TAYLOR, Samuel

Born in Croydon, on 15 August 1875, to a Sierra Leonean father and an English mother, Samuel Coleridge-Taylor became an outstanding musician and a distinguished composer. He studied at the Royal College of Music and later taught at and conducted the orchestra at the Croydon Conservatory of Music. His fame led to invitations to tour the United States which he did with great success in 1904, 1906 and 1910. These experiences increased his interest in his racial heritage and he vowed to do for African music what the celebrated Brahms had done for Hungarian music. He first rose to prominence when he produced his *Ballade in A Minor* in 1898. There followed such notable pieces as *Hiawatha's Wedding Feast*, *The Death of Minnehaha*, *Overture to The Song of Hiawatha*, *Hiawatha's Departure*, *24 Negro Melodies*, *Romance in G Minor*, *Violin Concerto in G Minor* and *Ballade in C Minor*. Coleridge-Taylor was the first British-born musician to include African, African-American and African-Caribbean elements in his melody. He consequently became extremely popular in the Western Hemisphere and served for years as a source of inspiration to African-American musicians and composers. He died on 1 September 1912.

COMPAORÉ, Blaise

Born on 3 February 1951 in Ouagadougou, Upper Volta, Blaise Compaoré is the founder and leader of the Congress for Democracy and Progress, his country's ruling party, and has been the president of Burkina Faso since 1987. His career began in the Voltaïc army where he rose to the rank of captain. He served as minister of justice during Thomas Sankara's presidency. In a bloody coup that killed Sankara, he emerged as president. This was the third successful coup in which Compaoré had been involved, but his own presidency provided Burkina Faso with a measure of political stability it had previously lacked. He gave the country democratic institutions and increased freedom of the press. He was re-elected several times, winning the general elections of November 2005 with more than eighty per cent of the popular vote.

CONSTANTINE, Learie

Sir Learie Nicholas Constantine was born in Diego Martin, Trinidad, on 21 September 1901. One of the most exciting cricketers of the inter-war years, he played brilliantly for Trinidad and the West Indies and was especially famous for his fielding and aggressive batting. He proved a great attraction as a professional for Nelson in the Lancashire League. After his retirement from the game, he qualified as a barrister and settled in England where he waged a vigorous campaign against racial prejudice. He became a member of the Race Relations Board, rector of St Andrews University and a governor of the British Broadcasting Corporation (BBC). Constantine was knighted in 1962 and was made a life peer in 1969 - a most unusual distinction for a black West Indian. He died on 1 July 1971. He had served briefly (1962-64) as high commissioner in London for Trinidad and Tobago. His legacy included such books as *Cricket and I* (1933), *Cricket in the Sun* (1948), *Cricketers' Carnival* (1949), *Cricket Crackers* (1951), *Colour Bar* (1954), and *The Young Cricketer's Companion* (1964).

CONTÉ, Lansana

Gen. Lansana Conté has been the president of Guinea since April 1984 when he toppled the previous régime in a military coup. Born in Moussayah Loumbaya, in 1934, he was educated at Dubréka Primary School and military schools in Côte d'Ivoire and Senegal. He enlisted in the French Army in 1955 and rose to the rank of captain in 1971 in the national army of Guinea. In 1975 he was appointed assistant chief of staff in the Guinean army. In 1984, Conté installed himself as president, suspended the constitution, denounced the human rights abuses of his predecessors and released 250 political prisoners. He began a programme to improve Guinea's economy and to encourage foreign investment by devaluing the currency and reducing government expenditure. He then initiated the transition to civilian, multi-party rule which permitted democratic elections every five years beginning in 1993. Conté's party has thus far prevailed in all of these contests.

COOK, Mercer

This educator, author and diplomat was born in Washington, D.C. in 1903. After teaching French at Howard University (1932-36) and Atlanta University (1936-43), he became supervisor of English at the University of Haiti. He returned to Howard University as full professor of French in 1945. In 1961, Cook was appointed US ambassador to Niger, and in 1964 became ambassador to Senegal and Gambia. His books included *Le Noir* (1934), *Five French Negro Authors* (1944), and *Militant Black Writers in Africa and the United States* (1969). He also produced a translation of Léopold Senghor's *On African Socialism* in 1964.

COOKE, Howard

His Excellency the Most Honourable Sir Howard Felix Hanlan Cooke served as Governor General of Jamaica from 1991 until his retirement in 2006. Born in the parish of St James on 13 November 1915, he was educated at elementary and private schools before attending Mico Training College and the University of London, England. Cooke taught at several schools in Jamaica before entering politics in 1938 as one of the founding members of the People's National Party (PNP). He was elected to the federal parliament of the British West Indies in 1958 and served from 1962 to 1967 as a member of the Jamaican Senate, over which he later presided (1989-91). Cooke was elected to the Jamaican House of Representatives in 1967 and held his seat until 1980. From 1972 to 1980 he was also a member of Michael Manley's cabinet. After many years of public service, he was knighted (KCMG) in 1991, the same year in which he was awarded the prestigious Order of the Nation (ON). He had previously been honoured with the title of Commander of the Order of Distinction (1978) and had received a Special Plaque in 1980 from the Commonwealth Parliamentary Association. During the 1980s, Sir Howard also served as Unit Manager of the Jamaica Mutual Life Assurance Society and Branch Manager of the American Life Insurance Company.

COOKE, Marvel Jackson

Marvel Jackson Cooke, a famous American journalist, was born in 1903 in Mankato, Minnesota. She began her career by writing for mainly black publications before becoming, in 1949, the first African-American woman to serve as a reporter for a mainstream white-owned newspaper, the *Daily Compass*. She later worked for a number of radical organizations. It was her compelling series, *I Was a Slave* for the *Daily Compass*, that drew public attention to the plight of underpaid domestics. Cooke died on 29 November 2000.

COOLS, Anne

Anne Claire Cools, who became in 1984 the first black person to be appointed to the Canadian Senate, was born in Barbados, West Indies, on 12 August 1943. She attended the Ursuline Convent and Queen's College, Barbados, before completing her education in Canada where her family immigrated in 1956. A graduate of McGill University, Montreal, Cools has devoted the bulk of her energies towards assisting battered women, families in crisis and families troubled by domestic violence. In 1974 she founded Women in Transition (WIT), one of the first shelters in Canada for battered women and opened a second such shelter in 1987. Cools has also served for many years as an instructor in social work at various institutions in Ontario, including the University of Toronto and Ryerson Polytechnical Institute (now Ryerson University). From 1980 to 1984, she served on the National Parole Board of Canada. She is now one of the most active, outspoken and controversial Canadian senators with an especially keen interest in gender and racial issues. She is currently the deputy chair of the senate standing committees on national finance, social affairs, science and technology. Senator Cools has been the recipient of several awards and honours, including the Spiritual Mother of the Year Award from NA'AMAT, the international Jewish Women's Organization that supports battered women's shelters in Israel. In 1997 she received the Outstanding Achievement Award in Politics from *Pride Magazine*. In 2001 she also won the Bob Marley Day Award for promoting equality, peace and harmony.

COOPER, Afua

Dr Afua Cooper is a well-known poet, sociologist and historian who emigrated from Jamaica to Canada in 1980, completed her PhD at the University of Toronto in 2000 and currently teaches at Ryerson University. She has published collections of verse and co-authored the first book on black women's history in Canada. In addition to articles in scholarly journals, her major works include *Breakin' Chains* (1983); *Red Caterpillar on College Street* (1989); *Memories Have Tongue* (1994); *Utterances and Incantations: Women, Poetry and Dub* (1999); *We're Rooted Here and They Can't Pull us Up: Essays in African Canadian Women's History* (1999); *The Underground Railroad: Next Stop, Toronto!* (2004) and *The Hanging of Angélique* (2006). Her albums include *Sunshine* (1989) and *Poetry is Not a Luxury* (1990). Dr Cooper won the *Casas de las Americas* prize for poetry in 1992 and the Joseph Brant Award for the best book on Ontario history in 1999.

CORNISH, Samuel

Samuel E. Cornish was an editor and a clergyman who left his mark on African-American life during the early nineteenth century. It was he who, in 1821, organized the first black Presbyterian church in New York City. He also helped to found, in 1827, the first black newspaper in the United States. Originally called *Freedom's Journal*, it was soon renamed *The Rights of All* but had to cease publication in 1829. Briefly during the 1830s, Cornish served as editor of another newspaper, *The Colored American*, in New York City. He was also one of the leaders of the first National Negro Convention which met in Philadelphia in 1830 and was very active for some years in the American Anti-slavery Society. Samuel Cornish died in 1859.

COUSSEY, James Henley

Sir James Henley Coussey was an eminent Gold Coast jurist who was the first native African to be appointed a judge without first having served as a colonial magistrate. He is best remembered as the chairman of the committee which made recommendations on which the Gold Coast constitution of 1951 was based. Born on 10 March 1895, Coussey was called to the bar in 1913 and became involved in local politics. Interested also in education, he served for years on the Achimota College Council. He was appointed judge of the Gold Coast High Court in 1943. After the Gold Coast disturbances of 1948, he was invited to head the royal commission which enquired into their causes. The report of the Coussey Commission led to the establishment of internal self-government and later to the independence of Ghana. Coussey also served as a member of the West African Court of Appeal. He died on 6 June 1958.

COX, Oliver

Dr Oliver Cromwell Cox, a noted sociologist, was born in Trinidad, West Indies, in 1901. He studied at Northwestern University and the University of Chicago (both in Illinois), emerging with his PhD degree in 1938. For some years, he taught at Wiley College, at the Tuskegee Institute and at Lincoln University. Chief among his works was the very important *Caste, Class and Race* (1948) in which he attacked the school of sociologists who viewed the black man as belonging to a caste. Cox was mainly concerned with the caste-class structure of American society. He died in 1974.

COX, Rita

Rita Cox, one of Canada's greatest story-tellers, has done much to illustrate the value of black oral traditions to thousands of listeners over the years. She is herself a noted author and has served for many years as the Head Librarian, Parkdale Branch of the Public Library in Toronto, Ontario. She was honoured in 1995 with a Canadian Black Achievement Award from Pride Communications.

CRICHLOW, Ernest

Ernest Crichlow, whose paintings did so much to establish African-American youngsters as characters in general children's stories, was born in New York City in 1914. One of the leading African-American artists of the twentieth century, Crichlow's work has frequently been exhibited in all parts of the United States. One of his best-known (and earliest) paintings was *Lend Me a Hand*. He is also remembered for his notable illustrations in Jerrold Beim's *Two is a Team*, a children's book published in 1945.

CROSTHWAIT, David

Born in 1898, David Nelson Crosthwait, Jr was responsible for about forty important inventions and became one of the most creative of all American engineers. An expert in heat transfer, air ventilation and central air conditioning, his patents dealt with heating systems, vacuum pumps, refrigeration methods and temperature regulation devices. During the 1920s and 1930s, he invented an improved boiler, a new thermostat control system and a new differential vacuum pump. In 1975, for his outstanding contributions to engineering technology, Crosthwait was awarded an honorary doctorate from Purdue University, the same institution from which he had himself graduated in 1919. After retiring from industry in 1969, he continued to share his knowledge by publishing several articles and manuals and by teaching a course in steam heating theory and controls at his alma mater. He died in 1976.

CROWTHER, Samuel

Revd Samuel Adjai Crowther of Nigeria is best remembered as the priest who broke through one of the most stubborn colour barriers by becoming the first black bishop of West Equatorial Africa in 1864. Born a slave around 1807 in Oshogbo, he was rescued by the British from a Portuguese ship in 1822 and taken to Freetown, Sierra Leone, where he proved himself an excellent student at Fourah Bay College. Following his graduation, he taught for a while before being ordained an Anglican priest in 1845. He was the first African to be ordained by the Church Missionary Society. Crowther then served for many years as a missionary in Abeokuta, Nigeria, preaching a simple gospel of black pride, freedom and dignity and thus alienated himself from the Anglican establishment during his last days. This respect for his roots was clearly reflected in *A Grammar and Vocabulary of the Yoruba Language*, which he published in 1852. He also wrote a *Journal of an Expedition Up the Niger and Tshadda Rivers* (1856) and co-authored (with J.C. Taylor) *The Gospel on the Banks of the Niger* (1859). Bishop Crowther died on 31 December 1891.

CUFFAY, William

William Cuffay was one of the leaders of Chartism, the first mass political movement of the British working classes. He was born in the West Indies in 1788 on a merchant ship, on which his father, a freed slave from St Kitts, was working as the cook. His family settled in Chatham, Kent, and he became a journeyman tailor. Furious at the treatment of unions and workers, he joined the radical Chartist movement in 1839 and was transported to Tasmania for twenty-one years when convicted in 1848 of conspiring to levy war against Queen Victoria. In that Australian colony Cuffay continued his crusade on behalf of trade unions and refused to return to England even after being pardoned in 1856. He was largely instrumental in persuading the Tasmanian authorities to amend the Master and Servant law. He died poor in the Tasmania workhouse in July 1870.

CUFFE, Paul

Paul Cuffe was born near New Bedford, Massachusetts, in 1759. He became a seaman at an early age and by the time he was twenty-five owned his own ship. He became a prosperous merchant and trader and eventually built up a major shipping company. Cuffe believed that Blacks might fare better in Africa and he transported many of them back to Sierra Leone. He also thought that such emigration might solve the problem of slavery. A civil rights activist, he campaigned vigorously for the abolition of slavery and equal rights for Blacks. He built a school on his farm in Massachusetts, hired his own teachers, and opened it to the public. He was also instrumental in forcing the state assembly to pass a law guaranteeing equal rights to free Blacks in Massachusetts. He died on 9 September 1817.

CUGUANO, Ottobah

Ottobah Cuguano was one of the harshest critics of slavery in the eighteenth century and the first African to demand publicly the total abolition of the trade and the freeing of all the slaves. Born in the late 1750s on the coast of what is now Ghana, he was kidnapped and taken to Grenada where he was sold into slavery when he was about thirteen years old. After being peddled around different islands in the Caribbean, his last owner took him to England in 1772 and set him free. He became baptised as a Christian in order not to be sold into slavery again and entered the service of Richard Cosway, principal painter to the Prince of Wales (later King George IV). Cuguano, a literate and eloquent speaker, immediately became one of the leaders of the black community in London. In 1787, with the help of Olaudah Equiano, another exceptional ex-slave, he published an important pamphlet, *Thoughts and Sentiments on the Evil and Wicked Traffic of the Slavery and Commerce of the Human Species*. He was the first writer in English to declare that enslaved Blacks had not only the moral right but the moral duty to resist enslavement, by all the means at their disposal. These thoughts did not endear him to Englishmen at large or even to the white abolitionists. In a shorter version of his *Thoughts*, he announced his intention of opening a school for Blacks but it is not clear if he ever succeeded in doing so. The date and details of his death are uncertain as nothing is known about Ottobah Cuguano after 1791.

CULLEN, Countee

The poet, Countee Cullen, is perhaps the best-known member of the Harlem Renaissance of the 1920s. Born on 30 May 1903 in Baltimore, Maryland, he received a BA from New York University in 1925 and his MA degree from Harvard University in 1926. For many years a teacher of French at Frederick Douglass High School, Cullen wrote several volumes of excellent poetry. These included *Color* (1925), *Copper Sun* (1927), *The Ballad of the Brown Girl* (1927), *The Black Christ and Other Poems* (1929), and *The Medea and Some Poems* (1935). A selection of his poems also appeared (posthumously) in 1947, in a volume entitled *On These I Stand*. Cullen died at the relatively young age of forty-two on 9 January 1946. His prizes and awards included the Witter Bynner Poetry Award in 1925, a Guggenheim Fellowship and a Spingarn Medal in 1928.

CURLING, Alvin

Born on 15 November 1939 in Kingston, Jamaica, Alvin Curling worked there in management of housing and land settlement before immigrating to Canada in 1965 and completing his education at Seneca College and York University in Toronto. For thirteen years after 1972, he served as Director of Student Services at Seneca College. He was also president of the World Literacy of Canada during 1981-84. Entering provincial politics in 1985, he established a record by garnering the most votes in a Canadian provincial election and won the Scarborough North seat for the Liberals in the Ontario legislature. Several subsequent re-elections made him one of the longest serving members in that parliament. He finally resigned his seat on 19 August 2005 to accept the appointment as Canada's ambassador to the Dominican Republic. In 1985 Alvin Curling became the first Black to hold a cabinet position in Ontario when he was created Minister of Housing. In 2003 he then became the first black speaker of the Legislative Assembly of Ontario. During the 1990s, as a member of the official opposition, he was the Ontario Liberal critic for housing, urban affairs, youth and employment, colleges and universities, the disabled and human rights. Curling's numerous honours and awards include the Order of Distinction from the Government of Jamaica in 2001.

DACKO, David

David Dacko had the dubious distinction of being twice deposed as the president of an African republic. Born in Moyen Congo, French Equatorial Africa, on 24 March 1930, he emerged as one of the political leaders of the former colony when it achieved its independence. When President Barthélemy Boganda died in a plane crash in 1959, Dacko installed himself as president of the Central African Republic which he declared a one-party state. His autocratic form of government in the midst of an economic crisis led to his deposition by Col. Jean-Bédel Bokassa who proclaimed himself Emperor and ruled even more autocratically than Dacko had done. In 1979, France intervened and restored Dacko to the presidency. But his second term was just as hapless as his first and it ended in 1981 when Gen. André Kolingba overthrew him in a bloodless coup. Dacko sought refuge in Cameroon where he died on 20 November 2003.

DADIÉ, Bernard

A prolific novelist, poet and playwright, Bernard Binlin Dadié was born in Assinie in the Ivory Coast in 1916, and educated in local schools before furthering his studies in Senegal. For many years he worked with the Institut Français d'Afrique Noire at Dakar before being appointed director of Fine Arts Research for the Ivorian government. He was later promoted to the office of director of cultural affairs for the Ivory Coast. Dadié's novels included *Climbié* (1953), and *Un nègre a Paris* (1959). Among his best plays were *Assémien Déhylé, roi du Sanwi*(1967); *Monsieur Thôgô-Gnini* (1970); *Les voix dans le vent* (1970); *Beatrice du Congo* (1971) and *Iles de tempête* (1973). His finest short stories appeared in *Le pagne noir: Contes Africains* (1970). He also wrote a number of folk tales in such collections as *Les belles histoires de Kacou Ananzé* (1963) and *Légendes africaines* (1966). In addition, Dadié was the author of *Patron de New York* (1964); *La ville où nul ne meurt* (Rome) (1968); *Carnet de prison* (1981) and at least two fine collections of poems, the first of which, *Afrique debout*, was published in 1950. He was one of the leading African writers of the French language.

DADSON, Joseph

Joseph E. Dadson Sr is an internationally renowned bio-medical engineer who emigrated from Ghana to Canada in 1962 and graduated from the University of British Columbia in 1968. In 1976, he helped to establish Medionics International in Toronto, where he invented the first portable Volumetric Peritoneal Dialysis machine. He invented a Quick Connect-Disconnect Cap, which not only reduced the incidence of peritonitis but decreased the cost of dialysis treatment and resulted also in greater convenience for the patient. Dadson then invented the disposable Y-Set that has become the standard in the industry, significantly reducing even further the incidence of peritoneal dialysis infection. His most recent invention is the miniature dialysis machine which incorporates a number of distinctive operating and diagnostic features. Dadson began his career as a technical administrator in the Nephrology Department at Toronto General Hospital before he entered the private sector. In 1997 he founded another company, Newsol Technologies, specializing in automated dialysis systems, including machines, disposable products and solutions. Dadson holds a number of important patents in Canada, Japan and the United States and is the recipient of numerous honours and awards.

DAIRO, I.K.

Isaiah Kehinde Dairo was the Nigerian musician and composer who revolutionized Yoruban juju music by introducing a broad range of rhythms and a number of western instruments. Born in 1930, he became leader of the 10-piece Morning Star Orchestra in 1957 and later renamed it the Blue Spots. His revolutionary use of the accordion and the electric guitar added a new dimension to the traditional music of the Yoruba. In 1963 he was the first African musician to be awarded an MBE. He died on 7 February 1996.

DAMAS, Léon

Léon Gontran Damas, unarguably the greatest poet produced by French Guiana, was born there, in Cayenne, on 28 March 1912. He attended local schools before going to the Lycée Schoelcher in Martinique, where he met Aimé Césaire for the first time. He then proceeded to Paris to study law and oriental languages, but soon decided to concentrate on his own writing. Along with Césaire and Léopold Senghor of Senegal, he was largely instrumental in launching the student newspaper, *L'Étudiant noir*, which did so much to promote the movement of 'négritude'. Damas was determined to popularize also the works of Francophone Blacks and succeeded in publishing in 1947 the very important *Poètes d'expression francaise 1900-1945*. He followed this up with *Nouvelle somme de poésie du monde noire* in 1966. For a brief period during the 1950s Damas served on the French National Assembly as a representative of Guiana. He also spent many years in North America, lecturing on African and Caribbean literature in such institutions as Georgetown University and Howard University. Although he spent most of his life abroad, he remained a fervent advocate of racial equality, social justice and Guyanese independence. His poetry appeared under such titles as *Pigments* (1937), *Poèmes nègres sur des airs africains* (1948), *Graffiti* (1952), *Black Label* (1956), and *Névralgies* (1964). Damas also wrote several short stories and essays. He died on 22 January 1978.

DANQUAH, Joseph Boakye

Dr Joseph Kwame Kyeretwi Boakye Danquah was born in Bepong, Gold Coast, on 21 December 1895. Educated at Basel Mission schools in the Gold Coast, he worked briefly as a barrister's clerk in Accra and as a clerk at the Supreme Court of the Gold Coast before studying law and philosophy at the University of London, England. A brilliant scholar, he won the John Stuart Mill Scholarship in 1925 and was called to the bar in 1926. In 1927 he was awarded his PhD. Danquah returned to practice law in Accra while taking an active interest in local politics. He joined the Gold Coast Youth Conference and, in 1931, founded the *Times of West Africa* which shortly became the most popular daily in Accra. A persistent critic of

British rule, he was instrumental in changing the name of the Gold Coast to Ghana after independence. He was elected to the Achimota College Council in 1939 and entered the Gold Coast parliament in 1951. He played a key role in the achievement of Ghanaian independence in 1957, but soon fell foul of President Kwame Nkrumah, whose autocratic rule he denounced. This led to his imprisonment on a few occasions and he eventually died in jail on 4 February 1965 after unnecessarily brutal treatment. Danquah is one of Ghana's most brilliant lawyers and scholars. His important books included *Akan Laws and Customs* (1928), *Cases in Akan Law* (1928), *The Akan Doctrine of God* (1944) and *Revelation of Culture in Ghana* (1961). He was also one of the earliest playwrights from black Africa, publishing two five-act dramas: *Nyankonsem* (Heavenly Tales), written in Akupem-Twi (1946) and *The Third Woman*, as well as another Twi play, *Biribi Wo Baabi* (There is More Beyond). An able poet, historian and dramatist, Dr Danquah wrote extensively on Ghanaian languages, culture and history. In 1967 the Ghana Academy of Arts and Sciences established the Joseph B. Danquah Memorial Lectures to be delivered annually every February.

DANQUAH, Mabel

Born Mabel Dove in the Gold Coast (now Ghana) around 1910, she married Joseph Boakye Danquah after studying in England and travelling extensively in Europe and the United States. Mabel Danquah eventually settled down in the Gold Coast and became editor of the *Accra Evening News*. She contributed several articles to the *West African Times* and wrote numerous essays and short stories under the pseudonym of Marjorie Mensah. Mabel Danquah became the first female member of an African parliament when she was elected in 1952 to the Gold Coast legislature. She was a truly outstanding author, journalist and politician.

DANTICAT, Edwidge

A popular Haitian-American author, Edwidge Danticat was born in Port-au-Prince on 19 January 1969 and emigrated to New York City with her parents in 1981. She graduated from Barnard College in 1990 and received an MFA from Brown University in 1993. Her master's thesis, which analyses the relationships between several generations of Haitian women, was published in 1994 under the title of *Breath, Eyes, Memory*. She also published a highly acclaimed novel, *The Farming of Bones*, in 1998. Danticat's works earned a warm reception from critics everywhere and became even more popular when *Breath, Eyes, Memory* was chosen in June 1998 by the Oprah Winfrey Book Club. Danticat's novels and short stories reveal a deep concern for the lives of women and address with sympathy and understanding such matters as power, injustice and poverty.

DA SILVA, Adhemar Ferreira

Adhemar Ferreira da Silva was the first Brazilian track star to win two gold medals in Olympic competition. Born in São Paulo on 29 September 1927, he became the world's outstanding triple jumper during the 1950s. He broke the world record seven times and won gold medals at the Helsinki Olympic Games in 1952 and the Melbourne Games in 1956. Between 1950 and 1956, he won 60 consecutive triple jumps. After moving the world record to 16.22 m (53 ft 2.75 in) in 1952 he broke his own records for the final time with a leap of 16.56 m (54 ft 4in) at the Pan American Games in Mexico City. After his retirement from athletics, da Silva worked as a film actor and appeared in *Black Orpheus* in 1962. He later served as Brazil's cultural attaché to Nigeria. He was also an accomplished sculptor. He died on 12 January 2001.

DATHORNE, O.R.

Dr Oscar Ronald Dathorne, a fine novelist, essayist and educator, was born in Georgetown, British Guiana, on 19 November 1934. He achieved his BA, MA and PhD from Sheffield University (England) before obtaining his Cert. Dip. Ed. from London University in England. He then taught in a number of universities in Africa and the United States. He also served briefly as UNESCO consultant to the government of Sierra Leone during the late 1960s. A prolific writer and busy editor, he published and edited a number of essays, articles, poems and short stories. Dathorne's earlier works also included such novels as *Dumplings in the Soup* (1963), *The Scholar Man* (1964) and *One Iota of Difference*. Among his later efforts are *Asian Voyages; In Europe's Image; Dele's Child; Dark Ancestor;* and *Imagining the World*. Dr Dathorne also founded the Association of Caribbean Studies which he has directed for years.

DAVID, Craig

Craig Ashley David was born in Southampton, Hampshire, on 5 May 1981 to a Grenadian father and an English mother. He is a British rhythm and blues singer who, although only twenty five (2006), has already sold 20 million albums. His biggest hits have been *Born to Do It* (2000), *Slicker Than Your Average* (2002) and *The Story Goes* (2005). Among his most popular singles are *Fill Me In* (2000), *7 Days* (2000), *Walking Away* (2001), *Rise and Fall* (2003) and *All the Way* (2005).

DAVIS, Allison

This very important educator and psychologist was born in Washington, D.C. in 1902. After graduating from Williams College (BA 1924), Howard University (MA 1925) and the University of Chicago (PhD 1942), he taught for many years at the University of Chicago where he eventually became the John Dewey Distinguished Service Professor of Education. Dr Davis was a member of the Conference to Ensure Civil Rights in 1965 and of the White House Task Force on the Gifted in 1968. He was the first academic in the field of education to become a Fellow in the American Academy of Arts and Sciences. In addition to numerous scholarly articles, Davis wrote or co-authored such books as *Children of Bondage* (1940), *Deep South: A Social Anthropological Study of Caste and Class* (1941), *Psychology of the Child in the Middle Class* (1960) and *Relationship Between Achievement in High School, College and Occupation: A Follow-up Study* (1963). These works were among the first to demonstrate the inadequacies of traditional IQ tests for measuring accurately the educational potential of disadvantaged children. Allison Davis died in 1983.

DAVIS, Benjamin O. Jr

General Benjamin Oliver Davis, Jr, the son of Benjamin O. Davis, Sr, was born on 18 December 1912 in Washington, D.C. Graduating from the US Academy at West Point in 1936, he was the fourth black student ever to do so. He transferred to the Air Corps in 1942, won his wings and became commander of the 99th Fighter Squadron which saw action in North Africa and Italy during World War II when he was awarded the Silver Star and the Distinguished Flying Cross. After the war, he was instrumental in desegregating the Air Force (1948). Davis was appointed commander of the 51st Fighter-Interceptor Wing during the Korean War (1952) and later became director of operations and training of the Far East Forces. In 1954, he was the first African-American ever to be promoted to the rank of Brigadier General in the Air Force. One year later he was promoted to the rank of Lieutenant General. After retiring from the Air Force in 1970, he served for some time as assistant secretary in charge of civil aviation security of the US Department of Transportation. He died on 4 July 2002.

DAVIS, Benjamin O. Sr

Benjamin Oliver Davis, Sr was born in Washington, D.C. on 1 July 1877. He attended Howard University before joining the US Army as a private in 1899 and serving for two years in the Philippines. He was then commissioned a second lieutenant in the cavalry. He served in various posts throughout the United States before his appointment as military attaché to the embassy at Monrovia, Liberia. During World War I, Davis rose to the rank of major and became a colonel in 1930. Ten years later he was promoted to the rank of brigadier general, the first African-American to rise to such heights in the US Army. After his retirement in 1941, he was frequently recalled to perform special tasks and served as special adviser to the commander of the European Theatre during World War II. He finally retired for good in 1948 after more than fifty years service. Among his many honours and decorations were the Bronze Star, the Distinguished Service Medal, and the French *Croix de Guerre*. By the time of his death on 26 November 1970, he had lived to see his son, Benjamin Oliver Davis, Jr., achieve similar distinctions in the US Air Force.

DAWSON, William

Born in Albany, Georgia, on 26 April 1886, William L. Dawson graduated from Fisk University in 1909 before earning a law degree from Northwestern University. He saw military service in Europe during World War I and began his political career in Chicago during the 1920s. He was elected to the US Congress as a representative and became the first Black to head a standing committee in the Congress. Dawson served as chairman of the House Committee on Government Operations and remained in Congress for fourteen years. He died on 9 November 1970.

DEAN, Mark

Dr Mark Dean is truly one of the outstanding scientists and inventors of the modern world. He has done most to transform the original computer, intended for use in factories and offices, into a smaller gadget that can be used comfortably in every household. The PC, now so commonplace, was his brainchild. Born on 2 March 1957 in Jefferson City, Tennessee, he achieved his BS in electrical engineering from the University of Tennessee in 1979, his MS from Florida Atlantic University in 1982 and his PhD from Stanford University in 1992. He has worked with IBM since 1980 and was named an IBM Fellow in 1995, the first African-American to be so honoured. He is currently Vice President of Performance for the RS/6000 Division in Austin, Texas. Dr Dean holds more than twenty US patents, including three of IBM's original nine PC patents. In 1997 he was inducted into the National Inventors' Hall of Fame, joining two other famous Blacks, George Washington Carver and Dr Percy Julian. In 1999, he led the team that built the first gigahertz (1000 MHz) chip capable of a billion calculations per second. He was mainly instrumental in starting the Digital Revolution that created Bill Gates and Michael Dell and creating literally millions of jobs in information technology.

DECARAVA, Roy

Roy DeCarava is an artist and photographer who has depicted life in Harlem, New York, with an uncanny realism that illustrates the condition of poor urban Blacks more graphically than prose or poetry could ever have done. In 1996 he exhibited over 200 photographs at New York City's Museum of Modern Art that addressed the realities of Harlem life from

1949 to 1994. This successful exhibition, entitled *Roy DeCarava: A Retrospective*, also included a number of remarkable jazz photographs. The exhibition travelled to major museums throughout the United States that year. Born in Harlem on 9 December 1919, DeCarava studied painting and printmaking at the Cooper Union School of Art, the Harlem Community Art Center and the George Washington Carver Art School, where he created images of black life. He switched to photography in the late 1940s and became (in 1952) the first African-American photographer to be awarded a Guggenheim fellowship. In 1955, in collaboration with Langston Hughes who provided the text, he published *The Sweet Flypaper of Life*, a collection of 140 pictures on daily life in Harlem. In that same year, DeCarava opened A Photographer's Gallery in New York City, aimed at stressing the links between art and photography and demonstrating that photography itself is an art. In 1963 he helped to found the Kamoinge Workshop, an association of African-American photographers based in Harlem and taught there for a few years. During 1969 to 1972, he was an adjunct instructor at the Cooper Union School of Art before teaching photography for several years at Hunter College. Himself a dedicated saxophonist, DeCarava has taken hundreds of jazz photographs, featuring such musical legends as Louis Armstrong, John Coltrane, Billie Holliday and Milt Jackson.

DELANY, 'Sadie'
Sarah Louise Delany was the first African-American teacher of home economics in white New York schools. With her sister Bessie, she co-authored in 1993 the autobiographical *Having Our Say: The Delany Sisters' First 100 Years*. This remarkable story was adapted into a Broadway play in 1995. The two sisters published another book, *The Delany Sisters' Book of Everyday Wisdom*, in 1994. Sadie Delany was born on 19 September 1889 in Lynch's Station, Virginia. She died in Mount Vernon, New York, on 25 January 1999 at the great age of 109.

DELGADO, Martín Morúa
Martín Morúa Delgado, whose mother was an African slave, was born in Cuba in 1856. Elected to his country's Congress in 1901, he rose to become the president of its Senate in 1909. He was held in such high esteem by his countrymen that its government gave him official recognition .by commemorating the centenary of his birth. In 1956, when statues were being sculpted in his memory, his complete works were reprinted in five volumes. Delgado was not only an important administrator but an accomplished novelist and journalist. His major works were *Sofía* (1891) and *La familia Unzúazu* (1901) which dealt with the inhumanity of slavery and its

toll on the society. He also founded and edited four newspapers: *La Revista Popular*, *La Nueva Era*, *El Pueblo* and *La Républica*. A staunch supporter of Cuban independence, he died on 28 April 1910. Ironically, the law which Delgado introduced banning political parties based on race and class led to the infamous purge of Blacks almost as soon as he was dead.

DE OLIVEIRA, João Carlos

Born on 28 May 1954, João Carlos de Oliveira was one of the greatest athletes thus far produced by Brazil. When he established a new world record with a triple jump of 17.89 m (58 ft 8.25 in) at the Pan American Games in Mexico City in 1975, he eclipsed the previous mark by an incredible 45 cm (17.7 in). His new standard remained untouched for ten years. He won gold medals in three consecutive world championships (1977, 1979 and 1981) but had to settle for bronze medals in the 1976 and 1980 Olympic Games. Sadly, de Oliveira's athletic career ended abruptly in 1981 when a serious automobile accident resulted in the amputation of his right leg. He died in São Paulo, Brazil, on 29 May 1999.

DEPESTRE, René

One of Haiti's finest poets, René Depestre was born in Jacmel on 29 August 1926. After attending the Frère Clément School of Jacmel and the Lycée Pinchinat at Port-au-Prince, he furthered his education in Paris where he also joined the French Communist Party. His revolutionary volume of verse, *Étincelles*, first published when Depestre was only nineteen years old, established him at once as a spokesman for the radical young generation. Even before his departure for Paris, he had taken an active part in the overthrow of President Élie Lescot in 1946. But his conversion to Communism won him few friends in Haiti and his works remained banned in that country for many years. He settled down in Cuba in 1958 and spent very little time in Haiti after 1946. His writing addresses Haiti's social, political and economic problems and the plight of oppressed Blacks all over the world. His poetry has appeared in many French and Spanish anthologies and collections. He is regarded by many as the main spokesman for the radical poets of the modern Pan-African world. Some of his finest verses can be found in *Gerbe de sang* (1946), *Végétation de clartes* (1951), *Traduit du grand large, poème de ma patrie enchaînée* (1952), *Minerai noir* (1957), *Journal d'un animal marin* (1964) and *Un arc-en-ciel pour l'occident chrétien poème mystère vaudou* (1966). He published his *Anthologie personelle* in 1993 and *Actes sud* which received the Prix Apollinaire. His novel, *Hadriana dans tous mes reves* won the *Prix Renandot* in 1988. He also wrote a Spanish novel, *El Paso Ensebado* (1975) and several articles, essays and short stories in both French and Spanish.

de SILVA, Jennifer Hodge

Jennifer Hodge de Silva was among the black pioneers in the Canadian film and television industry. Her work established the dominant mode in African-Canadian film culture while ranging as far as World War II, prison reform and Native peoples in Canada. Born in Montreal in 1951, she began her studies in that city but continued them in European academic institutions which left her with the ability to speak fluently in English, French, Italian and German and to take a more cosmopolitan approach on most matters. She later achieved degrees from Ryerson and York Universities in Toronto. Working first with the National Film Board in Montreal, she helped to direct and produce such films as *A Great Tree Has Fallen* (1973) and *Potatoes* (1979). She then joined the Canadian Broadcasting Corporation (CBC) as a producer in 1982. With her husband, Paul de Silva, she also founded Jenfilms Inc., the company that created such award-winning films as *Inside Stories* (1989) and *Neighbourhoods*. While working with the National Film Board, de Silva helped to direct and produce the memorable *Fields of Endless Day* (1978) generally considered one of the first substantive films about Black History in Canada. She also helped to create *Dieppe 1942* (1979); and *Home Feeling: Struggle for a Community* (1983) which deftly explored relations between the police and the black immigrant youth in Toronto's Jane-Finch neighbourhood. Still only thirty-eight, Jennifer Hodge de Silva died on 5 May 1989. She had been the recipient of numerous awards and honours.

de SOUZA, Isidore

Revd Isidore de Souza, an influential Benin religious leader, was born in Ouidah, Dahomey (French West Africa), on 4 April 1934. He entered the Roman Catholic ministry and rose to the rank of archbishop of Cotonou in 1991. He played a major role in Benin's transition to a multiparty democracy. He died on 13 March 1999.

DES'REE

Born Desiree Weekes to Barbadian parents in London, England, on 30 November 1968, Des'ree became one of Britain's most successful vocalists throughout the 1990s. Her pop/soul records sold millions of copies in Europe and the United States. Her most popular hit singles include *Feel So High* (1992), *You Gotta Be* (1994) and *Life* (1998). One of her albums, *I Ain't Movin* sold almost 2 million worldwide. Des'ree has also provided soundtrack material for the films *Clockers*, *Set It Off* and *Romeo and Juliet*. In 1999, she won a Brit Award for the British Solo Artist category.

DESSALINES, Jean-Jacques

This famous Haitian nationalist, who proclaimed his country's independence from France in 1804, was born in west Africa around 1758 and brought as a slave to the French West Indian colony of Saint Domingue. He joined the slave rebellion in 1791 and distinguished himself as one of the ablest lieutenants in Toussaint Louverture's army. After Toussaint's initial revolt had been suppressed, Dessalines renewed the attack on France in 1803 when Napoleon announced his intention to reintroduce slavery in the island. With British help, he drove the French from Saint Domingue and, on 1 January 1804, proclaimed himself governor-general of an independent country which he renamed Haiti, its original Arawak name. Dessalines was crowned Emperor Jacques I of Haiti in 1805. He renewed many of Toussaint's policies but was much more hostile to the white settlers whom he deliberately attempted to exterminate. He confiscated their estates and made it illegal for them to own property. Such drastic measures effectively prevented any renewal of white dominance over Haitian Blacks. When, however, Dessalines attempted to deal in like manner with the élitist mulattoes, he was killed trying to put down a revolt under the famous mulatto leader, Alexandre Sabès Pétion, on 17 October 1806. After his death, Pétion and the new black leader, Henri Christophe, agreed to divide Haiti between them, and a separate Santo Domingo came into existence as a result.

DETT, Nathaniel

Robert Nathaniel Dett was born in Niagara Falls, Ontario, on 11 October 1882. He was one of the pioneers of Negro spirituals and left a significant impression as choir leader, composer, pianist and music teacher. After attending Halsted Conservatory of Music, Oberlin College, Columbia University and the University of Pennsylvania, he wrote more than 100 musical pieces, using tunes from spirituals and black folk songs. Some of his original compositions included *Oh Holy Lord* and *Listen to the Lambs* that are still popular today. Dett taught music for twenty-one years (1913-34) at the Hampton Institute, Virginia, where he started the Musical Arts Society (a famous choir group), and for five years (1937-42) at Bennett College in Greensboro, North Carolina. He also wrote a seminal essay, *The Emancipation of Negro Music*, which won the prestigious Bowdoin Prize in 1921. He died on 2 October 1943 after having received honorary Doctor of Music degrees from Howard University and Oberlin College. His great opera, *The Ordering of Moses*, was performed by the National Negro Company at Carnegie Hall in 1951, posthumously adding to his lustre. His legacy included such other works as *The Chariot Jubilee* (1921), *Enchantment Suite* (1922), *Cinnamon Grove Suite* (1927) and *Topic Winter Suite* (1938).

DHLOMO, Herbert

The son of a Zulu preacher and the younger brother of Rolfus Dhlomo, Herbert Isaac Ernest Dhlomo was born in 1903 in Natal Province, South Africa. He was educated at local schools before earning his Teacher's Certificate from Adams College. He then taught for many years in Natal and later served as a librarian and assistant editor of *Ilanga lase Natal* in Durban. Dhlomo became a prolific playwright, producing such popular dramas as *The Girl who Killed to Save* (1935); *Shaka*; *The Living Dead*; *Cetywayo*; *Men and Women*; *Dingana*; *Moshoeshoe*; *Workers Boss Bosses*; *Ntsikana* and *Mofologi*. In addition, he wrote numerous beautiful poems, many of which first appeared in his *Ilanga lase Natal*. His best-known collection perhaps was *The Valley of a Thousand Hills*, published in 1941. Herbert Dhlomo, who died on 20 October 1956, was a truly outstanding and versatile Zulu author.

DHLOMO, Rolfus

The elder brother of Herbert Dhlomo, Rolfus Reginald Raymond Dhlomo was born around 1901 at Siyamu, Natal Province, South Africa. Like his sibling, he became a prolific writer, but while Herbert published mainly in English, Rolfus specialized in Zulu historical novels. Following his graduation from local schools, he served for some years as a clerk before becoming assistant editor of *The Sjambok*. He then became assistant editor of *Ilanga lase Natal*, a Zulu newspaper, which he eventually edited from 1943 to 1960. During 1933-42 Rolfus Dhlomo was also the assistant editor of *The Bantu World*. He wrote literally hundreds of articles for these papers in both English and Zulu. His great novel, *An African Tragedy*, published in 1928, was one of the earliest books produced in English by an African author. His major works included *Izikhali Zanamuhla* (1935), *U-Dingane ka Senzangakhona* (1935), *U-Shaka* (1936), *Ukwazi kiyathuthukisa* (1936), *U-Mpande ka Senzangakhona* (1936), *U-Nomalanga ka Ndengezi* (1946), *U-Cetshwayo* (1952), and *U-Dinuzulo ka Cetshwayo* (1968).

DIKE, Kenneth Onwuka

Dr Kenneth Onwuka Dike is one of the greatest among African historians and academics. Born on 17 December 1917, in Akwa, eastern Nigeria, he was educated in Nigeria, England and Scotland. His doctoral thesis, *Trade and Politics in the Niger Delta, 1830-85*, became a classic. He taught for some years in Ibadan and then at the West African Institute of Social and Economic Research. He became the first director of the Nigerian National Archives before being appointed a professor at the University College of Ibadan in 1956. Two years later he was named principal of that institution and became its vice-chancellor in 1963 when it was granted full university status. Dike was largely instrumental in the establishment of the

International Congress of Africanists in 1963, and in 1965 was elected chairman of the Association of Commonwealth Universities. He gave support to the Biafran cause during the civil war of the late 1960s and began to lay the foundations of a Biafran university at Fort Harcourt, but had to abandon this project when the secessionists lost the war. Dike then emigrated to the United States and served as the Andrew W. Mellon professor of African history at Harvard University. In his last years he returned to Nigeria as president of the Anambra State University. He died on 26 October 1983, having played the leading role in creating a generation of African historians who could interpret their own history without being influenced by Eurocentric approaches.

DINGISWAYO

Dingiswayo was a great Zulu warrior-king who carved out a sizeable empire in southeastern Africa for himself, his dynasty and his people during the first two decades of the nineteenth century (1807-17). He proved himself a brilliant general in warfare and an effective administrator in peacetime. His policy of absorbing the neighbouring Nguni peoples into a centralized state made him the suzerain over most of what is now northeastern Natal. When seemingly at his physical peak, however, he was assassinated by Zwide, chief of the Ndwandwe clan, who rebelled against his rule in Zululand. To this day, in many parts of Africa, Dingiswayo remains a legend. It was on the foundations laid by him that such famous Zulu emperors as Skaka and Cetshwayo built so spectacularly later on.

DINIZULU

Dinizulu was the last of the Zulu warrior-kings who dominated southeastern Africa for almost a century. He found it impossible to thwart the inexorable advance of the Europeans and, by the time of his death, on 18 October 1913, Zulu power had been completely eroded.

DIOP, Alioune

One of the most important figures in modern African literature, Alioune Diop was born in Saint-Louis, Senegal, in 1910. It was he who founded the journal *Présence Africaine* in 1947 and made it a leading voice of black African opinion during the period of independence. He opened his journal to the full range of African cultures and provided the young Francophone intellectuals with a very valuable forum. A French educated Catholic, Diop served as the Senegalese representative in the French Senate during 1946-48. In 1956 he organized in Paris the first World Congress of Black Writers and Artists, which was attended by such renowned authors as Aimé Césaire from Martinique, Léopold Senghor from Senegal, and Richard Wright from the United States. Diop later served as secretary-general of the Festival of Black Arts. He died on 2 May 1980.

DIOP, Birago Ismael

Born in Dakar, French West Africa, on 11 December 1906, Birago Ismael Diop was a veterinarian and diplomat who helped to shape contemporary literature by writing in French the African folktales and legends that he claimed he had heard from a griot, or story-teller. Diop was also known for his poems, the best of which appeared in the collection, *Leurres et lucurs* (1960). A brilliant student, Diop won a scholarship to the Lycée Faidherbe in Saint-Louis, the capital of French West Africa, when he was fifteen years old. He excelled in science but then took a second degree in philosophy (1928). After serving a year in the military, he attended the University of Toulouse, France, from which he graduated in 1933 as a doctor of veterinary medicine. He returned to Africa and served as a government veterinarian from 1934 to 1942. He also worked in the Ivory Coast, Mauritania and Upper Volta during the 1940s and 1950s. At the request of president Léopold Senghor, Diop entered Senegal's diplomatic service and was ambassador to Tunisia between 1961 and 1965. He, along with Senghor and Aimé Césaire of Martinique, did much to celebrate the traditional values of African life and to lead the movement generally known as 'négritude' ('Black is Beautiful') after World War II. His finest works perhaps were *Les Contes d'Amadou Koumba* (1947), *Les Nouveaux Contes d'Amadou Koumba* (1959, and *Contes et lavanes* (1963), which earned him the 1964 Grand Prix Littéraire d'Afrique Noire. Diop's autobiography, *La Plume raboutée*, was published in 1978. He died on 25 November 1989. His life and work reflected throughout the natural mingling of Islamic and local Wolof traditions.

DIOP, David

David Diop was one of the angriest and most talented of the French West African poets of the 1950s. His poems leave the impression that nothing good could ever have come from the European colonization of Africa. He not only denounced slavery but the suppression of African values and traditions. Diop called unequivocally for revolution to lead to a glorious African future. Though he himself grew up in France, where he was born in July 1927, his strong opposition to European society was reinforced by visits to Cameroon, Guinea and Senegal. He was also much influenced by the Martiniquan poet, Aimé Césaire. Diop's verses appeared mainly in *Présence Africaine* and in Léopold Senghor's *Anthologie de la nouvelle poésie nègre et malgache*. His only surviving collection, *Coups de pilon*, was published in 1956, before his life was tragically cut short by an airplane crash in 1960.

DIORI, Hamani

Hamani Diori, the first president of the independent Republic of Niger (1960-74), was born in Soudouré, Niger, on 6 June 1916. Educated in Dahomey (now Benin) and Senegal, he taught at schools in Niger and at the Institute of Overseas Studies in Paris during 1936-56. He was one of the founders of the Rassemblement Démocratique Africaine (1946) and founder of its local branch, the Niger Progressive Party (PPN). For many years he represented Niger in the French National Assembly and was chosen by the imperial government to serve as prime minister during the transition period leading up to Niger's independence (1958-60). In November 1960, after the first post-independence general elections, Diori was proclaimed president of the new republic. His reign, however, proved an unhappy one. He was neither able to stamp out corruption nor to cope effectively with the disastrous effects of the Sahelian drought of the early 1970s. He was deposed by a military coup in 1974 and imprisoned until 1980. Thereafter he remained under house arrest until 1987. He died on 23 April 1989.

DIOUF, Abdou

Abdou Diouf became president of Senegal on 1 January 1981 with the retirement of Léopold Sédar Senghor who had led Senegal to independence in the early 1960s. Diouf was born in Louga, northern Senegal, on 7 September 1935. Although a Muslim, he was educated in Saint Louis at the École Brière de l'Isle and the Lycée Faidherbe before completing his degree in public law in Paris. Entering the public service in 1960, he was soon appointed governor of the Region of Sine-Saloum and became director of the departmental staff of the Ministry of Foreign Affairs in 1962. A sequence of rapid promotions took Diouf all the way to the premiership of Senegal on 28 February 1970 when that post was first created by a revision of the constitution. For eleven years, Diouf served in the long shadow cast by Senghor, but he put this experience to good use by leaving his own stamp on Senegalese history when his turn came. Not only did he relax Senghor's laws against the establishment of new parties, but (almost at once) signed an important agreement with The Gambia, leading to the confederation of the two nations. He thus became the first president of Senegambia on 14 November 1981. He was re-elected president in 1983, 1988, and 1993. He played a key role in the affairs of the Organization of African Unity (OAU), serving twice as its chairman (1985-86 and 1992-93) and was also the chairman of the Economic Community of West African States (ECOWAS). Diouf was finally defeated in the general elections of 2000.

DISENGOMOKA, Émile Adolphe

Émile Adolphe Disengomoka was the first Congolese to achieve the degree of Régent Litéraire (the equivalent of an MA). The son of a Protestant priest, he was born on 31 March 1915 in Kingemba, a district in modern Zaire. After attending the Ngombe Lutête and the École de Moniteurs of Mazdia, he furthered his studies at the Evangelical Pedagogical Institute at Kimpese. He served for a while as a teacher and became headmaster of the Thysville Primary School. In 1949 he went to Belgium to pursue further studies and returned to the Congo in 1955 to assume the headship of the Institut Polytechnique Congolais. Apart from his teaching, Disengomoka was a member of the territorial council of Thysville, of the provincial Council of Léopoldville and the council of the Gouvernement Général. He is also remembered as perhaps the first Zairean novelist. He published *Ku Ntwala* (The Future) in 1942, *Kwenkwenda* (Where Shall I Go?) in 1943, and *Luvuvamu mu nzo* (Peace in the House) in 1948. Disengomoka also wrote several articles for *La Voix du Congolais* and a number of his poems appeared in *Minkunga mia kintwadi* in 1956. In addition, some fifteen of his important hymns were published. Disengomoka died on 15 March 1965.

DIXON, Dean

Dean Dixon was the first black man to achieve fame as a symphonic conductor. Born in New York in 1915, he studied at the Juilliard School of Music and received his BMus in 1936 before proceeding to Columbia University where he achieved his MA in 1939. He became the first African-American to conduct the NBC Symphony Orchestra and the New York Philharmonic. But, to make a successful career in this business, Dixon found it necessary to emigrate to Europe, where he served as the conductor of the Goteborg Symphony in Sweden from 1949 to 1960. He was later appointed conductor of the Hessian Radio Symphony in Frankfurt, Germany. Between 1960 and his death in 1976, Dixon frequently conducted at the Frankfurt Opera and with most of the major orchestras throughout Europe.

DIXON, George

Born on 29 July 1870 in Halifax, Nova Scotia, George Dixon was the very first black boxer to win a world championship. He claimed the vacant bantamweight (118 lbs) title in 1888 and defended it twice before dominating the featherweight (126 lbs) division throughout the 1890s. Dixon emigrated to the United States in 1887 to further his boxing career, which ultimately encompassed 158 recorded bouts, of which he won 86, and lost 25. The remaining 47 ended in questionable draws and no-decisions in an age when black boxers did not generally receive fair judgements from white officials. A very popular fighter in the United States, Dixon was generally known as 'Little Chocolate'. It is estimated that, in twenty years of professional boxing (1885-1905), he must have fought about 600 additional bouts of which no official record has been kept. Dixon died on 6 January 1909 and was inducted into Boxing Hall of Fame in 1956. He is unarguably the greatest boxer thus far produced by Canada.

DOMITIEN, Elisabeth

Elisabeth Domitien was the first woman to serve as prime minister of an African nation. She did so in 1975-76 during Emperor Jean-Bédel Bokassa's brief but stormy reign over the Central African Empire. Born in 1925, she began her political career in the Movement for the Social Evolution of Black Africa (MÉSAN), the country's only legal party at that time, and became its vice president in 1972. When Bokassa dissolved the republic and installed himself as emperor, he chose Domitien as his prime minister. But she disagreed with some of his dictatorial plans and was promptly fired together with all the members of her cabinet. When Bokassa's government was overthrown in 1979, Domitien was arrested and charged with covering up extortion committed by Bokassa during her tenure as prime minister. She served only a brief prison term but was prohibited from returning to politics. She remained a prominent figure, both as a former political leader and as a successful business woman. She died on 26 April 2005.

DOS SANTOS, Éduardo

José Éduardo dos Santos is the current President, Head of Government and Commander-in-Chief of the Armed Forces of Angola (2006). He succeeded Agostinho Neto on 10 September 1979. Born in Luanda on 28 August 1942, he joined Neto's party, the MPLA, in 1956 while he was still at school. He went into exile in 1961, seeking refuge in France, the Republic of the Congo and then the USSR (where he completed a degree in engineering). While abroad, he remained in close contact with Neto and became the party's vice president. An independent Angola then became embroiled in a lengthy and paralysing civil war between opposing nationalist forces that dwarfed everything else between 1975 and 2002. Dos Santos thus failed to solve internecine discord, to combat governmental corruption, reconstruct public infrastructure, draft a new constitution or to reduce control over the press. Only minimal progress has been made in these areas since the civil strife ended. He has promised to step down before the next elections, scheduled for late in 2006, but it is not certain that he will keep this promise.

DOUGLAS, Aaron
Born in Topeka, Kansas, in 1899, Aaron Douglas received his BA from the University of Kansas and his MFA degree from Columbia University. During 1928-1929, he studied in Paris on a Barnes Foundation grant. Douglas became a famous artist, eventually illustrating books by Countee Cullen, Langston Hughes and James Weldon Johnson. His work also appeared in such contemporary magazines as *American Mercury*, *Theatre Arts*, and *Vanity Fair*. He was among the first to apply the qualities of African sculpture to painting. He died in 1979.

DOUGLAS, Denzil
The Honourable Dr Denzil Douglas was sworn in as the second prime minister of St Kitts and Nevis on 7 July 1995 and was re-elected by a resounding majority in 2000. His party triumphed again on 24 October 2004. Born on 14 January 1953 in the village of St Paul's in the northern portion of St Kitts, he was educated at local schools before graduating from the University of the West Indies in 1984 with a medical degree. Following his internship in Trinidad in 1986, he returned to St Kitts as a practising physician and served as the president of the St Kitts-Nevis Medical Association. He also entered politics and became deputy chairman of the Labour Party which he soon restructured and re-energized. As prime minister, Dr Douglas plays an active leadership role in numerous regional and international organizations including the Association of Caribbean States (ACS), the Caribbean Community (CARICOM), the Caribbean Development Bank (CDB), the Eastern Caribbean Central Bank (ECCB), the International Monetary Fund (IMF), the Organization of American States (OAS), the Organization of Eastern Caribbean States (OECS), the World Bank and the Commonwealth of Nations.

DOUGLAS, Desmond
Born in Jamaica in 1956, Desmond Douglas emigrated to the United Kingdom with his parents when he was very young and was raised in Birmingham. He became the finest table tennis player ever produced by Great Britain, winning the national title no fewer than 14 times and rising to No. 3 in Europe and No. 7 in the world while at his peak. At the age of forty-five in 2001 he was still good enough to be ranked eighth in England. Douglas was awarded an MBE for his contribution to the growth of table tennis in the United Kingdom.

DOUGLAS, Rosie
Roosevelt Douglas was one of the most fascinating personalities in the history of Dominica. He appealed to the cause of the socialist radical

reformers and preached a brand of populism that attracted the younger voters. As the leader of the Dominica Labour Party, however, he had spent most of his political career in opposition as the United Workers Party became increasingly entrenched. Finally he was able to form a coalition with the moderate Dominica Freedom Party and win the elections of 31 January 2000. He pledged to tackle his country's social and economic problems with vigour and made state visits to Australia, Canada, Jamaica and Taiwan searching for means to improve Dominica's tourism industry and for any trading agreements from which the island might profit. Before any of his plans could bear tangible fruit, Rosie Douglas died suddenly on 1 October 2000. Born on 15 October 1941, he had earlier garnered considerable notoriety for his role in the Sir George Williams Computer Riot of 1969 while he was a student in Canada.

DOUGLASS, Frederick

Born a slave in Tuckahoe, Maryland, on 14 February 1817, Frederick Douglass became one of the most highly respected Americans during the nineteenth century and the epic story of his life still serves as a source of inspiration to countless African-Americans. After twenty years of slavery, he finally escaped and became an abolitionist lecturer during the 1840s. In 1847, at Rochester, New York, he became editor of an anti-slavery weekly, *The North Star*, which he kept alive for sixteen years. In 1848, he took a prominent part in the Seneca Falls Convention in New York which formally inaugurated the Women's rights movement in the United States. During the Civil War he recruited troops for the Union Army and worked tirelessly for a positive policy of Reconstruction when that struggle was over. The first African-American to be nominated as a vice-presidential candidate (1872), he was appointed marshal of the District of Columbia in 1877, and later served as the United States minister to Haiti. He did his best to improve the lot of Blacks and women in America and is now revered as one of the greatest Americans of his time. In 1956, more than sixty years after his death on 20 February 1895, a striking eight-foot bronze sculpture of Frederick Douglass was erected on the campus of Morgan State College in Baltimore, Maryland, to commemorate the words and deeds of this remarkable ex-slave. Part of his legacy was a classic autobiography, *The Life and Times of Frederick Douglass*, which remains essential reading for all students of Black History.

DOWNES, Marguerite

Major Marguerite A. 'Peggy' Downes was born in Dartmouth, Nova Scotia. She joined the Royal Canadian Army Service Corps Militia in Halifax in 1955 before transferring to the Toronto Reserves and rising all the way to the rank of major. She thus became the highest ranking black female officer in the Canadian Armed Forces Army Reserves in Ontario. After her retirement from the Reserves, Major Downes served as Commissionaire with the Superior Court of Justice and as aide-de-camp for many years to three Lieutenant Governors of Ontario. She was also the director and accompanist for the famous Toronto First Baptist Church Choir which has often been featured in film and on television.

DREW, Charles Richard

Dr Charles Richard Drew, one of the most famous of all black physicians, was born in Washington, D.C. on 3 June 1904. He attended Amherst College in Massachusetts where he was a star athlete in many disciplines. He received his MD from McGill University in 1933 and interned at the Montreal General Hospital in Quebec, Canada, where he pioneered in blood research. After five years of experimental work on the preservation of blood and its use for transfusions, he published his seminal *Banked Blood: A Study in Blood Preservation* (1940). He then launched his famous 'Blood for Britain' campaign which consisted of collecting and drying blood plasma to be used for transfusions on the battlefield. In recognition of these achievements, Dr Drew was awarded an honorary DSc from Columbia University. He served as the director of the American Red Cross Blood Bank in 1941, as assistant director of blood procurement for the National Research Council, and as chief surgeon of Freedman's Hospital in Washington, D.C. He was killed in an auto accident in North Carolina on 1 April 1950 while travelling to a medical conference at Tuskegee Institute. Dr Charles Richard Drew was among the first to insist that there was no scientific evidence indicating blood differences according to race. His contribution to the science of storing blood is incalculable. In addition to his classic text, his legacy included numerous scholarly papers and articles on the subject.

DUBÉ, John Langalibalele

Revd John Langalibalele Dubé, who became a great Zulu educator, statesman and novelist, was born near the Inanda Mission in South Africa on 22 February 1871. After attending the Inanda Mission school he furthered his education in the United States, achieving his BA from Oberlin College in 1893, and was ordained a priest in 1897. While in North America, he was much influenced by such black educators as W.E.B. Du Bois and Booker T. Washington. He determined to establish in South Africa a school of industrial arts similar to the Tuskegee Institute in Alabama. His herculean efforts finally resulted in the erection of the new Zulu Christian Industrial School in Natal in 1901. It evolved into the famous Ohlange Institute and was one of the first institutions of its type in South Africa to admit black female students. Dubé also helped in 1903 to found the *Ilanga lase Natal* (The Natal Sun) which was the first Zulu newspaper. It often came under fire from the authorities because of its outspoken advocacy of African rights but it survived for decades. He himself irritated the colonial administration by publishing his very critical book, *The Zulu's Appeal for Light and England's Duty*, in 1909. On 8 January 1912, Dubé was elected the first president general of the newly formed South African Native National Congress (ANC). He led this organization during it first five years. In 1914 he led a delegation to London to protest the Land Act of 1913 which placed the natives under very severe handicaps. The British press was sympathetic but the political leaders seemed totally indifferent. Dubé did not give up. He continued his attacks upon the racist system with his outspoken *Clash of Colour*, published in 1926. He was also one of the most active members of the Native Representative Council as Natal's representative after 1942. Apart from his political activism, Dubé was very anxious to preserve Zulu traditions and to promote native culture and values. He thus collected thousands of Zulu folk songs and folk tales and wrote often in the Zulu language. His major Zulu works included a novel, *Ujeqe insila ka Tshaka* (1933) and two biographies, *U-Shembe* (1935) and *Ukuziphaina kahle* (1935). Highly respected by both Africans and Europeans, Dubé received several awards and honours, including an honorary doctorate from the University of South Africa in 1936. He died on 11 February 1946.

DU BOIS, W.E.B.

This celebrated American author, editor and educator was born in Great Barrington, Massachusetts, on 23 February 1868. The son of a Haitian-born barber, Professor William Edward Burghardt Dubois was of Dutch, French and black ancestry but identified himself always with his African heritage. He achieved his BA from Fisk University in 1888 and his MA and PhD degrees from Harvard University (1891-95). The first Black to receive a doctorate from Harvard, he later studied at the University of Berlin and was awarded honorary degrees from Atlanta University, Howard University, Fisk University and Wilberforce University. Du Bois was a classics professor at Wilberforce University (1894-96) before teaching sociology at the University of Pennsylvania and then at Atlanta University, where he served as head of the Department of Sociology during 1933-44. One of the founders of the National Association for the Advancement of Colored People (NAACP) in 1909, Du Bois was for many years (1909-32) the editor of its publications, including *The Crisis*. He also edited the *Atlanta University Studies* (1897-1911), and the *Phylon quarterly review* (1940-44). In addition, he was editor-in-chief of the *Encyclopaedia of the Negro* (1933-45). From 1949 to 1954, he served as vice-chairman of the UN Council on African Affairs and was chairman of the Peace Information Bureau in New York City during 1950-51. A prolific writer, Du Bois produced numerous articles and books over an active academic career that spanned more than fifty years. His major works included *The Suppression of the African Slave Trade* (1896), *The Philadelphia Negro* (1899), *The Souls of Black Folk* (1903), *John Brown* (1909), *Quest of the Silver Fleece* (1911), *The Negro* (1915), *The Gift of Black Folk* (1924), *Darkwater Princess* (1928), *Then and Now* (1939), *Dusk of Dawn* (1940), *Color and Democracy* (1945), *The World and Africa* (1947) and *In Battle for Peace* (1952). Whether as editor, author, college professor or public lecturer, Du Bois consistently advocated the elimination of racial inequalities. He became a convert to socialism towards the end of his life, joined the communist party at the age of ninety-three, and spent his last days in voluntary exile in Ghana where he became a respected citizen and was awarded an honorary doctorate of literature by the University of Ghana. Dr William Du Bois died at ninety-five on 27 August 1963 and is revered as one of America's leading black scholars and political activists.

DUNBAR, Paul

Paul Laurence Dunbar is one of the best known of all African-American poets. He was born in Dayton, Ohio, on 27 June 1872. The son of former slaves, he started writing poems at the age of six and gave his first public recital at the age of thirteen. Dunbar attended Dayton's only high school and was its only black student in his graduating class. Lacking the money to further his education, he supported himself and his widowed mother by doing odd jobs. His first volume of poems, *Oak and Ivy*, appeared in 1893. Two years later he published *Majors and Minors*. He finally won national recognition with the publication of *Lyrics of a Lonely Life* in 1896. Paul Dunbar died at the age of thirty-four on 9 February 1906. Posthumously his collection of *Complete Poems* was published in 1913. It is sometimes forgotten that he also wrote excellent prose, including numerous short stories and several novels.

DUNBAR, Rudolph

This remarkable composer, conductor and clarinetist was born in British Guiana in 1917. He received his musical education at the Institute of Musical Art in New York City. He later studied in Paris and Leipzig. Thereafter he conducted several orchestras in Great Britain and the United States, including the NBC Symphony Orchestra and the London Philharmonic Orchestra. His compositions included the well-known *Dance of the 20th Century*. He was also the author of *A Treatise on Clarinet Playing*. Rudolph Dunbar is generally regarded as one of the finest musicians produced by the British West Indies.

DUNHAM, Katherine

Born in Chicago, Illinois, on 22 June 1909, Dr Katherine Mary Dunham became a renowned dancer, educator and choreographer. She studied anthropology at the University of Chicago and spent a year doing field work in the Caribbean on a Rosenwald Fellowship. This training provided her with the opportunity to observe West Indian dance forms and she was consequently able to display African and West Indian rhythms and movements before American audiences. Dunham danced and acted in such films as *Carnival of Rhythm* (1941); *Pardon My Sarong* (1942); *Stormy Weather* (1943); *Cuban Episode* (1944); the musical *Windy City* (1946), which she also choreographed; *Casbah* (1948); *Mambo* (1954); and *Música en la noche* (1958). During the 1940s, she founded the Katherine Dunham School of Cultural Arts as well as the Katherine Dunham Dance Company, which has performed in numerous countries. Many of her students have become prominent in the field of modern dance. In the 1970s, Dunham directed the Performing Arts Training Center and Dynamic Museum at Southern Illinois University and served as technical adviser for the John F. Kennedy Center for the Performing Arts in Washington, D.C. She also directed *Treemonisha*, a ragtime opera by Scott Joplin, at the Wolf Trap Farm for the Performing Arts in Virginia. For many years, Dunham conducted special projects for Chicago high school students. She also served briefly as artistic and technical director to the president of Senegal and was once an artist-in-residence at Southern Illinois University. She published four useful books: *Katherine Dunham's Journey to Accompong*,(1946) an account of her anthropological studies in Jamaica, on which her PhD from the University of Chicago was based; *Dances of Haiti* (1947); An autobiography, *A Touch of Innocence* (1959) and *Island Possessed* (1969). A biography by Terry Harnan, *African Rhythm-American Dance: A Biography of Katherine Dunham*, appeared in 1974. Over the years Katherine Dunham received scores of special awards including more than a dozen honorary doctorates from various American universities. She died in New York City on 21 May 2006 at the age of ninety-six.

DUPORTE, Melville

Dr E. Melville Duporte, a distinguished Canadian zoologist, was born in the small West Indian island of Nevis on 24 October 1891. He attended the Charlestown Primary School in Nevis and the St Kitts-Nevis Grammar School at Basseterre before furthering his education at McGill University in Montreal, Quebec. In 1913 he graduated at the top of his class and became the first ever McDonald College graduate to achieve an MA (1914) and a PhD (1921). He also became the first black person to teach at McGill University. After introducing several new courses in parasitology and insect morphology, he became head of his zoology department in 1955 at the age of sixty-four. Such was the respect in which he was held that, after his retirement in 1957, he was made professor emeritus of entomology at McGill University. Duporte continued his research on insects until 1980 and died on 31 July 1981 a few months before his 90th birthday. Although he did not publish a great deal himself (at a time when the mainstream presses were reluctant to promote the work of black scientists), he was recognized as a genius by all of his peers and colleagues, most of whose writings he inspired and sometimes even edited or co-authored. His honours and distinctions were consequently numerous. He received an honorary doctorate from Carleton University and the Quebec Entomology Society established a prize named for him after 1980. At McGill University the annual Dr E. Melville Duporte lecture is delivered in his honour and the department of entomology also presents the annual Dr E. Melville Duporte Award to encourage post-graduate study in that discipline. In 1981 a plaque was also erected in the McDonald College Library to commemorate his seventy years of service to McGill University.

DU SABLE, Jean-Baptiste
Jean-Baptiste Point du Sable, the first known settler in the area of Chicago, was born in Haiti around 1745. A courageous pioneer and entrepreneur, he purchased thirty acres of crown land in what later became Illinois in 1773. He participated briefly in the Revolutionary War as a spy for the British and later served as a liaison officer between the Port Huron Indians and white officials. He extended his Chicago holdings to more than 800 acres during the 1780s and 1790s. By the end of the eighteenth century, a mill, smokehouse, dairy, poultry house, horse stable, and barn were among the buildings on the fur-trading post that Du Sable had established there. But, on 7 May 1800, he suddenly sold his estate for the meagre sum of $1,200 and died a pauper in St Charles, Missouri, on 28 August 1818. It is believed that he was forced out of Chicago by white settlers who wanted the land for themselves. Today, however, a city plaque pays tribute to this remarkable pioneer and several schools and museums honour his name. On 25 October 1968, the state of Illinois and the city of Chicago recognized Jean-Baptiste Point Du Sable as the founder of Chicago.

DUVALIER, François
Dr François Duvalier, a former president of Haiti, was born in Port-au-Prince on 14 April 1907 and received his MD from the Faculty of Medicine, Haiti, in 1934. In 1943, he became director of the anti-yaws training centre of the American Health mission and served as head of the malaria control section in 1945. During the 1950s, Duvalier became increasingly involved in politics and eventually led the opposition to the government of President

Paul Magloire. Elected president in 1957, he pledged to end illiteracy, increase tourism and attract foreign capital. Within a year, however, he announced a state of siege and began ruling by decree. In 1964 he named himself president for life and strengthened his authority by creating a personal bodyguard of 'Tontons Macoutes' to discourage opposition. In 1970, he rewrote the Haitian constitution to ensure that his son, Jean-Claude, would succeed him as president for life. Despite his autocratic methods, François Duvalier enjoyed the support of the peasants who referred to him affectionately as 'Papa Doc'. He died on 21 April 1971. It is not very well known that he also left a solid body of literature on politics, sociology and medicine. Apart from his monumental *Oeuvres essentielles*, which appeared in four volumes in 1958, his miscellaneous writings included *Politique étrangère*; *histoire diplomatique* (1968), *Politique frontérale*, *géographie politique* (1968) and *Hommage au Marron Inconnu* (1969). He was also the co-author, among other works, of the important *Les tendances d'une génération* (1934), *Le problème des classes à travers l'histoire d'Haiti* (1948), and *L'avenir du pays et l'action néfaste de Mr Foisset* (1949). He was very influential in shifting Haitian literature and philosophy away from their French models by making local authors increasingly conscious of their debt to African patterns and influences.

EARLE, Gordon

Born in Halifax, Nova Scotia, on 27 February 1943, Gordon Earle has become a well-known Canadian administrator and politician. In 1997 he was the first black man from Nova Scotia to win a seat in the federal parliament and he served for three years as the spokesman for the New Democratic Party (NDP) on citizenship, multiculturalism, aboriginal affairs, national defence and veteran affairs. In 1968 Earle was the first person hired by the Nova Scotia Human Rights Commission and was instrumental in drafting that province's first Human Rights Act. He then served for ten years (1972-82) as Nova Scotia's assistant ombudsman. He did an excellent job as Manitoba's ombudsman during 1982-94 and returned to his native province after serving the maximum two terms. From 1994 to 1997 he was Nova Scotia's deputy minister of housing and consumer affairs. Earle and his wife are enthusiastic community servants who have provided Open Custody supervision for several young offenders.

EASMON, M.C.F.

Dr McCormack Charles Farrell Easmon was a noted Sierra Leonean physician who suffered from many years of racial discrimination in the colonial service because of his African descent. He left an enduring mark, however, as a curator and historian, having played the leading role in the founding in 1958 of the Sierra Leone National Museum which he served as its first curator. Born on 11 April 1890, McCormack Easmon became a prolific writer on Sierra Leone's culture and history, contributing numerous scholarly articles to *Sierra Leone Studies* and other journals. His best-known work perhaps was *The Sierra Leone Country Cloths*. He also wrote on medical subjects. Awarded an OBE in 1954, he served as the first director of the Bank of Sierra Leone (1963-67) while being secretary of the Royal Society for Tropical Medicine and Hygiene. Through his efforts and intensive research, some twenty national monuments were declared and developed. Dr Easmon died on 30 April 1972.

ÉBOUÉ, Félix

Adolphe Félix Sylvestre Éboué, the first Black to be appointed governor of a European colony, was born in Cayenne, French Guiana, on 26 December 1884. He attended local schools in Cayenne before completing his education in France and entering the French colonial service. In 1908 he was assigned as student-administrator in Oubangui-Chari (which later became known as the Central African Empire). After several promotions, Éboué was named secretary general in Martinique where he often served as acting governor and was then appointed to a similar post in the Sudan (now Mali) in 1934. In 1936 he became governor of Guadeloupe and was transferred to Chad in a similar capacity in 1938. Impressed by his patriotic fervour during World War II, the French government promoted Éboué to the office of Governor General of French Equatorial Africa in 1942. When he died on 17 May 1944, he received a hero's funeral and was deeply mourned both in Africa and in France. Always very interested in African culture and language, Éboué wrote frequently on these subjects. His seminal work, *Langues sango, banda, baya, mandjia: notes grammaticales, mots groupés d'après le sens, phrases usuelles, vocabulaire*, was published in Paris in 1918. Some of his other significant publications included *Les Peuples de l'Oubangui-Chari: essai d'ethnographie, de linguistique et d'économie sociale* (1933) and *Politique indigène de l'Afrique Equatoriale Française* (1942).

EDWARDS, Beresford

Born in Guyana, Beresford Edwards emigrated to the United Kingdom in 1960 and became a keen crusader for racial equality. Inspired by Marcus Garvey, he promoted the study of African history and served as the chairman of the Manchester branch of the Pan African Congress Movement (PACM). He was chairman of the Guyanese Association and a leading member of the West Indian Organizations' Coordinating Committee (WIOCC) which organized many youth projects, training seminars and Saturday Schools in Manchester. He was also the regional secretary for the Campaign Against Racial Discrimination (CARD) which urged the Government to pass the Race Relations Act in 1976. As a trade unionist, he fought his employers in the High Court for his right to work after he was made a victim of closed shop agreements. Edwards died on 15 March 2003.

EKWENSI, Cyprian

This noted Nigerian author was born at Minna on 26 September. 1921. Educated at local schools, Ibadan University, Ghana University and the Chelsea School of Pharmacy in London, England, he taught science at Igbobi College in Lagos before working for several companies including the Nigerian Broadcasting Corporation (as head of features). He also served in the federal ministry of information and for a short while was the chairperson of the Bureau for External Publicity in Biafra. During 1975-79, he was the director of Star Printing and Publishing. But Cyprian Odiatu Duaka Ekwensi is best remembered for his excellent literature. He is generally considered one of the most skilful African writers in depicting the feelings and dilemmas of rural natives in the face of modern urban complexities. He has published such fine novels as *People of the City* (1954), *Jagua Nana* (1961), *Burning Grass* (1962), *Beautiful Feathers* (1963), *Iska* (1966), *Africhaos* (1969), *Survive the Peace* (1976), *Divided We Stand* (1980), *Jagua Nana's Daughter* (1986) and *King for Ever!* (1992). He has also produced some first-class novelettes, including *When Love Whispers* (1947), *The Leopard's Claw* (1947), *Ikola the Wrestler* (1948), and *Yaba Roundabout Murder* (1964). Cyprian Ekwensi, who remains the outstanding chronicler of Nigerian city life, has also published numerous short stories, children's books and·a collection of Ibo folktales.

ELLINGTON, Duke

Edward Kennedy Ellington was born in Washington, D.C. on 29 April 1899. He became a legend in American jazz after forming his first band in Washington, D.C. in 1918 and another in New York City in 1922. For many years, he attracted several of the finest jazz musicians to his bands while also writing a large number of piano suites, including *Black, Brown and Beige* (1947), *Harlem* (1951) and *Blue Bells of Harlem* (1953). His bands enthralled audiences in such diverse settings as Carnegie Hall, the Cotton Club in Harlem, and Westminster Abbey in England. He himself composed over 900 songs, including such hits as *Mood Indigo*, *Don't Get Around Much Any More*, *Solitude*, and *Sophisticated Lady*. Duke Ellington was the recipient of numerous awards and honours, including the Spingarn Medal and the Grammy Award. He established a scholarship fund and Ellington Collection at Yale University, before dying, at the age of seventy-five, on 24 May 1974. His autobiography, *Music Is My Mistress*, was published in 1973.

ELLIS, Keith

Born in Jamaica on 25 April 1935, Dr Keith A.A. Ellis came to Canada as a student in 1956 and completed his BA at the University of Toronto before pursuing graduate studies at the University of Washington. He returned to the University of Toronto to teach Latin American literature and culture from 1963 until his retirement in 2000 when he was elevated to the status of Professor Emeritus. He is the outstanding authority on Nicolás Gillén, one of Cuba's most eminent poets. Professor Ellis made history in 1998 when he became the first Canadian to be awarded an honorary doctorate by the University of Havana. His major works include *Cuba's Nicolás Guillén: Poetry and Ideology* (1985); *Nicolás Guillén (1902-1989): A Life of Poetic Service* (1991); *Nicolás Guillén: New Love Poetry* (1994); *The Role of Science in Cuban Culture* (1995); and *A Cuban Poet at Niagara Falls* (1997).

ELLISON, Ralph Waldo

Ralph Waldo Ellison was born in Oklahoma City on 1 March 1914. After a brief attempt to study music at Tuskegee Institute, he turned to journalism and fiction, successfully editing the *Negro Quarterly* in the early 1940s. While serving in the Merchant Marine during World War II he began to write short stories. In 1952, he produced the much acclaimed *Invisible Man* which won a National Book Award and has since been judged by many critics as one of the most distinguished novels written in the 20th century. During the 1950s, Ellison lectured in Austria, Germany and Italy before returning to the United States to teach at Rutgers University and the University of Chicago. He was named Albert Schweitzer Professor of Humanities at New York University in 1970. He published two volumes of essays, *Shadow and Act* (1964) and *Going to the Territory* (1986). He died on 16 April 1994.

EMIDY, Joseph

Joseph Antonio Emidy was born in Guinea in 1775 and sold into slavery by Portuguese traders who took him to Brazil and then to Lisbon. As his musical talents were soon recognized, he was used by his master to entertain his guests. After a fine performance at the Lisbon Opera House in 1795, he was kidnapped by British sailors who took him to Falmouth where he was given his discharge in 1799. He made his living there by playing the violin and teaching music. He became leader of the Falmouth Harmonic Society and wrote many compositions which were much admired by his contemporaries. He was befriended in Falmouth by James Silk Buckingham who admired his music and became one of his many pupils. Buckingham tried vainly to find openings in London for his mentor but failed because of Emidy's colour. This accomplished and versatile musician was able to teach flute, violin, piano, pianoforte and guitar and to provide such services as tuning harps and other instruments for his clients in Falmouth and Truro. Had his background been different he would unquestionably have left a more significant mark on the history and development of British music. Joseph Emidy died on 24 April 1835.

ENWONWU, Benedict

Benedict Chuka Enwonwu was an outstanding Nigerian artist who gained international renown during the 1950s and 1960s for his figurative sculptures and paintings which effectively mixed traditional African elements with classical Western training. Born in Onitsha, Nigeria, on 14 July 1921, he attended local schools before winning a scholarship to study in England at Goldsmith College in London (1944), Ruskin College in Oxford (1944-46) and the Slade College of Art in London (1946-48). In 1946, Enwonwu took part in an international exhibition sponsored by the United Nations in Paris, France, and two years later staged a successful one-man exhibition in London. In 1957 Queen Elizabeth II posed for him for a bronze sculpture that graced the entrance to the Nigerian parliament building. He returned to Nigeria in 1959 as the official art adviser to the federal government. Twelve years later, he left this post to serve as a visiting professor of African studies at Howard University. After serving briefly as professor of fine arts at the University of Ife, Nigeria, he retired in 1975. He received an MBE in 1958 and the Nigerian National Merit Award in 1980. Enwonwu died on 5 February 1994. His legacy included the carved doors of the chapel for the Apostolic Delegation in Lagos and an elegant bronze figure of a woman donated by the Nigerian government to the UN headquarters in New York City in 1966.

EQUIANO, Olaudah

Olaudah Equiano was born into slavery around 1745 in Benin. At the age of twelve he was taken to the West Indies where he travelled widely with his master and received some education before being granted his freedom. Emigrating to England, he became an ardent abolitionist and lectured against the cruelty of British slave-owners in Jamaica. In 1789, with the encouragement of British abolitionists, Equiano published his famous autobiography, *The Interesting Narrative of the Life of Olaudah Equiano, or Gustavus Vassa, the African*. His graphic depiction of life in Benin became so popular that within five years it had already gone through eight editions in Britain and one in the United States. In his autobiography, and later in his *Miscellaneous Verses*, Equiano idealized the African past and showed a tremendous pride in his race, while attacking those Africans who had trafficked in slavery. In 1787, he helped Offobah Cuguano, another exceptional ex-slave, to publish an account of his personal experiences.

Equiano died on 31 March 1797, leaving an estate worth £950 – a considerable sum for those days. His autobiography was re-issued in 1966 with an introduction and detailed notes.

ESSY, Amara

Amara Essy of Côte d'Ivoire became the first secretary-general of the fifty-three-country African Union (AU) which was established in 2002 to replace the thirty-nine-year-old Organization of African Unity (OAU). He was asked to lead a much more powerful body than its predecessor which had perhaps been too respectful of the sovereignty of individual states. The AU was modelled after the European Union with plans to intervene in the internal affairs of countries to stop crimes against humanity. Born in Bouaké on 20 December 1944, Essy is a career diplomat who studied in Asia, Europe and South America, became fluent in several languages and achieved a degree in public law from the University of Poitiers in France. He served Côte d'Ivoire in many capacities during the 1970s and was appointed its representative to the UN in New York in 1981. Gaining respect for his diplomatic capabilities, he became vice-president of the UN General Assembly (1988-89) and its president (1994-95). He also served as president of the UN Security Council in 1990. During 1990-99, Essy was Côte d'Ivoire's minister of foreign affairs.

ESTE, Charles

Revd Charles Humphrey Este was born in Antigua, West Indies. He immigrated to Canada in 1913 and worked for many years as a shoe-shine boy in Montreal. From these humble origins he emerged as one of the truly influential religious leaders in Canada for more than fifty years. With much difficulty he completed a course of study at the Congregational College while still having to undertake sundry odd jobs to support himself. He graduated in 1925, was ordained a priest, and began his ministry at the Union United Church in Montreal, then the only black congregation in the United Church of Canada. Both from the pulpit on Sundays and in regular correspondence, he consistently prevailed upon businesses and governments to offer more employment opportunities to Blacks. These campaigns proved very successful and perhaps his greatest triumph came when the local hospitals and nursing schools began to accept and to train black nurses. He was also instrumental in the establishment of the Negro Community Centre in Montreal in 1927. Revd Este, who commanded the respect and admiration of all who knew him, died in January 1977.

EUSÉBIO

Eusébio Ferreira Da Silva was one of the world's greatest football players during the 1960s. Born on 24 January 1942 in Manfalala, Mozambique, his extraordinary skills attracted Portuguese scouts and he was hired by the Benfica professional team in Lisbon at the age of eighteen. He was only nineteen when he appeared in his first full international match for Portugal in 1961. Eusébio won the Jules Rimet Trophy in 1966 when he scored nine goals in the World Cup Finals in England. He was famous for his very hard kick and his remarkable ability to accelerate and to change direction suddenly without losing his speed or his balance. Eusébio is still perhaps the finest football player yet to represent Portugal.

EWARE THE GREAT
Eware the Great was the brilliant warrior-king who completed the transformation of the city-state of Benin into a sizeable empire during a most spectacular reign in the fifteenth century (1440-73). He made Benin one of the best governed kingdoms in western Africa by establishing a centralized system of commerce, law and politics. He built a number of good roads and erected strong walls around Benin city. He encouraged such handicrafts as ivory and wood-carving while promoting music by creating a national orchestra. Under his direction, religious and secular arts flourished while, in purely political terms, the hereditary monarchy became very powerful. Eware laid such solid foundations for his country's peace and security that Benin remained one of the most vital kingdoms in western Africa long after his death in 1473.

EYADÉMA, Gnassingbé
Born in the town of Pya on 26 December 1937, Gen. Gnassingbé Eyadéma was the president of Togo from 1967 until his death on 5 February 2005. He served in the French army during 1953-61 and participated in the military coups which torpedoed the régimes of Sylvanus Olympio in 1963 and Kléber Dadjo in 1967. He then won uncontested elections in 1972, 1979 and 1986. In 1993 and 1998, when Eyadéma was forced to democratize the electoral system, his margins of victory dwindled, but he was re-elected in 2003 with more than 57% of the popular vote. At the time of his death, he was the longest-serving head of state in Africa. He had served as the chairman of the Organization of African Unity (OAU) during 2000-2001. His lengthy tenure of the presidency provided Togo with a degree of political stability that it had never really known, but it was marred by personal extravagance of the most blatant kind. His totalitarian system drew frequent condemnation from Amnesty International and other groups and there were constant charges of corruption and mismanagement. On the credit side, Eyadéma helped to found the Economic Community of

West African States and was instrumental in several international agreements, notably the Lomé Convention of 1975.

FADUMA, Orishatukeh

Born William James Davies in British Guiana (West Indies) in 1860, he changed his name to Orishatukeh Faduma in 1887 as part of a personal revolt against all things European. His parents had been born in Nigeria but were repatriated to Freetown in the late 1860s. There William Davies attended the Methodist Boys' School before studying in England and becoming the first Sierra Leonean to achieve a degree from the University of London. Returning to Sierra Leone, Davies taught briefly and, in 1887, founded the Dress Reform Society fostering the wearing of African robes rather than European dress. Faduma emigrated to the United States in 1891 and studied divinity at Yale University. During 1895-1914 he served as principal and pastor-in-charge of Peabody Academy in Troy, North Carolina. Back in Sierra Leone during 1916-18 he was the principal of the United Methodist Collegiate in Freetown before being appointed Inspector of Schools (1918-23). Faduma then resettled in the United States, where he taught in various institutions from 1924 until his death on 12 January 1946. During a long and varied career, he had supported an unusual array of progressive organizations, including the American Negro Academy and the National Congress of British West Africa (NCBWA). Faduma wrote several articles and poems and remained to the end of his days a bitter opponent of European racism and injustice. Although he never swerved from the Christian faith, he particularly despised those Christians who behaved in a racist and an unchristian manner and he often attacked the church for fostering notions of European superiority.

FAGUNWA, Daniel

Chief Daniel Olorunfemi Fagunwa was a famous Nigerian educator and author who made an enormous contribution to the conservation and promotion of the Yoruba heritage by collecting and editing folk tales, which he translated into English, and by himself writing several books in the Yoruba language. Born in 1910, he was trained as a teacher and worked for many years for the ministry of education in Ibadan. Nigeria lost a priceless jewel when Fagunwa was killed in a car crash near the town of Bida on 9 December 1963. His best-known novel, *Ogboju ode Ninu Igbo Irunmale* (1939), was translated into English and published in 1968 as *The Forest of a Thousand Daemons*. His other works included *Alaye fun Oluko Nipa Lilo Iwe Taiwo ati Kehinde* (1949), *Irinago apa Kini* (1949), *Ireke Onibudo* (1949), *Irinkerindo Ninu Igbo Elegbeje* (1954), *Asayan itan* (1959), and *Adiitu Olodumare* (1961).

FANON, Frantz

One of the leading Francophone writers produced by the Caribbean, Frantz Omar Fanon was born in Fort-de-France, Martinique, on 20 July 1925. He attended the Lycée Schoelcher in Fort-de-France where he was taught (and very much influenced) by the legendary Aimé Césaire. He furthered his education in Paris, France, where he also fought during World War II. After the war, he studied medicine and psychiatry at the University of Lyon where he edited the black student newspaper. In 1953 he was appointed director of psychiatric services at Blida-Joinville Hospital in Algeria. In addition to his medical practice, Fanon was an activist who vigorously attacked Eurocentric orthodoxies and did much to illuminate the evils of racism and ethnic prejudices. He joined the Algerian liberation movement in 1954 and in 1956 became an editor of its newspaper, *El Moudjahid*, published in Tunis. In 1960, he was appointed ambassador to Ghana by the rebel Provisional Government. Fanon's famous book, *Peau noire, masques blancs* (Black Skin, White Masks), was published in 1952. He followed it up with such acrid and searching works as *L'An V de la révolution algérienne* in 1959, *Les Damnés de la terre* (The Wretched of the Earth) in 1961, and *Pour la révolution africaine* (posthumously) in 1964. These works were translated into several languages and left an indelible mark on twentieth century literature and thought. Fanon died on 6 December 1961 but he still remains the leading intellectual influence on the so-called Third World. As an internationally famous psychiatrist, he is also known for his theory that some neuroses are socially generated.

FARAH, Nuruddin

A son of the Somali poet and merchant, Aleeli Faduma, Nuruddin Farah, a famous Somali novelist, was born in the city of Baidoa in what was then Italian Somaliland. He studied in Ethiopia and at Mogadishu and Punjab University, learning both English and Italian. While in India he wrote his much acclaimed novel, *From a Crooked Rib*. His next literary success was *A Naked Needle*, published in 1976. His popular trilogy, *Sweet and Sour Milk* (1979), *Sardines* (1981) and *Close Sesame* (1983), then followed. But as most of his works seemed critical of Somali conditions under the rule of Muhammad Siad Barre, he was eventually forced into exile. For some years he then taught in Europe, North America and elsewhere in Africa. In 1998, he was awarded the prestigious Neustadt International Prize for Literature. He was only the second African writer, following Assia Djebar of Algeria in 1996, to receive this award, worth $40,000. Although his primary languages were Somali, Amharic and Arabic, Farah chose to write in English. His most recent novels include *Maps* (1986), *Gifts* (1992) and *Secrets* (1998). He is universally regarded as the most significant Somali writer in any European language.

FARMER, James

James Leonard Farmer, a distinguished civil rights leader in the United States after World War II, was born in Marshall, Texas, on 12 January 1920. After receiving a bachelor of chemistry degree from Wiley College and a divinity degree from Howard University, he refused to be ordained as a religious leader in a segregated society. He decided to devote his energies towards the elimination of racial discrimination and inequality. To this end, he formed (and presided over) the Congress of Racial Equality (CORE) in Chicago in 1942. He led non-violent protests and rallies for many years, utilising the strategies of passive resistance which became so popular and effective later on. Farmer served as professor of social welfare at Lincoln University during the late 1960s and was appointed assistant secretary of Health, Education and Welfare by President Richard Nixon in 1969. The author of numerous articles and essays, he also published *Freedom When?* in 1965. He was awarded the Presidential Medal of Freedom by President Clinton in 1998. He died on 9 July 1999.

FELA

Fela Anikulapo Kuti was a Nigerian musician and activist who is credited with having invented a modern African-based music called Afro-beat, a quaint fusion of American blues, jazz, and funk with traditional Yoruba sounds and rhythms. Born in Abeokuta on 15 October 1938, he was the son of feminist and labour activist, Funmilayo Kuti. He took lessons in piano and percussion before going to England to study classical music. He returned to Nigeria in the mid-1960s and formed his own band, 'Fela and Egypt 80', which made a tour of the United States in 1969 and became influenced not only by black American music but by the civil rights movement. He opened a night club in Lagos and used his music as a vehicle to protest oppression by Nigeria's military governments and became one of Africa's most celebrated stars. In Lagos, he also established a commune which he proclaimed the independent republic of Kalakuta. As head of the commune, he often provoked controversy by promoting indulgence in sex, polygamy and the use of marijuana. His night club and commune were frequently raided by the authorities who were anxious to find a pretext for placing Fela in jail. After one such raid in 1977 he was briefly imprisoned. In 1979 he formed a political party, the Movement of the People, and ran unsuccessfully for the presidency of Nigeria. He was jailed again in 1984 and in 1993. Fela died on 2 August 1997.

FENNELL, Rufus

Dr Rufus Leicester Fennell was born in the West Indies in 1888 and educated in the United States. He emigrated to the United Kingdom and practised as a dentist in Wales before enlisting in the British army and taking an active part in World War I. He served in Mesopotamia where he was injured thrice while attending thousands of wounded British soldiers. On his return from the battle-front, he drew attention to the shabby treatment of Britain's black soldiers by their white colleagues both in warfare and in the immediate post-war period. He did his best to solve the racial conflicts which flared up in Cardiff in 1919 and acted as the spokesman for the Blacks when the police and local authorities charged them as the instigators. He managed to see about 600 of them safely repatriated but still had cause to lament that, even in repatriation, they were still denied so many of the basic rights they had been promised.

FETCHIT, Stepin

This successful actor and comedian was born Lincoln Theodore Monroe Andrew Perry in Key West, Florida, on 30 May 1902. He became the first black actor to receive feature billing, appearing in many movies during the 1920s and 1930s. Although he always portrayed the stereotypical subservient black servant, he was the first to break down traditional barriers of segregation in American show business. He became a sensation with his motion picture début in *Old Kentucy* in 1927. A sequence of hits followed, including *The Tragedy of Youth* (1928), *The Big Fight* (1930), *Stand Up and Cheer* (1934), *Dimples* (1936) and *Miracle in Harlem* (1947). He came out of a lengthy retirement to appear in *Amazing Grace* in 1974. Fetchit died on 19 November 1985.

FIAWOO, Ferdinand Kwas

Dr Ferdinand Kwasi Fiawoo was an Ewe playwright, educator and politician who rose to prominence after World War II when elected Deputy Speaker of the Gold Coast Legislative Assembly in 1951. Born on 26 December 1891, he did much to popularize the Ewe language after producing his famous *Toko Atolia*, an Ewe drama, in 1932. He did his utmost to blend Christian education with the best in African culture and was awarded his PhD from the McKinley Roosevelt University in the United States in 1945. A member of the Akuffo-Addo Constitutional Commission which made proposals in 1968 for the reorganization of the Ghanaian republic, Fiawoo served on several other boards and committees during the 1960s. He died on 21 July 1969.

FIRMIN, Anténor Joseph

Anténor Joseph Firmin was born in Cap-Haïtien, Haiti, on 20 October 1851. He left his mark on that country as a statesman, biographer, journalist, scientist and historian. Following his graduation from local schools in Cap-Haïtien, he entered the teaching service and rose to the rank of assistant supervisor for all the schools of his native district. In 1878 he founded the newspaper, *Le Messager du Nord*. He went to France in 1884 and was accepted as a member of the Société d'Anthropologie. He returned to Haiti after President Félicité Salomon was overthrown and contributed to the formulation of the new constitution in 1889. He was then appointed minister of finance and foreign affairs. After serving for some years as Haiti's ambassador to France, Firmin lost his bid for the presidency of Haiti in 1902 and was exiled. He spent the remainder of his days in St Thomas, Virgin Islands, where he died on 19 September 1911. His major works included *De l'egalité des races humaines, anthropologie positive* (1885), *Lettres ouvertes aux membres de la Société de Législation de Port-au-Prince* (1904-1905), *Monsieur Roosevelt, Président des Etats-Unis et de la République d'Haiti* (1905), and *Lettres de Saint-Thomas; études sociologiques, historiques et littéraires* (1910). Firmin also wrote numerous essays and articles on Haitian politics and society.

FISHER, Rudolph

Born in Washington, D.C. in 1897, Rudolph Fisher became prominent in two separate fields. He was not only a successful physician who had graduated with honours from Howard University Medical College in 1927, but he became an important member of the famous Harlem Renaissance. He wrote two novels, *The Walls of Jericho* (1928) and *The Conjure-Man Dies* (1932). The latter was the first full-length detective novel by a black writer. Earlier, in 1923, the best known of Fisher's short stories, *The City of Refuge*, had appeared in *Atlantic Monthly*. The versatile Dr Rudolph Fisher died in 1934 at the young age of thirty-seven.

FITZGERALD, Ella

Ella Fitzgerald was a popular US singer of ballads and jazz who sold more than 40 million records during a career that spanned some six decades. Born on 25 April 1918 in Newport News, Virginia, she began as a dancer but changed disciplines after winning an amateur contest as a singer in 1934. She sang with the Chick Webb's orchestra from 1935 to 1939 (when Webb died) and then led the band herself until 1942. Later she toured internationally with such stars as Louis Armstrong, Duke Ellington, Dizzy Gillespie and Benny Goodman. Fitzgerald also appeared in films, most notably *Pete Kelly's Blues* in 1955. She won numerous Grammy Awards, was the 1979 recipient of the Kennedy Center Honors for lifetime achievement, and in 1987 was awarded the National Medal of Arts. She died on 15 June 1996 after struggling for several years with heart problems and diabetes.

FORDE, Freddie

Alfred N. Forde was an influential Barbadian administrator, editor, author, educator and diplomat. Born in Carrington Village, St Michael, in 1923, he was educated at St Giles' Elementary School, Combermere School and Harrison College before achieving his BA as an external student from London University in 1947. After teaching for many years in Grenada and Tobago in the West Indies, he returned to Barbados in 1957 to begin an outstanding career as an administrator in the civil service. He was the first Barbadian manager of the fledgling Caribbean Broadcasting Corporation (CBC) from 1965 to 1968, became the head of the Foreign Service department in the early days of Barbadian political independence, and eventually rose to the rank of permanent secretary in the prime minister's office in 1976. He then became a member of the United Nations Joint Inspection Unit in Geneva, a body which he chaired for some time. He was invited to serve as consultant when the African Caribbean and Pacific Secretariat in Brussels was being restructured. On returning to Barbados in the late 1980s he was appointed chairperson of the Combermere School Board of Management and director of the National Cultural Foundation. But it is as a writer that 'Freddie' will perhaps best be remembered. He did much to keep alive the literary journal, *Bim*, which he edited for some years and to which he contributed numerous poems and essays. He edited a *Talk of the Tamarinds: an Anthology for Secondary Schools* in 1971. He also wrote an excellent play, *The Passing Cloud*, published in 1966. Alfred Forde died on 13 March 1996.

FORTEN, James
James Forten was one of the first African-American business executives. Born in Philadelphia, Pennsylvania, in 1766, he managed to open his own sail-making shop in 1798. His personal fortune was estimated at more than $100,000 early in the nineteenth century. He devoted a great deal of energy as well as money to the anti-slavery movement and the cause of racial equality in the United States. He was also a supporter of the women's suffrage and temperance movements and founded the American Moral Reform Society in 1839 to promote all of these causes. James Forten died in 1842 but his descendants carried on his important work. His children remained active in the reform movement and it was his granddaughter, Charlotte Forten Grimké, who wrote *A Free Negro in the Slave Era*, which is still regarded as one of the most significant pieces of American literature.

FORTUNE, Thomas
Timothy Thomas Fortune, who was born a slave in Marianna, Florida, in 1856, became a very influential printer, journalist and author. He was associated with such newspapers as the *New York Age*, which he founded in 1879, the *Rumor*, which he and others bought in 1880, and the *New York Freeman*, which he served as publisher for some years after 1884. He also

spent time with the *Boston Transcript* and the *New York Sun*. In 1890, Fortune founded the National Afro-American League, a forerunner of the famous National Association for the Advancement of Colored People (NAACP). He was also instrumental in the establishment of the National Afro-American Press Association. A prolific writer, he produced numerous articles and pamphlets, as well as such books as *Black and White: Land, Labor, and Politics in the United States* (1884), *The Negro in Politics* (1886), and *Dreams of Life, Miscellaneous Poems* (1905). He died in 1928 after a prolonged struggle with mental illness, but is still remembered now as 'the dean of Negro newspapermen'.

FOSTER, Cecil

Born on 26 September 1954 in Barbados, West Indies, Cecil Foster immigrated to Canada in 1979 and has become one of this country's most respected authors on race relations. He was educated at Christ Church High School and Harrison College (Barbados), the University of the West Indies (Jamaica) and York University (Canada). While editing the *Contrast*, Canada's foremost black newspaper, he served as a reporter for the *Toronto Star* and the transportation expert and business reporter for *The Toronto Globe and Mail*. During the late 1980s he became a senior editor at *The Financial Post*. Foster, who has lectured at Ryerson University in Toronto, contributed regularly to *The Globe* and *Mail*, *The Toronto Star* and *Toronto Life* magazine. He also appeared frequently on CBC Radio's *Morningside* political forum and was the host of *Urban Talk* on CFRB Radio in Toronto. He is the author of three very fine novels, *No Man in the House* (1991), *Sleep on, Beloved* (1994) and *Slammin' Tar* (1998). He has also published *Caribana: The Greatest Celebration* (1995), *A Place Called Heaven* (1996) and *Island Wings* (1998).

FRANCO

Born L'Okanga La Ndju Pene Luambo Makiadi on 5 June 1938, in what was then the Belgian Congo, Franco was a brilliant Zairean jazz musician and composer. He was the leader of the African music scene for more than thirty years, blending the Latin American rhumba with jazz, gospel and traditional African melodies to create what became known as 'soukous'. He skilfully employed the elements of Lingala (a tonal language), the likimbi hand piano, horn, and guitar as background for the social themes of his lyrics which dealt with a wide range of social and political matters. One of the founders of TPOK Jazz, Franco wrote many successful songs, including *Independence Cha Cha* (1960), *Mario* (1985) and *Beware of AIDS* (1987). He recorded more than 100 songs and was named Grand Maître by president Mobutu Sese Seko. When he died on 12 October 1989, Mobutu declared four days of national mourning.

FRANKLIN, John Hope
One of the leading American historians of the last century, Professor John Hope Franklin taught at several universities, including Cambridge (England), and received more than thirty honorary degrees. Born in Oklahoma on 2 January 1915, he achieved his BA from Fisk University in 1935 before successfully pursuing graduate studies at Harvard University. He became chairman of the department of history at the University of Chicago in 1964, after having served in a similar capacity at the City University of New York for eight years. A prolific writer, his many books included *The Free Negro in North Carolina 1790-1860* (1943); *The Militant South 1800-1860* (1956); *Reconstruction: after the Civil War* (1961); *Color and Race* (1968); *The Historians and Public Policy* (1974); *Racial Equality in America* (1976); and *The Color Line: Legacy for the Twenty-first Century* (1993). His famous college textbook, *From Slavery to Freedom* (1948) achieved several editions. More than three million copies have been sold. During the 1970s, John Hope Franklin was elected president of the prestigious American Historical Association and served the Southern Historical Association in a similar capacity. In 1995 he was awarded the Presidential Medal of Freedom, the nation's highest civilian honour.

FRAZIER, Franklin
A truly outstanding sociologist, E. Franklin Frazier was born in Baltimore, Maryland, in 1894. After studying with much distinction at Howard University, Clark University and the University of Chicago, he taught for some years at Morehouse College and Fisk University and then served as head of the department of sociology at Howard University from 1934 to 1959. He published several important books, including *The Negro Family in Chicago* (1932), *Traditions and Patterns of Negro Family Life* (1934), *The Negro Family in the United States* (1939), *Negro Youth at the Crossways* (1940), *The Negro in the United States* (1949), *Black Bourgeoisie* (1957), *Race and Culture in the Modern World* (1962), and the *Negro Church in America* (1962). Professor Franklin Frazier died on 22 May 1962.

FUHR, Grant
Born in Spruce Grove, Alberta, Canada, on 28 September 1962, Grant Fuhr palpably demonstrated that Blacks are capable of performing brilliantly in one of the most demanding positions in one of the most challenging sports. After a stellar junior career in Victoria of the Western Hockey League (WHL), he was the first goal-tender to be drafted so high (8th overall) when chosen by the Edmonton Oilers of the National Hockey League (NHL) in the 1981 Entry Draft. He justified their confidence by leading them to no fewer than five Stanley Cups between 1984 and 1990.

He also led his country to an exciting Canada Cup triumph in 1987. In 1988 he was awarded the Vezina Trophy as the league's outstanding goal-tender and was selected to several NHL All-Star teams. By the time of his retirement in 2000, Grant Fuhr had become only the sixth goal-tender in NHL history to win more than 400 games. For almost twenty years he was, quite simply, one of the finest goalies in the world of ice-hockey.

FULLER, Hoyt
Hoyt William Fuller is best remembered as an important editor and publisher who gave great encouragement to promising, young African-American authors. Born in Atlanta, Georgia, on 10 September 1927, he graduated from Wayne State University with a BA in 1950. He worked for some years with the *Detroit Tribune* and other newspapers before serving as associate editor of the *Ebony* magazine from 1954 to 1957. After working as an African correspondent during 1957-60, he became the executive director of *Black World* (formerly *Negro Digest*) in 1961. When this magazine died in 1976, Fuller founded and became executive director of the literary journal, *First World*. He himself often wrote articles, under the pseudonym of William Barrow, for such publications as *The New Yorker*, *The New Republic*, and the *Christian Science Monitor*. He also published a book, *Journey to Africa*, in 1971. He was the founder of the Organization of Black American Culture in Chicago, Illinois, a nonprofit writer's workshop. Hoyt Fuller died on 11 May 1981.

FULLER, Meta
Meta Vaux Warwick Fuller is one of the leading sculptors and illustrators among all African-Americans. Born in Philadelphia, Pennsylvania, on 9 June 1877, she studied at the Pennsylvania Academy of Fine Arts and the École des Beaux-arts in Paris. One of the first American sculptors to use anti-slavery themes, her sculptures graphically expressed the suffering of black labourers. Fuller also produced portrait sculptures of such well known African-Americans as Frederick Douglass, Harriet Tubman and Sojourner Truth. Her sculptures were exhibited all across the United States and in Paris and many of them are currently on display in the collections of the San Francisco Museum of Fine Arts, of Howard University, and of the New York Public Library. She won many awards for her art, including the George K. Crozier First Prize for Modelling and the Battles First Prize for Pottery. Meta Vaux Warwick was married to Solomon C. Fuller, the eminent neurologist. She died in 1968.

FULLER, Mike
In January 2004, Michael Fuller took up his appointment as the Chief

Constable of Kent and thus became the first black man to assume such a role in the United Kingdom. His policing career began as a Met Cadet in 1975 and he served in a number of London communities. Winning a scholarship to study at Sussex University, he achieved a degree in social psychology and then earned a master's degree in business administration. He wrote the *Met's Action Plan* and proceeded to establish the Met's Violent Crime Task Force after the Macpherson Report had accused the London police of 'institutional racism'. He set up and commanded Operation Trident, the unit formed to tackle the serious issue of 'black on black' crime in London. Fuller was the founding chair of the Black Police Association and has mentored and supported many black police officers throughout his career.

FULLER, Solomon

A distinguished neurologist and psychiatrist, Solomon C. Fuller was born in Liberia in 1872. He emigrated to the United States to qualify himself as a physician and graduated with an MD from Boston University Medical School in 1897. He then pursued further research at the psychiatric clinic of the University of Munich, Germany. Dr Fuller returned to the Boston University Medical School in 1899 and taught neurology and psychiatry there for more than thirty years. He published numerous articles on psychiatry in a variety of scholarly journals before his death in 1953. He was married to Meta Vaux Warwick Fuller, the well-known sculptress.

GABRA HEYWAT BAYKADAGON

A distinguished Ethiopian political economist, who served briefly as an adviser to the great Emperor Menilek II, Gabra Heywat Baykadagon was born in 1888. He published an influential article, *Menilek and Ethiopia*, offering several constructive suggestions for basic fiscal and administrative reforms, reorganization of the armed forces, establishment of modern schools, and updating the legal code. Gabra also promoted religious toleration and the regular conduction of a population census. Unfortunately for Ethiopia, he died in the midst of an influenza epidemic (1919) when he was only thirty-one.

GABRA SELASSE WALDA ARAGAY

This noted Ethiopian civil servant, clergyman and historian was born around 1844 and became one of Emperor Menilek II's private secretaries during the 1870s. Accompanying Menilek everywhere, he kept a record of the major political and military events of the period. He was one of that ruler's principal advisers and played a prominent role in the reconstruction and administration of Ethiopia's churches. He was himself appointed head of the St Mary's Church in Addis Ababa. He died on 4 November 1912.

His important history was printed long after his death. It was published in French in 1930 but the Amharic original did not appear until 1966.

GAIREY, Harry

Harry Ralph Gairey Sr was born in Jamaica, British West Indies, on 29 August 1895. After spending some years in Cuba, he immigrated to Canada in August 1914 and became one of the leading civil rights activists in this country for what seemed like an eternity. A fervent advocate of racial equality and integration, he objected to the enlistment of Blacks during wartime without adequate compensation in times of peace. He succeeded in making his point during World War II when the Toronto City Council in Ontario finally passed legislation prohibiting discrimination on the grounds of creed, colour, race and religion. Gairey was instrumental, too, in persuading the federal government to liberalize its immigration laws during the 1950s and 1960s and played a key role in the assimilation and settlement of hundreds of West Indian domestics, nurses and students. To help newly arriving immigrants to settle down more comfortably in Toronto, he founded the West Indian Federation (WIF) Club in the 1950s. He died on 23 October 1993 at the great age of ninety-eight. Part of his legacy was the very informative *A Black Man's Toronto 1914-1980: The Reminiscences of Harry Gairey*, published in 1981. He was a recipient of the prestigious Order of Canada.

GAIRY, Eric

Sir Eric Matthew Gairy, who became the first prime minister of an independent Grenada in 1974, was born on 18 February 1922. After a brief teaching career in his native island, he worked in Aruba with Dutch oil refineries and became involved in the labour union movement. Following his return to Grenada in 1949, he continued to work as a union organizer and founded the Grenada Manual, Maritime and Intellectual Workers' Union in 1950. This organization was largely instrumental in doubling the wages of the farm workers within a short time. Gairy also founded the Grenada United Labour Party (GULP). Elected to the Legislative Council in 1951, he was named minister of trade and production in 1956 and became chief minister in 1961. After 1953, GULP became the dominant political force in Grenada. Gairy became the island's first premier in 1962 and retained that position until independence. A ruthless politician, he established a secret police force, upon which the power of his party was largely based. His 'Mongoose Gang' often terrorized his critics and some of his political opponents were frequently assaulted and beaten. There consequently developed a considerable opposition to his rule and his government was overthrown in 1979. Gairy sought refuge in the United States during 1979-83 while the New Jewel Movement (NJM), led by

Maurice Bishop, was in power. But neither he nor his party could regain their former appeal and GULP fared ill in the general elections of 1984, 1990 and 1995. Sir Eric Gairy died on 23 August 1997.

GANDANDA GIBANDA

Born around 1865, Gandanda Gibanda was a prominent Pende chief who was unjustly tortured by colonial authorities after the famous Pende Revolt of 1931 in what is now Zaire. He had ascended the throne in the early years of the twentieth century and was officially recognized by the Belgian government in 1920. The Belgians held him personally responsible for the rebellion of 1931 even though that uprising had been a spontaneous reaction to economic distress and Belgian oppression. The cruel manner in which Gandanda Gibanda was put to death was a graphic reminder of European arrogance and injustice and served as a fillip for further Congolese resistance.

GANS, Joe

Born Joseph Gaines on 25 November 1874 in Baltimore, Maryland, Joe Gans is still remembered as one of the greatest boxers in the history of the lightweight division. Because he was black, he was often compelled by promoters to carry less talented white fighters to more rounds than they would otherwise have lasted against him and sometimes he was actually required to lose. It is believed that Gans was also forced to fight at unnaturally low weights, which might well have contributed to his early death from tuberculosis. When he died on 10 August 1910 his death was treated by the press as a national calamity.

GARANG, John

John Garang was the Sudanese rebel leader and politician who was appointed to the post of first vice president after having founded and led the Sudan People's Liberation Army (SPLA) in twenty two years of war against the Sudanese government and then negotiating an end to that war. Born on 23 June 1945 in Wangkulei, Anglo-Egyptian Sudan, he graduated in 1969 from Grinnell College, Iowa, and returned to The Sudan to join the Anya Nya rebel group in the Christian section of the country. After the Addis Ababa agreement of 1972, Garang was among those rebels absorbed into the Sudanese army. He became a colonel and returned to the United States to upgrade his qualifications. The Sudanese government grew increasingly Islamist, however, and when Garang was sent in 1983 to put down a Christian uprising in the south, he joined the rebel forces and moulded them into the SPLA which, by 1991, had grown to 60,000 strong. To end the stalemate, a peace settlement was finally reached in January 2005 whereby

Garang was elevated to the post of first vice president of The Sudan. But he died soon after in a helicopter crash on 31 July 2005.

GARNER, Erroll

Erroll Louis Garner was born in Pittsburgh, Pennsylvania, in 1921. He became one of the most important jazz pianists and composers without the benefit of any formal training in music. He was the first jazz instrumentalist to give a solo recital in the United States. Garner appeared often on television and made many recordings. He achieved his greatest success with such popular tunes as *Laura and Misty*. He died in 1977.

GARRISON, Len

Leonard Garrison was a native of Jamaica who emigrated to the United Kingdom to further his studies. He gained a BA from Sussex University in African and Caribbean History, a diploma in Development Studies from Oxford University and an MA in Local History from Leicester University. He was a founding member of the International Social Group whose work led to the establishment of the Wandsworth Council for Community Relations. In 1977 he founded the Afro-Caribbean Resource Project (ACRP) to publish learning materials drawn from the black British experience for use in the school curriculum. He established the Black Young Writers' Award scheme which encouraged and exposed the talents of hundreds of young black writers, and co-founded the Black Cultural Archives (BCA) in 1981 to house documentary evidence of the black presence and struggle. Len Garrison represented Britain in the 1977 Festival of Arts and Culture in Nigeria. Later, as director, he set up the ACFF Education and Cultural Centre in Nottingham. He died in February 2006.

GARVEY, Marcus

Marcus Mosiah Garvey, who fought so single-mindedly for the cause of Pan-Africanism and universal Negro improvement, was born in Jamaica, British West Indies, on 17 August 1887. Largely self-educated, he travelled widely throughout the Americas and reached the conviction that Negro independence - at once economic, political and military - was the only method by which the Blacks could improve their lot. He therefore founded the Universal Negro Improvement Association (UNIA) in Jamaica in 1911. He formed another branch of this organization in Harlem, New York, in 1916 and began his famous 'Back to Africa' campaign. He also founded a newspaper, *Negro World*, to disseminate his views, and an African-American steamship company, called the 'Black Star Line', to facilitate the expected African-American exodus to Africa. He reached the height of his power in 1920, when he presided at an international convention in Liberty Hall, with delegates present from twenty-five countries. The affair was climaxed by a parade of 50,000 through the streets of Harlem, led by Garvey in flamboyant array. While more than one million Blacks joined his UNIA and chapters sprang up in almost every major city in the western hemisphere within about five years, most of Garvey's other projects failed. He was himself convicted (some say falsely) for mail fraud, jailed for two years, and then deported back to Jamaica as an undesirable alien. His efforts there after 1927 bore no better fruit and in 1935 he emigrated to England in despair. Life in London proved equally disappointing and he died there in undeserved obscurity on 10 June 1940. Marcus Garvey, however, is still revered as a national hero in his native island. He was perhaps too idealistic and visionary, but his star-crossed career served to focus international attention on the mistreatment of Blacks both in the old world and the new. His influence pervaded the great Harlem Renaissance of the 1920s in the United States, gave a tremendous stimulus to Caribbean independence movements during the inter-war years, and served as a source of inspiration to countless African nationalists long after the 'Black Moses' was dead.

GAYLE, Addison, Jr
Addison Gayle, Jr was born in Newport News, Virginia, in 1932. He became a teacher of English in New York City after studying at the City University of New York and the University of California at Los Angeles. A specialist in African-American literature, this noted critic and author has written several important books himself. Gayle's publications include *Black Expression* (1969), *The Black Situation* (1970), *Bondage, Freedom and Beyond: The Prose of Black Americans* (1971), *The Black Aesthete* (1971), *Oak and Ivy: A Biography of Paul Laurence Dunbar* (1972), *The Way of the New World: The Black Novel in America* (1975) and *Wayward Child: A Personal Odyssey* (1977). He died in 1991.

GEORGE, David
Born a slave in Virginia, David George escaped to live with Creek Indians before settling in Nova Scotia towards the end of the 1770s and becoming a Baptist preacher. He tried to find converts from both races in such cities as Fredericton, Horton, Liverpool, St John and Shelburne. Occasionally he ran foul of the locals and was often physically assaulted. In 1791, he was among those who organized immigrants to go to West Africa and thus played a prominent role in the settlement of the British colony of Sierra Leone.

GEORGE, Gbadebo
His Excellency Gbadebo Oladeinde George served as a career diplomat for Nigeria for more than thirty years before his retirement in 1990. He was originally a journalist who graduated from the University of Missouri in

1955. He was the first Nigerian correspondent in Ghana when that country won its political independence and he was in New York in 1960 when Nigeria became the 99th member of the United Nations. George entered the Nigerian public service in 1960 and served as external affairs officer in Cameroon, The Gambia, Ghana, Senegal and Zaire until 1974. During 1976-78 he served as Consul General of Nigeria in New York, and deputy permanent representative to the UN and to the UN Security Council. He was appointed Nigerian ambassador to Angola in 1978 and became dean of the Luanda diplomatic corps in 1983. Returning to Nigeria in 1984, he served for three years as the director of European affairs in Lagos. In 1987 he was appointed Nigerian High Commissioner to Canada, where he chose to reside after his retirement in 1990.

GHASSANIY, Muyaka bin Haji al
Muyaka bin Haji al-Ghassaniy of Mombasa, Kenya, was the first secular poet known by name to write beautiful poetry in the Swahili language. Born in 1776, he wrote numerous stanzas on a wide array of themes ranging from dialogue verse to love poems and from poems on domestic life to political commentary. Many of his works were collected and published in 1962 under the title of *Diwani ya Muyaka* (Poetry of Muyaka). They tell a great deal about life in Mombasa before and during Muyaka's time and show a general concern for the security and independence of the Mazuri people then under the suzerainty of the sultan of Muscat. He died in 1840.

GIBBS, Mifflin
Mifflin Wister Gibbs was born in Philadelphia, Pennsylvania, on 17 April 1823. Travelling west to San Francisco in search of fame and fortune, he was lucky enough to find both. Starting as a shoe-black, he was able to form a partnership in a successful shoe business. In 1855, he founded *Mirror of the Times*, the first black newspaper published in California. Moving north to British Columbia, Canada, Gibbs undertook a variety of enterprises as merchant, district councilman, and railroad builder. He provided the Blacks there with a voice in public affairs when he became chairman of the city's finance committee in 1866. He returned to the United States in 1869 to seek a career in law. He was admitted to the Arkansas bar and soon attained the office of municipal judge in Little Rock. Gibbs then occupied a number of federal posts under a lengthy succession of presidents. He served in turn, for instance, as registrar of US lands in eastern Arkansas, registrar of public moneys received, and as US consul in Madagascar. Gibbs published an interesting autobiography, *Shadow and Light*, in 1902. He died in 1915 at the age of ninety-two.

GIBSON, Althea

Althea Gibson was the first black tennis player to compete successfully in major international tournaments. Born on 25 August 1927, she attended Florida Agricultural and Mechanical University where she displayed unusual skills in tennis and golf. Following a brilliant amateur tennis career, she became (in 1957) the first African-American of any gender to win the US singles title at Forest Hills. She repeated her triumph in 1958, winning the prestigious Wimbledon singles titles in these two years as well. She became the first African-American to be voted American Female Athlete of the Year in 1957 and she won the award again the following year. As a professional, Althea won the world championship in 1960. Three years later, she also became a professional golfer. Her autobiography, *I Always Wanted to Be Somebody*, was published in 1958. Althea Gibson was elected to the National Lawn Tennis Hall of Fame in 1971. She died on 28 September 2003.

GIBSON, Leonard

Born in Athabasca, Alberta, Canada, in 1926, Leonard Gibson is an internationally famous dancer, choreographer and teacher. He began dancing at the age of five and performed as a self-taught tap dancer for many years. At the Katherine Dunham School of Dancing in New York in the 1940s he completed courses in ballet, tap, jazz, oriental percussion, costume and visual design. He was invited to perform as one of the dancers in the classic film, *Cleopatra*, and has performed, choreographed and directed for stage, film, television and radio. He also played a role in such films as *Fiddler on the Roof*, *West Side Story*, *Guys and Dolls*, *Hello Dolly*, *Finian's Rainbow* and Salome Bey's *Indigo*. His impact on the performing arts is incalculable, as many of his students have gone on to enjoy successful careers.

GIBSON, Truman

Truman Kella Gibson was born in Macon, Georgia, in 1882. After studying at Atlanta University and Harvard University, he became one of the shrewdest among African-American business executives. He was largely responsible for the establishment of the Supreme Life Insurance Company of America, one of the foremost black enterprises in the United States. Gibson served for many years as chairman and then as chairman emeritus of Supreme Life. He died in 1972.

GILL, Sarah Ann

The Rt Excellent Sarah Ann Gill was named one of the ten National Heroes of Barbados in 1998. She was thus honoured for the role she played in defending the Methodist Church and spreading the Methodist gospel of the equality of man under the fatherhood of God at a time when the white supremacists in the island held diametrically opposite views. As the Methodists gave staunch support to the anti-slavery movement, Sarah Ann Gill was subject to constant persecution and harassment. Even when her church was destroyed in 1823 she held prayer meetings in her own home in defiance of local authorities. Born on 16 February 1795, she lived to witness the abolition of slavery in 1834 and the abandonment of the Apprenticeship System in 1838 before dying, at seventy-one, on 25 February 1866. The Ann Gill Memorial Church was opened in her memory on 26 August 1990.

GILLESPIE, Dizzy

John Birks Gillespie, much better known as 'Dizzy', was a brilliant innovator and virtuoso who expanded the harmonic structure of jazz and played an important role in ushering in the style of bebop which flourished during the 1940s. Gillespie was an excellent trumpeter, composer and bandleader who left an enormous influence on such well-known jazz celebrities as John Coltrane, Miles Davis, Dexter Gordon and Thad Jones. Born in Cheraw, South Carolina, on 21 October 1917, Gillespie attended the Laurinburg Institute in North Carolina and became an accomplished musician by the time he was a teenager. He performed briefly with Teddy Hill's and Cab Calloway's bands before forming his own group in 1945. In such songs as *Night in Tunisia*, *Maneca* and *Con Alma*, he tried to assimilate African-Cuban elements into modern jazz. He continued to tour with various reorganized bands until a few months before his death on 6 January 1993. His autobiography, *To Be or Not to Bop*, was published in 1979.

GLASSPOLE, Florizel

Sir Florizel Augustus Glasspole served as Governor General of Jamaica from 1973 to 1991. Born in Kingston on 25 September 1909, he was educated at the Central Branch Primary School and Wolmer's Boys' School before attending Oxford University in England. From 1932 to 1944, Glasspole pursued an accountant's career while making significant contributions to the trade union movement in Jamaica. He presided over a variety of unions from the 1940s onwards and was elected to Jamaica's House of Representatives, where he sat for almost thirty years (1944-73) as a member of the People's National Party (PNP). Glasspole was among that small group of legislators who prepared the way for independence by helping to draft the new constitution in 1962. A regular member of PNP cabinets, he served as Minister of Labour (1955-57), Minister of Education (1957-62) and Leader of the House 1955-62 and 1972-73. During the course of a distinguished career in accounting, unionism and politics, Sir Florizel received many outstanding awards, including a knighthood in 1982, the Grand Cross of the Order of Merit from the President of the Federal Republic of Germany (1982), and the Venezuelan Order of the Liberator (1978).

GLISSANT, Édouard

Dr Édouard Glissant is one of Martinique's most famous authors. Born in Sainte-Marie on 21 September 1928, he was educated at the Lycée Schoelcher where he fell under the influence of Aimé Césaire. He proceeded to further his studies at the Sorbonne and the Musée de l'Homme in Paris. After achieving his doctorate in philosophy, he worked for some years at the Centre Nationale de la Recherche Scientifique in Paris. Glissant became very active in the Société Africaine de Culture and various left wing political groups in Paris. This brought him into conflict with the imperial authorities, especially during the Algerian war. He was forbidden during 1959-65 to return to Martinique or to travel to Algeria. Returning to Martinique in 1965, he began at once to participate in the development of a variety of cultural activities centred around the Institut Martiniquais d'Études (IME), a private secondary school, which he himself founded. Glissant is a prolific writer. His collections of poetry include *Un champ d'Iles* (1953), *La Terre inquiète* (1954), *Les Indes* (1956), *Le Sel noir* (1960), and *Poèmes* (1965). He also published two volumes of essays, *Le Soleil de la conscience* (1956) and *L'Intention poétique* (1969), and such fine novels as *La Lézarde* (1955), *Le Quatrième Siècle* and *Malemort* (1975). In addition, Glissant published a very good play, *Monsieur Toussaint*, which appeared in 1961.

GONSALVES, Ralph

Born on 8 August 1946, Dr Ralph Everard Gonsalves is the current prime minister of St Vincent and the Grenadines, a post he has held since winning the general elections by a landslide on 29 March 2001. His political career actually began when he was a student at the University of the West Indies at Mona in Kingston, Jamaica. It was he who, as President of the Guild of Undergraduates, led a memorable demonstration against the banning of a lecture that Professor Walter Rodney, an intellectual with well-known radical views, was scheduled to deliver. Gonsalves completed his PhD in political science before achieving a law degree at the Cave Hill Campus in Barbados. He returned home to practise law and then entered the political fray as a member of the Unity Labour Party. He led it to a stunning triumph that sent the New Democratic Party (NDP) packing in 2001. Gonsalves is also an accomplished author whose works include *The Spectre of Imperialism: the Case of the Caribbean* (1976); *The Non-Capitalist Path of Development: Africa and the Caribbean* (1981) and *History and the Future: A Caribbean Perspective* (1994).

GORDY, Berry, Jr

One of the most successful American business executives in the twentieth century, Berry Gordy, Jr was born in Detroit, Michigan, in 1929. A high-school drop-out, he was inducted into the US Army in 1951. His first venture, a record shop which he opened in 1953, failed miserably. His second did not. It was Gordy who founded the famous Motown Record Corporation in 1959 with William (Smokey) Robinson. By 1960, Motown had produced its first gold record and, within ten years, was grossing more than $50 million annually. Under Gordy's skilful guidance, Motown grew to become the largest black-owned American firm in annual gross income by 1975. Its most popular recording artists have included the Supremes, the Jackson Five, Marvin Gaye and Stevie Wonder.

GOURDINE, Meredith

Dr Meredith C. Gourdine was born in Newark, New Jersey, on 26 September 1929. An outstanding track and field athlete at Cornell University, he won a Silver Medal in the long jump competition at the Olympic Games in 1952. He was also an excellent physicist who pioneered research in electrogasdynamics, a way of producing high-voltage electricity from natural gas. He was instrumental in developing, among other things, an exhaust-purifying system for cars; equipment for reducing incinerator smoke pollution from older apartment houses; a technique for dispersing fog from airport runways; a method for computer chip cooling; and a system for production-line coating of metal products. Dr Gourdine established a research laboratory, Gourdine Laboratories, in Livingston, New Jersey, with a staff of over 150. He was the recipient of numerous patents and the author of many seminal articles. In 1991 he was elected to the National Academy of Engineering and in 1994 he was inducted into the Engineering and Science Hall of Fame in Dayton, Ohio. He died on 20 November 1998.

GQOBA, William

William Wellington Gqoba was born near Gaga in South Africa in 1840. He was a dominant literary figure among nineteenth century Bantu writers, whose poetry reflects the influence of missionaries on the Bantu people. A pastor and teacher, Gqoba was a noted translator of English and Xhosa. From 1884 to 1888, he edited the *Isigidimi samaxosa* (Kaffir Express) to which he contributed several articles on Xhosa history and culture. His fame as a poet rested to a large extent on two long and didactic poems, *The Discussion between the Christian and the Pagan* and *The Discussion on Education*. Gqoba died in 1888.

GRANT, Bernard

A British political activist and parliamentarian, Bernard Alexander Montgomery Grant was born in Georgetown, British Guiana, on 17 February 1944. Emigrating to the United Kingdom, he became an outspoken trade-union advocate and an ardent supporter of minority rights. He was the first black leader of a local British council authority (1985-87) and in 1987 won a seat in the House of Commons. Bernard Grant was a backbench (but vocal) Labour Party MP until his death on 8 April 2000.

GRANT, George Alfred

George Alfred Grant was born on 15 August 1878 and became one of the most prosperous of native African merchants during the twentieth century. He entered the timber business and began exporting mahogany in 1903. He opened branches in England and Germany and owned several motor launches. A firm believer in African independence, he served briefly on the Gold Coast Legislative Council during 1926-27. He died on 30 October 1956.

GRAVELY, Samuel

Samuel Lee Gravely was born in Richmond, Virginia, in 1922. A graduate of Virginia Union University, he was the first black ensign commissioned in the US Navy during World War II. He became the first African-American to command a US Navy ship, the USS *Falgout*, in 1962. In 1971, Gravely became the US Navy's first black rear admiral, and in 1973 was named commander of a flotilla of thirty ships.

GRIFFITH-JOYNER, Florence

Florence Griffith-Joyner was easily the most brilliant of all female athletes of the 20th century. Born into poverty in Watts, Los Angeles, on 21 December 1959, she began racing at the age of seven and reached her absolute peak in 1988 at the age of almost twenty-nine. She set two incredible world records in that year - 10.49 secs in the 100 metre dash and 21.34 secs in the 200 metre sprint. She won three gold medals and one silver for the United States in the Seoul Olympics that year, when she ran brilliantly as the anchor in the 4 x 400 relay (having never competed at that distance before). Her records have not yet been approached although it is almost twenty years since 'Flo-Jo' retired. Her sudden death on 21 September 1998, at the relatively young age of thirty-eight, rekindled allegations about her illegal use of performance-enhancing substances. These suspicions had surfaced in the late 1980s because of her unusually rapid improvement during 1986-88, her bulging muscles, and her sudden decision to retire from the track early in 1989 when mandatory random drug testing was introduced. It is not to be forgotten, however, that she passed every drug test she ever took, and made very positive contributions to the female techniques of starting and sprinting by studying very closely the methods of Ben Johnson (start) and Carl Lewis (form). Florence Griffith-Joyner, a flamboyant character noted for her facial beauty and outrageous running suits, was especially popular in the United States.

GRIZZLE, Stanley

Judge Stanley E. Grizzle was the first African-Canadian appointed as a citizenship court judge in Ontario in 1978. After serving for five years initially, he was reappointed in 1999. Born in Toronto, Ontario, of Jamaican parents in 1918, Grizzle has been at the forefront of the struggle for racial equality and human rights in Canada since 1938 when he was a founding member and secretary of the Young Men's Negro Association. He founded the Railway Porters' Trade Union Council in 1958 and was the driving force behind the Toronto Labour Committee for Human Rights during 1956-61. In 1959, Stanley Grizzle was one of the first Blacks to contest a seat for the Legislative Assembly of Ontario. He was a member of the delegation which went to Ottawa in 1954 to protest the racist immigration laws of the federal government and was a founding member and first president of the National Black Coalition of Canada in 1969. In 1960, he went to work for the Ontario Labour Relations Board and in 1978 became the first member of a trade union to be appointed a Judge in the Canadian Court of Citizenship. In 1959, he wrote a booklet, *Discrimination: Our Achilles Heel?*, which became immensely popular. Grizzle also published the autobiographical *My Name's Not George: the Story of the Sleeping Car Porters in Canada* in 1998. His many honours and awards include the Order of Ontario (1990) and the Order of Canada (1995).

GUILLÉN, Nicolás

Born in Camagüey, Cuba, on 10 July 1902, Nicolás Guillén was a social and political activist whose poems highlighted the worst evils of racism and snobbery then prevalent in his native island. He became a prominent spokesman for Cubans of African descent and a popular hero among revolutionaries in Europe and Spanish America. Published in 1930, *Motivos de son*, his first volume of poetry, made an enormous impact and is still widely regarded as one of the finest examples of black Latin American literature. His most famous collection of poems, such as *West Indies Ltd* (1934), *Cantos para soldades y sones para turistas* (1937), *España* (1937), *El son entero* (1947) and *La paloma de vuelo popular* (1959) have been widely translated, thus bringing the attention of a world-wide audience to the unique African-Cuban heritage that Guillén himself was attempting to preserve by founding the Society for Afro-Cuban Studies. He died in 1989.

GULAMA, Julius

Born in 1893, Julius Gulama was a paramount chief of Kaiyamba, a state in what is now Sierra Leone. He played a key role in developing the educational and political awareness among his people in the last decades before independence and was himself one of the main forces behind the formation of the Sierra Leone People's Party (SLPP) in 1951. Educated at the Evangelical United Brethren School at Rotifunk and the Albert Academy in Freetown, he worked briefly as a teacher and a civil servant before enlisting in World War I. Following his election as chief in 1928, Gulama instituted a number of useful and far-reaching reforms. He organized regular conferences with other chiefs to discuss matters of common concern and was also instrumental in founding the Protectorate Education Progress Union (PEPU). He took part in the activities of the Sierra Leone Organization Society (SOS). On 8 March 1951, however, Chief Julius Gulama died before most of his efforts could bear fruit.

GYLES, Carlton

Dr Carlton L. Gyles is a world famous microbiologist generally regarded as one of the leading experts on E. coli. He helped to discover the E. coli heat-labile enterotoxin and E. coli plasmids with genes for enterotoxin and drug resistance. He is also the first microbiologist to clone and sequence the gene for E. coli verotoxin 2e, to purify the edema disease toxin, and to develop a toxoid vaccine against edema diseases of pigs. Born in Jamaica, he immigrated to Canada in 1959 and completed his education at the Universities of Toronto and Guelph. Dr Gyles has published over 100 scholarly articles on such topics as the pathogenesis of E. coli infections, the role of verotoxins in disease and rapid methods for the detection of bacterial food-borne pathogens. From 1981 to 1986, he served as Dean of the Faculty of Graduate Studies at the University of Guelph. Among a host of honours and distinctions, he received the Beecham Award in 1990 from the Ontario Veterinary College for excellence in research.

EMPEROR HAILE SELASSIE

Born Ras Tafari Makonnen in the province of Harar on 23 July 1892, this revered Ethiopian ruler reigned as Emperor Haile Selassie I for more than forty years. He was the son of Ras Makonnen who had been one of Emperor Menilek II's ablest supporters. When he was only thirteen years old, his father appointed him governor of Gara-Muletta and Emperor Menilek II promoted him rapidly even after his father's death. Ras Tafari's political fortunes declined when Menilek II died in 1913 but he emerged as one of the most powerful figures in the nation after playing a key role in deposing Lej Iyasu, Menilek's successor, in 1916. He was instrumental in the pursuit of progressive policies after World War I, ensuring the eradication of slavery in Ethiopia and its admission to the League of Nations in 1923. He tried to establish modern schools patterned on western lines and to reorganize the Ethiopian army. But the whole period 1913-30 was characterized by unrest and violence which came to an end only with Tafari's elevation to the imperial throne in 1930. Forced into exile by the Italians in 1935, he returned to Addis Ababa in triumph in 1941. His principal aims were the modernization of Ethiopia and Pan-African unity and co-operation. He played a significant role in the fight for African independence and was the master-mind behind the Charter of African Unity which was signed in 1963. At home, however, Haile Selassie I was less successful. Liberals became more and more impatient with his reluctance to establish a constitutional monarchy, urban dwellers became increasingly dissatisfied with the slow pace of social and economic change, and he could do little to stem the tide of communism even though he had accomplished much by way of land and tax reforms. His régime was overthrown in the Revolution of 1974 and he died a prisoner on 27 August 1975. A source of inspiration to many African nationalists during the inter-war years when he achieved fame as a relentless opponent of Fascism, Haile Selassie I left an indelible mark not only on Ethiopia but on the whole of Africa. Rastafarians in Jamaica and elsewhere in the Caribbean still look upon him as their spiritual leader.

HALEY, Alex

Alex Palmer Haley was born on 11 August 1921 in Ithaca, New York. After working with the US Coast Guard during World War II, he became a free-lance writer, producing articles for *Playboy* and ghost-writing the *Autobiography of Malcolm X*. His career and fame as an author really hinged on the phenomenal success of *Roots: The Saga of an American Family*, which earned Haley a special citation from the National Book Award judges in 1977 and a Pulitzer Prize. It sold more than 5.5 million copies and was translated into thirty-seven languages. This best-seller was then dramatized in a television series that achieved unprecedented ratings, kindled an unusual interest in genealogy, and created a tourist boom for western Africa as other American Blacks sought to emulate Haley's search for his roots. Haley also published a novella, *A Different Kind of Christmas*, in 1988. He died on 10 February 1992.

HALL, Lloyd

Dr Lloyd Augustus Hall, a noted inventor and scientist, was born in Elgin, Illinois, on 20 June 1894. After graduating from Northwestern University in 1916, he served as sanitary chemist at the department of health laboratories in Chicago. In due course, he rose to the rank of chief chemist and research director of Griffith's Laboratories in that city. Hall held more than 100 patents in Canada, Great Britain and the United States and published more than fifty scientific papers on food preservation. During World War I he used his expertise as a chemist to help the United States Army ensure that explosives were made correctly and during World War II he solved many of the army's problems with the preservation of military food supplies. Still remembered everywhere as the Food Chemist, Hall made significant contributions to the meat-packing industry with his numerous recipes for curing salts, condiments, spices and flavours. He was awarded honorary doctorates from Virginia State University, Howard University and the Tuskegee Institute in Alabama. He died on 2 January 1971.

HALL, Stuart

Professor Stuart Hall, who was born in Kingston, Jamaica, on 3 February 1932, won a prestigious Rhodes Scholarship which took him to Oxford University where he achieved an MA. In the 1950s, he joined forces with other celebrated social historians to launch two radical socialist journals, *The New Reasoner* and *New Left Review*. He was invited to join the Centre for Contemporary Cultural Studies in Birmingham after the appearance in 1964 of the much acclaimed *The Popular Arts* which he had co-authored. He served as a professor of sociology at the Open University from 1979 to 1997. As one of the main proponents of reception theory, he has become a famous cultural theorist. Apart from seminal articles in various journals, his major works include *Situating Marx: Evaluations and Departures* (1972), *Encoding and Decoding in Television Discourse* (1973), *Policing the Crisis* (1978), *The Hard Road to Renewal* (1988), *Resistance Through Rituals* (1989), *The Formation of Modernity* (1992), *Questions of Cultural Identity* (1996), *Cultural Representations and Signifying Practices* (1997) and *Visual Cultural* (1999). Professor Hall currently sits on the Runnymede Trust's Commission on the Future of Multi-Ethnic Britain.

HALL, Wesley

Born on 12 September 1937, Revd Wesley Winfield Hall is one of the outstanding characters in the social history of Barbados. He first made a name for himself as one of the fastest and most feared bowlers in first-class cricket; he then entered the political field and served as a member of the Barbadian cabinet; he was an influential cricket administrator; and has finished up as an ordained Baptist priest. Hall captured 192 wickets in 48 Tests for the West Indies during 1958-71. He then served as a manager of West Indian touring sides as well as a selector. He was also the president of the West Indian Cricket Board (WICB) during 2001-2003. As a member of the Barbados Democratic Labour Party (DLP), he was for many years the minister of sport and tourism. An excellent and hilarious after-dinner speaker, he has made a huge contribution to Barbadian life and culture.

HALL, William
William Hall is justly famous for being only the third North American, and the first black man, to win the prestigious Victoria Cross, a British medal for outstanding valour during battle. Born in 1827 in Hants County, Nova Scotia, of refugee parents from the American southern states, he went to sea at an early age and then joined the Royal Navy. He distinguished himself in the Crimean War (1854-56), at the battles of Inkerman and Sebastopol, and in 1857 played a key role in the relief of the British garrison at Lucknow during the Indian Mutiny. Following his retirement from the navy in 1876, he returned to Nova Scotia where he was regarded as a local legend. Although he was given a carriage in the procession that honoured the Duke of York on his visit to Halifax in 1901, Hall was strangely buried in an unmarked grave when he died but three years later. In 1947, the Hantsport branch of the Canadian Legion erected a monument to him, and a branch of the Legion of Halifax was named for him.

HAMA, Boubou
One of the truly outstanding figures in the history of modern Niger, Boubou Hama was born in Fonéko, French West Africa, in 1906. A former president of the Niger National Assembly, he was also one of his country's finest writers who made an enormous contribution to the development of Nigerois culture and science. A Songhai Muslim, he trained as a teacher before entering politics in 1947 as a member of the Rassemblement Démocratique Africain. One of the finest orators in French West Africa, he became president of the National Assembly after Niger was proclaimed a republic in 1958. Overthrown in the military coup of 1974, he was held in custody until 1977 when the new régime bowed to public opinion throughout Africa and Europe and released him. Hama was one of the instigators of the UNESCO project to produce a history of Black Africa and himself inspired the systematic recording of Niger's oral culture. He won the Grand Prix Littéraire d'Afrique Noire for *Kotia-Nima*, a chronicle of his youth published in 1969. He continued to write during his imprisonment and after his release. He died on 30 January 1982.

HAMER, Fannie Lou
Fannie Lou Hamer's story is one of exceptional bravery and perseverance. In the face of the most violent resistance from the racists of Ruleville, Mississippi, she persisted with her crusade against racial inequality and injustice and eventually compelled the southern states to remove all barriers

to black voter registration. Born on 6 October 1917 in Ruleville, she grew up in a life of poverty and became very active in the US civil rights movement. Her attacks on Mississippi traditions led to her imprisonment and mistreatment at the hands of white neighbours and the local police. But by 1964 her persistence allowed her to become the first black woman from Mississippi to run for Congress. She also founded the Mississippi Freedom Democratic Party (MFDP) and in 1968 was invited to the Democratic Convention. A very eloquent speaker and effective community servant, she led many successful fund-raising drives to build a huge farm community to house and feed the needy of all races in her home district of Sunflower County. She also started a day care centre for the children of working mothers. Fannie Lou Hamer died on 14 March 1977 and was posthumously honoured by the state of Mississippi for her devotion to the struggle for human rights.

HAMILTON, Sylvia

Born in Beechville, Nova Scotia, Dr Sylvia Hamilton has become a highly respected Canadian film-maker and writer. After achieving her BA from Acadia University in 1972, she trained as a reporter and announcer and worked for private radio stations while freelancing for some years with the Canadian Broadcasting Corporation (CBC). During the 1980s she worked as a programme officer for the federal department of the secretary of state and rose to the rank of acting regional director. Through her films and her writing, Dr Hamilton has brought the life experiences of black Nova Scotians into the mainstream of Canadian arts. Her films include *Black Mother, Black Daughter* (1989); *Speak It: From the Heart of Black Nova Scotia* (1993); *Against the Tides* (1994); *No More Secrets* (1999) and *Portia White: Think on Me* (2000). These films have won numerous national awards. In 2001 Dr Hamilton received an honorary LLD from Dalhousie University, having been similarly honoured with a DLitt by St Mary's University in 1995. She has been very active in the Writers' Federation of Nova Scotia and the Canadian Independent Film Caucus. She is also an accomplished poet, whose verses have appeared in several anthologies. In addition, she has written many articles on women's studies.

HANDY, W.C.

Known almost universally as the 'Father of the Blues', William Christopher Handy was born in Florence, Alabama, on 16 November 1873. He was the first composer to recognize the importance of the blues and to write them down. His work helped develop the conception of the blues as a harmonic framework within which to improvise. He also composed many spirituals of his own. Handy moved to Memphis, Tennessee, and formed a band that played mainly at picnics, funerals and political campaigns. In 1912, he produced *Memphis Blues*, the first blues composition ever to be published. Handy died on 28 March 1958 after writing such pieces as *St Louis Blues* (1914), *Joe Turner Blues* (1915), *Beale Street Blues* (1917) and *John Henry Blues*. He was also the composer of several marches, including *Careless Love* and *Afro-American Hymn.*

HANI, Martin

Martin Thembisile Hani was a South African political activist who contributed significantly to the success of the African National Congress (ANC) and eventually was invited to participate in the negotiations which led to a relatively peaceful solution of the constitutional problems of the early 1990s. Born in Cofimvaba, South Africa, on 28 June 1942, he was educated at Fort Hare University (1959-61) and Rhodes University (BA, 1962). He abandoned an intended career in the priesthood to join the black struggle for social justice and political equality and became a member of the ANC Youth League. He underwent military training, fought with the black nationalists in Rhodesia (now Zimbabwe), became the leader of the military wing of ANC, and directed guerilla operations against South Africa from Lesotho and Zambia. Elected to the ANC executive council in 1974, Hani was foremost among those who endorsed using violence against civilian targets, as opposed to the more moderate tactics of the older leaders, such as Nelson Mandela and Oliver Tambo. After the ban on the ANC was lifted in 1990, however, he agreed to take part in the discussions for a peaceful transfer to majority rule. Hani was murdered in Johannesburg on 10 April 1993, after having escaped numerous previous assassination attempts.

HANLEY, Ellery

Ellery Hanley was born in Leeds in 1961 and became one of the outstanding rugby players of his generation. After a stellar career, he was appointed coach of the British national team in 1994, thus becoming the first Black to coach or manage a major national team in Great Britain. He had already created a sensation in 1985 when he transferred from Bradford Northern to Wigan for the then record fee of £150,000. Hanley played most of his games at stand-off and loose forward and was capped thirty-four times by Britain. Known as 'Mr Magic', he was the drawing-card wherever he performed. It was his inspiring play that allowed Wigan to dominate the sport during the late 1980s. At the age of thirty, he joined Leeds as captain and coach for £250,000 in 1991 and led them to two championship finals in 1994 and 1995. After scoring an amazing 428 tries in 498 matches in the English Rugby League, he played briefly in Australia before returning to England to serve as the coach of St Helens Rugby

League Football Club in 1999. He won numerous awards for his splendid play and was also the recipient of the MBE in 1990. Hanley was inducted into the Rugby League Hall of Fame in 2005.

HANSBERRY, Lorraine

A popular playwright, who flashed across the American literary scene like a proverbial meteor, Lorraine Vivian Hansberry was born in Chicago, Illinois, on 19 May 1930. Before she had reached the age of thirty five, she was dead. But her work lived on. She is still remembered for such plays as *A Raisin in the Sun* (1959) and *The Sign in Sidney Brustein's Window* (1965). The former enjoyed a longer run (19 months) on Broadway in New York than any previous play. When it was revived as a musical, *Raisin*, it won the Tony Award for best musical in 1973. Hansberry also wrote a few essays, poems and a book, *To Be Young, Gifted and Black*, which appeared posthumously (1969). *Les Blancs: The Collected Plays of Lorraine Hansberry* was published in 1972. She died on 12 January 1965.

HANSBERRY, William

William Leo Hansberry was born in Gloster, Mississippi, in 1894. After graduating from Harvard University, he served as professor of African history at Howard University for almost forty years. He was very instrumental in the founding of the African American Institute in Washington, D.C. in 1952. In 1964, he won the first Haile Selassie Prize Trust Award for his original work in African history, archaeology and anthropology. The University of Nigeria's Hansberry College of African Studies, where he once served as advisor and Distinguished Scholar, was named after him. His great work, *The William Leo Hansberry Notebook*, was published in two volumes posthumously: *Pillars of Ethiopian History* (1974) and *Africa and Africans as Seen by Classical Writers* (1977). He died in 1965.

HAREWOOD, Richard

Richard Alexander Harewood was born in Barbados in 1900. After serving in World War I, he emigrated to the United States and studied law. Establishing his private practice in Chicago in 1926, he became a prominent lawyer and judge in the state of Illinois. He served as assistant state attorney for Cook County during 1944-47 and as a member of the Illinois general assembly during 1937-38 and 1957-58. Harewood became a judge of Cook County Superior Court in 1962 before serving as a judge of the Circuit Court of Cook County in the 1970s.

HARLEM RENAISSANCE

This is the term commonly applied to that flourishing of black literature, especially poetry, which occurred in Harlem, an area in the northeastern portion of New York City, during the 1920s. About six square miles in extent, Harlem was one of the main residential areas for black Americans throughout the twentieth century. For the first time, during the 1920s, large numbers of black writers lived in close proximity to each other. Reacting in part to the large-scale oppression of Blacks after World War I and in part to the nationalistic teachings of Marcus Garvey, the African-American authors displayed an unusual degree of radicalism in their prose and verse. Their literature began to show a certain sense of black pride, interest in black history and culture, and a keen political and social awareness.

Foremost amongst the new breed of black writers was Langston Hughes (1902-67) who addressed his poetry specifically to black people, in a language and a mood that they could understand. Although other black writers, such as Countee Cullen (1903-46), Claude McKay (1891-1948) and Jean Toomer (1894-1967), wrote occasionally on social matters, they seemed more concerned with poetic beauty and form. The Harlem Renaissance also witnessed an outburst of black fiction from the pens of such gifted writers as Jessie Fauset, James Weldon Johnson, Nella Larsen, William Jourden Rapp, Wallace Thurman, and Walter White. An important anthology of this new realism and creativity is Alain Locke's *The New Negro* (1925). The Great Depression caused the Harlem group of writers to scatter during the early 1930s; many were forced to leave New York or to take odd jobs simply to survive.

HARRIS, Barbara

The Rt Revd Barbara Harris created history in February 1989 when she became the first woman of any denomination to be promoted to a bishopric in a Christian church. Born and raised in Philadelphia, Pennsylvania, she became a fervent social activist, consistently advocating gay rights and gender equality. She marched with Dr Martin Luther King, Jr in Selma, Alabama, in support of civil rights and registered voters in Mississippi. She worked as a public relations executive with Joseph V. Baker Associates and then with the Sun Oil Company before becoming director of the Episcopal Publishing Company. Born in 1931, she was already in her forties when she decided to enter the ministry. In 1980 she was ordained a priest and boldly used the pulpit as a forum for the expression of her progressive ideas. Needless to say, millions of Christians decried her appointment and mourned what they considered the death of their church. Male chauvinists lamented that there was no scriptural basis for female ordination in the first place. On the other hand, more progressive Christians looked favourably upon Revd Harris' consecration as a very significant milestone in the politics of race and gender.

HARRIS, Claire

Claire Harris was born in Trinidad in 1937. She studied at the University College of Dublin and the University of the West Indies before immigrating to Canada in 1966 and teaching English in Calgary until 1994. Generally considered one of Canada's most accomplished poets, she has published many collections of poems. Her first volume, *Fables from the Women's Quarters*, won the Commonwealth Award for Poetry for the American Region in 1984. Her 1992 volume, *Drawing Down a Daughter*, was nominated for the Governor General's Award for Poetry. Her *Travelling to Find a Remedy* won the Writers' Guild of Alberta Poetry Award in 1987. Claire Harris's work has been included in more than seventy anthologies and has been translated into German and Hindi. Her poems generally address the problems and injustices which Blacks and women have historically been forced to confront. In addition to her writing, Claire Harris worked as poetry editor for the now defunct Calgary journal, *Dandelion*, during 1981-89 and helped to found the all-Alberta magazine, *Blue Buffalo*, in 1983.

HARRIS, Patricia

The daughter of a Pullman-car waiter, Patricia Roberts Harris was born in Mattoon, Illinois, on 31 May 1924. A dynamic civil rights activist, she became the first black woman to hold a US cabinet post and/or to serve as a US ambassador. She graduated first in a class of ninety-four from George Washington University National Law Center in 1960 after having shone as a brilliant undergraduate student at Howard University. She lectured at Howard University during the early 1960s and later became dean of its School of Law. In 1965 Harris was appointed ambassador to Luxembourg where she spent the next two years. During 1977-79 she served as secretary of housing and urban development and then (1979-1981) as secretary of health, education and welfare. She returned to Howard University in 1981 as a full-time professor of law. During her career, Harris was active on numerous committees and commissions dedicated to the fight for civil rights. She died on 23 March 1985 after having been the recipient of several honorary degrees from a wide range of academic institutions.

HASTIE, William

Born in Knoxville, Tennessee, in 1904, William Henry Hastie was educated at Amherst College and Harvard University. During 1930-37, he taught in the School of Law at Howard University while working with the firm of Houston and Houston. He also served as assistant solicitor in the US Department of Interior during 1933-37. In 1937, Hastie became the first African-American to be appointed to a federal bench when he was made a judge of the US District Court for the Virgin Islands. He was appointed

Governor of the Virgin Islands in 1946, and three years later became a judge of the US Court of Appeals, Third Circuit, in which capacity he served until 1971. Hastie died in 1976. He is perhaps best remembered not only as being first African-American governor of the Virgin islands but for resigning his post as civilian aide to Secretary of War, Henry L. Stimson, in 1943 in protest over the mean-spirited segregation still prevalent in the US armed forces.

HAWKINS, Coleman

The virtual creator of the tenor saxophone for jazz, Coleman Hawkins was born on 21 November 1904 in St Joseph, Missouri. A child prodigy, he began to play the piano at four, the cello at seven, and the saxophone at nine. He became a professional in his teens and made his first recordings with Fletcher Henderson's orchestra in 1923. Hawkins created a positive impression in his tours throughout Europe and the United States and left a marked influence on scores of modern saxophonists. He was especially fine on slow ballads and his 1939 recording of *Body and Soul* remains one of the undisputed masterpieces of jazz. In 1944, he organized an all-star band for his first Bop recording sessions, and gave encouragement to such promising young performers as 'Dizzy' Gillespie and Charlie Parker. Hawkins died on 19 May 1969.

HAYFORD, J.E.C.

Joseph Ephraim Casely Hayford was an ardent African nationalist who contributed significantly to the evolution of Ghanaian independence. Born on 28 September 1866, he became an outstanding Gold Coast statesman, lawyer and journalist. Educated at the Wesleyan Boys' School at Cape Coast and Fourah Bay College in Freetown, Sierra Leone, he proceeded to study law at the Inner Temple in London, England, and economics at Cambridge University. He was called to the bar in 1896. He became principal of the Wesleyan High School in Accra and then accepted a similar post at the Wesleyan High School at Cape Coast. He ran the *Gold Coast Echo* for many years and was associated also with the *Gold Coast Chronicle* during the 1890s. He took over the *Gold Coast Leader*, an influential paper which consistently championed the cause of African political advancement. In addition, Casely Hayford helped Revd Attoh-Ahuma with the publication of the *Wesleyan Methodist Times*. A member of the Gold Coast Legislative Council from 1916 to 1925, he led a delegation to London in 1920 seeking self-government and other constitutional reforms. When this tactic failed, he appealed directly to the League of Nations and forced Great Britain to enact a number of changes. When a serious breach emerged between the rising intellectual African bourgeoisie and the traditional chieftains, it was

Casely Hayford who did most to bridge the gap during the 1920s. A prolific writer, his most important works perhaps were *Ethiopia Unbound* and *Gold Coast Native Institutions*. He died on 11 August 1930.

HAYNES, George

Born in Pine Bluff, Arkansas, in 1880, Dr George Edmund Haynes became (in 1912) the very first African-American to achieve the PhD degree from Columbia University. His thesis, *The Negro at Work in New York*, was immediately published by the Columbia University Press. Two years before, he had co-founded the National League on Urban Conditions Among Negroes. This organization survived him and became known as the National Urban League. While serving as chairman of the social sciences department at Fisk University (1910-21), Haynes organized a training centre for social workers, after having founded, in 1910, the Association of Negro Colleges and Secondary Schools. In 1921, he became a member of the President's Unemployment Conference. After extensive field work on the African continent, he ended his academic career on the staff of the City College of New York (1950-59). His books included *The Negro Newcomer in Detroit, Michigan* (1917) and *The Trend of the Races* (1922). He died in 1960.

HEAD, Bessie

Born Bessie Amelia Emery in Pietermaritzburg, Natal, on 6 July 1937, this South African author wrote novels which graphically illustrated the social and cultural problems by which her country was then bedevilled. Most of her writing drew on her own experiences as an outcast in a society that had placed her white mother in a mental asylum when she became pregnant for a Zulu stable boy. Educated in a mission orphanage, she worked for a while as a teacher and then as a journalist with the liberal magazine, *Drum*. She was briefly married to Harold Head (1961-64), but joined the African National Congress (ANC) and moved with her son to Botswana where she wrote such gripping novels as *When Clouds Gather* (1969), *Maru* (1971), *A Question of Power* (1973) and *Serowe, Village of the Rainwind* (1981). A collection of her short stories appeared in *The Collector of Treasures* (1977). Bessie Head died on 17 April 1986.

HEAD, Wilson

Dr Wilson A. Head, formerly a civil rights activist in the United States, immigrated to Canada in 1959 and played a prominent role in the history of his adopted country until his death on 7 October 1993. Among his accomplishments was the formation of the Urban Alliance on Race Relations (UARR) in 1975 which sought to bring all ethnic groups together in a mighty struggle for racial equality in Canada. The UARR soon became one of the most important forces in the improvement of race relations, especially in the province of Ontario. Dr Head was named an executive of the Metro Committee on Race Relations and Policing in Toronto. He was the recipient of the Harry Jerome Award and an honorary doctorate for his staunch opposition to racism. A noted educator, historian and sociologist, Dr Head's legacy included the much acclaimed *Adaptation of Immigrants: Perceptions of Ethnic and Racial Discrimination* (1981). A scholarship fund was established in his memory.

HEADLEY, George

The son of a Barbadian father and a Jamaican mother, George Alphonso Headley was born in Panama on 30 May 1909. He was one of the most brilliant batsmen that the sport of cricket has spawned thus far and is generally considered the 'Father of Caribbean batsmanship'. Headley was the first great black batsman in the West Indies which had become accustomed to patrician white batsmen and plebeian black bowlers. His first-class record was simply amazing. He ended his illustrious career with an average of almost 70 runs per innings and was the first West Indian batsman to exceed 2,000 runs in Test (international) cricket. He was also the first Black ever appointed to lead a West Indian Test team when he was named captain for the match against England at Barbados in January 1948. His Test average of 60.83 per innings is still the best ever achieved by a West Indian. George Headley, after whom a pavilion is named at Sabina Park in Kingston, Jamaica, was for many years a source of inspiration to young black West Indian cricketers. He died on 30 November 1983.

HEALY, James

Revd James A. Healy, who is best remembered as the first African-American Roman Catholic bishop in the United States, was born in Macon, Georgia, in 1830. His studies in divinity included stints at the Sulpician Seminary in Montreal, Quebec, and at a similar institution in Paris, France. He was ordained a priest at Notre Dame Cathedral in Paris in 1854. Returning to the United States, he served for many years as a pastor in Boston, before his elevation to the bishopric of Portland, Maine, in 1875. Bishop Healy was made an assistant to the papal throne by Pope Leo XIII, but died two months afterwards on 5 August 1900.

HECTOR, Tim

Born in Antigua on 24 November 1942, Tim Hector became one of the best known activists and journalists throughout the Caribbean. He was among those young radicals of the 1960s who vigorously confronted what they saw as corruption and irresponsibility in the post-colonial order. As editor and publisher of *Outlet*, a hard-hitting weekly newspaper, he constantly drew attention to governmental impropriety. To combat the ruling party that Vere Bird and his sons were leading to victory after victory in Antigua and Barbuda, he formed the Antigua/Caribbean Liberation Movement (ACLM). He then joined Baldwin Spencer in founding the United Progressive Party (UPP) in 1992 after a host of parties had failed to unseat the Birds. While Hector's involvement had much to with energizing UPP, he could not share in its triumph when it finally won the elections in 2005. He died on 12 November 2002.

HENDERSON, Fletcher

James Fletcher Henderson, eminent pianist and pioneer of large jazz orchestras, was born on 18 December 1898 in Cuthbert, Georgia. He was untypical of his black contemporaries in that he was conventionally educated, having majored in chemistry and mathematics at Atlanta University. He drifted into music, while trying to support himself as a graduate student in New York City, and founded his celebrated orchestra which attracted such great musicians as Louis Armstrong, Chuck Berry, Roy Eldridge and Coleman Hawkins. Henderson is important as the first orchestrator to use written arrangements without deflating the spirit of improvisation and it was he who paved the way for the great jazz orchestras of the 1930s. He played a prominent role in the success of Benny Goodman's famous band by serving for many years as its staff orchestrator. Henderson died on 29 December 1952.

HENRIQUE

The son of King Afonso I of Kongo, Dom Henrique was the first bishop of the Kongo Kingdom and the first African native to be promoted to this office by the Roman Catholic Church. Born around 1495, he was sent at a very young age to be educated in Portugal where he became a fine scholar of Latin and theology. He was ordained a Catholic priest and elevated to a bishopric in 1520. He returned to Africa in 1521 and served as Bishop of Umiac (in Tunisia). Dom Henrique was one of the first Christian converts and scholars in what is now Zaire. He died around 1526 when he was still a relatively young man.

HENRY, Lenny

Lenworth George Henry, a well-known British entertainer, was born to Jamaican immigrant parents in Dudley, West Midlands, on 29 August 1958. He studied at Bluecoat Secondary Modern School and Preston College and later obtained a degree in English Literature from the Open University. His earliest television appearances came on a talent show, *New*

Faces, a competition he won in 1975 and 1976. He anchored the Saturday morning children's show, *Tiswas*, during 1978-80. He participated in *The Black and White Minstrel Show* for five years and then joined the hugely popular sketch show, *Three of a Kind*. Even so, he is perhaps best known for *The Lenny Henry Show* and for his role in the television series, *Chef!*, during the 1990s. Henry played the lead character in the Hollywood film, *True Identity*, and also tried his hand at soul-singing. He has won many awards, including BBC British Personality of the Year and the Edric Connor Inspiration to Black People Award.

HENRY, Thierry

Born on 17 August 1977 of French West Indian stock in Paris, France, Thierry Henry has become one of the finest football players in the world. He was only fifteen when he began his professional career with the Versailles Football Club in 1992. His exceptional skills were so obvious that he was always in demand. Monaco snapped him up in 1995; he was transferred to Juventus for £9 million in 1998 and he finished up at Arsenal (England) in 1999. Thierry has been successful wherever he has played, leading Monaco to a French championship in 1997 and Arsenal to several titles during the past seven years. As a member of the French national squad during 1997-2006, he scored 36 goals in 88 international contests.

HENSHAW, James Ene

James Ene Henshaw was born in Calabar, eastern Nigeria, in 1924. A physician by profession, he was educated in Onitsha (Nigeria) and in Dublin, where he received his medical degree from the National University of Ireland. Dr Henshaw is more famous for his literature than his medicine and is one of the most accomplished of all Nigerian dramatists. One of his plays, *The Jewels of the Shrine*, won first prize in the All Nigeria Festival of the Arts in 1952 and was so popular that it went through nine printings within a very short while. Almost as successful were *Medicine for Love: A Comedy in Three Acts* (1964); *Dinner for Promotion* (1967); *Enough Is Enough* (1976) and *A Song to Mary Charles* (1985). The popularity of Henshaw's two excellent collections of plays, *This is Our Chance* (1957) and *Children of the Goddess and Other Plays* (1966), led other Nigerian playwrights to imitate his style and method.

HENSON, Josiah

Born a slave in Charles County, Maryland, on 15 June 1789, Josiah Henson eventually escaped to Canada where he played a prominent role in the establishment of Dawn, the name given to the attempt in the 1840s to plant a Negro colony in Canada West. He himself had settled down in Colchester, Ontario, in the 1830s, with a family of eight children, and did rather well as a tobacco farmer. During the rebellion of 1837 he fought for the imperial government, fearing that a successful rebellion might have led to a return to slavery. A converted Christian, he preached and lectured in many parts of North America and Great Britain, even though he had remained illiterate for most of his life. He became revered for his courage and loyalty and was often confused with Uncle Tom in Harriet Beecher Stowe's celebrated novel. Such was the impression he created on all races and classes that, when he died in May 1883, at the advanced age of ninety-three, some fifty wagons followed his hearse to the graveside. His house was opened as a museum in 1948 and the cemetery of the British-American Institute (which Henson had done so much to create) was restored by the Ontario Historic Sites Board. Henson thus remains one of the best known of all Canadian Blacks, even though Dawn and the British American Institute both failed. An autobiography, ghost-written by Samuel A. Eliot, a former mayor of Boston, was first published in 1849.

HENSON, Matthew

Matthew Alexander Henson, who explored the North Pole with Robert Peary in 1909, was born in Charles County, Maryland, in 1866. He went to sea at the age of twelve, and worked at a variety of odd jobs before accompanying Peary on a trip to survey a canal route through Nicaragua in 1887. This was the first of several expeditions made by the two explorers. But while Peary was lionized after 1909, Henson descended into oblivion until rescued by the Explorers Club which offered him a life membership in 1937. Two years later, he was awarded a master's degree by Howard University and in 1948 he received a gold medal from the Geographical Society of Chicago. Henson was honoured by President Harry Truman in 1950 and by President Dwight Eisenhower in 1954. In 1961, the state of Maryland finally passed a bill providing for a bronze plaque to be erected in its state house in Henson's memory - some six years after the great explorer had died at the age of eighty-nine. In 1912, Henson had published an autobiography, entitled *A Negro Explorer at the North Pole*.

HERBERT, Peter

Peter Herbert is a political activist and chair of the Society of Black Lawyers in the United Kingdom. He has consistently championed the cause of racial equality within the criminal justice system and the legal profession as a whole. Appointed to the Judicial Studies Board in 1991, he was involved in the first ever series of race awareness training programmes for judges. Currently he is a member of the Attorney General's Race Advisory Committee and has sat as an immigration judge since 1996. He was appointed an Employment Tribunal chair and a recorder in the Crown

Court. He also chairs the pan-London independent Race Hate Crimes Forum, helping to combat racial violence in that city and is a non-executive director of Ealing Health Authority. His concerns range from employment discrimination and human rights violations on the part of the police to deaths in custody and child care law. He was awarded the American Bar Association diversity award in 2002.

HERCULES, Felix

Felix Eugene Michael Hercules was born in Venezuela in 1888 and raised in Trinidad, where his father was a civil servant. He attended the Queen's Royal College and then taught in San Fernando before pursuing further studies at the University of London. While at school, he had founded the Young Men's Coloured Association; in London, he continued to promote the principle of racial equality and became editor of the *African Telegraph* in 1918. Hercules made a tour of the West Indies in 1919 to investigate conditions there and to recruit support for the Society of Peoples of African Origin. He continued to preach the gospel of racial equality and to seek an alliance of all peoples of African extraction in Africa, the Caribbean, Britain and the United States. He was one of the chief promoters of Pan Africanism and colonial independence in the inter-war period when he persisted with his crusade in the face of careful surveillance and constant persecution by the British authorities.

HERNÁNDEZ, Gaspar Octavio

Gaspar Octavio Hernández, a celebrated Panamanian poet, was born very poor on 4 July 1893. He had to leave school with only a third grade education after his mother's untimely death. Largely self-taught and self-made, he rose rapidly to the directorship of several literary and political newspapers and to be elected to civic office. A founding member of the Union Intelectual Latinoamericana de Panama, he is commemorated by a bust raised in his memory on Santa Ana Square in Panama City and a Day of Journalism named in his honour. Hernández was merely twenty-five years old when he died in 1918, but is now recognized as Panama's leading modernist poet, thanks in large part to the posthumous publication of his works, *Obras selectas*, in 1966.

HERUY WALDA SELASSE

Born in Shawa on 7 May 1878, Heruy Walda Selasse began his administrative career as one of the secretaries in the Ethiopian imperial service of Menilek II. He gained rapid promotion mainly because of his skills as a linguist. He was made director of the municipality of Addis Ababa in 1921 and presided over the special tribunal appointed to settle disputes between Ethiopians and foreigners. Before that he had been a member of several Ethiopian delegations, including the one to England for King George V's coronation in 1911. Heruy Walda Selasse became director-general of the foreign office in 1929 and took over the post of foreign secretary in 1930. In 1931, he was sent as ambassador extraordinary to Japan. In addition to his work as administrator and diplomat, he edited the Ethiopian civil and ecclesiastical codes and translated the New Testament into Amharic. A prolific writer, he published some thirty books, many of which were printed by his own press in Addis Ababa. They included histories, novels, poetry, hymns, travel books and translations and mainly stressed the social and religious responsibilities of Ethiopians. He died in exile on 19 September 1938 during the Italian occupation of Ethiopia (1935-41). His remains were brought back for a decent burial in Ethiopia in 1942. Heruy Walda Selasse won a host of awards and distinctions from several foreign governments during his brilliant career. He is generally considered the father of modern Amharic literature and is also believed to have translated the Bible into Ge'ez.

HIGGINBOTHAM, Leon

Aloysius Leon Higginbotham, Jr was born in Trenton, New Jersey, on 25 February 1928. After graduating from Antioch College in 1949, he studied law at Yale University and began his practice in Philadelphia, Pennsylvania, in the early 1950s. In 1956, he was appointed special deputy attorney general for Pennsylvania. Six years later, Higginbotham became the first African-American head of a federal regulatory commission when he was asked to chair the Federal Trade Commission. In 1964, he was sworn in as judge of the US District Court for the Eastern District of Pennsylvania. From 1989 to 1993, he served as chief judge of the US Court of Appeals and in 1995 was awarded the Presidential Medal of Freedom, the highest civilian honour in the United States. In addition to his work as a very successful lawyer and jurist, Higginbotham also wrote the much acclaimed *In the Matter of Color; Race and the American Legal Process: The Colonial Period* (1978). He died on 14 December 1998.

HILL, Dan

Born in Oakville, Ontario, on 3 June 1954, Dan Hill has become one of Canada's most famous singers and song-writers who has been producing hit songs to critical acclaim for more than thirty years. He has earned a Grammy Award and several number one songs, top ten records, Juno Awards, platinum albums and gold albums. His songs have been performed by such entertainers as George Benson, Celine Dion, Rod Stewart and Tina Turner. His greatest triumph, perhaps, was the CD *Falling Into You* which he wrote for Celine Dion in 1997. Hill himself sang the title song, *It's a Long Road*, for the Sylvester Stallone movie, *First Blood*. He also wrote a novel, *Come Back*. Dan is the son of Dr Daniel Hill, the famous civil rights activist, and brother of Lawrence Hill, a prolific writer on the history of Blacks in Canada.

HILL, Daniel

Dr Daniel Grafton Hill III was born in Independence, Missouri, on 23 November 1923. After graduating with a BA from Howard University in 1948, he moved to Canada to study sociology at the University of Toronto where he achieved his MA and PhD degrees. From 1955 to 1958 he was a researcher for the Social Planning Council of Metropolitan Toronto. He became the first full-time director of the Ontario Human Rights Commission in 1962 and was appointed the first Ontario Human Rights Commissioner in 1972. One year later he resigned to establish his own human rights consulting firm. Throughout the 1960s and 1970s, Dr Hill did his best to ensure that the Ontario Human Rights Code was implemented. He played a prominent role in persuading the federal and provincial governments of Canada to liberalize their laws in such a manner as to make them less blatantly racist. He ensured that literally hundreds of allegations of racism were thoroughly investigated. Racist landlords and employers were frequently exposed by the vigilance of his commission. He also introduced a Training Manual on Race Relations for the Toronto Metropolitan Police. He founded the Ontario Black History Society (OBHS) in 1978 and presided over it until 1983. From 1984 to 1989 he served as the Ontario Ombudsman, the first Black to hold this position. He was the author of *Negroes in Toronto: A Sociological Study of a Minority Group* (1960) and *The Freedom Seekers: Blacks in Early Canada* (1981). Dr Hill was the recipient of many honours, including honorary doctorates from St Thomas University in 1986 and the University of Toronto in 2001. He received the Order of Ontario in 1993 and the Order of Canada in 1998. The Dr Daniel G. Hill Community Service Award was established by the OBHS in 1993 and the Dr Daniel G. Hill Scholarship and Support Fund was established by the Faculty of Social Work at the University of Toronto in 1994. He died on 26 June 2003.

HILL, Errol

Born in Trinidad, West Indies, on 5 August 1921, Errol Gaston Hill was one of the finest among Caribbean playwrights, poets, actors and directors. A graduate of the University of London (England) and the Yale School of Drama (United States), he served as a leader in the extra-mural department of the University College of the West Indies from 1953 to 1965. During the late 1960s he taught at the University of Ibadan in Nigeria and the City University of New York. He then became a most active professor of drama at Dartmouth College, New Hampshire. A prolific researcher and writer, he authored no fewer than 33 entries in *The Cambridge Guide to World Theatre* (1988) and 83 entries in *The Cambridge Guide to American Theatre* (1993). He also wrote eleven plays and produced/directed 120 performances in England, Nigeria and the United States. Hill received numerous awards, including the prestigious Humming Bird Gold Medal from the Government of Trinidad and Tobago in 1973, the Presidential Medal from Dartmouth for outstanding leadership and achievement in 1991and the Robert Lewis Medal for Lifetime Achievement in Theater Research from Kent State University in 1996. His best known plays perhaps are *The Ping Pong: a backyard comedy* (1955), *Man Better Man* (1965), *Broken Melody: a family drama in one act* (1966), and *Dance Bongo* (1970). He contributed several poems to various collections and journals and was an influential editor of the *Bulletin of Black Theatre* during the 1970s. Hill also published *The Trinidad Carnival: Mandate for a National Theatre* in 1972. He died on 15 September 2003.

HILL, Lauryn

Lauryn Hill established an enviable record in 1999 when she was nominated for ten Grammy Awards and won no fewer than five for her multi-platinum album, *The Miseducation of Lauryn Hill*. She had earlier performed with a group known as the Fugees. Her style, which is a quaint mixture of hip-hop and mainstream popular music, is often classified as 'neo-soul'. Born on 26 May 1975 in South Orange, New Jersey, Hill is not only a singer and songwriter but has sometimes appeared in the US television soap-opera, *As the World Turns*, and once acted alongside Whoopi Goldberg in the film *Sister Act 2: Back in the Habit*.

HILL, Lawrence

Son of the late Dr Daniel Hill and brother of Dan Hill, the popular Canadian singer, Lawrence Hill was born in Oakville, Ontario. He is a prolific writer of both novels and non-fiction. He has also been a journalist and a teacher of creative writing. In addition, he was a writer and media relations officer for the Ontario Ministry of Economic Development, Trade and Tourism (1995-98) and a Senior Writer for various Ontario government communications branches. Hill has also led cultural exchanges in Cameroon, Mali and Niger and has done volunteer work for the Ontario Black History Society and the Writers' Union of Canada. His two most successful novels were *Some Great Thing* (1992) and *Any Known Blood* (a best seller in 1997). His non-fiction includes *Trials and Triumphs: the Story of African-Canadians* (1993); *Women of Vision: the Story of the Canadian Women's*

Negro Association (1996) and *Black Berry, Sweet Juice: on Being Black and White in Canada* (2001). Hill holds a BA in economics from Laval University in Quebec and an MA in creative writing from the John Hopkins University in Baltimore.

HINES, Earl

Considered by many to be the greatest of jazz pianists, Earl Kenneth 'Fatha' Hines was born in Duquesne, Pennsylvania, on 28 December 1905. He pioneered the trumpet-style piano solo by producing hornlike solo lines in octaves with his right hand while stating the harmony with his left. This method influenced several generations of jazz pianists, including such musical giants as Dizzy Gillespie, Charlie Parker, Joe Sullivan and Jess Stacy. For a while Hines played with Louis Armstrong's band, and together they produced such classic recordings as *Louis Armstrong/Earl Hines* in 1927 and *Weather Bird* in 1928. Hines led his own band during 1928-47, recording several solo hits. He continued to tour Europe, Japan and the United States during the 1950s and 1960s. He died on 22 April 1983.

HINTON, William

One of the most highly respected of African-American physicians, Dr William Augustus Hinton was born in Chicago on 15 December 1883. After graduating from Harvard Medical School in 1912, he served at the Massachusetts General Hospital before becoming director of the Boston Dispensary Laboratory in 1916. In 1949, he was appointed professor of preventive medicine and hygiene at Harvard Medical School, the very first Black to become a professor at that institution. He was also the first Black to publish an academic textbook (*Syphilis and Its Treatment*). Dr Hinton became world famous for his work in venereal diseases. He developed the Hinton test for detecting syphilis and was also instrumental in developing the Davies-Hinton tests of blood and spinal fluid for the detection of syphilis. He died on 8 August 1959.

HOLMAN, Carl

Moses Carl Holman was a prominent civil rights leader who gave effective direction to the National Urban Coalition during the last two decades of his life. Born on 27 June 1919 in Minter City, Mississippi, he graduated magna cum laude from Lincoln University in 1942, earned an MA from the University of Chicago in 1944 and a master of fine arts degree from Yale University in 1954. Holman taught for some years at Clark College, Atlanta, before joining the staff of the United States Commission on Civil Rights in 1962. From 1971 to 1988, as president of the National Urban Coalition, he advocated programmes in housing, education, employment opportunities and job training. He also developed programmes to improve the scientific, mathematical and computer skills of minority and female children. He always emphasized the need for a mutual partnership between industry and government to foster inner-city development. He died on 9 August 1988.

HOLMES, Wendell

Dr Dwight Oliver Wendell Holmes was born in Lewisburg, West Virginia, in 1883. A graduate of Howard University and Columbia University, he became a respected educator and administrator. He served Howard University for many years, first as dean of its College of Education and then as dean of its Graduate School. He became the first black president of Morgan State University in Baltimore, Maryland. He wrote an important book, *The Evolution of the Negro College* (1934) and was for many years a contributing editor to the *Journal of Negro Education* and the *Negro College Quarterly*. Dr Holmes died in 1966.

HOLNESS, Renn

Dr Renn O. Holness is professor of Neurosurgery and director of Surgical Education in the Department of Surgery at Dalhousie University. In 1992 he became the first neurosurgeon to perform fetal issue transplants for Parkinson's disease. Born in Jamaica, he achieved the degrees MB and BS from the University of the West Indies in 1968 and pursued his postgraduate research in the United Kingdom before immigrating to Canada in 1972. Dr Holness returns often to the Caribbean to perform delicate operations and to assist in the training and the examination of medical students and neurosurgical trainees. He is actively involved in the medical education of developing countries and often arranges to bring patients to Halifax for critical surgery. He has written many seminal articles in medical journals and sits on the editorial board of the *Canadian Journal of Neurological Sciences*. He was honoured as a distinguished alumnus by the University of the West Indies when it celebrated its 50th anniversary in 1998.

HONWANA, Luís

One of Mozambique's outstanding short-story writers, Luís Bernardo Honwana was born in Lourenço Marques in 1942. He created a very favourable impression with his collection of short stories, *Nós Matamos a Cao-Tinhosa* (1964), in which he displays considerable skill in depicting the flaws and ironies of village life in his native country without being overly didactic. Honwana's literary career was interrupted in 1967 when he became a political prisoner at a time when Mozambique was still being governed harshly by Portugal.

HOPE, John

The son of a white father and a black mother, John Hope was born on 2 June 1868 in Augusta, Georgia. With his white skin, auburn hair and blue-grey eyes, he could easily have passed for White, but he identified himself as one of the Blacks, especially after he was robbed of his family's inheritance by white executors following his father's death. He advocated a liberal arts education for Blacks at a time when Booker T. Washington was emphasizing the value of technical and practical training. Hope became president of Atlanta Baptist College in 1906, when he was one of the first African-Americans to head a college of this size and importance. He served as YMCA secretary with Negro soldiers in France during World War I and was so appalled by the treatment of the Blacks that he helped to establish the Commission on Interracial Co-operation, over which he also presided. Hope was appointed the first president of Atlanta University in 1929 and served in that position until his death on 20 February 1936. He was also one of the founders of the Niagara Movement, a forerunner of the National Association for the Advancement of Colored People (NAACP).

HORTON, J.A.B.

Dr James Africanus Beale Horton was one of the first African physicians to serve as a regular officer in the British Army. Born near Freetown, Sierra Leone, on 1 June 1835, he was educated at the Church Missionary Society Grammar School and Fourah Bay Institution before studying medicine in England, where he qualified as a doctor in 1859. That same year he returned to Sierra Leone to join the British Army medical services as a staff surgeon. Largely because of his colour and race, Dr Horton was shifted to several parts of British West Africa during 1859-75 with little chance of meaningful promotion. Even so, he distinguished himself in 1869 fighting an outbreak of cholera in the Gambia, and in 1871 trying to combat a smallpox epidemic at Mumford. He was finally promoted to the rank of surgeon-major in 1875 and retired from the army in 1880. Dr Horton made significant contributions to African education and the study of African diseases. His *Political Economy of British West Africa* (1865) and *West African Countries and Peoples* (1868) urged the British government to pay more serious attention to the important matter of education and proposed a scheme for the establishment of a West African university. Horton also established a commercial bank to assist local entrepreneurs in Sierra Leone and offered scholarships for promising Africans to study abroad. When he died on 15 October 1883 he left a substantial portion of his estate to further scientific education. This bequest was subsequently used to endow three scholarships at the Sierra Leone Technical School. Horton is remembered not only as a physician and philanthropist, but as a keen critic of European racism even though most of his recommendations for the improvement of Sierra Leone were based on European models.

HOUPHOUËT-BOIGNY, Félix

Dr Félix Houphouët-Boigny, the first president of independent Côte d'Ivoire (1960-1993) was Africa's longest-serving head of state when he died in office on 7 December 1993. Born Dia Houphouët, on 18 October 1905, into a family of local chieftains in Yamoussoukro, he trained as a doctor and practised as a physician during the 1930s. In 1940 he inherited his father's cocoa and coffee plantations in Yamoussoukro and returned there to assume the role of chief of the canton. In 1945 he was elected to the French National Assembly and immediately persuaded that legislature to abolish the much-hated practice of forced labour in the colonies. As a keen supporter of independence he helped to negotiate its eventual terms with the French government and was elected president of the new republic in 1960. By openly rejecting communism, he was able to gain generous material aid from the western countries and to play a key role in the upgrading of his country's agriculture. But his paternalistic style led to much dissatisfaction in his later years and he was forced in 1990 to allow multi-party elections for the first time. There was also some criticism of his willingness to spend some $200 million on the erection of a huge basilica in Yamoussoukro, Notre Dame de la Paix, at a time when Côte d'Ivoire itself was in the throes of economic distress. He is nevertheless remembered as the nationalist leader whose guidance provided Côte d'Ivoire with three decades of political stability and with substantial economic growth during much of his early reign.

HOUSTON, Charles

The son of a prominent Howard University professor, this outstanding lawyer and educator was born in Washington, D.C. in 1895. After graduating from Harvard Law School in 1923, Charles Hamilton Houston divided his time and energy between university teaching and private practice. He and his father established the famous firm of Houston and Houston in 1924 while he was serving as a law instructor at Howard University. He rose to the rank of vice-dean at that School of Law during the early 1930s, while also serving as a member of the board of education of the District of Columbia. In 1944 he was appointed to the President's Committee on Fair Employment Practices. Houston served on several national organizations and committees but is best remembered for his work as counsel for the National Association for the Advancement of Colored People (NAACP). He did as much as any other single individual to demolish the old walls of racial segregation and discrimination in American education, housing and employment. A tireless supporter of the civil rights movement, he was posthumously awarded the Spingarn Medal by the NAACP. Charles Houston died in 1950.

HOWELLS, Rosalind

Baroness Rosalind Patricia-Anne Howells was elevated to the peerage as Baroness Howells of St David, of Charlton in the London Borough of Greenwich in 1999. Born in Grenada, West Indies in 1931, she emigrated to the United Kingdom and served for some years as the director of the Greenwich Racial Equality Council and a Community and Equal Opportunity Worker. An active campaigner for justice in the field of race relations, she is a trustee of the Stephen Lawrence Trust and has worked with the London Voluntary Services Council, the Carnival Liaison Committee and the Greater London Action in Race Equality. She was the first black woman to sit on the Greater London Council's Training Board, the first female member of the Court of Governors of the University of Greenwich and was the vice-chair of the London Voluntary Services Council.

HOYTE, Desmond

Hugh Desmond Hoyte became the second president of Guyana after the sudden death on 6 August 1985 of Forbes Burnham, whose socialist system he gradually dismantled. Born on 9 March 1929, he was educated at St Barnabas Anglican School and Progressive High School before studying law in London, England. He set up his private practice in British Guiana (as it then was) in 1960 and soon became one of the leaders of the Guyana Bar Association. As a member of Burnham's People's National Congress (PNC), he entered parliament in 1968 and was appointed home affairs minister in 1969 and finance minister in 1970. In August 1984, Hoyte was made first vice-president and prime minister. He remained president of Guyana from 1985 until his PNC party lost the general elections of 1992. Thereafter he remained a formidable force while in opposition and did much to prevent the People's Progressive Party (PPP) from making retrograde constitutional changes. He died on 22 December 2002.

HUBBARD, William D.

William deHart Hubbard was born in Cincinnati, Ohio, on 25 November 1903. He was a great American track star who specialised in the sprints and the jumps and competed in the Olympic Games of 1924 and 1928. His long jump victory in the Paris Games of 1924 made him the first black athlete to win an Olympic gold medal in an individual event. Hubbard tied the world records in the 60 and 100 yard dashes and established a new mark for long jumpers when he leapt 25'10.75" in 1925. After his graduation from the

University of Michigan, he worked for the Cincinnati Recreation Commission. In 1942 he was appointed Race Relations Advisor for the Federal Public Housing Authority that provided better housing for minorities. In 1957 Hubbard was voted into the National Track Hall of Fame. He died on 23 June 1976.

HUBBARD, William P.

William Peyton Hubbard was born in Toronto, Ontario, in 1842. From a livery boy in one of his uncle's stables he rose to become an important member of the Toronto City Council and to serve as deputy mayor in the absence of Toronto's chief officer. Hubbard, who was largely self-taught in finance and law, became a successful real estate agent before entering politics and being elected an alderman in 1894. He retained his seat on the council for many years. He helped to plan the city's parks and served during 1904-1907 as the city comptroller. He was held in such high respect by his peers that a portrait of him was placed in the Toronto city chambers in 1914. William Hubbard died in 1935. In his honour, Hydro One awards scholarships to two black students each year to study power-related industries at universities and colleges.

HUGHES, Langston

One of the greatest of all African-American poets and playwrights, James Langston Hughes was born in Joplin, Missouri, on 1 February 1902. He became a truly prolific writer and critic. His first book of poems, *The Weary Blues*, appeared in 1926. One year later, he published another collection, *Fine Clothes to the Jew*. His latest verses appeared in *The Panther and the Lash* (1967). His first book of short stories, *Ways of White Folk*, was published in 1935. He also wrote a number of plays, including *Scottsboro Limited* (1932) and *Mulatto* (1935). His best-known novel perhaps was *Not Without Laughter* (1930). Altogether, Hughes published ten volumes of poetry and more than sixty short stories, while producing a variety of dramas, anthologies and operas. He also wrote two autobiographies: *The Big Sea* (1940) and *I Wonder as I Wander* (1956). His daily column, *Simple Says*, ran in the *Chicago Defender* from 1940 until 1962. In 1960, Hughes was awarded the Spingarn Medal by the NAACP as 'Poet Laureate of the Negro race'. He died on 22 May 1967. He is fondly remembered as one of the leading authors in the Harlem Renaissance.

HURSTON, Zora Neal

Zora Neale Hurston was born in Eatonville, Florida, on 7 January 1903. She attended Morgan State University, Howard University and Barnard College during the 1920s, specializing in folklore studies. She continued to pursue folklore studies while travelling extensively through the British West

Indies, Haiti, Florida and Louisiana during the 1930s. She eventually wrote several volumes of folklore, including *Mules and Men* (1935). Her other books included such novels as *Jonah's Gourd Vine* (1934), *Their Eyes Were Watching God* (1937), and *Seraph on the Suwanee* (1948). She also published an autobiography, *Dust Tracks on the Road*, in 1943. Apart from being one of the leading black female writers of the 20th century, Zora Neale Hurston wrote several radio scripts for a station in Cincinnati, Ohio, and served towards the end of her career as a drama instructor at North Carolina College. She died on 28 January 1960.

HUSBANDS, Clifford

His Excellency Sir Clifford Straughn Husbands has been the Governor General of Barbados since 1996. Born at Morgan Lewis Plantation on 5 August 1926, he was educated at Parry School and Harrison College before teaching for three years at Parry School. He then studied law at the Middle Temple in London, England, and was called to the bar in 1952. He returned home to practise law and acted briefly as deputy registrar. During 1954-60, Sir Clifford held various legal appointments in Antigua, Grenada, Montserrat and St Kitts. Moving back to Barbados in 1960, he assumed duties as assistant to the attorney general and legal draftsman. He became a Queen's Counsel (QC) in 1968, judge of the Supreme Court in 1976, acting Chief Justice and occasionally acting Governor General. In 1986 he was awarded the Gold Crown of Merit by the Government of Barbados and in 1989 was named a Companion of Honour. He was elevated to a knighthood in 1996 when he succeeded Dame Nita Barrow as the island's Governor General.

HUTTON-MILLS, Thomas

Born in 1865, Thomas Hutton-Mills became an eminent Gold Coast politician and lawyer. Educated at Duker School in Accra and the Wesleyan School in Freetown, Sierra Leone, he went to England to study law in 1891 and was called to the bar in 1894. He practised law briefly in the Gambia and eastern Nigeria before settling down in Accra, where as a young man he had taken part in the famous riots of 1885. Always keenly interested in education and politics, Hutton-Mills became a member of the Aborigines' Rights Protection Society (ARPS), was appointed an unofficial member of the Gold Coast Legislative Council and served also on the Accra Town Council at the end of the 1890s. He played a leading role in the meeting of the National Congress of British West Africa (NCBWA) to discuss common problems facing the Gambia, the Gold Coast, Nigeria and Sierra Leone. His agitation was partly responsible, too, for the founding of Achimota College in the Gold Coast in 1927. Working closely with nationalists like

Casely Hayford, Hutton-Mills was one of the great leaders of British West Africa throughout the early portion of the 20th century. He was also an active sportsman who played cricket and tennis to a high standard, representing the Gold Coast in a cricket match against Nigeria in 1905 when he was already in his fortieth year. He died on 14 March 1931.

IBAKA

A truly remarkable African who rose from slavery to become one of the wealthiest merchants engaged in the Zaire River trade in the nineteenth century, Ibaka was born around 1820. He took his name from his master, a powerful chief who had done much to establish the kingdom of Bolobo. When the original Ibaka died, his head slave took over all of his master's enterprises and claimed the throne for himself. Easily defeating all rival claimants, he exercised complete control over the kingdom of Bolobo. Ibaka then sought to strengthen himself against his neighbours by allying with the Europeans when they arrived in the region in the early 1880s. He is thus remembered as one of the African chiefs who accepted the arrival of the Europeans and tried to use them to augment his own political prestige and material wealth. But far more significant was his ability to rise from the very lowest to the very highest rung of his own society. Ibaka's courage and shrewdness, never in doubt, came to serve as a source of inspiration to millions of disadvantaged Africans. He died around 1889.

IDRIS ALOOMA

Idris Alooma was one of the greatest monarchs in the history of northwestern Africa. It was during his reign (1570-1602) that the kingdom of Kanem-Bornu reached the height of its power. A convert to Islam, he bureaucratized his government and placed it on firm Islamic foundations. He established a high court of law and staffed it with professional judges who dispensed Muslim law. He also equipped his army with Turkish muskets and employed Turkish advisers to defeat his neighbours during the period when the Songhai Empire had begun to decline. Idris Alooma is a classic example of a Renaissance African prince who effectively employed many of the systems and strategies then prevalent in western Europe. He used diplomacy and warfare to expand and centralize his empire, ensuring that all authority came to revolve around the monarchy at the expense of local chieftains. An excellent administrator, he delegated power to efficient bureaucrats and advisers but ensured that they were all responsible only to him.

IEN, Marci

Marci Ien was born in Toronto in 1969 and graduated as a journalist from Ryerson University (Toronto) in 1991. Hired immediately by Ontario

Network Television (ONTV), she worked as a week-end newswriter and was shortly promoted to general assignment reporter with occasional anchoring duties. In 1995 her news serial, *Journey to Freedom*, a look at Canada's role in the Underground Railroad (which operated during the 19th century), won her a News Directors' Award for Excellence. In 1997 she became a member of Canadian Television (CTV)'s news team in Atlantic Canada. She then returned to Toronto to anchor CTV Newsnet, that national network's 24-hour cable news service.

IGWEMEZIE, Jude

Dr Jude O. Igwemezie is an expert in structural mechanics, stress and failure analysis, design, testing and assessment of railway engineering structures, and derailment investigations. During the past twenty years or so, he has written or co-authored more than sixty articles, reports and miscellaneous publications on railway track, bridge structures and vehicle components. He has thus made significant contributions to the railway industry and was the first engineer to develop a methodology for setting railhead wear limits. A holder of several important patents, Dr Igwemezie has, among other things, designed derailment containment barriers for residential areas; designed the high relief joint-bar that allows more rail wear for several North American railroads; developed a formula for estimating the design load of concrete ties used on open deck railway bridges; developed a relationship between dynamic load that will cause rail to fracture and rail temperature, residual stresses, railhead defect size and rail fracture toughness; developed a standard for residual stress in rails; and designed special tie plates that fasten rail joints to wood ties, to reduce insulated and non-insulated joint damage. Most of these innovations have proved useful to railway companies all across North America. Born in Nigeria, Jude Igwemezie emigrated to Canada in 1978 and completed his education at McGill University, graduating with a PhD in engineering in 1988. He is the founder (1992) and chief executive officer of such businesses as ARRT, a railway consulting, engineering and research company; the UniP Tie Company (1994) to market the UniP steel tie and fastener he invented for use of heavy haul and light rail track and NorFast Inc., created in 1998 to market his premium elastic rail fasteners. A renowned specialist in the field of derailments, he has often appeared as an expert witness in litigations in Canada and the United States. Dr Igwemezie was given the Harry Jerome Award for Professional Excellence in 2001. His steel tie and fastener also won a Canadian Design Engineering Award in 1997.

INCE, Paul

Born in Ilford on 21 October 1967, Paul Emerson Carlyle Ince became the first black football player to captain an England team. In a long career that has so far stretched over more than two decades, he has played for six English sides and an Italian club, Inter Milan (during 1995-97). His longest stint was 281 matches with Manchester United during 1989-95. He played 53 matches at the international level. A thoughtful player, Ince was the acknowledged leader in most of the teams for which he performed.

ISAAC, Julius

Born in Grenada, West Indies, The Hon Mr Justice Julius Alexander Isaac immigrated to Canada in 1951 and studied law at the University of Toronto. After practising privately for some years, he served as chief adviser to all federal prosecutors and adviser on criminal matters with other countries. In 1989, he was appointed Chief Justice of Toronto's Supreme Court and, two years later, became Chief Justice of the Federal Court of Canada. One of the highest ranking black jurists in the history of Canada, Justice Isaac was appointed a supernumerary judge with the Federal Court of Appeal in 1999. He was awarded honorary doctorates by the University of Windsor in 1994 and the University of the West Indies in 2000. He also received one of Canada's Governor General 125th Anniversary Medals in 1992, a Silver Jubilee Award of Grenada in 1999 and the Order of Canada in 2006.

IYASU I

Known as Adyam-Saggad I during his reign (1682-1705) as Emperor of Ethiopia, this remarkable ruler has since come to be remembered as Iyasu the Great. Born in 1658, he became a truly brilliant general who extended the borders of Ethiopia in all directions. He was also a gifted administrator who built churches and schools and tried to reconcile the sectarian differences which then divided his kingdom. Very tolerant in matters of the faith, he arranged (and presided over) several councils during his reign. Grief stricken over the loss of his favourite concubine in 1705, he suddenly abdicated. One year later, he was assassinated (on 13 October 1706). He left a lasting impression on Ethiopian history and religion.

JABAVU, Davidson

Davidson Don Tengo Jabavu, a famous Xhosa scholar, journalist and statesman, was born in Healdtown, South Africa, on 20 October 1885. The son of John Tengo Jabavu, an influential South African journalist and politician, he was educated in local schools and in England, where he achieved his BA from the University of London in 1912 and a Dip Ed in 1914 from Birmingham University. Jabavu became an excellent musician and linguist and was fluent in such languages as English, Sotho, Tswana and

Xhosa. He visited the United States in order to examine the educational institutions for Blacks there. Returning to South Africa in 1915, he became the first lecturer at the Native College of Fort Hare (now Fort Hare University), where he taught Bantu languages from 1916 to 1946. He also served for many years as the secretary of the College Senate as well as a warden of one of the men's halls of residence. He was promoted to the rank of professor in 1942. Jabavu, meanwhile, had succeeded his father as editor of *Imvo zabantsundu* (Opinion of the Blacks) which John Tengo Jabavu had founded. He also helped to establish the All-African Insurance Company just before his death. Always anxious to bridge the gulf between the races, he worked hard with the Joint Councils of Europeans and Natives and the South African Institute of Race Relations (1932-59). Such was the universal respect in which Jabavu was held that he received an honorary doctorate from Rhodes University in 1946; a medal was struck in his honour by the Royal African Society and a memorial stone was erected on his grave at Middlerift, Cape Province, after his death in 1959. Jabavu also made a substantial contribution to South African literature with such major works as *The Black Problem* (1920), *Bantu Literature* (1921), *The Life of John Tengo Jabavu* (1922), *What Methodism Has Done for the Natives* (1923), *The Segregation Fallacy* (1928), and *The Influence of English on Bantu Literature* (1943).

JABAVU, John Tengo

John Tengo Jabavu, a noted South African journalist, teacher and politician, was born in Healdtown on 11 January 1859. He achieved a Government Teacher's Certificate in 1875 and taught at Somerset East School during 1876-81. After contributing several articles to the *Cape Argus*, he was named editor of *Isigidimi sama Xosa* (1881-83). In 1884 he founded the Xhosa newspaper, *Imvo zabantsundu* (Opinion of the Blacks) at King William's Town and served for the next three or four decades as its managing editor, chief reporter, advertising salesman, copyreader, composer and clerk. It was the first newspaper to be established and run completely by an African native. Jabavu must have written more than 2,000 articles of all kinds to keep it afloat. Very devout in matters of the faith, he remained a staunch member of the Wesleyan Conference and was instrumental in founding a Night School for adults in King William's Town in 1891. His role in the founding of the Native College at Fort Hare in 1916 was so substantial that for many years it was simply known as Jabavu's College. In his later years, however, his reputation among South African Blacks was considerably undermined by his decision to support Afrikaner politicians out of his pronounced dislike for Cecil Rhodes. But he was eulogized in a most fulsome manner by the South African prime minister, Jan Christian Smuts, when he died on 10 September 1921. A well-written biography of him was published by his son, Davidson Don Tengo Jabavu, in 1922.

JABAVU, Noni

Daughter of the famous John Tengo, Noni Helen Nontando Jabavu was born on 20 August 1919 in Cape Province, South Africa. After attending local schools, she completed her education in England where she became a film technician and married an English film-director. She wrote two well-known novels, in which she was among the first of the Commonwealth authors to mix formal English with local idioms. Her *Drawn in Colour, African Contrasts* (1960) and *The Ochre People: Scenes from a South African Life* (1963) included several dialogues in the Xhosa dialect.

JABBAR, Kareem Abdul

Born Lew Alcindor of Trinidadian parents in New York City on 16 April 1947, Kareem Abdul Jabbar was the dominant figure in professional basketball for almost two decades (1970-89). Though raised as a Roman Catholic, he converted to Islam and changed his name in 1971. Standing 7 ft 2 in tall, Jabbar was a simply imposing figure on the court and proved himself an outstanding player at every level. After leading the UCLA Bruins to three successive NCAA championships during 1965-67, he left an amazing record of achievement with the Milwaukee Bucks and the Los Angeles Lakers. When he retired in 1989, Jabbar held the National Basketball Association (NBA) records for games played (1,560), minutes played (57,446) and points scored (38,387).

JACKSON, Colin

Born on 18 February 1967 in Cardiff, Wales, Colin Ray Jackson attended Llanedeyrn High School where he excelled in many sports. He became one of the finest hurdlers in the history of athletics and established two long-standing records: 7.30 secs for the 60 metre indoor event in 1994 (which still stands) and 12.91 secs for 110 metre at the World Championships at Stuttgart in 1993 (which lasted until 2006). His triumphs in 110 metre competition included four consecutive Gold Medals in European Championships, two Gold Medals in World Championships and two Gold Medals in Commonwealth Games. His Achilles heel was Olympic competition, in which he managed to garner only one Silver Medal (at Seoul in 1988). Jackson was honoured with the award of the MBE in 1990 and the CBE in 1992. He now works as a sports commentator for the British Broadcasting Corporation (BBC).

JACKSON, Jesse

Revd Jesse Louis Jackson, a prominent civil rights leader and clergyman, was born in Greenville, South Carolina, on 8 October 1941. Educated at the Agricultural and Technical College of North Carolina and the Chicago

Theological Seminary, he was ordained a Baptist minister in 1968. Jackson gained fame as the protégé of Dr Martin Luther King Jr who had successfully organized Operation Breadbasket in Chicago during the early 1960s. This was an alliance of black businessmen and clergy for the purpose of promoting job opportunities for Blacks with firms doing business in the black community. Its purpose also was to provide sales outlets for merchandise produced by Blacks. The project was so successful that the idea gradually spread to other urban centres across the United States, with Jackson serving as national director from 1967 to 1971. He founded another economic programme, People United to Save Humanity (PUSH) in the early 1970s. After Dr King's assassination in 1968, Jackson emerged as the most eloquent of the young political activists, preaching a gospel of moderation, sobriety and self-help. He campaigned on behalf of many black leaders seeking political office and made a significant contribution to Harold Washington's election as mayor of Chicago in 1983. In the 1980s, too, he worked tirelessly to increase voter registration of Blacks while he himself sought the Democratic nomination for president in 1984. His participation in the presidential campaigns raised issues of importance to minorities and ensured that the eventual winner could not afford to neglect the growing political activism among US Blacks. Even though he made a number of blunders during the campaign, he at least succeeded in reinforcing his reputation as one of the nation's most eloquent public speakers and breaking the taboo against a Black running for president. He remains one of the most important figures on the North American political scene.

JACKSON, Mahalia

This outstanding gospel singer became a symbol of black protest through her association with the civil rights movement during the 1960s. Mahalia Jackson was born in New Orleans, Louisiana, on 26 October 1911. She rose to prominence as a singer in the 1930s when she took part in a cross-country gospel tour. In 1934, she made her first recording, *God Gonna Separate the Wheat from the Tares*. In 1945, her *Move On Up a Little Higher* became the first gospel record to sell more than a million copies. Later Jackson records also sold in the millions as they were very popular in both hemispheres. This led to her first appearance at Carnegie Hall on 4 October 1950, which was a sellout. Mahalia Jackson toured Europe and the United States with consistent success after that and became known worldwide as the 'Queen of the Gospel Song'. She died on 27 January 1972.

JACKSON, Maynard

Maynard Holbrook Jackson was born in Dallas, Texas, on 23 March 1938. Entering Morehouse College at the age of fourteen he received a BA in 1956 and earned his LLD with honours from the North Carolina Central University School of Law in 1964. Jackson was elected vice-mayor of Atlanta in 1969 and became, in 1973, the first black mayor of that city. He was re-elected in 1977 but was debarred by law from seeking a third term in 1981. In that year, he successfully promoted the candidacy of Andrew Young, Jr. He served as mayor again during 1990-94. A liberal Democrat, who always received support from white voters because of his moderation, Jackson worked tirelessly to bridge the differences between the races in Atlanta. His notable achievements included the implementation of many affirmative-action policies, especially the pioneering programme which reserved a portion of government contracts for minority businesses and firms, and the expansion of Hartsfield Atlanta International Airport. He also helped to bring the Olympic Games to Atlanta in 1996. Jackson died on 23 June 2003.

JACKSON, Ovid

A native of Guyana, Ovid Jackson immigrated to Canada in 1965 and completed his education at the University of Windsor. He worked for some years in Owen Sound, Ontario, as a technical teacher and automotive specialist. In 1974 he was elected alderman of Owen Sound and then served as mayor of that city from 1983 until 1993 when he was elected to the federal parliament. He has been the representative of Owen Sound in Ottawa ever since. As a Liberal member of parliament he has served on several standing committees and as parliamentary secretary to the president of the Treasury Board. Jackson was awarded a Governor General 125th Anniversary Medal in 1992.

JACKSON, Richard

Dr Richard Lawson Jackson is Professor Emeritus of African-Hispanic Studies at Carleton University, where he taught Spanish for more than thirty years until his retirement in 1995. Born in the United States, he completed his education at Ohio State University before immigrating to Canada in 1963. He is one of the outstanding experts in Spanish literature in the New World and has played a key role in the founding of such periodicals as the *Afro-Hispanic Review*, *Callaloo* and the *Journal of Caribbean Studies*. He is the author of several books, including *The Black Image in Latin American Literature* (1976); *Black Writers in Latin America* (1979); *Black Writers and the Hispanic Canon in Latin America* (1997); and *Black Writers and Latin America: Cross-Cultural Affinities* (1998).

JAJA

Born around 1821, Jaja was the king of Opobo in what is now part of Nigeria. He was fiercely opposed to British interference with his country's trade and commerce and he attempted therefore to boycott British goods and to prohibit their trade with the palm-oil produced by his own people. The British government retaliated by kidnapping Jaja and deporting him to the West Indies. He spent some time in Barbados, where he became a local celebrity, and was only allowed to return to west Africa when he became critically ill. The British relented too late, as Jaja died on the way back home in 1891. King Jaja's career bears eloquent testimony to the cruelty of British methods in dealing with African sovereigns with whom they signed agreements and made promises that they never intended to keep. Jaja remains a national hero in Nigeria and his memory lives on in Barbados where he features in a popular folk-song.

JAMES, C.L.R.

Arguably the brightest scholar thus far produced by Trinidad and Tobago, Cyril Lionel Robert James was born in Tunapuna on 4 January 1901. Educated at Queen's Royal College in Port-of-Spain, he taught in his native country from 1918 to 1932 before emigrating to England. There he distinguished himself as a music critic and cricket correspondent for the *Manchester Guardian*, an eloquent lecturer with Marxist tendencies, and a political activist advocating decolonization and social justice. James gave fervent support to the independence movements in Africa and the Caribbean and produced such seminal works as *The Life of Captain Cypriani* (1932), later reprinted as *The Case for West-Indian Self-Government*, and a classic, *The Black Jacobins* (1938), a powerful Marxist study of the Haitian revolution of the 1790s. Moving to the United States, James wrote numerous articles for radical and socialist periodicals and was expelled for his communist sympathies in 1953. Returning to Trinidad, he helped Dr Eric Williams establish the People's National Movement (PNM) as the most vibrant political organization there and became secretary of the West Indies Federal Labour Party (1958-60). After quarrelling with Williams, he went back to England where he spent most of his remaining days. In 1963, James produced another classic, *Beyond a Boundary*, which many scholars still regard as the finest piece of cricket literature. His other works included a novel, *Minty Alley* (1936), *World Revolution* (1937), *Mariners, Renegades and Castaways* (1953), *A History of Pan African Revolt* (1969), *Notes on Dialectics* (1971), *Nkrumah and the Ghana Revolution* (1977) and *Cricket* (1986), a collection of essays written during 1935-85. James died on 31 May 1989.

JAMES, Daniel, Jr

Brigadier General Daniel 'Chappie' James, Jr was born in Pensacola, Florida, on 11 February 1920. After graduating from Tuskegee Institute in 1943, he was commissioned a second lieutenant in the US Air Force. During the Korean War he flew more than 100 combat missions and, in 1957, was promoted to the post of chief air staff officer. In 1966, James was appointed deputy commander for operations, Eighth Tactical Fighter Wing, Thailand, and led more than seventy missions over North Vietnam. In 1970 he became the first black brigadier general in the US Air Force and, for the next five years, was the spokesman in the Pentagon for the secretary of defence. In 1975 he was appointed commander in chief of the North American Air Defence Command, responsible for all US and Canadian air space defence forces. He had then become the highest ranking black officer in the US armed forces. A few weeks after seeking early retirement, James died of a heart attack on 25 February 1978.

JAMES, June

Dr June Marion James was born in Trinidad, West Indies, on 23 June 1939. She received her elementary and secondary training in the Caribbean and completed her medical studies at the University of Manitoba, Canada. Remaining in Winnipeg ever since her graduation in 1967, she has specialized in paediatrics and immunology and is one of the best-known allergy specialists in Canada. Dr James has published numerous articles in medical journals and has presented a number of papers to professional audiences on such problems as drug therapy for asthma, immunotherapy and clinical immunology. She was elected as Councillor of the College of Physicians and Surgeons of Manitoba in 1994 and was its president during 2001-02. She has served on several professional boards and committees, including the Medical Advisory Board of the Manitoba Lung Association, the Manitoba Drug Standards and Therapeutic Committee, the Board of Trustees of the United Way, and the board of governors of the Manitoba Museum of Man and Nature. Apart from her duties as a professor of medicine at the University of Manitoba, she is also the medical director of the Family Asthma Programme and a specialist staff consultant, Health Sciences Centre, Winnipeg. Dr James is best known, however, as a dedicated community servant with an active involvement in a wide range of organizations promoting racial equality and women's rights. As president of the Harambee Housing Corporation, she was able to achieve funding of $5 million for a 54-unit housing co-op, which provided affordable accommodation to a culturally diverse population. She has presided over such organizations as the Museum of Man and Nature, the Manitoba Museum Foundation, the Canadian Automobile Association, United Way Board of Trustees and the University of Manitoba Alumni Board. She has bombarded the federal and provincial governments with lively briefs on such issues as pension reform, daycare reform, workplace and employment standards for domestics in Canada, and human rights legislation. She was a nominee for the Citizen of the Year Award in 1981, when she was chosen the YWCA Woman of the Year. Her numerous awards include the Schering Fellow Travel Award (1975), the Cross of Lorraine from the Canadian Lung Association Asthma Program (1980), the Canada 125th Anniversary Medal (1992), the Queen's Golden Jubilee Medal (1993), the Citation for Citizenship from the federal government of Canada (1993), the Physician of the Year Award from the Manitoba Medical Association (2000) and the Order of Manitoba (2004). In addition to these honours and distinctions, Dr June Marion James has received medals and plaques from such organizations as the Citizenship Council of Manitoba, the Black History Month Celebration Committee of Winnipeg and the Congress of Black Women of Canada.

JAMMEH, Yahya

His Excellency Alhagi Yahya Alphonse Jemus Jebulai Jammeh, the President of The Gambia, was born in the Foni Kansala District on 25 May 1965. After studying at Gambia High School, he joined the national army and rose to the rank of colonel. He took control of the country in a military coup in 1994 and was elected as president in controversial circumstances in 1996. He founded the Alliance for Patriotic Reorientation and Construction as his political party and was re-elected in 2001. His government has been marred by allegations of corruption and autocracy as he has muzzled the press and dealt severely with his critics.

JANVIER, Louis-Joseph

Born in Port-au-Prince on 7 May 1855, Louis-Joseph Janvier became one of Haiti's finest and most prolific authors. He was also a diplomat, lawyer and physician. Educated at the Lycée Pétion in Port-au-Prince, he won a scholarship to France where he studied medicine and graduated as a doctor in 1881. Having also achieved diplomas in law, political science, economics and finance, he was attached to the Haitian legation in London, England, where he served in turn as secretary, chargé d'affaires, and minister during 1889-1904. He was appointed chancellor at the Haitian legation in Paris and then returned to Haiti after an absence of thirty years and campaigned unsuccessfully for the office of mayor of Port-au-Prince. Dr Janvier was an influential writer of both fiction and non-fiction. His major works included a novel, *Une chercheuse* (1889); a critical commentary, *L'évolution littéraire en Haiti* (1883); a travel brochure, *Promenade au Quartier Latin* (1883); an attempt to promote his country's tourism, *La République d'Haiti et ses visiteurs* (1840-1882), *réponse à Victor Cochinat* (1883); such polemics as *Les détracteurs de la race noire et de la République d'Haiti* (1882), *L'égalité des races* (1884), *Les affaires d'Haiti 1883-1884* (1884), and *Haiti aux Haitiens* (1884); seminal studies on Haiti's government, such as *Les Constitutions d'Haiti, 1881-1885* (1886) and *Du gouvernement civil en Haiti* (1905); a sociological study, *Le vieux piquet, scènes de la vie haitienne* (1884); a report on Haitian education, *La caisse d'épargne et l'école en Haiti* (1906); a medical treatise, *De la phtisie pulmonaire* (1881); and biographies of such former Haitian heroes as Louis Boisrond-Tonnerre, Henri Christophe, Jean-Jacques Dessalines and Toussaint Louverture. Janvier died on 24 March 1911.

JASPER, Lee

Lee Jasper, who was raised in Oldham, is a crusader for racial equality in Britain and the senior policy advisor on equalities to the mayor of Greater London. As such he is responsible for the development, enactment and promotion of equalities policies for the Greater London Authority (GLA). Previously he had been the director of the 1990 Trust, a leading policy organization on issues affecting African, Asian and Caribbean communities in the United Kingdom and Europe. For some years Lee was senior policy advisor to the Inner London Education Authority (ILEA) and director of development, the Mangrove Trust. He continues to sit on numerous boards and committees dealing with racial issues. He is also the president of the National Black Students Alliance and the deputy representative of the United Kingdom on the European National Anti-Racist Network. In 1998 he won a Premiere Community Award from Britain's largest black newspaper, *The Voice*, for his work in race relations.

JAWARA, Dawda

Sir Dawda Kairaba Jawara was the first president of the Republic of The Gambia. The son of a Mandinka trader, he was born on 16 May 1924 and was educated at Achimota College (Ghana) and the University of Glasgow (Scotland), where he qualified as a veterinary surgeon in 1953. He entered politics in 1959, won a seat in the legislature in 1960, and became minister of education. When his party won the elections in 1963, Jawara became The Gambia's first prime minister and led his country to independence in 1965. He was knighted in 1966. When a republican constitution was adopted in 1970, he became president. His ruling People's Progressive Party won three successive elections after independence so that by the end of the 1970s The Gambia had become one of the most stable democracies on the African continent. In 1981, however, Jawara came perilously close to being overthrown by a military coup, but was saved by Senegalese intervention. He and Abdou Diouf, president of Senegal, then agreed to establish the confederation of Senegambia with Diouf as president and Jawara as vice-president. Although the official language of the Gambia was English and French that of Senegal, their populations had always been closely related ethnically.

JEAN, Michaëlle

Her Excellency the Right Honourable Michaëlle Jean, Governor General
and Commander in Chief of Canada was installed in this office on 27
September 2005, thus becoming the first black woman to be honoured in
this fashion. She was born in Port au Prince, Haiti, on 6 September 1957
and immigrated to Canada with her parents in 1968. She achieved degrees
in Hispanic Languages and Literature from the University of Montreal
before pursuing further studies in European universities and becoming
fluent in five languages. After working for some time at Employment and
Immigration Canada and with Quebec shelters for battered women,
Madame Jean turned to journalism and became host and anchor with
Radio-Canada during the 1990s. She also participated in a number of
documentary films. By 2004 she was hosting her own very popular show,
Michaëlle, featuring a series of in-depth interviews with experts, enthusiasts
and visionaries. She has received several prestigious honours and awards for
her journalism and was almost everywhere regarded as an excellent choice
to be Queen Elizabeth II's representative in Canada.

JEMISON, Mae

On 12 September 1992, Dr Mae Carol Jemison became the first African-
American woman launched into space when she joined the seven-member
crew of the space shuttle *Endeavour*. Born in Decatur, Alabama, on 17
October 1956, she entered Stanford University at the age of sixteen on a
National Achievement Scholarship. In 1977 she entered Cornell University
Medical School, having already, by the age of twenty, achieved both a BS in
chemical engineering and a BA in African-American studies. She obtained
her MD in 1981 and then worked (1983-85) as the Area Peace Corps
Medical Officer for Sierra Leone and Liberia. While in Africa, Dr Jemison
pursued research on hepatitis B vaccine, schistosomiasis, and rabies. In
1985, she returned to the United States and worked as a general
practitioner in Los Angeles while attending graduate engineering classes.
Accepted into the National Aeronautics and Space Administration (NASA)
space programme, she was assigned to STS-47 Spacelab-J, a joint US-
Japanese mission. As the space mission specialist, she was responsible for
conducting research on space motion sickness and how it could be avoided.
She was also involved in bone cell research and oversaw an experiment that
studied the effect of weightlessness on the development of frogs from eggs
to tadpoles. The mission in 1992, which spent 190 hours in space, was
NASA's most successful one up to that time. Dr Jemison retired from NASA
in 1993 and founded the Jamieson Group, Inc., located in Houston, Texas,
to research, develop and implement advanced technologies suited to the
social, political, cultural and economic context of developing countries. She

is currently a member of the Dartmouth faculty in the department of Environmental Studies Programme. She is also the host of and a technical consultant to *World of Wonders*, a series seen weekly on the Discovery Channel. She has numerous awards, distinctions and honorary doctorates and was inducted into the National Medical Association Hall of Fame.

JENNINGS, Marlene

A native of Montreal, Marlene Jennings became, in 1997, the first black woman to win a seat in the Canadian parliament as a Quebec representative. She was re-elected in 2000 to represent the riding of Notre-Dame-de-Grace-Lachine. In 2001 she was appointed parliamentary secretary to the Minister for International Co-operation. She also served on several standing committees and was secretary of the National Liberal Caucus during 1997-2001. Jennings is a lawyer by profession and was called to the Quebec bar in 1988. She served on the Quebec Police Commission during 1988-90 and then as deputy commissioner for police ethics in the province of Quebec. She has made numerous public presentations on policing, police ethics, race relations and minority women's rights.

JENNINGS, Thomas

Born in 1791, Thomas Jennings was the very first African-American to receive a patent. He did so in 1821 when he patented the first dry-cleaning process. He also did so illegally since, as a slave, he was the property of his owner who then had the legal right to the fruits of his labour, both manual and intellectual. It was not until 1861 that the Confederate States of America granted patent rights to slaves and the federal government waited until 1870 before passing a patent law granting all Americans, including Blacks, the rights to their inventions. Even so, Jennings was allowed to sell his patent rights and to use the assets to purchase the liberty of himself and his family. He thus became a free tradesman and operated a dry cleaning business in New York City. His income went mostly to support the activities of the abolitionists. In 1831 he became assistant secretary for the First Annual Convention of the People of Color in Philadelphia, Pennsylvania. As is the case with most American Blacks of his vintage, he simply vanished from the historical records after that.

JEROME, Harry

Born in Prince Albert, Saskatchewan, on 30 September 1940, Henry Winston Jerome is remembered as one of Canada's finest athletes. He achieved his BSc and MA from the University of Oregon which he attended on a track scholarship during 1958-62. In 1962 he anchored his team to a world record in the 4 x 100 yard relay during the NCAA finals. Jerome represented Canada in three Olympic competitions and at one time held no fewer than seven world records in the sprints. Following his retirement from the track, he became a highly respected teacher in Vancouver, B.C., and served for several years as a Sport Canada consultant. He was inducted into the Canadian Sports Hall of Fame and was a recipient also of the Order of Canada in 1971. After his early death, on 7 December 1982, Harry Jerome was honoured by the establishment by the Black Business and Professional Association of coveted scholarships in his name to recognize black academic achievement, leadership and community service. A Harry Jerome International Track Classic, a prestigious track and field meet held annually in Burnaby, British Columbia, is named in his honour. The Stanley Park sea wall in Vancouver is graced with a nine foot bronze statue of him. In 2001 he was inducted into Canada's Walk of Fame.

JOHN, Errol

One of the most famous of all Trinidadian actors and playwrights, Errol John was born in Port-of-Spain on 20 December 1924. His best-known work was the compassionate but humorous *Moon on a Rainbow Shawl* which won him *The Observer's* prize for the best new playwright in 1957 and a Guggenheim fellowship in 1958. This play has been performed in many parts of the world, including Argentina, England, Hungary, Iceland and the United States and is still used as a classic text in West Indian schools. Some of his other plays included *The Tout* (1966), *Force Majeure* (1967) and *The Dispossessed*. John founded the Whitehall Players in Port-of-Spain during the early 1950s but spent most of his life in London, England, where he once portrayed Othello. He also had supporting roles in some Hollywood films, including *The African Queen*, *Heart of the Matter*, *The Nun's Story* and *Sins of Rachel Cade*. He died on 10 July 1988.

JOHNSON, Beverley

Born in Kingston, Jamaica, on 1 August 1940, Beverley C.H. Johnson immigrated to Canada in 1973 and worked from that year until 1991 as the first Human Rights Intake Officer at the Ontario Human Rights Commission. Throughout the 1990s she served as the first Human Rights Officer with the Ontario Public Service Employees' Union and held thus post until her retirement in 2005. She became the first black woman to be appointed to the Ontario Judicial Appointments Advisory Committee. A vigorous community servant and political activist, Beverley Johnson has been involved in a variety of causes. She is a founding member of the Congress of Black Women (Toronto Chapter), the Ontario coalition of Visible Minority Women and the Coalition of Black Trade Unionists. She is the first woman to chair the Caribbean

Cultural Committee and is a lifetime member of the Toronto Metro Children's Aid Society.

JOHNSON, Charles Spurgeon

Charles Spurgeon Johnson, one of America's most eminent sociologists and educators, was born in Bristol, Virginia, on 24 July 1893. He was educated at Virginia Union University and the University of Chicago. He first came to prominence in 1919 when he co-authored the report of the Governor's Committee to Investigate the Chicago Riots. That report, entitled *The Negro in Chicago*, was published as a book in 1922. In 1921, Johnson became director of research and investigation for the National Urban League and founded the league's journal, *Opportunity*. He moved on to Fisk University where he served as chairman of the department of social sciences from 1928 to 1946 and developed the Fisk Institute of Race Relations. In 1946, he was appointed the first black president of Fisk University, a post he was destined to hold until his death on 27 October 1956. In addition, he was an active participant in numerous government projects and committees throughout his career. In 1930, Johnson was one of three experts chosen by the League of Nations to investigate charges of slavery in Liberia. One year later, he was a consultant to President Hoover's Conference on Home Building and Home Ownership (Negro Housing Committee). In 1934, he served on the Tennessee Valley Authority and as a consultant to the US Department of Agriculture, Farm Tenancy Committee during 1936-37. In 1946, he was one of the US delegates to UNESCO and a member of the group sent to Japan by the US Department of State to reorganize that country's educational system. Johnson was a prolific writer as well. Apart from his study of the Chicago riots, his major books included *The Negro in American Civilization* (1930), *The Economic Status of the Negro* (1933), *Shadows on the Plantation* (1934), *The Collapse of Cotton Tenancy: 1933-1935* (1935), *The Negro College Graduate* (1936), *Growing Up in the Black Belt: Negro Youth in the Rural South* (1941), *Patterns of Negro Segregation* (1943), *To Stem the Tide: A Study of Racial Tensions in the United States* (1944), *Education and the Cultural Crisis* (1951), and a *Preface to Racial Understanding* (1953). Charles Spurgeon Johnson received honorary doctorates from Columbia University, Harvard University, Howard University, the University of Glasgow (Scotland) and Virginia Union University.

JOHNSON, Georgia

Born Georgia Douglas Camp in Atlanta in 1886, this eminent writer and activist was one of the first African-American women to gain general recognition as a poet. Educated at Atlanta University and the Oberlin Conservatory of Music, she became a pioneer in many civic and women's movements. In 1928, she wrote a tragic play, *Plumes*, which was performed in New York City. She left four volumes of excellent poetry: *The Heart of a Woman* (1919), *Bronze* (1920), *An Autumn of Love* (1929) and *Share My World* (1962). Georgia Douglas Johnson died in 1966.

JOHNSON, Jack

John Arthur Johnson, who became the first black man to hold the world's heavyweight boxing championship, was born in Galveston, Texas, on 31 March 1878. He won the title by knocking out Tommy Burns on 26 December 1908, and held it until 5 April 1915 when he was knocked out by Jess Willard in 26 rounds at the age of thirty-seven. Jack Johnson fought professionally until 1928 and engaged in exhibition matches as late as 1945. He died in an automobile accident on 10 June 1946. He left a chequered legacy. While there is no question that he was an excellent boxer, he became one of the most unpopular of all champions by taunting the White world to the point where a big campaign was set underway in several quarters of the globe to find a 'White hope' to wrest the title from him. Johnson's arrogance and extravagance did not sit well with a public accustomed to viewing Blacks as docile and subservient.

JOHNSON, James Weldon

This poet, lyricist, lawyer, song-writer, government official and teacher was born in Jacksonville, Florida, on 17 June 1871. After studying at Atlanta University and Columbia University, he was admitted to the Florida bar in 1897, becoming the very first black lawyer in that state. Already, in 1895, he had founded *The Daily American*, the first black daily newspaper in the United States. For some years at the beginning of the 20th century, Johnson collaborated with his brother in writing musical comedies and light operas. Their best-known song was *Lift Every Voice and Sing* which came to be generally regarded as black America's national anthem. In 1902, he wrote the popular song, *Under the Bamboo Tree*, which sold more than 400,000 copies. Johnson's song-writing ended when he was appointed US consul to Venezuela in 1906. Three years later he was transferred to Nicaragua where he served until 1912, before being posted to the Azores. Returning to the United States, he became editor of the *New York Age* and devoted a great deal of his time and energy to the National Association for the Advancement of Colored People (NAACP) and helped it to become the strongest civil rights organization in the United States. In 1920, Johnson travelled to Haiti to investigate charges that US troops were abusing the black natives there, and boldly reported that this was indeed the case. He also spent two years in Washington, D.C., vainly trying to persuade the federal government to abolish the cruel practice of lynching that had become so prevalent in the southern states. He served periodically at New York University and at Fisk University as a literature instructor, before dying in a car crash in Wiscasset, Maine, on 26 June 1938. James Weldon Johnson is best remembered for his lyric poetry, especially his *God's Trombones: Seven Negro Sermons in Verse* (1927). He also wrote a novel, *The Autobiography of an Ex-Colored Man* (1912) as well as *Black Manhattan* (1930), the history of black theatre in New York. In addition, he edited several books, including *The Book of American Negro Poetry* (1922) and *Negro Spirituals* (1925). He was the recipient of many prestigious awards, including honorary doctorates and the NAACP Spingarn Medal for outstanding achievement.

JOHNSON, John Harold

One of the most famous and most successful of all American editors and publishers, John Harold Johnson was born in Arkansas City on 19 January 1918. After studying at the University of Chicago and Northwestern University's School of Commerce, he worked with the Supreme Liberty Life Insurance Company from 1936 to 1942. In 1942, he founded *Negro Digest*, which he later renamed *Black World*. It was patterned after *Reader's Digest* and focussed on events within the African-American community. Within one year the *Negro Digest* had 50,000 paid subscribers. He launched *Tan Confessions* in 1950 and later changed its name to *Black Stars*. But his greatest legacy was *Ebony*, a slick picture magazine, which he founded in 1945 and which still remains the leading African-American publication. In 1951, he introduced the news-weekly, *Jet*, another successful venture. Johnson then established the Johnson Publishing Company which began publishing books in 1962, in addition to its weekly and monthly magazines. The Johnson Publishing Company is one of the biggest of all business enterprises in black America. In 1982, Johnson became the first African-American to appear on *Forbes* magazine's list of the 400 richest Americans. In 1996 he was awarded the Presidential Medal of Freedom. He died on 8 August 2005.

JOHNSON, Linton Kwesi

Linton Kwesi Johnson was born in Chapelton, Jamaica, on 24 August 1952 and emigrated to the United Kingdom with his family in 1963. He attended Tulse Hill secondary school and later studied at Goldsmith's College, University of London. His career as a reggae dub poet began even before he left school when he joined the Black Panthers and helped to organize a poetry workshop within the movement. In 1977 he was awarded a C. Day Lewis Fellowship, becoming the writer-in-residence for the London Borough of Lambeth. He then went to work as the Library Resources and Education Officer at the Keskidee Centre, the first home of black theatre and art. Johnson's poems first appeared in the journal, *Race Today*, in 1974. An astonishing series of collections followed. Most of Johnson's verse is political, dealing mainly with the black experience in the United Kingdom. LKJ Records, his own record label, was launched successfully in 1981 and became the home to several other reggae performers. As a recording artist, he released a CD and (for the first time ever) a DVD in 2004, entitled *LKJ Live in Paris* with the Dennis Bovell Dub Band. Revered as the world's first great reggae poet, Johnson has received a host of honours and distinctions, including the XIII Premo Internazionale Ultimo Novecento from the city of Pisa for his contribution to poetry and popular music (1990); the Premo Piero Ciampi Citta di Livorno Concorso Musicale Nazionale in Italy (1998); an honorary fellowship from his alma mater, Goldsmiths College (2003) and a Musgrave Silver Medal from the Institute of Jamaica for distinguished eminence in the field of poetry (2005). He was also made an Associate Fellow of Warwick University (1985), an Honorary Fellow of Wolverhampton Polytechnic (1987) and an Honorary Visiting Professor of Middlesex University (2004).

JOHNSON, Michael

No track-and-field star dominated international competition as completely as did Michael Duane Johnson during the period 1992-99 when he won no fewer than fourteen gold medals. In 1995 he became the first athlete to win both the 200 metre and the 400 metre sprints at a single world championship. He repeated this feat at the Atlanta Olympics one year later. Born on 13 September 1967 in Dallas, Texas, Johnson became an outstanding track star at Baylor University and anchored the United States 4 x 400 metre relay team to a gold medal triumph at the Barcelona Olympics in 1992. Johnson's most impressive single performance came at Atlanta in the 200 metre final when he established an amazing world record of 19.32 seconds. He also holds the world record in the 400 metre race with an extraordinary time of 43.18 seconds.

JOHNSON, Mordecai

Mordecai Wyatt Johnson was born in Paris, Tennessee, in 1890. After graduating from Morehouse College, the University of Chicago and Howard University, he served as a teacher of English at Morehouse College and as a pastor of Baptist churches in New York and West Virginia. Meanwhile, he founded a local branch of the National Association for the Advancement of Colored People (NAACP) in Charleston and became instrumental also in the establishment of the Southwestern Annual Student Conference. In 1926, Johnson became the first African-American president of Howard University which simply flourished under his direction. During his tenure, that institution witnessed a revolution not only in its physical plant but in its scholastic standing. Johnson retired early in the 1960s and an administration building on that campus was named after him in 1973. Much earlier, his good work as a university administrator had been recognized by the award of a Spingarn Medal in 1929. He died in 1976.

JOHNSON, Obadiah Alexander

Dr Obadiah Alexander Johnson was a Sierra Leonean physician who eventually distinguished himself as one of the leading medical practitioners in Lagos, Nigeria. Born at Hastings in 1849, he was educated at the Christian Missionary Society Grammar School, at Fourah Bay College and at medical schools in London (England) and Edinburgh (Scotland). He served as assistant colonial surgeon in Sierra Leone (1887-89) before emigrating to Lagos where he served in a similar capacity during 1889-97. In 1901 Johnson was appointed to the Lagos Legislative Council and remained a member of that body until 1913. After practising medicine in Lagos for many years, he retired and moved to England, where he died in 1920. But he never forgot his roots. He bequeathed the majority of his books and £5,000 to Fourah Bay College in Freetown, Sierra Leone, for the founding of a science chair there.

JOHNSON, Robert

Born on 8 April 1946 in Hickory, Mississippi, Robert L. Johnson graduated from the University of Illinois in 1968 before achieving a master's degree from Princeton University. He moved to Washington, D.C. and worked for the Corporation for Public Broadcasting, the Urban League, and a local congressional delegate. In 1976, he established the Black Entertainment Television (BET) to exploit a huge market that had hitherto been untapped. BET gradually developed into a giant corporation and by 1991 was the first black-controlled company to be listed on the New York Stock Exchange. Johnson and his partners sold BET to Viacom in 2001 for some $3 billion while he was kept on at BET as CEO. This sale made him the first African-American to become a billionaire. He was wealthy enough to purchase a new National Basketball Association (NBA) franchise, the Charlotte Bobcats, for $300 million in 2003. He is the first African-American to own a major league sporting franchise.

JOHNSON-SIRLEAF, Ellen

In December 2005, Ellen Johnson-Sirleaf became the first African woman to win a presidential election when she was chosen president of Liberia. Born in 1939, she had earlier served as finance minister during William Tolbert's presidency in the 1970s. Her severe criticisms of Samuel Doe's administration led to her imprisonment and exile in the following decade. During the period of her exile, she served as a senior loan officer of the World Bank; vice-president of the Citibank in Nairobi, Kenya; founding member of the International Institute for Women in Political Leadership; vice-president of Equator Bank in Washington, D.C. and director of the Regional Bureau for Africa at the UN Development Programme. She returned to Liberia in 1996, at the conclusion of a seven-year civil war, assumed the leadership of the Unity Party and challenged Charles Taylor in the presidential campaign of 1997. Taylor won that election and promptly accused her of treason, compelling the 'Iron Lady' (as she became widely known) to flee once more. After Taylor's expulsion from Liberia, Johnson-Sirleaf finally led the Unity Party to victory at the polls and was officially sworn in as Liberia's president on 16 January 2006. She has pledged to undo the mischief caused by many years of civil anarchy and governmental corruption. Her writings include *From Disaster to Development* (1991) and *The Outlook for Commercial Bank Lending to Sub-Saharan Africa* (1992).

JOHNSTON, James Robinson

James Robinson Johnston is nowadays referred to as 'The Martin Luther King of Nova Scotia'. The first locally trained black lawyer from the Maritimes, he graduated from Dalhousie Law School in 1898 and opened his law office in Halifax, Nova Scotia, in 1900. He became a highly respected member of the community at a time when the bulk of the white residents still firmly believed that Blacks were incapable of serious thought. He was honoured many years after his death by the senate of Dalhousie University which passed a resolution in 1991 establishing an endowed James Robinson Johnston Chair in Black Canadian Studies.

JONES, Claudia

Claudia Jones was born in Port-of-Spain, Trinidad, in 1915 and emigrated with her family to the United States in 1924. Despite tuberculosis and other medical problems, she became a vigorous defender of civil rights, joined the American Communist party, was jailed briefly for her outspoken views and subsequently deported in 1955. She sought asylum in the United Kingdom where she resumed her crusade on behalf of racial equality. In the United States, Jones had been the editor of 'Negro Affairs' for the Communist newspaper, *The Daily Worker*, and had developed into an eloquent speaker and influential journalist in support of the disadvantaged Blacks. In England, she founded and edited *The West Indian Gazette* which became crucial in her fight for equal opportunities for the members of the African-Caribbean community. Her lasting legacy was the Notting Hill Carnival which she launched in 1959. These early celebrations were held in halls and were epitomised by her favourite slogan, 'A people's art is the genesis of their freedom'. She died in 1964.

JONES, Ethelred Nathaniel

Much better known as Laminah Sankoh, Revd Ethelred Nathaniel Jones was one of the most fearless Sierra Leonean nationalists during the colonial period. It was he who founded the Sierra Leone People's Party (SLPP) in 1948. Born on 28 June 1884, Jones was educated at Fourah Bay College and Wycliffe College, Oxford, where he studied theology and philosophy. His experiences of overt racism at Oxford so embittered him that he rejected his British name and chose a Temne one (more in keeping with his heritage), before returning to Sierra Leone in 1924. Sankoh spent several years in the United States, teaching at Tuskegee Institute and Lincoln University. A brief trip to England in the 1930s gave him an opportunity to support the West African Students' Union. When he finally settled back down in Sierra Leone during the 1940s, Sankoh embarked on social and political activities of all kinds. He became actively involved in the reconstruction of the Freetown City Council and was elected a member in 1948. He also served as president of the Freetown Adult Education Committee. In the meantime, he founded the Sierra Leone Aro Society, while editing a Freetown daily, the *African Vanguard* which he himself had done much to create. Disillusioned by the rampant racism within all European sects, he founded his own People's Church which focussed mainly on African approaches to God while remaining basically Christian in doctrine. Sankoh wrote several pamphlets, promoting Sierra Leonean unity and independence, and initiated the People's Forum which became immensely popular. He died poor on 29 March 1954 but received a decent and honourable funeral. His career left an indelible mark on Sierra Leonean life, culture, politics and religion.

JONES, Eugene Kinckle

Son of a slave father and freeborn mother, Eugene Kinckle Jones was born in Richmond, Virginia, in 1885. A graduate of Virginia Union University and Cornell University, he had been active in many university-related activities. He helped to organize the Alpha Phi Alpha fraternity which soon developed into a nationwide association. Jones taught briefly at Louisville University and Louisville's Central High School, but most of his energy was devoted to the National Urban League which expanded under his direction to include more than forty branches across the United States. For thirty years (1911-1941) he served as its executive secretary. One of the most influential civil rights leaders of his generation, Jones did his utmost to bring African-Americans into the fold of the American Federation of Labour and acted throughout the 1930s as a consultant to several government commissions, securing the appointment of Blacks to a number of federal agencies and commissions. He died in 1954.

JONES, Frederick

An exceptionally versatile and imaginative inventor, Frederick McKinley Jones was born into poverty in Cincinnati, Ohio, on 17 May 1892. His schooling was most irregular, especially after he became orphaned at nine years of age, but he shortly proved himself an expert mechanic. He learnt not only to fix cars but to build them and had built a number of racing cars by the time he was nineteen. During World War I, Jones served in the United States Army as an electrician and rose to the rank of sergeant. When he returned home, he began building radio station transmitters and also invented a way to put sound to movies. His first patent, however, was for a ticket machine used by movie houses. Emerging with the revolutionary notion that electricity ought to be able to provide cool air as easily as it was producing heat, he then designed air cooling units for trucks moving food products to the market. He joined with Joseph Numero, a manufacturer, to establish a huge factory making cooling units for trucks, trains, ships and planes. This made it possible for the first time to ship all kinds of food over very long distances. During World War II, cooling units designed by Jones were used by the United States Army to store blood and medicines as well as military food supplies. Altogether Jones patented over sixty inventions by the time of his death on 21 February 1961. This unusual genius completely transformed the food transport industry.

JONES, Lionel

Mr Justice Lionel. L. Jones was appointed a judge of the Provincial Court of Alberta in 1977 and promoted to the office of Justice of the Court of Queen's Bench in Alberta in 1995. A native of Edmonton he completed his education at the University of Alberta achieving a BA in 1960 and an LLB in 1963. He began his law career as a Crown Counsel for the Attorney General of Alberta in 1964 and eventually retired in 2001. He occasionally lectured to university students, justices of the peace and the RCMP on law-related topics.

JONES, Marion

Marion Jones, an outstanding American athlete, was born in Los Angeles, California, on 12 October 1975. She dominated the women's sprints between 1997 and 2001 and became, in 2000, the first woman in history to win five track-and-field medals at a single Olympic Games. Her first international triumph came in 1997 when she won the 100 metre dash in the time of 10.83 secs. In addition to being one of the members of the team that won the 4 x 400 metres relay at the Sydney Olympics, she won the 100 metres in 10.75 sec and the 200 metres in 21.84 sec. She also captured bronze medals in the long jump and the 4 x 100 metres relay. In 1998, Jones had become the first American woman to be ranked number one in three track-and-field events simultaneously: the 100 metres, the 200 metres and the long jump.

JONES, Oliver

Born in Montreal, Quebec, of Barbadian parents on 11 September 1934, Dr Oliver Theophilus Jones became one of the finest jazz pianists that Canada has ever produced. His public career began at the age of five when he performed at the Union United Church in Montreal. After many years in Puerto Rico where he worked as a musical director, he returned to Canada to produce a glorious sequence of albums after 1983, the year in which he launched Just in Time Records. These records garnered three Felix Awards as best jazz albums of the year in 1989 (*Just Friends*), in 1994 (*Just 88*) and in 1995 (*Yuletide Swing*). He also won the Composer of the Year Award from *Jazz Magazine* in 1996. Jones, who appeared in several international festivals before his retirement in 1999, performed in such places as Africa, Australia, Europe, New Zealand and South America. He received the Order of Quebec in 1994 and the Order of Canada in 1996 and has been the recipient of several honorary doctorates from reputable universities.

JONES, T.F.E.

Thomas Freeman Edward Jones, who was born in Abakampa, just east of Cape Coast, in 1851, became a wealthy merchant and a founding member of the Aborigines' Rights Protection Society (ARPS). It was he who led its deputation to England in 1898 to protest the Lands Bill of 1897 (which had left the local Blacks at a serious disadvantage). He also travelled to London in 1912 to oppose the Forest Lands Bill of 1911. Thanks in no small measure to the vigorous criticism of the ARPS, both of these unpopular and unjust measures had to be withdrawn. Jones sat on the Cape Coast Town Council from 1907 to 1924, where he found a forum for the expression of local African views. One of his major interests was education and he played an important part in bringing about much progress in this area. He was also a local preacher who gave staunch support to the Methodist Church of Cape Coast. He died on 18 July 1924.

JOPLIN, Scott

This creative composer and pianist made little impact during his lifetime even though his music was recognized as revolutionary and influential many years after his death. Born in Texarkana, Texas, in 1868, he began earning his living at the age of fourteen playing the piano in the saloons of several southern towns. The founder of ragtime, he wrote such hits as *Maple Leaf Rag* (1899), *Original Rag* (1901), *Palm Leaf Rag* (1907), *Fig Leaf Rag* (1908) and *Stoptime Rag* (1910). Still popular today, too, are his *Binks' Waltz* and *Cleopha*. Scott Joplin, who died on 1 April 1917, is now generally regarded as one of the greatest innovators in the history of American music. In 1976, he was awarded the Pulitzer Prize posthumously for the ragtime opera, *Treemonisha*, which he had composed some sixty years earlier.

JORDAN, Archibald Campbell

This outstanding Xhosa novelist, poet, scholar and educator was born at Mbokothwane in Cape Province, South Africa, on 30 October 1906. After attending Mbokothwane Higher Mission School, St Cuthbert's Higher Boarding School, and St John's College at Umtata, he proceeded to Fort Hare University where he achieved his BA and to the University of South Africa where he earned an MS. Jordan then taught for eight years (1936-44) at the Bantu High School at Kroonstad in the Orange Free State. Having by this time completed his MA, he was appointed a lecturer at the University of Cape Town where he served for seventeen years (1944-61). In 1956 Jordan finally achieved his PhD. He emigrated to the United States in 1962 and lectured at the University College of Los Angeles and then at the University of Wisconsin (1963-68) where he was promoted to a full professorship in the department of African Languages and Literature in 1964. He held that post until his death on 20 October 1968. Jordan's first novel, *Ingqumbo Yeminyanya* (The Death of the Ancestral Spirits) is still generally considered the classic of modern Xhosa writing. Much of his prose as well as his verse, however, was left unpublished at his death and he is perhaps best remembered for his *Practical Xhosa Course for Beginners* which was published in 1965 and is still very popular. He also wrote a series of articles entitled *Towards an African Literature* in the periodical *Africa South*. They threw much useful light on Xhosa proverbs, riddles and traditional praise poems and did much to promote the work of previous Bantu writers.

JORDAN, Barbara

Born in Houston, Texas, on 21 February 1936, Barbara Charline Jordan received a BA from Texas Southern University in 1956 before proceeding to Boston University to study law. In 1959 she began her practice in Houston and became administrative assistant to a county judge there. In 1966 she was elected to the Texas State senate, becoming the first African-American to sit in that house since 1883. After serving on many major senate committees, she was named president of that body in 1972. In that same year she was elected US Representative from the 18th Congressional

District of Texas. She won a seat on the House Judiciary Committee and was considered a possible vice-presidential candidate for the 1976 election. After serving three terms in the House, however, she decided to take up a position as ethics professor at the Lyndon B. Johnson School of Public Affairs at the University of Texas. Jordan chaired the US Commission on Immigration Reform and is best remembered for her stirring opposition in 1995 to a proposal to deny citizenship to children born in the United States to illegal immigrants. She died on 17 January 1996.

JORDAN, June

One of the most prolific African-American writers, who authored more than two dozen books that included poetry, collections of essays and short stories and novels, June Jordan was born in Harlem, New York, on 9 July 1936. She was educated at Barnard College in New York City before beginning her teaching career at City Colleges of New York in 1966. She served as a professor of African-American Studies at the University of California, Berkeley, from 1989 to 2002. Her major works included three collections of essays: *Civil Wars* (1981); *On Call* (1985); *Technical Difficulties: African-American Notes on the State of the Union* (1992); a poetry collection, *Some Changes* (1971); a children's book, *Who Look at Me* (1969) and a novel, *His Own Where* (1971). Jordan's writing dealt mainly with the problems facing women, the poor and the disadvantaged. She died on 4 June 2002. Her last collection of essays, *Some of Us Did Not Die*, was published posthumously.

JORDAN, Michael

Michael Jeffrey Jordan is regarded by many pundits as the greatest basketball player who has ever lived. Born in Brooklyn, New York, on 17 February 1963, he became a basketball star at every level even before being drafted third overall by the Chicago Bulls of the National Basketball Association (NBA) in 1983. Chosen Rookie of the Year in 1985, he proceeded to lead the NBA in scoring for seven consecutive seasons during 1987-93 while taking the Bulls to three successive championships during 1991-93. When he first announced his retirement from professional basketball in 1993 he had accumulated a record individual average of 32.3 points a game in regular NBA competition. Affectionately known as 'Air Jordan', because of his apparent ability to suspend himself aloft while executing marvellous plays, he was chosen the league's most valuable player (MVP) in 1988, 1991 and 1992. He led the United States to Olympic championships in 1984 and 1992. Jordan came out of retirement in 1995 to lead the Chicago Bulls to three more titles (1996-98) and to enhance his already monumental reputation. In 1996, he was chosen the league's Most Valuable Player (MVP) for the fourth time in both the regular season and the playoffs and broke Wilt Chamberlain's record by achieving his eighth NBA scoring title. Perhaps the highest paid athlete in the history of professional sports, Jordan is reputed to have earned more than $36 million (mainly in endorsement fees) in 1993 alone. In 1997, he is said to have signed for more than $30 million to play one more year for the Bulls whom he led to their sixth NBA championship in eight years. He was one of the most popular sports stars in the world and drew fans to games throughout the United States. He came out of retirement again (in 2001) to play for the Washington Wizards, of which he was a part-owner.

JORDAN, Vernon

A noted lawyer and civil rights leader, Vernon Jordan was born in Atlanta, Georgia, on 15 August 1935. After graduating from Howard University in 1960, he rendered yeoman service to the National Association for the Advancement of Colored People (NAACP) and the National Urban League (of which he became executive director in 1973). In 1970 he became executive director of the United Negro College Fund and later president of the National Urban League. He served for some years as the legal counsel for the Washington D.C. office of the law firm of Akin, Gump, Strauss, Hauer and Feld. As one of President Clinton's closest friends, he became one of Washington's most influential power brokers during the Clinton administration. He is currently a partner in the investment firm of Lazard Frere and Company in New York. Jordan has received numerous awards and honours, including the Alexis de Tocqueville Award from the United Way of America in 1977. In 2001 he published his much acclaimed autobiography, *Vernon Can Read!* He has also authored a weekly column syndicated to more than 300 newspapers and serves frequently as a television guest and commentator. He remains active on various corporate boards and has had several presidential appointments.

JULIAN, Percy

Dr Percy Lavon Julian, an eminent American scientist, was born in Montgomery, Alabama, on 11 April 1899. He received degrees from DePauw University and Harvard University before achieving his PhD from the University of Vienna, Austria, in 1931. After lecturing in chemistry at Howard and DePauw Universities, he joined the Institute of Paper Chemistry in Wisconsin, having already attracted international attention by discovering from his soybean research the chemical to cure glaucoma. Julian later became director of research on soya products for the Glidden Company of Chicago. It was there that he successfully developed new processes for paints and perfected a method of extracting sterols from soybean oil for the manufacture of sex hormones. Steroids, derived or synthesized from a soya base, dramatically lowered the cost of treating arthritis and other diseases. During World War II he developed a special foam that could be used to extinguish fires quickly. In 1954 he founded Julian Laboratories, Inc. with branches in Chicago, Mexico City and Guatemala. He then successfully developed synthetic cortisone. In 1964 he founded the Julian Research Institute, after having sold his plants for more than two million dollars to such pharmaceutical giants as Smith, Kline and French and Upjohn Company. Percy Lavon Julian was one of the outstanding chemists of the 20th century. He contributed numerous papers to scholarly journals and registered more than 100 patents. He was also active in the civil rights movement and contributed generously to promote its goals. He was awarded the Spingarn Medal in 1947. Julian died on 19 April 1975.

JUMINER, Bertène

Born in Cayenne on 6 August 1927, Dr Bertène Juminer has become one of the greatest figures in the modern history of French Guiana. He is not only a physician of international repute but he is also a much acclaimed novelist, playwright and short-story writer. He completed his secondary education at the Lycée Carnot in Guadeloupe and proceeded to the University of Montpelier in France where he achieved a medical degree in 1953. He returned briefly to Guyane to work at a hospital in Saint-Laurent, Moroni, before leaving for the Institut Pasteur in Tunis. There followed a sequence of appointments at medical schools in Iran, Senegal and France. In the field of medicine he has written more than 100 scientific articles in a wide range of scholarly journals. In addition Juminer has published several essays and short stories as well as such novels as *Les Bâtards* (1958), *Au seuil d'un nouveau cri* (1963), *La Revanche de Bozambo* (1968) and some fine plays, including *De Dunkerque à Maripassoula?* (1962) and *L'Archiduc sort de l'ombre* (1970).

JUST, Ernest

Dr Ernest Everett Just was born in Charleston, South Carolina, on 14 August 1883. After graduating from Dartmouth College in 1907 he joined the faculty of Howard University and remained there until his death on 27 October 1941. In 1916 he received his PhD in physiology and zoology from the University of Chicago. His major interest was the fertilization of marine eggs, on which subject he published more than fifty scholarly papers between 1912 and 1937. His two important books, *Basic Methods for Experiments in Eggs of Marine Animals* and *The Biology of the Cell Surface*, appeared in 1939. Just served for many years as vice-president of the American Zoological Society. He was awarded the Spingarn Medal in 1915.

KABBADA, Mikael

Mikael Kabbada was a distinguished Amharic playwright, poet and diplomat. Born in Ethiopia on 2 December 1915, he became one of Emperor Haile Selassie's protégés and was offered many important ministerial posts at home before his appointment as the Ethiopian ambassador to the Vatican in the early 1950s. Kabbada was a most prolific writer whose works have been translated into many languages, including English and French. Among his major plays were *Prophecy Fulfilled* (1934), *The Storm of Punishment* (1949), *Hannibal* (1949), *Kaleb* (1957) and *Achab* (1961). His histories included *Ethiopia and Western Civilization* (1942), *Great Men* (1944), *Alexander the Great* (1948), *The Modernization of Japan* (1954), *Old Ethiopian Paintings* (1962) and *Story and Parable*. Kabbada also wrote some delightful poems in such collections as *The Light of Intelligence* (1934), *Beyond Pardon* (1937), *Poetry* (1957) and *Romeo and Juliet* (1954).

KABBAH, Ahmed

Ahmed Tejan Kabbah, the president of Sierra Leone, was born of Muslim parentage on 16 February 1932 in Kailahun District in the eastern section of his country. He graduated with a degree in economics from the University College of Aberystwyth in Wales in 1959 and later qualified as a lawyer. Kabbah served for many years as a District Commissioner in most parts of Sierra Leone and as a permanent secretary in various ministries. He was also an international civil servant for almost two decades. He headed the UN Development Programme (UNDP) in such African countries as Lesotho, Tanzania, Uganda and Zimbabwe. He was also directly responsible for co-ordinating UN assistance to liberation movements like the African National Congress (ANC) and the South West African People's Organization (SWAPO). He then held a number of senior administrative positions at the UNDP headquarters in New York. Following the 1992 military coup in Sierra Leone, Kabbah was asked to chair the National Advisory Council to facilitate the restoration of constitutional rule. He became more involved in Sierra Leonean politics and assumed the leadership of the Sierra Leone People's Party (SLPP) which triumphed in 1996 in the first multi-party elections held there in twenty three years. In keeping with his philosophy of 'inclusion', Kabbah formed a broad-based government with members from most of the parties as well as 'technocrats' in civil society. He also signed a peace agreement with the rebel forces, led by Foday Sankoh, in an attempt to bring an end to the civil war which had already resulted in hundreds of civilian casualties. But the rebels engineered another military coup in 1997, forcing Kabbah into exile in neighbouring Guinea. He was restored in 1998 by troops representing the Economic Community of West African States (ECOWAS) and re-elected in 2002. He continues to struggle with Sierra Leone's grave social and economic problems and has sought to address the issue of corruption by inviting the British to aid in the establishment of an anti-corruption commission. President Kabbah has been awarded an honorary doctorate by the University of Sierra Leone in Freetown and a similar honour from the Southern Connecticut State University in the United States in recognition of his effort to bring peace to his country.

KABILA, Laurent

Laurent-Désiré Kabila, a former president of the Democratic Republic of the Congo (DRC), was born in Katanga province, Belgian Congo, on 27 November 1939. After studying in France and Tanzania, he returned home and joined forces with Patrice Lumumba, the Congo's first prime minister in the age of independence. He then led a long and relentless revolt of Lumumba's supporters against Mobutu's régime after Lumumba was ousted in 1961 and later assassinated. Eventually, his troops forced Mobutu Sese Seko to flee from Zaire in 1997. Kabila promptly installed himself as president, rejected the name of Zaire which Mobutu had given the country in 1971, and proceeded to rule the Congo as dictatorially as his predecessors had done. He banned all political parties, imprisoned journalists and human rights workers and appointed his relatives to positions of authority. He thus had to spend the next few years fighting against Zairean rebels who found support from within his country as well as from Rwanda and Uganda. Kabila's troubles ended with his own assassination in January 2001.

KAGAME, Abbé Alexis

This Rwandan poet, historian and ethnographer was born in Buriza in 1912. The son of Pierre Bitahurwina, deputy chief of the Tutsi, Abbé Alexis Kagame was educated in local schools and at the Pontifical Gregorian University at Rome. Ordained a priest in 1941, he became an ardent Catholic clergyman but still remained keen on the language and culture of his people. He thus wrote mainly in the Rwandan language in which he published several short stories as well as poems. His major works included a history, *Iganji Karinga*, published in 1943 and three volumes of poetry, *Isoko y'amäjyambere* (1949-51). In 1952 Kagame wrote *Le code des institutions politiques du Rwanda*, a lively defence of the Tutsi feudal system. He also produced his own French translations of his poems (1952-55) in *La divine pastorale: I and II - Veillées; III - La naissance de l'univers*. In addition, he produced a few critical commentaries in French on the literature of the Tutsi. But some western critics still regard his doctoral thesis, *The Bantu-Rwandese Philosophy of Being*, which was published in 1956, as his most important work. Abbé Alexis Kagame died in 1981.

KAGWA, Apolo

Sir Apolo Kagwa was the katikiro (chief minister) of Buganda from 1890 to 1926 and the leading figure in the semi-autonomous development of the Bugandan people under British rule. A devout Anglican, Kagwa was the leader of the Protestant faction in the Bugandan civil wars, 1888-92. He became katikiro when Mwanga was restored to the Bugandan throne in 1890 and became increasingly powerful as the reign progressed. When Mwanga fled in 1897, the new kabaka was only an infant and Kagwa served as regent until 1914. His constant support of the British imperial government earned him the latter's gratitude and he was granted a knighthood. Kagwa ruled Buganda competently for many years until a quarrel erupted between himself and the kabaka which led to his resignation. He died shortly afterwards in February 1927.

KAI SAMBA I

A vigorous and progressive paramount chief of Nongowa, a state in southeastern Sierra Leone, Kai Samba I played an important role in both local and national politics. He pioneered the development of agriculture in his district and transformed his capital, Kenema, into a prosperous urban centre. Born in 1902, he was educated at the Bo Government School before joining the civil service as a clerk in 1924. He was installed as chief of his state on 17 February 1942 and became deputy president of the Kenema District Council. Very active also in the Protectorate Assembly, Kai Samba became a member of the Sierra Leone Legislative Council. He is especially remembered for modernizing and developing the Kenema district. He re-planned the town and left it with better roads, a good sanitation system, a modern hospital with a full-time medical officer and a park with recreational facilities. He was also instrumental in building the Kenema Government Secondary School in 1952. Kenema remains a lasting monument to this unusual chief. In 1950 Kai Samba was awarded the King's Medal for African Chiefs (KMAC). He died on 3 January 1956.

KAJIGA BALIHUTA

An outstanding Zairean churchman, author and philosopher, Revd Kajiga Balihuta was born in Rugu in 1922. A staunch Catholic, he entered seminaries in Rwanda and was ordained a priest in 1953. He became professor of languages and history at the Migeri-Katana Catholic School and was later appointed Inspector of Catholic Education in the diocese of Goma. Apart from his work as priest and administrator, Kajiga Balihuta made significant contributions to scholarship. His works included *Conscience Professionelle* (1963), *Pour Une Langue Nationale Congolaise* (1967), *Initiation à la Culture Ntu: Grammaire Swahili* (1967), *Langue d'Enseignement et Culture Nationale*

(1971), *Lugha Ya Kiswahili* (1972), and *Dictionnaire Swahili-Français, Français-Swahili* (1975). These publications made an invaluable contribution to Zairean language and philosophy. Kajiga was a keen advocate of the adoption of a national language and tried his best to promote the use of Lingala and Swahili. He felt that Africans would learn a lot more quickly if taught in languages they understood. Zaire lost not only a philosopher, but also a linguist, educator, psychologist and humanist when Kajiga Balihuta died on 3 January 1976. He had served with much distinction as a member of the Société des Linguistes du Zaire and as a regular consultant to the Société des Historiens Zairois.

KANYIMBU NEWEJ MPEMB
Born at the beginning of the eighteenth century, Kanyimbu was a great military leader who extended Lunda influence over a vast area in what is now southeastern Zaire and northern Zambia. He tried to consolidate his gains by setting up a permanent capital at Lunde, near Lake Mweru. But he faced much opposition to his imperial designs and even his own ambitious sons plotted to usurp his authority. He was still, however, one of the most powerful rulers in tropical Africa when he died around 1760.

KAPEND TSHOMB, Joseph
Joseph Kapend Tshomb was a very successful Congolese entrepreneur who rose from poverty to become one of the wealthiest African merchants of his day. Born in 1889, he established a modest firm at Sandoa in 1924 and nurtured it into a very prosperous enterprise. When he died in 1950 he had become one of the richest Africans in the Congo. He is perhaps best remembered as the father of Moise Thsombe, a Zairean president during the 1960s.

KAPWEPWE, Simon
Simon Mwansa Kapwepwe was a Zambian political leader who played a key role in the African independence movement after World War II. Born on 22 April 1922 in Chinsali, Northern Rhodesia, he taught for some years before becoming actively involved in politics. Like Kenneth Kaunda, he was a Bemba and a keen supporter of African nationalism. He was initially a member the African National Congress (ANC), but joined Kaunda's breakaway party, the Zambia African National Congress, in 1958. Two years later, they founded the Independence Party (UNIP) which won a large majority in the elections of 1964. Kapwepwe then became independent Zambia's first foreign minister (1964-67) and served as vice-president under Kaunda during 1967-70). Disillusioned with Kaunda's policies and attitude, Kapwepwe resigned from the government and formed his own opposition

United Progressive Party (UPP). The UPP was soon banned and Kapwepwe placed under detention. In 1977, he rejoined UNIP, the only legal party since the early 1970s, but its national council disqualified his intended candidacy for the 1978 presidential election. He died on 26 January 1980.

KASAVUBU, Joseph

Born around 1913 at Kinkuma-Dizi, near Léopoldville in the Belgian Congo, Joseph Kasavubu became a staunch advocate of Congolese independence and is remembered as the first president of the republic of Congo, now known as Zaire. Educated at the Kizu Mission School and Mbata Kiela Minor Seminary, he proceeded to the Scheut Seminary at Kabwe studying to become a priest. He abandoned the priesthood, however, and worked for many years as a civil servant in Léopoldville. Keenly interested in the rights of Africans living under colonial government, he joined many of the progressive and radical movements then emerging in the Congo and distinguished himself by asserting the right of the Africans to possess their own land. This agitation eventually forced the Belgian government to initiate changes, especially after the riots of 1959. An independent Congo, however, witnessed considerable internal strife in the early 1960s and Kasavubu was himself ousted from the presidency in 1965 after he had dismissed Patrice Lumumba, the first Congolese prime minister, in 1961. He retired quietly to his farm at Boma thereafter and died on 24 March 1969. Kasavubu had to cope with insurmountable problems during the early days of Zairean independence. He tried valiantly to mediate between ambitious politicians and rival ethnic factions. He failed then but is remembered now for his patience and sagacity.

KAUNDA, Kenneth

The son of mission teachers, Kenneth David Kaunda was born at Lubwa (in Northern Rhodesia) on 28 April 1924. He abandoned a teaching career to become a full-time nationalist political organizer determined to destroy the racist system which then prevailed in his country. Despite repeated imprisonments and exile, he became the leader of the United National Independence Party (UNIP) in 1958. When Zambia became independent in 1964, Kaunda was elected its first president. A firm believer in nonviolence and in nonracial societies, he tried his utmost to prevent open warfare in southern Africa and to bring a halt to the racist systems prevailing in Angola, Mozambique, Rhodesia and South Africa. In 1970, as chairman of the Organization of African Unity (OAU), he led a delegation of African foreign ministers to Bonn, London, New York, Paris and Rome urging Western governments to observe a total arms embargo on Portugal and South Africa. The failure of this programme led Kaunda to give active support to various liberation movements in the region and this inevitably involved Zambia in direct military confrontation with its neighbours. To cope with such pressures on his borders and with political violence at home, he also imposed single-party rule on his country in 1973. But by the end of that decade, Zambia was facing economic collapse, disruption of its communication routes to the sea, and the hostility of its most powerful neighbours. Despite these serious problems, Kaunda retained the presidency of his country until his resignation on 6 January 1992. When Kaunda later attempted to win back his seat in 1996, he was barred on constitutional grounds.

KAY, Janet

Janet Kay, who was born in London to Jamaican immigrant parents, became famous as the first British black female to have a reggae song at the top of the British charts. Her first really big hit was the song, *Silly Games*, which rose to the number two position in 1979. Thereafter her songs regularly did very well indeed. Her first album, *Capricorn Woman*, was also a smash hit in the reggae market. Janet Kay has been a very successful singer and songwriter, whose recordings have been especially popular in Japan.

KAY, Ulysses

Universally regarded as the most important African-American composer of classical music, Ulysses Simpson Kay was born in Tucson, Arizona, on 7 January 1917. He began as a jazz saxophonist but soon turned to piano, violin and composition. He graduated from the University of Arizona with a BA in 1938 and furthered his education at the Eastman School of Music, the Berkshire Music Center and Columbia University. In 1968 he was appointed professor of music at Lehman College of the City University of New York and was named distinguished professor of music there in 1972. Kay composed literally hundreds of choral, chamber and film pieces, including *Sinfonietta* (1940), *Five Mosaics* (1940), *Oboe Concerto* (1940), *Piano Sonata* (1940), *Danse Calinda* (1944), *Of New York Horizons* (1944), *A Short Overture* (1947), *The Juggler of Our Lady* (1962), *Fantasy Variations* (1963), *Umbrian Scene* (1964), *Theatre Set* (1968), *Jubilee* (1976) and *Frederick Douglass* (1991). His orchestral compositions included *Symphony* (1967) and *Southern Harmony* (1975). *The Song of Jeremiah* (1945) was perhaps his finest sonata. Ulysses Kay died on 20 May 1995.

KEINO, Kipchoge

Born in 1940, this uncoached Nandi athlete from Kenya surprised the sporting world during the 1960s by establishing a host of records for distance races ranging from 1,500 to 5,000 metres. His time of 7:39.6 for

3,000 metres, set on 27 August 1965, stood unchallenged for almost a decade. In the 1968 Olympics at Mexico, he won the 1,500 metre run in 3:34.9 in what is still generally considered an incredible feat at that altitude. In the 1972 Olympics at Munich, Keino captured the gold medal in the difficult 3,000 metre steeplechase. He gave a distinct fillip to athletics in his native country and it was his outstanding career that began the tradition of Kenyan excellence in distance races. In 1987 he shared *Sports Illustrated* magazine's 'Sportsman and Sportswoman of the Year Award' with seven others, characterised as 'Athletes Who Care', for his work with orphans. He currently runs a charitable organization for orphans on his farm in western Kenya and is president of the Kenyan Olympic Committee. In 1996, he was inducted into the World Sports Humanitarian Hall of Fame.

KEITA, Fodeba

Fodeba Keita was born in 1921 in Guinea. He became a successful poet, song-writer, playwright and choreographer. Educated in Guinea and Senegal, he later studied law in Paris, France. It was he who organized the world-famous 'Ballet Africain' which became an important National Dance Troupe when Guinea achieved its political independence in 1957. Keita was a fine composer and musician and wrote a number of memorable songs which were translated into French but known at home mainly in the local Malinké tongue. Keita was invited by President Sékou Touré to serve his country and was given many significant ministerial positions during the late 1950s and early 1960s. But he apparently fell foul of the president and mysteriously vanished in the late 1960s. His supporters are still not sure whether he is languishing in jail or has been executed. His best-known works were *Poèmes Africaines* (1950), *Le Maître d'école* (1953), *Minuit* (1953), and *Aubé Africain* (1965).

KEITA, Modibo

Born at Bamako in the French Sudan, on 4 June 1915, Modibo Keita became the first president of the Republic of Mali in 1960. A Muslim and graduate of what is now the University of Dakar, Senegal, he became a committed African nationalist and founded the Union Soudanaise in 1945. One year later, this militant West African anticolonial movement merged with the Rassemblement Démocratique Africain. A member of the government of the French Sudan in 1948, Keita also sat as a deputy and vice-president of the French National Assembly in Paris during 1956-1958 and was appointed state secretary for overseas territories in 1957. After briefly crusading for the short-lived Federation of Mali (and Senegal), he served as Mali's president until ousted by a military coup in 1968. Keita died on 16 May 1977.

KEÏTA, Seydou

Perhaps the most famous of all African photographers, Seydou Keïta was born in 1923 in Bamako, in what was then the French Sudan. Using a camera that his uncle had given him in 1945, he soon made a name for himself because of his flattering pictures. A portrait by Keïta became a status symbol throughout Bamako and he was appointed state photographer in 1960 when Mali won its political independence. He worked as the official government photographer until 1977. His portraits became the focus of exhibitions at the Cartier Foundation in Paris and the San Francisco Museum of Modern Art as well as galleries in Los Angeles, New York and St Louis. His photographs document an important period of transition in Mali's history when the country was adjusting to its newly won independence. Keïta died on 21 November 2001. Earlier that same year the Seydou Keïta Foundation was established in Bamako to preserve his work and to support young African artists.

KENNEY, John Andrew

Dr John Andrew Kenney was born in Albemarle County, Virginia, on 11 June 1874. After graduating with his MD from Leonard Medical School of Shaw University in 1901 he became the resident physician of what is now Tuskegee Institute in Alabama. He also served in that town as director of the John A. Andrew Memorial Hospital. While there, he founded the *Journal of the National Medical Association*, which he edited for thirty-two years. After threats from the local Ku Klux Klan, Dr Kenney moved to Newark, New Jersey, where he established the Kenney Memorial Hospital. He died on 29 January 1950.

KENYATTA, Jomo

A strident Kikuyu nationalist, Jomo Kenyatta was born in 1893 and educated in a Church of Scotland mission school. He worked for some years as a civil servant in Nairobi while taking an active interest in local politics. In 1928 he took over the leadership of the Kikuyu Central Association which was advocating a greater degree of equality and autonomy for Africans. During the 1930s, Kenyatta studied in the United Kingdom and travelled extensively in Europe before returning to Kenya in 1946 to resume his assault on British colonialism. He became one of the driving forces behind the independence movement and spent some time in prison as a result. In 1961, he was elected president of the Kenya African National Union (KANU) and emerged as the unchallenged messiah when his country achieved political independence in 1963. From 1964 he served as president of Kenya until his death on 22 August 1978, by which time he was renowned as the elder statesman of Africa, a stabilizing influence in world affairs and a sincere friend of the west. Kenyatta was highly respected in Africa where he was known to be a firm champion of democracy and self-determination, but he failed to unite the divisive factions and ethnic groups within his own republic and left his successors with very serious internal problems. On the credit side, he also left them with his classic sociological study, *Facing Mount Kenya*, published during the 1930s.

KÉRÉKOU, Mathieu

Major Ahmed Mathieu Kérékou was born on 2 September 1933 in Kouarfa in the northwest of Dahomey (whose name he later changed to Benin). After studying in military schools in Mali and Senegal, he served in the army and rose to the rank of major. He seized power on 26 October 1972 and installed himself as president. Proclaiming Benin a Marxist-Leninist state, he nationalized the banks and the petroleum industry and banned all political parties except his own, the Parti de la révolution populaire du Bénin. In 1980, he was elected president by the Revolutionary National Assembly. Kérékou's initial programmes failed to solve Benin's economic woes and he had to revisit them towards the end of his career, especially since the state sector was plagued by inefficiency and corruption. He closed many of the state-run companies and accepted the IMF structural adjustment programmes which called for severe reductions in government spending. But these policies also failed and Benin was bedevilled with various strikes during the 1990s. Kérékou abandoned Marxist-Leninism, liberalized the constitution to permit a multi-party democracy and promptly lost the elections of 1991. His successor, Nicéphore Soglo, fared no better during his tenure and Kérékou was returned to power in 1996. He won the general elections again in 2001 but the constitution prohibited him from running again in 2006. His legacy is a chequered one. While he provided Benin with a peaceful transition from military to civilian rule after 1990, he failed to solve its grave economic problems.

KHAKETLA, Bennett

Bennett Makalo Khaketla was born in Basutoland (now Lesotho) in 1915. He was a Southern Sotho poet, playwright, scholar, educator and journalist who taught at St Patrick's School in Bloemfontein from 1932 to 1939. He achieved his BA from the University of South Africa in 1942 and then taught for some years at Betshabelo High School and the Bantu High School. He returned to Basutoland in 1949 and, with Ntsu Mohhehle, founded the outspoken journal, *Mohlabani* (The Soldier), in 1956. In 1957 Khaketla was elected to the executive council of the Basutoland African Congress and soon became deputy president of the Basutoland Congress Party. In 1960 he was elected to the Legislative Council of Lesotho. He then founded his own Basuto Freedom Party aimed directly at the immediate achievement of political independence from Britain. Always interested in the traditional culture and values of his people, Khaketla published his *Sebopheho sa puo*, a very important grammar of the Sotho language, in 1957. He also wrote a number of plays including *Moshoeshoe le baruti* (1947), *Tholoana tsa sethepu* (1954), *Tholoana tsa boikakaso* (1954) and *Bulane* (1958). His major novels included *Meokho ea thabo* (1951), and *Mosali a nkhola* (1960). He also published some fine poetry in *Lipshamate* (1954) and a popular song, *Likenkeng*. Khaketla is best remembered as a fervent Southern Sotho nationalist determined to throw off the European yoke and to give his native language a certain measure of respectability. He died on 9 January 2000.

KHAMA III
Sometimes called Khama the Great, this king of Bechuanaland (now Botswana) sided with the British to help destroy the great Matabele Empire that had recently been established in southern Africa. Born around 1837, Khama converted to Christianity in 1860 and succeeded to the kingship in 1875 after a very exhausting civil war. In 1885, seeking British support to strengthen his own position against internal enemies as well as the dangerous Matabele, he had Bechuanaland declared a protectorate of the British Empire. He secured British assistance to secure his northern borders from attacks by Lobengula's kingdom in what is now Zimbabwe and his eastern borders from the Boer republic of the Transvaal. Khama lent reinforcements to the British expedition that finally crushed the Matabele altogether in 1893. This programme allowed him to survive for many years with his kingdom intact, albeit as an adjunct to a European colonial system. Khama the Great died, much revered both in England and Bechuanaland, on 21 February 1923.

KHAMA, Seretse
Born on 1 July 1921, the heir to the paramount chieftaincy of the Bamangwato in Bechuanaland, Sir Seretse Khama created a stir in 1948 by marrying a white English woman without the chief's consent. It took eight years before he was forgiven by his uncle, Tshekedi Khama, and could return home from Oxford University where he had gone to study. Forced to renounce his local chieftaincy, Khama established the Democratic Party and campaigned for Bechuanaland's independence. When his party won the elections of 1965, he changed the name of the former British protectorate and became the first prime minister of the new republic of Botswana in 1966, the same year in which he received a knighthood. He carefully steered Botswana through the first fourteen critical years of its independence, achieving two of his major goals: free universal education and the

diversification of the economy. He remained a staunch opponent of such systems as apartheid but his primary concern always was the economic prosperity of his country. Sir Seretse Khama died on 13 July 1980.

KIBAKI, Mwai

Mwai Kibaki became only the third president of Kenya on 30 December 2002. It was his third bid for the presidency and his success on this occasion was largely due to the fact that a recent change in the constitution had prevented Daniel arap Moi (who had been president since 1978) from seeking re-election. The former ruling party, the African National Union of Kenya (KANU) had dominated Kenya's politics since the achievement of independence in 1963. To combat the strength of KANU, Kibaki skilfully forged an alliance with the veteran politicians who had fallen foul of arap Moi or had become critical of his programmes. His new party is known as the National Rainbow Coalition (NARC). A member of the Kikuyu people, Emilio Mwai Kibaki was born on 15 November 1931 in Gatuyaini, a village in central Kenya. He was educated at Makerere University in Uganda and the London School of Economics in England. He was active in the Kenyan struggle for independence and served in KANU under Moi's leadership, occupying several key positions, including the vice-presidency. But he became increasingly disenchanted with Moi in the early 1990s, seceded from KANU and founded the Democratic Party when political parties were legalised. It was under the banner of the Democratic Party that he lost the presidential elections in 1992 and 1997. Kibaki pledged in 2002 to eliminate government corruption and to promote constitutional reforms. He dismissed several officials suspected of fraud and bribery but his campaign was undermined by the lingering suspicion that leading members of his cabinet were themselves guilty of serious malpractices.

KIDJO, Angélique

Born on 14 July 1960 in Ouidah, Dahomey (now Benin), Angélique Kidjo has become one of Africa's most famous and popular singers and is well-known as an international pop diva for her ability to fuse Latin American and West African rhythms and styles. Her successful albums, such as *Pretty* (1988), *Logozo* (1991), *Ayé* (1993), *Fifa* (1995), *Oremi* (1998), and *Black Ivory Soul* (2002) are a remarkable blend of jazz, hip-hop, funk, Zairean rumba, samba, salsa, gospel, zouk, Cameroonian makossa and traditional Beninese music. Her albums have a special appeal to listeners in most parts of the world as they are sung in English, Fon (her native tongue), French and Yoruba. The lyrics of all of her songs deal with such universal themes as homelessness, the environment, freedom and integration. An outspoken advocate for the need of an education,

Angélique Kidjo was named by UNICEF in July 2002 as one of its special ambassadors.

KIGERI IV

The career of that great Rwandan Mwami, Kigeri Rwabugiri, helps to explain some of the major difficulties facing east Africa today. During the second half of the nineteenth century, this outstanding Tutsi ruler ruthlessly transformed his small kingdom into a major state in the Lake Kivu area by repeatedly embarrassing his neighbours in Ankole, Bukiga, Burundi and Kigezi. The Hutu and others suffered greatly at his hands. Using European firearms, for which he had skilfully negotiated, Kigeri IV considerably extended his domains and left a legacy of violence and mistrust from which the region has not yet recovered. He showed excellent military and administrative skills in his marvellous feats of conquest and centralization, but his empire was much too unwieldy to be kept intact after his death. The Europeans managed to impose a semblance of order and unity for a while (1890-1960), but troubles inevitably arose almost as soon as they departed.

KIMBA, Evariste

Evariste Kimba was born on 16 July 1926. He became an influential Congolese journalist while working for the *Essor du Congo*. Elected to parliament in 1960, he refused to participate as he felt that the interests of the Katangans had not been adequately considered. He campaigned vigorously for an independent Katanga and served during 1960-63 as that region's foreign minister when, under the presidency of Moise Tshombe, it had seceded from the Congolese Republic. He was appointed prime minister of the reunited territory on 13 October 1965 but was ousted within weeks. Kimba eventually paid the supreme penalty for his resistance to Joseph Mobutu. He was hanged for treason on 2 June 1966.

KIMBANGU, Simon

Born at Nkamba on 24 September 1889, Simon Kimbangu became a famous Congolese religious leader whose following continued to increase rapidly long after he himself had died in 1951. Educated at the Baptist Missionary Society School in Ngombe-Lutete, he worked for many years as a Baptist evangelist. In 1918, Kimbangu received several visions asking him to proclaim the gospel. Establishing his own separate church in 1921, he preached very widely throughout the Congo and seems to have had considerable success as a faith healer. His native village of Nkamba was called the New Jerusalem by his thousands of devoted African followers, who came to pay him homage from as far away as Angola. While his theology was basically Baptist, he identified God with Nzambi, the African

Supreme Being, and thus made a strong appeal to Africans far and wide. The Kimbangu phenomenon disturbed the Belgian authorities because of increasing absenteeism from work and the threat it posed to Roman Catholicism. The constant flow of pilgrims to Nkamba, many of whom were seeking cures for various diseases, also appeared to pose a health hazard. Kimbangu was consequently arrested and condemned to death for 'having disturbed the security of the state and the public peace'. This verdict produced such an uproar throughout the Congo that the King of Belgium thought it prudent to commute the sentence to life imprisonment. Simon Kimbangu therefore remained in an Elisabethville jail until his death on 12 October 1951. He continued his saintly conduct even in prison, where he showed kindness and compassion to inmates and authorities alike. He became renowned for his courage, piety and unselfishness. The ban on Kimbanguism remained in force until 1959, when Kimbangu's son, Joseph Diangienda, succeeded in reviving the movement (which had endured much division and sectarian strife in the interim). Kimbanguism was recognized during the period of independence as a major Zairean religious organization. It became a very important one indeed, operating schools and a seminary and developing ambitious programmes of social services in Lower Zaire. Simon Kimbangu is still revered as a prophet in many parts of Africa and the Kimbanguist Church of Zaire, recognized now by both Congos, was admitted to the World Council of Churches in 1969 with a membership numbering about 1,000,000.

KIMPA VITA
A legendary Zairean figure, born Dona Beatriz around 1685, Kimpa Vita founded a religious sect known as the Antonians early in the eighteenth century. Its goal was to restore the ancient glories of Kongo and to Africanize Christianity. Many Congolese flocked to hear the sermons of Kimpa Vita. This aroused the animosity of the Capuchin Missionaries who found her guilty of heresy and had her burnt at the stake on 2 July 1706. Despite her early death, she played a major role in the renewal and reunification of the Kongo Kingdom and inspired a host of messianic movements, including Kimbanguism. Simon Kimbangu, the famous Congolese prophet of the twentieth century, has frequently been regarded as the spiritual and political descendant of the martyred Kimpa Vita.

KING, Angela
Ms Angela Evelyn Vernon King was appointed in March 1997, by the UN secretary-general, Kofi Annan, as Special Adviser on Gender Issues and Advancement of Women. This made her one of the highest-ranking administrators in the United Nations Secretariat. She chaired the Inter-

Agency Committee on Women and Gender and Equality and served as head of the Division for the Advancement of Women for several years. Prior to this promotion, Ms. King had demonstrated unusual gifts as an administrator, having served since 1987 at the director level in the Office of Human Resources Management, as Director of Recruitment and Placement and Director of Staff Administration and Training. She was also one of the key representatives at the Fourth World Conference on Women at Beijing in 1995. During 1992-94, Ms King headed the UN Observer Mission in South Africa and was only the third woman to have led a United Nations peace and security mission. Born in Jamaica, West Indies, on 28 August 1938, Angela was educated at Wolmer's and St Hilda's High Schools before completing two degrees at the University of the West Indies (BA Hons) and the University of London (MA). She entered the Jamaican diplomatic service in 1962 and joined the United Nations Secretariat in 1966, working on matters relating to human rights and social development. Particularly keen on gender issues, she participated actively in the first two UN conferences on the status of women (in Mexico City in 1975 and Copenhagen in 1980). A founding member of the Group on Equal Rights for Women, she chaired for several years the high-level Steering Committee on Improving the Status of Women in the Secretariat. She retired from her various UN duties in 2004. Ms. King was honoured as one of its most distinguished graduates when the University of the West Indies celebrated its 40th anniversary in 1988. Some thirty years before, she had been the very first woman to be elected President of the Guild of its undergraduates.

KING, Kanya

Kanya King is the founder of the Music of Black Origin (MOBO) Awards which have become an established part of the British music scene. She started to develop MOBO in January 1996 by mortgaging her house and raising sponsorships through several companies. From modest beginnings, the show is now broadcast to about sixty countries and the awards themselves are much coveted by British artists. Prior to the establishment of MOBO, Kanya was a senior researcher for Carlton Television, where she was a founding member of the Crystal Rose Show. She is currently developing MOBO into a major communications company and has been awarded an MBE in recognition of her achievements.

KING, Martin Luther, Jr

The outstanding leader of the civil rights movement in the United States during the 1950s and 1960s, Dr Martin Luther King, Jr was born in Atlanta, Georgia, on 15 January 1929. He attended Booker T. Washington High School, Morehouse College and Crozer Theological Seminary before completing his PhD in 1955 at Boston University's School of Theology. In that year, he accepted the pastorship of the Dexter Avenue Baptist Church in Montgomery, Alabama. He soon became the voice of the growing non-violent civil rights movement which was spreading throughout the United States. After leading the famous Montgomery bus boycott, which began in December 1955 and forced the American courts to rule against segregated seating on municipal buses, King took part in numerous protest marches, culminating in the celebrated 'March on Washington' in 1963. In 1957, he founded the Southern Christian Leadership Conference (SCLC) aimed at educating Blacks in the techniques of demonstrating, protesting and boycotting peacefully. His tactics drew international attention to racial inequality and injustice in the United States and compelled the federal government to implement a series of progressive laws during the 1960s. In 1964, he was chosen Man of the Year by *Time* magazine and was also awarded the Nobel Peace Prize. At thirty- five years of age he was then the youngest recipient of this prestigious distinction. He had earned it not only because of his philosophy of non-violence at home but partly because of his urgent demands for an end to the war in Vietnam and the admission of China to the United Nations. On 4 April 1968 Dr Martin Luther King, Jr was assassinated. Several memorials have since been established to honour his memory and 15 January has been declared a national holiday in the United States. No other American hero has ever been honoured in this way. His influential writings included *Stride Toward Freedom* (1958), *Strength to Love* (1963), and *Why We Can't Wait* (1964).

KING, Oona
Oona King became only the second black woman to be elected to the British House of Commons when she was elected to represent Bethnal Green and Bow in 1997. Born in Sheffield on 22 October 1967 she was raised in Camden and educated in Chalk Farm, London. She achieved degrees from the University of York and the University of California at Berkeley. She then worked as a researcher for the Socialist Group of the European Parliament and as a trade union officer for the GMB (Britain's General Union), representing low-paid workers in the public sector. A member of the Labour Party since the age of fourteen, she was on the European Parliament's Economic and Monetary Affairs Committee and served as a political assistant to Glyn Ford and later Glenys Kinnock. King lost her seat in 2005 and is now pursuing a career in the media.

KINNEY, James
James A.R. Kinney, born in 1878 in Yarmouth, Nova Scotia, was the first black graduate of the Maritime Business College. He became the chief

spokesman in eastern Canada for black racial pride during the first half of the 20th century. In 1921 he was instrumental in founding the Nova Scotia Home for Colored Children, having persuaded the provincial government to purchase over 200 acres for a farm and to provide funds for a building. He superintended this home until his death in 1940. Kinney had hoped, somewhat optimistically, to establish in Canada an institution similar to the Hampton Institute that had grown up in the United States.

KITAWALANS

The Kitawala (or Watch Tower) Movement was an interesting twentieth-century African phenomenon. It was a response to the native yearning for equality and freedom from European domination. It was promoted by local millenarian preachers who successfully merged Christian concepts with traditional African values. The European theology gave a respectable religious base to their political and economic aspirations. Their native congregations related readily to the basic Christian principle of the equality and brotherhood of all men under the fatherhood of God. The Kitawalans founded a host of African-run separatist churches, stressing a post-colonial future after a gigantic struggle between the European forces of evil and the African forces of good. They drew attention to the blatantly unchristian conduct of the invaders and preached a simple gospel of divine retribution. They spoke persuasively of a Last Judgement in which the oppressed Africans would be preferred over the acquisitive Europeans. Most of the leaders of the movement, like John Chilembwe, Simon Kimbangu and Hanoc Sindano, were imprisoned or executed by the imperial governments, but even harsh official persecution failed to check the movement's growth in the Congo, Nyasaland, and Rhodesia. The Kitawalans played a very prominent role in the evolution of modern African nationalism.

KIWELE, Joseph

Born at Mpala in 1912, Joseph Kiwele is generally regarded as the greatest of all African musicians and composers. Educated at Lusaka and at the seminary of Baudouinville, he furthered his studies at the Academy of Liège in Belgium. He returned to the Congo to teach in the province of Katanga in 1941. Also interested in politics, he was elected as a member of the provincial assembly of Katanga and served, from July 1960 until his death, as minister of education and culture for the state of Katanga. He was also president of the State University of Elisabethville at the time of his death. Among Kiwele's greatest compositions were *Missa Katanga*, *La Katangaise*, and *Te Deum Bantou*. He also collected and wrote down several traditional songs of the Yeke. He died on 15 November 1961.

KLY, Yussuf

Dr Yussuf Kly is a popular professor of international law, justice studies and social policy at the University of Regina in Saskatchewan, Canada, where he has taught since 1989. A native of the United States, he received his first degree from the University of Iowa in 1960 before pursuing his postgraduate studies at the Universities of Montreal and Laval in Quebec. His major works include *The Anti-Social Contract* (1979); *International Law and the Black Minority in the United States* (1990); *A Popular Guide to Minority Rights* (1995); and *Societal Development and Minority Rights* (1997). The last two of these each won an award as the Outstanding Book on Human Rights in the United States. Dr Kly has lectured on minority rights to universities and institutes in Algeria, Canada and the United States. He has also contributed numerous articles to scholarly journals on the subject of social justice. It was he who founded the International Human Rights Association of American Minorities in 1988.

KNIGHT, Beverley

Beverley Anne Knight was born in Wolverhampton on 22 March 1973 and has become a critically acclaimed British soul singer, songwriter and record producer. Although her career began only in 1994, she has already been the recipient of a Lifetime Award at the Urban Music Awards (2004). She is well-known for such hit singles as *Greatest Day*, *Shoulda Woulda Coulda* and *Come as You Are* as well as her very popular albums. Many critics consider her one of Britain's greatest soul singers. In 2006 she starred in BBC1 music TV show, *Just The Two of Us*, and is the host of the BBC Radio 2 show, *Beverley's Gospel Nights*, which explores the origins and impact of gospel music. Beverley Knight is an ambassador for a multitude of charities, such as Christian Aid and the Terrence Higgins Trust. She was awarded an MBE in 2006 for her charitable work and her contribution to music.

KOBIA, Samuel

Revd Samuel Kobia is a Kenyan Methodist minister who was elected general secretary of the World Council of Churches (WCC) in January 2004. Born in Miathine, Meru, on 20 March 1947, he was educated at St Paul's United Theological College in Limuru, Kenya; the Christian Theological Seminary in Indianapolis, Indiana; and Fairfax University in Baton Rouge, Louisiana. He also received a diploma in urban ministry from McCormick's Theological Seminary in Chicago, Illinois, and a master's degree in city planning from the Massachusetts Institute of Technology. Kobia served as the WCC's executive secretary for urban rural mission during 1978-87 and was director of church development activities with the National Council of Churches of Kenya, of which he became the general secretary in 1990. In 1993 he was appointed executive director of the WCC's Unit III – Justice, Peace and Creation. He directed the global ecumenical organization's Cluster on Issues and Themes from 1999 to 2002 and served as director and special representative for Africa in 2003. As general secretary of the WCC, Kobia immediately began to deliver strong messages to Kenya, the rest of Africa, and the wider world. He denounced corruption, injustice and the increasing incidence of rape on the African continent. In March 2004, he met with the leaders of sixteen African-American denominations in Washington, D.C., and challenged them to address such issues as HIV/AIDS and the role of the Unites States as the sole remaining super power, whose arrogance he deplored. Two months later he met with Kofi Annan, the UN Secretary-General, to discuss the situation in Iraq, the Israeli-Palestinian conflict and the role of religion in political affairs. He publicly chided the United States for the blatant misuse of religion in mobilising for war, depicting all Muslims in a negative manner and presenting God in partisan terms.

KOK III

Adam Kok III was the famous south African monarch who led the people of the Griqua nation from their home in the Orange Free State to found a new nation, Griqualand East, on the east coast of South Africa. Born in 1811 near Kimberley, South Africa, Adam Kok succeeded to the throne in 1837. Threatened by constant Dutch aggressions, he sought an alliance with the British who had recognized his sovereignty in 1848 and encouraged his great two-year trek to the east. Adam Kok then aided the British in a campaign to subdue the Hlubi rebels in Natal in 1874 but the ungrateful British rewarded him by annexing Griqualand East as well. Kok III died on 30 December 1875.

KOONTZ, Roscoe

Roscoe L. Koontz is one of the world's most renowned health physicists. He was born in St Louis, Missouri, and educated at Tennessee State University and the University of Rochester. He designed a pinhole gamma ray camera and collimator and also helped to design and fabricate automatic air and water sampling equipment and radiation activity devices. He played a major role in developing the procedures and guidelines now commonly followed by health physicists. He is responsible for many of the techniques now used to protect people from the hazards of ionizing radiation.

KORSAH, Kobina Arku

Sir Kobina Arku Korsah, the first African Chief Justice in the history of the Gold Coast, became in due course the first Chief Justice of an independent

Ghana in 1957. Born at Salpond, just east of Cape Coast, on 3April 1894, he was the son of a prosperous merchant. Educated at Mfantsipim School in Cape Coast and Fourah Bay College in Sierra Leone, he graduated with a BA in 1915. He furthered his studies at Durham University, England, achieving a BCL degree in 1917 before earning his LLB from London University in 1919. Returning to the Gold Coast, he specialized in commercial law, but his keen interest in politics led him to participate quite actively in public affairs. He became a key member of the Aborigines' Rights Protection Society (ARPS) and of the National Congress of British West Africa (NCBWA). He was one of the mediators of the quarrel between the rising native intelligentsia and the traditional African chieftains in the late 1920s. This breach seemed at that time to threaten the whole African independence movement. Korsah went to London in 1934 to protest against the unpopular Sedition and Waterworks Bills, forcing the colonial government to withdraw them. He gained an enviable reputation as a debater in the Gold Cost Legislative Council and was appointed to the three-man committee in 1942 to draft a new constitution for the colony. Although their recommendations were rejected at that time, they formed the basis of similar suggestions which elicited more positive results in 1951 when self-government for the Gold Coast became a reality. Korsah was appointed a puisne judge in 1945 and held that post until his promotion to the office of Chief Justice in 1956. He originally gave support to Kwame Nkrumah's Convention People's Party (CPP) which led Ghana to independence, but fell foul of that autocratic president and was dismissed in 1963. He was kept under house arrest until 1966 when Nkrumah was ousted. He died on 25 january 1967. Sir Arku Korsah is remembered as one of the brightest jurists produced by Ghana. He was the recipient of several honours, including an OBE in 1937, and a knighthood in 1955. In 1960 he became a Knight of the British Empire (KCMG).

KOUNTCHÉ, Seyni

Gen Seyni Kountché was the Niger army officer who overthrew the government of Hamani Diori in 1974 and took control of his country until his death on 10 November 1987. Born at Fandou on 1 July 1931, he was educated at French army schools at Kati (Mali) and at St Louis (Senegal). He joined the French colonial army in 1949, served in Indochina and Algeria, and rose to the rank of sergeant in 1957. Following Niger's achievement of political independence in 1960, Kountché transferred to the army of his native country and obtained a sequence of promotions in the next few years, culminating in his appointment in 1967 as deputy chief of staff of the Niger armed forces. In 1973, he became chief of staff and assumed power one year later when he deposed the president in a military coup. His government was characterized by a certain no-nonsense firmness and a fair degree of economic progress. He made Niger self-sufficient in grain and increased its wealth by developing uranium mining. He maintained good relations with France, and visited both China and the United States. Kountché's thirteen-year reign as president of Niger was one of the longest in modern African history.

KUFUOR, John

The son of Asante royal parents, John Kofi Agyekum Kufuor, the current president of Ghana, was born on 8 December 1938 in Kumasi, the second largest city in Ghana. Educated at Prempeh College (Kumasi) and in Great Britain, he was called to the bar at Lincoln's Inn in London before achieving a master's degree in philosophy, politics and economics from the University of Oxford in 1964. Returning to Ghana, Kufuor launched his political career in 1967 and by 1969 was a minister in Kofi Busia's government. He retired from politics after Busia's overthrow in 1972 but helped to draft the constitution of the third republic in 1979. He left politics again after disagreeing with what he regarded as Jerry Rawlings' autocratic conduct and policy. Kufuor spent the 1980s as a private citizen and did not return to politics until democracy was restored to Ghana. He helped found the New Patriotic Party (NPP) in 1992 and opposed Rawlings (unsuccessfully) for the presidency in 1996. When the NPP won the general elections in 2000, he was sworn in as president of Ghana, promising to focus sharply on education and the economy. After his first year in office, the national currency stabilized and investment in the country increased. Kufuor formed commissions to investigate the alleged misdeeds of previous rulers and was able to boast in 2005, at the end of his first term as president, that his government had established multiparty democracy, reduced ethnic and political tensions, overhauled the national communications and transportation infrastructures and revamped the education system.

KUWA MEKKI, Yousif

Yousif Kuwa Mekki, a dynamic Sudanese educator and politician, was born in August 1945 in Al-Akhwal and became famous for leading a guerrilla rebellion on behalf of non-Muslim Blacks in southern Sudan against the Islamic fundamentalist rulers based in the north of the country. He had begun his career as a teacher after studying history and political science at the University of Khartoum. In 1981 he was elected to the regional assembly and became the charismatic leader of the Sudan People's Liberation Army (SPLA) when the civil war erupted between the north and the south. Kuwa Mekki died in Norwich, England, on 31 March 2001.

KWAKU DUA I

A noted nineteenth century Asante ruler, Kwaku Dua I was born around 1797 and reigned efficiently during 1834-67. His famous motto was 'Peace, Trade and Open Roads' even though he had enjoyed a very successful military career in his youth. He sought accommodation with the British and aimed at commercial and economic prosperity rather than military glory or territorial expansion. He revised the fiscal system to ensure that taxes fell most heavily on his richest subjects and encouraged Christian missionaries to establish stations and schools at Kumasi and elsewhere. He also sent the children of Asante nobles to be educated in Europe so that his people might profit from European ideas and innovations. He is, however, remembered as a very strict and sometimes cruel monarch who brooked no resistance to his authority. Many critics of his régime were summarily executed. Still, his wise policy of consolidation kept his kingdom intact in the face of potential challenges from African neighbours and European imperialists. Kwaku Dua I died on 27 April 1867.

LADIPO, Duro

Duro Ladipo was a distinguished Nigerian playwright, actor and producer who did a great deal to popularize the folk operas and traditions of the Yoruba people. Born in Yorubaland in 1931, he helped to found the Mbari Mbayo Club in Oshogbo. He also founded the Duro Ladipo Theatre Company and became its director. His three early plays, *Oba Moro* (The King of Ghosts, 1962), *Oba Koso* (The King Did Not Hang, 1963) and *Oba Waja* (The King is Dead, 1964) have become classics of the Yoruba stage and have introduced Yoruba dramatic ideas and conventions to a worldwide audience. A later work, *Eda*, gave further evidence of the validity of his decision to intellectualize Yoruba folk-opera. Ladipo had begun as a composer of Yoruba church music in Oshogbo, Nigeria, and it was his successful adaptation of Bible stories for the stage that led him to found his own theatre group in 1962. The most popular of his productions was *Oba Koso*, which won the Nigerian federal government award for the most significant contribution to culture in 1963, was highly successful at the Berlin Theatre Festival in 1964, and was presented at the Commonwealth Theatre Festival at London, England, in 1967. Duro Ladipo died in 1978.

LAFONTANT, Jewel

Born in Chicago in 1922, Jewel Stradford Lafontant-Mankarious became, in 1955, the first black woman ever to be named an assistant US attorney for the Northern District of Illinois. She eventually served as director of several executive boards, including Trans World Airlines, Jewel Companies, and the United Nations Association. In 1969 she became vice-chairman of the US Advisory Commission on International Education and Cultural Affairs, and served during 1970-72 as a member of the President's Council on Minority Business Enterprise. After spending a year as a member of the US delegation to the United Nations, she was appointed to the position of deputy solicitor-general of the United States in 1973, thus becoming one of the highest ranking African-Americans in Washington, D.C. She later became the United States Coordinator for Refugee Affairs and was named by President Bush as Ambassador at Large in 1989. She died in 1997.

LA GUMA, Alex

Born in Cape Town on 20 February 1925, Justin Alexander La Guma was a fervent defender of black African nationalism who ran foul of the apartheid system in South Africa and had to spend most of his later years in exile in England and in Cuba. Educated at the Cape Technical College and the London School of Journalism, he worked at several odd jobs before establishing himself as a gifted writer of novels and short stories. He was a member of the editorial board of the Afro-Asian Writers' Bureau and deputy secretary-general of the Afro-Asian Writers' Association. His work, banned in South Africa, drew on his experiences in the townships and in prison. His bitter criticism of his country's racist régime led to occasional detention and imprisonment before he departed for London in 1966 and then for Havana, where he represented the African National Congress (ANC). La Guma's novels included *A Walk in the Night* (1962), *And a Threefold Cord* (1964), *The Stone Country* (1967) and *Time of the Butcherbird* (1979). He won the Afro-Asian Award in 1969. He died on 11 October 1985.

LAINE, Cleo

Dame Cleo Laine, Lady Dankworth DBE was born on 28 October 1927 in Middlesex to a Jamaican father and English mother. She has enjoyed a wonderful career as singer and actress and, such is her versatility, she remains the only person to have received Grammy nominations in the jazz, popular and classical music awards. In 1983 she became the first British artist to win a Grammy Award as the best jazz vocalist. In 1979 she was made an Officer of the Order of the British Empire (OBE) for her services to music. This was upgraded in 1997 to Dame Commander of the British Empire (DBE). The US recording industry honoured her in 1991 with a Lifetime Achievement Award and the Worshipful Company of Musicians did likewise in 2002. Dame Cleo Laine was made an ambassador for SOS Children's Villages UK in recognition of her support for the Cambridge-based charity. She has also received honorary doctorates from Berkbee College of Music (Boston), Cambridge University, University of Luton, the Open University and the University of York.

LAMMING, George

One of the greatest of all West Indian authors, George William Lamming was born on 8 June 1927 in Barbados, where he was educated at Combermere School (1939-45). He taught for some years in Trinidad before emigrating to the United Kingdom where he published his much acclaimed first novel, *In the Castle of My Skin*, in 1953. He has lectured in places as far apart as Australia, Denmark, India, Tanzania and the United States and has also served as a visiting professor in several North American universities. Lamming was one of the founders of the Labour College of the Barbados Workers' Union and a recipient of the Writers Award from the Association of Commonwealth Literature in 1976. Some of his other works are *The Emigrants* (1955), *Of Age and Innocence* (1958), *Season of Adventure* (1960), *Water with Berries* (1971), and *Natives of My Person* (1972). In 1995 Lamming was honoured by the Combermere School Old Scholars' Association (CSOSA) for his sterling contribution to the Combermere community when that institution celebrated its 300th anniversary.

LAMMY, David

David Lindon Lammy is a promising young Labour politician who is expected by many to become the first black prime minister of Britain. At twenty seven, he was the youngest campaigner to win a seat in the House of Commons in 2000 and to be re-elected in 2005. Born in a working-class area of London on19 July 1972, he graduated with a law degree from the School of Oriental and African Studies in London and then became the first black Briton to achieve an MA from the Harvard Law School. He has practised as a lawyer in London and in California, specialising in medical ethics, negligence and commercial litigation. Always interested in politics, he secured a position on the Greater London Assembly (GLA) with a portfolio for culture and arts in 1997. His major political concerns are education, social inclusion, economic affairs and international development. Lammy is a member of the All-party Group on Rwanda and the Prevention of Genocide, the British-Caribbean All-party Group and the All-party Group on AIDS.

LANE, William Henry

William Henry Lane, much better known as 'Master Juba', has been recognized as one of the finest dancers of all time. The creator of professional tap dancing, he gave performances all over Europe and was acknowledged the dancing king of the world when he bested the famous white dancer, King Diamond, in a series of competitions in1845. Born in 1825 in Rhode Island, he began his career as a performer in local saloons, playing the banjo and the guitar and imitating the moves of the best dancers of his time. He eventually settled in London, England, where he performed with a major dance company and established his own studio. In 1848 he danced at Vauxhall Gardens and before Queen Victoria at Buckingham Palace. His famous 'Juba' dance was a mixture of the African shuffle and slide and the European jig, reel and clog steps. He emphasized rhythm and percussion over melody and was well versed in improvisation. He was perhaps the first to add syncopation to his dancing. William Henry Lane died, at the tender age of twenty seven, in 1852.

LANGSTON, John

John Mercer Langston, an eminent lawyer, educator and statesman, was born in Louisa, Virginia, in 1829. A former slave, he graduated from Oberlin College in 1849, the theology school there in 1852 and the law school at Elyria, Ohio, in 1854. He became, in turn, Ohio's first black lawyer, the first president of Virginia State College, and then Virginia's first black congressman. In 1869, Langston was appointed dean of the law department of Howard University, a post he held until 1876 while also serving as a member of the District of Columbia Board of Health He later became minister resident and consul general to Haiti and chargé d'affaires to Santo Domingo. Langston died in 1897.

LANSANA, David

Born on 27 March 1922, David Lansana became the first African native to be commissioned into the Royal Sierra Leone Military Forces and in due course became also the first Sierra Leonean brigadier-general. Educated at Central School in Sierra Leone before completing his studies in England, he enlisted as an officer cadet in 1947 and was commissioned five years later. In 1965 Lansana was promoted to the rank of force commander of the Royal Sierra Leone Military Forces. Following the general elections of 1967, he declared martial law because of the indecisive nature of the results and the general mood of uncertainty throughout the country. But he was arrested by his own officers. After order was apparently restored, however, he was given a diplomatic appointment in New York. Charged with plotting against the government later on, he was convicted of treason and executed on 19 July 1975.

LARA, Brian

Born in Cantaro, Trinidad, on 2 May 1969, Brian Charles Lara shocked the sporting world in 1994 by eclipsing two of cricket's most cherished records in the space of fifty days. On 18 April he scored 375 runs against England in a single Test innings at Antigua to erase the mark of 365 not out that Sir Garfield Sobers had set in 1958, and on 6 June against Durham at

Birmingham, he scored 501 not out for Warwickshire in the English County Cricket competition. This surpassed the previous first-class world record of 499 established by Hanif Mohammad of Pakistan in 1959. In April 2004, after his previous record had been broken by Matthew Hayden of Australia, Lara became the first cricketer to register 400 runs in a Test innings and in November 2005, he broke all existing records for most runs in a Test career. He is a stylish left-handed batsman who is considered by many to be the greatest thus far produced by the West Indies and one of the best that the world has yet seen. His three centuries against Australia in 1999 are thought by most pundits to be among the finest innings ever played. He remains the only batsman thus far who has scored several double centuries, a triple century, a quadruple century and a quintuple century in first-class cricket.

LATIMER, Lewis

One of America's outstanding scientists and inventors, Lewis Howard Latimer, the son of former slaves, was born in Chelsea, Massachusetts, on 4 September 1848. After serving in the Union Navy in the early 1860s, he studied drafting. In 1881, he invented and patented an incandescent light bulb with a carbon filament which permitted bulbs to be safer while lasting longer and shining more brightly. He then joined the Edison Company as an engineer and supervised the installation of the electric light system in cities as far apart as Montreal (Canada), London (England), New York and Philadelphia (United States). In 1890, Latimer wrote the first textbook used by the Edison Company, *Incandescent Electric Lighting*, after having been employed by Alexander Graham Bell to make patent drawings for the first telephone in 1876. He also served for many years as chief draughtsman for General Electric and Westinghouse companies. His other patented inventions include the first water toilet for railroad cars (1874), and a forerunner of the air conditioner (1886). Lewis Latimer will long be remembered for making possible the widespread use of electric light both in public and in private homes. This very gifted electrical engineer died on 11 December 1928.

LATINO, Juan

Memorialized by the great Spanish writer, Miguel de Cervantes, in his popular *Don Quixote*, this former African slave was born perhaps in Guinea around 1515 and is best remembered for his classic poem, *Austrias*, which he wrote to celebrate the Spanish naval victory over the Turks at Lepanto in 1571. He and his mother were slaves in the household of Dona Elvira, the daughter of Gonzalo Fernandez who was then Spain's most famous general. He taught himself to read and write while serving as a companion to the general's young grandson. With his youthful master, he attended the

University of Granada and achieved his BA in 1546. A brilliant student, he changed his name to Juan Latino and in 1557 joined the staff at the University of Granada where he rose to the rank of professor and was accorded the signal honour of delivering the Latin address to open the academic session in 1565. Juan Latino, who was also an accomplished musician, wrote several epics in Latin before ill health forced him to retire in 1586. He is believed to have survived as a highly respected intellectual in Spain until 1606 when he was more than ninety years old.

LAWRENCE, Richard

Richard Lloyd Lawrence was born in Toronto, Ontario, in 1926. Following his graduation from high school at Central Tech, he studied at Howard University where he received the American Institute of Architects Award and the Senior Medal for Excellence in Design when he graduated in 1955. He returned to Toronto to design several buildings of note and is remembered as the first native black architect in the city. He died in 1975.

LAYE, Camara

Camara Laye is one of the best and most influential among the African Francophone novelists. The son of a Malinké goldsmith, he was born in Kouroussa in French Guinea on 1 January 1928 and was trained in Conakry and in France as an engineer. While studying in France, he created quite a sensation with his first novel, *L'enfant noir*, which appeared in 1953 and yielded its author the prestigious Prix Charles Veillon in 1954. Translated into English as *The Dark Child* in 1955, it became a classic at once and has been standard fare for courses in African literature and culture ever since. Almost as successful as his first masterpiece was his second effort, *Le regard du roi*, which he published in 1954. These two literary triumphs earned him a post as attaché at the ministry of youth in Paris. Returning to Guinea just after his native country had won its political independence from France in 1957, he was named director of the Study and Research Centre in the Ministry of Information at Conakry. But, like so many other independent and progressive thinkers, he fell foul of the president, Sékou Touré, and found himself more or less under house arrest after 1960. His bitter experiences in those days are clearly reflected in his later writing after he managed to escape from Guinea in 1965. The tone of his acrid *Dramouss*, in which he severely censured the modern African political leaders ensured that he would have to remain in exile - at least until after Touré's death. He then worked for many years with the Institut Français d'Afrique Noire (IFAN) in Dakar, Senegal, where he sought refuge. He died there on 4 February 1980. His nostalgic novels deftly investigated the African psychology while leaving very interesting glimpses of passing local traditions.

LEE, Canada

Born Leonard Lionel Cornelius Canegata in New York City on 3 May 1907, this talented actor became one of the first African-American film stars. As Canada Lee, he tried his hand at music, horse racing and boxing before finding his proper niche. He achieved little success in these fields, although he did win the national amateur lightweight boxing title in the early 1920s. His acting career began in 1934 when he appeared in *Brother Mose*. Thereafter he played a variety of roles in such films as *Banquo*, *Haiti* and *Stevedore*. In 1941, Lee's career reached its peak when he portrayed Bigger Thomas in Orson Welles' production of Richard Wright's *Native Son* which enjoyed an unusually long run. In 1944, he took part in another important film, *Lifeboat*. Lee appeared on Broadway and was frequently heard on radio programmes during the 1940s. His radio work, especially after World War II, reflected a keen interest in the plight of American Blacks. He died on 9 May 1952.

LEE, Joseph

A noted American inventor, master chef and businessman, Joseph Lee was born in Charleston, South Carolina, on 19 July 1849. He began his career as a menial in a local bakery where he learnt to bake bread and to cook. His life changed forever when he invented a bread crumb machine and followed it up with a bread-making machine which brought him a small fortune. By 1900 he owned the Woodland Park Hotel in Newton, Massachusetts. In 1902, he also opened the Lee Catering Company to cook and deliver food to wealthy patrons. He died around 1905, but his fame lives on. The baking industry has never been the same after the invention of Lee's machines. Ever since then, bread has been baked more efficiently and more rapidly with the use of fewer hands.

LELEKA

Born in 1905, Leleka became one of the greatest chiefs of the Giri River region in what is now northwestern Zaire. He provided his kingdom with efficient administration and actively worked for the economic development of the area for almost fifty years. He mediated disputes between Protestants and Catholics within his realm, supervised the construction of new roads, encouraged the building of schools and dispensaries, and promoted the growth of trade and agriculture. He remained in office from 1929 to 1973. But so scrupulous and unselfish was Chief Leleka that he died a poor man in 1975.

LE MAR, Angie

Angie Lemar is an accomplished and popular comedienne, actress and director who is generally known as Britain's First Lady of Black Comedy.

She has won numerous awards, such as BECA's Best Stand Up Female (2000), BECA's Most Original Material (2001), Men and Women of Merit (2002) and the prestigious European Federation of Black Women in Business (EFBWO) in 2002. Angie has thrilled thousands of fans whether live on stage, on radio or on television. She has starred in such TV shows as *The Real McCoy* and *Get Up, Stand Up*. She has also presented *The Saturday Morning Show* on Choice FM. She was the first British black performer to appear at Harlem's legendary Apollo Theatre and she made history in London's West End with the first sell-out show by a female black entertainer.

LEONARD, Sugar Ray

One of the finest boxers of all time, Ray Charles Leonard was born in Wilmington, North Carlina, on 17 May 1956. After a spectacular amateur career, which culminated in an Olympic Gold Medal in 1976, he won professional world championships in several weight divisions, ranging from welterweight to light heavy, during 1978-97. He won 36 of his 40 professional fights and lost only three. Sugar Ray, who was inducted into the International Boxing Hall of Fame in 1997, is now involved in the TV reality series, *The Contenders*.

LEROY, Félix Morisseau

Félix Morisseau Leroy, a noted Haitian journalist, educator and author, was born in Grand-Gosier on 13 March 1912. Educated in Jacmel at Condorcet Leroy's school and the Lycée Pinchinat, he furthered his studies in Port-au-Prince and graduated with a law degree. He joined the teaching staff at the Lycée Pinchinat and later became the chef-de-division at the ministry of public instruction. Leroy then attended Columbia University in the United States before serving as director general of Education in Haiti. Always keen on journalism, he was a chief editor of *Sud-Ouest*, a local Jacmel newspaper, and a contributor to many other papers while also editing *Le Matin*. After working with the United Nations Economic and Social Council (UNESCO), he emigrated to Senegal and worked for the ministry of culture in Dakar. Leroy's importance as an author lies in his ability to combine formal French with Haitian colloquial and rustic dialects. He tried his utmost to demonstrate that the creole language used by the bulk of the Haitians ought to be accepted as a language in its own right. His major works included a novel, *Récolte* (1946); *Plénitude* (1940) and *Gerbe pour deux amis*, collections of poetry in French written with Roussan Camille and Jean F. Brierre (1945); and *Diacoute I* (1953) and *Diacoute 2* (1972), collections of poetry in creole. Leroy also wrote several plays, essays and short stories in French and creole. Many of his writings have been translated into English.

LEWIS, Allen

Like his brother, the famous economist, Sir Arthur Lewis, Sir Allen was born in St Lucia, British West Indies, and educated in local schools. He completed his law studies at the Inns of Court in London, England, and became a famous jurist and statesman in his native island. He served for many years as a puisne judge of the Supreme Court of St Lucia, was a member of the City Council in Castries (the capital city), and also of the colony's Legislative Council. The founder of the St Lucia Labour Party and the St Lucia Workers' Union, Allen Lewis played a notable part in the successful promotion of universal suffrage and collective bargaining in St Lucia. He was appointed president of the senate and a judge of the Supreme Court of the West Indies during the period of the British West Indian Federation (1958-62). In 1962 he was appointed a judge of the Supreme Court of Jamaica, and then chief justice of the newly created West Indies Associated States Supreme Court. In 1974, Sir Allen Lewis became Governor of St Lucia and assumed the office of Governor General when that island achieved its political independence in 1979. He served until 1987. The recipient of numerous honours and distinctions, he was awarded the Coronation Medal in 1953. In 1968 he was made a Knight Batchelor. In 1975 he became a Knight of the Order of St John of Jerusalem. In 1977 He was awarded the Jubilee Medal, and in 1979 he was made Knight of the Grand Cross of the Order of St Michael and St George (KCMG). In 1974 the University of the West Indies conferred on him the honorary degree of Doctor of Laws and one year later appointed him its Chancellor. He held that post for fourteen years. Sir Allen Lewis is one of the most important figures in the history of St Lucia. As its governor, he took an active interest in every department of the life of the people and was especially keen on education and voluntary organizations. He died in February 1993.

LEWIS, Arthur

Sir William Arthur Lewis was one of the brightest scholars produced by the West Indies. Born in Castries, St Lucia, on 23 January 1915, he achieved his PhD from the London School of Economics in 1940. After lecturing at the University of London from 1938 to 1947, he was appointed to the prestigious Stanley Jevons Chair in Political Economy at the University of Manchester in 1948. After 1957, Lewis served as the deputy managing director of the United Nations Special Fund for Economic Development. As the founder of the Caribbean Development Bank in 1970, he acted as its first president during 1970-73 while still serving as a consultant to the United Nations and many governments in the West Indies. He developed the famous 'Lewis Model' which was first enunciated in his classic *The Theory of Economic Growth* (1955). Lewis argued that India's failure to industrialize effectively reflected the lack of a solid agricultural base and concluded that the transition from an agrarian to an industrialized economy depended more on cheap labour than on conventional capital. In 1959 he was appointed principal of the University College of the West Indies and served as its first black vice-chancellor during 1962-1963. He joined the staff of Princeton University in 1963 and did not formally retire from it until 1983. In 1979 Sir Arthur Lewis became the first Black to receive a Nobel award other than the Peace Prize when he shared the prize in Economic Science with Theodore W. Schultz of the United States for research into the economic development of less developed countries. He was chairman of the Caribbean Research Council during 1985-91. His other books included *Economic Survey 1918-1939* (1949), *The Evolution of the International Economic Order* (1978), and *Racial Conflict and Economic Development* (1985). Lewis was named an honorary member of the American Academy of Arts and Sciences in 1962 and was knighted in 1963. Among his numerous honours were honorary doctorates from Bristol University (England), the University of Toronto (Canada) and the University of the West Indies (Jamaica). He died on 15 June 1991.

LEWIS, Carl

F. Carlton Lewis is one of the greatest athletes that the world has known. Born on 1 July 1961 in Birmingham, Alabama, he was the third of four athletic children produced by two professional track coaches. He created a sensation in 1983 by becoming the first athlete since 1886 to win the 100 metre and the 200 metre sprints and the long jump at the US national outdoor championships. Carl Lewis dominated the long jump competition at the international level for almost two decades and won the Olympic gold medal in that event in 1984, 1988, 1992 and 1996. Had it not been for the US boycott of the Moscow Olympics in 1980, he might well have become the first athlete to win an event in five consecutive Olympic competitions. Lewis also won the 100 metre dash at the Olympics in 1984 and 1988. Altogether Lewis, who won more medals in important international track and field competitions than any other male athlete, finished his career with nine Olympic gold medals to share the world record with Paavo Nurmi, Finland's celebrated distance runner. He also earned a silver medal in the 200 metre final at the Seoul Olympics in 1988. Carl Lewis will long be remembered as the most consistent long jumper in the history of athletics. He exceeded 28 feet more often than anyone else.

LEWIS, Daurene

Dr Daurene Lewis, a native of Nova Scotia, became the first black woman in Canada to be elected to municipal office when she served as councillor in

Annapolis Royal from 1979 to 1984 and as deputy mayor during 1982-84. She then became in 1984 the first black woman in North America to be elected mayor. She was the mayor of Annapolis Royal (Nova Scotia) from 1984 to 1988. During 1998-2001, she was the Executive Director of the Centre for Women in Business at Mount St Vincent University. In 2002 she was appointed principal of the Halifax Campuses, Nova Scotia Community College, and thus became the first black woman to hold such a post in that province. A nurse by training with over thirty years experience in health care, she also achieved an MBA from St Mary's University in 1997 and was awarded an honorary doctorate by Mount St Vincent University in 1993. An enthusiastic activist and community servant, Dr Lewis has received numerous other awards and distinctions, including the Global Citizen Award from the United Nations Fiftieth Anniversary Canada Committee in 1995 and the Order of Canada in 2002.

LEWIS, Denise

Born in West Bromwich on 27 August 1972, Denise Lewis made a name for herself by winning the Gold Medal in the heptathlon at the Sydney Olympics in 2000. She was named Britain's Female Athlete of the Year in 1996, when she was Britain's only female Olympic athletic medallist; in 1997 when she won the Silver Medal in the World Championships; and in 1998 when she triumphed at both the Commonwealth and European Games. Lewis was awarded the MBE in 1999 and the OBE in 2001 for her contributions to athletics.

LEWIS, Edmonia

Born around the mid-1840s, Edmonia Lewis was one of the earliest African-American women to earn fame as a sculptor. She attended Oberlin College and Edmund Brackett's studio in Boston before completing her art studies in Rome. It was her Italian training which led her to adopt the neoclassical style while specializing in portrait busts. Her most famous sculptures included a bust of Col Robert Gould Shaw, a Civil War hero; a medallion head of John Brown, the famous abolitionist; a plaster portrait of Charles Sumner; and the mother-and-children group, entitled *Forever Free*. Edmonia Lewis' work was exhibited in several cities during the nineteenth century and continued to be much admired long after her death in 1890.

LEWIS, Lennox

When Lennox Lewis won the undisputed heavy-weight championship of the boxing world on 13 November 1999 by defeating Evander Holyfield, he became the first British undisputed champion of that division for more than a hundred years. Although he had won a gold medal for Canada at the 1988

Olympics in Seoul, he had shortly returned to the United Kingdom where he had been born of West Indian parents on 2 September 1965. Lewis was one of the best of the heavyweights in the generation which followed Muhammad Ali, George Foreman and Joe Frazier. He retired from the ring in 2004 with a record of 41-2-1. His two losses came against Oliver McCall in 1994 and Hashim Rahman in 2001. He avenged both of these indignities as well as the controversial draw with Holyfield in March 1999. His victories included 32 by knockout. In 1999 he was voted the BBC Sports Personality of the Year.

LEWIS, Reginald

It is hard to believe that Reginald F. Lewis, the famous US lawyer, financier and philanthropist, was only fifty years old when he died on 19 January 1993. Born in Baltimore, Maryland, on 7 December 1942, he earned a degree from the Harvard Law School in 1968 and worked for some years with the firm of Paul, Weiss, Rifkind, Wharton and Garrison. He later became a key partner (1970-73) in Murphy, Thorpe and Lewis, the first black law firm on Wall Street. In 1973, he founded his own law firm, Lewis and Clarkson, which specialized in venture capital projects. Among his most lucrative deals was the purchase of the McCall Pattern Company in 1983 from which he made a personal net profit of $50 million when he sold it four years later. After his purchase of Beatrice Companies in 1987, he became one of the richest businessmen in North America and formed his own concern, The Lewis Company (TLC), then the largest single enterprise owned by an African-American. Having amassed a private fortune in excess of $400 million by the early 1990s, he donated huge sums to Virginia State University and Howard University and became the most generous of all donors to the Harvard Law School when he offered it $3 million in 1992.

LEWIS, Samuel

Sir Samuel Lewis was a distinguished Sierra Leonean lawyer who became a firm supporter of British imperialism while wishing also for African social justice and equality. The son of a prosperous trader, he was born on 13 November 1843 and attended the Church Missionary Society Grammar School before assisting in his father's firm until 1866. Lewis studied law in England and returned to practice in Freetown in 1872. Almost at once he was appointed acting attorney general. Establishing a fine reputation as an excellent advocate, he defended difficult cases all across British West Africa. He became permanent unofficial member of the Sierra Leone Legislative Council in 1882 and succeeded in winning the members of that body the right to receive information, debate bills and propose amendments. Thus the Sierra Leone Legislative Council, which had been little more than an advisory body in the past, gradually became an effective organ for the dissemination of African middle-class views. Lewis also played a significant role in the founding of the Freetown Municipal Council and became the first mayor of Freetown in 1896. He published three pamphlets on Sierra Leonean affairs during 1881-85 and is remembered as one of the pioneers of African nationalism despite his pro-British sympathies. Sir Samuel Lewis died on 9 July 1903.

LIVINGSTONE, Kay

One of Canada's leading actresses, radio hosts and social activists, Kay Livingstone devoted her life to the promotion of racial and gender equality. She was one of the leaders of the Canadian Negro Women's Association (CANEWA), founded in 1951. She persuaded this organization, and others like it, to involve themselves directly in politics in order to achieve their basic goals. She was among those who contributed enormously to Canada's more progressive civil rights and immigration legislation after World War II. Born in 1918, in London, Ontario, she studied at the Royal Conservatory of Music in Toronto and the Ottawa College of Music. In Ottawa, she began a career as a radio host in the 1940s with *The Kathleen Livingstone Show* before moving to Toronto and hosting programmes on several stations including the Canadian Broadcasting Corporation (CBC). Her community service included leadership roles in the Canadian Council of Churches, Heritage Ontario, the Legal Aid Society, the National Black Coalition of Canada, the United Nations Association and the YWCA. In her last years, Kay worked as a consultant for the Privy Council of Canada, travelling the country in preparation for a conference on 'Visible Minorities' (a term she is generally credited with coining). She died in 1975. In her honour, the Kay Livingstone Visible Minority Women's Society has been founded to provide educational funding for deserving young women.

LLOYD, Clive

One of the greatest captains in the history of Test cricket, Clive Hubert Lloyd was born in British Guiana on 31 August 1944. A brilliant left-handed batsman and fielder, he scored over 31,000 runs at almost 50 per innings, and took 377 catches in a first-class career that spanned more than twenty years (1963-86). In 110 Tests for the West Indies, he scored 7,515 runs (aver: 46.67), including 19 centuries, and held 90 catches. He is remembered as one of the most successful Test captains of all time. He led the West Indies in a record 74 matches, including 27 successive games without defeat, and to a record 36 victories as against 12 losses. In one golden spell during 1984-85 he led the West Indies to an unprecedented 11 consecutive victories against Australia and England. No other country had previously won more than eight straight Test matches. Lloyd, who played for many years for Lancashire in the English County Cricket championship, settled down in England after his retirement but he has occasionally served the West Indian Cricket Board (WICB) as the manager of its Test teams.

LOBENGULA

The son of the great Matabele chief, Mzilikazi, Lobengula proved himself a worthy successor and might have completed his father's work of expansion and centralization had it not been for European interference in the regions now occupied by South Africa and Zimbabwe. Born around 1836, Lobengula succeeded to the Matabele throne upon his father's death in 1868. He restored stability after two years of civil strife and proceeded to strengthen his empire by means of effective warfare and shrewd diplomacy. He managed to extend the boundaries of his chieftaincy and to create a highly centralized state which the Europeans did not succeed in overpowering until 1893. While many other African warrior-kings had alienated themselves irrevocably from their subject peoples and their neighbours, Lobengula managed to gain the support even of the Sothos and other groups whom he had promised security, justice and good government. He made the error, however, of making too many concessions to the South African Company in the hope that the British would help him solidify his position. But the latter were more interested in exploiting the diamond mines near Bulawayo than in strengthening Matabele rule in the area. Unscrupulously breaking their agreements, the British eventually destroyed that southeastern African empire by force. Lobengula died, a disappointed man, in 1894. The knowledge that administrative skill had kept the Matabele Empire in tact long after other native systems had crumbled before the inexorable European advance provided little consolation.

LOCKE, Alain

Dr Alain Leroy Locke, an eminent scholar and educator, was born in Philadelphia, Pennsylvania, on 13 September 1886. After graduating with his BA and PhD degrees from Harvard University in 1910, he joined the faculty at Howard University and remained there for more than forty years. A prolific writer, Locke published numerous articles and several books, including *The New Negro* (1925), *The Negro in America* (1933), *The Negro and His Music* (1936), *Negro Art: Past and Present* (1936), and *The Negro in Art* (1941). He edited the *Bronze Booklet* studies of cultural achievements by Blacks. For almost two decades he annually reviewed literature by and about Blacks in *Opportunity and Phyton*, and from 1940 until his death he regularly wrote about Blacks for the *Britannica Book of the Year*. Locke's greatest contribution here was that of a promoter and interpreter of black culture, but he also left an enviable reputation as one of the finest American minds of the twentieth century. A philosopher of no mean distinction himself, he was a humanist intensely concerned with aesthetics. He termed his philosophy 'cultural pluralism' and emphasized the necessity of determining values to guide human conduct and interrelationships. Chief among these values was respect for the uniqueness of each personality, which can develop fully and remain unique only within a democratic ethos. Locke was (in 1907) the first Black to be awarded a Rhodes Scholarship. In 1945 he was elected the first black president of the largely white American Association for Adult Education. He died on 9 June 1954.

LOGAN, Rayford, W.

This outstanding African-American historian was born in 1897 in Washington, D.C. He received his BA and MA from Williams College before completing his PhD at Harvard University in 1936. After teaching at Virginia Union University and Atlanta University, he moved to Howard University in 1938 and became head of the history department there four years later. Logan served for some years as the editor of the *Journal of Negro History* and the *Negro History Bulletin*. His books included *Diplomatic Relations of the United States with Haiti* (1941), *The Negro and the Post-War World, A Primer* (1945), *The African Mandates in World Politics* (1948), and *The Negro in American Life and Thought; The Nadir 1877-1901* (1954). Dr Logan died in 1982.

LONGANI

This famous Congolese chief rose from humble origins to control several Lega and Basile clans. Largely because of his ability to speak both Swahili and English, he was employed for many years as an interpreter and came to be trusted by the Europeans who installed him as the chief of the great Wamuzimu kingdom in 1931, when he was already more than seventy years old. As an agent of the colonial administration, he promoted the interests of the Europeans in Africa and consolidated his own position in the Congo with European support. But his authority waned as he grew older and more feeble. His empire literally crumbled from the 1950s onward. He had himself struggled to bring previously decentralized peoples under a single, western-supported government structure. He died at the age of about 104 on 14 July 1964, much saddened by the fact that even independence had failed to bring unity and co-operation to Zaire.

LOUIS, Joe

Born Joseph Louis Barrow in Lafayette, Alabama, on 13 May 1914, Joe Louis became one of the most popular and one of the greatest heavyweight boxers in the history of the sport. He held the championship for twelve years after knocking out James Braddock on 22 June 1937 and defended his title 25 times, scoring 21 knockouts. His most memorable triumph came in 1938 when he demolished Max Schmeling, the German champion, in less than three minutes to make a mockery of Adolf Hitler's theory of Aryan supremacy. Known affectionately as the 'Brown Bomber', he became a symbol of resistance to Nazism and gave several exhibitions to millions of soldiers during World War II. He was much less successful in his later years, however, losing to Ezzard Charles and Rocky Marciano when his skills had diminished. In 1954, he was elected to the Boxing Hall of Fame, having established a professional record of 65-3. But he fell on hard times after his retirement, being unable to account for much of the $4 million he had earned in the ring, or pay the huge sum of back taxes which the Internal Revenue Service calculated that he owed. Joe Louis died on 12 April 1981 and was buried at the Arlington National Cemetery at the request of President Ronald Reagan.

LOUVERTURE, Toussaint

Arguably the most important name in the entire history of the Republic of Haiti belongs to Pierre François Dominique Toussaint Louverture. Born into slavery in Cap-Français, Saint Domingue (now Haiti) on 20 May 1743, he was freed by his owner, Baron de Libertad, in 1777 at the age of thirty-four. He entered the French colonial service and rose to the rank of governor general of Saint Domingue after having shown exceptional military skills in thwarting the British and Spanish troops when they attempted to invade the island during the French revolutionary period. But Toussaint annoyed Napoleon by attempting to apply the revolutionary ideals to Saint Domingue, by uniting the whole island, and ultimately promulgating a new constitution calling for self-government. Louverture was captured by the French and taken to France where he died on 7 April 1803. But the foundations he had laid for the emancipation of the slaves and the independence of Haiti were too solid to be undone and the Haitians were able to proclaim their independent republic on 1 January 1804.

LOVELACE, Earl

Earl W. Lovelace is a West Indian novelist, poet, playwright, educator and civil servant who is largely self-taught but has himself been invited often to lecture at North American universities. Born in 1935 in Scarborough, Tobago, he worked briefly with the *Trinidad Guardian* before becoming a forest ranger. He created quite a sensation with his first novel, *While Gods Are Falling*, which won a British Petroleum prize of $5,000 in 1964. Another successful novel, *The Schoolmaster*, appeared in 1968. In 1997 Lovelace won the Commonwealth Writers Prize and was named Express Individual of the

Year for his latest novel, *Salt*. He has also published several poems and articles. He was invited to join the staff at Pacific Lutheran University on the west coast of the United States in September 1998.

LULE, Yusufu

Born in Kampala, Buganda, on 10 April 1912, Yusufu Kirolde Lule was a prominent Ugandan academic and politician. A graduate of Fort Hare University College, South Africa, and of the University of Edinburgh, Scotland, he became the first African lecturer at Makerere University College, Uganda. Just prior to Uganda's achievement of political independence, Lule was one of three African ministers in the colonial government and he was appointed chairman of the Uganda Public Service Commission in 1962. In 1964 he became principal of Makerere College which by this time had become affiliated with the University of East Africa. Leaving Uganda in 1970, Lule served for two years as assistant secretary-general in charge of education on the Commonwealth Secretariat in London, England. During 1972-79 he was secretary-general of the Association of African Universities before heading the Uganda National Liberation Front aimed at the overthrow of President Idi Amin's repressive régime. With Tanzania's aid, the rebels expelled Amin and Lule was chosen to lead a provisional government in April 1979, but within less than ten weeks he was himself ousted and returned in exile to England where he died on 21 january 1985. Lule's career illustrates the difficulties facing Uganda, where conflicting personalities and ethnic groups have vied for power and influence ever since the achievement of political independence in 1962.

LUMUMBA, Patrice

Patrice Emery Lumumba was an ardent Congolese nationalist who strove vainly in the early days of independence to prevent ethnic conflict and regional fragmentation. He became the first prime minister of the Congo in 1960 but was overwhelmed by labour unrest, bureaucratic collapse, military mutinies and international interference. He came, nevertheless, to be seen as a heroic martyr who died for his country. Born on 2 July 1925, he was largely self-taught after completing his primary education at a Catholic mission school. He read widely in such fields as economics, law and philosophy. He served as a special correspondent for several newspapers, including *La Croix du Congo* and *La Voix du Congolais*. Lumumba was a fervent Pan-Africanist and supported numerous cultural, educational, political and professional groups. His tenure of office as prime minister, however, proved disastrous. He was dismissed after a clash with Joseph Kasavubu, the president of the new republic. Within a few months he was also assassinated. Lumumba died on 17 January 1961 but became, in death, a powerful anti-imperial symbol. He was proclaimed an official National Hero of Zaire and an African Martyr in 1966.

LUTHULI, Albert

Chief Albert John Mvumbi Luthuli was the famous Zulu nationalist who won the Nobel Peace Prize in 1960 for his nonviolent campaign against the South African system of apartheid. Born in Rhodesia in 1898, and educated in local mission schools and trained as a teacher, he taught Zulu history and literature at the American Mission School for several years. He was elected chief of the Abasemakholweni in Natal in 1936. He joined the African National Congress (ANC) and helped to organize nonviolent resistance to the government's racist programme. In 1952, when he disobeyed the government's order to abandon the ANC, he was promptly stripped of his chieftainship. Four years later, he was placed under house arrest for his bold criticism of the cruel Western Areas Removal Scheme which left the natives under undue and unreasonable handicaps. His critical speeches in 1959 led to further restrictions and he was imprisoned again in 1960 when he publicly burnt his pass book and called for a day of national mourning in memory of those killed on 28 March during a peaceful demonstration at Sharpeville. In 1960, the ANC was outlawed, the same year in which Luthuli was elected its president. After having been legally confined to his farm in Groutville since 1959, he was grudgingly given permission by the government to go to Oslo in 1961 to receive the Nobel Prize that he had been awarded the year before. Still banned from an active public life, Luthuli spent his last days on his farm where he died on 21 July 1967, after having published his autobiography, *Let My People Go*, in 1962. During his enforced retirement, he had continued to write polemics and to advocate a multi-racial society with justice and equality for all citizens.

MAATHAI, Wangari

In 2004, Dr Wangari Muta Maathai, a Kenyan environmentalist and advocate for women's rights, became the first African woman to receive a Nobel Prize for Peace. She was the founder and leader of the Green Belt Movement which, among other things, had been responsible for planting more than 30 million trees in Kenya and elsewhere in Africa. Born on 1 April 1940 in Nyeri, she studied in the United States and achieved a master's degree from the University of Pittsburgh in 1966. Returning to Kenya, she completed her PhD in veterinary medicine at the University of Nairobi in 1971, becoming the very first woman in eastern Africa to receive a doctorate. In 1976, Dr Maathai was appointed head of the department of veterinary anatomy at the University of Nairobi. She joined the National Council of Women of Kenya and presided over this group during 1981-87.

In 1977 she founded the Green Belt Movement for the dual purpose of preserving the land from deforestation and empowering African women. Gradually the Movement became involved in a wide variety of activities ranging from environmental education to the development of life skills for women and the training of workers in other African countries. A vigorous critic of governmental incompetence and corruption, she often ran afoul of Daniel arap Moi, the president of Kenya. For her temerity, she was harassed and physically abused and, on one occasion, actually imprisoned. She also advocated the cancellation of the debts of poor African nations. When Mwai Kibaki replaced Moi as president in 2002, Dr Maathai, who had just been elected to the national legislature, was appointed minister for the environment, natural resources and wildlife. Her writings included *The Green Belt Movement: Sharing the Approach and the Experience*, published in 1988.

MACHEL, Samora

Samora Moises Machel emerged as the leader of the nationalists in Portuguese Africa after the assassination of Eduardo Mondlane in 1969. He became the military commander of the Front for the Liberation of Mozambique (FRELIMO), founded in 1962, and was elected its president in 1970. He led Mozambique into independence in 1975 and was its first president. Born on 29 September 1933 in Gaza Province, southern Mozambique, and largely self-taught, he began his career as a male nurse before crossing into Tanzania to join Mondlane's guerillas and to distinguish himself as a military leader. Although an avowed Marxist and fervent critic of apartheid, Machel soon discovered the need for pragmatism while leading his fledgling state. To counter internal opposition and avoid difficulties with the South African régime during a time of economic hardship, he was compelled to sign the Treaty of Nkomati with President Botha in 1984. This effectively deprived the guerillas of the African National Congress (ANC) from using Mozambique as a base. Machel took aid for his impoverished country from wherever he could find it: the West and the communist bloc as well as from South Africa. On 19 October 1986, he died in a plane crash for which many Mozambicans blamed the South African government, although the latter strenuously denied any involvement in the tragedy.

MAGLOIRE, Paul

The son of a Haitian general, Paul Magloire was born in Cap-Haitien on 19 July 1907 and entered his country's army at a young age. By the late 1940s he had risen to the rank of general, in which capacity he engineered the overthrow of President Dumarsais Estimé's government in 1950 and established himself as ruler. His own regime fell victim to a military coup in

1956 and Magloire went into exile in New York. He did not return to Haiti until 1986 and died there on 12 July 2001. During his reign, Magloire developed tourism, tried to modernize Haiti and cultivated harmonious relations with the United States, but his régime was undermined by economic distress and corruption scandals.

MAGOGO, Princess Constance

Princess Constance Magogo Sibilile Nantithi Ngangezinye kaDinzulu kaSenzangakhona was born in 1900 in Nongoma, Natal, South Africa. A member of the Zulu royal house, she was easily the greatest living authority on Zulu music. Although she knew no English and was a keen upholder of Zulu traditions, she was a committed Anglican. Not only was her theoretical knowledge of Zulu music unmatched, but she was also an outstanding singer with a vocal range that could span three octaves, and a fine performer with the ugubhu musical bow. She advised on music for the film *Zulu* in 1963 and on many broadcasts and recordings of Zulu music. Princess Constance, who died on 21 November 1984, was a granddaughter of the great King Cetshwayo and the mother of Chief Gatsha Buthelezi of KwaZulu who became a fervent African nationalist.

MAHONEY, Mary

Mary Eliza Mahoney was a black American nursing pioneer. Born in 1845 in Roxbury, Massachusetts, she began her career as a maid at the New England Hospital for Women and Children and fulfilled her dream of becoming a full-fledged nurse when she graduated from the New England Hospital nursing programme in 1879. She was the main source of inspiration for other African-Americans who steadily began to enter the profession. In 1908 she was largely instrumental in forming the National Association of Colored Graduate Nurses. Ten years after her death, on 4 January 1926, this association established the Mary Mahoney Award, a medal given in her honour for outstanding service.

MAÏNASSARA, Ibrahim

A Nigerois soldier, diplomat and politician, Ibrahim Baré Maïnassara was born in Maradi, Niger, on 9 May 1949. He enlisted in the national army and rose rapidly through the ranks during the reign of President Seyni Kountché, whose Presidential Guard he commanded. He served as Niger's ambassador to France during 1988-89 and as its ambassador to Algeria during 1990-92. Appointed chief of the Nigerois army in 1995, he orchestrated a military coup on 27 January 1996 and placed himself at the head of the newly formed National Salvation Council. His repressive actions, however, soon led to his own assassination on 9 April 1999.

MAKONNEN ENDALKACHEW

An eminent Ethiopian civil servant, artist and philosopher, Makonnen Endalkachew was born in Shawa on 16 February 1890. He became a devoted courtier of Emperor Haile Selassie and a prolific author. He wrote more than twenty books on mainly religious and moral subjects, but they also included an autobiography, a memoir, a philosophical treatise, a novelette, some novels and at least two histories. He also published several plays. His abundant literature revealed an unmistakable conservatism as he seemed to venerate the feudal aristocracy and to yearn for a return to mediaeval systems. Makonnen Endalkachew first rose to prominence during the reign of Empress Zawditu and received frequent promotions under Haile Selassie. He served, for instance, as minister of commerce (1926-31), Ethiopian envoy to the League of Nations and ambassador to London (1931-33). He then became mayor of Addis Ababa and held the rank of general during the Ethiopian war with Italy before joining his emperor in exile in the United Kingdom. After the withdrawal of Italian troops from Ethiopia, Makonnen Endalkachew served as minister of the interior (1941-43), prime minister (1943-57) and president of the senate (1957-61). He died a much respected scholar and statesman on 27 February 1963. He had been awarded an OBE in 1924. One of the most famous of all Amharic writers, most of Makonnen's major works were translated into several European languages, including English.

MAKONNEN, Ras Tefari

Born George Thomas Nathaniel Griffith in British Guiana early in the twentieth century, this social activist, philanthropist and businessman chose the name of Ras Tefari Makonnen after emigrating to the United Kingdom in 1937. During 1927-34 he lived in the United States where he studied agriculture and animal husbandry at Cornell University. He also spent two years in Copenhagen before being expelled for publicising the fact that the Danish government was manufacturing mustard gas. Makonnen studied history at the University of Manchester and lectured for the Co-operative Union. He then opened a chain of successful restaurants, some of which were used as meeting places for the growing number of African and Caribbean associations then spreading in Britain. He provided these movements with much needed funding and sometimes paid their legal fees when they were persecuted by local authorities for alleged offences. He famously brought over the celebrated lawyer, Norman Manley, to defend a Jamaican immigrant who was accused of murder. The Pan African Congress of 1945 was staged in Manchester with Makonnen's money. One of the staunchest supporters of the African nationalist movements during the inter-war years, Makonnen befriended such rising young militants as

Jomo Kenyatta and Kwame Nkrumah who were then studying in England. He went to Ghana as one of Nkrumah's advisers when the former Gold Coast won its independence and was accepted by Kenyatta when forced into exile after the fall of Nkrumah's government in 1966. Makonnen spent his last years as a citizen of Kenya. His autobiography, *Pan-Africanism from Within*, was published in 1973.

MAKONNEN WALDA MIKAEL

Father of Emperor Haile Selassie and son of Walda Mikael Malakot, a prominent Ethiopian military leader, Ras Makonnen was one of the ablest Ethiopian generals and administrators of the nineteenth century. Born on 8 May 1852, he was appointed governor of Harar in 1887 and extended the borders of Ethiopia towards the east at the expense of the Somali. In 1889 he was sent to Rome to negotiate the Treaty of Wechalé with the Italians against whom he fought with particular valour in 1895-96 because he was convinced that they had breached their agreement. His role in the Ethiopian victory over the invaders was significant. Makonnen had a certain tolerance for foreigners and did not hesitate to recommend the use of European ideas for the betterment of Ethiopia. This was an attitude which his son was later to emulate. When seemingly at the peak of his career, Makonnen Walda Mikael died on 22 March 1907.

MALCOLM X

Born Malcolm Little in Omaha, Nebraska, on 19 May 1925, this charismatic and influential civil rights leader became a convert to Islam after a youthful life of crime and imprisonment. As an apostle of Elijah Muhammad, the leader of the Black Muslim sect in the United States, he established a mosque in Philadelphia, founded the newspaper, *Muhammad Speaks*, and made impassioned pleas for racial separation, black self-defence and non-participation in white society or religion. His radicalism disturbed the majority of white liberals and other civil rights advocates, but his wonderful oratorical gifts won him a very large following. After his expulsion from the Black Muslim movement in 1963, Malcolm X formed two nationalist groups of his own: the Muslim Mosque and the Organization of Afro-American Unity. Following a pilgrimage to Mecca in 1964, he changed his name to Al Hajj Malik Shabazz and modified his views to encompass the possibility that all white people were not evil and that the African-American cause could profit from the help of world organizations. He was assassinated on 21 February 1965. Most of his public speeches, as well as his *Autobiography of Malcolm X*, were published posthumously. His unusual personal magnetism was reflected in the fact that some 20,000 people attended his funeral in New York City. He remained a major ideological hero throughout the United States, especially among black youth, for many years after his death.

MALULA, Joseph-Albert

Cardinal Joseph-Albert Malula was a courageous and unorthodox Zairean prelate who managed to incur the wrath of both Africans and traditional Roman Catholics. Born on 17 December 1917 in Léopoldville, Belgian Congo, he was ordained in 1946, named archbishop of Kinshasa in 1964, and cardinal in 1969. He sought a meaningful synthesis of Christian and African elements in the church but clashed with President Mobutu Sese Seko when the latter proclaimed that all Zairean children be given local African names at the time of their baptism. Cardinal Malula rejected the use of non-Christian names as well as the planned restrictions on religious education in Zaire. Mobutu retaliated by confiscating the cardinal's official residence in January 1972. Malula fled to Rome where he remained for five months until Mobutu relented under pressure from the Pope. Returning to Zaire, Malula continued to advocate greater cultural pluralism in the church and antagonized many Roman Catholic leaders by his incorporation of local tribal elements into the Zairean mass. He died on 14 June 1989.

MANDELA, Nelson

Born on 18 July 1918 of royal stock in Tembuland, Transkei, Nelson Rolihlahla Mandela became, in 1994, the first black president of the Republic of South Africa after a life of much toil and suffering. He was educated at a Methodist missionary school in Transkei before graduating from Fort Hare University in South Africa. He then studied law at the University of Witwatersrand in Johannesburg. After qualifying, Mandela entered a law partnership with Oliver Tambo and together they founded the African National Congress (ANC) Youth League in 1944. For many years, Mandela advocated a policy of non-violent resistance to the system of apartheid, but he was so appalled by the Sharpeville Massacre of 1960 and the banning of the ANC that he began to promote a programme of active military opposition to the South African régime. This led to a life sentence in prison in 1964. But even in jail Mandela remained the acknowledged leader of the ANC, the country's oldest black nationalist organization founded in 1912, and was elected its president-general. His release in 1990 met with rapturous welcome from people of all races all over the world and he immediately strengthened the position of the ANC by visiting such capital cities as London, Ottawa, Stockholm and Washington, D.C., leaving a positive impression by the moderation of his language and the regality of his bearing. Mandela persuaded the ANC to abandon the military struggle and agreed to work with white South Africans in a spirit of friendship and co-operation. His pragmatism had much to do with the results of the 1994 elections which, for the first time in South African history, were run on the lines of universal suffrage. His ANC party won 62.7% of the votes and he was accordingly installed as president. His tenure of office (1994-99) witnessed much needed reform, such as the establishment of a full democracy in 1996 and the passage of civil rights legislation that dismantled the bulk of the apartheid system. In his presidential address at the opening of parliament in February 1997, Mandela was able to claim that his ANC government had made significant progress in the fields of nutrition, health care, education, housing, and provision of water and electricity. Already nearly two million hectares of land had been redistributed and more than one million households had been given access to clean piped water since 1994 while almost one million electricity connections had been effected in the mean time. Some of the more militant South African Blacks, however, lamented the persistence of economic disparity and the more conservative Afrikaners much regretted the loss of their former privileges.

MANDRANDELE TANZI

One of the leading politicians and administrators of independent Zaire, Mandrandele Tanzi was born on 20 March 1933. Educated at the College Notre Dame in Dungu, he studied political science and administration at the Lovanium University in Léopoldville, now Kinshasa. He rose so rapidly in the Zairean civil service that, by 1964, he had become an administrator of Louvain University, director of the National Bank, and a director of the National Institute for Agronomic Research. In addition he served as the president of the Société de l'Uélé, president of the Congolese Trust Company, and a member of the Government Commission for Air Congo. He also served as a national senator. He died on 12 February 1974, still not yet forty-one. A close associate of Mobutu, he had been the leading theorist of the Mouvement Populaire de la Révolution (MPR).

MANGOAELA, Zakea

Zakea Dolphin Mangoaela was born in Cape Province, South Africa, in 1883. Educated in local schools and at the Basutoland Training College, he taught for some years in Lesotho. He was a Southern Sotho poet, teacher, scholar and translator who produced three graded readers, including the famous *Lipaliso tsa Sesotho* in 1903. Mangoaela later taught at the Koeneng Mission School during 1907-10 before joining the teaching staff at Morija. His *Tsoelopela ea Lesotho* appeared in 1911. One year later came his collection of Sotho tales and folklore, *Har'a libatana le linyamat'- sane*. In 1921 he published the very first Southern Sotho songs in *Lithoko tsa marena a Basotho*. Mangoaela died on 25 October 1963.

MANKABA, David

David Mankaba was a noted Zimbabwean musician who played bass guitar for the Bhundu Boys, a five-piece band that popularized African pop music in Britain and North America in the late 1980s with a unique style of very fast, highly percussive dance music known as 'jit-jive'. Born in Southern Rhodesia in 1959, Mankaba was a member of the Ndebele-speaking community while the others in the group were Shona. In the early 1980s the Bhundu Boys developed an upbeat dance music rooted in the traditional music of the Shona people. They had several hit records in Zimbabwe before touring the United Kingdom with considerable success in 1986, when they were invited to join the US singer, Madonna, in her concert at Wembley Stadium. In that same year they produced their best-selling album, *Shabini*. Mankaba died on 27 June 1991 after being the first African public figure to speak openly about his struggle with AIDS. By so doing, he drew international attention to the problem of this disease in Africa.

MANLEY, Michael

This famous son of a famous father (Norman Washington Manley) was born in Kingston, Jamaica, on 10 December 1923. Michael Norman Manley followed in his father's footsteps and became one of his country's leading politicians. Educated at Jamaica College, Kingston, and the London School of Economics in England, he saw action in World War II as a Royal Canadian Air Force pilot. For some years after the war, he worked as a freelance journalist for the British Broadcasting Corporation (BBC) before returning home as co-editor of *Public Opinion*, a Jamaican newspaper. Like his father, Michael became closely associated with the labour union movement and gave strong support to the National Workers' Union (NWU) in a successful strike against Aluminum Co. of Canada (Alcan) in 1953. Michael Manley became first vice-president of the NWU as well as president of the Caribbean Bauxite and Mine Workers' Union and established an enviable reputation as perhaps the most skilful union negotiator in the Caribbean. He soon rose also to the leadership of the People's National Party (PNP) and led it to a resounding victory in 1972. In 1973 he was one of the founders of the Caribbean Community and Common Market (CARICOM) and he cultivated close relationships with Cuba and the socialist countries of eastern Europe and the Far East. After two terms in office, however, he suffered two defeats at the polls in the 1980s. His party recovered to win the elections of 1989 and Manley served as prime minister again for three years until forced by ill health to resign in 1992. He died on 6 March 1997. One of the most popular of all Jamaican heroes, he was affectionately known as 'Joshua'. He was one of the most eloquent speakers in the Western Hemisphere and a most prolific writer. His works included *The Politics of Change: A Jamaican Testament*; *A Voice at the Workplace: Reflections on Colonialism and the Jamaican Worker*; *Up and Down the Escalator: Development and the International Economy*; *Search for Solutions* (a collection of speeches); *Jamaica: Struggle in the Periphery*; *Global Challenge: From Crisis to Cooperation; Breaking the North-South Stalemate* (Report of Socialist International Commission chaired by him); *Poverty of Nations* (based on a series of lectures delivered at Columbia University); and *A History of West Indies Cricket*. When the Sir Frank Worrell Memorial Cricket Lecture Series was established by the Centre for Cricket Research (CCR) in Barbados, Manley was invited in 1994 to deliver the inaugural address.

MANLEY, Norman

Norman Washington Manley is one of the greatest politicians in the history of Jamaica, West Indies. Born in the parish of St Andrew on 4 July 1893, he was a brilliant scholar-athlete who won a Rhodes Scholarship to Oxford University in England and qualified as a lawyer. He began his political career after the Jamaican labour riots of 1938 by founding the People's National Party (PNP), campaigning for social, economic and constitutional reforms. He became chief minister of Jamaica in 1955 and was that colony's first premier after the achievement of ministerial government in 1959. Manley was also a keen advocate of Caribbean unity and lost the elections of 1962 when his opponents campaigned masterfully in the rural districts on the policy of seceding from the recently-established British West Indian Federation. He died on 2 September 1969. Still remembered as one of Jamaica's greatest citizens, Norman Washington Manley has been named one of his country's six National Heroes.

MANNING, Patrick

Born on 17 August 1946, Patrick Augustus Mervyn Manning is the current prime minister of Trinidad and Tobago, minister of finance, and leader of the People's National Movement (PNM). He also served as prime minister during 1991-95 and was leader of the Opposition from 1986 to 1991 and from 1996 to 2001. He has been a member of parliament since 1971 and is currently the longest-serving member of the House of Representatives. He has been the leader of the PNM since 1987. Manning was educated at Presentation College in Trinidad and the University of the West Indies in Jamaica. After graduating in 1969, he returned to Trinidad and worked as a geologist for Texaco. Two years later he entered parliament and served as parliamentary secretary in various ministries before his promotion to the cabinet in 1981. When the PNM suffered a resounding defeat in 1986, Manning became the leader of the Opposition which had been reduced to three members. So far his terms in office have been marred by increased crime rates and accusations of incompetence and corruption. But the increased revenues from high petroleum and natural gas prices have allowed Trinidad and Tobago to substantially reduce income taxes and re-institute free university education.

MANSA MUSA I

Mansa Musa I was arguably the greatest emperor of Mali which dominated much of western Africa during the fourteenth century. Ruling from 1312 to 1337, he literally carved out, around the great Niger River, an empire the size of all of western Europe. A brilliant general, he defeated all of his immediate neighbours and brought their lands directly under his own control. He also established a highly centralized system of government, religion and commerce. Accepting the Muslim faith, he made the Mali Empire an important Islamic stronghold on the African continent. Arabic became the official Mali language and the Muslim scribes began to teach most of the new subjects how to read and write in that language. Mansa Musa made Timbuktu one of the academic centres of the world and many Muslim scholars travelled there to study. By the time of his death in 1337, he had made Mali one of the most powerful and influential empires in the world. He controlled the lands of the Middle Niger, absorbed into his empire the trading cities of Timbuktu and Gao, and imposed his rule on such south-Saharan cities as Walata, as well as on the salt deposits of Taghaza to the north. He extended the eastern boundaries of his empire as far as Hausaland, and to the west he invaded Tekrur and the lands of the Fulani and Tukulor. In Morocco, Egypt and elsewhere, Mansa Musa established ambassadors and imperial agents and on his return from a pilgrimage to Mecca (1324) established Egyptian scholars both in Timbuktu and Gao. He was, in short, one of the greatest of all warrior-kings in the history of Africa.

MANTANTU DUNDULU

Mantantu Dundulu is best remembered as the first Protestant Christian in the Congo and the African who did most to help the English missionaries establish a school in San Salvador and the Baptist Missionary Society at Malebo. Born around 1865, Mantantu Dundulu was also an important African linguist and translator. He helped compile a dictionary and a grammar of the Kongo language. His Bible, published in Kikongo, appeared in 1926. He died in 1938.

MANZANO, Juan Francisco

Juan Francisco Manzano was born a slave in Cuba towards the end of the eighteenth century. After teaching himself to read and write, he became the first black author to publish a book of poetry in Cuba. His first volume of poems, *Poesías líricas*, was published in Havana in 1821. After gaining his freedom, he also produced his *Autobiografía* (published first in English in 1840) and *Zafira*, a play, in 1842. Manzano died in 1844. He is historically significant as being among the earliest of black Latin American poets.

MAPFUMO, Thomas

Thomas Taferenyika Mapfumo has done as much perhaps as any other single individual to popularize Zimbabwean music. A noted singer and composer, he is also remembered as a staunch African nationalist who rallied Blacks around the independence movement through the power of his music. Born in 1945 in Marondera, Rhodesia, he began his musical career at the age of sixteen with a band called the Cyclones. He also sang with such groups as the Springfields and the Cosmic Dots. He revolutionized Rhodesian music during the 1970s by writing the lyrics of his songs in Shona, the language of the majority of black Zimbabweans. He also tried to strike a balance between western and traditional Shona models, rhythms and sounds. One of the main features of his style was the use of the mbira, an African hand piano with a gourd resonator fitted with a set of metal keys that were plucked with the thumbs. The drums also played an important role, since their complicated rhythms were intended to represent the stamping of dancers' feet. In 1976, Mapfumo formed his own Acid Band whose music successfully combined pop and tradition while the lyrics provided much social and political commentary. The white minority government considered his albums a threat and banned them from the Rhodesian airwaves. The administration, however, could not keep Acid Band's music out of the discos. The 1977 album, *Hokoyo!*, meaning 'Watch out!', was particularly critical of the régime. Mapfumo's lyrics led to his imprisonment for ninety days before that year had ended, but no sooner was he released than he began to produce his defiant sequence of Chimurenga songs that became identified with the Shona struggle for freedom. When Zimbabwe achieved its political independence in 1980, Mapfumo was considered to have played no small part in the saga. He formed another band, Blacks Unlimited, which successfully toured Europe and the United States chanting powerful lyrics that spoke eloquently to the struggle against war, the scourge of the AIDS epidemic in Africa, and the loss of traditional culture. Their most recent hits include *Toi Toi* (2003), *Choice Chimurenga* (2004) *and Rise Up* (2006).

MARAN, René

Born on 5 November 1887 of French Guyanese parents in Fort-de-France, Martinique, René Maran spent most of his early life in Gabon and in

Bordeaux, France. He graduated from the Lycée de Talence in Bordeaux in 1909 and, like his father, entered the French colonial service. He spent the next fourteen years (1909-23) in various African colonies but retired prematurely from the service and spent his last days in France concentrating mainly on his writing. He published a long list of successful novels, including *Batouala* (1921), *Djouma, chien de brousse* (1927), *Journal sans date* (1927), *Le coeur serré* (1931), *Le livre de la brousse* (1934), *Bêtes de la brousse* (1942), *Mbala, l'éléphant* (1942), *Un homme pareil aux autres* (1947) and *Bacouya, le cynocéphale* (1953). In 1921, Maran became the first black African to win the Prix Goncourt for his *Batouala*. He also wrote poetry in such collections as *La maison du bonheur* (1909), *La vie intérieure* (1912), *Le visage calme* (1922), *Les belles images* (1935), and *Le livre du souvenir: Poèmes* 1909-57 which won the Grand Prix de Poésie de l'Académie Française in 1958. Maran's short stories appeared in such publications as *Le petit roi de chimérie; contes* (1924) and *Peines de coeur* (1944). He also wrote some useful biographies, including *Livingstone et l'exploration de l'Afrique* (1938), *Les pionniers de l'Empire* (1943), *Savorgnan de Brazza* (1951), *Félix Eboué: grand commis et loyal serviteur 1885-1944* (1957), and *Bertrand du Guesclin; l'épée du roi* (1961). One of the most prolific and influential of the Francophone black writers, Maran also wrote numerous essays and articles. He died in Paris on 9 May 1960.

MARGAI, Albert

Sir Albert Michael Margai was one of the political leaders who played a prominent role in Sierra Leone's achievement of political independence. He succeeded his brother, Sir Milton Margai, as prime minister in 1964. Born in Bonthe, on 10 October 1910, he was educated in local schools before completing a law degree in London, England, and being called to the bar by the Middle Temple in 1947. He returned to Sierra Leone to practice law and to participate in local government. He helped his brother form the Sierra Leone People's Party (SLPP) and was elected by the Protectorate Assembly to a seat in the Legislative Council. He served in the early 1950s as minister of education, minister of local government and minister of social welfare before breaking away from the SLPP and, with Siaka Stevens, creating the People's National Party in 1957. Reconciling with Sir Milton in 1960, he was appointed minister of finance and became prime minister upon his brother's death in 1964. He was knighted in 1965, but ousted by a military coup on 21 March 1967 when attempting to create a one-party state with increased executive powers for the president. Sir Albert Margai died on 18 December 1980.

MARGAI, Milton

Sir Milton Augustus Strieby Margai was an outstanding political leader, a much acclaimed surgeon and a pioneer in medical welfare. His moderate approach had much to do with the alliance between the educated élite and the traditional chiefs which resulted in the formation of the Sierra Leone People's Party (SLPP) and led directly to the achievement of political independence. Born on 7 December 1895, Margai was educated at the Evangelical United Brethren School in Bonthe and at the Albert Academy in Freetown. He then attended Fourah Bay College before proceeding to King's College Medical School, Newcastle-on-Tyne, England, to study medicine. He returned to Sierra Leone in 1927, was appointed a medical officer in the colonial service in 1928, and served all over Sierra Leone during the next twenty two years. As a doctor, Margai tried his utmost to modernize midwifery and published a simple handbook, *A Primer of Midwifery*. In 1950 he retired as a senior medical officer and devoted the rest of his life mainly to politics. He became very active in the affairs of the Protectorate Education Progressive Union (PEPU) and the Sierra Leone Organization Society (SOS). He founded and edited the *Sierra Leone Observer* and became the first president of the SLPP. He served on Sierra Leone's legislative and executive councils and in 1952 headed the departments of health, agriculture and forestry. Chosen chief minister in 1954, he became prime minister in 1961 when Sierra Leone gained its independence. Sir Milton Margai was knighted in 1959 and awarded an honorary degree by Durham University in 1963. He died on 28 April 1964.

MARLEY, Bob

Robert Nesta Marley was one of the greatest singers and composers produced by the West Indies. Born in St Ann, Jamaica, on 6 February 1945, he made reggae internationally popular and became an ambassador for his country and its music. He made his first record in 1961 and formed the famous group, The Wailers, with Bunny Livingstone and Peter Tosh in 1963. Their finest records perhaps were *Burning, Catch a Fire, Exodus, Kaya, Natty Dread*, and *Rastaman Vibration*. Although Marley tried to stay aloof from local politics, he thought it necessary to bring together the country's two rival party leaders at a 'peace concert', following the violence that had accompanied the general elections of 1976. When this concert eventually took place in 1978, with Michael Manley and Edward Seaga joining Marley on stage in a dramatic show of unity, it produced a sobering effect even on the ghettos of Kingston. Marley was himself invited to attend the Zimbabwe independence celebration in 1980 and he made a successful appearance at Harlem's Apollo Theatre that same year. But he was struck down by cancer on 11 May 1981 shortly after receiving the Jamaican Order of Merit. Bob Marley's uncompromising lyrics, which are still popular with the younger reggae singers, set the tone for the assertion of black consciousness during the 1970s.

MARRYSHOW, Theophilus

Theophilus Albert Marryshow left a profound imprint on West Indian politics and literature. Born on 7 November 1887 in Grenada, he was compelled by the poverty of his parents to leave school at a young age and become apprenticed as a carpenter. Finding too little satisfaction in that occupation, he went to work as an office boy for the *Grenada Federalist*. From such lowly beginnings, he rose to the rank of editor of the *Grenada Chronicle* in 1909 and managed, six years later, to help found the *West Indian*, a literary journal, which did much to encourage and promote young Caribbean authors. Marryshow contributed liberally to this magazine, writing poems as well as political and social commentary. He was a fervent advocate of racial equality and regional autonomy and devoted most of his life to promoting the concept of a free and independent West Indian federation. When this idea finally became a reality in 1958, Marryshow was appointed a member of the federal senate. Always active in local politics, he had become in 1925 one of the first elected members of Grenada's Legislative Council. He served on that body for thirty-three years. He died in 1958, but is still remembered as one of the most important individuals in the history of Grenada. A collection of his political articles, entitled *Cycles of Civilization*, was published in 1973 by the Afro-American Institute.

MARSALIS, Wynton

Wynton Marsalis was born in New Orleans, Louisiana, on 18 October 1961. An excellent trumpeter and composer, he is generally considered one of the most prominent jazz musicians of the modern era and is unarguably the greatest African-American instrumentalist in classical music today. He became the first musician ever to win Grammy awards for both jazz and classical music. He made his first public appearance at the age of fourteen when he played Haydn's *Trumpet Concerto* with the New Orleans Philharmonic Orchestra. Four years later, he made an impressive début with Art Blakey's Jazz Messengers. By 1981 Marsalis was attracting attention in the jazz world with his exceptional technique and deft improvisation as a trumpeter. In 1983, he demonstrated his versatility by releasing two bestselling records, *Think of One* (jazz) and *Trumpet Concertos* (classical). His growing reputation as a composer has led to numerous commissions to create major compositions for many of the leading bands and orchestras. His *Fiddler's Tale* (1998) was a great success. In 1997, Marsalis became the first jazz musician to win a Pulitzer Prize in music for his epic oratorio, *Blood on the Fields*, on the subject of slavery. He emerged as one of the most notable leaders of New Orleans in the wake of Hurricane Katrina when he tried valiantly to promote the rebuilding process. He has won a huge number of awards and distinctions and is the recipient of several honorary doctorates. He has already (2006) toured thirty countries on six continents, selling almost five million of his recordings worldwide.

MARSHALL, Malcolm

One of the greatest fast bowlers in the history of international cricket, Malcolm Denzil Marshall was born in Barbados, West Indies, on 18 April 1958. He captured 376 wickets in 81 Test matches at an average of less than 21 runs each. In a first-class career that lasted from 1977 to 1996, he took 1,651 wickets (av: 19.10) in 408 matches. An accomplished batsman and brilliant fielder, Marshall also scored over 11,000 runs and took 145 catches. He died on 4 November 1999 while serving as a coach for the West Indies side at the 1999 World Cup. Very popular wherever he played, he was a fine ambassador for the sport.

MARSHALL, Thurgood

Born in Baltimore, Maryland, on 2 July 1908, Thurgood Marshall was one of the most influential civil rights leaders in the United States in the inter-war years. After graduating with high honours from the Howard University School of Law in 1933, he established a successful private practice in Chicago while serving as special counsel to the National Association for the Advancement of Colored People (NAACP). He played a prominent role in removing racial barriers to further education in several states and also did most to win Blacks the right to vote in primary elections in Texas. Marshall was appointed a judge on the US District Court in 1961 and was named US solicitor general in 1965. Two years later he was made an associate justice of the US Supreme Court, the first African-American to be so honoured. A brilliant advocate as well as jurist, Marshall was awarded the Spingarn Medal in 1946. In 1950 he went to Korea to investigate the treatment of Blacks in the United States Army. One of the most liberal judges in North American history, his efforts succeeded in eliminating racial discrimination in voting, housing, and public facilities. He strengthened the constitutional safeguards against illegal searches and seizures in the home, struck down the traditional loyalty oaths for teachers, and curbed the power of immigration authorities to deport aliens summarily. He died on 24 January 1993. Such was his impact on the community that two sizeable biographies of Thurgood Marshall appeared within a few months of his death: Carl T. Rowan, *Dream Makers, Dream Breakers* and Michael D. Davis and Hunter R. Clark, *Thurgood Marshall.*

MARSHALL, Valin

Dr Valin G Marshall is an important pioneer in the field of soil zoology who has focussed for almost forty years on the impact of environmental changes on biological diversity of forest ecosystems. Born in Grenada, West Indies, he immigrated to Canada in 1955 and completed his education at McGill University. He worked for thirty-one years with the Canadian Forest Service in British Columbia and is currently a Research Associate in the Centre for Economic Development and Applied Research at Royal Roads University. The author of numerous articles in scientific journals, Dr Marshall has identified and described many soil animal species, a number of which have now been named after him. He is currently investigating the taxonomy and ecology of Canadian soil fauna with special reference to the native and introduced earthworms of British Columbia, the biology of the yew mite, and the impact of forest clearing on soil fauna. He has also devoted much energy to the study of Blacks in western Canada and is one of the founders of the British Columbia Black History Awareness Society.

MASCOLL, Beverley

Born in Halifax, Nova Scotia, in 1942, Dr Beverley Mascoll was awarded the Order of Canada in 1998 for outstanding entrepreneurship and assisting Canada's youth. She was the president of the Beverley Mascoll Beauty Supply Ltd (Toronto), one of Canada's largest distributors and manufacturers of black beauty products. She established the Beverley Mascoll Community Foundation which provides post-secondary scholarships to promote the advancement of women and to assist in the development of youth and children. A graduate of York University (Toronto), she was actively involved in the fundraising campaign for the establishment of the James Robinson Johnston Chair, the first chair in Black Canadian Studies at the University of Dalhousie. Keenly interested in the professional education of her customers, she promoted and held a series of seminars for professional hair stylists, beauty schools and consultants representing the beauty industry. Beverley Mascoll received numerous awards, including an honorary doctorate from Ryerson University in 1999 and a similar honour, posthumously, from the Mount Saint Vincent University. She died in 2001.

MASIRE, Quett

Quett Ketumile Joni Masire was the natural and obvious successor to Sir Seretse Khama as president of Botswana in July 1980. He had been vice-president and finance minister under Khama for almost twenty years. Born on 23 July 1925 at Kanye, Bechuanaland, he became a teacher and then a journalist. Always active in politics, he served on his local council and then on the legislative and executive councils under the British administration. In 1962, he was one of the founding members of the Botswana Democratic Party (BDP) which Seretse Khama led to triumph in a series of general elections afterwards. In 1965, Masire served as deputy prime minister of what was then the British protectorate of Bechuanaland and when Botswana achieved its political independence in 1966, he became its first vice-president. Like Khama, he remained an unrelenting critic of the racist systems prevailing in southern Africa, and served during the early 1980s as the chairman of the association of nine African states (Angola, Botswana, Lesotho, Malawi, Mozambique, Swaziland, Tanzania, Zambia and Zimbabwe) that were committed to lessening their economic dependence on South Africa. In 1992, Masire began to use his second name (Ketumile) and was knighted one year later. Sir Ketumile Masire led Botswana through very difficult times until his resignation in 1998 and proved himself one of modern Africa's most durable and successful rulers. After his resignation, he remained active in diplomacy and served as a mediator in the civil war in the Democratic Republic of the Congo.

MATE KOLE, Emmanuel

Born on 7 February 1860, Nene Sir Emmanuel Mate Kole was an influential paramount chief of Manya Krobo, a state about fifty miles north of Accra. He became the first literate ruler of his kingdom, having been educated at Usu Salem Middle schools and at the Akuporon Seminary. During 1880-91 he taught at various Basel Mission schools in what is now Ghana before being elected konor of Manya Krobo in 1892. A consistent ally of the British, he fought on their side during the Asante War of 1895-96 and again offered them material aid during World War I when he sent more than 400 soldiers to fight against Germany in Togo. The British rewarded him with a knighthood in 1930 and he used their alliance to keep his kingdom intact during a very critical period in West African history. Mate Kole was very interested in agriculture, education, law and public works and did his utmost to promote them during his tenure. He acquired substantial areas of land from neighbouring people to establish more than 200 farming villages between 1892 and 1914. Manya Krobo was thus able to produce large quantities of cocoa, maize and palm oil. The Gold Coast government awarded Mate Kole the first agriculture medal in West Africa. He gave staunch support to the Basel missionaries in their educational and religious activities. He established local courts to ensure that disputes were fairly settled without resort to violence. In addition, he built about 100 miles of roads by communal labour to improve communications within his kingdom. In 1911, Mate Kole became the first paramount chief to be appointed to the Gold Coast Legislative Council. He also served on the

Cocoa Advisory Board. He died at Odumase in 1939 and is remembered as a shrewd native ruler who did not hesitate to employ European alliances, models and techniques to advance the cause of his people.

MATZELIGER, Jan

The son of a Dutch father and a black Surinamese mother, Jan Ernst Matzeliger was born on 15 September 1852 in Paramaribo, Dutch Guiana (now Surinam). He migrated to the United States and settled down in the small town of Lynn, Massachusetts, where he worked in a shoe factory. In those days, shoes were made laboriously by hand, but Matzeliger revolutionized the industry by patenting his famous shoe lasting machine that mechanically shaped the upper portions of shoes. He publicly launched his invention on 29 May 1885. To everyone's amazement, it allowed Matzeliger to make seventy-five pairs of shoes that day. His machine won swift acceptance and shortly supplanted all previous methods. This device meant that shoes could be manufactured much faster and more inexpensively. Matzeliger died at the age of thirty-seven on 24 August 1889. He was the recipient of several posthumous awards and distinctions and a statue was built in his honour in Lynn, Massachusetts, many years after his death.

MAY, Joseph Claudius

Born on 14 August 1845, Revd Joseph Claudius May became a prominent Sierra Leonean preacher, journalist and educator and was the first principal of the Wesleyan Boys' High School in Freetown. He founded the influential *Sierra Leonean News* which endured for more than sixty years. May was educated mainly in England where he spent many years. He returned to Sierra Leone in 1870 and was ordained in 1880. He established the *Methodist Herald* and *West African Educational Times* in 1882. He served on the Board of Education and was for several years the chief examiner for the civil service in the colony. His newspapers served for many decades as the mouthpiece of West Africans dissatisfied with British administration. May died on 14 October 1902.

MAYES, Joe

Joe Mayes was a Baptist preacher in Tennessee towards the end of the nineteenth century. He moved to Oklahoma where he headed a small congregation for some years until tempted by the offer of cheap land to emigrate to western Canada. He led his congregation north to Saskatchewan and settled in 1910 in the region which later became known as Eldon, some fifty miles north-west of North Battleford. By the 1920s Mayes' Baptists had established a fairly vibrant settlement, with the church as the focal point of their community. The Mayes family has remained a highly respected force in the region with sons and grandsons doing extremely well. Joe's son, Murray, opened an automobile body shop in North Battleford, and one of his grandsons, Reuben, who became a professional football player, also obtained a degree in administration. Joe's widow, Mattie, lived on until well into the 1950s.

MAYNARD, Frank

Born in Barbados, West Indies, on 19 September 1941, Frank A. Maynard was educated at Combermere School (Barbados) and the Royal College of Music (London) before immigrating to Canada. Following his graduation from Ryerson Polytechnic Institute and the University of Toronto in 1965, he entered the Ontario provincial service and rose rapidly to the rank of supervisor of administration in the department of treasury and economics. He moved to Winnipeg, Manitoba, in 1969 as director of personnel management in the department of health and social development. He quickly established an enviable reputation as one of the most efficient administrators in the public service and in 1981 was appointed executive director, administrative services, Manitoba Health. Later that same year he became assistant deputy minister of health and from 1988 to his retirement in December 1994 he served as deputy minister in this department. Notwithstanding the frequent change of governments and shuffling of cabinets, Maynard had thus been one of the chief bureaucrats in the provincial ministry of health for more than thirteen years. He was the first black administrator to rise to such heights in Manitoba. He is now president of the Population Health Institute of Canada and serves often as a consultant whose advice is much sought after by corporate businesses.

MAZRUI, Ali

Professor Ali Al'Amin Mazrui is perhaps the finest scholar thus far produced by Kenya. Born in Mombasa on 24 February 1933, he was educated in local schools and at the Universities of Manchester and Oxford in England. He returned to Africa as a teacher and became head of the department of political science at Makerere University and then the dean of its Faculty of Social Studies. He was also associate editor of *Transition* and then of *Mawazo*. Mazrui emigrated to the United States and served as Director, Center for Afro-American and African Studies at the University of Michigan (1978-81). In 1991, he was appointed Director, Institute for Global Cultural Studies, State University of New York. His scholarly articles are mainly on political science and appear in several journals, but he has also published a very fine novel, *The Trial of Christopher Okigbo* (1971). Mazrui is much better known for his non-fiction which includes *Towards a Pax Africana* (1967), *The Anglo-African Commonwealth* (1967), *On Heroes and Uhuru-*

Worship (1968), *Violence and Thought* (1969), *Africa since 1935: Vol. VIII of UNESCO General History of Africa* (1993; *Swahili, State and Society: The Political Economy of an African Language* (1995); *The Power of Babel: Language and Governance in the African Experience* (1998); *The Titan of Tanzania: Julius K. Nyerere's Legacy* (2002); *Black Reparations in the Era of Globalization* (2002); and *The African Predicament and the American Experience: A Tale of Two Edens* (2004). He also co-edited *Protest and Power in Black Africa* (1970). Dr Mazrui has been the recipient of numerous honours and awards

M'BA, Léon

Léon M'Ba became the first president of Gabon in February 1961 shortly after that country had gained its political independence from France. Born in 1902, in what was then known as French Overseas Territory, M'Ba assumed the leadership of the Gabonese independence movement while still recommending an alliance with France. He was ousted by a military coup d'état in January 1964 but was quickly reinstated by the French with whom he had earlier signed an assistance treaty. He remained in office until illness forced him to resign in August 1966. He died on 28 November 1967 in Paris, France, where he had gone for medical treatment.

MBASOGO, Teodro

Born on 5 June 1942 in the Akoakam-Esangui district of Mongomo, Teodro Obiang Nguema Mbasogo has been the president of Equatorial Guinea ever since he deposed and killed his uncle, Francisco Macías Nguema, in a military coup on 3 August 1979. Although his rule has been described as cruel and repressive, he has survived for more than twenty-five years. He promulgated a new constitution in 1982 but his own party has still dominated all subsequent elections. The constitution has also left the president with very wide powers, including the right to rule by decree. Mbasogo began his career in the military and attended the prestigious General Francisco Franco Military Academy in Spain from which he graduated in 1965. After his return home, as one of Nguema's relatives, promotion was so rapid that he had become Lieutenant Colonel by 1979. The discovery of oil in his country within the last few years has allowed him to solve a variety of economic problems that had dogged the footsteps of his predecessors.

MBEKI, Govan

Govan Archibald Mvuyelwa Mbeki, an ardent nationalist and political activist, was born on 9 July 1910 in Nqamakwe, South Africa. As a teacher, writer, labour organizer and editor of the *New Age*, he was one of the important leaders in the struggle against apartheid. He joined the African National Congress (ANC) in 1935 and rose to the rank of national chairman in 1956. He was imprisoned in 1963 on the charge of plotting to overthrow the government and was not released until 1987. His best-known book, *South Africa: The Peasant Revolt*, written surreptitiously while he was in jail, was published in London in 1964. Mbeki won a seat in the country's first multi-racial parliament in 1994 and had the great satisfaction of seeing his son, Thabo Mbeki, elevated to the presidency in 1999. He died at Port Elizabeth on 30 August 2001.

MBEKI, Thabo

On 10 May 1994, Thabo Mbeki became the first deputy president in the first democratically elected government of South Africa. Born in Idutwya, Transkei, on 18 June 1942, he attended Lovedale Secondary School in Alice and joined the African National Congress (ANC) Youth League in 1956. Leaving South Africa illegally in 1962, he studied at the University of Sussex, England, from which he achieved an MA in economics in 1966. He worked for the ANC in London (1967-70) and then underwent military training in the Soviet Union. Mbeki moved swiftly up the ANC hierarchy, becoming the youngest member of its national executive council in 1975 and serving (1978) as political secretary to Oliver Tambo, its president. During the 1970s he undertook missions for the ANC in Botswana, Nigeria and Swaziland in order to work with black youth who had left South Africa. Throughout the 1980s he also helped to pave the way for the negotiations with the white minority government that led to a peaceful constitutional settlement in 1991. In 1993 he was elected to succeed Tambo as chairperson of the ANC and he succeeded Mandela as president in 1999. His party was re-elected in 2004 by a resounding majority. In that year, Mbeki was able to boast that, under the ANC, South Africa had enjoyed not only political stability but considerable economic growth. Since 1994, the government had built 1.6 million homes and 56,000 new classrooms and had delivered potable water to 9 million people and sanitation to 6.4 million people.

MBITI, Samuel

One of Africa's greatest philosophers and theologians, Dr John Samuel Mbiti was born in Kamba Country, Kenya, on 30 November 1931. Educated at Alliance High School (Kenya), Makerere College (Uganda), Barrington College (United States) and Cambridge University (England), he studied theology and was ordained in 1960. He taught at Makerere College, where he became head of the department of religious studies and philosophy. Mbiti has published more than 400 scholarly articles and reviews on African theology and religion. He also produced such seminal studies as *African Religions and Philosophy* (1969), *New Testament Eschatology in an African Background* (1970), and *Concepts of God in Africa* (1975). This creative Kenyan also wrote stories in the local Kikamba dialect as well as beautiful poetry in English. Among his works, for instance, were *Mutanga na ngewa yaka* (1954), *Akamba Stories* (1966) and *Poems of Nature and Faith* (1969). Dr Mbiti has served as director of the Ecumenical Institute of the World Council of Churches in Geneva, Switzerland; and a visiting professor at numerous universities in Africa, Australia, Canada, Europe and the United States. He is now teaching Christianity and African religions at the University of Bern, Switzerland.

M'BOW, Amadou Mahtar

In 1974, Amadou Mahtar M'Bow became the first African to be elected director general of the United Nations Educational, Scientific and Cultural Organization (UNESCO). The son of a farmer, he was born on 20 March 1921 in Dakar, Senegal. During World War II he became the first black technical sergeant in the history of the French Air Force. After the war, he studied geography and history at the University of Paris, was elected president of the Federation of Black African Students in France, and by 1950 had established himself as a Marxist student leader. After his graduation, M'Bow was assigned to teach at a secondary school in isolated Rosso, Mauritania, as the authorities considered him a threat to their administration in Senegal which was still a French colony at that time. In 1953, however, he was appointed head in Senegal of a programme in fundamental education sponsored by UNESCO. When Senegal achieved its political independence in 1960, M'Bow served as minister of education and later as minister of youth and culture. In the late 1960s he headed Senegal's delegations to UNESCO general conferences and was a member of that body's executive board, chairman of the group of African members, and head of the caucus of its seventy seven 'third world' members. In 1970, he was named assistant director general for education and four years later was elected secretary general. In 1980 he was re-elected unanimously, but steadily lost the support of western delegates who feared that he was too partial in his treatment of African and Communist interests. By 1984, the United States had become so dissatisfied with his management of UNESCO that they withdrew from the organization and the United Kingdom threatened to follow suit. In 1987, Federico Mayor Zaragosa, a Spanish biochemist and politician, succeeded M'Bow as secretary general of UNESCO just when it appeared that an East-West split might lead to a total collapse of the organization.

MBOYA, Thomas

An eminent Kenyan politician and ardent Pan-Africanist, Thomas Joseph Mboya was among the leaders in the struggle for African independence after World War II. A member of the Luo, he was born on 15 August 1930 in eastern Kenya. Mboya began his career as a sanitary inspector in Nairobi and became involved at once in the trade union movement. From 1953 to 1963 he was general secretary of the Kenya Federation of Labour. One of the most eloquent supporters of Jomo Kenyatta's party, he was one of the first eight Africans to be elected to the Legislative Council in 1957. He became minister for justice and constitutional affairs when Kenya became self-governing in 1963. After independence in 1964, he was appointed minister for economic planning and development. As secretary-general of the Kenya African National Union (KANU), of which he had been a founder-member in 1960, Mboya was everywhere considered Kenyatta's natural successor, when, on 5 July 1969, he was assassinated in Nairobi. His death exacerbated tensions between the Kikuyu and the Luo in Kenya.

MCCALLA, Val

Val McCalla was born in Jamaica, West Indies, on 3 October 1943 and educated at Kingston College. He emigrated to the United Kingdom in 1959 and spent a few years in the Royal Air Force before working part-time for *East End News*, a radical community newspaper. It was this experience which inspired him to establish his own newspaper, *The Voice*, in the early 1980s. From modest origins, it grew into a powerful medium, shortly becoming easily the most successful and by far the most influential black newspaper in Europe. It sold more than 53,000 copies each week and served as the mouthpiece for the African-Caribbean community in London. *The Voice* quickly established itself as a major campaigner against all forms of racism. For local authorities and private sector organizations concerned about employment equity, it became a valuable recruitment tool and led also to pages of job advertising. Many of the younger black journalists now working in the mainstream media started their careers with *The Voice*. Val McCalla died on 22 August 2002. He is reported to have left a private fortune worth in excess of £10 million in addition to a stable of race horses.

MCCOY, Elijah

This celebrated inventor was born in Ontario, Canada, on 2 May 1843. Although his parents were runaway slaves from Kentucky, they were determined that he should be properly educated and sent him to Scotland to study engineering. Elijah McCoy returned to the United States with an engineering degree but found companies unwilling to hire him because of his colour. He worked for some years as a fireman with the railroad until he started the Elijah McCoy Manufacturing Company in Detroit, Michigan, in 1870. Two years later, he patented his automatic lubricator cup which

enabled machines to run for indefinite periods without having to be stopped
for constant oiling. He then invented and patented the lubricator cup for
steam engines and his device came at once to be used on railroads and
steamships. McCoy received over fifty patents altogether, including ones for
such gadgets as an ironing table and a lawn sprinkler. He died in 1929. His
invention of the lubricator cup gave birth to the phrase, 'The Real McCoy'
which has kept his memory alive until this very day.

MCCURDY, Howard

Born on 10 December 1932 in London, Ontario, Dr Howard McCurdy has
already left an indelible mark on Canadian education and politics. For many
years (1959-84), he was a professor of biology at the University of Windsor,
Ontario. He was also an active member of Canada's federal parliament
(1979-93) and one of the driving forces within the ranks of the New
Democratic Party (NDP). An eloquent speaker, he has constantly promoted
the principles of social justice and racial equality. He has also shown a
genuine interest in women's issues. In 1989 he campaigned vigorously but
in vain for the leadership of the NDP. That party would obviously have
done much better in subsequent general elections had it paid more attention
to his claims. Now retired from active participation in politics, Dr McCurdy
continues to consult, write and pursue research. His writings so far include
over fifty scientific publications in the field of biology and about a dozen in
the areas of politics and human rights. He has received numerous honours
and awards, including the Canadian Centennial Medal, 1967; the Black
Achievement Award for Politics, 1976; the Queen's Silver Jubilee Medal,
1977; the Person of the Year Award, 1986; and the J.S. Woodsworth Award
for Human Rights, 2001.

MCDONALD, Trevor

Sir Trevor McDonald was born in Trinidad on 16 August 1939 and
educated at Naparima College in San Fernando. He worked with the BBC
World Service in the West Indies as a producer for several years before
emigrating to the United Kingdom in 1969. He left BBC Radio in 1973 to
join Independent Televison News (ITN) as a reporter. He rose steadily
through the ranks to become diplomatic editor and newscaster. He
presented *The News at Ten* from 1991 to 1999 and then *The ITV News at Ten
Thirty*. He also hosted the popular current affairs programme, *Tonight with
Trevor McDonald*. He has presented the National Television Awards ever
since their inception in 1995. His clear and confident delivery has made him
one of British television's most trusted reporters and he has won more
awards than any other British broadcaster. In December 2005, he presented
his last ITV News bulletin but did not have any plans to retire completely

from television. In 1992, he received an OBE and a knighthood in 1999. Sir Trevor McDonald is famous for being the first black news anchor in the UK. An accomplished author, he has written *Viv Richards: The Authorised Biography* (1984); *Clive Lloyd: The Authorised Biography* (1985); and the autobiographical *Fortunate Circumstances* which was published in 1993.

MCFARLANE, Clare

An outstanding Caribbean poet, author, anthologist and critic, John Ebenezer Clare McFarlane, who founded the Poetry League of Jamaica in 1923, was born in that island in 1894. He devoted most of his life to the promotion of Jamaican poetry in particular and literature in general. His *Voices from Summerland*, published in 1929, was the first anthology of Jamaican verse. He also edited *A Treasury of Jamaican Poetry*, published in 1949. Some of his own work had already appeared in *Beatrice* (1918) and *Poems* (1924). McFarlane's miscellaneous prose writings included *Sex and Christianity* (1934), *Jamaica's Crisis* (1937), *The Freedom of the Individual* (1940), *The Challenge of our Time* (1945), *A Literature in the Making* (1956), and *The Magdalen: A Story of Supreme Love* (1960). He was awarded the Musgrave Silver Medal in 1935 and the Musgrave Gold Medal in 1958 for the encouragement of Jamaican poetry. McFarlane died in 1962.

MCGRATH, Paul

Paul McGrath is famous for being the first black football player to captain an Irish team in international competition. In 1985, he won his first cap for Ireland and eventually played in 83 international matches altogether. McGrath is generally considered the greatest of all Ireland's football stars. He helped his country to the European Championships in 1988 and to the World Cup in 1990 and 1994. He also played for Manchester United and Aston Villa in the English Premier League before retiring from football in 1998.

MCKAY, Claude

Claude McKay was born in Jamaica, British West Indies, on 15 September 1890. Emigrating from his native island, he travelled extensively throughout Europe before settling down in the United States, where he attended Tuskegee Institute (1912) and Kansas State Teachers College (1912-14). Moving to New York City in 1914, he became editor of *The Liberator* and *The Masses*, two radical magazines. McKay wrote excellent poetry as well as prose during the inter-war years. His works included *Home to Harlem* (1928), *Banjo* (1929), *Ginger Town* (1932), *Banana Bottom* (1933), *A Long Way From Home* (1937), and *Harlem: Negro Metropolis* (1940). With the publication of two volumes of poetry, *Spring in New Hampshire* (1920) and *Harlem Shadows* (1922), McKay emerged as the first and most militant voice of the Harlem Renaissance. A collection of Selected Poems also appeared posthumously in 1953. During World War II, McKay became a convert to Roman Catholicism and worked with a Catholic youth organization in Chicago for some years before his death on 22 May 1948. It is not often remembered that, prior to settling down in the United States in 1912, McKay had written two volumes of Jamaican dialect verse, *Songs of Jamaica* and *Constab Ballads*. These were the forerunners of the dialect poems of Louise Bennett and others.

MCWATT, Faye

The Hon Madame Justice Faye E. McWatt was appointed to the Ontario Superior Court of Justice in 2000. Born in Guyana, she immigrated to Canada in 1963 and completed her education at the universities of Western Ontario (BA, 1978) and Ottawa (MA, 1981 and LLB, 1984). She was an assistant Crown Attorney in Ontario during the late 1980s and served on two important Royal Commissions as counsel. She was appointed director on the Ontario Heritage Foundation in 1992 and, in 1995, became the Standing Agent for the Attorney General for the Toronto/Brampton Regions.

MÉNDEZ, Arnaldo

Arnaldo Tamayo Méndez was born in Guantánamo, Cuba, on 20 January 1942. He graduated from the Air Force Academy and became a pilot in the Cuban Air Defence Force. In 1978, he was selected for training as part of the seventh international programme for Intercosmos. Along with the Soviet cosmonaut, Yuri Romanenko, Arnaldo was launched into space on 18 September 1980 as part of the Soyuz 38 from Baikonur Cosmodrome. He thus became the first Black, the first Cuban, and the first person from a country in the Western Hemisphere other than the United States to travel into space. For eight days and nights, he and his Soviet partner, making 124 orbits of the earth, conducted experiments in an attempt to discover the causes of space sickness. Following his career as a cosmonaut, Méndez was made director of the Military Patriotic Educational Society in Cuba. He was also promoted to the rank of brigadier general and became director of the International Affairs in the Cuban armed forces.

MENGHISTU, Lemma

Lemma Menghistu was an Ethiopian writer of fine poetry and witty, satiric plays in Amharic (the modern language of Ethiopia). Born in Addis Ababa in 1925, he was educated in local Muslim schools before completing his studies at the London School of Economics in England. After graduating in 1953, he entered the public service and then became first secretary at the Ethiopian embassy in India (1957-63). His best known plays, which he also translated into English, were *Snatch and Run, or Marriage by Abduction* (1963) and *Marriage of Unequals* (1970). Menghistu also wrote critical essays in both Amharic and English in which he examined the difficulty of reconciling traditional values and customs with modern Western ideas. Lemma Menghistu died in July 1988.

MENILEK II

Born on 17 August 1844, Emperor Menilek II was the son of King Hayla Malakot of Shawa. Energetic, wise and progressive, he became one of the greatest of all Ethiopian rulers. His career began inauspiciously as his father was killed in battle with Emperor Tewodros who annexed Shawa and sent him into captivity. In 1865, Menilek managed to escape. He recaptured Shawa and eventually claimed the imperial throne for himself in 1889. His reign began in some disorder but he succeeded in quelling the nobles and establishing a firm control over the entire kingdom which he considerably expanded at the expense of most of Ethiopia's neighbours. His skill in warfare allowed him to defeat the Italians decisively in the war of 1895-96. This marked the first occasion on which African soldiers had prevailed against Europeans over an extended campaign. Menilek's armies crushed the Italians at Adwa, Alage and Maqalé. By 1896, Menilek's empire stretched from Sudan in the west, to Kenya in the south and the Somalilands in the east. But he failed to acquire a port and Ethiopia thus remained landlocked until the incorporation of Eritrea in 1952. The latter portion of Menilek's reign was devoted chiefly to peaceful and constructive endeavours. He erected schools and churches, established a few industries and a printing press, and founded a modern hospital. He reorganized the administration of Ethiopia into provinces, each with its own governor, but owing an allegiance to the emperor. He stationed troops at strategic points to discourage rebellion and, in 1907, restructured the central administration further by creating ministries in the European model. Menilek II died on 12 December 1913 leaving an enviable reputation as a soldier and statesman.

MENTEWAB

Born Walatta Giyorgis in 1706, this Ethiopian empress preferred to be called Mentewab, 'the beautiful queen'. She was the mother of Iyasu II with whom she reigned as co-ruler since he was only six years old on his accession to the imperial throne in 1730. Her policy of conciliating the nobles ensured a generation of peace and tranquillity for Ethiopia, but at the expense of central authority since the provinces became increasingly autonomous. When Iyasu II died in 1755, Mentewab somehow managed to remain co-ruler while her grandson was a minor. But her intrigue eventually produced civil strife and Ethiopia disintegrated during the last years of her life which she spent in virtual captivity after Mikael Sehul had usurped the throne. Empress Mentewab died on 27 June 1773. She left a reputation for patronizing the arts and building an unusual number of churches.

METCALFE, Ralph

Born in Atlanta, Georgia, on 30 May 1910, Ralph H. Metcalfe enjoyed two successful careers. He was a world-famous track star during the 1930s, when he represented the US in two Olympic competitions, and later became an eminent politician. Completing his MA at the University of Southern California in 1939, he coached athletics and taught political science at Xavier University for a few years before entering politics. After serving on Chicago's city council from 1955 to 1971, he gained election to the US House of Representatives in 1972 and remained a member of that legislature until his death on 10 October 1978. His major legacy was the Ralph H. Metcalfe Foundation in Chicago.

MILLER, Billie

Billie Miller was born in Barbados on 8 January 1944. She attended Queen's College before studying law in England and becoming the very first lady barrister produced by her native island. A fiery and eloquent politician, she has retained her seat in the Barbadian legislature for many years and has occasionally served as acting prime minister. One of the leaders of the Barbados Labour Party (BLP), she has held several important portfolios, including minister of education (1981-85) and minister of foreign affairs and deputy prime minister (1999-2003).

MILLER, Kelly

A truly outstanding sociologist and educator, Kelly Miller was born in Winnsboro, South Carolina, in 1863. A scholarship took him to Howard University where he achieved his BA, MA and LLB degrees. He also undertook postgraduate studies in mathematics at John Hopkins University. He enjoyed a remarkable career as author, teacher and administrator at Howard University from 1890 to 1935. Two of his early articles brought him lasting fame: 'Education of the Negro' in *US Bureau of Education Report* (1901) and 'Enumerations of Errors' in *Negro Population in Scientific Monthly*, (February 1922). His important books include *Race Adjustment* (1910), *Out of the House of Bondage* (1914), *An Appeal to Conscience* (1918) and *The Everlasting Stain* (1924). Kelly Miller died on 29 December 1939.

MINGUS, Charlie

This creative jazz bass player, bandleader and composer was born in Nogales, Arizona, in 1922. Known as a 'hard Bop' performer, he played with such famous jazz musicians as Louis Armstrong, Duke Ellington, Stan Getz, Charlie Parker and Art Tatum. One of jazz's most original bassists, he was also a successful composer. Two of his best-known pieces were *Meditations on Integration* and *The Mingus Dances*. Charles Mingus died in 1979. His autobiography, *Beneath the Underdog*, was published in 1971.

MINK, James

James Mink was the son of former slaves who had come to Upper Canada with their loyalist owners from New York around 1800. He became one of Toronto's wealthiest Blacks in the 1840s when he was the owner of the Mansion Inn and Livery on Adelaide Street. His business prospered to such an extent that he was able to open two additional stables. His stage coaches carried passengers and mail from Toronto to Kingston where his brother, George, also kept a livery service. For many years the Toronto City Council used Mink's livery stables but the advent of the Grand Trunk railway put an end to the expansion of his business. He retired quietly and comfortably to a huge mansion in Richmond Hill.

MIRAMBO

Mirambo was a very successful Nyamwezi warrior-king in eastern Africa during the 1870s. He united the various Nyamwezi clans into a powerful kingdom and gained a strategic control of the old traditional Arab trade routes. He established his new capital at Urambo (now in Tanzania) and it quickly became a major trading centre. Mirambo's success was based on his skill as a negotiator which allowed him to acquire large supplies of firearms and his ability to exploit the ruga-ruga, the much dreaded Ngoni mercenary warriors from the south. His rise to power severely checked Arab expansion in Buganda and other regions of eastern Africa. After Mirambo's death in 1884, however, his kingdom rapidly disintegrated in the face of the relentless European advance.

MITCHELL, Arthur

Arthur Mitchell was born in New York City in 1934. After studying dance at the School of American Ballet, he developed into one of the finest ballet dancers and artistic directors in North America. When he made his début with the New York City Ballet in 1955, he became the first black dancer in the United States to perform with a major classical ballet company. He soon became the principal dancer of that body before forming his own interracial American Dance Company in 1966. Mitchell also founded the National Ballet Company of Brazil and acted for years as its choreographer and artistic director. He later created the Dance Theatre of Harlem to teach children of all races the art of classical ballet.

MITCHELL, Clarence

Clarence M. Mitchell, Jr was born in Baltimore, Maryland, on 8 March 1911. He graduated from the University of Maryland Law School with both LLB and JD degrees in the early 1930s before undertaking graduate studies in social work at Atlanta University and the University of Minnesota. Despite his admission to the Maryland bar, Mitchell worked mainly as a journalist and civil servant while devoting his major energies to the National Association for the Advancement of Colored People (NAACP) during the 1940s. From 1950 to 1978, he served as the NCAAP's main lobbyist in Washington, D.C. and won the respect of both the Democrats and Republicans. His efforts were largely responsible for the progressive civil rights legislation that followed World War II and he played a significant role in the passage of the Fair Housing Act of 1968. He was rewarded with the Spingarn Medal in 1969. He retired from the NCAAP in 1978 and entered private practice. Mitchell died on 18 March 1984, much lamented by all ethnic groups in the United States. Known for his discipline, respect, courtesy and quiet persistence, Clarence Mitchell was sometimes referred to as the '101st senator'.

MITCHELL, Keith

Keith Claudius Mitchell has been the prime minister of Grenada since 1994. Born on 12 November 1946, he attended local schools in his native island before completing his education at the University of the West Indies and the American University. He returned home to lead the New National Party (NNP) which has won three consecutive elections (1994, 1999 and 2003) so far. But his majority has now dwindled to one seat. He is a very active member of CARICOM and one of the keenest supporters of West Indies cricket.

MITCHELL, William

Revd William M. Mitchell is best remembered for his influential book, *The Under-Ground Railroad*, published in 1860. A free Negro, he had been a slave driver before converting to Christianity and emigrating to Toronto in 1855. He served as an agent for the American Baptist Free Mission Society and played a role in helping American slaves to escape to Canada from southern plantations during the middle of the nineteenth century.

MLAMBO-NGCUKA, Phumzile

In 2005, Mrs Phumzile Mlambo-Ngcuka became the first black woman to be appointed deputy president of South Africa. Born on 3 November 1955, she obtained a bachelor's degree in social science and education from the National University of Lesotho in 1980 and a master's degree in philosophy from the University of Cape Town in 2003. During 1981-

83, she taught in Kwa-Zulu, Natal, before moving to Geneva to serve on the World Young Men's Christian Association (YMCA) Board. From 1990 to 1993, she was director of the World University Services. She started and managed her own management consulting company, Phumlela Services, during 1993-94. Elected to the national legislature in 1994, she chaired the Public Service and Administration Portfolio Committee and was deputy minister of trade and industry during 1996-99. Phumzile served as a member of the executive committee of the African National Congress (ANC) and acted briefly in 2004 as minister of arts, culture and technology and was minister of mines and energy during 1999-2005. She led the Southern African Development Community mission to observe the Zimbabwe parliamentary elections. Phumzile Mlambo-Ngcuka was awarded an honorary doctorate by Wits Technikon in 2003.

MOBUTU SESE SEKO

Joseph-Désiré Mobutu was born at Lisala in the Belgian Congo on 14 October 1930. He studied at Congolese and Belgian schools before becoming a journalist and joining Patrice Lumumba's Mouvement National Congolais. When the Congo achieved its independence in 1960, he served first as defence secretary and then as chief of staff of the Congolese Army. Five years later, he staged a military coup from which he emerged as the most powerful figure in the country. He transformed his ill-trained troops into a modern, well-disciplined force and created his own political party, the Mouvement Populaire de la Révolution. A tough and sometimes ruthless leader, Mobutu embarked on a series of radical reforms, including the nationalization of the Union Minière, a powerful Belgian mining corporation. In 1971, in a campaign to promote the 'authentic African personality', he changed his country's name to Zaire and his own to Mobutu Sese Seko. He also called upon all Zaireans to de-europeanize their names. His whole reign was marked by civil strife and he significantly added to his own problems by opposing Agostinho Neto's Marxist movement in Angola, which became a base for most anti-Mobutu campaigns after 1975. For more than thirty years he ruled Zaire with absolute power, taking full advantage of the support he received from the western powers who viewed him as a bulwark against communism in Africa. He outlawed all political parties except his own and amassed a huge personal fortune at the expense of the country's treasury and natural resources. In 1996, while undergoing cancer treatment in Switzerland, Mobutu was finally overthrown by rebel forces led by Laurent Kabila. He abandoned the strife-torn country to the rebels and sought refuge in Morocco, where he died on 7 September 1997.

MODJADJI V

Born in the late 1930s in Northern Province, South Africa, Modjadji V, who died on 28 June 2001, was South Africa's last reigning queen. Believed to have been endowed with magical rain-making powers, she was revered as the Rain Queen of the Bantu-speaking Lovedu people. As their Rain Queen, she served as their spiritual and religious leader while her brother handled most of the political and administrative details. She had ascended the throne after her mother's death in 1982. Modjadji V, like all of her maternal predecessors, had been respected and consulted by tribes and national leaders throughout the region. Even Nelson Mandela, the former president of South Africa, is reported to have sought her sagacious counsel.

MOFOLO, Thomas

Thomas Mokopu Mofolo was one of the greatest of South African vernacular novelists who created a great impression with his classic, *Chaka*, in 1925. He is generally regarded as the first important African novelist of the twentieth century and foremost among Bantu writers. Although he published very little in his last thirty years, he is still considered the greatest of all Lesotho's authors. Born in the Mafeteng District of Lesotho on 2 August 1875, he was educated in local schools in the Qomoqomong Valley and Masitise as well as at the Morija Bible School and the Basuto Training College. He taught for several years at various schools in southern Africa before working at the Morija Book Depot as a proofreader and secretary. Writing in his native dialect, Mofolo had produced another successful novel, *Moeti oa bochabela*, in 1906. His much acclaimed *Pitseng* appeared first in 1910 in serialized form and was largely an account of his own childhood and education in Lesotho. Mofolo devoted a great deal of his energy, however, to commerce and politics, in both of which he ultimately failed. In 1916 he bought his own steam engine and milling plant, becoming one of the very first Africans in northern Lesotho to do so. In 1922 he set himself up as an independent Labour Agent recruiting workers for the diamond mines, sugar plantations and larger farms. He then opened a branch of the Labour Office at Teyateyaneng. Abandoning all of his earlier enterprises, Mofolo invested in a trading store in Bokong in 1928 and seemed to prosper for a while. But he never really could recover from the effects of the racist Land Bill of 1914 which literally nullified his purchases of real estate in Griqualand East without any compensation. He was reduced to seeking odd jobs to survive and, when his health eventually failed, he died penniless on 8 September 1948. His Sotho works have since been translated into English.

MOI, Daniel Arap

When the legendary Kenyan president, Jomo Kenyatta, died in 1978,

Daniel Toroitich arap Moi emerged as his obvious successor, having served as his deputy since 1966. Born of peasant stock in the Baringo District, on 2 September 1924, he was educated at local mission schools before qualifying as a teacher in 1945. Entering politics in 1950, he became a member of the Legislative Council in 1955 and served in the late 1950s as minister of education and then as minister of local government. Seceding from Kenyatta's party, the Kenya African National Union (KANU), Moi founded the Kenya African Democratic Union (KADU) to promote the interests of minority groups, like the Tugen (to which he himself belonged). After independence, Moi's party agreed to work in cooperation with Kenyatta's and Moi became one of the leaders of the cabinet. As soon as he took over the reins in 1978, he launched a determined campaign against corruption, inefficiency, illiteracy and unemployment. But his campaign ultimately languished and these problems still remain largely unsolved. Moi, however, retained his control over Kenya largely by governing in an autocratic manner and browbeating his critics, who were generally divided among themselves. In 2002, when his political opponents finally united against his government, he handed over power to Mwai Kibaki in a peaceful transition that followed the victory of the National Rainbow Coalition (NARC) over the KANU. While Moi's domestic policy was chequered, his foreign policy was more progressive and enlightened. He consistently promoted the principle of African co-operation and gave vigorous support to the Organization of African Unity (OAU) over which he twice presided. Even when Kenya was bedevilled by economic woes of its own, Moi frequently became involved in mediation between contending African nations while sending peace-keeping forces to Angola, Chad, Congo, Eritrea, Liberia, Sierra Leone and other parts of the world. He is now trying to establish a foundation to help solve on-going conflicts in Africa and to combat the scourge of HIV/AIDS.

MOKHEHLE, Ntsu

An educator and politician, Ntsu Mokhehle was born in Teyateyaneng, Lesotho, on 26 December 1918. He graduated with honours in 1946 from Fort Hare University and earned a master's degree in parasitology in 1949. He was working as a teacher when he founded the Basutoland Congress Party (BCP) in 1952 in opposition to British colonial rule. When the Basutoland National Party (BNP) gained control in 1966 on Lesotho's achievement of political independence, Mokhehle led the opposition party which appeared on the threshold of victory in 1970. Fearing defeat, the prime minister, Leabua Jonathan, declared a state of emergency, suspended the constitution, banned opposition newspapers and arrested the opposition leaders. Mokhehle's party led an unsuccessful revolt in 1974 and he was forced to flee to South Africa. In exile, Mokhehle continued to lead the resistance against unconstitutional government and civilian rule was finally restored in 1993. The BCP won all sixty-five legislative seats and Mokhehle became prime minister. To thwart rebellion within the BCP's ranks, he formed a new party in 1997, the Lesotho Congress for Democracy (LCD). Despite his avowed concern for democracy and good government, Mokhehle left Lesotho plagued by factionalism and violence when he died on 6 January 1999.

MONDLANE, Eduardo

Dr Eduardo Chivambo Mondlane was one of the most effective guerilla leaders engaged in Mozambique's struggle against Portugal for political independence during the 1960s. Born to a peasant family in 1920, he studied at local mission schools and in South Africa before completing his PhD in sociology at Northwestern University in Illinois. After teaching for some years in the United States, Mondlane joined the staff of the United Nations Trusteeship Council. Then, at the age of forty-one, he returned to eastern Africa to head FRELIMO (the Front for the Liberation of Mozambique), into which he breathed new life and vigour. Establishing his military headquarters in Tanzania, he began a patient and determined assault upon the Portuguese forces in Mozambique in 1964. Described as one of Portugal's most wanted men, he was killed in a bomb blast in Dar es Salaam, Tanzania, on 3 February 1969. Mondlane's role in the eventual emancipation of Mozambique, however, was pivotal.

MONK, Thelonius

Thelonius Sphere Monk was a creative jazz pianist and composer. Born in Rocky Mount, North Carolina, on 10 October 1917, he began playing the piano at a very early age. Along with such jazz greats as Charlie Christian (guitarist), Kenny Clark (drummer), Dizzy Gillespie (trumpeter) and Charlie Parker, he pioneered the revolutionary bebop music jazz form of the 1940s. Among his better known jazz compositions were *Blue Monk*, *Round About Midnight*, *Epistrophy*, *Ruby*, *My Dear*, *In Walked Bud* and *Straight, No Chaser*. A leader of small jazz bands that gave successful concerts worldwide during the 1950s and 1960s, Monk exerted a powerful influence on modern jazz musicians. He died on 17 February 1982.

MONTAGUE, Kenneth

Dr Kenneth Montague is a dental surgeon who has been rated the Best Dentist in Toronto by *NOW* magazine in two consecutive years (1995, 1996). Born in Windsor, Ontario, in 1963, he completed his DDS at the University of Toronto in 1987 and has been in private practice since 1992. He not only provides his patients with relaxing music, but issues a seasonal newsletter, entitled *Word of Mouth*, aimed at educating them in the better care of their teeth. In 1986, he organized a professional excursion to Jamaica to initiate a programme for the provision of dental care to disadvantaged children in the rural districts.

MOODY, Harold

Dr Harold Moody was born in Kingston, Jamaica, on 8 October 1882. He emigrated to the United Kingdom 1904 and completed his medical studies at King's College in 1910. As no hospital would accept him because of his colour, he started his own private practice in Peckham in 1913. To combat the racism which he and others encountered in London, he co-founded the League of Coloured Peoples in 1931 which began a serious campaign for racial equality by publishing its own journal, *The Keys*. Moody continued his crusade during the Second World War when he denounced segregation in the armed forces while he himself worked for the civil defence in Peckham. The League of Coloured Peoples organized a three-day conference in London in 1944 and drew up a series of resolutions foreshadowing those of the Pan African Conference held in Manchester in 1945. Dr Moody died on 24 April 1947. He was one of the earliest black civil rights activists in the United Kingdom.

MOORE, Archie

Born Archibald Lee Wright in Benoit, Mississippi, on 13 December 1913, Archie Moore changed his name when he was being raised by an aunt and an uncle after his parents separated. He became one of the finest professionals in the history of boxing, winning at least 194 of an estimated 228 bouts. He captured the light heavyweight title on 17 December 1952 and held it until 1962 and was almost fifty when he fought against Cassius Clay in a much publicized encounter. After retiring from the ring, he founded the Any Boy Can (ABC) Club for the benefit of inner city youth. He played a minor role in the 1960 motion picture, *The Adventures of Huckleberry Finn* and, in the same year, published his autobiography, *The Archie Moore Story*. In the 1980s he worked for the Los Angeles branch of the US Department of Housing and Urban Development. He died on 9 December 1998 in San Diego, California.

MOORE, Donald

Donald Willard Moore was born in Barbados, British West Indies, on 2 November 1891. He immigrated to Canada in 1913 and almost at once set out to improve the circumstances of black Canadians. He played a key role in the establishment of the Negro Citizenship Association (NCA) in 1951 which did much to persuade the Canadian government to open its doors to black people from the West Indies. Along with other black activists like Harry Gairey and Stanley Grizzle, he opened a hostel in Toronto to aid newly-arrived immigrants and played no small part in their assimilation and integration. For more than seventy years, Moore strove valiantly for human rights in Ontario and was a most deserving recipient of the Order of Canada. Much loved and revered by Toronto's black community, he died at the advanced age of 102 on 22 August 1994. His legacy includes *Donald Moore: An Autobiography*, published in 1985.

MOORE, Richard

Richard B. Moore was born in Barbados, British West Indies, in 1893. After working briefly as a junior clerk in Bridgetown, the island's capital, he emigrated in 1909 to New York, where he worked tirelessly for the next six decades on behalf of African-American consciousness, Pan-Africanism, and Caribbean freedom and nationhood. A noted journalist, essayist, historian, and activist, he was a key figure in the development of radical politics in Harlem, and it was he who first proposed the use of the term 'Afro-Americans' to distinguish them from other Blacks. After his death in 1978, his huge and unique private library of black history and literature was purchased by the Lions' Club of Barbados.

MORGAN, Garrett

This remarkable inventor was born in Paris, Kentucky, on 4 March 1875. Without any formal training beyond the level of the fifth grade, he developed a belt fastener for sewing machines in 1901, and won a national prize in 1914 for his new breathing helmet and smoke protector. This latter device was successfully used on the battlefield during World War I. Morgan opened his own sewing machine business and started a tailoring shop in 1909 with thirty-two workers making dresses, suits and coats. Having discovered a mixture that straightened hair, he opened the G.A. Morgan Hair Refining Company in 1913. In that same year, he invented an automatic stop sign to aid in the movement of traffic. His traffic signals are now used all over the world. During the 1920s, he founded *The Cleveland Call*, one of the most durable of all African-American newspapers. Garrett A. Morgan died in 1963 at the age of eighty-eight.

MORRIS, Bill

Sir William Morris OJ was born in Jamaica in 1938 and educated at the Mizpah School in the parish of Manchester before emigrating to the United Kingdom with his family in 1954. He started working for a Birmingham engineering company while attending Handsworth Technical College as a part-time student. He joined the Transport and General Workers' Union

(TandG) in 1958 and rose steadily within the union ranks to become a member of its executive council. In 1973 he became a full-time union official and in 1979 was appointed national secretary for the Passenger Services Trade Group, responsible for leading national negotiations in the bus and coach industries. In 1986 he became deputy general secretary and was elected general secretary of the T and G in 1991, becoming the first black man to lead a trade union in Great Britain. He was re-elected in 1995 and held the post until his retirement in 2003. Sir Bill has been active in many capacities as a member of the Employment Appeals Tribunal; member of the Commission for Racial Equality; non-executive director of the Bank of England; chancellor of the University of Technology in Jamaica; member of the Board of governors of South Bank University; patron of a number of charities, including the National Black Boys Can Association; member of the Royal Commission on the Reform of the House of Lords; and a trustee of the Prince of Wales Youth Business Trust. He is a Fellow of the Royal Society of Arts and the City and Guilds of London Institute and he holds honorary degrees from a number of British universities. He was awarded the Order of Jamaica in 2002 and received a knighthood in 2003. In April 2006 he was elevated to the peerage of the United Kingdom.

MORRIS, Mervyn

One of the best known critics, poets and educators in the Caribbean, Dr Mervyn Morris was born in Jamaica in 1937. A brilliant Rhodes scholar, he was educated at Munro College, the University of the West Indies (Jamaica) and Oxford University (England). He returned to Jamaica in the early 1960s to join the staff of the University of the West Indies where he has served as assistant registrar, warden of Taylor Hall, and professor of English. He is currently Professor Emeritus of Creative Writing and West Indian Literature. Apart from editing several anthologies of Jamaican poems, he is himself a distinguished poet whose greatest efforts include *The Pond* (1973); *On Holy Week* (1975); *Shadow Boxing*; and *Examination Centre*. He has also written numerous books of literary criticism, the most recent being *Making West Indian Literature* (2005). In addition, Morris has written a number of articles on a variety of subjects ranging from Caribbean literature to West Indian student life in Britain and the Black Power movement in the United States. His awards and distinctions include the prestigious Musgrave Silver Medal from the Institute of Jamaica in 1976.

MORRISON, Toni

Born Chloe Anthony Wofford in Lorain, Ohio, on 18 February 1931, Toni Morrison became one of America's most distinguished writers during the

1970s and 1980s. She graduated from Howard University with a BA in 1953 and achieved her MA from Cornell University in 1955. She then taught briefly at Texas Southern University and Howard University, where she met and married Howard Morrison, a Jamaican architect. In 1964, she got a divorce, resigned from Howard University, and moved to Syracuse, New York, where she served as an editor for Random House. Morrison's first novel, *The Bluest Eye*, was published in 1969 with considerable success. Her second, *Sula*, was nominated for the 1975 National Book Award in the fiction category. Her *Song of Solomon*, a bestseller, won the National Book Critics Circle Award for fiction in 1978, and was the first novel written by a black author to be chosen as a full selection of the Book-of-the-Month Club since Richard Wright's *Native Son* in 1941. In 1996, when it was Oprah (Winfrey)'s Book Club second book-of-the-month selection, an additional 870,000 copies were sold. Morrison's fourth novel, *Tar Baby*, won its author a place on the cover of *Newsweek* during 1981. But none of this could compare with the reception of *Beloved* in 1988. This novel not only won the Pulitzer Prize but was nominated for the National Book Award, the National Book Critics Circle Award, and the Ritz Hemingway Award. Morrison has also written one play, *Dreaming Emmett*. In 1993, she won the Nobel Prize for Literature for her collected works. Since then she has enhanced her reputation with *Paradise* (1998) and *Love* (2003). In recent years, with her son Slade Morrison, she has also produced a number of children's books. She served as the Robert F. Goheen Professor of Humanities at Princeton University during 1989-2006.

MORTON, Ferdinand Joseph

A noted composer and pianist, 'Jelly Roll' Morton was born in New Orleans, Louisiana, on 20 September 1885. He is best remembered as one of ragtime's greatest exponents but he also made a significant contribution to the evolution of modern jazz. He wrote more than 120 songs and hundreds of recordings. He did more than any other single individual to document and preserve much of early jazz. He died in 1941.

MOSHOESHOE I

Moshoeshoe the Great is the famous Sotho warrior-king who founded the kingdom of Basutoland in the nineteenth century and protected it from the aggressions of both African and European predators in southeastern Africa for about fifty years (1820-70). Born around 1786, Moshoeshoe was the son of a lesser chieftain but soon distinguished himself as a daring warrior and astute statesman by first dominating and then uniting the various Sotho communities in the region into a centralized system with his headquarters at Thaba Bosiu. By playing off the Boers and the British against each other,

Basutoland retained its independence, sovereignty and integrity until 1868 when Moshoeshoe finally had to seek British protection to counter the aggressiveness of the Boers. The great emperor died on 11 March 1870 and Basutoland did not regain its political independence until 1966 when it changed its name to Lesotho and restored Moshoeshoe's great-grandson to his rightful inheritance. Moshoeshoe I is a good example of superior administrative, diplomatic and military skills at work in pre-colonial Africa.

MOSHOESHOE II

Constantine Bereng Seiso assumed the title of Moshoeshoe II when he became the first king of independent Lesotho in 1966. Born on 2 May 1938 in Thabang, Basutoland, he was a descendant of the famous Moshoeshoe who had founded the Sotho kingdom of Basutoland in the nineteenth century. Educated locally at Roma College and in Great Britain, he claimed his royal birthright when he succeeded to the paramount chieftaincy in 1960 and was proclaimed king when Basutoland won its political independence and changed its name to Lesotho. But Moshoeshoe II faced enormous difficulties from the start. While he had no interest in becoming a mere figurehead, Sotho democrats were anxious to create a constitutional monarchy after the British model. He also had to face opposition from the republic of South Africa. He was twice placed under house arrest by his prime minister, Lebua Jonathan, was twice sent into exile, and was once deposed. But Moshoeshoe remained so popular with his Sotho people that he had to be reinstated as king of Lesotho in 1995. He died on 15 January 1996.

MOTHOPENG, Zephania

Zephania Lekoane Mothopeng was a South African activist who helped to found the Pan-African Congress (PAC) and advocated a united African continent called Azania and controlled by the indigenous African peoples. Born on 10 September 1913 in Vrede, Orange Free State, he was educated at Adams College in Natal and taught for many years at Orlando High School in what would later become Soweto. 'Zeph', as he was generally known throughout South Africa, was an active member of the ANC Youth League and was elected president of PAC in 1986 even while serving a jail sentence for his political activities. Fired from his teaching position in South Africa in 1953, he taught briefly in Lesotho before returning to South Africa to work as a law clerk in Johannesburg during 1956-59. After that, Mothopeng spent most of his days in prison or detention without trial, as he continued to defy the racist régime. When charged in 1976 under the new Terrorism Act, he refused to testify in a court whose authority he rejected. In 1988 he was released for medical reasons and permitted to travel to Britain for cancer treatment. He died on 23 October 1990.

MOTLEY, Constance Baker

Constance Baker Motley was born in New Haven, Connecticut, on 14 September 1921. She received her BA from New York University in 1943 and her LLB from Columbia University in 1946. She then devoted her major energies to the cause of the National Association for the Advancement of Colored People (NAACP) and was one of the leading civil rights advocates throughout the 1950s and 1960s. Constance Baker Motley was elected to the New York State Senate in 1964, becoming the first African-American woman to achieve that distinction. In 1965 the New York City Council elected her Manhattan borough president and she was named judge of the US Supreme Court for the Southern District of New York in 1966. She was appointed chief judge of the court in 1982 and senior judge in 1986. She died on 28 September 2005.

MPADI, Simon-Pierre

Simon-Pierre Mpadi was a messianic Zairean religious leader who established a separatist Church in what was then the Belgian Congo in the 1930s. Born around 1900 in Madimba territory, he became a convert to Christianity and was an officer in the Salvation Army. In 1936, frustrated by the blatant racism of the white Christians, he became a follower of Simon Kimbangu and, in 1939, established a branch of Kimbangu's church which he called Mission des Noirs. His strident criticisms of European colonialism led to his deportation from both the French and Belgian Congos during the 1940s and he eventually disappeared altogether in the early 1950s. His followers assumed that he was assassinated and he became another martyr in the long line of Kitawalan prophets. Mpadi's mission was thus a brief one but it had significant effects on the growth of nationalist political and cultural feelings in the Belgian and French Congos. Like the Kitawalan preachers of his generation, he spoke in terms of European eternal suffering for their cruel treatment of the meek Africans who were destined to inherit the earth.

MPETHA, Oscar

Oscar Mafakafaka Mpetha was an outspoken advocate of racial equality and collective bargaining in South Africa for more than fifty years. He was the founder of South Africa's trade union movement and became famous for his efforts on behalf of the mainly black Food and Canning Workers' Union during the 1940s. Born in Transkei on 5 August 1909, he qualified as a road master and began working as an assistant foreman. In 1940 he organized and led a movement calling for higher wages for road labourers. He also made a name for himself as a vocal critic of apartheid and as one of the leaders of the African National Congress (ANC). Following the Sharpeville Massacre, Mpetha was detained for four years. During the

1970s he was repeatedly held in detention for his trade union activities and was once imprisoned for five years for terrorism. After his own discharge from prison in 1989, he fought valiantly for Nelson Mandela's release in spite of his own poor health. He died on 15 November 1994.

MPEZENI

Mpezeni was one of the southern African rulers who found it difficult to retain the independence and integrity of their kingdoms in the face of European and other pressures towards the end of the nineteenth century. Born around 1830, he was the son of the great Ngoni king, Zwangendaba, who died in 1848. Mpezeni was caught in the middle of European competition for control of southeastern Africa, and his unwillingness to grant land and mineral concessions to European colonists earned him their enmity. At Zwangendaba's death, the Ngoni empire split into five major groups under different sons of the old emperor. Mpezeni led his group to what is now southern Zambia where they were undisturbed by external threats until late in the 1890s. He tried to play off Britain, Germany and Portugal against each other but he was ultimately overwhelmed by the British in 1898. His people had retained their independence long after the bulk of other Africans had lost theirs. Mpezeni died on 21 September 1900.

MPHAHLELE, Ezekiel

Dr Ezekiel Mphahlele was arguably Black Africa's leading literary intellectual using the English language. Born on 17 December 1919 in Pretoria, South Africa, he was educated in local schools, at St Peter's Secondary School in Johannesburg and at Adams' College in Natal. He achieved a Teacher's Certificate in 1940 and taught English and Afrikaans for some years in one of the largest secondary schools in Johannesburg. But in 1952 he was dismissed for taking part in a protest against the unpopular Bantu Education Act which not only promoted further segregation but seemed deliberately calculated to place additional handicaps upon the black majority. Banned from teaching in South Africa, Mphahlele turned to journalism and literature. He served as the literary editor of *Drum* while contributing articles to *African Writing Today*, a journal which he himself began to edit in 1955. Having to support himself by writing, he proceeded to publish a sequence of excellent books, including *The African Image* (1962) and two autobiographical novels, *The Wanderers* (1971) and *Down Second Avenue* (1971). His short stories also created a very favourable impression, with the best of them appearing in *Man Must Live and Other Stories* (1947), *The Living and the Dread and Other Stories* (1961) and *In The Corner* (1967). He also edited such influential anthologies as *Modern African Stories* (1966) and *African Writing Today* (1967). Some of his finest essays also appeared in the collection, *Voices in the*

Whirlwind and Other Essays (1972). Mphahlele was invited to lecture in several universities in Africa, Europe and the United States during the 1960s and he also served as director of the African programme at the Congress for Cultural Freedom in Paris. With Ulli Beier and Wole Soyinka, he co-edited the influential literary journal, *Black Orpheus*, published in Ibadan, Nigeria. He edited the periodical, *Africa Today*, in 1967, and founded Chemchemi, a cultural centre in Nairobi, Kenya, for artists and writers in 1963. While in exile, Mphahlele earned a PhD from the University of Denver and taught at the University of Pennsylvania. He eventually returned to South Africa and joined the University of Witwatersrand where he served as a professor in the Department of Comparative and African Literature during 1977-87. His later novels included *Chirundu* (1979) and *Father Come Home* (1984). He also published the autobiographical *Afrika My Music* in 1984. His most recent scholarly writing included *Poetry and Humanism: Oral Beginnings* (1986), *Echoes of African Art* (1987) and *Renewal Time* (1988).

MQHAYI, Samuel

Samuel Edward Krune Loliwe Mqhayi is easily the most famous of all Xhosa poets. Born in Cape Province, South Africa, on 1 December 1875, he was the son of Ziwani, a noted scholar of all Bantu languages, and the grandson of Mqhayi who had been a chief of the Amarica clan of the Xhosa people. He studied at Lovedale and trained as a teacher before teaching at the West Bank Location in East London. For many years Mqhayi served as the sub-editor of *Izwi labantu* (The Voice of the People). For a while he also edited Jabavu's *Imvo zabantsundu*. His fame, however, rested upon the instant success of his first Xhosa novel, *Ityala lamaWele*, published in 1914. A prolific writer of both poetry and prose, Mqhayi authored such fine biographies as *U-bomi bom-Fundisi u J.K. Bokwe* (1925), *U-Sogqumahashe* (1927), and *Isikhumbuzo sika Ntsikana* (1930). His autobiography, *U-Mqhayi wase- Ntab' ozuko*, appeared in 1939. Some of his most beautiful poetry was published in such works as *Ama-gora e-Mendi* (1920), *I-Bandla labantu* (1923), *Imihobe nemi-Bongo* (1927), *Yoko-Fundwa ezikolweni* (1937) and *I-Nzuzo* (1942). He also translated several European works into the Xhosa language. Mqhayi died on 29 July 1945.

MSIRI

Msiri, also known as Ngelengwa or Mwenda, was one of the most successful African rulers during the nineteenth century. He began his reign towards the end of the 1850s with a few Nyamwezi subjects in southern Katanga and, within less than two decades, had succeeded in taking over most of the valuable copper region from its previous Lunda owners. During the 1880s, Msiri not only ruled directly over a very large kingdom but also received tribute from neighbouring areas. His prosperity was largely based on the copper trade but he dealt with ivory and slaves as well. Msiri used these resources to purchase firearms which he saw as absolutely necessary to his military strength. He refused to negotiate with the Europeans when they discovered that his kingdom was rich in minerals. They therefore encouraged local rebellions against him and he was assassinated on 20 December 1891. While employing older Lunda methods of state building, Msiri also created new political titles and ceremonies and made important changes in customary law. He was also instrumental in introducing into Katanga sweet potatoes, small pox vaccination, and a technique for making copper wire. King Msiri of Katanga serves as another classic example of African military and administrative genius on the eve of European colonization.

MSWATI

Sometimes known also as Mswazi, this great south African monarch was one of the sons of the famous King Sobhuza I of Basutoland. Born around 1820, Mswati earned significant fame himself by founding the kingdom of Swaziland. His reign began in 1840 and he gradually extended his sway over the Bantu clans in eastern South Africa. Reorganizing the Ngwane along the lines of the successful Zulu regimental castes, he made them one of the most powerful nations in southern Africa. By the mid-century Mswati's empire stretched across the regions now known as Zimbabwe and Mozambique. He died in 1868 but not before sowing the seeds of Swaziland's destruction. Unaware of the dangers involved, he ceded territory to the Boer settlers in the Transvaal in 1845 and in 1864 aided them in conquering the Poko nation. The Boers repaid the great Mswati by depriving the Swazi of their independence in 1894.

MSWATI III

Born on 19 April 1968, the current King of Swaziland was the second of the sixty-seven sons fathered by Sobhuza II. When his father died in 1982, two relatives served as queen regents until he became of age. He was crowned king in April 1986, thus becoming the youngest reigning monarch. Mswati III is also Africa's last absolute hereditary ruler. He rules by decree and is strongly opposed to the democratization of his country although he did restore the national parliament which his father had dissolved. His reign has been marred by exceptional personal extravagance in the midst of Swaziland's abject poverty.

MUGABE, Robert

One of the most effective African nationalist leaders in the period after World War II, Robert Gabriel Mugabe played a significant role in the establishment of an independent Zimbabwe in 1980. He was one of the leaders of the Patriotic Front of Zimbabwe and president general of the Zimbabwe African National Union (ZANU). Born in Kutama on 21 February 1924, he was trained as a teacher in a Roman Catholic school before furthering his studies at the University of Fort Hare in South Africa. A militant radical, although he distanced himself from Marxism, Mugabe was an outspoken critic of the racist régimes in Rhodesia and South Africa. He therefore spent some years in voluntary exile in Ghana during the late 1950s. In 1960 he returned to Rhodesia and helped Revd Ndabaningi Sithole form ZANU as a breakaway from Joshua Nkomo's Zimbabwe African People's Union (ZAPU). In 1964, he was arrested for 'subversive speech' and imprisoned until 1974. While in a Rhodesian jail, Mugabe acquired three law degrees by correspondence courses and managed to lead a coup deposing Sithole as ZANU's leader. Under his direction, ZANU won a clear majority in elections held to determine Rhodesia's future. He consequently became prime minister of the new republic of Zimbabwe in April 1980. Mugabe has dominated Zimbabwean politics ever since. When Canaan Banana, the country's first president, resigned on 31 December 1987, he succeeded to the presidency and the office of prime minister was abolished. Mugabe proceeded to make Zimbabwe more or less a one-party state, to confiscate several estates previously owned by white farmers for redistribution among the Blacks, and to treat his opponents harshly. His autocratic methods have produced much criticism (both from within Zimbabwe and without) but he has shown tremendous resilience as a political leader over the past twenty-six years.

MUHAMMAD, Elijah

Born Elijah Poole in Sanderville, Georgia, on 7 October 1897, this religious leader converted to Islam during the 1930s and succeeded Wali Farad in 1934 as the high priest of the Black Muslim sect in the United States. His policies of strict racial separation were modified as he grew older but nevertheless ensured that the Black Muslims remained outside the mainstream of the US civil rights movement. Elijah Muhammad died on 25 February 1975.

MUNFORD, Clarence

Dr Clarence Joseph Munford is Professor Emeritus of Black Studies at the University of Guelph, where (in 1969) he introduced the first courses in Black History in an Ontario university. A native of the United States, he immigrated to Canada in 1966 after completing his doctorate at the University of Leipzig in Germany. A keen scholar and activist, he developed a theory of human history from a black perspective which he called 'civilizational historicism', the hallmark of his award-winning books *Black Ordeal* (1992); *Race and Reparations: A Black Perspective for the Twenty-first Century* (1997); and *Race and Civilization: The Rebirth of Black Centrality* (2002). He is also one of the leaders in the campaign for reparations to African-Americans for the ills of slavery. He was honoured in 1995 by the students at the University of Guelph with the opening of the Munford Centre, a race relations resource facility committed to the destruction of racism in Canada and elsewhere.

MURPHY, Isaac

Isaac Murphy was the outstanding American jockey of the nineteenth century. Born in 1856 in Fayette County, Kentucky, he became the first to ride three Kentucky Derby winners (1884, 1890 and 1891) and the first to win two of those classics in succession. In his long career (1873-96), Murphy rode 628 winners, including four of the first five runnings of the American Derby in Chicago, Illinois (1884-88). He was so successful indeed that white Americans concluded that black jockeys were endowed with some natural and unfair advantages. Racial discrimination consequently forced all black jockeys off the US track for the next several decades. He died on 12 February 1896, but not until 1955 was he elected to the National Museum of Racing Hall of Fame, Saratoga Springs, New York. One year later, he was chosen a member of the Jockeys' Hall of Fame, Pimlico, Maryland.

MURRAY, Pauli

This amazing and versatile woman left her mark in American history as an educator, scholar, lawyer, poet, priest and civil rights activist. Dr Anna Pauline Murray was born in Baltimore, Maryland, on 20 November 1910. She studied at the City University of New York, Howard University and the University of California before eventually achieving her DJS from Yale Law School. After having been denied entry to the University of North Carolina Law School because of her race, she became the first African-American to achieve a doctorate in law from Yale. She helped to found the Congress of Racial Equality (CORE) in the early 1940s and was a key contributor to the early civil rights movement. In 1961, she was appointed by President Kennedy to his Committee on Civil and Political Rights. She wrote several books, including *Proud Shoes: The Story of an American Family* and *The Constitution and Government of Ghana* (1956). Two autobiographies were published posthumously: *Song in a Weary Throat: An American Pilgrimage* (1987); and *The Autobiography of a Black Activist, Feminist, Lawyer, Priest and Poet* (1989). She also left for posterity a beautiful collection of poetry, entitled *Dark Testament and Other Poems*. Murray was named the Outstanding Educator of America in 1971, and in 1973 became the Louis Stulberg Professor of law and politics at Brandeis University. She was the first black attorney general of California and one of the co-founders of the National Organization for Women (NOW). At the ripe age of sixty-seven Murray became (in 1977) the first woman to be ordained in the Episcopal Church. She died on 1 July 1985. In 1990, the Pauli Murray Human Relations Award was established in her honour to commemorate her life work.

MUSARURWA, Willie

Wirayi Dzawanda Musarurwa was the defiant Zimbabwean journalist who campaigned against oppression by both the Rhodesian white minority government and the post-independence black majority government of Zimbabwe, led by Robert Mugabe. Born in Zvimba Reserve, Southern Rhodesia, on 24 November 1927, Musarurwa was certified as a teacher and attended Princeton University in the United States before achieving a degree in journalism through a University of South Africa correspondence course. He became the editor of several black publications, including *African Weekly* and the *African Daily News*, and through these newspapers gave strong support to the nationalist campaign of Joshua Nkomo's Zimbabwe African People's Union (ZAPU). His editorials led to his detention, without charge or trial, by the government from 1965 to 1974. After his release, Musarurwa joined Nkomo in exile in Zambia and in 1979 he represented ZAPU at the Zimbabwean independence talks in London, England. In 1981, he was named editor of the *Sunday Mail* but was dismissed by the government for writing critically about ZANU and Mugabe's policies. Musarurwa died on 3 April 1990.

MUSEVENI, Yoweri

Yoweri Kaguta Museveni has been president of Uganda since 1986. A participant in the upheavals that brought an end to the regime of Idi Amin in 1979 and to that of Milton Obote in 1985, he has brought relative stability and economic growth to a country that has endured decades of government mis-management and internecine strife. Born in Ntungamo in 1944, he attended local schools before entering the University of Dar es Salaam in Tanzania to study economics and political science under leftist radicals like Guyana's Walter Rodney and became attracted to Marxism. In 1970, he joined Obote's intelligence service but fled to Tanzania with other exiles afer Amin's coup d'état. There he built up a powerful rebel force that succeeded, with the help of other rebels, in toppling Amin's government. In the chaos that ensued, Museveni emerged as the ruler of a new political party, the Uganda Patriotic Movement (UPM), and a military force, the National Resistance Army (NRA). When this combination triumphed in 1986, Museveni tried to restore some semblance of democracy by establishing

Resistance Councils at the local level and he promised to restore security and respect for human rights. He also initiated economic policies designed to combat hyperinflation and the balance of payments. Abandoning his Marxist ideals, he embraced the structural adjustments advocated by the World Bank and the International Monetary Fund (IMF). He was re-elected president of Uganda in 2001 and ran successfully again in 2006, in defiance of the new constitution which had prohibited a third term. His legacy has thus far been chequered. While his tenure has witnessed some useful economic reforms and one of the most effective national responses to HIV/AIDS in Africa, he has failed to check the ethnic conflicts within the republic or to refrain from intervening in conflicts in the Democratic Republic of the Congo, Rwanda and The Sudan. The north of Uganda is still plagued by rebellion and genocide. His democratic system has been impaired by the prolongation of the presidential term, the stringent laws governing the formation of parties and the harassment of his opponents.

MUTESA I

Born around 1838, Mutesa I was the most famous and the greatest of all the kabakas of Buganda in the region that now forms part of Uganda. He carved out an imposing empire for himself in eastern Africa during the second half of the nineteenth century. By 1870 he had established himself as an absolute ruler over many ethnic groups by curbing the power of their priests and undermining the authority of their local chieftains. His system was a highly centralized one, based on an administrative hierarchy and a well-equipped army, both responsible only to him. But Mutesa's successes hurt eastern Africa in the long run since they made the region more vulnerable to European penetration during the 1880s and afterwards. His creation of a powerful Buganda (1856-84) had been accomplished largely at the expense of his immediate neighbours, some of whom (like Bunyoro) were severely crippled. While this is true, Mutesa's career provides graphic evidence of excellent military and administrative skills on the part of some African rulers prior to the days of European colonization.

MUTESA II

Sir Edward Frederick William Walugembe Mutebi Luwangula Mutesa, the 36th kabaka of Buganda, was born in Mengo, near Kampala, on 19 November 1924. He became the first president of an independent Uganda in 1963, but his whole political career illustrates the difficulties and dilemmas of modern Ugandan history. While disavowing British claims to supremacy over his people, he feared that the integrity and independence of Buganda might be compromised by an artificial Ugandan unity when the British withdrew. He had studied for a few years at Cambridge University after his installation as kabaka in 1942, but he returned to Buganda to defend his traditional rights (and those of his people) when the colonial government seemed bent on unifying Uganda by means of a popularly elected assembly. His opposition to this policy led to his deportation by the British in 1953. Mutesa II relented, adopted a more progressive approach, returned to Uganda in 1955, was awarded a knighthood, and was elected president. But he became increasingly isolated as he could be trusted neither by the traditionalists nor the left-wing Pan-Africanists. His basic objective was to establish a separate and independent Buganda over which he could exercise the royal prerogative that he had inherited. Mutesa therefore did his best to frustrate the programmes of Milton Obote, the newly elected president of a united Uganda, and was consequently ousted in 1966. He died in exile in London, England, on 21 November 1969.

MUZOREWA, Abel

President of the United African National Council (UANC), Bishop Abel Tendekayi Muzorewa was generally considered one of the most moderate Rhodesian black nationalist leaders during the 1970s. Unlike other militant Blacks, he seemed prepared to establish a free and democratic Zimbabwe by means of peaceful negotiation with the white minority. Born in Umtali on 14 April 1925, Muzorewa was educated at Methodist schools in Rhodesia and at theological colleges in the United States. He became a bishop of the United Methodist Church after working for some years as a lay preacher and a teacher. Bishop Muzorewa emerged as a political figure in the early 1970s when the imprisonment or execution of the majority of black Rhodesian leaders had created a vacuum. He founded the UANC in 1971 and mobilized resistance against the one-sided agreement that the Rhodesian and British governments had reached without any consultation with the Blacks. His campaigns were largely responsible for bringing Ian Smith's unpopular system to an end and he became the first black prime minister of Rhodesia when his party won 51 of the 100 parliamentary seats in the elections of 1979. He promptly negotiated an end to the Rhodesian civil war, granted the former rebels an amnesty and called another general election in March 1980 to allow the previously banned political parties to compete. The result was a resounding triumph for the Zimbabwe African National Union (ZANU) led by Robert Mugabe, who replaced Muzorewa as Zimbabwe's leader ever since.

MWANAWASA, Levy

Levy Patrick Mwanawasa was sworn in as president of Zambia on 2 January 2002. A member of the Lenje tribe, he was born in Mufulira in Northern Rhodesia on 3 September 1948. He was educated at the Chiwala

Secondary School and the University of Zambia, from which he emerged in 1973 with a law degree. For some years he practised law in Ndola and became the vice-chairman of the Law Association of Zambia in 1982. In 1985-86, he served as Zambia's solicitor general. In 1990, Mwanawasa joined Frederick Chiluba's newly formed party, Movement for Multiparty Democracy (MMD), which won the election in 1991. He was appointed vice-president when Chiluba took over the presidency from Kenneth Kaunda. But he resigned in 1994, claiming that his colleagues were irresponsible and greedy and that he was being marginalised by the president. Surprisingly, in 2001, he was adopted as MMD's candidate and succeeded Chiluba as president. He promptly launched a campaign against the corruption of his predecessors, and dismissed several military, political and administrative leaders. His anti-corruption campaign, which continued throughout his tenure, won high praise from foreign observers. He also gained IMF approval by following a programme of fiscal restraint. These policies, however, were not always popular among his own countrymen and the civil servants, in particular, were continually threatening to go on strike for higher salaries.

MWINYI, Ali Hassan

When Julius Nyerere finally decided to retire from active politics, after leading Tanzania for twenty-four years, Ali Hassan Mwinyi became that country's second president in 1985. Born at Kivure on 8 May 1925, he was trained as a teacher in Zanzibar before completing his studies in England. He served as principal of Zanzibar's Teacher Training College for many years before entering the public service in the ministry of education in 1964. For the next twenty years he performed in the long shadow cast by President Nyerere who eventually handpicked him as his successor. Mwinyi's presidency was a time of hardship for Tanzania as it coincided with economic collapse following many years of drought. The spiralling cost of oil and manufactured goods, at a time when the price of Tanzania's agricultural exports kept falling, created almost insoluble difficulties, and these were made much worse for a number of years by the constant fighting against Idi Amin's régime in Uganda. Mwinyi was eventually replaced as president of Tanzania by Benjamin Mkapa after the elections of October 1995. During his tenure of the presidency, the socialist policies of Julius Nyerere were reversed, multi-party politics were reintroduced, import restrictions were relaxed and private enterprise was encouraged. Many observers, however, still argue that he failed to implement a proper and disciplined money policy and thus contributed to rampant inflation. There are allegations, too, that he failed to eliminate government corruption and widespread tax evasion.

MZILIKAZI

Born around 1790 near Mkuze, in what is now South Africa, Mzilikazi was the famous warrior-king who founded the powerful Matabele Empire by dint of his military genius and administrative brilliance. Originally one of Shaka's vassals, he revolted against that Zulu overlord and led his small Kumalo tribe on a northward trek of about some 500 miles towards the region now known as Zimbabwe. By about 1840 he had established a highly centralized (albeit multi-ethnic) empire that was strong enough to keep even the Boers at bay. Mzilikazi was generally friendly towards the Europeans but when the latter discovered that there was gold in Matabeleland that spelt doom for the natives. When the great emperor died on 5 September 1868, the frantic rush had already begun and even the considerable talents of his son, Lobengula, could not save the Matabele Empire from European depredation in the 1890s.

NANKA-BRUCE, Frederick

Dr Frederick Victor Nanka-Bruce was one of the first natives of the Gold Coast to be trained as a physician in a western university. Born on 19 October 1878, he also became an influential publisher and journalist who participated most actively in the politics of his day. Educated at the Accra Government School and the Wesleyan Boys' School in Lagos, Nigeria, he proceeded to the University of Edinburgh (Scotland) to study medicine and graduated in 1907. Returning to the Gold Coast to practice, he did yeoman work during the plague of 1908. He helped to revive the *Gold Coast Independent* in 1918 and founded the *Daily Echo* in 1935. Nanka-Bruce gave whole-hearted support to liberal ideas and opposed all of the oppressive legislation passed by the imperial parliament in the early years of the 20th century. He served briefly as a member of the Gold Coast Legislative Council but influenced national politics mainly through his very popular newspapers. He died on 12 July 1953.

National Association For The Advancement Of Colored People

Founded in 1909, the National Association for the Advancement of Colored People (NAACP) has remained the most important and influential organization promoting African-American interests and aspirations. It has consistently aimed at the establishment of a truly democratic society in the United States and the elimination of racial inequality and segregation. It has gathered its strength in large part from the fact that it remained highly centralised from the very beginning, maintaining strict control over its numerous local branches. Supported by white liberals and the bulk of black intellectuals, it has managed to play a significant role in the gradual emancipation of American Blacks during the twentieth century. Its vigilance and determination have brought an end to such cruel practices as lynching, especially in the southern states, and have secured the appointment of African-Americans to a number of federal boards and committees. The role of the NAACP in persuading the federal government to pass a series of progressive Civil Rights bills during the 1950s and 1960s was crucial. The NAACP has also encouraged black excellence by awarding annually its prestigious Spingarn Medal to outstanding African-American citizens.

NDADAYE, Melchior

Melchior Ndadaye became the first Hutu president of Burundi in June 1993 after that country's first free elections in twenty-six years. His triumph marked the temporary end of centuries of Tutsi domination over the Hutu. Born in Muramvya on 28 March 1953, he had spent many years as a refugee in neighbouring Rwanda after the massacre of some 200,000 Hutu in 1972. Ndadaye studied at the teacher training college in Butare, Rwanda, and served as a teacher and part-time university lecturer there. He returned to Burundi in 1984, studied banking, and became a training manager with the Savings and Credit Co-operative before being appointed adviser to the Rural Development Ministry. From 1989 to 1993 he worked at the Meridien BIAO bank. When elected president, Ndadaye appointed a Tutsi woman to be prime minister, established a broadly based government, and pledged to work for national reconciliation and an extension of individual liberties. But such a promising beginning was sadly erased when he was killed in a bloody coup on 21 October 1993.

NDEBELE, Nimrod

Born on 12 October 1913 in Natal Province, South Africa, Nimrod Njabulo Ndebele was the first Zulu playwright. In addition to local primary schools, he attended St Peter's High School in Johannesburg and Adams' College before earning his BA in 1948 from the University of Witwatersrand by correspondence. From 1945 to 1953, he taught at Madibane High School in Johannesburg and then served as principal of Charterston High School (1953-57) before being appointed inspector of schools for the Middelburg Circuit. His *Ugubdudele namazimuzimu* was the first drama written and published in Zulu (1941). Composed in the 1930s, it had won the Esther May Bedford Prize for drama in 1937. It was republished as Volume VI of the Bantu Treasury Series in 1959. Nimrod Ndebele died in 2000.

N'DOUR, Youssou

The innovative Senegalese musician, Youssou N'Dour, was born in Dakar, French West Africa, on 1 October 1959. In 1979 he formed a group with which he recorded three albums and one hit single, *Xalis*. They then relocated to Paris, France, in 1984 under the name of Le Super Étoile de Dakar now consisting of fourteen members including guitarists, saxophonists, and percussionists. N'Dour's music was a quaint blend of traditional Senegalese and European sounds: a combination of salsa, soul and disco, highlighted by his own trademark wailing tenor. This distinctive feature attracted the attention of the American singer, Paul Simon, who invited N'Dour to participate in his *Graceland* album of 1986. N'Dour also took part in Amnesty International's 'Human Rights Now!' world tour of 1988. His style of mbalax became so widely popular in the late 1980s that he is often credited with inventing 'Afro-pop' as it is called in the West. His albums include *Nelson Mandela* (1986), *Immigrés* (1988), *The Lion* (1989), *With Eyes Open* (1992), *Djamil* (1996), *Joko: The Link* (2000), *Le Grand Bal à Bercy* (2001), *Nothing in Vain* (2002), and *Kirikou* (2004). In addition to his French and English songs, N'Dour has also recorded albums in his native Wolof dialect. He is not only a powerful cultural icon in Senegal, his fame has spread worldwide. He wrote and performed the anthem for the 1998 Football World Cup; and won an American Grammy Award, for his CD *Egypt*, in 2005. Youssou has recently opened his own recording studio, Xippi, and his own record label, Jololi.

NETO, Agostinho

The son of an Angolan Methodist pastor, Dr Antonio Agostinho Neto was born near Luanda on 17 September 1922. A brilliant student at the Correia High School in Luanda, he won a scholarship to study medicine in Portugal. There he showed much talent as a Portuguese poet, although his verses displeased the authorities as they were bitterly critical of the Portuguese colonial system. He returned to Angola as a doctor in 1959 and was arrested in June 1960 for his unrelenting opposition to the government. When his patients protested his arrest, the police opened fire and killed some thirty of them. Neto spent the next two years in detention in Cape Verde and in Portugal, but managed to write some more satirical verses and to escape to Morocco where he joined the Movimento Popular de Libertaçio de Angola (MPLA). Although a committed Marxist, he sought support from both the east and the west when he was elected president of the MPLA. When Angola achieved its political independence on 11 November 1975, Dr Neto was proclaimed its first president. In 1976, he signed a Soviet-Angolan treaty of friendship and co-operation, but refused to allow the Soviets to dominate the affairs of the MPLA. In 1977, he also cemented Angola's cordial relations with Cuba by visiting Havana. He died on 10 September 1979. Neto's legacy included some fine verses in *Colectânea de poemas*, published in 1961.

NETTLEFORD, Rex

Professor Rex Milton Nettleford, who was appointed chancellor of the University of the West Indies in 1998, is a distinguished Jamaican citizen who has excelled as a choreographer, dancer, essayist, editor and educator. Born in 1933, he was educated at Cornwall College, the University College of the West Indies (Jamaica) and Oxford University (England). He has published numerous articles in a wide range of scholarly journals, dealing mainly with Jamaican ethnicity and culture. His major works include *Mirror Mirror Identity: Race and Protest in Jamaica* (1970) and *Caribbean Cultural Identity: The Case of Jamaica* (1978). Nettleford, however, is much better remembered as the individual who organized the Jamaica Dance Company which has left a significant imprint on the cultural life of the Caribbean. He has succeeded wonderfully well in linking African culture and Jamaican folklore in his dancing, choreography and design. A political scientist as well as an artist, his introductions to the speeches of Norman Manley (which he edited in 1971) and to *Jamaica In Independence: Essays on the Early Years* (which he edited in 1989) are invaluable sources for students wishing to understand the roots of the Jamaican cultural heritage.

NGALIEMA

A former Tio slave, born around 1850, Ngaliema rose to become the richest and most powerful merchant at Malebo Pool in the late nineteenth century. Acting first as a middleman between the Bobangi traders and the caravan leaders from the lower Zaire River region, he became rich as a dealer in ivory and was able to purchase slaves and caravans of his own. Ngaliema became the local chieftain and made himself total master of Kintambo. Arming his soldiers with rifles, he succeeded in dominating his neighbours. He also hoped to profit from an alliance with the Europeans when the latter began their infamous scramble for Africa. But European competition ultimately reduced Ngaliema's authority and he lived to regret his decision to allow the white men to settle on his territory. His commercial and political empire disintegrated during the 1890s and he himself died around 1900. But his memory has been kept alive by the modern government of Zaire which created a monument of him and renamed 'Mount Stanley' Mount Ngaliema in honour of a great merchant and a shrewd administrator.

NGAN KABI

This powerful queen mother of the Bantote clan played an important role in the revival of Nunu fortunes in the lower Kasai River region during the second half of the nineteenth century. As the mother of Bokoko, the reigning chief of the Bantote, Ngan Kabi exerted enormous influence over political and economic affairs. She herself actively participated in the great

Zaire River trade and was able to purchase guns and slaves. She remained on good terms with neighbouring chiefs as well as the European missionaries. Eventually the Europeans greatly undermined her authority, but she is still fondly remembered by Zairean nationalists as an enlightened ruler whose reign witnessed considerable Nunu economic prosperity. Ngan Kabi died in 1892.

NGUEMA, Francisco

Francisco Macías Nguema was the first post-colonial leader of Equatorial Guinea from 1968 until his overthrow eleven years later. Born on 1 January 1924, he rose to the position of mayor of Mongomo under the Spanish colonial government and was later elected to the territorial parliament. After his election as president in 1968, he subjected the country to the worst forms of autocratic government. It is claimed that about one third of Equatorial Guinea's population fled to neighbouring countries to escape his tyranny. He declared himself president for life in 1972 but was overthrown by his nephew, Teodoro Obiang Nguema Mbasogo, in a military coup. He was convicted of genocide and executed on 3 August 1979.

NGUGI, James

Born in Limuru, Kenya, on 5 January 1938, James Thiong'o Ngugi is generally considered the major Anglophone native writer from East Africa. He was educated at Makerere University in Uganda and the University of Leeds in England. For some years he edited *Penpoint*, a student journal that gave great encouragement to young East African authors and he also served as the first editor of *Zuka: A Journal of East African Creative Writing*, an important English language review, published in Dar es Salaam in Tanzania. Ngugi went to the US in 1970 as a lecturer in African Literature at Northwestern University in Illinois. His fine novels include *Weep Not, Child* (1964), *The River Between* (1965), *A Grain of Wheat* (1967), and *Petals of Blood* (1977). *Weep Not, Child*, the first novel in English by an East African, won prizes at the Festival of Negro Arts in Dakar (Senegal) and the East African Literature Bureau. Ngugi has also written such superb plays as *The Black Hermit* (1968) and *This Time Tomorrow*, as well as a number of short stories. The turning-point of his life came with the publication in 1977 of *I Will Marry You When I Want*, a play in which there were criticisms of the government. He was promptly imprisoned for one year without trial and dismissed permanently from his post as a professor at the University of Nairobi. Further harassment of himself and his family after his release forced him into voluntary exile from Kenya in 1982, swearing never to return so long as arap Moi remained in office. His later writings include

Decolonising the Mind: The Politics of Language in African Literature (1986), *Moving the Centre: The Struggle for Cultural Freedom* (1993), *Penpoints, Gunpoints and Dreams: The Performance of Literature and Power in Post-Colonial Africa* (1996) and *Wizard of the Crow* (2006).

NICOL, Abioseh

One of the greatest minds thus far produced by western Africa, Davidson Sylvester Hector Willoughby 'Abioseh' Nicol was a distinguished Sierra Leonean diplomat, scholar, physician and medical researcher. Born in Freetown, Sierra Leone, on 14 September 1924, he earned several degrees from London and Cambridge Universities in England. By the time he was thirty years old, he had achieved doctorates in both medicine and biochemistry. He conducted research on the chemical structure of insulin in the human body and wrote seminal papers on the subject. In 1957 he was made a fellow of Christ's College, Cambridge, the first black African to achieve this distinction. Dr Nicol returned to Sierra Leone in 1958 as a senior pathologist, but was soon appointed principal of the Fourah Bay College in Freetown. His diplomatic career began in 1969 with his appointment as Sierra Leone's ambassador to the United Nations. In 1970 he became president of the UN Security Council and served from 1972 to 1982 as executive director of the United Nations Institute for Training and Research. From 1983 to 1987 he was president of the World Federation of UN Associations. Among his most important works, apart from his numerous scholarly articles, were *Two African Tales* (1965), and *The Truly Married Woman, and Other Stories* (1965). He also edited *Paths to Peace: The UN Security Council and Its Presidency* (1981) and co-edited *Creative Women in Changing Societies: A Quest for Alternatives* (1982). In 1952 he won the Margaret Wrong Prize and Medal for Literature in Africa. Dr Nicol died on 20 September 1994.

NKABINDE, Simon

An accomplished Zulu singer, Simon Nkabinde, better known as 'Mahlatini', was born in Newcastle, Natal, in 1938. As the lead vocalist for the Zulu music group, 'Mahlatini and the Mahotella Queens', he became a popular proponent of the deep-voiced 'groaning' style of black South African singing. His band produced a number of very popular recordings, including such CDs as *Thozokile* (1988), *The Lion Roars* (1991), *King of the Groaners* (1993), *Isomiso* (1994), *Stoki Stoki* (1996), and *Best of Mahlatini and the Mahotella Queens* (1998). Often called the 'Lion of Soweto', he frequently performed dressed in the traditional regalia of Zulu chieftains. Nkabinde died on 27 July 1999 in Johannesburg.

NKANGA LUKENI

Sometimes known as Garcia II, this great Mani Kongo chief, who ruled from 1641 to 1661, was able to exploit the rivalry between the Dutch and the Portuguese to restore some of the former authority of the Kongo Kingdom. Although remaining Catholic, Nkanga allied with the Dutch to combat the influence of the Portuguese missionaries. He also appealed to the Vatican to help stabilize his dynasty. His efforts ultimately failed as Portuguese influence increased in the Kongo after his death, but he did manage for a time to free himself and his people from Portuguese tutelage and control.

NKEITA, Kwabena

Professor John Hanson Kwabena Nkeita is an outstanding Assante-Twi scholar, novelist, playwright, composer and musicologist. Publishing numerous seminal books in both English and Twi, he has already left a huge impact on West African music and literature. After attending local primary schools in Mampong, Gold Coast, where he was born on 22 June 1921, he studied at the Akropong Teachers' Training College and, in 1944, was invited to teach the Twi language at the School of Oriental and African Studies in London, England. Nkeita returned to Ghana in 1949 to join the staff at the Akropong Teachers' Training College before going to the University of Ghana at Legon, where he shortly became director of the School of Music and Drama at the Institute of African Studies. He has done extensive research on West African music and has built up an excellent collection of tapes at the University of Ghana at Legon. Some of his important contributions to musicology have appeared in *African Music in Ghana* (1955), *Drumming in the Akan Communities of Ghana* (1955), *Funeral Dirges of the Akan People* (1955), and *Folk Songs of Ghana* (1963). These works are generally regarded as among the best authentic collections of oral traditions produced by African scholars. Nkeita has also written a successful novel, *Kwabena Amoa* (1953); some fine poetry in *Anwonsem 1944-1949* (1952) and *Akwansosem bi* (1967); and a much acclaimed play, *Ananwoma* (1951), which went through six editions within the space of twelve years. As a world-renowned composer, he has written extensively for both western orchestral and traditional African instruments. He serves on the advisory panels of numerous organizations and has lectured in several universities in Africa, Asia, Europe and North America. He is currently Emeritus Professor and Director of the International Centre for African Music and Dance and is a member of the International Council of Music and of the International Commission for a Scientific and Cultural History of Humanity.

NKOMO, Joshua

Joshua Mqabuko Nyongolo Nkomo was one of the leading African nationalists who spearheaded the Zimbabwe independence movement during the period 1957-79. Born on 19 June 1917, the son of a cattle rancher in Matabeleland, he was educated at the best black colleges in South Africa and obtained a BA degree. After serving for some years as a social welfare officer, he helped to organize the first African railway workers' union and in 1957 became president of the African National Congress (ANC). When that organization was banned, Nkomo took over the leadership of the Zimbabwe African People's Union (ZAPU). Having denounced the all-white Rhodesian Front in 1965, he was imprisoned until 1974. He again took over the leadership of ZAPU when he was released and played a key role in the dismantling of the racist system in Rhodesia. When Robert Mugabe's party, the Zimbabwe African National Union (ZANU), won the general elections in 1980, Nkomo was offered a place in the cabinet and served as minister of home affairs but friction between himself and the prime minister led to his demotion in the very next year and his exclusion from the cabinet altogether in 1982. ZAPU then became Zimbabwe's chief opposition party. Nkomo remained its leader and was for many years the most outspoken critic of Mugabe's régime, even though ZANU and ZAPU agreed to unite just before the general elections of 1989. Partly to muzzle him, Mugabe made Nkomo vice president in 1990, a post with influence but with limited power. Nkomo died on 1 July 1999 in Harare.

NKOSI, Lewis

This noted editor, critic, playwright and short-story writer was born in 1936 in Natal, South Africa, and educated in local Zulu schools before studying for one year at the M.L. Sultan Technical College in Durban. He joined the staff of *Ilanga lase Natal* in 1955 and wrote articles for the *Drum* while working also for the *Golden City Post*, a Sunday newspaper in Johannesburg. When he accepted a Nieman Fellowship to study journalism at Harvard University in the United States during 1961-62, the South African government barred Nkosi from returning home. He sought refuge in London, England, and became editor of *The New African*. Trying to support himself on the strength of his writing, he began to publish articles in several journals. His *Home and Exile*, a collection of essays published in 1965, won an award at the first World Festival of Negro Arts in Dakar, Senegal, in 1966. He also published *The Transplanted Heart* (1975) and *Mask and Tasks: Themes and Styles of African Literature* (1981). Apart from numerous essays and short stories, Nkosi also produced a very good play, *The Rhythm of Violence*, published in 1964; and two novels, *Mating Birds* (1986) and *Underground People* (1993). He was for many years a free-lance journalist in London and once served as host-moderator for a National Educational Television (New York City) series on modern African writers. During most of the 1990s, Nkosi was professor of English at the University of Wyoming in the United States.

NKRUMAH, Kwame

Born on 21 September 1909, Francis Nwia Kofie Kwame Nkrumah was the charismatic nationalist who led the Gold Coast to its political independence in 1957 and changed its name to Ghana. An able political organizer, who did most to expel the British from West Africa after World War II, he left a chequered legacy. Some see him as the great Ghanaian liberator who did most to modernize Ghana and to promote the Pan-African ideal. Others regard him as an arrogant dictator who sowed the seeds of future political chaos in Ghana by undermining the very democratic institutions he had done so much to create. Kwame Nkrumah was educated at the Government Training College in Accra and at Achimota College where he was much influenced by Dr James Aggrey. He received his Teacher's Certificate in 1930 and taught briefly at several local schools before leaving for the United States to pursue further studies at Lincoln University and the University of Pennsylvania. He achieved his BA in 1939, a degree of Bachelor of Theology in 1942 and an MA in 1943. During the early 1940s he served as a part-time lecturer at Lincoln University and helped to form the African Students' Association of America and Canada as well as the African Studies Association. Nkrumah left the United States to study law in London, England, where he came under the influence of George Padmore, the famous Trinidadian political activist, who sparked his interest in African decolonization. This resulted in the publication of *Towards Colonial Freedom*. Returning to the Gold Coast in 1947, Nkrumah launched himself into the independence struggle and became general secretary of the recently founded United Gold Coast Convention (UGCC). But he was too impatient with the moderates among the African intelligentsia and soon founded his own party after the Accra Riots of 1948. His People's Convention Party (CPP), with its aggressive brand of populism, appealed at once to the African grassroots and performed surprisingly well in the general elections of 1951. Rejecting the moderate recommendations of the Coussey Commission, Nkrumah demanded complete and immediate self-government for the Gold Coast. He became the first premier of the Gold Coast and forced the British to grant his country full independence in 1957. By 1960 he had created a new republic with himself as president. He tackled many problems in a forthright manner. New elementary and secondary schools were promptly built and university education considerably expanded; new roads were constructed and a new port was opened at Tema, just east of Accra; the Adomi bridge was opened in 1956;

a national shipping line, the Black Star Line, was established in 1958; a new airline, Ghana Airways, was established also; and the great Volta Dam, providing electricity for all of Ghana's needs, was constructed and formally opened in 1966. In 1962, he was awarded the Lenin Peace Prize as a leader 'in the struggle against colonialism'. But the problems facing Nkrumah proved almost insoluble. Despite his efforts to improve Ghana's industry and agriculture, they languished in large part because of bad planning, corruption, and ill fortune. Cocoa prices fell too sharply at a time when that crop remained the nation's most important export. Money could not therefore be raised to complete the projects that were so vital. To make matters worse, Nkrumah was unable to deal fairly with constructive criticism. He punished severely all of those who disagreed with him. His dictatorial manner led to the departure from the CPP of some of the best brains in Ghana and at least two prominent Ghanaian nationalists who had supported Nkrumah staunchly during the 1950s, died in prison in the decade that followed. His popularity inevitably declined and the final result was his own overthrow in 1966. He had done a great deal to inspire other Africans in their quest for self-determination but had tarnished his own image by his autocratic attitude in Ghana. He left his country in a state of disorder from which it has not yet recovered, but yet his name is still legendary throughout Africa and beyond. He also left posterity with a number of important books, including *Ghana: The Autobiography of Kwame Nkrumah* (1957), *I Speak of Freedom* (1961), *Africa in the Struggle Against World Imperialism* (1962), *Africa Must Unite* (1963), *Consciencism: Philosophy and Ideology for Decolonization with Particular Reference to the African Revolution* (1964), *Neo-Colonialism: The Last Stage of Imperialism* (1965), *Challenge of the Congo* (1967), *Handbook of Revolutionary Warfare: A Guide to the Armed Phase of the African Struggle* (1968). Nkrumah died in exile in Conakry, Guinea, on 27 April 1972. His latest works were largely intended to answer his various critics and to defend the policies he had pursued in Ghana. Such was his reputation beyond the boundaries of his native country that, in 1966, he was actually invited by Sékou Touré, without any sign of protest, to rule as co-president of Guinea, where he was warmly welcomed after his overthrow.

NTSIKANA

A legendary figure in the modern history of southern Africa, Ntsikana was born in Transkei in the early 1780s. He experienced a number of visions after his conversion to Christianity and concluded that it was his divine mission to found his own Baptist church at Makanzara. There he composed his own sacred songs and hymns for his followers and preached an ethical religion stressing the relationships between man and man and striving to produce an effective synthesis of European and African ideas. He had remarkable success as a faith healer and attracted a sizeable congregation of Xhosa people, in whose language he sang and preached. His hymns were not immediately recorded but were memorized by his followers. Although his missionary work was cut short by his early death (in 1820), Ntsikana left a lasting impression on a wide range of South African Blacks. A collection of Xhosa hymns, presumably composed by him, was eventually published around 1840, and a fine biography, *Ibali lika Ntsikana*, written in Xhosa by John K. Bokwe, was published in 1904. These along with numerous other memoirs, articles and books have nourished the legend of Ntsikana right up to the present day.

NUJOMA, Sam

After spending twenty nine years in exile, Samuel Daniel Shafiishuna Nujoma returned in triumph to Namibia in September 1989 and led his South West Africa People's Organization (SWAPO) to victory in the UN-supervised elections. He thus became Namibia's first president when South Africa relinquished control over the territory in 1990. Born to a poor peasant family in Ovamboland, on 12 May 1929, Sam Nujoma spent his early years tending his parents' few cattle and goats. Leaving school at an early age, he worked for some time as a railway dining car steward. When one of his colleagues was sent home without compensation after a serious accident, he decided to form a union for railwaymen but was promptly sacked. He became the first president of SWAPO when it was founded in 1960 and retained that title even after he was banished by the South African government. A pragmatist, Nujoma pledged in 1990 to work for national reconciliation. He initiated a land reform plan which called for redistribution from Whites to Blacks on a gradual and long-term basis. He was re-elected president in 1994 and 1999. He was barred from another term by the constitution but remained the party leader of SWAPO after stepping down as president in 2005.

NXUMALO, James

A distinguished Zulu educator, novelist and scholar, James Alfred Walter Nxumalo was born in Natal Province, South Africa, on 16 January 1908. He attended St Chad's College and Adams' College, where he achieved a Teacher's Certificate, and became principal of the Ethaleni Training College. After completing his BA from the University of South Africa, he became supervisor of schools for the Dundee Circuit in 1950. In 1955 he was appointed inspector of Bantu education for all of Natal. An eminent Zulu scholar, Nxumalo produced an important Zulu grammar, *Umtapo wolwazi lwesiZulu*, in 1951. Then came *Isangoma somcwebo wolimi lwesiZulu* (1951), *Igugu likaZulu* (1953), and *Umthombo wegugu likaZulu* (1953). He also wrote a novel, *UZwelonke*, in 1950. Nxumalo did much to encourage the use of Zulu in Bantu schools and to formalize it as a modern African language. Like other modern African educators, he remained convinced that Africans would learn much faster if taught in their native tongues rather than in the language of former European imperialists.

NYANDORO, George

George Bodzo Nyandoro was one of the African nationalist leaders who contributed significantly to the overthrow of the white minority régime in Rhodesia. Born on 8 July 1926, in the Marandellas district of Southern Rhodesia, he was a member of the Shona ethnic group and the grandson of the leader of the unsuccessful revolt against the British in 1896-97. After training as a bookkeeper, he became involved in the trade union and independence movements and was secretary-general of the British African National Voice Association. In the 1950s he helped to found the African National Youth League and began to tour the rural areas inciting resistance to the restrictive land laws. In 1959 he was arrested and detained without trial for four years. In 1964 Nyandoro moved to Zambia to give support to the outlawed Zimbabwe African People's Union (ZAPU), but he seceded from this party to form his own Front for the Liberation of Zimbabwe in 1971. In 1979, however, he returned home to take a ministerial post in Bishop Abel Muzorewa's transitional government. When Robert Mugabe, the new prime minister, refused to offer him a place in the cabinet of 1980, Nyandoro left the political arena altogether and became a successful businessman. He died on 24 June 1994.

NYERERE, Julius

The son of Burito Nyerere, a Zanaki chief in the Northern Province of Tanganyika, Julius Kambarage Nyerere was born on 13 April 1922. He became a Roman Catholic and studied at the Makerere College in Uganda and the University of Edinburgh in Scotland, where he became (in 1949) the first Tanganyikan student to earn a British degree. He taught for some years at St Mary's Mission School in Tabora, before becoming seriously involved in local politics. In 1954 he was elected president of the Tanganyika African National Union (TANU) which shortly dominated the elections just before Tanganyika achieved its political independence. Nyerere therefore became the first prime minister of an independent Tanganyika in 1961 and was elected Tanganyika's first president in 1962. He signed the Act of Union with Zanzibar in 1964 and became also the first president of Tanzania. Committed to the principles of African independence and majority rule, he remained a staunch critic of the racist and colonial systems in Angola, Mozambique, Rhodesia and South Africa.

He also supported the right of the Ibo people to establish their own Biafran republic if they so wished and he denounced the autocratic methods of Idi Amin in Uganda. The latter responded by accusing Nyerere of harbouring Ugandan enemies and invaded part of Tanzania in 1978. Despite these and other difficulties, Nyerere remained at the Tanzanian helm until his voluntary retirement on 5 November 1985 and continued to play a prominent role in his country's politics for several years afterwards. It is not often remembered that he was also a Swahili scholar of no mean distinction. He translated William Shakespeare's *Julius Caesar* (1963) and *Merchant of Venice* (1969) into Swahili and himself wrote *Uhuru na Ujama* which was translated into English and published as *Freedom and Socialism* in 1968. Nyerere also published *Democracy and the Party System* in 1965. His writings, which appear in both English and Swahili, are mostly collected essays based on his experiences in African politics. He died on 14 October 1999.

NZEKWU, Onuora

Born on 19 February 1928 in Kafanchan, Nigeria, Onuora Nzekwu was one of the finest west African authors. He produced three excellent novels in the 1960s which clearly illustrated the frustrations and dilemmas facing young Africans trying to merge modern European and urban concepts with traditional native and rural values. His *Wand of Noble Wood* (1961) stressed the futility of western pragmatic approaches to the problems created by traditional African religious beliefs. In *Blade Among the Boys* (1962) traditional notions ultimately prevailed again over half-absorbed European and Christian values. A similar message was delivered in his *Highlife for Lizards* (1965). Nzekwu also wrote (with Michael Crowder) a popular children's book, entitled *Eze Goes to School*, published in 1963. A sequel of this work, *Eze Goes to College*, was published in 1988. Foundation grants enabled Nzekwu to travel and lecture in many parts of Europe and North America. As one of the first generation of African writers in English, he helped pioneer a new vision of African literature.

NZINGHA

One of the most remarkable of all African women, Queen Nzingha was the great ruler of the kingdom of Ndongo in southwestern Africa during the period 1613-63. To escape from the relentless Portuguese advance into southwestern Africa during the second decade of the seventeenth century, Nzingha moved eastward with her followers, conquered the state of Matamba and developed it into a powerful slave-trading centre. She is best remembered for her determination to thwart the Portuguese by seeking the help even of the Protestant Dutch and inspiring her people by personally leading her soldiers into battle. Nzingha managed to preserve the independence of Ndongo throughout her long reign, but no sooner was she dead in 1663 than the Portuguese prevailed. She left an enormous impact on what is now Angola by converting to Catholicism and introducing European values to that part of the African continent. One of her last acts was to request the Pope to send missionaries to convert and to educate her subjects. Her determination to maintain the political independence of her people while imitating certain elements of European culture presented her, like most of the progressive African nationalists then and since, with an interesting dilemma.

NZO, Alfred

A South African nationalist and statesman, Alfred Baphethuxolo Nzo was born in Benoni on 19 June 1925. He served as secretary-general of the African National Congress (ANC) during 1969-91 and as South Africa's first black foreign minister in the post-apartheid era. Like most of his contemporaries, he was arrested in 1963 for his resistance to the apartheid régime and was exiled in 1964. Nzo represented the ANC in Egypt and India before establishing that organization's headquarters in Tanzania during his tenure as secretary-general. He returned to South Africa in 1990 when the ban on the ANC was lifted and served in President Mandela's cabinet during 1994-99. Alfred Nzo died in Johannesburg, South Africa, on 13 January 2000.

OBASANJO, Olusegun

A Nigerian military and political leader, Olusegun Obasanjo was born in Abeokuta, just north of Lagos, on 5 March 1937. Raised as a Christian, he attended Baptist Boys' High School and later worked for a year as a teacher before joining the national army in 1958. Rising quickly through the ranks, he played a major role in the defeat of the Biafran troops during the civil war of 1967-70. At one stage, during Nigeria's protracted time of troubles, General Obasanjo served as interim president and became (in 1979) the first Nigerian military leader to cede power to civilian rule. During the 1980s and early 1990s he retired from the army and worked as a diplomat, holding various positions through the UN and other organizations. He returned to Nigeria to lead the People's Democratic Party which won the general elections by a huge margin in 1999. He was thereupon declared president and vowed to establish a democratic, transparent and corruption-free Nigeria. He promptly ensured the passage of anti-corruption laws with severe penalties for proven embezzlement and dismissed many of the old military leaders with political connections. In 2000, for instance, he established a permanent watchdog group, the Independent Corrupt Practices and Other Related Offences Commission while a Human Rights Violation Investigation Commission continued to look into alleged abuses committed by former military governments. Obasanjo was re-elected in 2003 when democratic elections were held as he had promised, but Nigeria continues to be disturbed by ethnic and other conflicts during his tenure.

OBESO, Candelario

Born in 1849, Candelario Obeso was a famous novelist and educator who wrote language texts and grammars for English, French and Italian which were adopted for use in schools in his native Columbia. He also authored arithmetic texts as well as a three-act play, entitled *Secundino el zapatero*. In addition, he published several translations from Longfellow, Hugo and Musset. He is best remembered, perhaps, for three works in particular: *Lecturas para tí*, a collection of verse and prose; *Cantos populares de mi tierra*, a novel depicting Negro life and language in Columbia; and *Lucha de la vida*, a long and partly autobiographical poem. It is difficult to believe that Obeso was only thirty-five years old when he died on 1884. In his short life, he had not only been a prolific writer but one of the few Blacks to have served in Columbia's military and diplomatic service.

OBETSEBI-LAMPTEY, Emmanuel

Emmanuel Odarkwei Obetsebi-Lamptey was one of the so-called 'Big Six' jailed by the British government in 1948 after the Accra Riots that triggered off a chain of events leading ultimately to Ghana's independence. A fearless and outspoken critic of the colonial administration, Obetsebi-Lamptey also became vigorously opposed to Nkrumah's autocratic system. The son of an Accra businessman, he was born on 26 April 1902 and sent to the Wesleyan School and the Kumasi Government School in Accra before proceeding to study law in the United Kingdom. After receiving his LLB from the University of London in 1939, he returned to take part in Gold Coast politics and made a name for himself by his virulent attacks on the imperial authorities. He was returned unopposed to the Gold Coast Legislative Council as a member for the Accra municipal area and became one of the founders of the United Gold Coast Convention (UGCC) in 1947. Despite his well-known radicalism, Obetsebi-Lamptey was appointed to the Coussey Committee in 1949. Thereafter his main criticisms were reserved for Kwame Nkrumah who responded by having him sent to jail, where he spent his last years before dying on 29 January 1963. He was constantly suspected by Nkrumah, even while in prison, of masterminding plots to oust the president of the new republic.

OBOTE, Milton

Apollo Milton Obote, who became president of Uganda in 1966, was born of peasant parents in the district of Lango on 28 December 1925. After a brief stay at Makerere College, from which he was expelled for his political activities, he spent many years in voluntary exile and did not return to Uganda until 1957. By 1958 he had become a member of the Legislative Council and one year later had established himself as the leader of the Uganda People's Congress (UPC). Allying with the more conservative Buganda party, he was able to make himself prime minister of Uganda in 1962 and to lead his country to political independence in 1963. Obote was a staunch Pan-Africanist and a pragmatist in politics, but he soon discovered that Uganda, with its various ethnic divisions and traditions, was a very difficult country to govern. A conflict between himself and the kabaka of Buganda severely weakened his position and permitted his government to be toppled by a military coup, led by Idi Amin, in 1971. Obote spent eight years in exile in Tanzania where he reorganized the UPC and developed a sizeable military force. With the help of the Tanzanian government, he succeeded in overthrowing Amin, restoring civilian rule, and calling a general election which the UPC easily won. He thus became, in December 1980, the first African leader to regain his presidency through an electoral process after having been deposed by a military coup. Obote, however, suffered the indignity of being overthrown a second time by another military coup on 27 July 1985. His second stint was marred by a deadly guerilla war and charges of human rights violations. While still in exile, he died on 10 October 2005 in Johannesburg, South Africa.

OCANSEY, Alfred John

Born in 1879, Alfred John Ocansey was a successful Gold Coast businessman who established a huge commercial enterprise with branches at Accra, Akuse, Dodowa and elsewhere. His Ocansey Stores dealt in all kinds of merchandise, including even cars and tyres. He introduced the cinema into the Gold Coast and operated a chain of theatres. He also became a prominent Accra cocoa merchant who strove to organize the cocoa industry in such a way that Africans would market their own produce and control their own trade. He became an executive member of the working committee of the Gold Coast Economic Conference of 1930. It was largely due to his efforts that the Gold Coast and Asante Cocoa Federation was formed in 1930. Ocansey also published the *Gold Coast Spectator* and was proprietor of the *African Morning Post*. These newspapers became notorious for their vicious attacks on colonial government and on the European race generally. Altogether, Alfred John Ocansey, who died in 1943, was a man of many interests and talents who exercised a significant influence on West African national life during the first half of the twentieth century.

OCLOO, Esther

Esther Afua Ocloo was an innovative Ghanian entrepreneur who pioneered the practice of microlending, providing tiny loans to small home-based businesses, usually those run by women in developing countries. Born in Peki-Dzake, Gold Coast, on 18 April 1919, she began as a street vendor of homemade orange marmalade and gradually expanded her business to form Nkulenu Industries. She studied in Accra and later went to the United Kingdom to study agriculture, food technology and useful handicrafts. In 1979 she became the co-founder and head of Women's World Banking. In 1990 she shared with Olusegun Obasanjo of Nigeria the prestigious Africa Prize worth $100,000. Esther Ocloo died in Accra, Ghana, on 8 February 2002.

ODHIAMBO, Thomas

Thomas Risley Odhiambo, one of Africa's greatest scientists, was famous for his research into non-chemical methods of agricultural insect control and was a pioneer in the promotion of indigenous African scientific education and research. Born in Nyanza Province, Kenya, on 4 February 1931, he was educated at Makerere University College (Uganda) and Queen's College, Cambridge. He was the founding director general (1970-94) of the multi-disciplinary International Centre of Insect Physiology and Ecology, based in Nairobi. He became the first dean of the University of Nairobi's department of agriculture and was the founding president of the African Academy of Sciences. Among his numerous awards and distinctions was the African Prize for Leadership for the Sustainable End of Hunger in 1987. Thomas Odhiambo died on 26 May 2003.

ODINGA, Oginga

Oginga Odinga was one of the Kenyan nationalists who led the independence movement against Britain during the 1950s when he was a firm supporter of Jomo Kenyatta and the Mau Mau organization. But, after serving as the vice-president of Kenya in the early 1960s, he broke away from the administration and became the controversial leader of the opposition party, the Kenya People's Union (KPU). He denounced Kenyatta's pro-western policies and sought support from the Communist bloc, describing himself as an African socialist. Part of the problem sprang from the fact that while Kenyatta's party generally supported Kikuyu interests, Odinga felt that his Luo compatriots were disadvantaged. Born in central Nyanza in 1912, Odinga was educated at a local mission school and at Makerere University College. Following his graduation he served as a teacher and a headmaster until the late 1940s. Always keen on politics and on African civil rights, he became a member of Kenya's Legislative Council in 1957 and made a mark as a fiery debater. His support of Kenyatta's government waned, however, after a demotion in the party hierarchy early in 1966. In 1969 the KPU was banned and Odinga was placed in detention.

When he tried to rejoin KANU, his efforts to campaign for presidential election were effectively blocked by Kenyatta and he was expelled from the party altogether in 1982. In 1991 he founded another opposition party, the Forum for the Restoration of Democracy, and placed third in Kenya's first multiparty presidential election in 1992. Odinga died on 20 June 1994. His autobiography, *Not Yet Uhuru*, was published in 1967.

OFFIAH, Martin

Martin Offiah, who was born in London on 29 December 1966, became one of the greatest rugby league players in the United Kingdom. In a career that lasted fourteen years, he accumulated an astounding 501 tries for teams in England and Australia. He scored 26 tries in 33 matches for Great Britain and five in eight for England. He was awarded an MBE in 1997.

OFORI ATTA I

Born on 11 October 1881, Nana Ofori Atta I became one of the most influential chiefs of the Gold Coast. Educated at Basel Mission schools and the Basel Mission Theological Seminary at Akuporon, he had originally intended to become a priest. His reign began in November 1912 and he was nominated a member of the Gold Coast Legislative Council in 1916. An excellent debater and orator, he was one of the most eloquent champions of the cause of the traditional West African chiefs. He helped the British carry out their policy of indirect rule largely because he feared that the emerging African nationalists, with their agitation for civil rights and democratic institutions, might pose a greater danger to traditional authority. He was therefore violently opposed to such movements as the Aborigines' Rights Protection Society (ARPS). He was rewarded with a knighthood in 1927. But he reconciled his differences with the nationalists during the 1930s and began to give support to some of their progressive recommendations. He supported the Gold Coast Youth Movement, the Cocoa boycott of 1937-38, and the movement for a more democratic constitution. Nana Ofori Atta I also founded the Abuakwa State College as the first secondary school in his state. He died on 20 August 1943 at Kyebi, his capital.

OGOT, Grace

Born on 15 May 1930 in the Central Nyanza District, Kenya, Grace Akinde Ogot is one of the most successful and certainly one of the most versatile of all East African women. She has already left her mark on public health, journalism, business, literature, politics and diplomacy. She received her early education in Butere High School and Ng'uja Girls' School in Kenya before going to England to train as a nurse. Following her graduation she worked as a script writer and announcer for the British Broadcasting Corporation (BBC)'s

East African Service in London during 1955-58. She then returned to Kenya to serve, in turn, as a headmistress of a secondary school and as Community Development Officer in Kisumu. She later became nursing sister and midwifery tutor at Maseno Hospital in Nyanza before working as a public relations officer for Air India in Nairobi. In 1984 she became one of only a handful of African women to serve as a member of a national parliament and was the only female member of Daniel arap Moi's cabinet. Since then she has represented Kenya as an ambassador to the United Nations and UNESCO. Grace Ogot is also regarded as one of Africa's most accomplished writers. She published a very successful novel, *The Promised Land*, in 1960, and a fine collection of short stories, *Land Without Thunder: Short Stories*, in 1965.Her other publications include *The Strange Bride*, *The Graduate*, *The Other Woman*, *The Island of Tears* and *Miaha*. Examples of her work have also appeared in *Pan African Short Stories* (1963) and in various issues of the magazine, *Black Orpheus*. She remains perhaps the finest and best-known among all female East African writers with her works appearing in both English and Luo. She was a founding member of the Writers' Association of Kenya. In addition to all of this, Grace Ogot became the very successful proprietress of Lindy's of Nairobi.

OGUNDE, Hubert

Hubert Ogunde, a famous Yoruba playwright, musician and theatre-manager, was born in western Nigeria on 31 May 1916. He organized the African Music and Dance Research Party in the early 1940s and in 1945 established the Ogunde Concert Party which toured widely in Africa and the United Kingdom after World War II. This was the first professional theatrical company in Nigeria. Ogunde wrote Yoruba songs for his group and founded the Mbari Mbayo Club in Oshogbo in 1962. An innovative pioneer in the field of Nigerian folk opera, he succeeded wonderfully well in merging traditional Yoruba folk songs with Christian elements in his compositions. He also wrote some fine Yoruba plays, including *Yoruba Ronu* (1964), *O tito koro* (1965), *Aropin n't'enia* (1967) and *Ologbu dudu* (1967). His better known English plays included *Garden of Eden*, *Nebuchadnezzar's Feign*, *Journey to Heaven* and *Tiger's Empire*. Occasionally, his plays offended the political authorities and were banned. Ogunde died on 4 April 1990.

OGUNMOLA, Kola

Ekemezi Kolawole Ogunmola, a famous Nigerian actor, mime and playwright, was born on 11 November 1925. He refined Hubert Ogunde's techniques and helped to develop further the modern Yoruba folk opera that his mentor had pioneered. Whereas Ogunde had allowed his cast to improvise most of the dialogues, Ogunmola wrote more structured dramas, the majority of which were gentle social satires. This was perhaps because of the more formal training he had received at the University of Ibadan (Nigeria) School of Drama. His finest works perhaps were *Love of Money* (first performed in 1950) and *The Palmwine Drinkard* (1963). Ogunmola wrote several plays ranging in theme from biblical story to fairy tale to satires on current politicians, but is still best remembered for his brilliant acting. In 1947, he founded the Ogunmola Travelling Theatre with which he toured several countries until his death in 1973.

OGUNYEMI, Wale

Generally regarded as one of the most important Yoruba playwrights, Wale Ogunyemi was born in western Nigeria in 1939. He was a scholar who published both in English and his native tongue. Among his most popular plays were *Born with Fire on His Head* (1967), *Be Mighty, Be Mine* (1968), *Eshe Elegbara* (1969), *Ijaye War: A Historic Drama* (1970), and *Obaluaye* (1972). Ogunyemi, who was also a charismatic actor on stage and television, died in 2001.

OKARA, Gabriel

Born in Ijaw County in 1921, Gabriel Imomotimi Gbaingbain Okara was a renowned Nigerian poet and novelist whose major works have been translated into several languages. His great novel, *The Voice*, which was published in 1964, appears to have been translated literally into English from his native Ijaw dialect and its style is thus considered by many critics to be as beautiful as it is bizarre. Okara, in fact, was largely self-taught and became a bookbinder after leaving school at an early age. He began his literary career as a poet and one of his early poems, *The Call for the River Nun*, won an award at the Nigerian Festival of Arts in 1953. Okara tried to incorporate African thought, religion, folklore and imagery into both his prose and his poetry and always gave the impression of thinking primarily in Ijaw before translating his ideas literally into English. He also included a great deal of verse into his prose writing. During the 1960s, Okara served as information officer for the Eastern Nigeria Government Service in Enugu and he later toured the United States with two other accomplished Nigerian novelists, Chinua Achebe and Cyprian Ekwensi, lecturing at various universities. In 1979 he won the Commonwealth Poetry Prize. He has also written such children's books as *Little Snake and Little Frog* (1981) and *An Adventure to Juju Island* (1981). Most of works display a deep respect for traditional Yoruba values and disillusionment with the moral bankruptcy of post-colonial Africa.

OKIGBO, Christopher

Christopher Okigbo was born near Onitsha, in eastern Nigeria, in the early 1930s. He was a promising poet whom many critics regard as one of Nigeria's finest. Educated at Government College in Umuahia and the

University College in Ibadan, he worked briefly as a civil servant before teaching at Fiditi, near Ibadan. He was killed in action during the Nigerian civil war in 1967. Okigbo's best poetry appeared in *Heavensgate* (1962) and *Limits* (1964).

OKRI, Ben

Ben Okri was born in Lagos, Nigeria, in 1959 and emigrated to the United Kingdom where he studied at the University of Essex. He has become known as one of the finest novelists produced by his native country and has received honorary degrees from the University of Westminster (1997) and the University of Essex (2002). In 2001 he was awarded an OBE for his contribution to English literature. He is a vice-president of the English Centre for the International PEN, an association of writers with 130 branches in over 100 countries. He is also a member of the United Kingdom's Royal National Theatre. Okri's novels include *Flowers and Shadows* (1980); *The Landscapes Within* (1981); *Incidents at the Shrine* (1986); *The Famished Road* (1991); *Songs of Enchantment* (1993); *Astonishing the Gods* (1995); *Dangerous Love* (1996); *Infinite Riches* (198); and *In Arcadia* (2002). He is an accomplished poet whose collections of poems may be found in *An African Elegy* (1992); and *Mental Flight* (1999). He has also written essays and short stories in such collections as *Stars of the New Curfew* (1988) and *A Way of Being Free* (1997). His best known work, *Famished Road*, won the 1991 Booker Prize.

OLATUNBOSUN, Olufemi

Professor Olufemi Olatunbosun is chair of the Department of Obstetrics, Gynaecology and Reproductive Sciences at the University of Saskatchewan. Born in Nigeria, he completed his education in Canada and returned to his native country to teach medicine at the University of Ife. He also taught in Saudi Arabia during 1989-92. Dr Olatunbosun joined the staff of the University of Saskatchewan in 1992, rising to the rank of full professor in 1999. In 2000 he was appointed Chief of Obstetrics and Gynaecology at Saskatoon District Health He has been responsible for a number of discoveries and innovations, including the use of the Olatunbosun technique in advanced cervical dilation, and the procedures he recommended for prolonging the gestation of multi-fetal pregnancy and increasing fetal salvage rates have now become standard practice. One of his most recent recommendations is that DNA testing be performed on prospective sperm donors to reduce the risk of cervical cancer in the recipients. He has published many seminal articles in medical journals and is the recipient of several awards for the excellence of his teaching.

OLATUNJI, Babatunde

Babatunde Olatunji, a Nigerian-born musician, introduced the rhythms and sounds of African drumming to the North American audience in the 1960s and significantly influenced a whole generation of jazz and rock bands. Born in Ajido on 7 April 1927, he immigrated to the United States in the 1950s and formed an African drum and dance group in New York City. His first album, *Drums of Passion*, was released in 1959. Five years later, with John Coltrane, he opened the Olatunji Center for African Culture in New York City. As late as the 1990s, Olatunji was still performing with a variety of well-known bands. With one of them, Drums of Passion, he released the popular album, *Love Drum Talk*, which was nominated for a Grammy Award in 1997. Olatunji died on 6 April 2003.

OLDFIELD, Bruce

Bruce Oldfield, who was born on 14 July 1950, has become one of Britain's most famous fashion designers. He specializes in couture evening wear and has designed gowns for British royalty, Hollywood actresses and much of the European aristocracy. He attended St Martin's School of Art in 1973, started his ready-to-wear label in 1975 and his couture label in 1978. In 1980 he was awarded an OBE for his services to the fashion industry. He is a committed supporter of Barnardo's children's charity, having been himself a Barnardo baby.

OLIVER, Donald

Senator Donald H. Oliver, a native of Wolfville, Nova Scotia, is a successful Canadian author, businessman, farmer, lawyer, politician and teacher. A keen supporter of the federal Progressive Conservative Party, he served as its director of legal affairs from 1972 until 1988. In 1990 he was appointed to the Canadian Senate, where he has been very active, serving on several of its standing committees. Senator Oliver practised law in Halifax during 1965-90 and also taught part-time at Dalhousie University for fourteen years. He has served on many boards and committees and remains a valued consultant, advisor and director of many companies.

OLIVER, Pearleen

Born Pearleen Borden in New Glasgow, Nova Scotia, she married Dr William Oliver in 1936. She was a noted civil rights activist and one of the influential leaders of the Nova Scotia Association for the Advancement of Colored People (NSAACP). This distinguished historian of the black experience in her native province was the first black graduate of New Glasgow High School in 1936. Forty years later, she became the first woman to be elected moderator of the African United Baptist Association of Nova

Scotia. In 1981 she received the first Woman of the Year Award from the YWCA, and in 1990 was the recipient of an honorary Doctor of Letters degree from St Mary's University in Nova Scotia. A similar honour was bestowed upon her by Mount St Vincent University in 1993. Her major works include *A Brief History of the Coloured Baptists of Nova Scotia, 1782-1953* (1953); *A Root and a Name* (1977); *From Generation to Generation* (1985); and *Song of the Spirit* (1994).

OLIVER, William

Revd William Percy Oliver was born in Wolfville, Nova Scotia, on 11 February 1912 and was educated at Acadia University where he obtained BA and BD degrees. He succeeded Revd William A. White as pastor of the famous Cornwallis Street Baptist Church in 1936. During World War II, he served as a chaplain to black regiments and in 1948 he introduced black voices for the first time to the CBC's trans-Canadian programmes. Oliver promoted black credit unions, adult education, and closer contacts with black academic institutions in the United States. He founded the Nova Scotia Association for the Advancement of Colored People (NSAACP) in 1945, the Black United Front (BUF), and the Society for the Protection and Preservation of Black Culture in Nova Scotia. The Baptist Church prospered under Oliver's direction and on one occasion, in 1951, he baptized sixty five persons in the largest such ceremony known to black Canadians up to that time. He constantly urged industry, service institutions and the government to grant more nearly equal opportunities for employment. He publicly denounced racial discrimination in the job market and persuaded the leading hospitals in Halifax to admit black women to nurses' training in 1945. In 1952 he finally managed to persuade that city to appoint black teachers for the first time. Oliver received many honours and distinctions, including an honorary doctorate from King's College, Halifax; the Order of Canada (1984); a Human Relations Award from the Canadian Council of Christians and Jews (1985); and the Distinguished Service Award of the Alumni of Acadia University (1988). He was a firm believer in gradualism, denouncing any form of militancy. He thought that Canadian Blacks were largely responsible for their own upliftment and could gain the respect of their white counterparts only by making every effort to upgrade their skills, their morals and their character. He died in May 1989.

OLWENY, Charles

Dr Charles Lwanga Mark Olweny was born and educated in Uganda, where he qualified as a physician at the Makerere Medical School. He taught medicine at Makerere University in Kampala from 1969 to 1984 and served as the Director of the Uganda Cancer Institute during 1973-84. He became an important consultant with the World Health Organization (WHO) and worked in such African countries as Zambia and Zimbabwe. From 1985 to 1990, he worked in Australia as Senior Director, Medical Oncology, Royal Adelaide Hospital and Clinical Professor, Department of Medicine and Surgery, at the University of Adelaide. Dr Olweny immigrated to Canada in 1990 to assume the position of co-director of the WHO Collaborating Centre for the Quality of Life in Cancer Care. He then joined the Faculty of Medicine at the University of Manitoba in 1997. He continues to publish important articles in medical journals on such topics as bioethics, Burkitt's lymphoma, hepatocellular carcinoma, Hodgkin's disease, Karposi's sarcoma and the quality of life. A keen community servant, he has made vital contributions to such ethnic organizations as the Council of African Organizations of Manitoba, Friends of Makerere in Canada and the Ugandan Canadian Association of Manitoba.

OLYMPIO, Sylvanus

Sylvanus Olympio, who was elected the first president of independent Togo in 1961, was born in Dahomey in September 1902. A member of the Ewe people, he was educated in German and British mission schools in Togoland before completing his degree in economics at the University of London, England. Returning to Togo, he joined the United African Company (UAC), a coastal trading chain, and succeeded largely on the strength of his ability to speak fluently such languages as English, Ewe, French, German and Portuguese. These skills also made Olympio an influential politician and he shortly became leader of the Comité de l'Unité Togolaise after World war II. He was elected president of the first territorial assembly in 1946 and it was he who headed the UN trust government of Togoland, as prime minister and minister of justice, during 1958-60 just before Togo achieved its political independence. Olympio declared himself President of Togo for life in 1962 but was assassinated by military insurgents on 13 January 1963. He had created enormous problems for himself by attempting to unite the Ewe people, who were divided by the boundaries of British and French Togoland; by making Togo a one-party state; and by governing, in the opinion of his critics, much too autocratically. Sylvanus Olympio is thus remembered, sadly, as the first presidential victim of a wave of African military coups during the 1960s.

OMAR, Dullah

Abdullah Mohamed Omar was a South African lawyer, activist and politician, who rose to a position in President Nelson Mandela's cabinet after the apartheid system had been dismantled. Born on 26 May 1934, he qualified as a lawyer and set up his own private practice in 1960 since he was ineligible to join an established firm. He defended victims of apartheid in political trials and allied himself with the progressive nationalist movements of the day. He was therefore frequently arrested, his passport was revoked and his movements were restricted by the government. After 1994, however, he was free to join the new government. He was appointed minister of transportation by President Thabo Mbeki in 1999 after having served during 1994-99 as minister of justice. Omar died on 13 March 2004.

O'NEAL, Duncan

The Rt Excellent Dr Charles Duncan O'Neal, who was named a National Hero by the Barbados government in April 1998, was one of the most outspoken critics of oligarchical snobbery and injustice in his native island during the inter-war period. Born on 10 November 1879, he attended the Parry School and Harrison College in Barbados before completing his education at Edinburgh University in Scotland. He qualified as a medical doctor and practised privately in Newcastle in the north of England before returning to the West Indies in 1910. After working for some time in Dominica and Trinidad, he finally settled down in Barbados in 1924. While in Britain he had fallen under the influence of Keir Hardie, the famous socialist, and had been much involved in local politics. Dr O'Neal took his fiery brand of democratic socialism back to Barbados and denounced the white oligarchy in a series of blistering speeches and pamphlets. Among other things, he called for a total restructuring of the electoral pattern, better wages for manual labourers, a superior system of public health, and more educational opportunities for the disadvantaged. Towards the end of 1924, he founded the Democratic League, a new political party aimed at Blacks, but he was universally branded a dangerous Communist and could not therefore gain election to the colonial legislature until 1932. In the meantime, however, more moderate Blacks had joined his party and were winning seats in the House of Assembly. Although he spent only four years in that chamber he left an indelible mark. He persuaded the local parliament to abolish child labour and to improve (albeit slightly) the plight of plantation workers. Dr O'Neal died on 20 November 1936. He had done more perhaps than any other single individual to arouse the Barbadian community from its long slumber and to pinpoint the basic reforms of which his native island then stood in dire need. The Charles Duncan O'Neal Bridge in Bridgetown commemorates his name and his portrait appears on the Barbados $10 note. His Democratic League eventually formed the basis of the Barbados Labour Party which became one of the most powerful organizations in Barbadian life and politics.

O'NEAL, Shaquille

One of the greatest basketball players of all time, Shaquille Rashaun O'Neal was born on 6 March 1972 in Newark, New Jersey. A huge and powerful man, over 7 ft. tall and weighing in excess of 300 pounds, he is nevertheless extremely quick and agile. Ever since his days at the Louisiana State University, he has been a dominant figure in the sport, averaging over 27 points and 12 rebounds per game. He took the Los Angeles Lakers to successive NBA championships early in this century, silencing those critics who had complained about his failure to win the big games while playing for the Orlando Magic during the 1990s. He then played a significant role in the success of the Miami Heat after leaving the Lakers.

OPOKU WARE

Opoku Ware, who ruled during 1720-50, was perhaps the greatest of all Asante warrior-kings. Under his leadership the Asante became the predominant power in the Gold Coast. A brilliant general, he soon annexed such states as Ahafo, Aowin and Sehwi. He conquered Akyem in 1742 and shortly became the overlord of such neighbouring principalities as Accra, Adangme, Akuapem, Akwamu and Kwamu. He then conquered the Dagomba to the north and, by 1746, had made the Asante Empire the main source of gold, ivory and slaves in the Gold Coast. During his later years, Opoku Ware devoted his major energies to internal administration and proved himself as great a governor as he had been a general. He strengthened the monarchy by making all the nobles and Kumasi chiefs directly responsible to him. Thus he not only saved the Asante state from disintegration but added significantly to its economic power in his thirty years at the helm. The Asante Empire reached its fullest extent during his remarkable reign.

ORTIZ, Adalberto

Adalberto Ortiz is universally considered the finest of all African-Ecuadorian authors. His reputation is largely based on the novel, *Juyungo*, a veritable classic, published in 1943. His works included numerous short stories, essays and at least one other important novel, *El espejo y la ventana*, which appeared in 1967.

OSAGYEFUO KUNTUNKUNUNKU II

Born Alex Agyeman at Kibi, Gold Coast, on 22 February 1942, he assumed the title of Osagyefuo Kuntunkununku II on ascending the throne in 1976 as Okyehene (ruler) of Akim Abuakwa in Ghana. The son of a wealthy businessman (who had married a royal princess), he studied medicine in eastern Europe and continued his practice as a physician even after his assumption of kingly duties. He remained very interested in public health and hospital modernizations. He died on 17 March 1999.

OSAM-PINANKO, Frank

Revd Dr Frank Ata Osam-Pinanko was the first African minister of the African Methodist Episcopal Zion (AMEZ) Church of the Gold Coast. Born in 1875, he taught briefly in Wesleyan Schools at Winneba and Dixcove before attending Livingstone College in North Carolina during 1899-1903. He returned to the Gold Coast in 1903 to establish an AMEZ church and a school at Cape Coast and was ordained a deacon in 1910. He was awarded an MA from Livingstone College in 1912 and a DD in 1928. During 1920-24 he served as general superintendent of the AMEZ Mission in the Gold Coast and later became general manager of AMEZ schools. The founding of the Aggrey Memorial College at Cape Coast in the 1950s was largely a result of his vision. Very interested also in the public life of the Gold Coast, Osam-Pinanko was a member of the Aborigines' Rights Protection Society (ARPS) and of the National Congress of British West Africa (NCBWA). He died in 1945.

OSEI BONSU

Born in 1779, Osei Bonsu was the greatest of the nineteenth century Asante warrior-kings. He began by crushing a Muslim rebellion in the northwest of his kingdom and then treating them with great tolerance and respect. He defeated the Fante and brought them under Asante rule. By 1800 the Asante had therefore captured most of the area now known as Ghana. When the British tried to unite the other West African chiefs against the Asante in the early 1820s, Osei Bonsu triumphed again. Sir Charles McCarthy, the governor-in-chief of the British West African colonies, was actually killed in that attempt. Osei Bonsu rebuilt the city of Kumasi, his capital, and administered a huge empire (much larger than present-day Ghana) with considerable tact and skill. He established an efficient central bureaucracy recruited by merit, and a fine system of communications. Although he resisted British attempts to infiltrate western Africa, he admired European manners and technology and wished his sons to be trained in England. The great Osei Bonsu died in 1824.

OSEI TUTU

Osei Tutu was the founder of the Asante nation early in the eighteenth century. He established his capital at Kumasi and unified the bulk of the Asante under his leadership. They were thus able to defeat their powerful and dangerous Denkyira neighbours to the south in the wars of 1699-1701. During Osei Tutu's reign as Asantehene (king of all the Asante), the area of

Asante dominion approximately tripled. It was he who left them with the famous Golden Stool, on which all subsequent Asante kings were enthroned. He did much to centralize the Asante political system without destroying the traditional powers of local chieftains. He thus set the pattern for much of later Asante government and administration. He was the first of the Asantehene to transform the kingdom from a loose confederation into a solid union. Osei Tutu was killed in warfare in 1712, but his work of conquest and centralization was effectively continued by such gifted successors as Opoku Ware (1720-50) and Osei Bonsu (1798-1824).

OTOMFUO OKOPU WARE II

Otomfuo Okopu Ware II became the fifteenth Asantehene (paramount chief) of the Ashanti people in 1970 and ruled over the everyday spiritual and cultural life of that ancient kingdom until his death at Kumasi, Ghana, on 26 February 1999. Born on 30 November 1919, he studied law and qualified as a barrister.

OTTEY, Merlene

One of the greatest female athletes that the world has known, Merlene Ottey-Page was born in Jamaica on 10 May 1960. She became the first woman to reach the final in any event in five consecutive Olympics when she won a silver medal in the 200 metre sprint at Atlanta in 1996. Her greatest disappointment was her failure to achieve an Olympic gold medal in an otherwise brilliant career that spanned more than twenty years, but she did manage to eclipse the women's record of seven track and field medals (silver and bronze) in Olympic competition when she won her eighth (a silver) in 2000 as a member of the Jamaican 4 x 100 metre relay. She was involved in several close finishes at the international level before claiming victory outright in the 200 metre sprint in the world outdoor championships in 1993 and 1995. In five World Championships during 1983-97, she won thirteen medals: three gold, four silver and six bronze. Ottey, who continued to compete internationally until she was more than forty years old, received many honours and awards and remains one of Jamaica's most prized and decorated heroines. She finished her career, however, running in the colours of Slovenia in the Athens Olympics in 2004. She is the first athlete to participate in seven consecutive Olympic Games; the first female Caribbean athlete to win an Olympic medal; the first female to win an Olympic medal at the age of forty; and the first female athlete to break seven seconds in the 60 metre indoor sprint. Ottey was named an Officer of the Order of the Nation by the Jamaican government in1980 and was declared an Ambassador at Large for her country in 1993.

OUSLEY, Herman

Baron Ousley of Peckham Rye in Southwark was raised to the peerage in 2001. Born in Guyana in 1945, he emigrated to the United Kingdom with his family when he was eleven years old. He was educated at William Penn School and Catford College, where he gained a diploma in municipal administration. He was appointed as the first principal race relations advisor in local government and served as head of the Ethnic Minority Unit of the Greater London Council (GLC). He later became chief executive of the London Borough of Lambeth and of the Inner London Education Authority (ILEA). He was the first black person to hold such a post. In 1993 he became the executive chairman of the Commission for Racial Equality (CRE) and held that position until 2000, doing a great deal to restore CRE's waning credibility. Lord Herman Ousley is often required to chair independent inquiries into racism and is actively involved in the work of many voluntary organizations, including the Institute of Race Relations and the Ethnic Minority Foundation. He is currently the managing director of Different Realities Partnership Ltd, a consultancy specializing in equality, diversity, and people management studies. He is the recipient of eight honorary degrees.

OWENS, Jesse

Born in Danville, Alabama, on 12 September 1913, James Cleveland Owens was one of the most famous track stars in the history of athletics. He was arguably the greatest athlete of the first half of the twentieth century. After an outstanding athletic record at East Technical High School in Cleveland, Ohio, he attended Ohio State University and achieved his BA in 1937. He established a magnificent array of world records in the long jump and the sprints, which remained intact until long after World War II. His long jump world record of 26 ft 8¼in, for instance, was not eclipsed until 12 August 1960. It had lasted for 25 years, 79 days. More than any other single individual, Owens helped to demolish Adolf Hitler's myth of Aryan supremacy by winning no fewer than four gold medals at the Berlin Olympics in 1936. Despite his BA and his reputation, however, Owens became a forgotten man almost as soon as his Olympic records were set. He was forced to take odd jobs to make ends meet and to accept money to race against cars, horses, and dogs. He languished in oblivion and frustration until rescued by President Gerald Ford who awarded him the Presidential Medal of Freedom in 1976. Three years later, President Jimmy Carter presented him with a Living Legacy Award. In his later years, Owens served as a public relations officer making numerous inspirational speeches and undertaking goodwill tours to India and the Far East for the US Department of State. He died on 31 March 1980 but still remains a legend in North American history and serves as an inspiring role model to countless modern athletes in all parts of the world. He wrote two autobiographies: *Black-think: My Life as Black Man and White Man*, and *I Have Changed*.

PADMORE, George

Born Malcolm Ivan Meredith Nurse in Trinidad, West Indies, in 1903, he changed his name to George Padmore in the 1930s and played an active role in developing Pan-African and black labour movements during the inter-war years. Often called the 'father of African emancipation', he was a close associate and adviser to Kwame Nkrumah in the early days of Ghanaian independence. Padmore pursued a degree in political science at Fisk University in the United States during 1924-27 before studying law at New York University and Howard University. He became an ardent socialist and led many organizations aimed at converting American students to communism. In 1929 he travelled to Germany to attend the second congress of the League Against Imperialism and helped to plan a Black Workers' Conference. He then went to Moscow to prepare for service with the Comintern. The Soviet leader, Josef Stalin, sent him on a mission to China to report on the progress of the Communist Party there. Padmore became secretary of the International Trade Union Committee of Negro Workers (ITUCNW) in 1931 and then moved to Hamburg, Germany, to edit the *Negro Worker*. His activities as a communist agent led to his arrest, imprisonment and deportation to the United Kingdom in 1933. There, he formed the International African Service Bureau in 1936 with another Trinidadian political activist, C.L.R. James, and devoted the rest of his life to the emancipation of the African colonies. Padmore spearheaded the Pan-African Congress which met at Manchester in 1945 and later served as Nkrumah's special adviser. When he died in London on 23 September 1959, his ashes were interred in Christiansborg Castle, Accra, on 4 October. But his special relationship with Nkrumah had caused such resentment among Ghanaians that the Padmore Library in Accra that was named after him was renamed the Research Library on African Affairs after Nkrumah's overthrow in 1966. Padmore's legacy included such works as *The Life and Struggles of Negro Toilers* (1931), *How Britain Rules Africa* (1936), *Africa: Britain's Third Empire* (1939), *How Russia Transformed her Colonial Empire* (1943), *The Gold Coast Revolution* (1953) and *Pan-Africanism or Communism* (1956).

PAIGE, Satchel

Robert Leroy Paige, universally known as 'Satchel', was born on 7 July 1906 in Mobile, Alabama. He was a phenomenal right-arm pitcher who would surely have become one of the greatest in the game had his colour not excluded him from the major leagues until he was forty two years old. Prior to his belated entry into the majors, he had claimed a minor league record of 2,000 wins, 500 losses and 100 no-hitters over a period of twenty years. As a rookie in 1948, he sparked the Cleveland Indians to an American League pennant and a World Series triumph. Known for his precision and his stamina, Paige was able to pitch three scoreless innings for the Kansas City Athletics against the Boston Red Sox as late as 1965, when serving as a reliever at the age of fifty-nine. Thirty years earlier, he had been known to pitch every day for 29 consecutive days. Satchel Paige was eventually inducted into the Baseball Hall of Fame in 1971. He died on 8 June 1982.

PARKER, Charlie

Born in Kansas City, Kansas, on 29 August 1920, Charles Christopher Parker is considered by most jazz experts as perhaps the greatest jazz improviser and one of the finest of alto saxophonists. He began his professional career at an early age, playing with such great stars as Kenny Clark, 'Dizzy' Gillespie and Thelonious Monk. After spending six months in Camarillo State Hospital, California, for treatment of narcotics addiction, Parker resumed his musical activities in 1947 and recorded a number of hits. Among his best known pieces were *Hot House*, *Salt Peanuts*, *Now's the Time* and *Billie's Bounce*. By the time of his early death on 12 March 1955, he had become a source of inspiration to countless musicians and his style was imitated by many of the great jazz pianists and trumpeters of the 1940s and 1950s.

PARKS, Gordon

Gordon Parks, who became (in 1941) the first photographer to win a Rosenwald Fellowship and the first African-American to direct full-length films for a major studio, was born in Fort Scott, Kansas, on 30 November 1912. After poverty had forced him to leave school at an early age, he did a variety of odd jobs before becoming a photographer and gradually establishing a national reputation in this field. This rested, in part, on the publication of his first two books, *Flash Photography* (1947) and *Camera Portraits: Techniques and Principles of Documentary Portraiture* (1948). Between 1950 and 1952 he served as a staff photographer for *Life* and *Time*. He directed such films as *Flavio* (1964), *Shaft* (1971), *The Super Cops* (1974) and *Leadbelly* (1976); and wrote six autobiographical novels, *The Learning Tree* (1963), *A Choice of Weapons* (1967), *Born Black* (1971), *To Smile in Autumn* (1979), *Voices in the Mirror* (1990), and *A Hungry Heart* (2005). Gordon Parks was an exceptionally gifted individual who shone in a variety of fields. In addition to film-directing, literature and photography, he also left his mark on music. An excellent pianist, he wrote compositions for jazz as well as serious classical music, including several concertos. Among his numerous awards were a television 'Emmy', Photographer of the Year (1960), and a Spingarn Medal in 1972. Parks died on 7 March 2006.

PARKS, Rosa

Rosa Louise Parks was an American civil rights activist who became a symbol of the power of non-violent protest when she refused to give up her seat to a white man in the segregated South. Her action led to the famous bus boycott in Montgomery, Alabama, in 1955-56. This was one of the vital sparks that ignited the civil rights movement. Born in Tuskegee, Alabama, on 4 February 1913, she attended Alabama State Teachers College briefly before working as a seamstress. She became involved in the activities of the National Association for the Advancement of Colored People (NAACP) and served as the secretary of its Montgomery chapter from 1943 to 1956. When she refused to surrender her seat in 1955, she was arrested and fined. The boycott which followed lasted more than one year and in 1956 the US Supreme Court ruled that Montgomery's segregated bus seating was unconstitutional. She moved to Detroit and continued to work with the NAACP and other civil rights groups. The Southern Christian Leadership Council established the Rosa Parks Award in her honour in 1979 and the NAACP awarded her its Spingarn Medal. In 1987, she co-founded an institute to help educate young people and teach them leadership skills. Her autobiography, *Rosa Parks : My Story*, appeared in 1993. She received the Presidential Medal of Freedom in 1996 and the Congressional Gold Medal of Honor in 1999. She died on 24 October 2005.

PATASSÉ, Ange-Félix

Ange-Félix Patassé was born on 25 January 1937 in Paoua, the capital of Ouham Pendé in French Equatorial Africa. After attending local schools, he completed his education in France where he specialized in zootechnology. He joined the Central African civil service in 1959 as an agricultural engineer and was appointed minister of agriculture in 1965. During the reigns of David Dacko and Jean Bédel Bokassa, he occupied several important posts and was named prime minister in 1976 when Bokassa declared himself president of the Central African Republic. Patassé was forced to spend several years in exile in the chaotic period which followed the collapse of Bokassa's government in 1979. He returned to the Central African Republic in 1992 as leader of a new party, the Movement for the Liberation of the Central African People (MLPC). He won the election of 1993 and became the first president in the nation's history to gain power by means of a fair and democratic election. But his first term was marred by serious mutinies in the army which quite adversely affected the economy. He was re-elected in 1999 but was ousted in a bloodless coup in 2003 and had to return forthwith into exile once more.

PATTERSON, Frederick Douglass

Dr Frederick Douglass Patterson, who won the US Presidential Medal of Freedom in 1987, made a significant contribution to the education of Blacks as the president of Tuskegee Normal and Industrial Institute (1935-53) and as the founder in 1944 of the United Negro College Fund, which boasted forty-two member colleges and aided some 45,000 students with an annual income of $42 million by 1988. Born on 10 October 1901 in Washington, D.C., Patterson received a PhD in veterinary medicine (1923) and an MSc (1927) from Iowa State College before earning a second doctorate from Cornell University. He taught at Virginia State College before joining the staff at Tuskegee Institute in Alabama in 1928. He served for seven years as director of its School of Agriculture and then became that institution's third president. In the 1970s, Patterson also devised the College Endowment Fund that depended on private donations which were matched by federal funds. Patterson died on 26 April 1988.

PATTERSON, Orlando

Horace Orlando Patterson was born in Jamaica, West Indies, on 5 June 1940. Educated at Kingston College, the University College of the West Indies (Jamaica) and the London School of Economics (England), he taught briefly at the University of the West Indies before joining the staff at Harvard University in the United States. Patterson is an internationally renowned sociologist whose major works include *The Sociology of Slavery* (1967); *An Analysis of the Origins, Development and Structure of Negro Slave Society in Jamaica* (1968); *Ethnic Chauvinism: The Reactionary Impulse* (1977); *Slavery and Social Death: A Comparative Study* (1982); and *Freedom in the Making of Western Culture* (1991) which won the National Book Award for non-fiction that year. He is also an accomplished writer of fiction and has published such novels as *The Children of Sisyphus* which won the first prize at the Dakar Festival of Negro Arts in 1965, *An Absence of Ruins* (1967) and *Die the Long Day* (1972). Patterson has received many notable awards and honours, including the Distinguished Contribution to Scholarship Award of the American Sociological Association in 1983 and the Ralph Bunche Award of the American Political Science Association for the best scholarly work in pluralism. He is also a Fellow of the American Academy of Arts and Sciences.

PATTERSON, P.J.

Percival Noel James Patterson, a former prime minister of Jamaica, was born there on 10 April 1935. Educated at Calabar High School (Kingston) and the University College of the West Indies (Jamaica), he entered politics shortly after his graduation with an English honours degree in 1958. He became a stalwart within the People's National Party (PNP) and succeeded

Michael Manley as its leader and as prime minister of Jamaica when the very popular 'Joshua' retired, for health reasons, on 30 March 1992. Patterson was re-elected four times, after pledging himself in 1992 to maintain the PNP policy of deregulation, divestment of state enterprises, and encouragement of private initiative. On this platform, his party triumphed in the general elections of March 1993 by the margin of 52-8 seats. The margin was significantly reduced in the three succeeding elections, but Jamaica enjoyed fourteen years of relative tranquillity and economic growth with 'P.J.' at the helm. He resigned from the leadership of the country in 2006 and was succeeded by Portia Simpson-Miller, the first woman to serve as Jamaica's prime minister.

PAYNE, Clement

The Rt Excellent Clement Osbourne Payne was declared a National Hero by the Barbados Government in April 1998. He was born in Trinidad in 1904 of Barbadian parents who moved back to Barbados when he was four years old. Educated at the Bay Street Boys' (elementary) School, he worked for some years as a junior clerk before returning to Trinidad in 1927. Largely self-taught and widely read, Payne became a fiery, persuasive orator championing the cause of the down-trodden and drawing attention to the oppressive nature of colonialism. A staunch advocate of human rights and social justice, he encouraged the growth of militant trade unionism in Trinidad and eventually provided the spark that triggered the Bridgetown riots of 1937 when the local authorities attempted to put an end to his activism there. Payne died at the young age of thirty-seven in 1941 but is everywhere remembered as one of the individuals who did most to bring about change in the modern British West Indies. The various riots he inspired forced the imperial parliament to establish the famous Moyne Commission to investigate the cause of so much unrest. The Commission eventually reiterated most of the points that Payne himself had been making. The Clement Payne Cultural Centre has recently been erected in Barbados to honour his memory and there is a Clement Payne Memorial Bust in Golden Square, Bridgetown, the island's capital.

PAYNE, Daniel

Revd Daniel Alexander Payne, an eminent American clergyman, educator and historian, was born in Charleston, South Carolina, in 1811. After attending the Lutheran Theological Seminary in Gettysburg, Pennsylvania, he was ordained a Lutheran minister in 1839 and became one of the leaders of the African Methodist Episcopal (AME) Church, rising to the rank of bishop in 1852. He was instrumental in raising the educational level of AME ministers and in purchasing Wilberforce University for that church in

1863. Bishop Payne served as the university's first president for the next sixteen years. He was very active during the American Civil War (1861-65) in promoting the abolition of southern slaves and the rights of Blacks generally. His books included *Recollections of Seventy Years* (1883) and *The History of the A.M.E. Church from 1816 to 1856* (1891). He died in 1893.

PAYTON, Walter

One of the greatest performers in the National Football League (NFL) in North America, Walter Jerry Payton was born in Columbia, Mississippi, on 25 July 1954. An exceptionally gifted running back, he set the then NFL record for most career yards rushing (16,726) and most career carries (3,838). He once ran for 275 yards in a single game against Minnesota. He also set a team record for pass receptions on behalf of the Chicago Bears and threw eight touchdown passes. He played in nine Pro Bowls during 1975-87 and was elected to the Football Hall of Fame in 1993. At the time of his death on 1 November 1999, Payton held or shared no fewer than eight NFL records.

PELÉ

Born Edson Arantes do Nascimento in Minas Girais, Brazil, on 21 October 1940, Pelé emerged as one of the greatest stars in the history of international football. He was only seventeen when he helped Brazil win the World Cup in 1958. He was held in such high regard that Italian clubs were prepared to offer as much as $1.2 million for his services in 1967. His Brazilian team, Santos, declined these offers since Pelé was such a huge attraction at home. In 1969 he scored his 1,000th goal and in 1970 led Brazil to its third championship in World Cup competition. He retired in 1974 but remains a legend in his native country. During his eighteen year career, Pelé scored 1,216 goals in 1,253 games, including a record eight goals in one match for Santos in 1964. He signed a reported $7 million contract with the New York Cosmos of the North American Soccer League in June 1975, but failed to make soccer a popular major-league sport in the United States. In the early 1970s he was thought to be the world's wealthiest and most celebrated athlete, with an annual income in excess of $2 million.

PENNINGTON, James

Revd James W.C. Pennington was born a slave in Maryland in 1809. He escaped to Pennsylvania where he was befriended by a Quaker who taught him to read and write. In 1828 he moved to New York and worked as a blacksmith He audited courses at Yale University during 1834-39, thus becoming the first black man to attend classes at that institution. He was then ordained and became a priest, teacher, abolitionist and author. Revd

Pennington represented Connecticut at the World's Anti-Slavery Convention in London, England, in 1843 and continued to work for black civil rights until his death in 1870. Pennington published *The Origin and History of the Coloured People* in 1841 and *The Fugitive Blacksmith*, an autobiography, in 1859. In 1849 the University of Heidelberg awarded him an honorary doctorate of divinity.

PÉREC, Marie-José

Marie-José Pérec was born in the French West Indian island of Guadeloupe on 9 May 1968. Recruited by a French coach, who took her to the mainland, she became France's greatest track star during the 1990s. Pérec accomplished the unusual double by winning both the 200 metre and 400 metre women's sprints at the Atlanta Olympics in 1996. Her time of 48.25 secs was an Olympic record for the women's 400 metres. She dominated these two events for much of the 1990s, winning them both at the world outdoor championships of 1991 and 1995 and triumphing in the 400 metre sprint in the 1997 world championship. Pérec was adoringly called the 'Gazelle' by her thousands of fans in France, where she was acknowledged as one of the nation's most special celebrities and heroines.

PETERS, Thomas

Born around 1738, Thomas Peters was a courageous African-American slave who escaped and eventually became a leader of black emigrants from Nova Scotia to Sierra Leone. Running away from slavery during the American War of Independence, he fought for the British Army and became a sergeant in the regiment known as the Black Pioneers. He was among those Loyalists who sought refuge in Nova Scotia when the war was over. Distressed by the degree of racial prejudice the Blacks encountered there, he sought (and was granted) permission to resettle in West Africa. He thus played a role in the history of the United States, Nova Scotia and Sierra Leone. The migrants Peters took to West Africa had much to do with the success of the Sierra Leone settlement at the end of the eighteenth century.

PETERSON, Oscar

One of Canada's most proficient and famous musicians, Oscar Emmanuel Peterson was born in Montreal, Quebec, on 15 August 1925. He began to play the piano at the age of seven and became noted for his ability to play with blazing speed and authority in all jazz piano styles. After attending the Montreal Conservatory of Music for one year, he studied privately with the Hungarian pianist, Paul de Marky. In 1939 he won a Canadian Broadcasting Corporation (CBC) amateur contest. Peterson played with the Johnny Holmes Orchestra from 1944 to 1949 and was invited to play at the Carnegie

Concert Hall with Norman Granz's touring concert unit in 1949. In 1952 he formed his own little band, the Oscar Peterson Trio, which made several successful tours of Europe. In 1959 he opened the Advanced School of Contemporary Music in Toronto but had to close it four years later because of the heavy demands of his concert tours. In 1985 he founded the Oscar Peterson Scholarship for Jazz Studies at York University in Toronto, where he was named adjunct professor of music. In 1987 he received the Roy Thomson Hall Award for his outstanding contribution to the musical life of Toronto. In 1973 he was made an Officer of the Order of Canada, and in 1989 the French government made him an Officer of the Order of Arts and Letters. Peterson, who is a thirteen-time winner of the Down Beat Award for best jazz pianist of the year, is also a composer. His best-known pieces include *Canadiana Suite* (1963), *Royal Suite* (1981) and *Africa Suite* (1983). An Oscar Peterson Scholarship has been established at the Berklee School of Music in Boston and an Oscar Peterson Day has been proclaimed in Baltimore and Florida. In 1997 he received a Grammy Award for Lifetime Achievement and an International Jazz Hall of Fame Award. His numerous other awards and distinctions include the Governor General's Performing Arts Award (1992); the Glenn Gould Prize (1993); the award of the International Society for Performing Artists (1995); the Loyola Medal of Concordia University (1997); the Praemium Imperiale World Art Award (1999); the UNESCO Music Prize (2000); and the Toronto Musicians' Association Musician of the Year Award (2001). During 1991-94 he was Chancellor of York University (Toronto) and in 2004 the City of Toronto named the courtyard of the Toronto-Dominion Centre Oscar Peterson Square.

PHILLIPS, Trevor

Trevor Phillips was born in London, England, on 31 December 1953 to parents of Guyanese origin. He is currently (2006) the chairman of the Commission for Racial Equality (CRE). He has recently been appointed the head of a new organization, the Commission for Equalities and Human Rights, established to address such issues as ethnic and gender equality and the rights of the disabled. Phillips was educated at Queen's College in Guyana and Imperial College, London, where he studied chemistry. He has had a varied career in both media and politics, working initially as a researcher for London Weekend Television (LWT) before being promoted to head of current affairs. He produced *The London Programme* and worked on projects for the BBC. He became one of a small number of black senior executives of major British broadcasting organizations. With his brother, Michael Phillips, he wrote *Windrush: Irresistible Rise of Multi-racial Britain* (1998). This was the basis of the interesting series that was created by his independent production company, Pepper Productions, which chronicled the history of black people in Britain over the last fifty years. Entering politics, he was elected a member of the Greater London Assembly (GLA) in 2000 and served as its chair until February 2003. He has been chair of the Runnymede Trust and commissioner for a number of other charities.

PINDLING, Lynden

One of the most significant personalities in Bahamian history, Sir Lynden Oscar Pindling was born on 22 March 1930 in Nassau, The Bahamas. He served as premier and prime minister of The Bahamas for twenty five years (1967-92), guiding that nation through its early stages of independence after 1973. Pindling was re-elected on five occasions and his reign witnessed the establishment of the tourist industry in the midst of considerable economic growth He was a founding member of the Progressive Liberal Party (PLP) in 1953. It suffered defeat for the first time in almost thirty years when it lost the general elections of 1992 in the midst of an unusual economic depression and rumours of corruption.Pindling died in Nassau on 26 August 2000.

PITT, David

Lord David Pitt of Hampstead was the longest serving black British parliamentarian who was granted a life peerage in 1975 and served in the House of Lords until his death in London on 18 December 1994. His civil rights leadership was unparalleled in post-war Britain. His whole career was devoted to the cause of racial equality in the United Kingdom and elsewhere. Born in Grenada in 1913, he attended Grenada Boys' Secondary School and won the prestigious Island Scholarship which took him to the University of Edinburgh, Scotland, where he qualified as a medical doctor. After graduating with honours, he returned to the West Indies in 1938 and practised medicine in St Vincent and Trinidad. Pitt was elected to the borough council of San Fernando (Trinidad) and served as its deputy mayor. In 1943, he founded the West Indian National Party and was its president until 1947. His party advocated independence for Trinidad in a British West Indian Federation, but could make no headway given the temper of the times. In frustration, he emigrated to England and established a medical practice in London that he ran for more than thirty years. In the 1950s his was the loudest voice deploring the treatment of black immigrants. He became the first chair of the Campaign Against Racial Discrimination (CARD). He failed in his bid to win a parliamentary seat in 1959 but was elected to the London City Council (LCC) in 1961. When this body was absorbed by the Greater London Council (GLC) in 1964, he became the deputy chair in 1969 and the chair in 1974. The first black man to hold this post, he paved the way for the multi-racial politics for which the GLC became known. After his elevation to the peerage in 1975, he continued his crusade on behalf of the African-Caribbean community in Britain. He was at the helm of the Community Relations Commission from 1968 to 1977 and played a key role in the 1976 legislation outlawing racial discrimination in housing, employment, education and services. He joined with three of the first black members of parliament, Diane Abbott, Bernie Grant and Keith Vaz, to form the well-known lobbying group often referred to as the Black Caucus. One of his greatest achievements, however, was his election as president of the British Medical Association from 1985 to 1986, a position seldom achieved by general practitioners.

PITT, Romain

The Hon Mr Justice Romain W.M. Pitt, who has been practising law since 1965, was appointed to the Superior Court of Ontario in 1994. Born in Grenada, he emigrated to Canada in 1954 and completed his education at the University of Toronto. He became the first black lawyer in Canada to be appointed from private practice to a superior provincial court. A founding director of Caribana (an annual Caribbean festival in Toronto), he also assisted in the formation of the Sickle Cell Association of Ontario. He was a recipient of a Governor General 125th Anniversary Medal in 1992.

PLÁCIDO

Gabriel de la Concepción Valdés, a Cuban author who wrote under the pseudonym of Plácido, was born in 1804. His poetry stressed the unjust nature of Cuban society and led to his execution on charges of treason in 1844. His numerous poems are now widely translated and admired. Many critics consider him the forerunner of modern African-American literature.

PLAATJE, Solomon

Solomon Tshekiso Plaatje was a truly exceptional individual. Born into poverty in the Orange Free State, South Africa, in 1878, he left school at an early age and largely by teaching himself, while doing a variety of odd jobs, became an eminent Tswana scholar, novelist and statesman. A brilliant linguist, he made himself proficient while still quite young in Afrikaans, English, High Dutch, German and French, while also learning to speak Sotho, Tswana, Xhosa and Zulu. He was working full-time as a postman when he passed the Cape civil service certificate examination in 1895. His knowledge of both European and African languages then allowed him to serve as an interpreter and clerk in the Mafeteng magistrate's office. During the Boer War he was an interpreter and signalman for the British Army while also serving as a war correspondent. From 1901 to 1908 he edited the weekly journal, *Koranta ea beloana* (The Tswana Gazette). Moving to

Kimberley in 1912, he published and edited a new paper, the *Tsala ea batho* (Friend of the People). He was elected the first secretary-general of the African National Congress (ANC), then more generally known as the South African Native National Congress. He was a member of the small delegation which travelled to Great Britain in 1914 vainly protesting against the racist policies of the South African government. While his colleagues returned home at once, Plaatje stayed on, lecturing and writing until the end of World War I. He travelled widely throughout Europe and North America at that time, trying to draw international attention to the plight of South African Blacks and he also attended the first Pan African Congress organized by W.E.B. Du Bois at Paris in 1919. Returning to Kimberley in 1920, Plaatje founded the Brotherhood Society dedicated to the improvement of race relations in South Africa and was instrumental in forcing the government to improve working conditions in the mines and on the plantations. He also toured the Congo during the 1920s and created a positive impression on the Congolese. Such was the respect in which he came to be held in Kimberley that, in celebration of his 50th birthday in 1928, he was rewarded with a plot of land purchased by local Blacks out of gratitude for his efforts on their behalf. Plaatje died on 19 June 1932. His legacy included several scholarly works, such as *Native Life in South Africa* (1916), *Sechuana Proverbs with Literal Translations and Their European Equivalents* (1916), and *A Sechuana Phonetic Reader*. His fine novel, *Mhudi*, appeared in 1930 and a more serious pamphlet, *The Mote and the Beam*, in 1920. Plaatje also translated several Shakespeare plays into Tswana.

POITIER, Sidney

This famous American actor, film director and activist was born in Miami, Florida, on 20 February 1927 and raised mainly in Nassau in the Bahamas. His Excellency Sir Sidney Poitier KBE consciously defied racial stereotyping and gave a new dramatic credibility for black actors to mainstream film audiences in the Western world. After many odd jobs in Miami and New York City as well as a stint in the US Army, he became the janitor of the American Negro Theatre. It was there that he learnt the trade that changed his entire life. Beginning with many small parts in Broadway plays, he shifted to motion pictures and became an important film star and remained one of the finest in the world for almost forty years. He performed brilliantly in such movies as *Cry, the Beloved Country* (1952); *The Blackboard Jungle* (1955); *Edge of the City* (1957); *The Defiant Ones* (1958); *Porgy and Bess* (1959); *A Raisin in the Sun* (1961); *Lilies of the Field* (1963); *The Greatest Story Ever Told* (1965); *To Sir, With Love* (1967); *Guess Who's Coming to Dinner* (1967); *For the Love of Ivy* (1968); *They call Me MISTER Tibbs* (1970); *Let's Do It Again* (1975); *Shoot to Kill* (1988) and *The Jackal* (1997). For his stellar performance in *Lilies of the Field*, Poitier became the first African-American to win an Academy Award as best actor. He has also directed such films as *Buck and the Preacher* (1972); *A Warm December* (1973); *A Piece of the Action* (1977); *Stir Crazy* (1980); *Fast Forward* (1985); and *Ghost Dad* (1990). As the son of Bahamian parents, he was knighted by Queen Elizabeth II of England in 1974. The Bahamian government also appointed him a non-resident ambassador to Japan and to the United Nations. Poitier was the recipient of numerous awards, including the Lifetime Achievement Award from the Screen Actors Guild and an Honorary Academy Award for his lifetime achievement in the film industry from the Academy of Motion Picture Arts and Sciences.

PORTER, James Amos

James Amos Porter was born in Baltimore, Maryland, in 1905. He became a distinguished educator, painter and art historian. Educated at Howard University, Columbia University and New York University as well as at the Sorbonne (Paris, France), he eventually spent forty years as professor of art at Howard University where he left an indelible influence on more than one generation of African-American artists. His own work included *Woman Holding a Jug*, a well-known portrait; *Cuban Bus*; and a portrait of his wife, *Dorothy Porter*, who was herself a famous librarian. A foremost authority on African, Cuban and Haitian art, Porter also published *Modern Negro Art*, a standard reference work, in 1943. He died in 1971.

POTTER, Philip

Born in Roseau, Dominica, on 19 August 1921, Revd Philip Alford Potter became the third general secretary of the World Council of Churches (WCC) in 1972. He had received his BD from the University of London in 1948 and his master of theology in 1954. A Methodist, Potter began attending meetings of the WCC as early as 1948 and consistently called for a restructuring of its committees to allow a greater degree of involvement from the developing countries. He also saw the Christian church as an integral force in society with important social and political responsibilities. He served as a Methodist pastor in Haiti from 1950 to 1954, secretary of the WCC's youth department from 1954 to 1960, and field secretary for Africa and the West Indies for the British Methodist Missionary Society from 1960 to 1967. When Potter was elected to guide the WCC in 1972, that organization then comprised more than 260 Anglican, Orthodox and Protestant churches in ninety countries and territories, representing more than 400 million Christians.

POWELL, Adam Clayton, Jr

Himself the son of a distinguished clergyman and author of the same name, Revd Adam Clayton Powell, Jr became an important religious and political leader. Born in New Haven, Connecticut, on 29 November 1908, he was educated at Colgate and Columbia Universities before receiving his DD from Shaw University. After serving for some years as a minister of the Abyssinian Baptist Church in New York City, he was elected to the New York City Council in 1941 and to the US Congress in 1945, retaining his seat in that legislature for eleven consecutive terms. Always a staunch supporter of civil rights legislation, he was able to promote the African-American cause even more effectively while serving as chairman of the House Committee on Education and Labor from 1960 to 1967. Powell was largely instrumental in the passage of such bills as the 1961 Minimum Wage Act, the Manpower Development and Training Act, and the anti-poverty legislation. He died on 4 April 1972. Five years earlier, he had published a book of sermons, entitled *Keep the Faith, Baby!*

POWELL, Colin

Gen Colin Luther Powell, the son of Jamaican immigrants, was born in New York City on 5 April 1937. He graduated from the City College of New York in 1958 and was commissioned a second lieutenant in the US Army. He served in Vietnam in 1962-63 and 1968-69. In 1971 he received an MBA from George Washington University. Powell commanded a battalion in South Korea in 1973-74 and worked in the Pentagon in 1974-75. He was promoted to the rank of colonel in 1975 and studied at the National War College before achieving the rank of major general in 1979 when he became senior military assistant to the secretary of defence. He commanded the 4th Infantry Division at Ft Collins, Colorado, in 1981-83. In 1986, Powell became a lieutenant general assigned to the V Corps in Europe. In 1987 he became secretary of defence and in 1989 took over the Army Forces Command. Four months after being made a four-star general in April 1989, he was appointed chairman of the Joint Chiefs of Staff, thus becoming the first black officer nominated to the highest military post in the United States. He then played a leading role in the invasion of Panama in December 1989 and of Iraq in the following winter. Powell retired from the army in 1993 and became more active in politics. Appointed secretary of state in President Bush's administration (2001), he is one of the leading forces in the Republican government although his support of abortion rights and affirmative action has often placed him at variance with the majority of his party. In 2004 he was replaced by Condoleezza Rice as secretary of state.

PREMPEH I

This Asante ruler is best remembered for his cruel maltreatment at the hands of the British authorities during the twentieth century. Born around 1872, he ascended to the throne in 1888 and quickly subdued rival claimants while expanding Asante power in all directions. This success alarmed the British, especially since Prempeh I refused to accept a British resident in Kumasi, declaring that the Asante would remain independent as of old and on friendly terms with all Europeans. The British therefore sent several hostile expeditions to Kumasi in the 1890s and banished Prempeh to the Seychelles Islands in 1901. He was not allowed to return to Kumasi until 1924. Eventually the British discovered that it was almost impossible to govern the Asante indirectly without Prempeh's co-operation - such was the respect in which he was held by the West Africans. He was therefore restored in 1926. Prempeh I died in 1931. His career illuminated the cruelty, injustice and arrogance of the British authorities during the colonial period.

PRESCOD, Samuel Jackman

The Rt Excellent Samuel Jackman Prescod was named one of the ten National Heroes of Barbados in 1998. Born of mixed parentage in 1805, he became a vigorous proponent of social justice and racial equality. He denounced slavery and the apprenticeship system with equal violence and played no small part in the abandonment of the latter (in 1838) after a four-year experiment. He subjected all the class legislation to very critical analysis and urged the ex-slaves, mulattoes and poorer Whites to co-operate to compel the wealthy and selfish élite to modify the one-sided political, economic and social structures of the day. For a while he succeeded in forming a Liberal Party in the House of Assembly after becoming, in 1843, the first Black to be win a seat in a Barbadian election. Almost all of the progressive legislation passed for the next quarter of a century bore his stamp. His newspaper, *The Liberal*, which he personally edited and published after 1837, became a powerful medium for the diffusion of his philosophy and ideas. These were very radical in the context of their time. He believed, for instance, in such principles as universal suffrage, a national system of free education, a fiscal system that bore less heavily on the masses and a more humane master-servant relationship. His newspaper became a driving force in the development of black consciousness and black empowerment. Prescod died in 1871 after years of distinguished service in the House of Assembly and as a judge in the island's Court of Appeal. His image on the Barbados $20 bill serves as a lasting memorial to a hero whom many historians regard as perhaps the greatest Barbadian of them all.

PRESTON, Richard

Revd Richard Preston was born a slave in Virginia, in the United States, but escaped in 1822 to join his mother in Nova Scotia, Canada. After attending a Baptist school there, he furthered his education in England and was ordained a priest in 1832. Returning to Halifax, he organized an abolitionist society and founded Baptist churches in Annapolis, Bear River, Digby, Hammond's Plains, Salmon River and Weymouth. In 1842, he organized an Anglo-African Mutual Improvement and Aid Association, and in 1846 he also established a Negro Abolition Society. In 1854 he convened a conference of Nova Scotian black ministers in Granville Mountain which directly led to the establishment of the African Baptist Association of Nova Scotia. Preston thus created a viable and lasting church organization while stressing interracial cooperation. Most of his other projects, however, ultimately languished. He died in 1861.

PRICE, George Cadle

George Cadle Price, who served as the head of the Belizean government from 1961 to 14 December 1984, was born in Belize City, British Honduras, on 15 January 1919. He was educated at the Holy Redeemer Parish School and St John's College in Belize City before furthering his education at the St Augustine Seminary at Mississippi (United States). Returning to British Honduras in 1940, Price worked briefly as a librarian before serving as a private secretary from 1942 to 1955 to Robert Sidney Turton, one of the first elected members to the British Honduras Legislative Council. In 1947, Price was elected a member of the Belize City Council, on Turton's prompting, and in 1950 became a founding member of the People's United Party (PUP). The PUP, campaigning for a more liberal franchise and a greater degree of local autonomy for British Hondurans, gradually became the most vibrant political organization in the colony. In 1961, when British Honduras was allowed internal self-government, the PUP won its first truly general elections and Price became its first chief minister. He assumed the title of premier when a ministerial system was introduced in 1964 and he became the country's first prime minister when it achieved its political independence in 1981 and changed its name to Belize. Price offered Belize effective leadership during some of its most critical years and taught his community a great deal about political agitation and organization. He was replaced as prime minister by Manuel Esquivel in 1984, but he resumed the post in 1989, serving until 1991 when his party lost the elections again. In 1982 he became a member of the United Kingdom's Privy Council and in 2000 was the first person to receive Belize's highest honour, the Order of National Hero, for the prominent role he played in leading his country to independence.

PRICE-MARS, Jean

Generally acknowledged as Haiti's brightest scholar, Jean Price-Mars was born in Grande Rivière du Nord on 15 October 1876. He studied at Cap-Haïtien at the Collège Grégoire and at the Lycée Pétion of Port-au-Prince before completing his education at the Universities of Haiti and Paris, France. He pursued a medical degree while also studying the social sciences, especially anthropology which was quite new in those days. Following his graduation he was invited to join the diplomatic service and spent some time representing Haiti in places as far apart as Berlin (Germany) and Washington, D.C. (United States). While in the USA he was often shocked by the American attitudes towards Blacks and was much influenced by such African-American intellectuals as W.E.B. Du Bois and Booker T. Washington. Returning to Haiti, Price-Mars was a professor of secondary education from 1918 to 1930, became a senator and helped to found the Institut d'Ethnologie of Haiti of which he became the first director. He wrote prolifically on many subjects and went far towards giving the Haitians a sense of pride in their African heritage which had hitherto been seen as inferior to the civilization promoted and encouraged by the French. His works, in fact, had a world-wide impact as they helped to inspire such Francophone Blacks as Aimé Césaire, Birago Diop and Léopold Senghor in their promotion of 'négritude'. Price-Mars' germinal ethnographic essays included *Ainsi parla l'oncle* (1928), *Une étape de l'évolution haitienne* (1929), *Formation ethnique, folklore et culture du peuple haitien* (1939), *De Saint Domingue à Haiti, essai sur la culture, les arts et la littérature* (1949), *Le processus d'une culture* (1952), *L'Afrique noire et ses peuples* (1952), *Les survivances africaines dans la communauté haitienne* (1953), and *Le bilan des études ethnologiques en haiti et le cycle du nègre* (1954). On education, Price-Mars produced such studies as *La vocation de l'élite* (1919) and *Le problème de l'analphabétisme et sa solution* (1943). He wrote, in addition, such important biographical works as *Le sentiment de la valeur personelle chez Henri Christophe en fonction de son role de chef* (1934), *Jean-Pierre Boyer Bazelais et le drame de Miragoâne* (1948), *Silhouettes de nègres et de négrophiles* (1960), *Vilbrun Guillaume Sam, ce méconnu* (1961), and *Anténor Firmin* (published posthumously in 1978). Price-Mars also wrote some excellent history in *Le sentiment de la liberté chez les nègres de Saint Domingue* (1939), *La contribution haitienne à la lutte des Amériques pour les libertés humaines* (1942), and *La République d'Haiti et la république Dominicaine, 2 vols* (1953). He wrote countless articles on a variety of subjects and left dozens of manuscripts with unfinished novelettes and short stories. When he died on 1 March 1969 at the advanced age of ninety-two, Haiti had lost arguably its greatest and most versatile genius.

PRIMUS, Pearl

Pearl Primus was born in Trinidad, British West Indies, on 29 November 1919. She moved with her family to the United States when she was three, received a BSc from Hunter College in New York City, and then encountered difficulties finding a suitable job because of her colour. This drove her into a dancing career, for which Blacks were then thought to be best suited. She became a renowned dancer, choreographer and teacher, pioneering the use of African elements in her works and leaving a significant influence on such famous dancers and choreographers as Alvin Ailey and Donald McKayle. Her first major work, *African Ceremonial*, was performed in 1944 and won her a Rosenwald fellowship which allowed her to do extensive research in Africa. Eventually in 1978 she achieved a PhD in African and Caribbean studies. In the late 1940s, she created *Strange Fruit*, depicting a woman's reaction to lynching, and *The Negro Speaks of Rivers*, portraying the harsh realities of life along the Mississippi. Another classic, *Michael, Row Your Boat Ashore*, dealt in 1979 with the mother of a church-bombing victim in Birmingham, Alabama. After dancing and choreographing until 1980, Primus directed a Black Studies programme at the State University of New York at Buffalo. Her numerous awards included the National Medal of the Arts in 1991. She died on 29 October 1994.

PURVIS, Robert

Born on 4 August 1810 in Charleston, South Carolina, Robert Purvis became one of the driving forces behind the abolitionist movement in the United States. After graduating from Amherst College, he helped William Lloyd Garrison establish the American Anti-Slavery Society and signed its *Declaration of Sentiments* in 1833. He also helped to establish the Library Company of Colored People in that year. In 1838 he drafted the famous *Appeal of Forty Thousand Citizens Threatened with Disfranchisement* in support of a movement to repeal the recent law which barred Blacks from voting. In 1836, he visited England to do some lobbying on behalf of the American Anti-Slavery Society. Throughout his adult life, he was very active in the Underground Railroad and is thought to have assisted about 9000 slaves in gaining their freedom. Robert Purvis died on 15 April 1898.

QOBOZA, Percy

This South African journalist was one of the most outspoken critics of apartheid and one of his country's most influential black newspaper editors. Born in Johannesburg on 17 January 1938, Qoboza studied theology in Basutoland (now Lesotho) before turning to journalism and writing for the *World* in 1963. He became the editor in 1974 and transformed the *World* into the largest circulation black newspaper in South Africa. In 1975 he was awarded a Nieman fellowship at Harvard University and he returned home with a much more hostile attitude towards the racist government of his country. His support for the Soweto rebellion led to the banning of his newspaper in 1977 and to his own imprisonment without charge or trial until 1978. His case attracted worldwide attention and he was awarded the Golden Pen of Freedom by the International Federation of Newspaper Publishers. Qoboza worked briefly as editor of the *Post* and, when that too was shut down by the South African government, he accepted a position as guest editor of the *Washington Star* in the United States. In 1985, he returned to South Africa as the editor of the *Johannesburg City Press*. He died on 17 January 1988 (his 50th birthday).

QUAISON-SACKEY, Alex

Born on 9 August 1924 at Winneba in the Gold Coast, Alex Quaison-Sackey attended Achimota College before furthering his studies at Oxford University in England. He was one of the first diplomats appointed by Ghana after that country achieved its political independence in 1957. He served in the Ghanaian High Commissioner's Office in London (England) and in 1959 was assigned to the United Nations as Ghana's chief delegate. At the age of forty, he became (in 1964) the youngest man ever elected president of the UN General Assembly and the first African native to fill that post. He was also Ghana's ambassador to Cuba from 1961 to 1965. He served as foreign minister briefly under Kwame Nkrumah but disappeared from Ghanaian politics after Nkrumah's overthrow in 1966. He later wrote a memoir, entitled *Africa Unbound*. Quaison-Sackey died in 1992.

QUAQUE, Philip

Revd Philip Quaque was the first African to be ordained as a priest in the Church of England. Born in 1741, he was the son of a Fante chief in the Gold Coast and was taken to England to be trained as a missionary at the expense of the Society for the Propagation of the Gospel (SPG). In 1765 he was ordained first as a deacon and then as a priest and was sent as a missionary, catechist and teacher back to his native country. He then spent the next fifty years in the service of the SPG, preaching in the Gold Coast. His son, Samuel Quaque, who was also educated in England, assisted him in his later years. Revd Philip Quaque died in 1816.

QUARLES, Benjamin

One of the most prolific writers among African-American historians, Dr Benjamin Quarles was born on 23 January 1904 in Boston, Massachusetts. Altogether, in a span of more than fifty years, he produced 10 books, 23 articles, 70 shorter pieces, 11 chapters in books, 26 encyclopaedia entries, 5 documentary sources, 12 introductions to reprints, and 170 book reviews. He received his BA from Shaw University in 1931, and his MA and PhD degrees from the University of Wisconsin. Following stints as a lecturer at Shaw University and Dillard University, he became professor of history and chairman of the department at Morgan State College in Baltimore, Maryland. In addition to the numerous articles he published in scholarly journals, Quarles wrote such well-known books as *Frederick Douglass* (1948), *The Negro in the Civil War* (1948), *The Negro in the American Revolution* (1961), *Lincoln and the Negro* (1962), *Blacks on John Brown* (1972), *Black History's Antebellum Origins* (1979) and *Black Mosaic* (1988). Most of these important works have enjoyed multiple editions. Professor Benjamin Quarles died, at the age of ninety-two, on 16 November 1996.

QUARTEY-PAPAFIO, Benjamin

Dr Benjamin William Quartey-Papafio was a noted Gold Coast physician and administrator during the early years of the twentieth century. Born in Accra on 25 June 1859, he was educated at schools in Sierra Leone and universities in the United Kingdom where he qualified as a medical doctor in 1886. He became the first African physician to be appointed to the colonial medical service, but was consistently denied promotion on purely racial grounds. He therefore retired from the colonial service in 1905 and entered politics, serving on the Accra Municipal Council during 1909-12. An influential leader of the Aborigines' Rights Protection Society (ARPS), Quartey-Papafio was one of its delegates who went to London in 1912 to lobby against the Forest Lands Bill of 1911. He was appointed to the Gold Coast Legislative Council in 1919 and became one of the most vocal advocates of social, political and economic reforms. He had earlier helped to found the Accra Grammar School in the 1890s. Quartey-Papafio died on 14 September 1924, shortly after having been awarded an OBE.

QUIST, Emmanuel

Born at Christiansborg on 21 May 1880, Sir Emmanuel Charles Quist became the first native president of a legislative body in British colonial Africa. He served as president of the Gold Coast Legislative Council during 1949-50 and 1951-57. The son of Revd Carl Quist, he was educated at Mission Schools in Christiansborg and Akuporon. He taught briefly in the Gold Coast before studying law in the United Kingdom. After being called to the bar in 1913, Quist established a successful practice in Accra where he became the first African to be appointed a Crown Counsel. In 1948 he acted as a puisne judge. He also served on the Accra Town Council during 1919-29 and on the Gold Coast Legislative Council from 1925 to 1934. When the Gold Coast Legislative Assembly came into being in 1951, Quist became its first speaker. He died on 28 February 1959. His career had been truly brilliant, marked by the award of the OBE in 1942 and a knighthood in 1952.

RAINY, William

Born in Dominica, British West Indies, around 1819, William Rainy emigrated to Sierra Leone and worked in the customs department during 1844-47. He then studied law at the Inner Temple in the United Kingdom and returned to Freetown to practice in 1850. He became a distinguished barrister devoted to fighting against racial prejudice in West Africa and was for many years the leading organizer of local petitions protesting against the arrogant conduct of colonial officials. Rainy also established a number of newspapers, including *The Sierra Leone Observer*, *The African Interpreter and Advocate*, and *The West African Liberator*. In 1867 he served as Sierra Leone's first delegate at the Anti-Slavery Conference held in Paris, France. This consistent and passionate defender of African rights died in 1878.

RAMAILA, Epafras

Revd Epafras Mogagabise Ramaila is considered by many to be the father of Sepedi (Northern Sotho) literature. Born on 30 January 1897 in Transvaal, South Africa, he was educated at the Botshabelo Mission Station and the Mission's Training School. Following his graduation as a teacher and an evangelist in 1915, he taught for five years at the Lydenburg Mission School and was then appointed principal of the Saron Lutheran School in the Rustenburg District. He administered other schools in Transvaal before being ordained in 1944. Ramaila was a prolific writer who contributed numerous essays and articles to a variety of journals while editing the magazine, *Mogwara wa babaso*, for several years. His major works included such stories as *Molomatsebe* (1951) and *Taukobong* (1953); a novel, *Tsakata* (1953); a biography, *Tsa bophelo bya moruti Abraham Serote* 1865-1930 (1931); two historical studies, *Ditaba tsa South Africa* (1938) and *Setloxo sa batau* (1938); and some excellent poetry in *Direto* (1956) and *Seriti sa Thabantsho* (1960). Ramaila died on 28 August 1962.

RANDOLPH, A. Philip

Asa Philip Randolph, who made an enormous contribution both to the civil rights struggle and the trade union movement in the United States, was born in Crescent City, Florida, on 15 April 1889. He worked at a series of odd jobs while studying at the City College of New York. He then taught for some years at the New York Rand School of Social Science. An ardent socialist, Randolph helped to found the weekly, *Messenger*, in 1917 and began to deliver socialist messages in a series of lectures all across the country. In 1925 he organized the Brotherhood of Sleeping Car Porters (BSCP) which succeeded, after ten years of determined effort, in negotiating a collective bargaining agreement with the Pullman Palace Car Company. He was also instrumental in persuading President Franklin D. Roosevelt to form the Fair Employment Practice Committee (FEPC) in 1941. In 1942, he was himself appointed to the New York Housing Authority. Appalled by the blatant discrimination in the US Armed Forces even during World War II, Randolph founded the League for Nonviolent Civil Disobedience in the Armed Forces in 1947. When the American Federation of Labor (AFL) merged with the Congress of Industrial Organizations (CIO) in 1955, he was appointed to the AFL-CIO executive council. In 1957 he became vice-president of the union and in 1960 founded the Negro American Labor Council, over which he presided until 1966. He was also the founder and president of the A. Randolph Philip Institute of New York City aimed at increasing the educational and employment opportunities for minority youth. One of Randolph's greatest triumphs came on 28 August 1963 when he acted as director of the historic 'March on Washington' which involved more than 200,000 people and was easily the largest civil rights demonstration in US history. He died on 16 May 1979, highly respected by all segments of American society. His numerous honours and distinctions included an honorary doctorate from Howard University in 1941, the NAACP Spingarn Medal in 1942 and the prestigious Medal of Freedom from President Lynden B. Johnson in 1964.

RANSOME-KUTI, Funmilayo

Funmilayo Ransome-Kuti was an ardent Nigerian activist, nationalist, feminist and teacher who challenged both the imperial and post-colonial governments of her day in a relentless quest for racial, gender and ethnic equality and for social justice. Born in Abeokuta, on 25 October 1900, she first came to prominence when she formed the Abeokuta's Ladies Club while serving as the head teacher of the Abeokuta Girls' Grammar School in the 1920s. This gradually evolved into the Abeokuta's Women's Union (AWU) over which she presided until her death some fifty years later. The AWU became a huge due-paying organization with some 20,000 members and led a memorable anti-tax protest in 1947. In time it became the Nigerian Women's Union (NWU), prosperous enough to hold a two-day conference in 1953 which attracted over 400 delegates from fifteen provinces. Funmilayo also gave great support to the West African Students' Union (WASU) which operated in the United Kingdom during the inter-war period, acting with her husband as its agents in Nigeria raising funds and distributing its pamphlets. She herself made a visit to England in 1947 and made a number of speeches radical enough in a feminist sense to upset some of her Nigerian brethren. By publicly denouncing the corruption of succeeding military administrations, she suffered constant persecution and harassment. Eventually, on 18 February 1978, her home was raided by the police and armed forces. She and her family were severely beaten and the property was razed to the ground. Left in shock, one of Nigeria's greatest female champions lost her fighting spirit and died a few weeks later.

RAWLINS, Micheline

When the Hon Madam Justice Micheline Rawlins was appointed to the Ontario Court of Justice in 1992, she became the first black woman to receive such an appointment in that province. She had previously worked for six years as Assistant Crown Attorney in Kent County, Chatham, Ontario. Born in Montreal, Quebec, she received a BA from McGill University in 1974 and an LLB from the University of Windsor in 1978. She sat on the Windsor Board of Education during 1982-84 and on the Board of Governors of the University of Windsor during the 1990s. Madam Justice Rawlins also served as the Ontario Court of Justice representative on the National Judicial Council Advisory on Education and co-chaired the Ontario Court of Justice Conference on Race Relations in 1996. She is the recipient of several honours and awards.

RAYMOND, Claude

A Haitian military leader, Claude Raymond was born in 1929. He rose to the rank of general in the national army and was its chief of staff during the reign of François Duvalier. He was appointed defence and interior minister by 'Papa Doc's' son, Jean-Claude Duvalier. When the latter was forced into exile in 1986, Raymond was rejected as a presidential candidate and later arrested on suspicion of plotting to overthrow the new government. He died in prison in Port-au-Prince on 9 February 2000. He had been held without trial, despite insufficient evidence, and in the face of international protests for many years.

RAYMOND, Julien

Julien Raymond, the distinguished Haitian lawyer, administrator and author, is often called the 'Father of French Negro Writers'. Born of a free and well-to-do family in Cap-Français (now Cap-Haïtien) in 1743, he was sent to France at a young age to receive his education. Graduating as a lawyer, he practised privately in Paris before returning to Saint Domingue (now Haiti) to fight for the civil and political rights of the free Blacks. In 1796 he was chosen a member of the third Civil Commission to apply the revolutionary French decrees in Saint Domingue. On 7 October 1801 he died during Toussaint Louverture's government after having made a significant contribution to the

Haitian independence movement during the 1790s. He was the author of numerous addresses, papers, essays and public letters.

REDMAN, Don

Donald Matthew Redman was born in Piedmont, West Virginia, on 29 July 1900. A brilliant saxophonist and composer, he became a very important pioneer figure in the evolution of the large jazz orchestra. A child prodigy, he played the trumpet at three, joined a band at six, and studied composition, harmony and all the orchestral instruments while still very young. Following his graduation from the Boston and Detroit conservatories, he made his first recording in 1923 in the Fletcher Henderson orchestra. The first important composer/arranger in jazz history, Redman achieved fame in the 1920s as a brilliant instrumentalist on several types of saxophone, and he recorded with Louis Armstrong and other great stars of the period. During the 1940s he led one of the greatest of all black orchestras, and in the following decade served as musical director to the singer-actress, Pearl Bailey. In 1954, he appeared in her Broadway musical, *House of Flowers*. Redman's major compositions included *Cherry* and his well-known theme song, *Chant of the Weeds*. He died on 30 November 1964.

REGIS, Gregory

The Hon Mr Justice Gregory Regis was appointed to the Ontario Court of Justice in 1999 and presides in the Durham Region. Born in St Lucia, West Indies, he emigrated to Canada in 1974 and completed his education at Ryerson University, where he achieved a degree in journalism, and at York University in Toronto, where he gained his LLB. After working as a journalist with the Canadian Broadcast Corporation (CBC) in both radio and television, he was admitted to the Ontario bar in 1985. He served as the executive director of the Jane-Finch Legal Clinic for some years before joining the Ontario Ministry of the Attorney General as an assistant crown attorney. A former chair of Caribana (the Caribbean annual festival in Toronto), Mr Justice Regis has given yeoman service to several community organizations in Ontario.

REID, Ira

Dr Ira de Augustine Reid was born in Clifton Forge, Virginia, in 1901. After graduating with his BA from Morehouse College and MA from the University of Pittsburgh, he worked for some years with the New York Urban League before completing his PhD at Columbia University in 1939. Reid became an eminent sociologist who wrote a number of important books on black America. His major publications included *The Negro*

Population of Denver (1929), *Social Conditions of the Negro in the Hill District of Pittsburgh, Pennsylvania* (1930), *The Negro in New Jersey* (1932), *The Problem of Child Dependency Among Negroes* (1933), *The Negro Community in Baltimore* (1935), The *Urban Negro Worker in the United States* (1938), *The Negro Immigrant* (1939), and *In a Minor Key: Negro Youth in Story and Fact* (1940). Ira Reid died in 1968. He had served as chairman of the department of sociology and anthropology at Haverford College in Pennsylvania from 1947 to 1966.

REINDORF, Carl Christian

Born on 31 May 1834, Dr Carl Christian Reindorf became an eminent Gold Coast evangelist, scholar, physician, trader and historian. He is best remembered as the author of the classic *A History of the Gold Coast and Asante* which was published in 1895. During the 1860s he ran a prosperous coffee farm near Aburi. He then served as headmaster of the Osu Middle School from 1866 to 1869. He started the Basel Mission in Accra in 1883 and wrote a number of Christian hymns in Ga, also producing a translation of his seminal work in that African language. In 1912 he helped to produce the first Ga Bible. Reindorf died on 1 July 1917 after a truly exceptional career in which he achieved success in a wide range of fields.

REMOND, Lenox

Charles Lenox Remond was born in Salem, Massachusetts, in 1810. Establishing a fine reputation as an eloquent speaker in his youth, he was recruited in the early 1830s by the Massachusetts Anti-Slavery Society on whose behalf he delivered a number of fiery speeches at public meetings across the north-eastern United States. In 1840 he went with William Lloyd Garrison as a Massachusetts delegate to the World's Anti-Slavery Convention in London, England. He remained in the United Kingdom for nineteen months lecturing about the evils of slavery. Remond, who was the first black American public speaker on abolition, tended to be more militant than his white colleagues and called unequivocally for slave uprisings to compel and secure emancipation. During the Civil War, he recruited black soldiers for the Union Army and later became a clerk in a Boston custom house. He died in 1882.

REMOND, Sarah Parker

Born in Salem, Massachusetts, on 6 June 1826, Sarah Parker Remond was the younger sister of Charles Lenox Remond. Like him, she became a vigorous agent of the Massachusetts Anti-Slavery Society and was the first black female abolitionist to make a lecture tour of the United Kingdom. After touring the United States with great success for two years, she emigrated to England in 1859 and raised huge sums not only for the anti-slavery movement but for the union cause in the American Civil War of 1861-65. While there, she also resumed her studies at the Bedford College for Ladies (now part of the University of London). Leaving England in 1866, Remond travelled to Italy where she spent the remainder of her life. She entered the Santa Maria Nuova Hospital in Florence as a medical student at the age of forty-two. She then practised medicine there until her death on 13 December 1894.

REVELS, Hiram

Born a free man in Fayetteville County, North Carolina, on 1 September 1822, Revd Hiram Rhoades Revels became the first African-American to serve in the US Senate when he was elected to that body in 1870. Educated at a seminary in Indiana and at Knox College in Galesburg, Illinois, he was ordained a priest in the African Methodist Episcopal (AME) Church in 1845. He worked among Blacks in the Midwest and elsewhere for a few years before settling in Baltimore, Maryland, where he was a pastor and a principal of a school for Blacks. During the Civil War, Revels recruited Blacks for the Union cause and himself served as chaplain of a regiment. After the war, he did his utmost to eliminate racial discrimination and injustice and, although he remained a senator only for one year, had much to do with the defeat of an amendment that would have ensured segregation in the public schools of the District of Columbia. In 1876, he became editor of the *Southwestern Christian Advocate*, but devoted most of his later years to Alcorn State University in Lorman, Mississippi, which he served as president. Hiram Revels died on 16 January 1901.

RICE, Condoleezza

Condoleezza Rice is an accomplished administrator, educator, diplomat and scholar. She was born in Birmingham, Alabama, on 14 November 1954. She completed her education at the Universities of Denver and Notre Dame, achieving a PhD in international studies in 1981. She lectured at Stanford University during the early 1980s and won an award for the excellence of her teaching. In 1986 she became an assistant to the Joint Chiefs of Staff on nuclear strategy and later served as a special assistant to the president. Returning to Stanford in 1991, Rice proved herself an effective provost by balancing the university's budget while revamping the curriculum for undergraduates. She left that institution in 1999 to serve as foreign policy adviser to the Bush campaign and was named head of the National Security Council upon his election as president. She was the first woman to hold this office. She has become the president's principal adviser on foreign affairs and, in 2004, succeeded Colin Powell as secretary of state, becoming the highest ranking black woman in the history of the United States.

RICHARDS, Lloyd

Dr Lloyd Richards was born in Toronto, Ontario, on 29 June 1919 but moved with his parents to Detroit, Michigan, in his youth. He served in the United States Army Air Force during 1943-44 and was one of the first black pilot-trainees. He completed his studies in drama when the war was over and became a Master Teacher in the actor training programme at New York University's School of Arts. He later served as a professor of theatre and cinema at Hunter College, New York, before being appointed Dean of Yale University School of Drama in 1979. Dr Richards was the first black dean in the Ivy League schools and remained in that post until 1991. As dean at Yale and Artistic Director of the National Playwrights Conference at the Eugene O'Neill Memorial Theatre for thirty-eight years, he trained and influenced a number of famous playwrights, leaving an indelible impression on American drama and film. One of his greatest successes was the 1984 production of August Wilson's *Ma Rainey's Black Bottom*. He directed seven successive instalments of Wilson's multi-part chronicle of African American life, including *Fences*, *Joe Turner's Come and Gone* and *The Piano Lesson*. Among his numerous TV credits was *Roots: The Next Generation*. For many years Dr Richards was perhaps the most influential figure in modern American theatre. He was elevated by Yale University to the status of Professor Emeritus in 1991. The list of his other awards and distinctions is most extraordinary, including as it does almost twenty honorary doctorates. He received the National Medal of Arts from President Clinton and was inducted into Theatre Hall of Fame in 1990. *Fences* also won him a Tony Award as the best director in 1986. Lloyd Richards died on 29 June 2006. (his 87th birthday).

RICHARDS, Viv

Sir Isaac Vivian Alexander Richards, a famous cricketer who was born in Antigua on 7 March 1952, was one of the greatest batsmen that the world has yet seen. Playing for the West Indies during 1974-91, he amassed 8,540 runs, including 24 centuries, in 121 international contests. He was a most successful captain, leading his team to 27 victories in 50 Tests while losing only eight. He remains the only West Indian skipper never to have lost an international series. A brilliant fieldsman, Richards also held 122 Test catches.As a slow off-break bowler, he captured 32 wickets at this level of competition. In a first-class career that encompassed 507 matches, he scored over 36,000 runs at an average of almost 50 runs per innings and registered 114 centuries. He was chosen by *Wisden Cricketers' Almanack 2000* as one of the top five players of the twentieth century. Following his retirement, Sir Vivian became a cricket coach and commentator and was knighted for his services to the sport.

RICHMOND, Bill

Bill Richmond was the first black boxer to gain international recognition. Born a slave in New York in 1763, he was taken to England as a servant by the Duke of Northumberland who sent him to school in Yorkshire and apprenticed him to a cabinet maker in York. He later moved to London and became a famous pugilist. He won some historic fights against highly ranked boxers like Jack Carter, Jack Holmes, George Maddox and Yossoup, but his most memorable encounter was the loss to the future heavyweight champion, Tom Cribb, in 1805. Richmond used the earnings from his professional bouts to purchase a pub, 'The Horse and Dolphin', in Leicester Square. He also ran a boxing academy and sometimes took part in exhibition matches in London. He died on 28 December 1829.

RILEY, Betty

Born in 1930 in Montreal, Quebec, Betty Riley became a pioneer in TV production featuring Blacks in Canada, and has been honoured by the cities of Montreal and Windsor as well as various levels of government for her important contributions. She began her career in television in 1970, by producing her own programme, *Black Is*, to provide information on black history, politics and culture. She founded the first ever Black Youth Television Network (BYTN) in 1973 to teach black youth how to work with TV equipment and to acquire knowledge about producing and directing. This programme encouraged a number of young Canadian Blacks to consider careers in photojournalism. In 1972, Riley also produced a radio programme at McGill University called *Black Speaks* to provide training in the use of this medium. She was the co-founder and executive director of the Black Community Communication Media Inc. in 1975, and organized the first national Black Media Conference in Canada two years later. Returning to school at the age of fifty, Riley graduated from the University of Windsor with a degree in communication studies in 1984. Remaining in Windsor, Ontario, she created a TV programme, *Building Together*, which ran for three years and allowed youth of diverse cultural backgrounds to work with TV equipment and production. She received a Silver Jubilee Award in 1977 and was proclaimed Windsor's Woman of the Year in 1987. Her numerous honours also included a Governor General 125th Anniversary Medal in 1992.

RILLIEUX, Norbert

Norbert Rillieux was born in New Orleans, Louisiana, on 17 March 1806. After attending local schools he completed his education in France, where he qualified as an engineer. A brilliant student, he was invited to join the teaching staff at L'École Central in Paris in 1830. While there, he earned an international reputation by publishing several scholarly articles on the steam engine. In 1834, Rillieux returned to New Orleans where, after much trial and error, he eventually patented his multiple-effect vacuum evaporation process for refining sugar. He installed this system on many plantations in the United States during the next few years. When he could not, on purely racial grounds, persuade the local government in 1854 to accept his revolutionary method to rid New Orleans of mosquitoes, he left his native town in a huff and returned to France. There, in 1881, he perfected the modern system of refining sugar. His basic technique is now also used to manufacture condensed milk, glue and gelatin. Rillieux died in Paris at the age of eighty eight on 8 October 1894.

RIVE, Richard Moore

Richard Moore Rive was one of black South Africa's most important short-story writers whose works did much to reveal the injustices of the apartheid system. Born in Cape Town on 1 March 1931, he first distinguished himself as a champion hurdler before proceeding to achieve degrees from the University of Cape Town (South Africa), Columbia University (United States)and the University of Oxford (England). He taught at South Peninsula High School and Hewat Training College in Cape Town, while travelling extensively and lecturing in many parts of Europe and the United States. Rive's first novel, *Emergency*, achieved international acclaim when it appeared in 1964 detailing the racial strife which had exploded into violence in the black township of Sharpeville in 1960. It was banned for a time by the South African government.The autobiographical *Writing Black* (1981) and *Buckingham Palace, District Six* (1986) also described in graphic detail the immediate results of governmental cruelty. His best-known collections of short stories were *African Songs* (1963), *Quartet: New Voices from South Africa* (1965) and *Advance, Retreat* (1983). In 1967 he also edited *Modern African Prose*, an anthology of short stories by nineteen African authors. Rive was found murdered in his home in Athlone, South Africa, on 4 June 1989. His books are now required texts in many parts of Africa and have been translated into several languages.

ROBERTS, Louis

Professor Louis W. Roberts was born in Jamestown, New York, on 1 September 1913 and was educated at Fisk University and the University of Michigan. A professor of mathematics and physics at Howard University during the 1940s, he held eleven patents for electronic devices and is the author of important research papers on electromagnetism, optics and microwaves. For many years he served as director of research for Microwave

Associates and director of Energy and Environment at the Transportation System Center in Cambridge, Massachusetts. He also founded and presided over a microwave company of his own. He died on 3 November 1995.

ROBERTS, Thomas Webb

Thomas Webb Roberts was born of middle-income parents in Black Rock, St Michael, Barbados, West Indies, on 27 April 1880. He attended Harrison College and became, in 1897, the very first black student to win the prestigious Barbados Scholarship. This took him to Oxford University, England, where he qualified as a barrister before entering the British Colonial Civil Service. Posted to Ceylon (now Sri Lanka), he eventually became a high court judge. A fine right-handed batsman, Roberts played an important part in the development of cricket in Ceylon both as a player and as an administrator. This distinguished jurist and sportsman served for many years as a source of inspiration to black students in the Caribbean. He died in London, England, on 13 July 1976 at the age of ninety-six.

ROBESON, Paul

This famous actor, singer and political activist was born in Princeton, New Jersey, on 9 April 1898. He was educated at Rutgers University where he received his BA in 1919 after having distinguished himself as an honour student, a football star and an award winner in oratory. He then proceeded to study law at Columbia University where he earned his LLB. As there were then more opportunities for North American Blacks in entertainment than in law, Robeson soon made a name for himself by his performances on the stage in such productions as *All God's Children Got Wings* (1924), *Emperor Jones* (1924), *Showboat* (1925), *Taboo, The Hairy Ape* and *Othello* (1930). His characterization of the title role in Othello in London, England, won high praise indeed, as did the North American production in 1943, which set a new and long-standing record run for a Shakespeare play on Broadway. Robeson starred also in a number of films, including *Sanders of the River* (1935), *Show Boat* (1936), and *The Proud Valley* (1940). He spent most of the 1930s travelling across Europe, denouncing Nazism, entertaining the Loyalist troops during the Spanish Civil War, supporting the Committee to Aid China, and serving as the chairman of the Council on African Affairs. After World War II, Robeson campaigned vigorously for African-American rights but his movements were much restricted by authorities who suspected him of Communist sympathies and revoked his passport in 1950. He was also banned from the stage until 1958. In 1952 he received the Stalin Peace Prize. Between 1958 and 1963, he lived in the Soviet Union where he learned to speak several languages, including Russian and Chinese. Returning to the United States in 1963, he continued his support of the civil rights movement and took part in the Selma, Alabama, March of 1965. Robeson died on 23 January 1976. His autobiography, *Here I Stand*, was published in 1958.

ROBINSON, A.N.R.

The Honourable Arthur Napoleon Raymond Robinson, who rose to the presidency of the republic of Trinidad and Tobago in 1997, was born in Calder Hall, Tobago, on 16 December 1926. Educated at Bishop's High School in Tobago, he obtained his LLB in 1949 from the University of London, England, as an external student. He also completed an MA in philosophy, politics and economics at the University of Oxford, England, in 1955. Returning to Trinidad, Robinson became a founding member of the People's National Movement (PNM) in 1956 and served that party with much distinction for the next fourteen years. In 1958 he was elected to the federal parliament of the British West Indies as a representative of Tobago and became the deputy political leader of the PNM after the dissolution of the British West Indian Federation. Robinson was appointed the first minister of finance of independent Trinidad and Tobago in 1962 and served as minister of external affairs from 1967 to 1970. Philosophical differences with the prime minister, Dr Eric Williams, forced Robinson to secede from the PNM and establish his own party, the Democratic Action Congress, in 1970. In 1985, he convinced the major opposition parties to join a coalition, the National Alliance for Reconstruction (NAR), which won the general elections in 1986. For the next five years Robinson was the first non-PNM prime minister of the republic. The courage and dignity he displayed during the attempted coup of 1990 won him the respect of the majority of his people. He is also well-known for his support of the International Criminal Court and the Caribbean Court of Appeal. He strengthened the position of Tobago within the unitary state by establishing the Tobago House of Assembly in 1980. The Honourable Arthur N.R. Robinson has received a number of awards and distinctions, including an honorary doctorate of laws from the Obafemi Awolowo University of Nigeria, the prestigious Simon Bolivar Award from Venezuela, the Presidential Medal of Honour from the Lutheran University of California, the Distinguished International Criminal Law Award of 1977 and the Distinguished Human Development Award of 1983. He is the author of two books, *The New Frontier and the New Africa*, and *The Mechanics of Independence*.

ROBINSON, Eddie

Edward Gay Robinson, a sharecropper's son, was born on 13 February 1919 in Baker, Louisiana. He became the most successful coach in US College football when, in 1985, he broke Bear Bryant's record of 323 victories. By this time he had sent two of his former players at Grambling State College to the Pro Football Hall of Fame, and no fewer than 211 of them to the National Football League (NFL). Robinson was not only famous for coaching a poor black team to incredible successes on the football field but for his influence as a teacher and role model. He coaxed them through their classes at a remarkable 80% graduation rate. He taught them how to speak in public, how to behave like gentlemen, and how to make a contribution to fields beyond football.

ROBINSON, Frank

Born in Beaumont, Texas, on 31 August 1935, Frank Robinson became the first African-American (in 1975) to be appointed manager of a major-league baseball team. He had been an outstanding player during 1956-74, winning the Most Valuable Player award in both the American and National Leagues. He led the Cincinnati Reds to one pennant in 1961 and the Baltimore Orioles to another in 1966. He ended with a career batting average of .298 and 574 home runs.

ROBINSON, Jackie

John Roosevelt Robinson, born in Cairo, Georgia, on 31 january 1919, is remembered as the first African-American baseball player to be drafted into the major leagues. He appeared for the Brooklyn Dodgers in 1947 and paved the way for countless other Blacks since. Jackie Robinson was educated at Pasadena Junior College and the University of California at Los Angeles where he displayed exceptional skills as an all-round athlete. After serving in World War II in the United States Army, he played professional baseball with the Kansas City Monarchs of the Negro American League. After signing with the Dodgers, he led them to six pennants and one world championship in ten seasons (1947-56), during which he achieved a career batting average of .311, with 734 RBIs and 137 home runs. In 1962 he was inducted into the Baseball Hall of fame. Following his retirement from baseball, Robinson became a keen spokesman and fund-raiser for the civil rights movement. He died, much lamented, on 24 October 1972. His autobiography, *I Never Had It Made*, was published posthumously.

ROBINSON, Sugar Ray

Born Walker Smith Jr in Ailey, Georgia, on 3 May 1921, Sugar Ray Robinson is widely recognized as, 'pound for pound', the greatest boxer of all time. As an amateur, he completed an amazing record of 85-0, including 69 wins by knock out, before turning professional in 1940. He became the first boxer to win a divisional world championship five times when he defeated Carmen Basilio for the middleweight title in 1958. He was also welterweight champion of the world during 1946-51. When he finally retired in 1965, he finished with a record of 175 wins, including 110 knock outs. The majority of his 19 losses had come during the period of his decline after 1958. Robinson was inducted into the International Boxing Hall of Fame and is featured on a 2006 Unites States postage stamp. He died on 12 April 1989.

RODNEY, Walter

When, on 13 June 1980, Walter Anthony Rodney was assassinated, the academic world lost one of its most promising Marxist historians. Born in Guyana and educated at the University of the West Indies, he became an expert in imperial and African history and wrote very critically of European programmes and methods during the age of colonization. He also criticized very harshly the autocratic behaviour of Forbes Burnham, the president of Guyana, and paid the supreme penalty with his life. Suspected of communist sympathies, Rodney was once forbidden to land in Jamaica, where he was scheduled to deliver a speech (1968). His legacy includes such seminal works as *A History of the Upper Guinea Coast 1545-1800* (1970), *How Europe Underdeveloped Africa* (1971), and *A History of the Guyanese Working People 1881-1905* (1981).

ROHLEHR, Gordon

Gordon Rohlehr was born in Guyana in 1942 and is a graduate of the University of the West Indies (Jamaica) and Birmingham University (England). A professor of West Indian Literature at the St Augustine Campus (Trinidad) of the University of the West Indies, Dr Rohlehr is a leading authority on Caribbean folk-songs and oral traditions. He has written several articles and essays on these subjects and is also the author of *Pathfinder: Black Awakening in the Arrivants of Edward Kamau Brathwaite* (1981), *My Strangled City and Other Essays* (1990) and *Calypso and Society in Pre-Independence Trinidad* (1990).

RONALDINHO

Born Ronaldo Assis de Moreira on 21 March 1980 in the Restinga district of Porto Alegre in Brazil, Ronaldinho is generally considered the finest football player of his generation. After playing briefly with Gremio in the Brazilian league, he signed with the French side, Paris Saint-Germain (PSG), in 2001. He was bought from PSG by FC Barcelona for £18 million in 2003 and led that club to five championships in Spanish and European contests in the next three years, scoring 41 goals in 96 games during 2003-06. In 2004, he was adjudged the FIFA Player of the Year and the UEFA Champions League Best Forward of the Year. In 2005 he was voted the

FIFPro World Player of the Year, the European Footballer of the Year, the FIFA Player of the Year, the UEFA Champions League Best Forward of the Year and the World football Player of the Year. He gained selection to the Brazilian team at the age of nineteen after having starred in the Under-17 World championship (which Brazil won) in Egypt in 1997. He made useful contributions to Brazil's triumph in the Copa America 1999, the World Cup of football in 2002 and the Confederations Cup in 2005. In his first 68 international matches, he scored 27 goals for Brazil during 1999-2006. One of the most marketable athletes in the world, Ronaldinho's advertising campaigns and sponsorships have generated almost $58 million annually.

RONALDO

Ronaldo Luiz Nazario de Lima was born in Itaguai, Brazil, on 22 September 1976. He is one of the greatest football players in the history of the sport. He gained selection to his country's team at the age of only eighteen and by 2006 had scored 62 goals in 97 international contests. He played brilliantly for such clubs as Cruzeiro (Brazil), PSV Eindhoven (The Netherlands), Barcelona, Internazionale and Réal Madrid (Spain). He has scored more goals in World Cup football competition (15) than any other player. He has won numerous individual awards, including three FIFA World Player of the Year awards (1996, 1997 and 2002) and has led Brazil to two World Cup championships (in 1994 and 2002).

ROTINI, Ola

Emmanuel Gladstone Olawale Rotini, a noted Nigerian playwright and director, was born in Sapele, Nigeria, on 13 April 1938. Travelling to the United States on the strength of a government scholarship in 1959, he studied fine arts at Boston University and writing at Yale University. While in North America, he wrote *To Stir the God of Iron* (1963) and *Our Husband Has Gone Mad Again* (1966). After achieving his MA from Yale, Rotini returned to Nigeria and lectured at Obafemi Awololo University in Ife-Ife and at the University of Port Harcourt. He was the author of several fine plays, in which English and Nigerian cultural forms and expressions were incorporated. The most important of these works perhaps were *The Gods Are Not to Blame* (1968); *Ovonramwen Nogbaisi* (1971); and *Hopes of the Living Dead* (1985). Rotini taught briefly at Macalester College in St. Paul, Minnesota, before his death in Ife-Ife, Nigeria, on 18 August 2000.

ROUMAIN, Jacques

Born of well-to-do parents in Port-au-Prince on 4 June 1907, Jacques Jean-Baptiste Roumain is one of Haiti's most important writers. After attending local primary schools, he was sent at an early age to France, Spain and

Switzerland to complete his education. Returning to Haiti in 1927, he founded two important journals, *La Revue Indigène* and *La Trouée 559*, in order to promote indigenous Haitian literature. Strongly opposed to the long American occupation of Haiti, he became a bitter critic of the government and was consequently exiled in 1934 after having founded the Communist party of Haiti. After making peace with the new régime, he served in Mexico as Haiti's chargé d'affaires, but he died at the age of thirty-seven on 18 August 1944. Roumain's numerous writings, which consistently reflected a strong socialist bias, were mainly aimed at drawing attention to the plight of transplanted Africans in the New World and promoting the African roots of West Indian and Latin American heritage. His major novels were *La montagne ensorcelée* (1931) and *Gouverneurs de la rosée* (1944). He also wrote two popular stories, *La Proie et l'ombre* (1930) and *Les Fantoches* (1931). Some of his excellent poetry appeared in the classic *Bois d'ébène* (1939) and in several anthologies, many of them published after Roumain's early death. His output of scholarly articles on the subject of racial inequality was simply prodigious.

ROWAN, Carl T.

Carl Thomas Rowan was born in poverty on 11 August 1925 in Ravenscroft, Tennessee. He joined the US Navy and, at nineteen, became one of the youngest African-Americans to be appointed a commissioned naval officer. In the years following World War II, he received his BA from Oberlin College in Ohio and his MA in journalism from the University of Minnesota. After working for some years with the *Minneapolis Tribune*, he entered the federal service in 1961 as deputy assistant secretary for public affairs. In 1963 he was appointed US ambassador to Finland and then served as head of the US Information Agency, thus becoming the first African-American to join the National Security Council. Rowan was also a writer of some renown. His books included *South of Freedom* (1953), *The Pitiful and the Proud* (1956), and *Wait Till Next Year* (1960). He remained a staunch advocate of civil rights, although he was careful to warn North American Blacks that 'there is a vast difference between being courageous and being pugnacious.' He was a panellist on the weekly television show, *Inside Washington*, from 1967 to 1996. Rowan died in Washington, D.C. on 23 September 2000.

RUBADIRI, David

Born in Liuli, Malawi, on 19 July 1930, Dr David Rubadiri became in 1964 his country's first ambassador to the United States. In that year, too, he appeared on the National Educational Television (New York City) *African Writers of Today* series. He studied English literature at Makerere University College in Uganda, and at Cambridge University in England. While pursuing graduate studies at Makerere in the late 1960s, he published (with David Cook) an anthology, *Poems from East Africa*, aimed at presenting the works of East African writers to a larger audience. Rubadiri was himself an accomplished poet, with the bulk of his verses dealing with the themes of race and racism. He also wrote a play, *Come to Tea* (1965), and a novel, *No Bride Price* (1967). As a young student, he had been very active in Malawi's nationalist cause during the late 1950s. After leaving his diplomatic post in New York in 1965, Rubadiri taught at Makerere University (1968-75), the University of Nairobi (1976-84) and the University of Botswana (1984-97). He was reappointed Malawi's ambassador to the United Nations in 1997 and was named vice-chancellor of the University of Malawi in 2000. His later publications include *Growing up With Poetry: An Anthology for Secondary Schools* (1989). He received an honorary doctorate from the University of Strathclyde in 2005.

RUCK, Calvin

The Hon Calvin W. Ruck was appointed to the Canadian senate in 1998 after many years of vigorous activism on behalf of minority rights and racial equality in Nova Scotia. Born in Sydney on 4 September 1925, he worked for many years with the Dominion Steel and Coal Corporation and the Canadian National Railway (CNR). In 1968 he joined the provincial civil service as a community development officer and was appointed a Commissioner of the Supreme Court in 1971. He also served at that time as a Human Rights Officer with the Nova Scotia Human Rights Commission. During 1986-90 he worked as a Community School Coordinator. As an enthusiastic member of the Nova Scotia Association for the Advancement of Coloured People (NSAACP), he convened public meetings in the 1950s and 1960s to inform residents of their rights and methods of obtaining them. He mounted campaigns against local businesses in Dartmouth, Nova Scotia, which refused to provide services to Blacks, and initiated a Stay in School Project for black students. In 1987, after many years of research, Ruck finally published *Canada's Black Battalion, 1916-1920*, in which he drew attention to the shabby manner in which the black soldiers were treated both by the Government and their own white colleagues. This was followed by *The Black Battalion, 1916-20: Canada's Best Kept Military Secret*. As a result of this crusade, a monument to the battalion was erected on the waterfront of Picou, Nova Scotia, in 1993. Dr Ruck's awards and distinctions include an induction into the Black Wall of Fame Society in 1981; a Harry Jerome Award in 1987; a Governor General 125th Anniversary Medal in 1992; an honorary LLD from Dalhousie University in 1994; the Order of Canada in 1994; and an honorary LLD from the University of King's College in 1999. He died in Ottawa, Ontario, on 19

October 2004. The Calvin W. Ruck Scholarship in his honour has been established by the Maritime School of Social Work at Dalhousie University (where, in 1979, he had achieved a diploma at the age of fifty-four).

RUCK, Winston

Winston Ruck is an ardent Canadian political activist who deservedly won the Tom Miller Human Rights Award in 1990. Twenty years earlier, he had been elected president of the United Steel Workers of America, Local 1604. By this time he had already given thirty-seven years of faithful service to the Sydney Steel Plant in Nova Scotia. He was for a long time the executive director of the Black United Front of Nova Scotia.

RUDOLPH, Wilma

Wilma Glodean Rudolph has remained an enormous source of inspiration to Blacks, women, and the disadvantaged everywhere because of her courage and tenacity in the face of overwhelming difficulty. She overcame crippling childhood illnesses to become the first American woman to capture three track-and-field gold medals at a single Olympics. Born on 23 June 1940, in Clarksville, Tennessee, she conquered polio, scarlet fever, double pneumonia, and the temporary paralysis of her left leg to play basketball at a very high level and to become the fastest woman on earth. She attended Tennessee State University during 1957-61 and was the Amateur Athletic Union 100 yard dash champion from 1959 to 1962. At the Rome Olympics in 1960, Rudolph won the 100 metre dash and the 200 metre dash, before anchoring the US 4 x 100 metre relay team to victory in a world record time of 44.4 seconds. She was named Female Athlete of the Year by the Associated Press and the most outstanding athlete of the year by the European Sportswriters' Association. Her accomplishments that year (1960) included a world record time of 22.9 seconds in the 200 metre dash that was destined to last several years. Following her retirement from the track, Rudolph established a foundation for underprivileged children, served as a goodwill ambassador to French West Africa, coached briefly at DePauw University and held various corporate business positions. She was inducted into the US National Track and Field Hall of Fame in 1974. Three years later her inspirational autobiography, *Wilma*, was published and made into a television movie. She died on 12 November 1994.

RUGAMBWA, Laurien

One of the most famous of all African black Catholic priests was His Eminence Laurien Rugambwa of Tanzania. Born on 14 July 1912, he became the first black bishop of Rutabo in 1953, just ten years after his ordination, and was promoted to a cardinalate in 1960, becoming the first

African native to achieve this distinction. He also served as archbishop of Dar-es-Salaam from 1968 to 1992. He died on 8 December 1997.

RUSSELL, Bill

The first African-American to coach a major-league professional athletic team was William Felton Russell, one of the greatest basketball players of the 20th century. Born in Monroe, Louisiana, on 12 February 1934, he led the University of San Francisco basketball team to two national titles before playing on the successful US team that took part in the 1956 Olympics. Bill Russell then became an important member of the Boston Celtics, winning the National Basketball Association (NBA) Most Valuable Player award no fewer than five times in his nine seasons (1957-66). He served as head coach of the Celtics during 1966-69 and was later appointed head coach and general manager of the Seattle Supersonics in 1973. He was also among the first African-Americans to become a television commentator on basketball. Russell revolutionized basketball by perfecting the art of shot-blocking and rebounding and by demonstrating the importance of defence. In 1967 the Associated Press (AP) named him one of the five members of its All-America collegiate team for the preceding twenty years; and later the AP selected Bill Russell the outstanding basketball player of the 1960s.

RUSSWURM, John Brown

Born in Jamaica, British West Indies, in 1799, John Russwurm enjoyed a most unusual career. He received his early education in Canada before entering Bowdoin College in Maine from which he graduated with a BA in 1826, becoming one of the earliest Blacks to achieve a degree in the United States. He helped to found and edit *Freedom's Journal* in New York City, one of the first African-American newspapers. Campaigning for the resettling of American Blacks in Africa, he emigrated himself to Liberia where he became superintendent of schools, founded the *Liberia Herald* and served as colonial secretary. He was appointed governor of the Maryland Colony at Cape Palmas (later incorporated into Liberia) and held that post until his death in 1851.

SADE

Born Helen Folasade Adu in Ibadan, Nigeria, on 16 January 1959, this popular British singer has made an indelible impression on music lovers across the world with her sensual voice and exotic looks. Her music is a curious blend of soul, funk, jazz and African-Cuban rhythms. Her very first album, *Diamond Life* (1984) won a Grammy Award and *Promise* (1985) enjoyed equal success. Also successful were *Stronger than Pride* (1988), *Love Deluxe* (1992), *Lovers Rock* (2000) and *Lovers Live* (2002). After studying for three years (1976-79) at Central St Martin's College of Art and Design in London, England, Sade first worked as a menswear designer and did some modelling. She only turned to singing after an agreement to stand in temporarily as a substitute as lead singer for Arriva, a funk band that some of her friends had put together. She has already sold more than 50 million albums worldwide.

SADLIER, Rosemary

Rosemary Sadlier is an activist and historian dedicated to emphasizing the role of Blacks in Canadian history and has thus far published two books on the subject: *Leading the Way: Black Women in Canada* (1994) and *Mary Ann Shadd: Publisher, Editor, Teacher, Lawyer, Suffragette* (1995). She has also written *Harriet Tubman and the Underground Railroad* (1996). Born in Toronto, Ontario, Sadlier received a BA from York University and a BEd and MSW from the University of Toronto. As president of the Ontario Black History Society (OBHS), she persuaded the cities of Ottawa and Toronto to proclaim 1 August Emancipation Day; urged Toronto to officially recognize 26 December as the beginning of Kwanzaa; persuaded the federal government to declare Black History Month (February) a national event in Canada; and secured political and public support for the creation of a Museum of African-Canadian History. In 1994, she hosted six episodes of *Blacks in Ontario* on Rogers TV and was the executive producer for *Black History Bytes*, which was aired on many TV stations across Canada. Sadlier, who worked for some years with the Women's Bureau, was also a member of the Ontario Ministry of Education Advisory Panel examining the new curriculum. She remains involved with a number of community organizations, especially those dealing with the mentally challenged.

ST JOHN, Bernard

Sir Harold Bernard St John was a Barbadian politician who served as prime minister during 1985-86 and was leader of the Barbados Labour Party (BLP) during 1970-71 and 1985-87. Born in Christ Church on 6 August 1931, he was educated at Harrison College and the University of London where he was trained as a lawyer. He joined the BLP in 1959 and was elected to the House of Assembly in 1966. Between 1971 and 1976 he served as a member of the Senate. He held several ministerial posts when his party was in power and became deputy prime minister in the early 1980s. When J.M.G.M. Adams suddenly died in 1985, he became prime minister but the BLP lost the election that followed one year later. When his party won the election of 1994, St John did not return to the Cabinet, opting instead to serve as a backbencher. He was knighted later that year. He died on 29 February 2004. St John's best work was done while he was minister of tourism. He helped significantly to develop the tourism industry in Barbados and to promote the integration of the regional economy.

ST OMER, Garth

Garth St Omer is a noted Caribbean novelist. Born in St Lucia in the mid-1930s, he is a graduate of the University College of the West Indies but has spent most of his life in Africa, France and the United States. He received a PhD from Princeton University in 1975 and taught English Language and Literature for some years at the University College of Santa Barbara. His major works include *Shades of Grey* (1968), *A Room on the Hill* (1968), *The Lights on the Hill* (1969), *Another Place Another Time* (1969), *Nor Any Country* (1969) and *J. Black Bam and the Masqueraders* (1972). St Omer also published a much acclaimed novella, *Syrop*, in 1968. He received the Gold Medal of Merit from the Government of St Lucia in 2001.

SALKEY, Andrew

Felix Andrew Alexander Salkey was born in Panama of Jamaican parents on 30 January 1928. He spent a great portion of his life in England, where he studied at the University of London and achieved his BA in 1955. In that year he won the Thomas Helmore Poetry Prize for his Jamaica Sympathy which was eventually published as *Jamaica* in 1973. After producing a very successful novel, *A Quality of Violence*, in 1959, Salkey wrote an extraordinary number of poems, radio plays, short stories, travel journals, children's tales and novels, while serving as a radio interviewer for BBC World Service. He was a contributing editor to the influential journal, *Savacou*, and the editor of several anthologies, including *West Indian Stories* (1960), *The Poetry of the Caribbean* (1973), and *Writing in Cuba Since the Revolution* (1977). From 1976 until his death on 28 April 1995, he was a professor of English at Hampshire College in Amherst, Massachusetts. Salkey's contribution to West Indian literature was incalculable. Apart from advertising the work of promising Caribbean writers in his collections, he encouraged them to contribute to *Savacou* and often promoted their efforts by interviewing them on the British Broadcasting Corporation (BBC). He was among those authors who pioneered the use of West Indian dialect in their fiction and is perhaps best remembered for his two volumes of stories about the Caribbean folk character, *Anancy*.

SAMPSON, Edith

Edith Spurlock Sampson was born in Pittsburgh, Pennsylvania, on 13 October 1901 and became a distinguished lawyer, judge and diplomat. She received her LLB from John Marshall Law School in 1925 and her LLM from Loyola University in 1927. Admitted to the Illinois bar, she established a thriving private practice in Chicago and served also as a referee of the Cook County Juvenile Court. In 1947 she was appointed an assistant state's attorney and in 1950 was the first woman ever to become a member of the US delegation to the United Nations. In 1962 she was elected associate judge of Chicago's Municipal Court and, two years later, was elected associate judge of the Circuit Court of Cook County. She died in 1979.

SAMPSON, Magnus John

Born on 17 May 1900, Magnus John Sampson became a Gold Coast author and politician of some standing. Educated at Winneba and at Fourah Bay College in Sierra Leone, he completed his studies at Durham University (England) where he gained the MA degree. He then taught briefly before entering politics. He served in 1949 on the famous Coussey Committee and became a member of the Gold Coast Legislative Assembly when it was first created in 1951. His most important books were *Gold Coast Men of Affairs, A Political Retrospect of the Gold Coast 1860-1930*, and *West African Leadership*. Sampson died on 27 July 1958.

SANCHO, Ignatius

Ignatius Sancho was born on a slave ship in 1729 and was bought as a toy by three English maidens when he was two years old. Teaching himself to read and write when he was very young, he was soon employed as a butler by the Duke of Montagu who was much impressed by his precocity. Sancho wrote poetry, two stage plays, and a theory of music dedicated to the Princess Royal. He was also an accomplished composer with three collections of songs, minuets and other pieces for violin, mandolin, harpsichord and flute (all published anonymously). He left the services of the Duke and Duchess of Montagu in 1773 and opened a grocery shop in Charles Street, Westminster, with the legacy he inherited from them. Two years after his death in 1780, his correspondence was published by a certain Miss Crewe. *The Letters of the Late Ignatius Sancho* quickly went into its fifth edition. He thus became the first African writer to be published in England with a best-seller. Sancho was very concerned about the plight of slaves and fervently besought his white friends and benefactors to have the cruel practice abolished. His life and writings served as positive proof that an untutored African could possess the talents and abilities equal to any European. Such was the respect in which he was held that the great Gainsborough painted a portrait of him in 1768.

SANDERSON, Tessa

Born in St Elizabeth, Jamaica, on 14 March 1956, Tessa Sanderson emigrated to the United Kingdom and became a world-class javelinist and heptathlete. When she won the Gold Medal in the javelin competition at the Los Angeles Games in 1984 she became the first British black female athlete to win an Olympic gold. In that discipline she remained highly competitive until 1996 and participated in a no fewer than six Olympic Games. After her retirement, she presented the sports news on Sky Television for over two years and currently runs her own sports management company. Particularly interested in sports development for youth, she has worked for a number of children's charities. Sanderson was awarded an OBE in 1998 for her charitable activities and her contribution to sport.

SANDIFORD, Erskine

Sir Lloyd Erskine Sandiford, who became the fourth prime minister of Barbados in 1987, was born on 24 March 1937. Educated at Coleridge Parry School and Harrison College, he won the prestigious Barbados Scholarship in 1956 and proceeded to study English Language and Literature at the University College of the West Indies from which he graduated in 1960. He gained a postgraduate degree in economics and government from Manchester University, England. He then taught briefly in Barbados and Jamaica before entering politics in 1966 as personal assistant to the Barbadian prime minister, Errol Barrow. He was appointed to the senate in 1967 and became minister of education and community development. During the years when his party was out of office (1976-86), he acted as deputy parliamentary opposition leader and was selected deputy prime minister in 1986. When Barrow died suddenly on 1 June 1987, Sandiford succeeded him as prime minister and held that post until 1994. In the general elections of 1991, he led his Democratic Labour Party (DLP) to an impressive triumph, but was unfortunate enough to encounter a serious and prolonged economic slump which demanded the pursuit of unpopular policies in order to balance the national budget. This led to the defeat of his party after eight years in power, but Sandiford had the satisfaction of knowing that his austere programme set the stage for the economic recovery that Barbados enjoyed during Owen Arthur's tenure as prime minister. His name is generally associated with the constructive social and economic reforms enacted by the DLP since 1966. He has also served on the boards of governors of the World Bank, the International Monetary Fund, the Inter-American Development Bank and the Caribbean Development Bank. He was appointed a Privy Councillor by the Queen of England and awarded the honour of the Order of the Liberator from the government of Venezuela. He was knighted in 2002. An excellent cricketer in his youth, Sandiford was one of the finest schoolboy batsmen in the Caribbean during the early 1950s.

SANKARA, Thomas

Capt Thomas Isidore Noël Sankara was born on 21 December 1949 in Yako, Upper Volta. He attended local schools before pursuing military studies in Madagascar. After returning home in 1972, he fought in a border war between Upper Volta and Mali. He was appointed secretary of state for information in the military government in September 1981 but resigned in April 1982 because of what he considered its anti-labour drift. After another coup, Sankara was made prime minister in January 1983 but was dismissed and placed under house arrest after disagreeing with the president's autocratic views. In August 1983, he emerged as president of Upper Volta following a military coup led by Blaise Compaoré.Sankara's policy was geared towards fighting corruption, promoting reforestation, averting famine, and making education and public health real priorities. He suppressed many of the traditional powers of the local chiefs, including their right to levy tribute payments and demand obligatory labour. In 1984, he renamed the country Burkina Faso, gave it a new flag and wrote a new national anthem for it. He brought women into the cabinet and made improving the status of women one of his goals. His government was also one of the first in Africa to publicly recognize AIDS as a major threat to the whole continent. These programmes did not sit well with the more conservative leaders in the army and Sankara was assassinated in yet another bloody coup on 15 October 1987.

SANTAMARIA, Ramon

Ramon 'Mongo' Santamaria was a Cuban-born American conga drummer who became a Latin jazz giant during the 1970s when the popularity of salsa music was at its height. Born in Havana on 7 April 1922, he was a well-known percussionist before immigrating to the United States in 1950. His recorded music was an attractive combination of African-Cuban and Latin American beats and sounds. Several of his hit songs were the result of his clever addition of Latin beats to pop and soul music tunes. He is best remembered for *Watermelon Man*, released in 1963. Santamaria died in Miami, Florida, on 1 February 2003.

SARBAH, John

Born around 1834, John Sarbah became one of the wealthiest African merchants in the Gold Coast and one of the first African members of the Gold Coast Legislative Council. He taught briefly at the Methodist Mission School before entering business and opening a huge store in Cape Coast. Eventually he established as many as ten branches in various towns in West Africa, trading in palm oil and rubber with British firms in London,

Liverpool and Manchester. Sarbah became rich enough to educate his sons in England. His businesses continued to flourish for many years after his death in 1892.

SARBAH, John Mensah

Born at Cape Coast on 3 June 1864, John Mensah Sarbah was the son of John Sarbah, a wealthy Gold Coast merchant. He became an influential African nationalist and left an indelible imprint on Ghanaian life, law, politics and education. He was educated in England where he studied law at Lincoln's Inn and qualified as a barrister in 1887, becoming the first Gold Coast African to do so. Returning to Cape Coast, Sarbah shortly built up a very lucrative practice while also participating actively in public affairs. He helped to found the Aborigines' Rights Protection Society (ARPS) and was prominent among those who agitated for the withdrawal of the notorious Lands Bill of 1897. Keenly interested in African education, he founded the Dutton Scholarship at Taunton School in Somerset, England, in memory of his younger brother, John Dutton Sarbah, who had died there in 1892. He helped to revive the Collegiate School in Cape Coast and contributed to the creation of the important Mfantsipim School there in 1904. Sarbah House was eventually named there after him. The University of Ghana also named Mensah Sarbah Hall after him some fifty years after his death A member of the Gold Coast Legislative Council from 1901 to 1910, Sarbah was keenly interested in African rights and did much to thwart colonial laws which seemed to violate them. He even saw the need for interpreters in the colonial courts since many Africans were not sufficiently competent in English to defend themselves and he very strongly advocated the use of the vernacular in local court cases. This outstanding Gold Coast citizen was as much interested in language as he was in law, politics and education. He published *Fante Customary Laws* (1897), *Fante Law Reports* (1904) and *The Fante National Constitution* (1906). Much of his work is still seen as indispensable in today's Ghana. His interest in agriculture also led to the publication of his seminal article, *The Palm Oil and Its Products*, in 1909. He encouraged farmers to grow cocoa and even gave them loans for this purpose. A good Christian, too, he bought a pipe organ for the Methodist Church at Cape Coast. John Mensah Sarbah was much lamented when he died on 27 November 1910. It is hard to believe that he was only forty-six.

SARO-WIWA, Ken

Kenule Beeson Saro-Wiwa is going to be remembered, sadly, more for the circumstances surrounding his death than for his courageous work as an environmentalist and as one of Nigeria's foremost authors. Born on 10 October 1941, near Port Harcourt, he was educated at Government

College in Umuahia and the University of Ibadan. He taught briefly in the late 1960s before fighting against the Biafrans in the civil war and then working as a government administrator. In 1973 he gave up his civil service appointment to concentrate on his writing. He created quite a sensation in 1985 with *Sozaboy*, a novel written in pidgin English and satirizing the corruption of Nigerian society. During the 1980s, too, he produced a very popular television series, *Basi and Company*, using comedy to illuminate the cultural, social and economic ills of Nigeria. During the 1990s Saro-Wiwa decided to devote the bulk of his energy to the cause of the Ogoni, a minority people, whose lands and lives had been much disturbed by the activities of the Anglo-Dutch petroleum company, Shell. He drew international attention to the environmental damage inflicted on Ogoni lands by this corporation and argued that the locals were inadequately compensated. He was also bitterly critical of the Nigerian military régime. For his pains, Saro-Wiwa was publicly hanged on 10 November 1995. His execution sparked a wave of international protests and demands for economic sanctions against Nigeria. But nothing came of these reactions. Shell announced its commitment to an even more substantial natural-gas project in the area and Nigeria lost a courageous patriot and a most gifted journalist, playwright, novelist and poet who has apparently died in vain.

SASRAKU I

Nana Ansa Sasraku I was the ruler who created the powerful state of Akwamu in western Africa during the seventeenth century. He inherited a very small kingdom but left it considerably enlarged when he died in 1689. Using Nyanawase as a base, Ansa conquered the neighbouring states and controlled the major trade paths leading to Accra. He inadvertently contributed also to the founding of the mighty Asante empire by his kindnesses to the young Osei Tutu in the 1680s. It was his Akwamu advisers who assisted Osei in establishing Kumasi as the centre of the Asante state.

SARTSA DENGEL

One of the great Ethiopian warrior-kings, Sartsa Dengel was born around 1550. He ascended the throne in 1563 when still quite young but succeeded in safeguarding himself and preserving the integrity of his realm for more than thirty years. He had at first to contend not only with rival claimants but with the Turks as well. He finally reduced the Turks to submission in the late 1580s. But with most of his energies devoted to self-defence, his reign witnessed little by way of constitutional advance. Sartsa Dengel died on 2 September 1597.

SAVAGE, Augusta

Augusta Christine Savage was born in Green Cove, Florida, in 1900. She became one of America's most famous sculptresses after studying in New York, Paris and Rome. The first director of the Harlem Community Art Centre, she was commissioned in 1939 to create the harp-shaped sculpture, *Lift Every Voice and Sing*, that gained her instant international fame. Augusta's ability to manipulate stone, plaster and bronze won her numerous awards and her work is still exhibited in such places as Morgan State University in Maryland, the National Archives in Washington, D.C., and the New York Public Library's Schomburg Collection. Augusta Savage died in 1962.

SAVIMBI, Jonas

A member of the Ovimbundu tribe, Jonas Malheiro Savimbi was born in Munhango, Angola, on 3 August 1934. He studied medicine in Lisbon, Portugal, where he met Agostinho Neto and joined the independence movement. Accepting funding and military aid from China, he then founded his own party, the National Union for the Total Independence of Angola (UNITA). He returned home with a small militia and quickly gained popular support in the eastern portion of the country. After independence was achieved in 1975, Savimbi's UNITA waged a civil war with the Popular Movement for the Liberation of Angola (MPLA), the ruling party led by Neto. A peace agreement resulted in democratic elections in 1992 to determine the winner. When the MPLA won, Savimbi refused to accept the results and continued his guerilla warfare until killed by government troops on 22 February 2002.

SCHOLES, Theophilus

Dr Theophilus Edward Samuel Scholes, an outstanding physician, activist, author and missionary, was born in Jamaica in the 1850s. He studied medicine in London and Edinburgh, while training as a missionary physician, before working for five years in the Congo. He then sought a second medical degree in Brussels, Belgium, during 1890-94 and worked briefly in Nigeria. Dr Scholes finally emigrated to the United Kingdom in the late 1890s where he spent the last forty years of his life. While practising medicine there, he wrote three very critical studies of British racism and imperialism: *The British Empire and Alliances* (1899); *Chamberlain and Chamberlainism* (1903); and *Glimpses of the Ages* (1905-06). The third of these publications drew graphic and painful pictures of the shabby treatment meted out to black medical students in the United Kingdom. Dr Scholes died in the late 1930s.

SCHOMBURG, Arthur

Born in San Juan, Puerto Rico, in 1874, Arthur Alfonso Schomburg was a voracious collector of African-Americana. Long before his death in 1938, Schomburg had amassed more than 5,000 volumes, 3,000 manuscripts, 2,000 etchings, and several thousand pamphlets, comprising the most extensive library of African-American history and culture. This collection was purchased in 1926 by the Carnegie Corporation and given to the New York Public Library where Schomburg himself served as its curator. It became known, after 1973, as the Schomburg Collection of Negro Literature and History. Schomburg's interest in African-American culture was first kindled at St Thomas College in the Virgin Islands where he made a special study of Negro literature. After teaching in the Caribbean for several years, he moved to the United States and helped to found the Negro Society for Historical Research in 1911. In 1922 he became the head of the American Negro Academy. Schomburg also wrote numerous articles for newspapers and magazines and contributed regularly to *The New Negro*, edited by Alain Locke.

SCOTLAND, Patricia

Patricia Janet Scotland, Baroness Scotland of Asthal, was born in Dominica on 19 August 1955 and moved with her family to the United Kingdom when she was three years old. In 1991 she was the first black female to be appointed a Queens Counsel (QC) and in 1997 became the first black female peer in the United Kingdom House of Lords. Patricia was educated at the University of London where she received a law degree in 1976, specializing in family and children's law. In 1994 she was named a Millennium Commissioner and a member of the Commission for Racial Equality. In 1999 she was made a judge and became parliamentary undersecretary of state at the Foreign Office and the Commonwealth Office. In 2001 she was named parliamentary secretary in the Lord Chancellor's department and a member of the Privy Council. Two years later, she was appointed minister of state for the Criminal Justice system and law reform at the Home Office. Baroness Scotland has held many distinguished positions, such as chair of the Caribbean Advisory Group; Dominican representative of the Council of British Commonwealth Ex-Services League; member of the Lawyers' Christian Fellowship; member of the BBC World Service Consultative Group; Honorary Fellow of Wolfson College, Cambridge; and patron of the Women and Children's Welfare Fund. She has also received numerous awards, including an honorary degree from the University of Westminster.

SCOTT, Arleigh

Sir Arleigh Winston Scott was the first native Governor General of Barbados. He served in this capacity from 1967 to 1976. Born in 1900, he was educated at St Giles Boy's School and Harrison College before studying medicine at Howard University in the United States and the University of Edinburgh in Scotland. He returned to the United States for further study and became a visiting ophthalmic surgeon to Harlem Hospital in New York. In 1943, Dr Scott settled back down in Barbados where he pursued a very successful practice, establishing Woodside Memorial Clinic, a valuable nursing home. An active community servant, he gave his services without charge to the Children's Goodwill League and gave frequent lectures on public health He occasionally taught hygiene to some of the primary schools in the Bridgetown area and gave annual check ups to the pupils of Combermere School. He was a member of the national Senate from 1964 to 1967 and in 1966 was appointed to the Privy Council of Barbados. He succeeded Sir John Stow as Governor General on 18 May 1967 when he was also offered a knighthood. As Governor General, Sir Winston won the respect and affection of the nation by the quiet dignity with which he performed his duties. On 9 August 1976, he died suddenly while in office.

SEACOLE, Mary

Born Mary Grant to a Scottish father and a Jamaican mother in Kingston, Jamaica, in 1805, this pioneering nurse became a heroine, albeit unsung, during the Crimean War (1853-56) when, at her own considerable risk and expense, she nursed hundreds of British soldiers on the field of battle. She returned to England destitute and in ill health after the war. Her plight was highlighted by William Russell, the war correspondent for *The Times*, who had witnessed first-hand her bravery and skill in the Near East. Money was raised for her through a military festival held over four nights at the Royal Surrey Gardens. She was awarded a Crimean Medal, the French Legion of Honour and a Turkish medal. Despite this brief fuss and flurry, however, Mary Seacole sank promptly into oblivion and died in obscurity in1881. She had inherited her nursing skills from her mother who practised traditional Jamaican medicine while caring for sick and injured British soldiers stationed in the island. By travelling widely, Mary learnt how to combine Jamaican and European methods of nursing and was well-known in the West Indies for her work during outbreaks of cholera. She was the first black woman to make her mark on English public life. She is still revered in Jamaica, where one of the halls on the Mona Campus of the University of the West Indies has been named after her. She published an autobiography, *The Wonderful Adventures of Mrs Seacole in Many Lands*, in 1857. The difference between her fate and that of her more famous contemporary, Florence Nightingale, epitomizes the gulf between the black and white races. The celebrated 'Lady of the Lamp' was given great support and encouragement by the British government, while Seacole's application to serve was summarily rejected. The one became an instant national heroine; the other remained a nonentity until rehabilitated more than a hundred years later.

SEALY, Joe

An internationally renowned pianist, composer and music director, Joseph Arthur Sealy was born in Montreal, Quebec, on 16 August 1939. He has become one of Canada's leading jazz musicians. He has performed throughout Canada, Europe and the United States and is perhaps best known for his *Africville Suite* which won a Juno Award. His major recordings include *Blue Jade*, *Clear Vision*, *Double Entendre*, *Dual Vision* and *Live at Errol's*. He has scored numerous works for film, radio and television and has also appeared in a number of films and TV shows, including *Brown Bread Sandwiches* and *I'll Take Manhattan*. As a stage actor, Sealy was featured in *Ma Rainey's Black Bottom* and *Lady Day at Emerson's Bar and Grill*. Among his many honours and distinctions was a Dora Mavor Moore Award for musical direction in *Ain't Misbehaving*. He is the founder and president of Seajam Recordings.

SEARS, Djanet

Djanet Sears is an award-winning Canadian playwright, actor and director. Her best-known plays include *Afrika Solo* (1989), *Harlem Duet* (1997) and *The Adventures of a Black Girl in Search of God* (2002). As playwright in residence in several institutions, she has tried to promote the works of Africans on the continent and in the diaspora. A founding member of the Obsidian Theatre Company, she has also been the driving force behind the AfriCanadian Playwrights' Festival. Sears won the Phenomenal Woman of the Arts Award in 1997 and the Governor General Literary Award for *Harlem Duet* in 1998.

SEKYI, William

William Essuman-Gwira Sekyi was one of the outstanding Gold Coast nationalists in the years leading up to the achievement of Ghanaian political independence. Born on 1 November 1892, he was educated at the Cape Coast Wesleyan Primary School and Mfantsipim School before studying philosophy at the University of London, England, from which he graduated in 1914. Sekyi then studied law at the Inner Temple in the United Kingdom and was called to the bar in 1919. He returned to the Gold Coast and became a prolific writer, distancing himself from the other African intellectuals by recommending a total separation of the races and urging his people to abandon European manners, speech and dress. An implacable foe of the British, he served as president of the Aborigines' Rights Protection Society (ARPS) from 1927 to 1950. He died on 5 October 1956.

SELLASIE, Sahle

Sahle Sellasie is an Ethiopian novelist and short-story writer in three languages: his native Chaha (an unwritten Semitic dialect hitherto), Amharic (Ethiopia's national language), and English. Born in Wardena in 1936, Sellasie finished his secondary education in Addis Ababa before studying law at Aix-en-Provence in France. He completed an MA degree in political science at the University of California, Los Angeles, in 1963. While at UCLA, he wrote *Shinega's Village: Scenes of Ethiopian Life in Chaha as a linguistic exercise.* When this work was translated into English by Wolf Leslau in 1964, it was the first Ethiopian novel to be published in the United States. In 1969, Sellasie produced an Amharic novel, *Wotat Yifredew,* and an English one, *The Afersata,* dealing with traditional techniques of crime detection in Ethiopia. He also wrote numerous articles and essays for various literary magazines.

SEMBENE, Ousmane

Born on 8 January 1923 in Ziguinchor, in southern Senegal, Ousmane Sembène was educated at the École de Céramique at Marsassoum before moving to Dakar and doing a variety of odd jobs. Drafted into the French Army during World War II, he remained in France after demobilization and became a militant trade unionist in Marseille, where he also established himself as an excellent writer. His major works included *Le Docker noir* (1956), *O pays, mon beau peuple!* (1957), *Les Bouts de bois de Dieu* (1960), *Voltaique: nouvelles* (1962), *L'Harmattan* (1964), *Mandat* (1965), *Xala* (1974), and *Le Dernier de l'empire* (1981). Sembène, however, is best remembered as the 'Father of African Cinema'. Having studied at the Moscow Film School during the 1960s, he returned to Senegal to produce a series of remarkable films, all intended as social commentary on life in Dakar, and most of them written in the Wolof language. His great film, *Le Noir de ...,* produced in 1967, created quite a stir by describing the virtual enslavement of an illiterate girl from Dakar employed as a servant by a French family. It was also the first ever produced by an African filmmaker. Sembène's *Mandabi* ('The Money Order'), a comedy of daily life and corruption in Dakar, created a precedent in 1968 by being the first movie to be filmed in an African language. His more famous *Ceddo,* produced in 1980, was actually banned in Senegal because of its criticism of the role of Islam in pre-colonial days. The government objected because it was itself then heavily dependent on Muslim support. Other Woloff films included *Camp de Thiaroye* (1987) and *Guelwaar* (1992). One of Sembène's most recent films, *Moolaadé*, won awards at the Cannes Festival and the FESPACO Film Festival at Ougadougou, Burkina Faso. Ousmane Sembène is considered one of the greatest authors of sub-Saharan Africa and the 'Father of African Film'. His writings and his films are all intended as constructive criticisms of the post-colonial order in Africa.

SEMOPA BAVON

Born around 1885, Semopa Bavon is remembered as a black apostle of the Giri River region of what is now Zaire. Born at Nioki, he was educated at the Colonial School at Nouvelle-Anvers and then at Bogbona before being sent as a missionary to the Giri River valley to counter the growing influence of the Protestant missionaries. He served as the chief Catholic catechist west of Mankanza for more than twenty years. Travelling widely, he converted hundreds of Congolese while freeing several slaves. He also settled many disputes between villagers and between ethnic groups. He died on 1 March 1933, after having earned the profound respect of Africans and Europeans alike.

SENGBE PIEH

Also known as Joseph Cinque, Sengbe Pieh was the courageous leader of the slave revolt on board the *Amistad* in 1839. This was an important event which produced the historic trial in the United States Supreme Court. This tribunal ruled that the mutineers had been taken against their will from Africa and were therefore free to return to that continent. Thanks to the zeal and determination of the American Abolitionists, they were shipped back to Freetown, Sierra Leone, aboard the *Gentleman* in 1842. This episode led in 1846 to the formation of the American Missionary Society which established a host of institutions throughout the United States and marked the beginning of American evangelical work in Africa. These missionary activities continued long after Sengbe Pieh himself had died in 1879.

SENGHOR, Léopold Sédar

Léopold Sédar Senghor is by far the most prominent figure in the history of modern Senegal. A brilliant scholar and successful politician, he led Senegal to its independence from France in 1960 and remained its revered president for twenty years. The son of a prosperous merchant, he was born on 9 October 1906 at Joal and educated at the Ngasobil Catholic mission and at Dakar before completing his studies in Paris, France. He was the first black student to earn the equivalent of an MA from the Sorbonne in 1933 and the equivalent of a PhD in 1934. While in France, Senghor helped to found the Association des Étudiants Ouest-Africains and contributed to *L'Étudiant noir*. From 1935 to 1938, he taught Greek and Latin at the Lycée Descartes and then served as an officer in the French Army during World War II. He founded a new party, the Bloc Démocratique Sénégalais (BDS) in 1948 and was elected a deputy of the French National Assembly for Senegal from 1946 to 1958. Senghor was appointed to some important parliamentary and administrative posts in France and Senegal during those years and became president of the short-lived Mali Federation in 1959. One of the most highly respected among the African Francophone authors, he continued to produce excellent poetry and prose even during his years as head of state after the proclamation of Senegal's independence. His best known works in verse were *Chants d'ombre* (1945), *Hosties noires* (1948), *Chants pour Naëtt* (1948), *Éthiopiques* (1956), *Nocturnes* (1961), *Poèmes* (1964) and *Lettres d'hivernage* (1973). His collected poems appeared in 1977 amidst much acclaim. Senghor also wrote serious prose as appeared, for example, in *Nation et voie africaine du socialisme* (1961), *Négritude, Arabisme et Francité* (1967) and *Les fondements de l'Africanité ou négritude et l'Arabité*. He did his best to gain recognition for black writers and artists and, along with Aimé Césaire and Léon Damas of the French West Indies, did most to create a positive image of 'negritude' in the inter-war years. These three outstanding scholars were the writers who first popularized the notion which, in English, came to be translated as 'Black is Beautiful'. Among his numerous awards, honours and distinctions, Senghor was received into the French Academy on 29 March 1984 to crown his brilliant literary career. He was the first Black to be thus honoured. He resigned from the presidency of Senegal on 31 December 1980 but remained a force in west African politics for some years afterwards. He had been the first black African political leader to hand over the reins of office in a peaceful transfer of power. He died on 20 December 2001 at the age of ninety-five.

SEY, Jacob Wilson

Born in 1832, Jacob Wilson Sey was a wealthy Gold Coast merchant who flourished during the second half of the nineteenth century. He made huge profits from the sale of palm oil and ploughed a good portion of his wealth into local projects and worthy causes. A staunch Methodist, he always contributed very generously to his church. The very first president of the Aborigines' Rights Protection Society (ARPS), founded in 1897, Sey financed its deputation to London in 1898 to challenge the Lands Bill that the imperial parliament had passed in the previous year. His death on 22 May 1902 was a severe blow not only to the ARPS in particular but to the Gold Coast in general.

SEYMOUR, A.J.

Born in Georgetown, British Guiana, on 12 January 1914, Arthur James Seymour was one of the acknowledged 'godfathers' of West Indian literature to which he made an enormous contribution by promoting the work of others in his influential literary journal, *Kyk-over-Al*. He encouraged West Indian authors by editing numerous anthologies of verse and short stories. He was also one of the main organizers of the Carifesta held in Guyana in 1972 when he took charge of the literary portion of the programme. He served for many years as the deputy chairman of the Guyana National History and Arts Council. He was honoured by the Guyana government in 1970 with the Golden Arrow of Achievement for his work in literature. An accomplished poet himself, Seymour published such collections as *Verse* (1937), *More Poems* (1940), *Over Guiana Clouds* (1944), *Sun's in My Blood* (1945), *We Do Not Presume to Come* (1948), *Leaves From the Tree* (1951), *Selected Poems* (1965), *Patterns* (1970), and *Tomorrow Belongs to the People* (1975). He also wrote several articles, short stories and (starting in 1976) five volumes of autobiography. With the help of the poet and novelist, Ian McDonald, he was able to revive *Kyk-Over-Al* in 1984. Seymour died on 25 December 1989.

SHAABAN, Robert

Sir Robert Shaaban was born in 1909 near Tanga in Tanzania. A truly brilliant Swahili poet, essayist and novelist, he is regarded by many critics as the most distinguished of all east African writers. His career represented a significant turning point in the evolution of Swahili language and literature. His numerous honours and distinctions included a knighthood and a Margaret Wrong Medal and Prize for literature. For many years, too, he served as chairman of the Swahili Committee in Dar es Salaam. It was Shaaban who introduced the essay (insha) into Swahili literature. His best known essays perhaps were *Pambo la lugha* (1947), *Kielezo cha fasili* (1954), *Insha na mashairi* (1959) and *Masomo yenye adili* (1959). Some of his finest poetry appeared in *Pambo la lugha* (1948), *Marudi mema* (1952), *Almasi za Africa* (1960), *Ashiki kitabu hiki* (1968), *Masomo yenye adili* (1968), *Utenzi wa Vita vya uhuru* (1968) and *Koja la lugha* (1969). Among his major novels were *Kusadikika, nchi iliyo angani* (1951) and Siku *ya watenzi wote* (1960). He wrote several novelettes, including *Adili na nduguze* (1952) and *Utoboro mkulima* (1968). Shaaban also published a biography, *Wasifu wa Siti Binti Saad, mwimbaji wa Ugoja* in 1955 and his own autobiography, *Maisha yangu na Baada ya miaka hamshini*, in 1949. He died on 20 June 1962. A fervent Muslim and African nationalist, Shaaban always lamented the cruelties of European colonialism and the tendency towards the suppression of African values and traditions. The first volume of his complete works, *Diwani ya Shaaban*, appeared in 1966.

SHADD-CARY, Mary Ann

Mary Ann Shadd-Cary is best remembered as the publisher of Canada's first anti-slavery newspaper and the first black newspaperwoman in North America. Born on 9 October 1823 in Wilmington, Delaware, she attended primary schools in Pennsylvania as it was then illegal to offer education to Blacks in her native state. She was only sixteen years old when she returned to Wilmington and opened a private school for black children. Her family immigrated to Canada in the early 1850s and she encouraged the immigration of other African-Americans to Canada by publishing a popular pamphlet, entitled *Notes on Canada*. She also founded *The Provincial Freemen* to advertise opportunities for Blacks in Canada and to provide them with the kind of forum not readily available at that time. Her newspaper became a powerful mouthpiece for the abolitionists as it ranted daily against the evils of slavery. In 1856 Mary Ann Shadd married Thomas Cary, a resident of Toronto, where she shortly opened an interracial school. During the American Civil War she returned to the United States to support the North in the belief that she was participating in a crusade against slavery. She became a recruiting officer and encouraged as many Blacks as possible to fight against the South. After the war, Shadd-Cary studied law at Howard University and became in 1883 only the second African-American woman to earn a degree in that discipline. She then devoted her major energies to the cause of gender and racial equality in the United States until her death, in Washington, D.C., on 5 June 1893.

SHAKA

One of the most brilliant of all Zulu monarchs, Shaka remains a legend throughout southern Africa to this day. Born around 1787, he usurped the throne from his half-brother, whom he killed in 1813. He then built up an almost invincible army which carried all before it in southern Africa and, by the time of his own death on 23 September 1828, had made the Zulu Empire one of the largest and most feared throughout the continent. A military genius, Shaka revolutionized warfare in southern Africa by discarding the traditional spear and employing the more wieldy and effective assegai, a much lighter and sharper weapon. He was such a fine tactician and strategist that his armies remained unbeaten for more than a decade. He overcame the Ndwande and the Qwabe clans, his two greatest foes, and overran the rest of the region now known as Natal. Shaka is reputed to have once quadrupled the Zulu population in a single year by incorporating remnants of clans his warriors had defeated. He also proved himself a skilful administrator by choosing his governors and military generals carefully to ensure their efficiency as well as their loyalty to him. Although he ruled for only fifteen years he left an enormous impact on the region. He created a mammoth empire and gave the Zulus a sense of pride and importance. Had he lived longer, he might well have been able to organize a much stiffer resistance to European infiltration in southern Africa. As it was, he left his own neighbours too feeble to cope with the pressure of Dutch and British enterprise in the decades that followed. Shaka apparently became insane in 1827 and was murdered by his half-brothers who feared for their own safety as well as the security of the Zulu kingdom.

SHAQQ, Hameed

Hameed Shaqq, better known as the 'Pan Piper', is a native of Trinidad and Tobago. He is an innovative, versatile and talented steel pan musician and composer whose repertoire includes jazz, blues, classical, pop, calypso and liturgical music. He immigrated to Canada in 1978 and has attempted to popularize steel band music by playing it in nightclubs, schools, community centres, libraries and parks and by teaching steel pan music and composition to students in the elementary schools of Toronto, North York, Scarborough and Etobicoke in Ontario. In the early 1970s, Shaqq toured Europe with the 'Solo Harmonites', a Trinidadian band, who thrilled audiences at the World Fair in Zurich in 1972 and the Music Festival in Spain in 1975. He has released a popular CD, *Plant Pan*, and an audio cassette, *Life on the Line*. He is also the writer/arranger of *Under the Mango Tree: A Caribbean Cultural Melée*, a celebration of West Indian music and dance which he produced in Trinidad in 1996.

SHAWARAGGAD GADLE

One of the most famous of Ethiopian women, Shawaraggad Gadle came to prominence during the Italian occupation (1935-41). She was very active in social work and helped to organize the Red Cross and the earliest women's associations in Ethiopia. Most of her life was devoted to charitable causes and she spent her private fortune on schools for the children of the poor. When she died in 1949, she was fittingly buried at the monastery of Dabra Libanos.

SHEARER, Hugh

Hugh Lawson Shearer was a Jamaican politician and trade union leader who served as the third prime minister of his native country during 1967-72. Born in Martha Brae on 18 May 1923, he joined the Bustamante Industrial Trade Union in 1941. He became a protégé of Sir Alexander Bustamante, Jamaica's first prime minister, who had also founded the Jamaica Labour Party (JLP). Shearer rose gradually to the leadership of both the union and the JLP and became prime minister upon the death of Sir Donald Sangster. During his tenure, Jamaica enjoyed considerable economic growth and a noticeable increase in schools. In 1978 he became president of the Bustamante Industrial Trade Union. He served as Jamaica's foreign minister during 1980-89 and in 1994 he became the first president of the Jamaica Confederation of Trade Unions. Shearer died in Kingston on 5 July 2004.

SHEMBE, Isaiah

Born in Natal, South Africa, during the early 1860s, Isaiah Shembe became a popular Zulu poet and a very influential religious leader. A most unusual seer, he travelled around southern Africa by foot and oxcart, preaching and baptising, and healing and purifying the bodies and souls of his followers. After becoming an ardent convert to Christianity, he seceded from his church in 1911 and founded his own mission, the Ama-Nazaretha, having been convinced by a series of visions that he was the reincarnation of Jesus Christ. His followers quickly accepted him as the second messiah and he was fervently worshipped by thousands of Zulus. He restored Zulu dances into his religious worship, accepted polygamy, and tried to effect a workable synthesis of Christian orthodoxy and Zulu traditions. In search of divine inspiration, he often climbed to the top of the mountain, Nhlangakazi, which he regarded as his sacred peak. He founded the holy city of the new Nazareth, called Ekuphakameni, some 18 miles from Durban. Shembe composed his own hymns, some 200 of them, and his enthusiastic apostles used them as the basis for *Izihlabelelo zaNazarethe*, an important Zulu hymnal, published in 1940. The great prophet himself died on 2 May 1935 and is believed to have risen again in 1939. His son, John Galilee Shembe, took over the leadership of his Nazarite Church in Natal and his followers, estimated variously from 10,000 to 80,000, continued to worship at Ekuphakameni and Mt Nhlangakazi for many years.

SHERWOOD, Anthony

Born in Halifax, Nova Scotia, and raised in Montreal, Quebec, Anthony Sherwood is one of Canada's most successful actors, having performed in more than thirty feature films. He is also a director, producer and writer. He wrote and directed such musical productions for the stage as *Ain't Got No Money*, *Once Upon a Stage*, *But I Was Cool* and *Razz M'Jazz*. He has created and produced several documentaries, including *Honour Before Glory*, based on the story of Canada's first and only all-black battalion in World War I. *His Music - A Family Tradition* won a Gemini Award in 1997. Sherwood has performed in such feature films as *Dirty Tricks* (1981), *The Guardian* (1984), *Eternal Evil* (1987), *Switching Channels* (1988), *Eddie and the Cruisers II* (1989), *Guilty as Sin* (1993), *Undue Influence* (1996) and *Freedom's Land: Canada and the Underground Railroad* (2004). For Black History Month in 1998, he produced and directed the series, entitled *Playin' 4 Keeps*, which was carried by national television in Canada. For six successive seasons, Sherwood portrayed the character of Dillon Beck in *Street Legal* and has guest-starred in more than forty TV shows. For five years, he hosted and narrated the series, *Forbidden Places*, which was nominated for best documentary series on Canadian TV for two years running. He is the recipient of many honours and awards.

SHORUNKEH-SAWYERR, Alfred

An eminent Sierra Leonean bookseller, printer, journalist and lawyer, Alfred James Shorunkeh-Sawyerr was born around 1861. He attended the Christian Missionary Society Grammar School in Freetown and then studied law in England where he was called to the bar at Grey's Inn in 1889. Returning home, he founded *Sawyerr's Advertising Medium* and the *Sierra Leone Ram* as well as *Saturday, Ho!* In 1911 he was appointed a member of the Sierra Leone Legislative Council on which he served until 1924. He died on 29 May 1929.

SIBTHORPE, A.B.C.

Aaron Belisarius Cosimo Sibthorpe was the first historian of Sierra Leone. Born around 1840, he was educated at the Christian Missionary Society Grammar School in Freetown and became a teacher. He wrote a *History of Sierra Leone* and a *Geography of Sierra Leone* in 1868. Both of these seminal texts went through numerous editions and revisions. He was a talented but generally unrecognized scholar. Sibthorpe also practised as a herbal doctor using medicines of his own concoction. He died on 20 June 1916.

SIMMONDS, Kennedy

Dr Kennedy Alphonse Simmonds has the distinction of becoming the first prime minister of St Kitts and Nevis, in the West Indies, when their political independence was achieved in 1983, after having been the last premier in their days of associated statehood with Great Britain. Born on 12 April 1936 in Basseterre, St Kitts, he was a scholarship student at the St Kitts-Nevis Grammar School before winning the prestigious Leeward Islands Scholarship in 1954. He studied medicine at the University College of the West Indies and graduated in 1962. Following his internship at the Kingston Public Hospital in Jamaica, he returned to St Kitts where he established a successful private practice. Entering politics, he became a founding member of the People's Action Movement (PAM) in 1965, but did not win a seat in the legislature until 1979 at a by-election to fill the vacancy created by the death of Robert Bradshaw, the former premier. Simmonds was re-elected in 1980, when he led a coalition of opposition forces to overthrow the Labour Party that had held power for thirty years. He remained prime minister of St Kitts and Nevis until 7 July 1995 after fifteen reasonably successful years in office. During his tenure, his nation experienced considerable economic growth as it became increasingly attractive as a tourist resort in the Caribbean. The Dr Kennedy A. Simmonds Highway, from Frigate Bay to Major's Bay in St Kitts, has been named after him. He resigned from the leadership of his party in 2000.

SIMMS, Glenda

Dr Glenda Simms was born in Jamaica, West Indies. After teaching there for some years, she immigrated to Canada and headed the Native Education Department of the Saskatchewan Indian Federated College. She later served as supervisor of Intercultural Education and Race and Ethnic Relations for the Regina Public School Board. Moving to Ontario, Dr Simms taught at Nipissing University in North Bay, before being appointed president of the Canadian Advisory Council on the Status of Women in 1989. A founding member of the National Organization of Immigrant and Visible Minority Women of Canada, she is also a former president of the Congress of Black Women of Canada. Dr Simms has received many honours and distinctions, including the Citation for Citizenship, the National Award from the Council for Multicultural and Intercultural Education, the University of Alberta Inter Amicus Human Rights Award and an honorary membership in the Federation of Medical Women of Canada. She has also been inducted into the North Bay Human Rights Hall of Fame.

SIMPSON-MILLER, Portia

The Most Honourable Portia Lucretia Simpson-Miller, ON, became only the second black woman, following Dame Eugenia Charles of Dominica, to assume the office of prime minister of a Caribbean country. She succeeded Perceval J. Patterson as the prime minister of Jamaica on 30 March 2006. Born in Woodhall, St Catherine, on 12 December 1945, she was educated at the Marlie Hill Primary School and St Martin's High School in Jamaica before proceeding to the Union Institute in Miami, Florida, to pursue a bachelor's degree in public administration. It was from that same academic institution that she later received an honorary doctorate. An active supporter of the People's National Party (PNP), she rose to the rank of vice-president in 1978. During Patterson's long tenure as prime minister, Portia Simpson-Miller held several important ministerial positions after 1989 and was one of the most popular members of the cabinet. She is well-known for her commitment to the alleviation of poverty and oppression. On 29 May 2006 she was invested with the Jamaican Order of the Nation.

SISULU, Walter

Walter Max Ulyate Sisulu, one of Nelson Mandela's most influential mentors, was born in Engcobo, South Africa, on 18 May 1912. He was a prominent member of the African National Congress (ANC) which led the fight against apartheid. Before joining the ANC in 1940, he had been involved in trade union activism for several years. In 1941, he encouraged Mandela to join the ANC and to take the lead in non-violent demonstrations, strikes and boycotts to protest South Africa's racist system. Along with Mandela and 154 others, he was arrested in 1956 and charged with treason. After a four-year trial, he was acquitted. Sisulu was arrested again in 1963 and sentenced to life imprisonment for plotting to overthrow the government. After his release from jail in October 1989, he served as deputy president of the ANC, but declined office when President Mandela was forming his cabinet in 1994. He remained one of Mandela's closest confidants until his death in Johannesburg on 5 May 2003.

SITHOLE, Ndabaningi

One of the most important among the Zimbabwean nationalists, Revd Ndabaningi Sithole was born in Matabeleland, Rhodesia, on 31 July 1920. He studied in local mission schools before completing his education in the United States at the Andover Newton Theological School in Massachusetts. He was ordained a minister and appointed principal of a primary school when he returned to his native country. A firm supporter of native rights, he joined the Zimbabwe African People's Union (ZAPU) in the early 1960s and advocated a strategy of nonviolent resistance to the colonial régime. But he soon became disillusioned with ZAPU and founded his own party, the Zimbabwe African National Union (ZANU). He also abandoned nonviolence as a strategy after the avowedly racist government, under Ian Smith, made its infamous unilateral declaration of independence in 1965. Publicly demanding the overthrow of Smith's régime, Revd Sithole was accused of treason and imprisoned in 1969. He continued to plot against the white minority government while in prison and played a key role in mobilizing black resistance to it during the 1970s. Released in 1974, he sought refuge in Zambia where he continued to plot against the government. He returned to Rhodesia in 1977 and was invited by the prime minister, along with Bishop Abel Muzorewa, to take part in the discussion of peaceful means of achieving a satisfactory settlement of the constitutional problem. Sithole had established a reputation as the leading intellectual among the black nationalists with the publication of his *African Nationalism* (1959) and *Roots of Revolution* (1977). Following the establishment of an independent republic of Zimbabwe in 1980, however, his influence became almost negligible as he found himself eclipsed by other black nationalists, such as Canaan Banana, Bernard Chidzero, Robert Mugabe and Joshua Nkomo. From 1983 to 1991, he lived in self-imposed exile in the United States. Sithole returned to Zimbabwe and headed a new party, ZANU-Ndonga, but was convicted of plotting to assassinate Mugabe in 1997. Three years later he was released from prison to seek medical treatment in the United States, where he died (in Philadelphia) on 12 December 2000.

SMALLS, Robert

Born a slave in Beaufort, South Carolina, on 5 April 1839, Robert Smalls became a naval hero for the Union during the American Civil War (1861-65) and went on to serve as a congressman from South Carolina during Reconstruction (1865-77). The young Smalls was taken by his master in 1851 to Charleston, South Carolina, where he worked as a hotel waiter, hack driver and rigger. Pressed into service by the Confederate Navy at the outbreak of the Civil War, he was forced to work as a wheelman aboard the armed frigate, *Planter*. On 13 May 1862, Smalls and twelve other slaves seized control of the vessel and succeeded in turning it over to a Union naval squadron in Charleston harbour. This exploit won Smalls instant fame throughout the northern states, and he was eventually promoted to the captaincy of the *Planter* in 1863, after a few more feats of daring. In 1865, he joined the state militia and was shortly promoted to the rank of major-general. Despite his limited education, Smalls rose rapidly in politics when the Civil War was over. From 1868 to 1870 he served in the South Carolina House of Representatives and from 1871 to 1874 in the state Senate. He was elected to the US Congress (1875-79, 1881-87), where he often spoke eloquently in favour of racial equality and social justice. In 1895, he delivered a memorable speech before the South Carolina constitutional convention in a valiant (but vain) attempt to prevent the virtual disenfranchisement of Blacks. Smalls spent his last years in Beaufort, where he served for a long time as port collector, working with white leaders to advance what he felt was the well-being of the whole community. The only blemish on his record was a conviction in 1877 for having accepted a bribe while he was a senator. He was pardoned by the governor. Smalls died on 22 February 1915.

SMITH, Bessie

One of the greatest women blues singers, Bessie Smith was born into a poor family in Chattanooga, Tennessee, on 15 April 1894. She began singing professionally from an early age, touring with such groups as Fats Chappelle's Rabbit Foot Minstrels and Florida Cotton Pickers. Eventually she formed her own band, the Liberty Belles, and became known as the

'Empress of the Blues'. She made several successful recordings with such great musicians as Louis Armstrong, Fletcher Henderson, Benny Goodman and Fats Waller. Her biggest hit, *Down Hearted Blues*, sold more than 2 million copies within a year. Smith starred in a short motion picture, *St Louis Blues*, in 1929. She died on 26 September 1937 from injuries sustained in a car accident. It is generally believed that, had Bessie been white, she would have received more prompt medical attention, saving her life. This became the subject of Edward Albee's play, *The Death of Bessie Smith*, in 1960.

SMITH, Emmitt

Emmitt James Smith was born in Pensacola, Florida on 15 May 1969. He excelled at football from early and was a star running back for the University of Florida during 1987-89. Drafted by the Dallas Cowboys of the National Football League (NFL), he won the Offensive Rookie of the Year Award in 1990 and in 1995 became the first player to rush for 25 touchdowns in a single season. In 2002, he broke the NFL rushing record when he eclipsed the mark of 16,726 yards that Walter Payton had set in 1987. By the end of the 2005-06 NFL season, Smith had accumulated 18,335 yards. He was voted Most Valuable Player in the NFL in 1992 and 1995. He leads all running backs with 166 career touchdowns and in rushing attempts with 4,409. Emmitt Smith was inducted into the College Football Hall of Fame in 2006.

SMITH, Ifeyironwa

Dr Ifeyironwa Smith is an author, researcher, teacher and a world-renowned expert in foods and nutrition. Born in Nigeria, she immigrated to Canada in 1997 after having served for many years as a Senior Lecturer at the Obafemi Awolowo University and a Consultant and Head of the Dietetic Unit at that institution's teaching hospitals. She has been a consultant in foods and nutrition to the International Foundation for Science and has written reports and recommendations for CareCanada, the West African Women's Association, the UN Development Fund for Women and the United Nation's Economic and Social Council (UNESCO). In addition to several scholarly articles, Dr Smith's research has also resulted in the publication of two seminal works: *Nutrition and Diet Therapy for Health Care Professionals in Africa* (1995) and *Foods in West Africa: Their Origin and Use* (1998).

SMITH, Zadie

Regarded as one of the finest young British novelists, Zadie Smith was born of mixed parentage in London in 1975. She studied English at Cambridge University and graduated with a BA in 1998. Her reputation is based on the remarkable success of her first two novels, *White Teeth* (2000) and *The*

Autograph Man (2002). She has already won numerous awards, including the Whitbread First Novel Award (2000), and the Jewish Quarterly Wingate Prize for Fiction. In 2003, she became a fellow at the Harvard University's Radcliffe Institute for Advanced Study.

SOBERS, Gary

The Rt Excellent Sir Garfield St Auburn Sobers was born in Barbados, West Indies, on 28 July 1936. An exceptionally gifted athlete, he represented his country in three different sports before he had reached the age of seventeen. He played cricket, football and basketball for Barbados in his youth, and became one of the island's finest golfers after he had passed the age of forty. It was as a cricketer that Sobers made himself world-famous. He was easily the most versatile bowler that the world has yet seen, capable of bowling his left-arm deliveries effectively in three different styles. He was the greatest batsman in the world while at his peak (1958-70). He was also one of the most brilliant all-round fielders in cricket's history. At the international level, Sobers scored 8,032 runs at an average of 57.78 per innings. His Test aggregate was then a world record. His 365 not out at Pakistan's expense in 1958 remained a world record for more than 36 years. He also captured 235 wickets (av: 34.03), and held 109 catches in 93 Test matches for the West Indies during 1954-74. These statistics explain why Sobers is universally recognized as the greatest all-rounder that the game of cricket has yet produced. He captained Barbados, Nottinghamshire and the West Indies and was knighted in 1975 for his services to cricket. Altogether, in 383 first-class matches, Sobers registered 28,315 runs (av: 54.87); 1,043 wickets (av: 27.74); and 407 catches. He was named a National Hero by the Barbados government in April 1998 and, in April 2002, a huge statue was erected in his honour in St Michael.

SOBHUZA I

King Sobhuza I is the great Swazi leader who founded an independent kingdom in what is now Swaziland early in the nineteenth century. Born in the 1780s, he succeeded to the chieftaincy of his Ngwane clan around 1815. A contemporary of the famous Shaka, he was forced by that Zulu warrior-king to lead his subjects to safety from their original homeland on the Pongola River in South Africa. By 1818, Sobhuza had established his new kingdom several miles away from its initial location but still found it necessary to protect himself and his people by contracting diplomatic marriage alliances with Shaka. In 1839, Sobhuza consolidated his position by defeating Skaka's successor, Dingane, in a pitched battle. His own policy of allowing conquered clans to be governed directly by their traditional chiefs gave his new nation the popularity and support necessary to enable it to survive the repeated dangers to which it was subject in those days from both African neighbours and European invaders.

SOBHUZA II

Born in Mbabane on 22 July 1899, Sobhuza II, King of Swaziland, established a remarkable record as the longest reigning monarch in the history of the world. He was the son of King Ngwane V, who died a few months after he was born. Sobhuza was thus the official ruler of Swaziland before the twentieth century had begun. His grandmother served as regent before he assumed the full reins of authority in 1921. He led his kingdom to independence in 1968, when a constitutional monarchy replaced the imperial administration, but in 1973 reverted to the traditional system of government in which he and his personal advisers exercised power. The political leaders were no longer elected, but the cabinet and the ministers were appointed by Sobhuza II himself. The latter's pragmatism provided Swaziland with an enviable measure of political stability until his death on 21 August 1982. He had reigned for more than sixty years and had officially held the throne for almost eighty-three.

SOBUKWE, Robert

Robert Mangaliso Sobukwe was a South African black nationalist who protested against the blatant injustices of the apartheid system and consequently spent many years in prison and under surveillance. Born at Graaff-Reinet, in Cape Province, on 5 December 1924, he was a graduate of Fort Hare University where he became secretary of the African National Congress (ANC) youth league. He later taught at Witwatersrand University and edited *The Africanist*. In 1958 Sobukwe seceded from the ANC to form the Pan-Africanist Congress (PAC) which sought to eliminate racism from South Africa by the use of nonviolent strategies. On 21 March 1960 when he and other Blacks demonstrated peacefully against the restrictive pass laws, police opened fire and killed more than sixty of them in the notorious Sharpeville Massacre. Sobukwe was arrested, charged with incitement to riot, and imprisoned until 1969. Even after he was released he was denied the right to emigrate to the United States where he was offered several opportunities to teach. He remained in South Africa, studied law and practised as a qualified attorney after 1975. He died on 27 February 1978.

SOGA, Tiyo

Tiyo Soga was an eminent Xhosa journalist, minister, translator, composer of hymns and collector of Bantu fables and customs. He is famous for having produced in 1866 an excellent translation of John Bunyan's *Pilgrim's Progress*, which had a profound influence on the evolution of the Xhosa language. Born around 1829 in Gwali, South Africa, Revd Soga belonged to the first generation of truly literate Xhosa speakers and was the first African minister to be ordained in Great Britain (Glasgow, 1856). During the 1860s, he contributed regularly to *Indaba* (The News), addressing a wide range of issues in a humorous and intelligent manner. He also composed a large number of Christian hymns in Xhosa, which continue to be sung in several South African churches today. Soga's influence upon subsequent generations of Xhosa writers is simply immense. Tiyo Soga died on 12 August 1871.

SOJO, Juan Pablo

Born in Curiepe in 1908, Juan Pablo Sojo is regarded by many literary critics as the first significant African-Venezuelan author. His best known novel, *Nochebuena negra*, first written in 1930, was finally published in 1943. It proved to be a cleverly crafted protest on behalf of the black peasantry in Venezuela. Sojo died in Caracas in 1948.

SOLANKE, Ladipo

Ladipo Solanke was born in Abeokuta, Nigeria, in 1884. He went to London, England, in 1922 to study law and became a barrister. He was the driving force behind the establishment in 1925 of the West African Students' Union (WASU) which became the main social, cultural and political focus for Africans in Britain for the next thirty years. During World War II, WASU constantly drew parliament's attention to African problems and became increasingly insistent upon the granting of colonial self-government. It also played a crucial role in the fifth Pan African Congress which met at Manchester in 1945. Solanke was a prolific writer and the first person to make a BBC broadcast in the Yoruba language. He was an outstanding figure in the nationalist awakening of Nigeria and its neighbouring countries. He died in London in 1958.

SOLOMON, Adam

Adam Solomon, better known as 'The Professor', was born in Mombasa, Kenya. A versatile musician who incorporates a number of African sounds and rhythms into his musical style, he immigrated to Canada in 1992 and formed the popular band, Tikisa, in 1995. They were much encouraged by the success of their first two CDs, *Safari* (1996) and *Tabia* (2001). Their *African Renaissance Blues* won a Juno Award in 2005. Adam Solomon himself sings in six languages, plays bass and rhythm guitar and plays the keyboard. In addition to performing, he has also developed a fine reputation as a teacher and has made a valuable contribution to programmes on African Heritage education in Canada.

SOSA, Tom

Thomas G. Sosa, a native of Trinidad and Tobago, immigrated to Canada in 1958 and completed his education at the Universities of Winnipeg, Manitoba, Toronto and Michigan. During 1964-71, he lectured at Ryerson Polytechnic (now Ryerson University) in Toronto. He served as Director of Student and Academic Services during 1971-77 and was then appointed Vice-President of Ryerson, perhaps the first Black to hold such high office in a Canadian university. From 1989 to 1993, he was the provincial deputy-minister of Mines and then of Skills Development. This gave him ample opportunities to promote programmes in education that catered to the needs of Blacks and other immigrants in Ontario. In addition to being a successful educator and administrator, Thomas Sosa was very actively involved in the community. He supported the Afropan Steelband, the Black Achievers Programme, the Subway Academy, the West Indies United Football Club and West Rouge Community Association. At various points, too, he served as chairperson of such organizations as the Canada Employment and Immigration Council, the Canadian Labour Market and Productivity Centre, the Law Society of Upper Canada, the Ontario Training Corporation, the Progress Career Planning Centre and the Society for Conflict Resolution in Ontario.

SOUTHWELL, Rustum

A native of St Kitts, a small island in the Caribbean, Rustum Southwell immigrated to Canada in 1972 and became one of the most successful businessmen in Nova Scotia. He owned and operated a Harvey's franchise and served as Chair of Harvey's Atlantic Franchise Association as well as Executive Director of the African Canadian Business Development Centre. In 1996, he was appointed founding Executive Director of the Black Business Initiative (BBI) which was funded by federal and provincial grants to create business opportunities for Blacks in Nova Scotia. Under Southwell's direction, the BBI has done extremely well. He continues to be an active community servant with his involvement in the affairs of the Black Employment Partnership committees, the African Heritage Month Committee and the Black Cultural Society.

SOYINKA, Wole

The first African writer to win the coveted Nobel Prize for Literature was the Nigerian playwright and poet, Akinwande Oluwole Soyinka, who was honoured with this distinction in 1986. The son of a school inspector, he was born near Abeokuta, in southwestern Nigeria, on 13 July 1934. He attended local schools and the Government College at Ibadan, before completing his education at Ibadan University in Nigeria and Leeds

University in England. It was during his stay in the United Kingdom that Soyinka established his reputation as a most promising dramatist with such fine plays as *The Invention* (1955), *The Lion and the Jewel* (1959), *The Swamp Dwellers* (1959), *The Trials of Brother Jero* (1960) and *The Strong Breed* (1960). These early plays were so successful that he was commissioned to write a serious drama to celebrate Nigeria's achievement of political independence in 1960. The result was the production in that same year of *The Dance of the Forest*. Returning to Nigeria, Soyinka served for a while as head of the English department at Lagos University and became research professor of drama at the University of Ife in 1972. But his poetry, novels and plays were all characterized by political satire and often therefore resulted in strained relations between himself and the Nigerian political leaders. Equally candid and critical is *The Open Sore of a Continent: A Personal Narrative of the Nigerian Crisis* (1997). Soyinka was actually imprisoned during 1967-69 for his violent criticism of the government's corruption. One of his plays, *The Road*, won first prize at the Dakar Festival of Negro Arts in 1960 and was successfully staged in London, England, in 1965.Another, *The Strong Breed*, was performed in London in 1968. Among his numerous other plays are *Camwood on the Leaves* (1960), *The House of Bandiji* (1962), *Blackout* (1965), *Madmen and Scientists* (1965), *Kongi's Harvest* (1967), *The Detainee* (1968), *A Play of Giants* (1984), *Requiem for a Futurologist* (1985) and *Death and the King's Horseman* (2002). As a poet, Soyinka is chiefly remembered for his *Idanre and Other Poems* (1965) and *Poems from Prison* (1969). His novels include *The Interpreters* (1965), *The Forest of a Thousand Daemons* (1968), and *Season of Anomy* (1973). He has also written several critical commentaries on African literature and theatre. A collection of his essays, especially cited by the Swedish Academy in 1986, is entitled *Myth, Literature, and the African World*. Soyinka is one of the finest of all African authors and arguably black Africa's most accomplished playwright. He is also one of the sternest critics of African misrule and corruption in the age of independence.

SPARKS, Corrine

The Hon Judge Corrine E. Sparks was appointed to the Nova Scotia Family Court in 1987 and thus became Canada's first black female judge. Born in Halifax, Nova Scotia, she received a BA from Mount St Vincent University in 1974 and an LLB from Dalhousie University in 1979. She worked for some years as an officer with the Nova Scotia Human Rights Commission before serving as a corporate manager with Turbo Resources in Alberta. In addition to her duties as a judge since 1987, Corrine Sparks has also been a lecturer with the National New Judges Training Programme and a lecturer with the Commonwealth Judicial Education Institute. In 1993, she was appointed a member of the Canadian Bar Association's Gender Equality

Task Force where, among other things, she completed a study on Women of Colour in the legal profession. In 1997 she was honoured by the Canadian Association of Black Lawyers as well as the Black Law Students of Canada. She was also honoured by the Congress of Black Women in 2002 and by the Elizabeth Fry Society in 2003. An ardent community servant, Judge Sparks has served on a number of boards, including the Nova Scotia Home for Coloured Children and the Canadian Mental Health Association.

SPARROW, Mighty

Born Slinger Francisco in Grenada in 1934, the Mighty Sparrow has dominated the field of Caribbean calypso for more than forty years. Moving early to Trinidad, he was the Calypso King in that island's annual carnival festival for an unconscionably long time. Sparrow, quite simply, is one of the outstanding musicians and singers produced by the West Indies thus far and has been churning out popular hits ever since his celebrated *Jean and Dinah* in 1956. He has toured successfully throughout Canada, Europe and the United States. Some of his most memorable songs include *Queen's Canary* (1957), *Leave the Damn Doctor* (1959), *Ten to One is Murder* (1960), *Wahbeen and Grog* (1962), *Dan is the Man in the Van* (1963), *Obeah Wedding* (1966), *Good Citizen* (1972), *Maharajhin's Sister* (1983), *Invade South Africa* (1986), *Rocking Soca* (1988), *Music to Wine* (1989) and *Let the Music Play* (1990). Sparrow's appeal lies in his ability to articulate the feelings of ordinary Trinidadians in their own language and cadence while offering half-serious and half-comic social commentary.

SPENCER, Baldwin

The Honourable Winston Baldwin Spencer has been the prime minister of Antigua and Barbuda since 24 March 2004 when he finally led his United Progressive Party (UPP) to victory over its perennial nemesis, the Antiguan Labour Party, led by Lester Bird. Spencer was born on 8 October 1948 and attended the Greenbay Primary School and the Princess Margaret Secondary School before furthering his education at the Coady International Institute (Canada), Oxford University (England) and Oslo University (Norway). Returning to Antigua, he offered strong leadership to both the UPP and the Antigua and Barbuda Workers' Union. He has also been an active community servant, supporting a variety of sporting organizations and presiding over the Caribbean Maritime and Aviation Council.

SPIKES, Richard

Richard Spikes was born around 1880. He was a truly gifted and creative engineer whose successful inventions included the railroad semaphore (1906); a beer keg tap 1910); the self-locking rack for billiard cues (1910); an automatic car washer (1913); automobile signals (1913); the continuous contact trolley pole (1919); a combination milk bottle opener and cover (1926); the automatic gear shift (1932); the automatic transmission (1933); the automatic shoe-shine chair (1939); a multiple barrel machine gun (1940); a horizontally swinging barber chair (1950); and an automatic safety brake (1962). Many of these inventions were a godsend to major companies. The beer keg tap, for instance was purchased by the Milwaukee Brewing Company, while the automobile directional signals shortly became standard equipment for all vehicles. His automatic safety brake was soon to be found in every school bus in the United States. For his innovative gear shifting and transmission devices, Spikes received over $100,000 - an enormous sum for an African-American in the 1930s. He died in 1962.

SPOTTSWOOD, Stephen Gill

Bishop Stephen Gill Spottswood was a prominent religious and civil rights leader who served for many years as the chairman of the board of directors of the National Association for the Advancement of Colored People (NAACP). Born in Boston, Massachusetts, on 18 July 1897, he was ordained in the African Methodist Episcopal Zion Church after graduating from the Gordon College of Theology (Boston) in 1919. He preached in a variety of churches before being promoted to a bishopric in 1952. Although he was generally regarded as a moderate, Bishop Spottswood was very actively involved in the civil rights movement and often joined picket lines, organized boycotts and initiated protests. He died on 1 December 1974.

SPRINGER, Hugh

Born in Barbados, West Indies, on 22 January 1913, the Rt Excellent Sir Hugh Worrell Springer was a distinguished Caribbean lawyer, statesman and educator who was elevated to the status of a National Hero by the Barbados Government in 1998. After attending Harrison College, he proceeded to Oxford University (England), where he graduated with a first-class BA in 1936. He then studied law at the Inner Temple and was called to the bar in 1938. He practised law very successfully in Barbados until 1947, when he was appointed the first registrar of the University College of the West Indies at Mona, Jamaica. As an administrator, he made an invaluable contribution to that institution over the next twenty-two years. In 1963 he became the first director of its Faculty of Education which shortly became one of the most important institutes in the region, training teachers from all across the Caribbean, and replacing the various ministries of education as the accreditation body for teachers. In 1954, Springer was awarded the Order of the British Empire (OBE) and was made a Commander of the British Empire (CBE) in 1963. In 1971, he was named Knight Commander of the Order of St Michael and St George (KCMG) for his service to higher education in Barbados and the Commonwealth In 1984, Sir Hugh Springer was appointed Governor General of Barbados. He died on 13 April 1994. In his younger days he had been a driving force behind the formation of the Barbados Labour Party (BLP) and the Barbados Workers' Union (BWU). But his work extended far beyond Barbados and the University of the West Indies. He served for many years as secretary to the Association of Commonwealth Universities and as chairman of the Commonwealth Human Ecology Council.

SRI II

Born Cornelius Kofi Kwakume in 1862, this paramount chief of Anlo in western Africa for almost fifty years distinguished himself as a statesman and innovator.   Educated at the Bremen Mission School at Keta, he assumed the title of Togbi Sri II in 1907 and spent the rest of his life trying to spread Christianity throughout his state and fighting against superstitious taboos. He represented the Ewe in the Gold Coast Legislative Council during 1916-38 and sat on the Eastern Provincial Council from 1926 to 1956, constantly promoting two causes in particular: Ewe unity and African independence. Eager to promote the material progress of his people, he felt that this could best be accomplished through co-operation with the British. For his efforts he was awarded the King's Medal for African Chiefs (KMAC) during World War I. He later received the Order of the British Empire (OBE) and Commander of the British Empire (CBE) from the colonial government. While well regarded by the British, Sri remained very popular also with the Africans. He died in 1956. His greatest disappointment was the failure of the Europeans after World War I to advance the cause of Ewe unity. The settlement of 1919 had left too many of his people outside the British colonial boundaries.

STEVENS, Siaka

Siaka Probyn Stevens, who became prime minister of Sierra Leone when he was sixty-two years old, was born in Tolubu on 24 August 1905. He began his career as a policeman but gradually became involved in labour politics and helped, in 1943, to found the United Mineworkers' Union. A staunch advocate of African nationalism and workers' rights and a powerful and persuasive orator, Stevens was elected to the colonial legislature in the early 1950s. He became minister of lands, mines and labour in 1953. But he soon quarrelled with the other members of the administration and established his own All People's Congress (APC) which became strong enough to win an electoral majority in 1967. Stevens, however, was promptly ousted by a military coup and went into exile. In 1968, he was restored by a counter coup and became Sierra Leone's first president when it declared itself a republic in 1971. After his re-election as president in 1976, he turned the country into a one-party state and reached the pinnacle of his career in 1980 when he was elected chairman of the Organization of African Unity (OAU) and presided over its summit meeting in Freetown. At the age of eighty, he resigned from the presidency in 1985 in favour of his hand-picked successor, Maj Gen Joseph Saidu Momoh. He died on 29 May 1988.

STOKES, Carl

Carl Burton Stokes is historically significant in that he became the first African-American to be elected mayor of a major US city when he won the mayoralty election in Cleveland, Ohio, in 1966. Born in that city on 21 June 1927, he had received his BS degree in law from the University of Minnesota in 1954 before completing his LLD in 1956. After serving for some years as probation officer for the Cleveland Municipal Court, he was elected to the Ohio State legislature as a Democrat in 1962. His voting record established him as a moderate although he was a consistent supporter of civil rights legislation. After two terms as mayor of Cleveland, Stokes joined the news staff of NBC-TV in New York and became that city's first black television news anchorman. Stokes later served as US ambassador to Seychelles. He died on 4 April 1996.

STUART, Moira

Moira Stuart, born in 1952, was the first black female newsreader on British television. She worked as a community announcer and newsreader for both BBC Radio 4 and Radio 2 before moving to television in 1981. Since then she has presented almost every news bulletin devised on BBC TV. She was voted Best Newscaster of the Year in 1988 by the TV and Radio Industries Club Awards, and in 1989 Best TV Personality by the Women of Achievement Awards. The Black Journalists' Association named her the Best TV Personality in 1994, and in 1997 she was adjudged the Best Media Personality by the influential black newspaper, *The Voice*. Stuart has served on various boards and panels, including Amnesty International, the Royal Television Society, United Nations Association, the London Fair Play Consortium and the Human Genetics Advisory Commission. She was awarded the OBE in 2001 and received an honorary doctorate from Edinburgh University in 2006.

SUNDIATA

Sundiata was the great west African monarch who founded the Sudanese empire of Mali in the thirteenth century and laid the basis for its future prosperity and political unity. A Mandingo from the small kingdom of Kangaba, near the present Mali-Guinea border, Sundiata was one of twelve brothers who were heirs to the throne of Kangaba. After his brothers were all killed by neighbouring enemies in Kaniaga, he exacted revenge by defeating them at the battle of Kirina around 1235. During the following decade or so, Sundiata extended his control over an extensive territory stretching as far north as the southern fringes of the Sahara desert, east to the Great Bend of the Niger River, south to the gold fields of Wangara, and west to the Senegal River. He moved his headquarters from Jeriba, the former capital of Kangaba, to Niani, which soon became one of the most important commercial centres in the Sudan. Sundiata died in 1255. The imperial system he established survived long after him because of his religious toleration, respect for conquered clans, and administrative competence. Mali remained the strongest force in western Africa until the emergence of the Songhai Empire during the fifteenth century.

SUNNI ALI BER
Sunni Ali Ber, who governed the Songhai from 1464 to 1492, was perhaps the most important among the rulers of that great empire in western Africa. It was he who founded the powerful dynasty that ruled over a vast territory during the fifteenth and sixteenth centuries. Establishing his headquarters at Timbuktu, the old Mali capital, he built up a strong army, excellent bureaucracy and centralized administration, bringing several neighbouring city-states under his personal direction. The remnants of the old Mali empire fell steadily under his own control and he was left in charge of most of the traditional trade routes linking the Niger River to Ethiopia and Egypt. He kept his new empire intact by treating his subject peoples humanely and offering them justice at home and protection from hostile neighbours. He encouraged education, trade, commerce and public works, building schools, canals and roads at what was a truly remarkable pace for the fifteenth century. Although not himself a Muslim, Sunni Ali Ber allowed the old Mali priests to keep the mosques open and his empire became famous for its Islamic culture as well as its military might. His sudden and mysterious death in 1492 was a great misfortune for western Africa but his solid foundations paved the way for the mighty deeds of the emperor Muhammad Touré (1493-1528) who followed him.

SUTHERLAND, Efua
Efua Theodora Sutherland was born, on 27 June 1924, in Cape Coast in what is now Ghana. She is generally seen as black Africa's most famous female writer. Educated at St Monica's School in the Gold Coast and the Universities of Cambridge and London in England, she returned to her native country in 1951 and helped to found the Writers' Workshop at the Institute of African Studies at the University of Ghana in Legon. She was

also instrumental in the founding of the Ghana Drama Studio and the Ghana Society of Writers. Sutherland played a key role, too, in the creation of *Okyeame*, an influential literary magazine, and for many years directed the University of Ghana's travelling theatre group, Kusum Agoromba. She published some fine plays, including *Anansegora* (1964), *Edufa* (1967), *Foriwa* (1967), *Vulture! Vulture!* (1968), *Tahinta* (1968) and *Nyamekye*. Her book of fairy tales and folklore in Ghana, *The Voice in the Forest*, was published in 1983. Sutherland also wrote several poems, essays and short stories. She died on 22 January 1996.

SWEENEY, Sylvia

Sylvia Sweeney was a superstar on the Canadian basketball team at the Seoul Olympics in 1988 when she was chosen the most valuable player in the whole competition. The same dedication and perseverance she displayed on the court has been much in evidence off it. She has become the president of Elitha Peterson Productions Inc., an innovative television production company. She has co-hosted the show, *POV: Women*, on the Women's Television Network and directed the popular programme *Hymn to Freedom*. She won an award for her documentary, *In the Key of Oscar*, which featured her uncle, Oscar Peterson, the celebrated Canadian musician. Sweeney is also a director of the Toronto Raptors, a team in the National Basketball Association (NBA).

SYLVAIN, Georges

Georges Sylvain was born in the Dominican Republic, on 2 April 1866, while his Haitian family was in exile. He completed his education in Paris, France, and returned to Haiti to practise law. In 1896 he founded the literary magazine, *La Ronde*, to which he contributed a number of articles. He served as Haiti's ambassador to Paris during 1909-11 and was among those intellectuals who condemned the American occupation of Haiti as a sudden loss of independence after 112 years of hard-earned freedom. Sylvain was a noted translator (in French and creole) as well as a competent historian. He also wrote several fine poems, most of which appeared in *Confidences et mélancolies: poésies 1885-1898* (1901). His two-volume study, *Dix années de lutte pour la liberté* (1915-1925) is still regarded as one of Haiti's literary classics. Many of his speeches and essays also appeared in print. Georges Sylvain died on 2 August 1925.

TACHIE-MENSON, Charles William

Born at Butre in the Gold Coast in 1889, Sir Charles William Tachie-Menson was educated at Shama Methodist School in Elmina. He enjoyed a brilliant career of public service in the Gold Coast, serving for many years on the Sekondi-Takoradi Town Council and the Gold Coast Legislative Council. He was a member of the Coussey Committee on Constitutional Reform which met in 1949. Tachie-Menson was also a very successful business executive, working for some thirty-five years after 1910 with the Elder Shipping Lines. He became a director of the West African Airways Corporation (1946-52), of the Gold Coast Development Board (1948-51), and of Barclays Bank D.C.O. He was also elected the first general president of the Gold Coast Trade Union Congress. Tachie-Menson was the recipient of several honours and distinctions, including the Order of the British Empire (OBE) in 1947, Commander of the British Empire (CBE) in 1955, and a knighthood (KCMG) in 1960. He died in London, England, on 17 October 1962.

TAMBO, Oliver

Oliver Reginald Tambo was born on 27 October 1917 at Bizana, Transkei, of humble parentage. He was educated at St Peter's Secondary School in Johannesburg and the University of Fort Hare (BSc, 1941). After teaching for a while at his old school, he studied law and entered private practice in a partnership with Nelson Mandela. Together they founded the African National Congress (ANC) Youth League in 1944. Tambo was elected secretary-general of the ANC in 1955 and his opposition to the apartheid régime led to his imprisonment during 1956-57. When the ANC was banned in 1960, he went into exile to lead it from foreign bases. He spent the next thirty years publicizing the black nationalist cause, promoting the international boycott of South Africa, and raising money to support the armed struggle against apartheid. His unrelenting assault on the racist government played a key role in its eventual collapse, and he returned in triumph to Johannesburg in December 1990. Tambo, however, had suffered a stroke in 1989 and the leadership of the ANC fell to Nelson Mandela while he was named honorary chairman. He died on 24 April 1993.

TANNER, Henry Ossawa

Born on 21 June 1859 in Pittsburgh, Pennsylvania, Henry Ossawa Tanner was the first African-American to be elected a full member of the National Academy of Design. He is remembered as one of North America's foremost painters whose work has been frequently exhibited all across the United States and Europe. After teaching for some years at Clark University in Atlanta, Georgia, Tanner moved to France in 1891. His works were much better received there than they had been in his native country and he became particularly famous for his successful biblical paintings. Among a host of prestigious awards and distinctions, he was made a Chevalier of the Legion of Honor in 1923. He died on 25 May 1937.

TASAMMA NADAW

Tasamma Nadaw was a noted Ethiopian political and military leader during the reign of Emperor Menilek II. He was instrumental in the conquest of the Galla and thus contributed to the expansion of the empire towards the east during the 1880s and 1890s. He participated actively, too, in the war against Italy in 1895-96 and helped to conquer Kaffa. He became one of Menilek II's most trusted advisers after the death of Ras Makonnen in 1905. Tasamma Nadaw died on 10 April 1911.

TAYLOR, Charles

Charles Ghankay Taylor was born on 28 January 1948 to a family of American-Liberians, the elite group descended from the freed slaves who had founded the country in the nineteenth century. Educated in the United States, he returned to Liberia and became an important administrator during Samuel Doe's presidency (1980-90). When he was accused by Doe of embezzlement, he fled to the United States and began to plot his accuser's overthrow. In 1989, he launched an armed uprising from Côte d'Ivoire which soon resulted in Doe's demise, but the civil war disintegrated into a violent conflict among several ethnic factions and it was not before 1997 that Taylor could contrive to win the presidency of the country. By 2003 his government had collapsed. Taylor sought refuge in Nigeria but found himself charged with crimes against humanity and now faces trial by a UN court in the Hague.

TAYLOR, Garth

Dr Garth Alfred Taylor was an ophthalmologist and a cornea specialist who served for many years as the Chief of the Department of Ophthalmology at Cornwall General and Hotel Dieu Hospitals. He was also a professor in the Department of Ophthalmology at Queen's University in Montreal. Born in Montego Bay, Jamaica, on 29 April 1944, he immigrated to Canada in 1976. He was the founder and director of Canadian Surgical Eye Expeditions (CANSEE), a voluntary organization that provides eye services to patients in developing countries. He was also a member of ORBIS, an international humanitarian organization that provides hands-on training to local eye doctors, nurses, technicians and health care workers, restoring sight to thousands in developing countries. Altogether he made over 100 such missions and performed more than 1,000 surgeries in about sixty countries. In addition, his scholarly papers made valuable contributions to the study of ophthalmology. Dr Taylor was totally dedicated to the elimination of preventable blindness around the world. He was the recipient of numerous honours and distinctions, including the Meritorious Service Medal from the Government of

Canada in 2001 and the Order of Distinction from the Government of Jamaica in 2004. He died in Ottawa, Ontario, on 19 November 2005.

TAYLOR, John

John David Beckett Taylor, Baron Taylor of Warwick, is a British politician and a member of the House of Lords. In 1996, he became the first Black to be named a life peer by the Conservative party. Born in Birmingham in 1952, he was educated at Moseley Grammar School and Keele University and worked for some years with the media. In 1990-91 he served as special adviser to the home secretary and the minister of state when his portfolio included inner cities, legal services and crime prevention. In his first year in the upper house, he skilfully piloted through the important Criminal Evidence Amendment Act. Lord Taylor is the vice-president of the British Board of Film Classification and vice-chairman of the All Party Parliamentary Media Group. He is a patron of various children's charities and vice-president of the National Small Business Bureau. He is chancellor of Bournemouth University and was awarded an honorary doctorate of laws by Warwick University in 1999.

TAYTU BETUL

This revered empress of Ethiopia was a very influential wife of Menilek II. Born around 1853, Taytu Betul played an important role in the reign of one of Ethiopia's most important monarchs. It was she who gave the name of Addis Ababa to Menilek's capital in 1887 and during her husband's last days she was the de facto ruler of Ethiopia. After Menilek's death in 1913, however, the Council of Ministers excluded her from its meetings and considerably reduced her influence. She died on 11 February 1918. Taytu Betel is remembered for having managed her own estates most astutely and for occasionally feeding the poor in Addis Ababa very sumptuously.

TAYYE GABRA-MARYAM

Alaqa Tayye Gabra-Maryam was a noted Ethiopian scholar, author, teacher and preacher. After attending an evangelical mission school at Monkula in the early 1870s, he returned to the province of Bagemder where he was born in 1858. He became proficient in the Ge'ez language and in the teachings of the Ethiopian Orthodox Church. He then taught for many years in Monkolu and published five books on religious subjects, but his most memorable work was a Ge'ez grammar which appeared in 1889. Such was his reputation for scholarship that Emperor Menilek II commissioned him to write a history of Ethiopia and recommended him to the German Kaiser when the latter needed an expert to catalogue Ethiopian manuscripts and to teach Ge'ez at the University of Berlin. Tayye Gabra-Maryam continued to serve the government after Menilek II's death and published a social history of Ethiopia in 1922. He died in 1924.

TERRELL, Mary Eliza Church

Mary Eliza Church Terrell was a prominent author and civil rights leader who, in 1895, became the first African-American woman to be appointed to a District of Columbia school board. She served with distinction on that body until 1911. She was born in Memphis, Tennessee, in 1863 and educated at Oberlin College, Ohio, where she achieved her BA in 1883 and her MA in 1888. From 1885 to 1887, she taught at Wilberforce University before marriage to one of the founders of the Robert H. Terrell Law School took her to Washington, D.C., where she became a charter member of the National Association of Colored Women. A staunch advocate of women's rights, she served as president of that organization from 1896 to 1901. At the International Conference of Women in Berlin in 1904, Mary Terrell amazed the audience by addressing them in English, French and German while eloquently advocating equality for women and Blacks. Not surprisingly, she was also one of the founders of the National Association for the Advancement of Colored People (NAACP) in 1909 and served as vice-president of the Washington branch for many years. In 1953, at the advanced age of ninety, she headed a group opposing segregation in the District of Columbia and helped to persuade the US Supreme Court to abolish it in the nation's capital. Her interesting biography, *A Colored Woman in a White World*, was published in 1940. Mary Church Terrell died on 24 July 1954 after a very long career of distinguished community and public service.

TEWODROS II

Born around 1818 as Kassa, the son of Haylu Walda Giyorgis (a governor of the province of Qwara), this Ethiopian emperor changed his name to Tewodros (meaning the elect of God) to reunify his people after he had himself rebelled against the incumbent emperor and established his own supremacy by a series of bold campaigns. Having cowed the nobility into submission, he was crowned king on 11 February 1855. He attempted many administrative and social reforms and put an end to the internal feuds that had bedevilled Ethiopia for more than fifty years. He appointed religious and political leaders whom he could trust and brought the whole administration as well as the Ethiopian Church more tightly under central control. He invited Europeans to assist with the building of roads and the manufacture of ships and generally ruled with much intelligence. But in the end he alienated himself from the Ethiopian élite, while also falling foul of the British government, and was ousted early in 1868 by a combination of British troops and rebellious aristocrats. He committed suicide shortly afterwards (13 April 1868). Tewodros II is remembered for being the first Ethiopian ruler to seek to modernize his country by using western models.

THOMAS, Horatio

Dr Horatio Oritsejolmi Thomas was the first Nigerian physician to become a fellow of the British Royal College of Surgeons. Born in Sapele, Nigeria, on 31 August 1917, he studied medicine in the United Kingdom and returned to practice in his native country. He lectured in surgery at the University of Lagos from 1949 until his promotion to a professorship there in 1962. In that year, too, he was appointed dean and provost of the university's College of Medicine. From 1972 to 1975 Dr Thomas served as vice-chancellor of the University of Ibadan. He was awarded the Commander of the British Empire (CBE) in 1963 and the Cross of Nigeria in 1965. In addition to publishing numerous papers in British and west African medical journals, he contributed to the classic *Diseases of Children in the Subtropics and Tropics* (1970). Dr Thomas died on 2 July 1979.

THOMAS, Nigel

Dr H. Nigel Thomas was born in St Vincent. He immigrated to Canada in 1968 and completed his education at Concordia University and L'Université de Montréal. For many years he taught at secondary schools in Quebec before becoming a professor of literature at L'Université Laval. He is the author of many publications, including novels, poems, critical studies and short stories. He is best known for his use of Caribbean folklore and his exploration of that region's complex social and cultural dynamics. His major works include *From Folklore to Fiction: A Study of Folk Heroes and Rituals in the Black American Novel* (1988); *Spirits in the Dark* (1993); *How Loud Can the Cock Crow?* (1996); *Moving Through Darkness* (1999); and *Behind the Face of Winter* (2001). Professor Thomas is the founder of the literary journal, *KOLA*, and was one of the co-founders of the Free South Africa Committee in Montreal.

THOMAS, Jesse

Jesse Thomas, who was born in McComb, Mississippi, in 1883, became a prominent civil rights leader rendering yeoman service to the National Urban League for many years. After studying at the Tuskegee Institute in Alabama and the New York School for Social Work, he served briefly as examiner in charge of the US Employment Service. From 1919 onwards, he became totally devoted to the affairs of the Urban League, organizing several branches in Arkansas, Florida, Georgia, Louisiana and Virginia. Thomas also helped organize the Atlanta University School of Social Work, aimed largely at the training of African-American social workers. When he joined the staff of the American Red Cross in 1940, he became the first African-American to work for that organization in a professional capacity. He died in 1972.

THOMPSON, A.W. K.

Born in 1880 at Winneba, Gold Coast, Augustus William Kojo Thompson became one of the staunchest supporters of African nationalism in the inter-war years. Educated at schools in Cape Coast, Accra and Nigeria, he studied law at Lincoln's Inn in the United Kingdom and was called to the bar in 1914. He set up his private practice in Accra where he became leader of the Manbii Party and a member of the Gold Coast Legislative Council. A relentless critic of British imperialism, he was a member of the committee established in 1934 to lead the Gold Coast agitation against two unpopular bills recently passed by the metropolis. His political career suddenly ended in 1944, however, when he was convicted of extortion. Kojo Thompson died on 26 February 1950.

THOMPSON, Daley

Born on 30 July 1958 in London, Francis Morgan Thompson, better known as 'Daley' Thompson, is a former British decathlete who won two consecutive Olympic Gold Medals (1980 and 1984) and broke the world record for the event four times. His best score was 8847 points, the record he set at the Los Angeles Games in 1984. It lasted for nine years as a world record and was not bettered in Olympic competition until 2004. Thompson was the first athlete to simultaneously hold Olympic, Commonwealth, European and world titles in a single event. Through his showmanship and ability, he almost singlehandedly transformed the decathlon into a competition of great international interest and importance. Altogether he won eight gold medals in international competition during the 1980s. Thompson was voted the BBC Sports Personality of the Year in 1982 when he was also awarded the MBE. He was awarded the OBE in 1983 and the CBE in 2000.

THORNHILL, Esmeralda

Born in Barbados, West Indies, Dr Esmeralda M.A. Thornhill has the distinction of being the first scholar appointed to the James Robinson Johnston Chair in Black Canadian Studies at Dalhousie University, Halifax, Nova Scotia. She is a noted lawyer, linguist, lecturer, writer and human rights activist who was instrumental in promoting the Black History Month concept in Quebec. She is a founding member of the Congress of Black Women of Canada, the Congress of Black Lawyers-Jurists of Quebec and the International Resource Network for Women of African Descent. She is also an accomplished poet whose works have been published in English, French and Spanish. Dr Thornhill remains a vigorous community servant committed to the principles of gender equality and social justice for minority groups. She received honorary doctorates from City University of New York in 1996 and Concordia University in 1997. She was also chosen Woman of the Year in 1991 by the Salon de la femme in Quebec.

THUKU, Harry

An ardent African nationalist, Harry Thuku was the founder of the Young Kikuyu Association which protested British imperialism in Kenya during the inter-war years. He was particularly concerned with social justice and economic empowerment and urged the imperial government to pass mild social and economic reforms to ease the burden of the Kenyan poor. Although he was asking for no more than reasonable and moderate legislation on such mundane issues as coffee and land, Thuku was imprisoned by the British. This inevitably led to the formation of much more militant organizations in Kenya, culminating in the emergence of the Mau Mau association during the 1940s and 1950s.

THURMAN, Howard

Revd Howard Thurman was a famous American mystic and theologian who received honorary degrees from a wide range of academic institutions and whose sermons appeared in many books and pamphlets. He was born in Daytona Beach, Florida, on 18 November 1900 and ordained a Baptist minister in 1925 after studying at Morehouse College, Atlanta, and the Rochester Theological Seminary. From 1931 to 1943, Thurman was a professor and dean of the chapel at Howard University. Later he served as professor at Boston University. A poet as well as an author, his major books included *The Greatest of These* (1944), *Meditations for Apostles of Sensitiveness* (1947), *Jesus and the Disinherited* (1949), *Deep is the Hunger* (1951), *The Inward Journey* (1961), and *The Luminous Darkness* (1965). His autobiography, *With Hand and Heart*, appeared in 1980. Thurman was profoundly influenced by Mohandas Gandhi, whom he met while on an 'evangelical' tour of India in 1935. He was so deeply moved by Gandhi's conviction that Christianity 'fostered segregation' that he eventually decided to found the Church for Fellowship of All Peoples in San Francisco in 1944, an interracial, nondemonational religious fellowship. For nine years he served as co-pastor of this church with Alfred Fisk until, in 1953, he became the first Black to be appointed a full-time faculty member at the Boston University School of Theology. Revd Thurman was committed to making Christianity 'live for the weak as well as the strong - for all peoples whatever their colour, whatever their caste'. He died on 10 April 1981.

TOBOKU-METZGER, Albert

A fervent African nationalist who played a significant role in the early years of the National Congress of British West Africa (NCBWA), Albert Emerick Toboku-Metzger was born at Kissy, Sierra Leone, on 14 October 1856. He attended the Christian Missionary Society Grammar School at Freetown and Fourah Bay College before teaching briefly at the latter institution. He then became the first Sierra Leonean graduate to enter the colonial service. His salary of £45 per annum was far below what any European civil servant would have accepted or been offered. Nor was it before 1908 that a promotion came in the form of an appointment as assistant district commissioner. Toboku-Metzger steered the NCBWA wisely through the 1920s while serving as president. Elected to the Legislative Council in 1924, he also served as a Justice of the Peace and was awarded the Member of the British Empire (MBE). In addition to his administrative and political activities, he wrote numerous articles for the *Sierra Leone Weekly News* and published *Historical Sketch of the Sierra Leone Grammar School, 1845-1935*, an important local history. He died on 20 July 1950.

TOLBERT, William Richard, Jr

William Richard Tolbert, Jr, the 19th president of Liberia, was born in Bensonville on 13 May 1913 of a prominent family of early settlers. He graduated from Liberia College in 1934 and worked for some years as a civil servant before being elected to the House of Representatives in 1943. In 1951, he was chosen by President William Tubman to be his running mate as vice-president, and served in this capacity for the next twenty years. When Tubman died in 1971, Tolbert succeeded him. The new president immediately put his personal stamp on Liberia by dismissing some important officials for corruption and inefficiency, setting up a commission to reorganize the civil service, depriving a company of the important rice monopoly it had long enjoyed under Tubman, establishing cordial relations with the USSR, and offering dual citizenship to African-Americans. A devout Christian, Tolbert had previously devoted most of his energy to the affairs of the Baptist Church. He was president of the Liberian Baptist Missionary and Educational Convention and of the Baptist World Alliance. His presidency, however, proved unsuccessful. He could neither eliminate corruption completely nor stabilize Liberia's economy. When he attempted to arrest the opposition leaders who had called for a general strike, he was assassinated in Monrovia, his capital city, on 12 April 1980.

TOMBALBAYÉ, N'Garta

N'Garta Tombalbayé was the first president of the independent republic of Chad. He was born at Bessada, in what was then known as French

Equatorial Africa, on 15 June 1918 and taught for some years before
entering politics. In 1947, he helped to found the Parti Progressiste
Tchadien and soon became its acknowledged leader. His party emerged as
the strongest political force in the colony and Tombalbayé became Chad's
first premier in 1959 with the introduction of internal self-government.
When the country achieved its political independence in 1960, he merged
the main opposition party with the Progressiste Tchadien and won the
presidency in an uncontested election. Tombalbayé's ruthless and autocratic
leadership, however, soon produced civil strife and he often had to employ
French troops to hold his Chadian opponents at bay. In an attempt to
'chadize' the country, he changed his own name from François to N'Garta
and renamed Fort-Lamy, the capital, N'Djamena in 1973. N'Garta was
assassinated on 13 April 1975 during a military coup.

TOSH, Peter

Born Winston Hubert McIntosh in Westmoreland, Jamaica, on 9 October
1944, Peter Tosh became one of the most famous Jamaican musicians. He
was a founding member of Bob Marley's reggae band, the Wailers, who
revolutionized West Indian music. He took part in the Jamaican 'Peace
Concert' of 1978 which Marley had intended to halt the violent feuds
between the political parties of the day. Tosh used this forum not only to
defend political freedom but to advocate the legalization of marijuana and
to denounce police brutality. With the Wailers he recorded such hits as *Catch
a Fire* and *Burnin'*; and his own albums included the very popular *Equal
Rights.* He was shot dead during an attempted robbery at his home in
Kingston, Jamaica, on 11 September 1987.

TOURÉ, Ahmed Sékou

After leading the independence movement against France for many years,
Ahmed Sékou Touré became the chief minister of Guinea in 1958 and then
served as the first president of that independent country from 1961 until his
death twenty-three years later. Born at Faranah, Guinea, on 9 January 1922,
he was educated in local Muslim schools and at the Georges Poiret
professional school in Conakry. He founded the first Guinean trade union
for postal workers and then became secretary of the Union Généralé des
Travailleurs d'Afrique Noire, a militant body seeking political independence
as well as the right to collective bargaining. He organized the first successful
strike in French West Africa when his union held out for seventy-six days.
Touré was also the founder, in 1946, of the Rassemblement Démocratique
Africain (RDA) which became the leading political party in French West
Africa. He was elected a deputy to the French National Assembly in 1956
and became secretary to the RDA's parliamentary group. An outstanding

orator of Marxist leanings and a firm believer in African independence, Touré became immensely popular in Guinea and throughout Africa. He enhanced his reputation in the 1960s by Africanizing the Guinean civil service, suppressing the traditional chieftaincy, nationalizing the financial institutions, and taking a consistently hostile stand against colonialism. But he lost a great deal of this respect later on when he became increasingly autocratic at home. His critics were brutally suppressed and many of them were executed. Touré was an ardent supporter of Ghana's president, Kwame Nkrumah, whom he granted asylum in 1966 and proclaimed co-president of Guinea. Touré died on 26 March 1984. It is sometimes forgotten that he was also a writer of some note. His legacy includes *La Révolution et l'unité populaire* (1946), and a collection of verse, *Les Poèmes militants* (1964).

TOURÉ, Amadou Toumani

Amadou Toumani Touré became president of Mali for the second time in May 2002. Born in Mopti, French Sudan, in 1948, he was educated originally to be a teacher but eventually attended military schools in France and the USSR and served in the Presidential Guard of Mali during the 1980s. In 1991, he led a coup that toppled Gen Moussa Traoré's oppressive government and served briefly in his place, restoring democracy to Mali. He re-established the constitution, permitted a general election in 1992 and gracefully retired when he lost it. He was only the second elected president since Mali's achievement of independence in 1960 who had voluntarily relinquished power. Touré devoted most of the 1990s to matters of public health, such as the eradication of Guinea Worm, the elimination of polio and other childhood diseases and the control of AIDS in Africa. Running as an independent, he won the presidential election in 2002. His tenure has been troubled by grave economic problems exacerbated by long periods of drought and an infestation of locusts (2003-04) which crippled Mali's agriculture.

TOURÉ, Muhammad

Emperor Muhammad Touré, who governed the huge Songhai Empire in northwestern Africa from 1493 to 1528, was one of the greatest rulers in that continent's history. His dominions included most of ancient Mali and a good portion of Hausaland. He created a vast bureaucratic network to help him administer this extensive territory and established ministries for the army, navy, fisheries, forests and taxation. He also divided the empire into provinces, each ruled by a governor whom he personally chose from among the royal family. Touré established large plantations and did his best to promote trade and commerce by introducing a standard system of weights and measures and appointing market inspectors to protect consumers. He even tried to improve the standard of education by transforming the mosque at Timbuktu into a famous academic institution. It was there that schools of law, theology, mathematics and medicine soon emerged. Touré created some friction among his more conservative subjects by promoting Islamic practices and beliefs but his vigorous and effective leadership helped to make the Songhai Empire one of the most vibrant forces in northwestern Africa for several generations. European historians, many of whom had previously believed that most of Africa had remained uncivilized until quite recently, now marvel at the efficiency and modernity of Muhammad Touré's administration.

TRICE, Virgil

Virgil Garnett Trice, Jr was born in Indianapolis, Indiana, on 3 February 1926 and spent most of his professional career developing nuclear energy before turning his attention to the management of radioactive waste that results from the generation of nuclear power. He was an important pioneer in both of these fields. After achieving degrees in industrial engineering from Purdue University and the Illinois Institute of Technology, he served as a chemical engineer at the Argonne National Laboratory from 1947 to 1971. He then worked as a nuclear waste management engineer for the Energy Research and Development Administration during 1971-77 and later became a senior programme analyst for the US Department of Energy until his retirement in 1992. Trice died on 31 October 1997.

TRUTH, Sojourner

Born a slave in Hurley, New York, in 1797, Isabel Baumfree became deeply religious after being freed by the New York Emancipation Act of 1827. In 1843, as a result of a religious vision, she changed her name to Sojourner Truth, left New York, and embarked on a mission to abolish slavery. She became the first outstanding African-American woman to speak out publicly against slavery and was one of the most eloquent among the abolitionists of her age despite her lack of formal training. She also helped many slaves who had escaped from the southern states. During the American Civil War, she gave staunch support to the northern cause and served as a nurse in the northern army. When the war was over, she remained for some years in Washington, D.C., lobbying valiantly (but vainly) for land grants in the west for freedmen and former slaves. She continued to advocate equal treatment for all Blacks and proved herself an equally staunch defender of women's rights. One of the most fiery and outspoken women of the nineteenth century, she died on 26 November 1883 after many decades of unselfish toil.

TSHOMBE, Moise

A Congolese political leader during the chaotic days of the early 1960s, Moise-Kapenda Tshombe served briefly as president of the secessionist state of Katanga and then as prime minister of the republic of the Congo. The son of Joseph Kapend, a prosperous merchant, he was born at Musumba, in Katanga, on 10 November 1919. He was educated at the Methodist Mission School near Sandoa and the Methodist Teacher-Training Institute in Kanene. He then went to Elisabethville to run his father's business which he took over as director after his father's death in 1951. Elected president of the African Chamber of Commerce at Elisabethville in 1951, he replaced Joseph Kapend on the provincial council during 1951-53. Tshombe then left the business to be run by his brothers while launching himself into local and national politics. Campaigning for the establishment of an independent Katanga, he broke away in the late 1950s from the other African nationalists who wanted to unify the Congo. This division produced much political unrest and disorder for most of the 1960s. Tshombe managed, in the midst of the confusion, to serve briefly as president of the unified republic before being overthrown by Joseph Mobutu in 1965. He fled to Spain where he continued to plot against the new régime, but was kidnapped and taken to Algiers, where he died on 29 June 1969.

TSHWETE, Stephen

Born in Springs, South Africa, on 12 November 1938, Stephen Vukile Tshwete became an important force in the African National Congress (ANC). He served for many years as the political commissioner of ANC's military wing and as a member of its national committee. He later held cabinet posts under Presidents Nelson Mandela and Thabo Mbeki. Like most of his contemporaries, Tshwete spent fifteen years in prison and five years in exile during the period of apartheid. He returned to South Africa in 1994 to serve as minister of sports and recreation. He developed so many opportunities for young Blacks that he was later promoted by Mbeki to the ministry of safety and security with the responsibility of reforming the national police force. He died in Pretoria on 26 April 2002.

TSIBOE, John Wallace

John Wallace Tsiboe was born on 21 September 1904 and became a firm supporter of Ghanaian political independence after World War II. In 1939 he founded the *Ashanti Pioneer* through whose pages he campaigned most vigorously for political reform and social justice. He was one of Kwame Nkrumah's supporters in the beginning, but became a harsh critic of that leader's policy and style later on. For this his newspaper was banned in

1962. Tsiboe seceded from the Convention People's Party (CPP) in 1957 and joined the United Party, serving for a brief period as its treasurer. Having fallen foul of Nkrumah he spent his last years in London, England, where he died on 10 September 1963.

TUBMAN, Harriet

Born a slave in Dorchester County, Maryland, in 1820, Harriet Ross Tubman became known as the 'Moses of her People' as a result of her courageous attempts to help hundreds of slaves in the southern states of America to escape. She was one of the most famous 'conductors' of the Underground Railroad which took slaves to their freedom in Canada. Tubman is reputed to have made nineteen dangerous trips back to the south to lead some 300 slaves to safety. This was an incredible feat, considering the passage of the cruel Fugitive Slave Act of 1850, which provided serious penalties for anyone caught assisting slaves to escape. During the American Civil War (1861-65), Tubman served the union troops in a number of capacities, including cook, laundress, scout, spy and nurse, and is reputed to have led the Union Army on a raid that freed more than 700 slaves. She devoted her last years to the establishment of a home for elderly and indigent African-Americans before dying, highly respected by white liberals and American Blacks alike, on 10 March 1913. She has become a legendary figure in North American history. Schools have been named in her honour and her story has been repeatedly told in a wonderful array of books and television programmes. In 1914 the city of Auburn, New York, where she spent her last years, placed a bronze tablet at the entrance to the Cayuga County Courthouse to commemorate her; and when a Harriet Tubman postage stamp was issued in 1978, it was the first in a Black Heritage (USA) series.

TUBMAN, William

William Vacanarat Shadrach Tubman is perhaps the most outstanding figure in the history of Liberia, over which he presided for twenty-seven years after an exceptional series of re-elections. A descendant of early American immigrants, he was born in Harper, Liberia, on 29 November 1895, and began his career as a teacher and a lawyer before becoming, at twenty three, the youngest Liberian ever elected to the Senate. In 1937 he became a judge and in 1944 was elected president. He held that office until his death, on 23 July 1971, in London, England. A skilful politician, he managed to mediate between the 'Americo-Liberians' and the more conservative native elements within his republic. He also succeeded in weakening the US economic monopoly by encouraging other countries to share in Liberia's trade and development. Tubman was perhaps fortunate to rule Liberia at a time of economic prosperity just after the discovery of huge deposits of high grade iron ore in the country, but it still required considerable skill on his part to maintain such a high degree of political stability while other African countries were enduring civil strife. He is perhaps best remembered for his progressive legislation which provided female residents of twenty-one years or older with the suffrage and property rights, and which considerably extended Liberia's system of public education.

TUCKER, Elrie

Dr Elrie C. Tucker is a highly successful businessman and an innovative medical specialist who has made significant contributions to the study and treatment of breast cancer. A native of Trinidad and Tobago, he immigrated to Canada in 1953 and completed his medical studies at McGill University in Montreal, Quebec, in 1961. It was while working at the Royal Victoria Hospital during 1963-66 that he began to use Lymphangiography as an aid to breast cancer diagnosis. From 1972 to 1980 he was the co-founder and president of the Breast Centre Group, Canada's largest cluster of breast cancer detection clinics. In 1978 he founded the Carolyn Birthing Centre, Canada's first medically supervised location for non-hospital births. In 1989, in Barbados and Montreal, he launched In Vivo Spectroscopy as a new diagnostic tool in the fight against breast cancer. An active community servant, Dr Tucker was a founding member and president of the Quebec Black Medical Association and a supporter of the Negro Community Centre. As a businessman, he founded (in 1973) the Tropical Air Services Ltd, a charter air service for the Caribbean with a fleet of ten light planes; he sold his majority share on 1979 but remained involved in the company until 1989. He has been the recipient of numerous awards for his contributions to the study of medicine.

TUDOR, Cammie

Sir James Cameron Tudor was born in Barbados, West Indies, on 18 October 1918. Educated at Harrison College and Oxford University, England, he achieved a BA in politics and economics in 1943 and an MA in politics and history in 1948. He had the distinction of being the first Black to preside over the Oxford Union. Returning to the West Indies in the late 1940s, Tudor taught briefly at Combermere School (Barbados) and Queen's College (British Guiana) before entering politics as a member of the Barbados Labour Party (BLP). In 1955 he was among those dissidents who seceded from the BLP and founded the Democratic Labour Party (DLP). Under Errol Barrow, he served for many years as minister of education and was instrumental in the establishment of free secondary and tertiary education for those children who were capable of passing entrance examinations. When Barbados achieved political independence in 1966, Tudor was its first deputy prime minister (1966-71) and later became the leader of the senate. He was minister of foreign affairs during 1986-89. From 1972 to 1975 he served as the Barbadian high commissioner to the United Kingdom and from 1990 to 1993 as the high commissioner to Canada. Tudor was also his country's representative to the United Nations in 1976. He was the recipient of a knighthood in 1987, the same year in which he was honoured by the government of Venezuela with the Order of the Liberator. He died in 1995. He will long be remembered as one of the island's most eloquent speakers.

TULL, Walter

The son of a Barbadian immigrant father and an English mother, Walter Tull was born in Folkestone, Kent, in April 1888. As both his parents died when he was very young, he was raised in a Methodist orphanage in Bethnal Green, London. After leaving school, he was apprenticed briefly as a printer but soon displayed exceptional skills as a football player. Walter Tull was the second Black to play football professionally in England, representing Tottenham Hotspur and Northampton Town's first XI between 1908 and 1914 with no little distinction. Just he was ready to sign with Glasgow Rangers, World War I broke out and he enlisted in the 17th battalion of the Middlesex Regiment with other football professionals. By 1916, shortly before he was invalided home, he was promoted to the rank of sergeant. Upon his recovery, he was sent to a cadet officer training school and returned to the battle front with the rank of second lieutenant in the 23rd Battalion of the Middlesex Regiment. Going to the Italian front in 1917, he led his men at the Battle of Piave and was highly praised in despatches for his 'gallantry and coolness ' under fire. He died while fighting bravely in France on 25 March 1918. Tull has the distinction of being the first black officer in the British army. As is customary with most black heroes, he descended immediately into oblivion until rescued in recent years by a British army desperate to bolster its equal opportunities initiative. A Walter Tull Memorial Match was played in 1997 and a Walter Tull Memorial Garden was opened in 1998 next to Northampton Town's Sixfields Community Stadium.

TURNER, Nat

Nat Turner was the leader of the most successful and dramatic slave rebellion in the United States. Although born a slave himself on 2 October 1800, he lived an ascetic life and felt divinely inspired to accomplish heroic deeds. An ardent Christian, he was much respected by his fellow slaves to whom he preached and whom he sometimes baptized. On 21 and 22

August 1831, he and a small army of about fifty rebels killed some sixty white Virginians before the insurrection could be put down. Turner was executed on 11 November 1831, after many 'suspicious' (but innocent) slaves were summarily put to death by nervous owners in the hysteria that followed. This revolt dispelled the myth of the docile, innocuous, stupid and contented slave and led to more rigid and brutal regulations governing slave conduct, especially in the southern American states. But Turner has ever since then been regarded as a hero and a martyr by black America.

TURPIN, Randy

Randolph Adolphus Turpin was Britain's first black boxing champion who dominated the middleweight division in Britain and Europe during the 1940s and 1950s. Born in Leamington Spa, England, on 7 May 1928, he turned professional in 1946 and won his first nineteen fights. He became the British middleweight champion in 1950 and the European champion in 1951. That year he also created history by defeating the immortal Sugar Ray Robinson to become middleweight champion of the world. As Robinson avenged this loss two months later, Turpin's reign was very brief. He retired with a record of 66 wins, 8 defeats and one draw. He committed suicide on 17 May 1966 when he was only thirty-eight years old. In 1979, a plaque was unveiled in his memory in Leamington Town Hall and in 2001 he was inducted into the American International Hall of Fame.

TUTU, Desmond

Born at Klerksdorp, Transvaal, of mixed Xhosa and Tswana parentage, on 7 October 1931, the Rt Revd Desmond Mpilo Tutu emerged as one of the most highly respected religious leaders in southern Africa. The son of a schoolmaster who taught in South African mission schools, he graduated with a BA from Pretoria Bantu Normal College and taught for a while before studying theology. In 1961 he was ordained an Anglican priest and in 1967 became a lecturer in a theological seminary in Johannesburg. Tutu then studied at the University of London, England, where he was awarded an MA, and served for a few years as associate director of theological education funds for the World Council of Churches. In 1975 he became the first black dean of Johannesburg; in 1976 he was promoted to the bishopric of Lesotho; and in 1978 became assistant bishop of Johannesburg. In that same year, Tutu was appointed general secretary of the South African Council of Churches. In this capacity, he showed himself a stern critic of apartheid and this led to the temporary withdrawal of his passport in 1981. But while denouncing racial discrimination, he always pleaded for moderation on the part of the Blacks. In 1982 he was awarded an honorary degree by Columbia University in the United States. Two years later, Tutu was awarded the Nobel Peace Prize for his non-violent resistance to apartheid and was promoted to the bishopric of Johannesburg shortly afterwards. He remains one of the most revered clergymen throughout Africa.

Underground Railroad

This complicated system of 'conductors', 'lines' and 'packages', which was neither underground nor a railroad, had to operate in secret as it blatantly contravened the Fugitive Slave Acts then operating in the American south. Established and supported by Abolitionists, Quakers, free Blacks and former slaves, it operated mainly during the period 1835-65 to help slaves escape from southern plantations. At its peak, the Underground Railroad extended throughout fourteen northern states and Canada, the country then regarded by American Blacks as the promised land (as it was beyond the reach of the slave hunters). Among the ex-slaves involved in this enterprise, by far the most famous was Harriet Tubman, who is reputed to have assisted more than 300 slaves in their attempt to reach Canada. Various routes were lines, stopping places were called stations, those who aided along the way were known as conductors, and their charges were packages or freight. Estimates of the number of slaves who reached freedom in this manner range from 40,000 to more than 100,000.

Universal Negro Improvement Association

The Universal Negro Improvement Association (UNIA) was founded in 1911 by Marcus Garvey, the Jamaican civil rights activist, who believed that Blacks could achieve equality only by becoming independent of white society and forming their own governments and nations. Its basic aims, as enunciated in its official mouthpiece, the *Negro World*, were to champion the cause of Negro independence in both a political and economic sense, to advocate self-determination, to instill racial self-help, and to inspire racial love and self-respect. The UNIA led to the 'Back-to-Africa' Movement during 1914-23. For a while it seemed to prosper, especially in the urban centres in the north of the United States, with up to 1,000,000 followers participating in its activities, which included colourful costumes and parades. But the UNIA soon languished for lack of funds as well as the whole-hearted support of African-American intellectuals who considered Garvey's schemes too visionary and impractical. Garvey himself was convicted of fraud in 1923 and deported from the United States after spending two years in prison. Even so, his message reached multitudes on both sides of the Atlantic and gave inspiration to a much more vigorous black nationalism which emerged in Africa, the Caribbean and the United States after World War II.

UPSHAW, Fred

Fred Upshaw was born in Halifax, Nova Scotia. He moved to Toronto, Ontario, where he completed his secondary education and became a registered nurse. After becoming president of the local branch of his union, he served several terms as the president of the Ontario Public Service Employee Union. He was the first black person (1990-95) to head a major Canadian union. During his tenure, the union won numerous benefits, including the right to strike for provincial civil servants, joint control of their pensions, and Employee Assistance Programmes to assist staff with personal problems. Fred Upshaw supported the principle of Employment Equity to ensure that Blacks and other 'Visible Minorities' were not discriminated against in the job marketplace. He has also been an active member of the Coalition of Black Trade Unionists and the Ontario Federation of Labour.

UPSHAW, Robert

Born in Cole Harbour, Nova Scotia, Robert Graham (Ted) Upshaw became, in 1999, the first black commissioned officer of the Royal Canadian Mounted Police (RCMP), attaining the rank of Inspector and placed in charge of the Cole Harbour detachment. An accomplished basketball player in his youth, he was a three-time all-Canadian player while at Acadia University, where he achieved his BA in 1981. He received an Award of Excellence from the Canadian Centre for Police Race Relations in 1999 and was inducted into the Acadia Sports Hall of Fame in 2002.

VALDÉS, José Manuel

Born in Peru in 1767, Dr José Manuel Valdés was an accomplished physician whose medical articles and theories gained the respect of European and American doctors. Prevented from joining the priesthood because of his colour, he contented himself with writing religious verses. His most memorable occur in the collection, the *Peruvian Psalter*, which appeared in 1833. The first black author to publish anything in Peru, Valdés, who died in 1844, is still remembered as one of the finest among the early black Peruvian poets. He also published a biography of Fray Martin de Porres, another black Peruvian.

VANCOL, Frantz

Frantz Vancol was born in Port-au-Prince, Haiti, but immigrated to Liberia in 1969 before going to the United States to complete his education. He studied business administration and cosmetology and then, in 1976, moved to Canada where he launched a chain of beauty shops, Les Jeunes Romantiques, introducing the Canadian market to the most popular hair and skin care products manufactured especially for Blacks. He founded

Tropica Inc., a wholesaler of tropical consumer products, and New York-New York, a retailer of foods and cosmetics and became the exclusive distributor of many specialized commodities. He also manufactured Quisqueya-boyo, a tropical flavoured soft drink. Vancol started the very first radio station managed by black communities in Canada. As a result of his efforts, many other ethnic beauty shops, retail stores, tropical soft drinks and radio stations gradually appeared all across his adopted country. One of the most successful entrepreneurs in Quebec, Frantz Vancol has supported many community activities that foster closer relations between the Francophone and Anglophone Blacks in Montreal.

VAN LARE, William Bedford

The son of a successful Keta merchant, William Bedford Van Lare was born on 7 September 1904. He attended the Bremen Mission School in Keta and Mfantsipim School in Cape Coast before studying law at the University of London, England. He was called to the bar at Lincoln's Inn in 1937. Van Lare, who soon made a name for himself as a brilliant advocate after returning to the Gold Coast, was appointed a magistrate in 1943 and became chairman of the Magistrates' Association. During 1948-50 he also acted as chief registrar for the West African Court of Appeal. He was made a puisne judge in 1952 and had become one of Ghana's senior jurists by 1957. At first a supporter of Kwame Nkrumah, he eventually objected to that ruler's high-handed treatment of the courts and resigned in 1963. After Nkrumah's overthrow, Van Lare was appointed Ghana's high commissioner to Canada in 1966 and was awarded the Grand Medal of the Republic of Ghana in 1967. After serving occasionally as one of Ghana's delegates to the United Nations, he died in Accra on 3 September 1969 and was given a state funeral.

VANN, Robert Lee

Robert Lee Vann became a qualified lawyer in 1909 after achieving his BA and LLD degrees from the University of Pittsburgh. But he made a name for himself in the field of journalism by helping to form the Pittsburgh Courier Publishing Company over which he eventually gained total control. His *Pittsburgh Courier*, which he edited after 1912, soon became the most widely circulated African-American newspaper. Apart from journalism, Vann also took an active interest in politics, giving support to the Republicans before shifting his allegiance in the 1930s to President Franklin Roosevelt who appointed him special assistant US attorney general in 1933. Vann gave up this post, however, to focus more single-mindedly on his newspaper after 1936. Born in 1887 in Ahoskie, North Carolina, he died on 24 October 1940.

VAUGHAN, Hilton

Born in Santo Domingo of Barbadian parents on 23 November 1901, Hilton Augustus Vaughan was educated at Combermere School and Harrison College in Barbados. He became a distinguished poet, historian, diplomat and jurist. He was for many years the editor of the *Barbados Recorder* which he freely used to disseminate his views on social justice and racial equality. Vaughan wrote several articles on Barbadian culture, politics and history, but - as a writer - is better known as a poet, having contributed numerous poems to various magazines and anthologies after publishing *Sandy Lane and Other Poems* in 1945. He was for many years a member of the national legislature, where he served as attorney general and as minister without portfolio. Vaughan was his country's first ambassador to the United States after Barbados' achievement of political independence (1966) and its permanent representative to the United Nations. He was also a competent and popular judge. He died in 1985.

VENETIAAN, Ronald

Ronald Runaldo Venetiaan was re-elected president of Suriname in 2005 to serve a third term. He had been president in 1991-96 and 2000-2005. Born on 18 June 1936, he is a mathematician by profession. In his first term as president, he implemented an austerity programme which was very unpopular but helped to stabilise Suriname's economy. When he returned to power in 2000, he found his good work undone. He inherited a devalued currency, high inflation, a collapsing health system and a bloated bureaucracy. Once again he had to cut public spending and introduce emergency measures to contain inflation and stabilise the exchange rate. He also restructured the banana industry with the help of international loans. His policies, however, have led to a dwindling of his party's seats in the legislature and his new minority government depends upon the co-operation of other parties.

VILAKAZI, Benedict

Dr Benedict Wallet Bambatha Vilakazi was an eminent Zulu novelist, scholar and teacher. Born in Natal Province, South Africa, on 6 January 1906, he was educated at St Francis College and the Roman Catholic monastery just outside Durban. After achieving his Teacher's Certificate in 1923, he taught at Marianville College and then at the Catholic seminary at Ixopo. Vilakazi completed his BA from the University of South Africa in 1934 and then earned an MA from the University of Witwatersrand, whose first successful black PhD candidate he became in 1946. Vilakazi was appointed senior lecturer in the department of Bantu Studies at the University of South Africa and served also as president of the Catholic African Teachers' Federation and editor of the *Catholic African Teachers' Review*. A prolific writer, he contributed several articles in both English and Zulu to such journals as *African Studies*, *Bantu Studies*, *The Native Teachers' Journal* and *The Forum*. He published numerous poems in *Ilanga lase natal*, *UmAfrika*, *The Bantu World*, and *The Star*. His *Inkondlo kaZulu* was the first collection of Zulu songs to be published. It was selected by Witwatersrand University in 1935 to be the lead volume of its *Bantu Treasury* Series. Vilakazi also produced a collection of Zulu verse in *Amal'eZulu* (1945). His novels included *Nje nempela* (1933), *Noma Nini* (1935) and *U-Dingiswayo ka Jobe* (1939). Vilakazi was prematurely struck down by meningitis on 26 October 1947. He was the first great expert on Bantu languages and one of the finest of all Zulu poets.

VINCENT, Sténio

Sténio Joseph Vincent was a famous Haitian statesman, scholar and journalist. Born in Port-au-Prince on 22 February 1874, he attended the Lycée Pétion, eventually qualified as a lawyer and served his country in a variety of capacities. He was secretary of school inspection in Port-au-Prince (1890), professor of literature at the Collège Louverture (1893-96), secretary to the Haitian legation at Paris (1896-99) and Berlin (1899-1900), division chief in the department of public instruction (1902), communal magistrate (1907-09), Haitian chargé d'affaires at the Hague (1916) and secretary of state for the ministry of the interior (1916). Vincent eventually became a senator and president of the senate in 1930. His glorious career in public service was crowned with his election as president of Haiti on 18 November 1930 and his re-election in 1935 for a second term of five years. Having consistently warned against the aggressiveness of the United States, he helped found the Patriotic Union which was largely instrumental in the recapture of Haiti's independence. Very keen on promoting Haitian literature and culture, Vincent was among the founders of such journals as the *République-Express* (1895), *L'Effort* (1902) and *Haiti-Journal* (1930). He was also the director of the first School of Commerce in Haiti. His numerous publications, on subjects ranging from politics to education and law, included *Choses et Autres* (1895), *Petite Histoire d'Haiti* (1895), *La Législation de l'Instruction Publique de la République d'Haiti, 1804-1895* (1898), *La République d'Haiti telle qu'elle est* (1910), *L'écolier haitien with Dantès Bellegarde* (1911), *L'année enfantine d'histoire et de géographie d'Haiti with Dantès Bellegarde* (1913), *Les grands jubilés du Barreau Haitien* (1928), *Efforts et résultats* (1938), and *En posant les jalons*, 5 volumes (1930-41). Vincent died on 19 July 1959.

WADE, Abdoulaye

Abdoulaye Wade, a Senegalese lawyer, educator and politician, was born on 29 May 1926. After studying in Senegal and France, he achieved his PhD in law and economics from the Sorbonne in 1970. For some years he practised law in France before returning to his native country and becoming a professor at the University of Dakar. He launched the Senegalese Democratic Party (PDS) in 1974 in opposition to Léopold Senghor's Socialist Party (PS) that had ruled Senegal ever since that country's achievement of political independence (1960). After twenty-six years and four unsuccessful bids for the presidency, Wade finally managed to win an election on 1 April 2000. He promised to improve literacy levels, to raise health standards and to alleviate poverty. But Senegal's sad economic situation and chronic ministerial discord have conspired to dog his footsteps.

WALATA PETROS

Born in 1594, Saint Walata Petros remains one of the very few Ethiopian women to have been sanctified. Her whole life was devoted to the promotion of the Ethiopian Orthodox Church against Roman Catholicism. Despite her banishment in 1617, she managed to establish seven religious communities in Jabal. After the death of the Catholic Emperor, Susneyos, the Orthodox Church was restored and Walata Petros was recalled in 1632. She spent the last decade of her life preaching and gathering new disciples all across Ethiopia. She died on 24 November 1643.

WALCOTT, Clyde

Sir Clyde Leopold Walcott, who was knighted for his services to cricket in 1993, was born in Barbados, West Indies, on 17 January 1926. Educated at Combermere School and Harrison College, he was one of the greatest schoolboy athletes in the history of Caribbean sport. He represented Barbados at both cricket and football before he was eighteen years old. He eventually became one of the most brilliant batsmen ever to play Test cricket for the West Indies. In 44 international matches Walcott registered 3,798 runs at an average of almost 57 per innings. Appointed Cricket Organizer and Coach on the Estates of the British Guiana Sugar Producers' Association in 1954, he broke down many of the ethnic and social barriers there to make that territory one of the most powerful in West Indies cricket. As an administrative leader after his retirement, Walcott's contributions to the Barbados Cricket Association (BCA), the Guyana Cricket Board of Control (GCBC), the West Indies Cricket Board of Control (WICBC) and the International Cricket Council (ICC) were substantial. In 1993, he became the first non-White president of the ICC. Off the cricket field, Walcott also enjoyed a distinguished career. He was for many years the chief personnel officer in the Barbados Shipping and Trading Company Limited (BS&T), by far the largest and most influential commercial institution in that island. He eventually became one of its first black directors and served for many years as president of the Barbados Employers' Confederation. Apart from his knighthood, Sir Clyde was the recipient of many honours and distinctions, including the Arrow of Achievement (AA) from the government of Guyana, the rank of Officer of the Most Excellent Order of the British Empire (OBE) from the government of the United Kingdom, and the Gold Crown of Merit (GCM) from the Government of Barbados. He died on 26 August 2006.

WALCOTT, Derek

Derek Walcott, who won the Nobel Prize for Literature in 1992, was born in St Lucia, West Indies, of mixed Barbadian parentage on 23 January 1930. He was educated at St Mary's College, Castries, and the University College of the West Indies, Jamaica, where he majored in French, Latin and Spanish. A Rockefeller Foundation grant in 1957 took him to New York City, where he attended directing classes and rehearsals at the Phoenix Theatre's repertory company. By the time he was thirty, he had published three volumes of poetry and established the Trinidad Theatre Workshop. His popular plays were also being performed throughout the West Indies and in England. Walcott's greatest work perhaps is his epic poem, *Omeros*, regarded by many as a modern Odyssey composed of sixty-four chapters and attempting to capture the experience of the Caribbean peoples while exploring several cultures. His other poetic works include *25 Poems* (1948), *In a Green Night: Poems 1948-1960* (1962), *Selected Poems* (1964), *The Castaway and Other Poems* (1969), and *Another Life* (1973). Among his best-known plays are *Henri Christophe* (1951), *In a Fine Castle* (1970), *The Dream on Monkey Mountain* (1971), *The Last Carnival* (1986) and *The Odyssey* (1992).

WALCOTT, Frank

The Rt Excellent Sir Frank Leslie Walcott was declared a National Hero by the Barbados Government in 1998. Born on 16 September 1916 in relative poverty, his formal education had to cease when he graduated from Wesley Hall Boys' (elementary) School in 1931. Thereafter he was largely self-taught and became quite widely read. After a series of odd jobs in Bridgetown, he worked as an assistant to Hugh (later Sir Hugh) Springer, then the general secretary of the Barbados Workers' Union (BWU). When Springer left Barbados in 1947, Walcott took over his duties and remained the leader of the BWU until his retirement in 1991. He made the BWU, which became an adjunct to the recently formed Barbados Labour Party (BLP), one of the strongest organizations of its kind anywhere. He aimed not only to increase the wages of workers but to promote all aspects of the workers' welfare such as diet, health and education. Hence his establishment of the Labour College in St Philip in 1968. He also brought all kinds of trades and professions under the umbrella of his union. In addition, he recognized the community of interests shared by workers everywhere. He himself became chairman of the Caribbean Area Division of the Inter American Regional Organization of Workers in 1952 and was the founding president of the Caribbean Congress of Labour from 1960 to 1991. He became one of the leaders of several international boards involving unions, including the American Institute for Free Labour Development and the International Labour Organization. For some years, too, he served as chairman of the World Employment Conference. Sir Frank was the recipient of many honours, including an honorary doctorate from the University of the West Indies in 1987 and a knighthood in 1988. A new building to house the National Insurance Department was named after him shortly after his retirement. He died on 24 February 1999.

WALDA GIYORGIS ABBOYE

One of Ethiopia's greatest generals and administrators, Walda Giyorgis Abboye is best remembered for the conquest of Kaffa in 1897. Born on 4 November 1851, he became governor of such important provinces as Amhara, Bagemder and Semén. After the death of Emperor Menilek II, he led the successful coup against Lej Iyasu Mikael in 1916 and was crowned king by Empress Zawditu just before his own death on 1 March 1918. Walda Giyorgis Abboye had by this time done enough to cement the position of Ras Tafari Makonnen who ultimately became Emperor Haile Selassie I in 1930.

WALKER, A.B.

One of the earliest advocates of Black Power was the barrister and journalist, Abraham Beverley Walker, who was born in British Columbia, Canada, and educated in the United States. He toured the southern states in the 1880s lecturing on 'the philosophy of race development from a Canadian standpoint'. In 1890, he moved to St John, New Brunswick, where, as the sole black lawyer in the Maritimes, he quickly became the intermediary between the black voters and the Conservative Party and helped Sir Charles Tupper to win the federal election of 1896. He had hoped to be named a queen's counsel for his efforts but was disappointed; he then threw in his lot with the Liberal Party but with no better results. In 1903, Walker launched *Neith*, an eclectic monthly magazine. He advocated colonization in Africa, where American, Canadian and Caribbean Blacks might live in interracial harmony under British rule. Following the early collapse of *Neith*, one of the best among early African-Canadian publications, Walker emigrated to Boston in 1905. He died in 1909.

WALKER, Madame C.J.

Born Sarah Breedlove in Delta, Louisiana, on 23 December 1867, this amazing business woman turned her invention of the metal heating comb and conditioner for straightening hair into a fabulous fortune and became America's very first black millionaire. After attending night school in St Louis, Missouri, she began as a door-to-door peddler of her cosmetic products. After patenting her special hairdressing and straightening comb in 1905, she steadily expanded her business, establishing branches in Denver (Colorado) and Pittsburgh (Pennsylvania), before building her own factory in Indianapolis to manufacture her hair preparations, facial creams and other products. In 1913, Madame Walker (as she was now known) established Lelia College (named after her daughter) in New York City, to train young women in the Walker beauty system and the use of Walker beauty products. This was the beginning of a chain of successful Walker salons throughout the United States. The Madame C.J. Walker Manufacturing Company grew to employ over 3,000 workers, attracting customers from all across the United States and the Caribbean. Madame Walker had become one of the foremost social leaders of her day by the time of her death on 25 May 1919. She is also remembered as a famous philanthropist who gave generously to the needy of Indianapolis, the National Association for the Advancement of Colored People (NAACP), the YMCA and the YWCA, and to homes for the aged. She awarded scholarships to young women at several high schools and colleges, while also supporting in a material sense the work of Mary McLeod Bethune and Ida B. Wells. Madame Walker is also reputed to have contributed over $100,000 on one occasion to build a girls' school in West Africa.

WALKER, David

David Walker was a controversial black abolitionist who called unequivocally for slave rebellions to bring a prompt and complete halt to the inhuman system of bondage. He was born in Wilmington, North Carolina, on 28 September 1785 of a slave father and a free mother. He grew up free, obtained an education, opened a secondhand clothing store in Boston, and travelled throughout the United States calling for the abolition of slavery. In 1829 he published his famous pamphlet, *Appeal ... to the Colored People of the World*, calling upon the slaves to revolt. The Appeal was promptly and loudly denounced by the slave-owners in the south and some of them actually put a price on Walker's head. The pamphlet was banned by a number of southern states and legislation was passed forbidding slaves to learn to read and write. Warned that his life was in danger, Walker refused to flee to Canada. He was murdered in Boston on 28 June 1830. Walker's pamphlet was widely reprinted and circulated after his death, but many Blacks and abolitionists rejected his bid for violence.

WALKER, Maggie Lena

Born of slave parents in Richmond, Virginia, in 1867, Maggie Lena Walker rose from such humble circumstances to become the very first female bank president in the United States. Following her graduation from high school, she taught for some years before taking charge of a black institution, the Independent Order of St Luke which she transformed, almost single-handedly, into the St Luke Penny Savings Bank. It shortly absorbed all of the black banks in Richmond under the title of the Consolidated Bank and Trust Company over which Maggie Lena Walker presided for many years. By 1924 it was catering to more than 100,000 customers. Walker also organized the Richmond Council for Negro Women which rapidly grew to 1,400 members. She led many successful fund-raising drives to purchase a farm for black girls and to build a nursing home and a community centre in Richmond. In the meantime she remained very active in the National Association for the Advancement of Colored People (NAACP) as well as the National Urban League. A tireless and effective community servant, she died in 1934. But her name still lives on in Richmond, Virginia, where a street, a theatre and a school have all been named for her. The Blacks in that city also inaugurated the 'Maggie L. Walker Month' (October). She was the recipient of several honours and awards, including an honorary degree from Virginia Union University.

WALKER, Rudolph

A native of Trinidad and Tobago, Rudolph Walker broke many barriers when he became the first black person to star in a major television series in Britain. Born on 28 September 1939, he emigrated to Britain in 1960 and established himself as a performer by working in various theatres across the country. His big break came in 1972 when he was cast as one of the main characters in the popular television series, *Love Thy Neighbour*. He later played the role of Patrick Trueman in the BBC soap opera, *The Eastenders*. He was awarded the OBE in 2006.

WALLACE-JOHNSON, Isaac

Isaac Theophilus Akuna Wallace-Johnson was a militant Sierra Leonean trade unionist, political activist and journalist. Born in Freetown on 6 February 1894, he was an ardent campaigner for African workers' rights and a firm believer in Pan-Africanism. After attending the Centenary Tabernacle School in Freetown, he entered the civil service in 1912 and was soon dismissed after leading a strike for better pay. He worked briefly with the United African Company (UAC) and then the Freetown City Council, but again he had to be discharged for encouraging his fellow-workers to strike for better working conditions. He therefore decided to become a sailor, publishing *The Seafarer*, an eclectic periodical. Moving to Nigeria, Wallace-Johnson organized that colony's first labour union, the African Workers' Union, in 1931 and became editor of the *Nigerian Daily Telegraph*, while writing also for the *Negro Worker*. Following his expulsion from Nigeria for his militancy, Wallace-Johnson went to the Gold Coast where he founded the West Coast Youth League and wrote articles for the *Gold Coast Spectator* and the *African Morning Post*. Finally resettling in Sierra Leone, he started no fewer than eight labour unions during the late 1930s. He was arrested for criminal libel and imprisoned for one year, using that opportunity to write a series of poems, *Prison in the Muse*, depicting the appalling conditions in the Freetown jail. These verses led to an official investigation and a few improvements. Upon his release from prison, Wallace-Johnson founded two more newspapers, the *African Sentinel* and *Africa and the World*, before helping to organize the Pan-African Congress that was held in Manchester, England, in 1945. He was elected to the Sierra Leone Legislative Council in 1951. When he died in a car crash in Ghana on 16 May 1965 and was buried in Freetown, his funeral drew the greatest crowd of mourners in the history of Sierra Leone. He is still revered as the father of African trade unionism. His frequent harassment at the hands of the colonial authorities had served to draw attention to the brutal nature of the British colonial system and had thus given a stimulus to the independence movements in Africa.

WALLER, Calvin

Born on 17 December 1937, Calvin Augustine Hoffman Waller rose to become one of the highest-ranking African-Americans in the United States Army. During the Persian Gulf War of 1991 he served under Gen Norman Schwarzkopf as deputy commander of the US forces. He died on 9 May 1996.

WALLS, Bryan

Dr Bryan Edmond Walls, the great-great grandson of John Freeman Walls, a refugee slave who arrived in the Windsor area of Ontario, Canada, in 1846 through the Underground Railroad, has been instrumental in increasing awareness of African Canadian history. Along with other members of his family, he has turned his ancestor's log cabin into the Underground Railroad Museum and the John Freeman Walls Historic Site. He is also a founding member of the North American Black Historical Museum in Amherstburg. In 1980, he published *The Road That Led to*

Somewhere, an historical novel based on the Walls's family history. He has helped to document Essex County's involvement with the Underground Railroad and produce a resource kit for use in schools. Born in Windsor, but raised in Puce, Ontario, Dr Walls completed his doctorate of dental studies at the University of Toronto in 1973. In addition to his practice as a dentist, he is the deacon of the historic First Baptist Church Puce, founded by his ancestors in 1846.

WALSH, Courtney

One of the greatest cricketers produced by the West Indies, Courtney Andrew Walsh was born in Kingston, Jamaica, on 30 October 1962. In a fabulous international career that lasted from November 1984 to May 2001, he captured the then world record 519 wickets in Test cricket, demolishing the old mark of 434 set by India's Kapil Dev. In 132 Tests, Walsh also became the first fast bowler to exceed 30,000 deliveries at this level. His wickets cost him less than 25 runs apiece and he also took 227 in one-day internationals for the West Indies. Towards the end of his career, he served as captain of the West Indies, the first fast bowler ever to do so. Although he was generally regarded as a feeble batsman, Walsh shared (with Guyana's Carl Hooper) the West Indian record of 106 for the tenth wicket partnership when he achieved his highest score in Test cricket (30) at St John's, Antigua, against Pakistan in May 1993.

WARD, Samuel Ringgold

Samuel Ringgold Ward was born into slavery in Maryland in 1817. His family escaped from their owners in 1820 and settled in New York, where the young Samuel was educated. He became a teacher and a priest. He later served as an agent for the *Colored American* and an editor of the *Farmer and Northern Star*. In the 1850s, Ward immigrated to Canada, where he founded the *Provincial Freeman*, an influential anti-slavery newspaper. A fiery lecturer for the Anti-Slavery Society, he was a firm advocate of equality and racial integration. He moved to Jamaica, British West Indies, where he died in 1864. His legacy included *The Autobiography of a Fugitive Slave*, which was published in 1855.

WARE, John

One of the generally unknown heroes still lurking, as it were, in the shadows of Canadian history, John Ware was one of the most proficient cowboys of his generation. A former slave, he was one of the pioneers who moved from Texas to Alberta in 1882 and tried to settle there with his young family. He was largely instrumental in introducing longhorn cattle to Canada and had much to do with the development of the rodeo in the Calgary area.

WASHINGTON, Booker T.

Booker Taliaferro Washington, one of the most celebrated educators among all African-Americans, was born a slave in Franklin County, Virginia, on 5 April 1856. His major legacy was the Tuskegee Institute in Alabama which he founded in 1881 and administered until his death. After his family's emancipation, Washington attended Hampton Institute where he learned to be a brick mason. Largely self-educated, he turned to teaching and served on the staff of Hampton Institute from 1878 to 1881. Much influenced by Samuel Chapman Armstrong, the founder of Hampton Institute, he tried to model his school at Tuskegee after the institution that his mentor had established. Hence his focus on practical and vocational disciplines. His school became famous for its training of African-American farmers, mechanics and tradesmen as well as teachers. By 1915, Tuskegee Institute had more than 100 well-equipped buildings, some 1,500 students, a faculty of nearly 200 teaching 38 trades and professions, and an endowment of approximately $2 million. In 1900, Washington organized a Negro Business League to help Blacks develop their own businesses. He also raised money to build schools for Blacks in rural areas. Firmly believing that economic and professional empowerment was the foundation of social and political status, and that African-American militancy would be counter-productive, he urged the Blacks of his generation to be less aggressive in their demands for immediate equality. Secretly, however, he spent large sums fighting against laws that denied civil rights to African-Americans. His moderate views, in the face of black restlessness and white injustice, assured Washington the support of white liberals and philanthropists and he became the foremost adviser to Presidents Theodore Roosevelt and William Howard Taft on racial problems. His influence resulted in the appointment of several Blacks to federal posts. Inevitably, however, the younger generation of black intellectuals, led by such scholars as W.E.B. Du Bois, became impatient with Washington's approach and he lost a good deal of his influence in his later years. Washington died on 14 November 1915. In addition to Tuskegee Institute he left a number of books for posterity. His major works included *The Future of the American Negro* (1899), *The Story of My Life and Work* (1900), *Up From Slavery* (1901), and *Working with the Hands* (1904). Washington's numerous distinctions and awards included honorary degrees from Harvard University (1896) and Dartmouth College (1901). On 4 July 1953, the United States government also honoured his memory by officially opening the Booker T. Washington Highway.

WASHINGTON, Harold

Harold Washington was elected Chicago's first black mayor on 12 April 1983. Born in that city on 15 April 1922, he obtained his BA from Roosevelt

University in 1949 and a law degree from Northwestern University in 1952. He practised law in Chicago for the next twelve years before entering the state legislature where he served during 1964-76. He was elected to the US Senate in 1976 and then became a member of the US House of Representatives in 1980. The mayoral contest in 1983 drew considerable national attention as it proved to be emotional and race-dominated. Washington was re-elected to a second term in 1987. He had become a folk hero to Chicago's black population and a symbol throughout the United States of urban black political power. He died on 25 November 1987.

WASHINGTON, Jackie

Jackie Washington is a popular singer, guitarist and pianist who was born in Hamilton, Ontario, on 12 November 1919 and first performed publicly at the age of five. He sang for many years with his brothers in southern Ontario nightclubs as a member of the 'Four Washingtons' but did not release his first album, *Blues and Sentimental*, until 1976. He made his film début in 1983 when he appeared in *Hank Williams -The Show He Never Gave*. One of his many recordings, *Where Old Friends Meet*, was nominated for a Juno Award in 1991. Jackie Washington, who had developed a repertoire of about 1300 songs by the turn of the century, was inducted into the Canadian Jazz and Blues Hall of Fame in 2002. Several Jackie Washington Awards have been created to honour this versatile and accomplished performer who has been a staple of the Canadian musical scene for more than eighty years.

WASHINGTON, Walter, E.

Walter Edward Washington, who served for many years as mayor of Washington, D.C., was born in Dawson, Georgia, on 15, April 1915. He graduated with a BA from Howard University in 1938 and received his LLD from the Howard University Law School in 1948. From 1941 to 1966, he gave staunch support to the National Capital Housing Authority which he served as executive director in the early 1960s. In 1966, Washington was appointed chairman of the New York City Housing Authority and in 1967 served the District of Columbia in a similar capacity. Elected mayor of Washington, D.C. in 1972, he was re-elected to a second four-year term in 1976. He was the first elected black mayor of a major American city. He is credited by many observers with diffusing racial tensions and preventing large-scale riots in the city following the assassination of Martin Luther King, Jr in 1968. After he lost the mayoral election in 1978, he returned to the practice of law in the Washington district. He died on 27 October 2003.

WATERS, Ethel

This distinguished actress and singer was born in humble circumstances in Chester, Pennsylvania, on 31 October 1896. She began her career as an entertainer by singing in night clubs before touring with Fletcher Henderson's Black Swan Jazz Masters. Waters made her Broadway début in 1927 when she appeared in the musical, *Africana*. This was the first of many Broadway appearances which led to a successful career as a film star. Her most important roles were played in *Tales of Manhattan* (1941), *Cabin in the Sky* (1943), and *Pinky*, which won her an Academy Award nomination in 1949. Waters later participated regularly in Billy Graham's evangelical crusades. Her autobiography, *His Eye Is on the Sparrow*, was published in 1951. She died on 1 September 1977.

WATSON, Andrew

The son of a wealthy Scottish sugar planter and a black Guyanese lass, Andrew Watson was born in Demerara in 1857. His father sent him to be educated in the United Kingdom at the exclusive King's College in London and at the University of Glasgow, where he studied philosophy, mathematics and engineering. His main interest, however, was football. He played for Maxwell F. C. when he was only nineteen years old before signing for Parkgrove F. C. as a player and secretary, thus becoming the first black football administrator in the United Kingdom. He soon joined Queen's Park - then Britain's biggest football club - and later became their secretary, leading them to several Scottish Cup victories. In 1884 he was the first foreign player ever to be invited to join the élite Corinthians. Although he represented Scotland in only three international matches, Watson was considered one of the finest footballers ever to play for that country. He emigrated to Australia and died in Sidney.

WEAVER, Robert Clifton

Dr Robert Clifton Weaver was born in Washington, D.C. on 29 December 1907. He became an eminent economist, educator and government official. After receiving his BA (1929), MA (1931) and PhD (1934) from Harvard University, he embarked on a lengthy and stellar career in public service. He was one of the young 'New Dealers' who advised President Franklin D. Roosevelt on minority problems and became the leader in what was then known as the 'Black Cabinet', a group of African-American intellectuals whom the federal government employed to help solve social, economic and racial problems. Weaver rose to the rank of secretary of Housing and Urban Development during President Lyndon B. Johnson's tenure and became the first African-American to serve in the US cabinet. He also wrote several important books, including *Negro Labor: A National Problem* (1946), *The*

Negro Ghetto (1948) *The Urban Complex* (1964) and *Dilemmas of Urban America* (1965). Weaver, who died in 1982, had also served periodically as a distinguished professor at the City University of New York and had been very active in the civil rights movement, serving for one year as the chairman of the National Association for the Advancement of Colored People (NAACP).

WEEKES, Anesta

Anesta Weekes is a young British barrister who has made significant progress since being called to the bar in 1981. She took silk in 1999 and was appointed a Bencher of Gray's Inn in 2003. As a lawyer and Queen's Counsel, her main area of practice is criminal law. She defends in all forms of criminal trials. She sits as a part-time chair of the Employment Tribunals and also as an arbitrator of the Commonwealth Secretariat Arbitral Tribunal. She has been a member of the Government's Review Committee on Gambling, and during 2000-03 was the vice-chair of the Bar Council's Equal opportunities Committee. Anesta Weekes was *The Times* runner-up Woman of the Year in 1999. She was a member of the team of lawyers sponsored by the British government to train South African lawyers in advocacy skills.

WEEKES, Everton

Sir Everton DeCourcey Weekes, born in Barbados on 26 February 1925, was one of the greatest cricketers in the world during the immediate post-war period. He scored 4,555 runs at an average of 58.61 per innings in 48 Tests for the West Indies during 1948-58. He also captained the Barbados XI with much distinction during 1959-64 and was the first Black to do so on a regular basis. In 152 first-class matches he recorded 12,010 runs at an average of 55.34 per innings and held 125 catches. Weekes is best remembered for two remarkable world records: five centuries in consecutive Test innings (1948-49), a mark that has not yet been approached; and seven successive Test fifties that has been equalled only once. A very popular player, who had risen from modest origins, he was a role model and a source of inspiration to hundreds of young West Indians. He became a coach and a commentator after his retirement from first-class cricket and was knighted for his services to the sport in 1995.

WELLS-BARNETT, Ida

A truly courageous civil rights leader, Ida B. Wells-Barnett was born in 1862 in Holly Springs, Mississippi. She began to teach in a country school at an early age and continued to do so while attending Fisk University during the summers. She lost her teaching job after becoming involved in a law suit by refusing to give up her seat in a railroad car designated for 'whites only'. She turned to journalism, writing first for an African-American weekly, *Living World*. In 1891, Wells became co-owner and editor of the Memphis weekly, *Free Speech*. But when she publicized the names of white murderers involved in lynchings, her printing press was destroyed and she had to flee to New York City. She then embarked on an intensive campaign against lynching, travelling all across the northern states of America and even lecturing twice in England. Following her marriage to Ferdinand Barnett in 1895, Wells moved to Chicago and headed an anti-lynching organization known simply as the Ida B. Wells Club. Three years later, she led a delegation to Washington, D.C. to protest against the cruel practice of lynching. She became the secretary of the national Afro-American Council in 1898 and later founded the Negro Fellowship League. In 1913, she was appointed adult probation officer in Chicago and was elected vice-president of Chicago's Equal Rights League in 1915. One of the foremost authorities on lynching, she shed much light on this sordid subject in *Southern Horrors* (1892) and *A Red Record* (1895). Ida Wells-Barnett died on 25 March 1931, highly respected by all segments of the American society. The recipient of many awards and distinctions during her lifetime, she was also honoured posthumously when a housing project in Chicago was named for her.

WESLEY, Charles Harris

Born in Louisville, Kentucky, on 2 December 1891, Dr Charles Harris Wesley became a noted historian, administrator and educator. He received his BA from Fisk University in 1911 and his MA from Yale University in 1913 before completing his PhD at Harvard University in 1925. For almost thirty years (1913-42), Wesley taught at Howard University where he rose to the rank of full professor. He then served as president of Wilberforce University during 1942-47 and president of Central State University from 1947 to 1965. At the advanced age of seventy four, he was made president emeritus of Central State while also accepting the post of director of the Association for the Study of Negro Life and History. Wesley's major publications included *Negro Labor in the United States: a Study in American Economic History, 1850-1925* (1927); *Richard Allen: Disciple of Freedom* (1935); *The Collapse of the Confederacy* (1938); *Neglected History* (1965) and *In Freedom's Footsteps* (1968). He also served as an editor on both the *International Library on Negro Life* and *History and the Negro History Bulletin*. Charles Harris Wesley died in 1987.

WEST, Dorothy

One of the last survivors of the Harlem Renaissance of the 1920s, Dorothy West, a noted American author, died at the age of ninety-one on 16 August

1998. Born in Boston on 2 June 1907, she began writing at the age of seven and her stories were already appearing in the *Boston Post* when she was fourteen. After her short story, *The Typewriter*, won a national competition in 1926, she moved to New York to further her literary career and wrote short stories for the *New York Daily News*. In 1934 she started the literary magazine, *Challenge*, to encourage young authors and rekindle the spirit of the Harlem Renaissance which seemed to have languished during the depression. Her first novel, *The Living is Easy*, was released in 1948; her second, *The Wedding*, did not appear until 1995 but it created a great stir in literary circles and was adapted into a television mini-series by Oprah Winfrey's production company in 1998. A collection of West's short stories and essays, *The Richer, the Poorer*, was published in 1995. Her works dealt mainly with the conflicts and aspirations of middle class African-Americans.

WESTMORELAND-TRAORÉ, Juanita

Born in Montreal in 1942, the Hon Judge Juanita Westmoreland-Traoré became, in 1999, the first Black to be appointed to the Court of Quebec. She serves in the Criminal and Penal Division. Previously she had been the dean of the Faculty of Law at the University of Windsor, Ontario, the first black Canadian to hold such a post. A distinguished lawyer, who received her doctorate from the Université de Paris, she began her career as an assistant professor at the University of Montreal in 1972. She was appointed Employment Equity Commissioner by the Government of Ontario in 1991 and spent the next four years directing the creation of the first Employment Equity Commission in Canada which investigated and monitored some 17,000 businesses. Most of her efforts, in this capacity, were devoted to building bridges between Quebec's diverse communities. Dr Westmoreland-Traoré also served as a consultant to the United Nations, assisting its National Commission on Truth and Justice in Haiti in 1995. Judge Juanita Westmoreland-Traoré was awarded honorary doctorates by the University of Ottawa in 1993 and the Université de Quebec à Montreal (UQAM) in 2001.

WHARTON, Clifton Reginald

After a brief career in law, Clifton Reginald Wharton became the first African-American diplomat to serve the US in important posts in Europe. Born in Baltimore, Maryland, in 1899, he received his LLB from Boston University in 1920 and his LLM in 1923. After practising briefly in Boston, he entered the US Foreign Service in 1925 and remained for more than twenty years the only African-American career diplomat. Beginning as a third secretary and vice-consul in Monrovia, Liberia, he rose to higher posts in West Africa and the Canary Islands and eventually was named consul general in Portugal in 1950. After serving as a consul general in Marseilles,

France, from 1953 to 1958, he was appointed US minister to Romania and, in 1961, became US ambassador to Norway. He died in 1990. He remains one of a mere handful of Blacks whose image appears on a United States postage stamp. He was the father of Clifton Reginald Wharton, Jr who was appointed president of Michigan State University in 1970.

WHARTON, Clifton Reginald, Jr

The son of an eminent US diplomat of the same name, Dr Clifton Reginald Wharton, Jr was born in Boston in 1926. After graduating with a BA from Harvard University in 1947, he received his MA from John Hopkins University in 1948 and his PhD in economics from the University of Chicago in 1958. In 1957 he joined the staff of the Agricultural Development Council of which he was named vice-president in 1967. Three years later, he became the first black president of Michigan State University and was thus the first African-American to serve as president of a major white university in the United States. He remained in that office until 1978, when he became chancellor of the State University of New York System. From 1987 to 1993 he was chairman and chief executive officer of Teachers Insurance and Annuity Association and the College Retirement Equities Fund, the largest pension fund in the world with assets in excess of $150 billion. Long active in US foreign policy, Wharton has held appointments under six presidents. He was a member of the presidential task force on Agriculture in Vietnam in 1966; a member of the advisory panel on East Asia and the Pacific of the US Department of State, 1966-69; a member of the presidential mission to Latin America in 1969 and of President Carter's Commission on World Hunger, 1978-1980. During 1976-83 he served as chairman of the board for International Food and Agricultural Development of the State Department's AID programme. President Bush appointed him to the Advisory Commission on Trade Policy and Negotiations in 1991; and in 1993 he served as President Clinton's deputy secretary, US Department of State. Dr Wharton has served as trustee (1970-87) and chairman (1982-87) of the Rockefeller Foundation. An outstanding black pioneer in four different fields (philanthropy, foreign economic development, higher education and business), Wharton has received the 1977 Joseph C. Wilson Award for achievement and promise in international affairs and the 1983 President's Award on World Hunger. He has been awarded more than sixty honorary degrees and in 1994 was the recipient of the American Council on Education Distinguished Service Award for Lifetime Achievement. An initial member of the Knight Commission when it issued its first report in 1991, Wharton began serving as its vice-chairman in 2005 and was appointed co-chairman of the Commission in May 2006.

WHEATLEY, Phyllis

Born in Senegal in western Africa around 1753, Phyllis Wheatley was brought to America as a slave and sold to John Wheatley of Boston in 1761. Treated more like a daughter than a slave, she quickly learned to read and write both English and Latin and became one of the earliest African-American poetesses of renown. Two of her best-known poems were *To the University of Cambridge in New England* (1767) and *On the Death of the Rev. Mr George Whitefield* (1770), a touring English evangelist who had touched the hearts of many Americans. Always frail and sickly, Phyllis Wheatley died in 1784. Her first volume of verse, *Poems on Various Subjects: Religious and Moral*, was published in London in 1773. Such were the doubts about the ability of Blacks and women to write poetry in those days that several prominent Boston individuals, including the governor of Massachusetts, thought it necessary to sign a statement at the front of this book to prove that Wheatley had actually written it.

WHITE, Carl

In 2001, Carl A. White, a native of St John, New Brunswick, became the deputy mayor of the City of St John and is the first Black to occupy this position. He was first elected to the city council of St John in 1998 and was re-elected in 2001. A very active community servant, he contributed to several organizations devoted to the principle of racial equality. He served as secretary of the Atlantic Multicultural Council (1983-86), as vice president and secretary of the Multicultural Association of St John (1983-87) and as a member of the City of St John Committee on Race Relations and Multiculturalism (1990-93). He has also been an officer with the New Brunswick Human Rights Commission since 1986.

WHITE, Charles Wilbert

This eminent African-American painter and graphic artist was born in Chicago in 1918. He studied at the Art Institute of Chicago, the Art Students League in New York City and the Taller de Grafica in Mexico. His best-known work perhaps is the huge mural at Hampton Institute, entitled *The Contribution of the Negro to American Democracy*. White's paintings have been exhibited all over Europe and the United States and many of them still remain in the collections of the Metropolitan Museum of Art, Howard University, the Library of Congress and Syracuse University. Charles White died in 1979.

WHITE, Clarence Cameron

Clarence Cameron White was one of the finest of all African-American violinists and composers. Born in Clarksville, Tennessee, in 1880, he attended Howard University and the Oberlin Conservatory of Music before furthering his musical studies in England and France. He became a popular music teacher in public schools in Washington, D.C. (1911-24), at West Virginia State College (1924-31) and at Hampton Institute (1931-35). White composed several pieces, including operas (*Ouanga*, 1932); pieces for the violin; and works for orchestra, band, organ and voice. He also arranged a number of African-American spirituals. Two of his finest compositions were *Symphony in D Minor* and *A Night in Sans Souci*. Clarence White died in 1960.

WHITE, Eartha

Born in 1876, Eartha M.M. White became a legend in Jacksonville, Florida, where she was known during the days of the Great Depression as the 'Angel of Mercy' because of her generous contributions to worthy and charitable causes. She had apparently made enormous profits from a series of small businesses and real estate investments. To honour her daughter, she established the Clara White Mission in 1928 which provided relief and social services to thousands of disadvantaged Blacks. Eartha White died in 1974 at the great age of ninety-eight.

WHITE, Portia

Born in Truro, Nova Scotia, on 24 June 1911, Portia May White, a truly brilliant contralto vocalist, was one of Canada's most famous singers for many years. She performed on major stages both at home and in the United States. As a successful musician and teacher, her popularity helped to open doors that had previously been closed to Canadian Blacks. A scholarship at the age of seventeen took her to the Halifax Conservatory of Music. After touring many parts of the world, she retired because of failing health and settled in Toronto, Ontario, where she trained most of Canada's top singers of the generation that followed. One of her last major concerts took place in Charlottetown, Prince Edward Island, when she was asked to perform for Queen Elizabeth II. Portia White died on 13 February 1968. She is still often referred to as Canada's Marian Anderson.

WHITE, Walter Francis

Born on 1 July 1893 in Atlanta, Georgia, Walter Francis White became one of most influential civil rights leaders and authors of the twentieth century. After graduating from Atlanta University in 1916, he worked for Standard Life Insurance Company while forming an Atlanta branch of the National Association for the Advancement of Colored People (NAACP). He was one of driving forces behind the NAACP throughout the inter-war years, working tirelessly to promote civil rights legislation that would abolish lynchings, poll taxes, segregation and discrimination. He remained the executive secretary of the NCAAP from 1930 until his death. White served as adviser to Presidents Franklin D. Roosevelt and Harry S. Truman and persuaded both administrations to be more liberal in the area of civil rights. During World war II, he was largely instrumental in the formation of the Committee on Fair Employment Practices. White was also a prolific writer, whose numerous books included *Rope and Faggot: A Biography of Judge Lynch* (1929), *A Rising Wind: A Report of the Negro Soldier in the European Theatre of War* (1945), *A Man Called White* (1948), and *How Far to the Promised Land?* (1955). He also wrote two novels: *Fire in the Flint* (1924), and *Flight* (1926). Walter White died on 21 March 1955.

WHITE, William

Born a slave in Virginia in 1874, Revd William Andrew White immigrated to Canada in 1898 and left his mark on Nova Scotia after completing his studies at Acadia University. He worked for a Baptist church in Truro for twelve years before serving as chaplain to a black battalion during World War I. In 1919, he became pastor of the Cornwallis Street Church and fostered the image there of the Mother Church of Negro Baptism in Nova Scotia. To combat the suffering resulting from the Great Depression, he launched a Five Year Programme to raise $2,500 annually to establish vocational schools for Blacks within the churches. He became universally recognized as the leader of Nova Scotia's Blacks regardless of their faith or heritage. He was awarded an honorary doctorate of divinity by Acadia University in 1936, becoming the first Canadian Black to be so honoured. A few weeks later he died, much lamented by all elements of society within the province. In 1941, Memorial Windows were unveiled in his Church to honour his memory.

WILKINS, Ernest, Jr

Professor Jesse Ernest Wilkins, Jr was born in Chicago, Illinois, on 27 November 1923. He is a distinguished mathematician, physicist and engineer. A schoolboy prodigy, Wilkins entered the University of Chicago at the age of thirteen and graduated with an A.B. in mathematics at the age of seventeen when he ranked in the top ten in Mathematics' famous undergraduate Putnam Competition. In 1942, at the age of nineteen, he became the seventh African-American to achieve a PhD in mathematics. After working for several years as a mathematician, Wilkins studied mechanical engineering, obtaining two more degrees (from New York University). In 1970 he was appointed distinguished professor of applied mathematics at Howard University. Wilkins made an immense contribution there by helping that institution to establish a PhD programme in mathematics, the first doctoral programme in that discipline at a Historically

Black College or University (HBCU). After retiring briefly from academia, he joined the staff at Clark Atlanta University as distinguished professor of applied mathematics and applied physics in 1990. Dr Wilkins was a joint owner of a company which designed and developed nuclear reactors for electrical power generation. He is a past president of the American Nuclear Society. His major achievements include the development of radiation shielding against gamma radiation and the development of mathematical models by which the amount of gamma radiation absorbed by a given material can be calculated. This technique of calculating radiative absorption is now widely used by researchers in space and nuclear science projects. In 1976, Professor Wilkins was inducted into the National Academy of Engineering. He has been the recipient of numerous honours and awards, including his election as a Fellow by the American Association for the Advancement of Science (1956), his election to the National Academy of Engineering (1976) and the Outstanding Civilian Service Medal (US Army, 1980). Very early in his career, he became the first Black ever to attend a White House cabinet meeting as a representative of a department when he was serving, in 1954, as assistant secretary of labour for international affairs. Dr Wilkins was also appointed to the 1958 Civil Rights Commission.

WILKINS, Roy

Roy Wilkins was born in St Louis, Missouri, on 30 August 1901. After graduating from the University of Minnesota with a BA in 1923, he served for eight years as the managing editor of the African-American weekly, the *Kansas City Call*. He became an active member of the National Association for the Advancement of Colored People (NAACP) and was appointed assistant executive secretary of that organization in 1931. In 1934 he took over the task of editing its official organ, the *Crisis*. In the meantime, Wilkins distinguished himself as a civil rights leader by writing important articles on racial issues for a variety of magazines and books and delivering lectures throughout the United States. His investigation of working conditions for Blacks in Mississippi in the 1930s prompted congressional action. During World War II he served as a consultant to the US War Department on the problems facing Blacks in the US Armed Forces and with W. E .B. Du Bois and Walter White he was a consultant to the American delegation at the founding conference of the United Nations in 1945. Wilkins was largely responsible for the Supreme Court decision in 1954 which undermined the traditional system of segregation in public schools. He succeeded White as the executive secretary of the NAACP in 1955 and gave it twenty-two years of effective leadership during a critical period of racial turbulence and mass protest. In the early 1960s, he helped draft President Kennedy's civil rights bill and helped organize the civil rights March on Washington. Wilkins was a firm advocate of racial equality and social justice but frowned upon violence and thus angered some of the more militant Blacks towards the end of his career. He died on 8 September 1981.

WILLIAMS, Castor

The Hon Judge Castor Williams was appointed to the bench as a provincial court judge in Nova Scotia in 1996. He had previously been a crown attorney. Born in Antigua, West Indies, he immigrated to Canada in 1970 and achieved a BA in 1973 and an LLB in 1976 from Dalhousie University. An active community servant, he was awarded a Governor General 125th Anniversary Medal in 1992. He is a founding member of the Joint Consultative Committee (JCC), which brings together major black organizations with a view to community economic development. He is the chairperson of the Black Learners' Advisory Committee and president of the Black Lawyers' Association of Nova Scotia.

WILLIAMS, Daniel Hale

One of the greatest surgeons in North American history, Dr Daniel Hale Williams was born in Hollidaysburg, Pennsylvania, on 18 January 1856. He began as a barber in Wisconsin before achieving his MD from Chicago Medical College in 1883. For many years afterwards, he served simultaneously as staff physician of the Protestant Orphan Asylum, surgeon at the South Side Dispensary, instructor at Chicago Medical College, surgeon of the City Railway Company, and staff member of the Illinois State Board of Health. In 1891 he was instrumental in the establishment of Provident Hospital, the first hospital founded and controlled by African-Americans. It was there that he successfully performed, in 1893, the very first open-heart operation. In the same year, he was appointed surgeon-in-chief of Freedman's Hospital in Washington, D.C. Such was Dr Williams' fame as a surgeon that he became a consultant to a number of medical institutions and was a visiting professor at Meharry Medical College at Nashville, Tennessee, in 1899. He also served as associate attending surgeon at St Luke's Hospital from 1907 to 1931. A founder and the first vice-president of the National Medical Association, he was the first African-American to become a fellow of the American College of Surgeons in 1913. Dr Williams died on 4 August 1931.

WILLIAMS, Eric

Perhaps the most outstanding personality thus far produced by Trinidad, Dr Eric Eustace Williams was born on 25 September 1911 and educated at Oxford University in England. After achieving his PhD, he lectured for some years in sociology and political science at Howard University in the

United States. In 1948 he was appointed to the Caribbean Commission which investigated the social and economic conditions within the region. Returning to Trinidad, Williams organized the People's National Movement (PNM) in 1955 and led the colony to independence in 1962. The PNM dominated local politics for many years and Williams was able to remain prime minister of the republic of Trinidad and Tobago from 1956 until his death on 29 March 1981. Apart from a brief flurry of 'Black Power' unrest in the early 1970s, Dr Williams provided Trinidad and Tobago with relatively stable government. But he failed to check rampant corruption within his own administration or to bridge the gap between the Blacks and the Browns in the republic. His autocratic style also offended many, both within his country and throughout the West Indies. A noted scholar, his numerous books included *The Negro in the Caribbean* (1942), *Slavery to Chaguaramas* (1959), *History of the People of Trinidad and Tobago* (1962), *British Historians and the West Indies* (1964), *Inward Hunger: The Education of a Prime Minister* (1969), *From Columbus to Castro: the History of the Caribbean, 1492-1969* (1970), and the classic, *Capitalism and Slavery*, which argued that emancipation had much more to do with simple economics than with humanitarianism.

WILLIAMS, George Washington

Born in Bedford Springs, Pennsylvania in 1849, Revd George Washington Williams became an eminent clergyman, historian, journalist, lawyer, state legislator and government official. Enlisting in the Union Army when he was only fourteen, he attained the rank of sergeant major during the American Civil War (1861-65). In 1874 he graduated from Newton Theological Institution and became a Baptist minister, preaching for a while in Boston. Moving to Washington, D.C. in 1875, Williams founded a journal, the *Commoner*. In 1876, he accepted a position as a pastor in Cincinnati, Ohio, where he began the study of law and was admitted to legal practice. In 1878, he worked with the US Department of the Treasury and then served briefly in the Ohio state legislature. In 1885, he was named US minister to Haiti. He died in Blackpool, England, in 1891 after having been in the service of the Belgian government for a few years. Incredibly, for a man who had played so many roles, he was only in his forty-second year. Eight years earlier, he had produced his famous two-volume study, *History of the Negro Race in America from 1619 to 1880*, the most careful work done up to that time on the black experience in North America. Williams was also the author of another significant book, *A History of the Negro Troops in the War of the Rebellion, 1861-65*, published in 1888.

WILLIAMS, Henry

Henry Sylvester Williams was born in 1869 in the small Trinidadian village of Arouca. He became famous for organizing the first Pan African conference which took place in London, England, in 1900 and for being the first black man to address the House of Commons on the evils of racism. He taught in elementary schools in Trinidad during 1886-91 before emigrating to the United States. Failing to find suitable employment there, because of his colour, he went to Nova Scotia to study law. Three years later he moved to the United Kingdom and completed his law degree. While there, he lectured frequently on the weaknesses of the Crown Colony system and advocated self-government for British colonies. He also founded the African Association and persuaded 37 delegates and 10 observers to attend an important three-day conference to address the problems of racial injustice and inequality. After the conference, Williams travelled around the West Indies establishing branches to fight for the emancipation of Africans both at home and in the diaspora. His experiences in South Africa, where he practised law during 1903-05, convinced Williams of the necessity to proceed with his crusade with even greater vigour. He returned to England and was elected to public office on the Marylebone borough council in 1906. Two years later, with a growing family now to support, he decided to move back home to Trinidad to practise law. He died there in 1911. His African Association proved to be the fore-runner of similar movements in the inter-war years and his gospel of Pan Africanism was wholeheartedly adopted by W. E .B. DuBois, Marcus Garvey and others.

WILLIAMS, Hosea

A civil rights leader and politician, Hosea Williams was a major figure in the struggle against segregation in the United States during the 1960s. He helped organize and lead such demonstrations as the 'Bloody Sunday' march in Selma, Alabama, in 1965, during which many peaceful marchers were brutally assaulted. He was also present when Revd Martin Luther King Jr was assassinated in Memphis, Tennessee, in 1968. Born in Attapulgus, Georgia, on 5 January 1926, Williams achieved a BSc from Morris Brown College and a master's degree in chemistry from Clark Atlanta University. When he worked in the Department of Agriculture in Savannah, Georgia, he was the first federally employed black research chemist in the American south. He was an enthusiastic member of the National Association for the Advancement of Colored People (NAACP) before joining King's Southern Christian Leadership Conference (SCLC) in 1963. He travelled widely throughout the United States recruiting volunteers and teaching the basic techniques of non-violent demonstration. Williams was elected to the Georgia state legislature in 1974 and served in it until 1985 when he was elected to a term on the Atlanta City Council. He was unsuccessful in his bid to become mayor of Atlanta in 1989 but served during the 1990s as a county commissioner. He remained an ardent worker on behalf of the homeless and the destitute until his death on 16 November 2000.

WILLIAMS, Lee

Lee Williams is best remembered as the black Canadian who was largely instrumental in bringing an end to racial discrimination in employment practices on the railroads. Born in Oklahoma in 1907, his parents immigrated to Saskatchewan when he was only three. He began working with the Canadian National Railway (CNR) as a sleeping-car porter in 1930. During the 1950s he waged a vigorous campaign to win his black colleagues the right to promotion as well as equality within the trade unions. His complaints impressed John Diefenbaker, the leader of the federal Conservative party, and his agitation resulted in the passage of the Fair Employment Practices Act (1960) which significantly improved working conditions for Blacks all across Canada. Williams himself rose to the rank of an executive officer within the railway union and ensured that Blacks were no longer confined to menial tasks on the trains. A long-time president of the local (Winnipeg) chapter of the National Black Coalition, his activism and community service had much to do with the gradual demolition of racial barriers in the province of Manitoba, where he resided from 1940 until his death in 2002.

WILLIAMS, Serena

One of the finest female tennis players of all time, Serena Williams was born on 26 September 1981 in Saginaw, Michigan. Showing exceptional talent from an early age, her father (Richard) was able to predict that she and her sister, Venus, would soon become the dominant women players in the world. His prophecies were fulfilled when Serena and Venus won eight of eleven major tournaments between June 2001 and January 2003. Serena herself has won seven major tournaments, including the US Open on two occasions. She was only eighteen when she claimed her first US Open title in September 1999. Her tennis is distinguished by powerful serves and ground strokes and incredible speed on the court. With her sister, she also forms one of the most proficient duos in the history of the sport and they won six major doubles championships between 1999 and 2002. Becoming increasingly pre-occupied with acting and her burgeoning business interests, her tennis has declined since 2003 and her days as a top professional in the sport appear to be numbered. Among other ventures, Serena Williams has established her own line of designer clothing called 'Aneres'.

WILLIAMS, Tonya Lee

Tonya Lee Williams is best known for her role as Dr Olivia Winters in *The Young and the Restless*. Born in England of West Indian parents, she immigrated to Canada in her youth and completed her education at Ryerson University in Toronto. She has appeared in many TV programmes, including *Hill Street Blues*, *Matlock*, *Street Legal* and *The Polka Dot Door*. She is the president and founder of Reel World Film Festival, dedicated to featuring films from diverse ethno-cultural communities. She is also president and founder of Wilbo Entertainment and the Publicity Group, which provide opportunities for promising artists in the entertainment industry. She was co-executive producer of the short film, *Maple*, which won an award in 2001. Williams has won many honours and distinctions, including the NAACP Image Award and Best Daytime Actress, 2000 and 2002.

WILLIAMS, Venus

Had it not been for her younger sister, Serena, Venus Williams would have been regarded all over the world as the greatest female tennis player of this generation. She quickly won two Wimbledon championships and two US Open titles but had to serve as runner-up in five other finals. Born on 17 June 1980 in Lynwood, California, Venus first came into prominence when, in 1997, she was the first unseeded US Open woman's finalist in the modern era. Her serve, often measured in excess of 120 miles per hour, and her exceptional agility and speed on the court have made her a most dangerous opponent. Because of their size, strength and athleticism, Venus and Serena Williams were almost invincible in women's doubles at the turn of the century. They generally avoid playing against each other on the professional circuit but have appeared together in five finals of major tournaments thus far. Venus prevailed in the first one, before Serena defeated her in four consecutive finals between June 2002 and January 2003. Like her younger sibling, Venus is becoming more and more a businesswoman than a tennis player. She is the founder and CEO of her interior design firm, 'V Starr Interiors', located in Jupiter, Florida.

WILLS, Dorothy

Dr Dorothy Abike Wills was born in the small Caribbean island of Dominica. She immigrated to Canada in 1952 and studied at Concordia, McGill and Mount St Vincent Universities before completing her PhD at Pacific Western University. She then taught at various levels before serving as Dean of the Faculty of Applied Technologies at Vanier College in Quebec from 1994 to 2000. In the 1980s, she helped to develop a Special Care Counselling Programme to meet the needs of First Nations people on the Khanawake Reserve in Quebec. She also developed a mentoring programme to help young Blacks cope with the education system in that province. From 1988 to 1994, she served on the Immigration and Refugee Board of Canada. An active community servant, Dr Wills was a founding member and executive secretary of the National Black Coalition of Canada. She has been the recipient of numerous awards, including honorary doctorates from Concordia University (1989) and Dalhousie University (1996); the Mount St Vincent Alumni Jubilee Award of Distinction; and the Order of Canada in 1989.

WILSON, Margaret Bush

Margaret Bush Wilson created history in 1975 when she became the first black woman to hold the post of president of the National Association for the Advancement of Colored People (NAACP). Born on 30 January 1919, she was educated at Talladega College in Alabama and Lincoln University School of Law in St Louis. She worked with the Missouri Office of Urban Affairs (1965-67), established the Model Housing Corporation in St Louis to obtain federal housing money for the black poor, served as deputy and then acting director of the St Louis Model Cities programme (1968-69), and was assistant director of St Louis Lawyers for Housing (1969-72). Wilson had for many years been a most active NAACP leader in St Louis before being elevated to the presidency of the national body.

WILSON, Salah

A native of Trinidad and Tobago, Anthony Salah I. Wilson immigrated to Canada in 1973 and has devoted his major energies to the promotion and teaching of steel band music in Montreal and Toronto. Towards these ends he established Pan Québec in 1992 and the Salah and Family Steelpan Music Academy in Montreal in 1996. A consummate musician, recording artist, arranger, composer, producer, author and educator, he teaches steel pan music to students of all ages and ethnic groups and holds workshops regularly. In 2001 he initiated Montreal's first International Steel Pan Festival. Almost incredibly, Salah Wilson persuaded Concordia University to accept the steel pan as a principal instrument of study and graduated from that institution in 1995 with a BFA, achieving a distinction in steelpan jazz, the first for any student anywhere. He published a popular text book, *Steelpan Playing with Theory*, in 1999.

WILSON, William Julius

Born on 20 December 1935 in Westmoreland County, Pennsylvania, Dr William Julius Wilson was educated at Wilberforce University (BA, 1958), Bowling Green State University (MA, 1961) and Washington State University (PhD, 1966). He taught at the University of Massachusetts at

Amherst from 1965 to 1971 before joining the sociology department at the University of Chicago where he became a full professor in 1975 and chairman of his department in 1978. Wilson left an indelible mark on American sociology by emphasizing the role of economics as a key cause of black poverty rather than the simple operation of racism. His first major study, *The Declining Significance of Race: Blacks and the Changing American Institutions* (1978) caused a sensation in the academic community by asserting that class divisions were more damaging than racial ones. In *The Truly Disadvantaged: The Inner City, the Underclass, and Public Policy* (1987), he strengthened his case by arguing that whereas civil rights legislation and affirmative action had served the educated black middle class, it had left the poor unaffected. These arguments led to the establishment in 1993 of the Center for the Study of Urban Inequality, an important research and policy-making foundation. In 1996, Wilson returned to the fray with another controversial study, *When Work Disappears: The World of the New Urban Poor*, suggesting that the disappearance of low-skilled manufacturing jobs and the flight of the urban middle class to the suburbs had, within the last generation or so, proved a greater detriment to the ghetto poor than had racism and/or other cultural pathologies. These works exposed Wilson to attack both from the right and the left. The conservatives opposed his call for programmes of national health care, education reform and government-financed jobs; while the liberals, including the bulk of African-American sociologists, were disturbed by his de-emphasis of race and by his consideration of the behavioural problems associated with poverty. Wilson became one of President Bill Clinton's main advisers on social policy but consistently maintained that the welfare reforms proposed by the cabinet were bound to fail unless they were directly concerned with increasing the job opportunities in the inner cities.

WINFREY, Oprah

From humble beginnings, Oprah Gail Winfrey has become arguably the brightest star in the television industry in the United States, if not the world. Born on 29 January 1954 on a farm in Kosciusko, Mississippi, she spent a chequered youth before winning a scholarship to Tennessee State University in 1972. After graduating in 1976, she moved to Baltimore, Maryland, to work for the American Broadcasting Company (ABC) as a reporter for the local evening news. She later became co-host of a morning talk show before moving to Chicago to become the anchor of the A.M. Chicago morning show in January 1984. By September 1985, it had become so popular that it was renamed *The Oprah Winfrey Show* and soon went into syndication on 138 stations. By 1987, such was its popularity and impact that *The Oprah Winfrey Show*, which now appeared in 180 cities, won three Emmy awards.

The show continues to receive excellent ratings and is considered the best of its kind on North American television. In 1996, Winfrey established 'Oprah's Book Club' to encourage all classes of Americans to read and write. Her monthly choices immediately dominated the best seller lists and an additional 10 million copies of her first eight selections were sold. Oprah persuaded the publishers to donate 10,000 copies of her book-of-the month selection to libraries and also bought film rights to a number of them to make the stories accessible to an even greater proportion of the population. Her own *Make the Connection*, written in collaboration with Bob Greene in 1996, sold over 2 million copies in that year alone. Oprah Winfrey, meanwhile, has appeared in a number of films, including *The Color Purple*, *Native Son* and *Beloved* and is one of the best-known and best-loved personalities in the western hemisphere. She established her own company, *Harpo Productions*, co-founded the women's television network, *Oxygen*, and publishes two magazines, *O, the Oprah Magazine* and *O at Home*. Early in 2006, it was announced that Winfrey had signed a $55 million three-year contract with XM Satellite Radio to establish a new radio station. According to *Forbes* magazine, she was the only black billionaire in the twentieth century and the richest black woman in American history. *Time* magazine has consistently ranked her among the world's most influential individuals. She has also established an enviable reputation for community service and her generous treatment of worthy causes.

WINT, Arthur

Dr Arthur Wint was born in Kingston, Jamaica, on 25 May 1920. He was educated at Calabar High School and Excelsior College before going to England and serving in the Royal Air Force during World War II. He stayed on in the United Kingdom to pursue medical studies at the University of London and qualified as a physician. Dr Wint eventually returned to enjoy a very successful and lengthy practice in Jamaica. Before settling back down in his native country, however, he established a great reputation as an athlete by winning the Olympic Gold Medal in the 400 metre dash in 1948. He was one of the best middle-distance runners in the world for many years. This popular physician made a noteworthy contribution to Jamaican athletics after his own retirement from the track by encouraging and coaching several generations of promising track stars. He was an enthusiastic community servant while often serving as a professional consultant to his government. Dr Wint also acted as Jamaica's High Commissioner to the United Kingdom during the 1970s. Among his many awards and distinctions was the Member of the British Empire (MBE) which he received in 1954. He died on 19 October 1992.

WONDER, Stevie

Despite being born black and blind in Detroit, Michigan, on 13 May 1950, Stevie Wonder had become a musical prodigy before he had reached the age of twenty-five. He was probably christened Steveland Morris (or Hardaway), but he had such great musical skills in his early childhood, that he was everywhere known as 'Little Stevie Wonder'. He excelled on the harmonica, drums and the piano by the time he was nine years old. By the age of twelve, he had written two concertos and recorded for Motown his first hit, *Fingertips*. After attending the Michigan School for the Blind, he churned out an incredible number of hits, selling more than 40 million records by the time he was twenty-four. Such was his status in the world of music that he was able to compel Motown to renegotiate his contract and give him total musical freedom. In 1974 alone, he won four major Grammy Awards and proceeded to win more awards for singing in 1975 and 1976 than any other singer had done in a whole life time. Wonder also appeared in such motion pictures as *Bikini Beach* and *Muscle Beach Party*.

WOOD, Wilfred

The Rt Revd Dr Wilfred Denniston Wood was born in Barbados, West Indies, on 15 June 1936. After leaving Combermere School in 1955, he emigrated to Britain, studied theology and was ordained a priest in the Anglican Church on 21 December 1962. He became the first black clergyman to be promoted to a bishopric over an English diocese when he was consecrated Bishop of Croydon in 1985. A devoted community servant, he began his career by doing some excellent work among the ethnic communities in the Shepherds Bush area of London. He soon came to wider attention by speaking out boldly against racial discrimination. He was a founding member of the Paddington Churches Housing Association, and was appointed the Bishop of London's race relations officer in 1966. In 1974, he joined the diocese of Southwark, where he stayed until his retirement in 2002. In 1977, he was appointed Rural Dean of Lewisham and became Archdeacon of Southwark. He remained a vocal champion of racial justice, launching several initiatives and serving on many committees. In 1968, his recommendations for the replacement of the National Committee for Commonwealth Immigrants (NCCI) with a Community Race Relations Commission were accepted and came to be known as the 'Wood Proposals'. In 1992, in collaboration with the Bishop of Liverpool, he put forward a new set of race equality principles for employers and they became known as the 'Wood-Sheppard Principles'. He was the moderator of the Southwark Diocesan Race Relations Committee; moderator of the World Council of Churches Programme to Combat Racism; president of the Royal Philanthropic Society; and chairman of the Tramlink Penalty

Fares Appeals Panel. In 2000, Bishop Wood was offered a knighthood for his contribution to race relations in the United Kingdom and in 2002 he was awarded an honorary doctorate by the University of the West Indies.

WOODRUFF, Hale

Hale Aspacio Woodruff, a distinguished educator, painter and printmaker, was born in Cairo, Illinois, in 1900. After training at several institutions in the United States, France and Mexico, he became an art instructor at the University of Atlanta where, in 1941, he introduced the important series of Atlanta University art shows. From 1946 until his retirement in 1968, he served as professor of art education at New York University while winning several awards and distinctions. Woodruff's works were exhibited throughout the United States and some of them are preserved in collections at New York University, the Library of Congress at Washington, D.C., and the Golden State Insurance Company in Los Angeles. Hale Woodruff died in 1979.

WOODS, Anne-Marie

Born in London, England, Anne-Marie Woods moved with her family to Trinidad and then to Dartmouth, Nova Scotia. She settled in Halifax and graduated from the Dalhousie Professional Actor Training Programme. She has become an actress, dancer, narrator, poet, singer and songwriter who first made a name for herself as the leader of 'Four the Moment', a capella group which produced three popular CDs and a video. In 1996, she founded the Imani Women's Artistic Project (IWAP), a professional interdisciplinary training programme for African Nova Scotian female youth. She has also taught at various locations, including Halifax Dance, Neptune Theatre School, the Nova Scotia College of Arts and Design, and Fresh Arts in Toronto, Ontario. In 2001, Anne-Marie Woods became the first black Canadian to perform at the prestigious National Black Theatre Festival, held every two years in North Carolina. Her *Waiting to Explode* was performed there to critical acclaim.

WOODS, Eldrick 'Tiger'

Eldrick 'Tiger' Woods was born in Cypress, California, on 30 December 1975. Demonstrating extraordinary golf skills at an early age, he was only five years old when he was featured in a golf magazine. He won his first US Junior Amateur title in 1991 and became in 1992 the first golfer to win it twice. In 1993 he won it again. He then proceeded to win three consecutive US Amateur titles during 1994-96. As a student at Stanford University, Woods also won the National Collegiate Athletic Association championship in 1996 just before turning pro. He made an immediate impact on the professional sport, winning two tournaments as a rookie before that year was over and then setting a record for tour earnings in 1997 with $2,066,833 (which he has broken with monotonous regularity since). One of his greatest triumphs came in April 1997 when, at the age of twenty one, he won the 61st Masters Tournament by a record 12 strokes and established a course record score of 18 under par for the event at Augusta. He was the first non-white golfer in history to win a major event. He established another incredible record when he won the 2000 US Open at Pebble Beach by fifteen strokes. The Tiger now owns the lowest career scoring average and the most career earnings of any player in PGA history. He has already accumulated almost $65 million in prize money in just over ten years. His charisma and dynamism attracted thousands of new enthusiasts to the sport and his ability to drive the ball huge distances from the tee added new dimensions to professional golf. This was recognized at once by a host of sponsors who offered him endorsement deals worth millions of dollars. Still only thirty, Woods has already won more than fifty tournaments, including twelve majors, and was the leading money winner on the professional circuit in seven of the past eight years. Woods has revolutionized the sport, making it immeasurably more popular and more lucrative than ever before.

WOODS, Granville T.

Born in Columbus, Ohio, on 23 April 1856, Granville T. Woods became a famous inventor and electrical and mechanical engineer. Beginning as a machinist and blacksmith, he worked as a railroad fireman and engineer for some years before taking courses in electrical and mechanical engineering in the late 1870s. Settling down in Cincinnati, Ohio, he founded the Woods Electric Company which manufactured and sold telephone, telegraph, and electrical instruments. Altogether, he registered more than fifty patents dealing with railroad telegraphs, electrical brakes and electrical railway systems. Woods' first patent was for a steam boiler furnace in 1884. One year later, he patented a telephone transmitter which was bought by Bell Telephone. But perhaps his greatest invention came in 1887 when he patented the induction telegraph system, a method of informing an engineer of trains immediately ahead and behind him. This led to much safer rail travel all over the world. Woods died in 1910.

WOODSON, Carter G.

One of the greatest of all African-American historians, Dr Carter Godwin Woodson was born in New Canton, Virginia, on 19 December 1875. The son of former slaves, he was largely self-taught as he was unable to attend school until he was twenty. In 1903, however, he received his LittB degree from Berea College in Kentucky and proceeded to achieve his BA (1907) and MA (1908) from the University of Chicago. In 1912 he was awarded a PhD from Harvard University. Woodson was the driving force behind the creation of the *Journal of Negro History* and remained its director/editor for thirty four years after the appearance of its first issue in 1916. It was the mouthpiece of the Association for the Study of Negro Life and History which Woodson had been largely instrumental in founding in 1915. After serving briefly as dean of the School of Liberal Arts of Howard University and as dean of West Virginia Collegiate Institute, Woodson organized the Associated Publishers, Inc. in 1922 to publish books about African-American history and culture that did not appeal to the mainstream publishers. In 1926 he inaugurated Negro History Week, which was extended into Black History Month (February) in 1976, for the basic purpose of focussing attention on black contributions to civilization. Generally regarded as the 'Father of Negro History', Woodson used his quarterly magazine and his press to publish many scholarly articles and volumes that would not otherwise have appeared in print. Among the most important books that he himself wrote were *The Education of the Negro Prior to 1861* (1915), *A Century of Negro Migration* (1918), and *The Negro in Our History* (1922), which remained for many years the standard text in African-American history. Carter G. Woodson died on 3 April 1950, while still working on a projected six-volume *Encyclopaedia Africana*.

WORRELL, Frank

Sir Frank Mortimer Maglinne Worrell was born in Barbados, West Indies, on 1 August 1924. He was educated at Combermere School (Barbados) and Manchester University (England). He was a brilliant cricketer who registered 15,025 runs, 349 wickets and 139 catches in 208 first-class matches during 1942-64. He was the first black player to be appointed captain of a West Indies cricket touring team and created such an impact on the Australian public during the 1960-61 season that they instituted a trophy, named after him, for which Australia and the West Indies have been contending ever since. He was instrumental in bringing the smaller Caribbean islands within the fold of the West Indies Cricket Board of Control (WICBC) and it was he who also taught the players to eschew their parochial differences and band together as a national unit. Thanks in large part to Worrell's influence, the West Indies abandoned what used to be styled 'Calypso Cricket' and steadily became the most clinically proficient team in the world. After his retirement from the game, he served as an administrator on the staff of the University of the West Indies (UWI) and was awarded a knighthood. One of the shrewdest of all cricket captains, and most elegant of all batsmen, Sir Frank Worrell died on 13 March 1967 and received a hero's funeral in Barbados. The respect in which he was held everywhere is reflected in the unusually wide range of honours and distinctions bestowed upon him in his last years as well as posthumously. He was awarded an honorary doctorate of law by Punjab University in India, where the government declared a Frank Worrell Day. He was elected to 'Black America's Hall of Fame' in the United States. A street in Radcliffe, Lancashire, England where he once played professional cricket, was renamed 'Worrell Close'. In Trinidad, the playing fields of the St Augustine Campus of the UWI have been called the Sir Frank Worrell Grounds. In Barbados, the Frank Worrell Memorial Gardens surround his burial site at the Cave Hill Campus of the UWI. The Frank Worrell Gate has been erected at Bank Hall, the home of his first cricket club, Empire. The Sir Frank Worrell Pavilion has been built at the Combermere School grounds at Waterford; and his picture, which was placed on a Barbadian stamp, now still appears on a Barbados five dollar bill.

WRIGHT, Ian

Ian Edward Wright is a former professional football player and is currently a television and radio personality in the United Kingdom. Born in Woolwich, London, on 3 November 1963, he first made a name for himself by scoring more goals for Arsenal than any player had previously done. His record of 185 goals has since been broken by Thierry Henry. Wright led Arsenal to their second Premier League championship and FA Cup double in 1997/98. A formidable striker, he also played 33 matches for England. He was inducted into the English Football Hall of Fame in 2005. After retiring from professional football in 2000, Wright joined the BBC and has presented TV shows such as *Friday Night's All Wright*, *The National Lottery Wright Around the World*, and *Friends Like These*; the radio programme, *Wright and Bright*, has also been immensely popular. In 2004 he became team captain on the BBC game show, *They Think It's All Over*. He is currently a football pundit on the BBC's *Match of the Day*. Wright was awarded the MBE in 2000 for his football achievements and remains one of the sport's most colourful characters.

WRIGHT, Louis Tompkins

Born on 23 July 1891 in La Grange, Georgia, Dr Louis Tompkins Wright was educated at Clark College in Atlanta and at Harvard University Medical School. After interning at Freedmen's Hospital in Washington, D.C., he served in the US Army Medical Corps during World War I and saw active service in France. Establishing his private practice in New York City in 1919, he was immediately appointed to a municipal position in Harlem Hospital, thus becoming the first African-American to serve in such a capacity. Remaining in Harlem Hospital from 1919 to 1949, he became its director of the department of surgery and president of the medical board. Wright headed the team that was the first to use Aureomycin, then known as the 'wonder drug'. He was renowned as an authority on head injuries and was the physician who introduced the intradermal method of vaccination. He is also famous for founding the Harlem Hospital Cancer Research Foundation. Dr Wright died on 8 October 1952. He was an outspoken civil rights activist who consistently denounced racial discrimination in the entertainment media, in hospital practices and in professional organizations.

WRIGHT, Richard

A prolific author, Richard Wright is famous for being the first African-American to write a novel that became a Book-of-the-Month-Club selection. Born into poverty on 4 September 1908 near Natchez, Mississippi, he worked briefly as the Harlem editor for the *Daily Worker*, a Communist newspaper. His *Uncle Tom's Cabin* appeared in 1938 and his even more successful *Native Son* was published in 1940. This was the landmark novel that catapulted him to fame. It was a bestseller and was staged successfully as a play on Broadway (1941) by Orson Welles. Wright's autobiography, *Black Boy*, was released in 1945. He then emigrated to France where he remained an expatriate until his death on 28 November 1960. *The Outsider*, published in 1953, was acclaimed as the first American Existential novel and warned that the black man had awakened in a disintegrating society not ready to encompass him. Wright's later works included *Black Power* (1954), *Savage Holiday* (1954), *White Man, Listen!* (1957), *The Long Dream* (1958), and *Pagan Spain*. *Lawd Today*, written much earlier, was published posthumously in 1963. Wright was among the first of the African-American writers to expose the hostility and alienation building up in the black ghettos of the urban centres in the northern states. *Native Son* is still universally regarded as the most influential single work in the black fiction of the United States. It set the stage for much of the polemical writing which appeared after World War II.

WRIGHT, Richard Robert

Richard Robert Wright was born in Dalton, Georgia, in 1855 and educated at Altanta University (BA 1876, MA 1879) and Wilberforce University (LLD, 1899). A noted educator, he served as president of the Georgia State Industrial College from 1891 to 1921 and developed it into a progressive academic institution. Wright then moved to Philadelphia and distinguished himself as an eminent banker. He organized the Citizens' and Southern Bank and Trust Company and, from 1925 to 1947, served as president of the National Association of Negro Bankers. Wright died in 1947.

WURIE, Alhaji Ahmadu

Born in Gbinti on 27 August 1898, this son of the paramount chief, Bai Sheka Bundu, became one of the foremost educators and politicians in Sierra Leone during the immediate post-independence period. Alhaji Ahmadu Wurie was educated at the Bo School in the Southern Province and was that school's first alumnus to succeed in the civil service entrance examination. He joined the Bo School staff in 1916 and was promoted to senior assistant master in 1925 and then became the first African native to serve as acting principal there during 1933-35. From 1935 to 1942 Wurie was the headmaster of Koyeima School and served the Kenema Secondary School in a similar capacity during 1952-62. In the interim, he was an education officer. Elected to parliament in 1962, he was appointed minister of education and later became minister of the interior. An author of numerous articles in Sierra Leone Studies, he was awarded an honorary doctorate by the University of Sierra Leone in 1973. He died on 13 June 1977.

YERGAN, Max

This noted educator and civil rights leader was born in Raleigh, North Carolina, in 1893. He graduated from Shaw University in 1914 and went to Kenya during World War I to organize the Young Men's Christian Association (YMCA) among regiments recruited by the British Army. He became the first African-American professor of black history in a major white university when appointed to such a position at City College of New York in 1936. Yergan, who earned the Spingarn Medal in 1933, was an ardent political activist who championed the cause not only of African-Americans but of African nationalists. He was for many years the president of the National Negro Congress and in 1962 served as chairman of the American Committee for Aid to Katanga Freedom Fighters. Max Yergan died on 11 April 1975.

YOHANNES IV

Born in 1831, this Ethiopian prince rebelled against Takla Giyorgis and successfully claimed the Ethiopian crown himself in 1872. He then tried his best to reunify the empire, conquering a number of internal and external foes within a short period. He brought the provinces of Bagemder, Gojam, Lasta and Semén firmly under his control and came to terms with the powerful and efficient Menilek who was then the governor of Shawa. Yohannes IV also repelled the Egyptians but was mortally wounded in a battle against the Mahdists. He died on 10 March 1889.

YOUNG, Andrew

Revd Andrew Jackson Young, Jr was born in New Orleans, Louisiana, on 12 March 1932. Educated at Dillard University, Howard University and Hartford Theological Seminary, he was ordained a priest in 1955 and served for two years as pastor of Congregational churches in Georgia. Between 1957 and 1961 he was associate director of the department of youth work of the National Council of Churches. Always active in the civil rights movement, he rose to the vice-presidency of the Southern Christian Leadership Conference (SCLC). In 1972, Young became the first African-American from Georgia in more than 100 years to be elected to the US House of Representatives. He was appointed the US ambassador to the United Nations in 1977, largely as a reward for his role in securing Jimmy Carter's election to the presidency in 1976. He committed the United States to the principle of black majority rule in southern Africa and supported the UN proposal of an embargo on arms shipments to South Africa. Young's conduct in the UN (1977-79) went far towards improving US relations with the developing countries. In 1979, however, he created quite a stir when, contrary to US policy, he met secretly with the representatives of the Palestine Liberation Organization (PLO) to discuss a forthcoming debate on Palestine. Yielding to pressure from Jews and other Americans, President Jimmy Carter had to ask for Young's resignation.

YOUNG, Coleman

Born in Tuscaloosa, Alabama, on 24 May 1918, Coleman A. Young is best remembered as the first African-American politician to be elected mayor of Detroit. He served in that capacity for an unprecedented five terms (1973-93) and helped to build biracial coalitions within the Democratic Party. He had earlier been elected to the Michigan state senate (1964) and been the Democratic floor leader there. To run Detroit during very difficult economic and racially divisive times for so long was a credit to his tact and skill. Young died on 29 November 1997.

YOUNG, Whitney M. Jr

This noted civil rights leader was born in Lincoln Ridge, Kentucky, on 31 July 1921. He served from 1961 until his death on 11 March 1971 as the executive director of the National Urban League. Whitney Moore Young, Jr was educated at Kentucky State College (BS, 1941) and the University of Minnesota (MA, 1947). During the 1950s, he lectured in social work at the University of Nebraska, Creighton University and Atlanta University. As executive director of the National Urban League during the 1960s, he greatly expanded its scope and functions, searching for strategies that would address most directly the problems facing African-Americans particularly in the fields of education and employment. Under his direction the organization grew from sixty to ninety-eight chapters and shifted its focus from middle class concerns to the needs of the urban poor. Young is generally credited with having persuaded corporate America and major foundations to aid the civil rights movement through financial contributions in support of self-help programmes for education, housing, jobs and family rehabilitation. He also helped to organize the great march on Washington, D.C. in 1963. Young was the president of the National Association of Social Workers, and the author of *To Be Equal*, a series of essays published in 1964, and *Beyond Racism: Building an Open Society* (1969). During the 1960s he was an influential consultant to both President John F. Kennedy and President Lyndon B. Johnson on racial matters. Young was the recipient in 1969 of the Presidential Medal of Freedom, the highest US civilian award, while the Whitney Young Magnet High School in Chicago was later named in his honour.

ZARE'A YA'EQOB

Zare'A Ya'Eqob was the greatest of all Ethiopian emperors during the so-called Middle Ages. He is especially noted for his piety, literary achievements, social reform and his attempts to reorganize the administrative structure of his empire. Born around 1399 in the area later known as Shawa, he found Ethiopia torn by civil and religious strife when he came to the throne in 1434. Zare'A Ya'Eqob gradually centralized the government of Ethiopia by curtailing the powers of the local governors and taking full control of military and fiscal matters. He built a large number of churches and monasteries but in the end he encouraged further conflict by too rigidly enforcing his own ecclesiastical rules and regulations. He himself wrote hymns and religious texts and encouraged translations of all kinds of religious works. He died in 1468.

ZAWDITU

This famous daughter of the great Emperor Menilek II was born in 1876. She became the first female ruler of Ethiopia by virtue of a fortunate marriage at the age of six to the son and heir of Yohannes IV. But her husband died in 1888 and Menilek II himself left no male heir. Ras Tafari Makonnen (later Haile Selassie I) and Zawditu conspired to overthrow Lej Iyasu in 1916 and Zawditu was proclaimed empress on 25 September that year. She then tried her best to restrict the growth of Ras Tafari's power and influence, but failed. Ras Tafari easily succeeded her as emperor when she died on 3 April 1930. Empress Zawditu was a skilful politician who succeeded in keeping Ethiopia relatively stable and united at a critical period in its history.

ZEPHANIA, Benjamin

Benjamin Obadiah Iqbal Zephania is a popular British Rastafarian novelist, playwright, dub poet and actor who was born on 15 April 1958 in Birmingham to Jamaican parents. His first book of poems, *Pen Rhythm*, was so well received in 1980 that three editions were quickly printed. His album, *Rasta*, gained him international prestige and topped the pop charts in Yugoslavia in 1983. A fervent advocate of racial equality, his poetry has mainly been critical of conditions in Britain and his second collection of poems, *The Dread Affair*, contained several verses attacking the British legal system. Other critical poems were included in the collection, *Too Black, Too Strong* (2001). Some of his poetry, such as appeared in *Talking Turkey* (1994) and *Funky Chickens* (1996), was written for children. He wrote two novels for teenagers, *Face* (1999) and *Refugee Boy* (2001). His most recent books include *We Are Britain!* (2002) and *Chambers Primary Rhyming Dictionary* (2004). In addition to his published writing, Zephania has produced numerous music recordings, including *Us and Dem* (1990) and *Belly of De Beast* (1996). He has also appeared as an actor in several television and film productions. His play, *Hurricane Dub*, was one of the winners of the BBC Young Playwrights Festival Award in 1998 and his radio play, *Listen to Your Parents*, won the Commission for Racial Equality Race in the Media Radio Drama Award in 2000. He also won the Portsmouth Book Award (for *Refugee Boy*) in 2002. Zephania has been writer-in-residence at the Africa Arts Collective in Liverpool and the creative-artist-in-residence at Cambridge University. He has been awarded honorary doctorates by the University of North London (1998), the University of Central England (1999), the University of Staffordshire (2002), London South Bank University (2003) and the University of Exeter (2006). In 1998 he was appointed to the National Advisory Committee on Creative and Cultural Education to advise on the place of music and art in the national curriculum and in 1988 Ealing Hospital named a ward after him. His utter contempt for empire and imperialism led him to reject the offer of the OBE in 2003. He was the first person to do so publicly and with such verve.

ZINSOU, Émile

Émile Derlin Zinsou, a Dahomeyan physician and politician, was born on 23 March 1918 in Ouidah, a cultural and religious centre in what was then French West Africa. Following his graduation from the Dakar Medical School, he pursued further research in France before practising in the Ivory Coast and in Dahomey. Zinsou began his political career in 1947 as a counsellor in the French Union and later became a senator, representing Dahomey in the French National Assembly, and serving as minister of commerce in 1957. He founded the Dahomean Progressive Union and became secretary-general of the Dahomean Progressive Party, formed in 1958. After Dahomey achieved its political independence in 1960, Zinsou held various government positions, including minister of foreign affairs and president of the Supreme Court. He also served briefly as ambassador to France. In 1968 he was designated president of Dahomey by the national army during a time of political turmoil, but was overthrown by the army chief of staff only two years later.

ZOBEL, Joseph

A gifted novelist, literary critic, poet and essayist, Joseph Zobel was born on 26 April 1915 in the Caribbean island of Martinique. He attended a local primary school before studying at the Lycée Schoelcher in Fort-de-France. After working briefly as a bookkeeper, he joined the teaching staff at the Lycée. In 1946, Zobel went to France to study dramatic art at the Sorbonne. After passing the French Radio Actors' examination, he took part in many radio plays. In the meantime, he wrote a novel, *La Rue cases-nègres*, which won the Prix de Lecteurs, awarded by a jury of a thousand readers. In 1953, he published another successful novel, *La Fête à Paris*. In 1957 Zobel moved to Senegal where he was appointed director of the Lycée of Ziquinchor and he later taught at the Lycée of van Vollenhoven in Dakar. He became cultural adviser to Radio Senegal in 1962 and began to direct the Senegalese Cultural Services which he was largely instrumental in organizing. Known as Martinique's best regionalist writer, Zobel's legacy includes such other novels as *Diab'la* (1946), *Les Jours immobiles* (1946), *Le Journal de Samba Boy* (1950) and *Intimités avec la terre*. He also wrote several short stories and poems. Some of Zobel's stories were published in *Laghia de la mort ou Qui fait pleurer le tam-tam* (1946) and *Le Soleil partagé* (1964). While most of his poetry appeared in various magazines and newspapers, a fine collection, *Incantations pour un retour au pays natal*, was published in 1965. Both his prose and poetry were characterized by a simple style as he deliberately sought to appeal to the 'petit peuple'. The day-to-day life of average Martiniquans is described in great and vivid detail, especially in his novels and short stories. Zobel died on 18 June 2006.

ZVOBGO, Eddison

Born on 2 October 1935 near Fort Victoria in Southern Rhodesia, Dr Eddison Zvogbo was one of the founding fathers of independent Zimbabwe. He was one of the founders of the National Democratic Party which predated the formation of the Zimbabwe African National Union (ZANU) in 1963. He left home to study in the United States and was jailed almost as soon as he returned in 1964. After his release in 1971, he went back to the United States where he completed his PhD at Harvard

University and became a law professor. In 1978 he joined Robert Mugabe in exile in Mozambique and acted one year later as the ZANU spokesman in the independence negotiations in London. After independence, Zvogbo served in Mugabe's cabinet from 1980 to 2000 but he grew increasingly critical of Mugabe's rule although he had himself been instrumental in making some of the constitutional changes which increased the president's power and authority. Dr Zvogbo died in Harare on 22 August 2004.

ZWANGENDABA

A monarch of incomparable stature, Zwangendaba was the great South African king (1815-48) who led his Ngoni people on a monumental migration of more than 1,000 miles, lasting more than twenty years. To escape from the enormous pressure being applied by the restless Zulus under Shaka, he brought his subjects from their original home near Swaziland to the western portion of what is now Tanzania and moulded them into one of the most powerful kingdoms in eastern Africa. Adopting the Zulu military organization and strategy that had defeated him early in his career, Zwangendaba brought captives into the Ngoni organization and gradually collected an efficient fighting force. Defeating other clans along the way, he moved his ever-increasing army northwards through what is now Malawi and eventually settled near Lake Tanganyika, establishing his headquarters at Mapupo. For about a decade he consolidated his holdings by setting up a centralized structure, having brought an end to the old Changamire empire in that region. When Zwangendaba died in 1848, however, his five sons divided the empire among themselves and resumed their travels, occupying areas in Malawi, Tanzania and Zambia. These divisions considerably weakened the Ngoni empire and made it much easier for the Europeans to dominate that portion of Africa in the generation following the great Zwangendaba's death.

SELECT BIBLIOGRAPHY

Alexander, K. and Glaze, A. *Towards Freedom: The African-Canadian Experience* (Toronto, 1996).

Bertley, L. W., *Canada and its People of African Descent* (Quebec, 1977).

Blackman, F. W. (Ed), *For the Love of Country: The National Heroes of Barbados* (Bridgetown, 2001).

Clay, W., *Just Permanent Interests: Black Americans in Congress*, 1870-1992 (New York, 1993).

Encyclopaedia Britannica (Chicago, 1978).

Encyclopaedia Britannica Year Book (Chicago, 1960-2006).

Fryer, P., *Staying Power: The History of Black People in Britain* (London, 1984).

Gates, H.L. and West, C., *The African American Century: How Black Americans Have Shaped Our Country* (New York, 2002).

Herdeck, D. E., *African Authors: A Companion to Black African Writing 1300-1973* (New York, 1973).

Herdeck, D. E.,*Caribbean Writers: A Bibliographical Critical Encyclopedia* (New York, 1978).

James, C. L. R., *The Black Jacobins: Toussaint L'Ouverture and the Santo Domingo Revolution* (London, 1938).

James, C. L. R., *A History of Negro Revolt* (London, 1938).

Lipschutz, M. R. & Rasmussen, K., *Dictionary of African Historical Biography* (University of California Press, 1989).

Livesey, R. & Smith, A. G., *Black Heritage* (Markham, 2006).

Low, W. A. & Clift, V. A., *Encyclopedia of Black America* (New York, 1984).

Mensah, J., *Black Canadians: History, Social Experiences, Social Conditions* (Halifax, 2002).

Sandiford, K.A.P., *A Black Historical Calendar* (Winnipeg, 1973-94).

Sealy, T., *Caribbean Leaders* (Kingston, 1991).

Swain, C., *Black Faces, Black Interests: The Representation of African Americans in Congress* (Harvard, 1993).

Taylor, S., *Many Rivers to Cross: The African-Canadian Experience* (Toronto, 1992).

Thompson, C., *Blacks in Deep Snow: Black Pioneers in Canada* (Toronto, 1979).

Walker, J. W., *A History of Blacks in Canada* (Hull, 1980).

Walker, J. W., *Les Antillais au Canada* (Ottawa, 1984).

Walker, J. W., *Racial Discrimination in Canada: the Black Experience* (Ottawa, 1985).

Williams, D. P., *Who's Who in Black Canada* (Toronto, 2006).

Winks, R., *The Blacks in Canada: A History* (New Haven, 1971).

INDEX